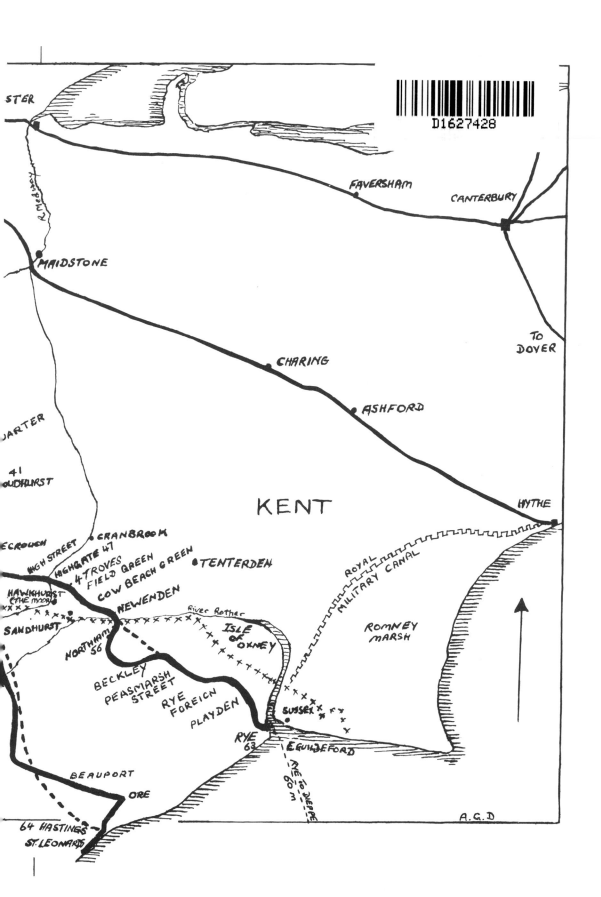

D1627428

STER

FAVERSHAM

CANTERBURY

R. Medway

MAIDSTONE

TO DOVER

CHARING

ASHFORD

UARTER

41
OUDHURST

KENT

HYTHE

ECROUCH   HIGH STREET   CRANBROOK

HIGHGATE 47

47 ROVES
FIELD GREEN   COW BEACH GREEN   TENTERDEN

ROYAL MILITARY CANAL

HAWKHURST
(THE MOOR)

NEWENDEN

River Rother

ISLE
OF
OXNEY

ROMNEY
MARSH

SANDHURST

NORTHIAM
56

BECKLEY
PEASMARSH
STREET   RYE
FOREIGN

PLAYDEN

SUSSEX

RYE
63

E GUILDEFORD

RYE TO DIEPPE

RYE TO
60 m

BEAUPORT

ORE

64 HASTINGS
ST. LEONARDS

A.G.D

THE POSTS OF
SEVENOAKS IN KENT

THE POSTS OF SEVENOAKS IN KENT

An Account of the Handling and Transportation of the
Written Communication of Sevenoaks District
(Westerham to Wrotham, Biggin Hill to Edenbridge)
on the Road to Rye and Hastings.

AD 1085 to 1985/6

by

Archie Donald

B.Sc(Econ) London, M.Ed. Dunelm
FCIS, FCCA, FCMA, FBIM, J.DIP.MA.

WOODVALE PRESS TENTERDEN KENT

First Published   1992

© Archie Donald 1992

ISBN   0 9512887 0 9

British Library Cataloguing in Publication Data

DONALD, Archibald G.

The Posts of Sevenoaks in Kent : An Account of the handling and transportation
of the Written Communication of Sevenoaks District (Westerham to Wrotham,
Biggin Hill to Edenbridge) on the Road to Rye and Hastings AD 1085 to 1985/6.

1. Kent, Local History
I. Title
942.23

Much of the material quoted here has originated in Post Office Archives and is subject
to Crown Copyright. It is reproduced here by kind permission of Post Office Archives.

Crown-copyright material in the Public Record Office is reproduced by permission
of the Controller of Her Majesty's Stationery Office.

Typeset and Designed by Angus Donald Design Assoicates, Tunbridge Wells, Kent
Printed by Mastercolour Limited, Tunbridge Wells, Kent

MCMXCII

COMMUNICATIONS in HISTORY

The Posts of Sevenoaks in Kent on the Road to Rye and Hastings

An analysis of the effect of National Policies projected
onto one local geographical area

For Mary

without whose direction this book could
well never have been completed

Acknowledgements

Copyright material is reproduced with permission of

Public Record Office, Post Office Archives, Controller of H.M. Stationery Office, Tonbridge/Sevenoaks Post Office Records, Kent County Archives, East Sussex Record Office, Trustees of the Stevenson Collection, Sevenoaks Library Kent County Council, Canterbury Cathedral City and Diocesan Record Office, Sevenoaks Chronicle, Gordon Anckorn, Richard Blake of Caterham, Chapman and Hall Ltd., Fine Art Graphics Bradford (Raphael Tuck), Illustrated London News, James Mackay, Motor, J. Salmon Ltd Sevenoaks,

to whom my grateful thanks are given.

Postal material not otherwise credited is that of the author.
Photographs are individually credited. A few of the early photographs were taken by photographers long gone and it has been impossible to trace them. My thanks to them for the record they left behind; and to Emma Colyer who did the word-processing.

Sevenoaks Postmasters

Main Post Stage at Chipstead

1589 Standing Post. **Edmond Thomas**
1597 Standing Post. No name known
1635 Posts open to Public. No name known
1660 Reorganised Posts open to Public. No name known
1665-1675 **Anthony ffuller**
1675-1676 **Richard Everes**t
1676 Closed

Sevenoaks Sub-Office under Chipstead

1635,1660 No names known
1669 Shown as sub-office on GPO's first published list

Sevenoaks Main Office

1676 June (24) - 1686 Robert **Hockham**
1687-1689 Edward **Kent** (Both General Post Letters and Bye Letters)
1689-1692 Robert **Hockham** (GP) Robert Verron (Bye) Robert Verron (Farm)
1692-1697 Robert **Hockham** (GP) John Brett (Bye) J.Brett & Anne Verron (Farm)
1697-1699 Daniel **Stephens** (GP) John Brett (Bye Letters and Farm)
1699-1711 John **Brett** (Tonbridge Branch Farmer)
1711-1716 John **Brett** (Tonbridge Branch Manager)
1717-1727 Richard **Adams** Crown Inn and William **Bayley**
1728   Richard **Adams** and Thomas **Adams** Crown Inn
1729-1738 Jane **Morley** Old Crown Inn
1739-1742 Thomas **Harrison**
1743-1748 Thomas **Barton** Crown Inn
8 April 1748-1762 Garnett **Loving** (died)
1762-1770 Mrs Elizabeth **Loving** (dismissed)
24 Jan 1770-1774 Mrs Elizabeth **Dransfield** (married P.Jones in 1774)
Dec 1774-1797 Philip **Jones** (but Elizabeth continued to do the office work until P.Jones died)
Dec 1797-1803 James **Hanson** Duke of Dorset Arms (Retired)
Aug 1804-1822 Joseph **Burrell** Wheatsheaf Inn (died)
18 Nov 1822-Feb 1837 Mrs Elizabeth **Burrell** Wheatsheaf Inn (died 3 Feb)
16 Feb 1837-1843 Thomas **Poulter** Probably Shambles to High St (died)
6 Sept 1844-1848 Henry **Morris** High Street (died)
7 Dec 1848-1879 Samuel Thomas **Hills** (died)
8 June 1879-1909 Frank Hooper **Hills** (died)
1 Mar 1909 Thomas Edmund **Miles** (from Warwick,subsequently retired)
1 Aug 1915 Thomas Henry **Barrow** (from Liverpool, on to Salisbury 8 Dec 1918)
12 Feb 1919 Robert Walter **Scott** (from Ipswich, on to Maidstone)
1 Oct 1925 Harry Edward **Cockrell** (from Redditch)
18 June 1929 **A.H.Trinder** (from Cirencester)
25 May 1933 **J.Warrior** (from Deal, subsequently retired) "Old John"
1 June 1937 **S.D.W. Wigger** (from Pontefract and Castleford, subsequently retired)
2 Oct 1944 **H.R.Ottaway** (from Bromley and Beckenham, subsequently retired)
14 Feb 1948 **J.R.Henderson** (from Dingwall, subsequently retired to Scotland)
20 July 1959 **A.F.Davis** (from Falmouth, on to Maidstone as Head P.M.)
15 Apr 1962 **D.E.Middleton** (to Bournemouth on promotion)
Oct 1970 **W.G.Orton** (ex Sevenoaks Assistant Postmaster,subsequently retired)
June 1978-88 William **Clancy** (from Crowborough, subsequently retired)

Places visited in the quest for information:

Archives and Record Offices

Post Office Archives St Martins-le-Grand, now at Freeling House Glasshill Street
Public Record Office Chancery Lane and Kew
House of Lords Record Office
Kent County Archives Maidstone
East Sussex Record Office Lewes
British Library London
British Library Newspaper Division Colindale
Canterbury Cathedral Library
Lambeth Palace Library
Guildhall Library
Sevenoaks/Tonbridge Local Postal Records
Royal Air Force Museum Library Hendon
Bruce Castle Museum Tottenham Haringey Public Libraries
    which houses the W.V. Morton collection

Libraries – with Local Studies Sections

Kent County Libraries	Kemsing
	Maidstone
	Otford
	Sevenoaks
	Springfield Maidstone
	Tonbridge
	Tunbridge Wells
	Westerham
	Wrotham & Boro Green

Bromley Library

Gravesend Library

East Sussex County Libraries	Brighton
	Hastings
	Rye

London	Westminster City Library
	Holborn Public Library
	Borough of Camden Library

Museums – with reference material

At   Battle
      Hastings
      Maidstone
      Sevenoaks
      Tunbridge Wells
      Tyrwhitt-Drake Museum of Carriages, Maidstone

Post Office Establishments

Sevenoaks Sorting Office
Mechanised Letter Offices at Tonbridge, Dartford and Canterbury
Redhill and Reigate Parcel Sorting Office at Salfords

It is astonishing how diffuse is the information relating to local postal operations. My thanks are given to the staff at all these institutions who answered questions and helped me in my search for specific information, not forgetting the many individuals who search for and locate documents, early letters and photographs needed for research and still in private hands.

Prefatory Note

As far as possible each chapter is a vignette of its period and the spelling of the time is adhered to. An attempt is made to represent to the reader the ethos of that period.

Letter writing may often be careless or untutored or hurriedly written and so in a freer and less formal style than the Courthand of the scholar. Some of the major changes are listed here; these are not mistakes in printing, but adherence to contemporary spelling. Extracts and quotations from documents are in most cases in italics with the original spelling, both the spelling of the times and the occasional spelling error, both retained. In early letters Capitals are frequently used within a sentence to give emphasis to the item under discussion. In the few extracts from the Peover Papers superscript letters and nunnation marks in contractions are retained.

Typical of 1400s, 1500s

One of the few remaining Saxon alphabet letters to persist throughout Norman times was the double letter 'th' written as 'þ'; thus 'þe' for 'the' and 'oþer' for 'other'. In handwriting to distiguish this 'þ', from the ordinary 'p' it began to be rendered as 'y', thus 'ye' for 'the' which can be seen, for example, in manuscript in 1413. (see Bibliography). When printing started in the late 1400s, 'ye' for 'the' became well-established.

Nunnation marks, tildes, ∞ or ‿ over a word indicate that it has been abbreviated and some letters left out. The reader is not expected to have any difficulty in supplying them himself.

Early missives, although in English, may contain letters formed in a manner to which we are now unaccustomed. A good example is the emphasis on the now defunct downward loop of the letter 'h' making it look like a 'g', thus '_ℎ_' becomes '_ℓ_' and 'the' becomes '_ℯ_' when written quickly.

Typical of 1500s, 1600s

ff for F, eg fflymwell
F for V

qu for k, eg pacquet
ie for y, eg daie, verie, praie, chronologie
final 'e' omitted, eg. com
additional e at the end of a word, eg poste, bee, doe, Courte

y for i, eg guyde
addicon for addition (phonetic)

superscripts and abbreviations
y^s this   Ma^ts Majesty's
wch which   wth with
yor your

use of 'u' and 'v'
haue have   remoueing removing
vse use
numerals: last i as j eg iiij = 4

Typical of 1700s, early 1800s

u missed out eg Honor
c for s eg Expence
I for E eg Inquiry, Imploy.

The long looped s.
Often the first s of two together is written with long loops, top and bottom eg *pafs* ;
Often printed as an f which it is not, eg pass as pafs

Early £10 was written 10L

Typical of early 1900s

£ - s - d (Pounds, shillings and pence) used until 1971 when it became £ – p
12d = 1 shilling; 240 pence or 20 shillings to £1
1/- (one shilling) = 5p ; 6d = 2½p
To convert Old pence d to New pence p, divide by 2.4
A guinea is 21/- or £1-1-0 or 252 old pence

Changes in Place Name spellings

Eaton Bridge   Edenbridge

Tubbs Hill   Tubs Hill

Tonbridge, Tonbridge Wells ⎫
Tunbridge, Tunbridge Wells ⎭

Logically both should be spelt the same way with either 'o' or 'u' but the difference now used (Tonbridge, Tunbridge Wells) helps to distinguish between the two similar names. At times the spelling was the reverse of what now obtains. The last Post Office official change of spelling to 'TONBRIDGE' in February 1893 was on petition from the local Chamber of Trade, leaving the Wells spelt as 'TUNBRIDGE WELLS'.

Other alternative spellings for villages are shown in the Appendix.

Foreword

As the present Postmaster at Sevenoaks, I am particularly happy to have been invited to provide a Foreword to Archie Donald's book 'Posts of Sevenoaks on the road to Rye and Hastings'.

In writing about the history of written communication in the Sevenoaks district, his chosen area for detailed research, Mr Donald reveals the complexity of the arrangements involved over a span of more than nine hundred years, although it is only the last three hundred and fifty years that a national postal system has been available to the public. His work covers the whole of this period thus giving the reader a background to the birth of a public postal system in this area and relating the national policy to the Sevenoaks Postal District, an area that straddles the second most historically important road in Kent, that from London to Rye and, thereafter, to Hastings.

The author has spent years recording and accumulating material and detailed information for this well researched book.He has spent many hours in Post Office Archives,London, and local post offices checking and re-checking historical records. References have been conveniently placed at the end of the text enabling the story to flow without interruption; a format that should make the book of immediate use to the social and local historian and more easily read as a story by the general reader. The social historian and the postal history enthusiast will find much previously unpublished detail that reveals the origin of practices still in evidence today.

For me, personally, the timing of the writing of Archie Donald's book has particular significance, for I shall, in all probability, be the last person, of a total of thirty two, to hold the title 'Postmaster of Sevenoaks'. In the near future, following re-organisation within the Post Office, the position will be designated 'Area Delivery Manager', and 'Branch Manager' status will be conferred on officers in charge of Counters at Crown Offices. The title 'Postmaster, Sevenoaks' will disappear and become but a line in the history of the posts in Sevenoaks.

Post Office
South Park
Sevenoaks
Kent
TN13 1AA

William Clancy
Postmaster
1986

Post Office Archives

Posts of Sevenoaks

Author's Introduction

Historically Sevenoaks stands on the road to Rye, an important road used as a link to the Continent: and so this book starts with an introduction to the Rye Road, considering its importance as a Continental link, later turning to its internal importance.

As Otford and subsequently Sevenoaks develop, the scene shifts to the local area's (Westerham and Edenbridge to Wrotham) communications concentrating on the transmission of written messages on paper (or vellum), that is, **letters**, including packets and parcels. Mostly this is the story of the 'Royal Mail' but there are many other facets to the story and these are touched on also.

Foxall and Spafford in their book about the Post Office Surveyors 'Monarchs of all they Surveyed' mention the different postal systems that developed in early days and these may be classed as:

Institutional Posts	Ecclesiastical Administration and Universities. Cinque Ports	Travelling monks, friars and lay messengers attached to orders and dioceses. Cinque port and university messengers persisted after 1538 dissolution of monasteries.
The Kings Post	Royal and Court Messenger System, which develops into 'Royal Mail' the Post system for the General Public.	Couriers, Heralds, Pursuivants. And still retains King's Messengers under the Foreign Office, and the Defence Courier System for Classified mail.
Merchants Posts	Hanseatic League Merchant Strangers Posts Merchant Adventures Posts	Early Merchant Posts messenger systems surpressed; now become Courier Services and Road services.
Judicial system of Communication	for delivery of writs, summonses etc	Own messengers.

all of equal importance in their respective ways. For a time all of them persisted and mention is made in this book of the first three but not the last, for Sevenoaks was not a municipal borough and never became a large judicial centre.

It was The King's Post that finally predominated – The Royal Mail. 'The King' was different in kind in that he 'owned' the road and could make the laws, set up 'stations' and make overriding regulations as to how affairs were to be conducted.

The book is written mainly in historical sequence. Each chapter is bound in by its history to what comes before and what follows after, but an attempt is made to capture the ethos of each period, and to make each chapter a separate vignette representative of its era, retaining typical spelling. The chronology at the beginning of each chapter links national postal events with local ones and the dates of a few relevant well known national historical events are interwoven to relate to a familiar structure. Each chapter includes examples of letters typical of its period, the basic research material.

At the core of the work is information gleaned from Post Office Records and my thanks go first of all to Jean Farrugia, Archivist, who looks after these records and ever seeks to add to them; together with the staff of the Search Room. And then to Peter Swann and his staff at Sevenoaks Library for information held locally.

Great thanks are due and given to earlier researchers in this field. Jeremy Greenwood, T E Smith, Michael English, Brian Austen, John Dann, Brian Smith, Cliff Boas, Douglas Wilson, Maurice Porter and to Martin Willcocks, and whilst I do not always agree with their conclusions, and perchance neither do they with mine, their earlier references give a good lead in to the source material; not forgetting Michael Jackson who gave me the initial impetus to begin. Other contributors to the detailed office data are given at the start to the Appendix.

A considerable number of libraries and archives have been visited. Wherever possible references have been given, hopefully without overburdening the text. Many of the archive quotations are given at some length as it is hoped the work may be useful as a local source book. There is a historical list of postmasters and much detail has been relegated to an appendix which also gives a list of local post marks. These lists have been developed over the years from the author's own material and in conjunction with the Kent Postal History Group and the Sevenoaks Philatelic Society. Additional information and/or corrected data will at all times be gratefully recieved (through the pulisher).

Throughout, 'current prices' are given as at February 1987 when a new Retail Price Index was started at 100 and need to be lifted yet further to the year of reading.

The penultimate Chapter 8, 1920-1985/6 may appear of a different order to the others. Census material is not available after 1881 and much, though not all, of detailed Post Office archival material is subject to the thirty year rule and is not available for inspection.

As a member of the Kent Archaeological Society and the Sevenoaks Society the whole is offered as a contribution to the Social History of Sevenoaks and its surrounding district.

Archie Donald
Halstead, Kent
1987

Chapter I
AD 1085-1625 Messengers and Pursuivants

Chipstead Stage and the Route to Rye in the 1500's

Continental Couriers and Posts

Orders for Kent. Regulation of Movement

The King's Posts

An analysis of Organisation along a Road and Development toward a Public Postal System carrying Letters

Early Travellers Road Books

Ecclestiastical Organisation based on Otford and the Development of Knole and Sevenoaks Town – a flashback (1085-1550)

Monarchs	Henry VII	(1485-1509)
	Henry VIII	(1509-1547)
	Edward VI	(1547-1553)
	Jane	(1553)
	(Phillipp &) Mary	(1553-1558)
	Elizabeth	(1558-1603)
	James	(1603-1625)

Chronologie

AD

1085	Otford Manorial Postal Duties - carrying letters of the Archbishop.
1086	Domesday Book published at Winchester.
1218	Early Papal letter to Aaron re Chapel of St Nicholas Sevenoaks.
1323	Early Westerham letter.
1324	Edward II Writ to Warden of the Cinque Ports to search for letters. Further writ 1326.
1347	Calais taken by English, held till 1558. (Dover Route)
1348	Black Death.
1362	English becomes official language in Parliament and Law Courts.
c1370	Edward II (1350-90) has fixed stations for horses when message carrying.
c1370	William, later Sir William Sennocke, found under a tree.
1377	Patent. Search for letters being brought into England.
1415	Agincourt. Henry VIII.
1418	Sevenoaks School founded by William Sennocke.
1450	Jack Cade rebellion, Battle of Solefields.
1456	Knole. Major part built by Thomas Bouchier Archbishop of Canterbury.
1476	Printing commenced in England.
1482	Edward IV lays 20 mile interval posts to North for fresh horses.
1512	Tuke (Sir Brian) in charge of King's Posts.
1526	Post House in London fixed at the Windmill in Old Jewry. Start of City Post.
1533	Tuke's report on the organisation of the King's Posts.
1534	Act of Supremacy - Henry VIII
1536/40	Dissolution of the Monasteries. Knole handed over to Henry VIII
1541	Act for Debarring of Unlawful Games in Public (Cards, dice, tennis, bowls etc).
1550	Death of Henry VIII Somerset is Protector
	Grant of Manor of Sevenoaks. Power-shift from Otford to Sevenoaks.
1555	Ordnounce for Order of the Posts between London and Dover.
	First Passenger Coach built in England for Duke of Rutland.
	Incorporation of Carters, the first Friendly Society.
1570	Wm Lambarde wrote 'A Perambulation of Kent' England's first local historian.
1571	Queen Elizabeth commissions first State Coach.
	Italian merchants Posts along the Rye Road well established.
1573	Queen Elizabeth passes through Sevenoaks on her way to visit Rye.
1574	Decree of Rye Assembly to stop landing of immigrants, but not 'common posts and messengers'.
1576	Opening of first London Theatre.
1577-80	Drake sailed the world. 6.4.1580 Earthquakes (Richter 6.6) epicentre in Channel 20m east of Rye.
1582	Pope Gregory inaugurates the (New Style) Gregorian Calendar. England adopts it in 1752.
1584	'Orders for Posts in Kent', relating to travel on roads.
	Merchants Strangers Post officially suppressed (but went on till 1600 or so)
1584-1623app.	Merchant Adventurers Post.
1585	Shakespeare settles in London.
1588	Spanish Armada.
1589	Letter from Thomas Randolph Controller of HM's Posts to mayor of Rye re Standing Posts.
	Queen's fish stolen from Ripiers while in transit.
1593	Parliament establishes the Statute Mile.
1596	Symondson's Map of Kent - with roads marked.
1597	Standing Post. Thomas Miller chooses Rye-London.
1598	Hertzner's ride from Rye to London.
1600	East India Company founded.
1603	'Orders for Thorough Posts and Couriers' riding on King's affairs.
	Petition from Mayor and Jurats of Rye to Sir John Stanhope re Standing Post.
	Tunbridge Wells Spring discovered.
1605	Oath of Allegiance (3 Jacobi I). In 1609 extended to all professional people.
1611	Plantation of Ulster - English and Scottish colonialists went to Ireland.
1613	Complaints against Postmaster for sending foreign packets via Rye.
1620/21	Master of the Rolls. A liste of Stages & Rates of Wages. Rye not mentioned.

Chapter I

AD 1085 -1625
Messengers and Pursuivants

Sevenoaks is situated about a third of the distance along the London-Rye road and the history of its Posts until the coming of the railways into Kent in the middle of the nineteenth century is intimately bound up with developments along this road. The Rye road along the Kent/Sussex border was the second most important road in Kent after the London - Canterbury - Dover road, the third being the London - Wrotham - Maidstone - Hythe road.

Roads each have their characteristics based on the trade and people that pass along them and the places they serve. For better or worse, the Rye road became known as the Ripier road, carrying the flourishing trade of sea fish from the coast and letters to and from the Continent through the port of Rye past Sevenoaks to London. Rye was not one of the original Cinque ports like Hastings, but joined the confederation at the same time as Winchelsea, the group then being known as the Cinque Ports and Two Ancient Towns. Rye was attached to Hastings, one of the original five towns.[1] Under Henry II Rye became a full member of the Cinque Ports independent of Hastings and later on 1st August 1449 Rye annexed Tenterden with its port of Small Hythe.

Rye had much trade through Dieppe to France. Rye boats were small but effective in action as when in 1546 *'William Blakye and others of Rye Had goods from the hoye Pellican of Antwerp including xii bales of madder belonging to Jasper Loscorte'*.[2] The excuse of the Rye boatmen for this act of piracy was that they thought England was at war with Antwerp at the time, an excuse embarrassing to the authorities, because often we were. Later when the port at Rye finally silted up and became more or less unusable the emphasis of the latter third of the route switched at Flimwell to Hastings, which then became the more important route, the A21 of the present day.

The earlier way south from Sevenoaks was along the Holmesdale valley to Ightham, skirting the iron age Hill Fort at Oldbury, then a sharp turn south along the River Bourne via Fairlawn and Shipbourne to Tonbridge. This was the Roman trackway that went on to Mark Cross and Heathfield of to-day.

About the tenth century a trackway was cleared through deep forest from Sevenoaks down Riverhill to Tonbridge making a much shorter direct route and once this way was clear it began to be well used. Tradition has it that Harold Goodwinson used it on his way to meet the Normans at Senlac (Battle).[3] There was a growing traffic to Normandy even before the Conquest, using the Hastings - Harfleur route.

Chipstead Stage and the Route South in the 1500s

At first the main centre of activity on the Rye road was not in Sevenoaks at all, but at Chipstead (Chepstow) a village about 3 miles to the N.W. where there was a convenient ford across the River Darenth. There was as yet no Longford Bridge and the nearest bridge at Otford required far too great a detour for this road,

But the few inches depth of water at Chipstead was of little consequence to the passage of animals and ridden horses. Another important road came from Otford Palace up Sepham Hill, along Otford Lane past Halstead and down a holloway to join the Rye road at Pratts bottom, an important route of an earlier period when Otford was the ecclesiastical and administrative centre of the district, of which more later.

Importance of the Fish Trade

From Rye through Chepstow a fish trade requiring quick transit grew up. Whereas carp a fresh water fish can be kept alive when being carried, for up to ten days if kept in damp straw and fed with a little bread soaked in milk, seafish do not stay alive long once caught. The London fish trade demanded a quick movement up from the South Coast and the ripiers of Rye developed just this. One day's journey by packhorse from the coast to Chepstow; their packtrains of small horses with panniers strapped across their back dominated the roadscene. When necessary the fish could be salted for preservation at Salters Heath and Mackerals Plain on the south bank of the river. It was sold, if not already sold, to London buyers at The Red Lion, now Southdown House, at Bessels Green. Then taken by the purchasers across the Darenth ford to London, again as quickly as possible.

With such a well established quick daily run, there was a great temptation to use these tradesmen to carry official mail even if it did smell a bit fishy by the time it reached London. It was cheap, regular and quick for the times. There are no records of letters being stolen by the ripiers and so this method of transit was used, frequently, and in spite of regular instructions that such methods were not to be used.

The fish trade was not free of problems and all did not run smoothly all the time. The Ripiers themselves were perhaps not as tough as history has made them out to be, for on one occasion the Queen's Provisions were stolen from them en route, requiring a letter to be sent to the Justices of the Assyses in the County of Kent requiring them to examine '*such persons as they should think were likely to take from the Ripiers that brought fyshe for her Majestie's dyett and provisions soe manie dorsers of fyshe . . . as they were coming from Rye*'.[4] And the local people set out to confound the Queen's buyer who was '*verie badly served*' in that much of the catch at Rye was often sold surreptitiously to London buyers. Finally in 1594 a letter had to be sent to the Corporation of Rye stating that the market had to be held within an hour of the boat's arrival and that the Queen's Yeoman Purveyor had to be given first choice.[5] Other goods passed and repassed along the road. John Dowse a freeman who made white felt hats in Rye was in the habit of sending them to London to be dyed and then returned. It was claimed that he should have free (of duties) passage for them.[6]

At this time the road carried little or no wheeled traffic. There were few carriages or carts, travellers went on horseback. Pack animals were used to carry goods and oxen often used in conjunction with horses to give staying power to the big teams hauling heavy weights. In the Tonbridge area roads were greatly damaged by the dragging of trees for the local charcoal burning industry. Coaches did not start to develop until after 1590 when a new method of suspension 'above the wheels' was invented. Although traffic along the Rye road was to a considerable extent that of the Ripiers with their packtrains carrying fish and other goods it is known now that Italian merchants' imports were at times landed at Rye and carried overland to London and that also there was a considerable passage of couriers and messengers along the road.

Refugees and Business Couriers from the Continent

The early 1570s saw a great flux of refugees into Rye, so much so that the position was reached where the Mayor and Jurats had to state that all such persons called '*passengers*' in Rye and Dieppe '*shall orderly take their turns without enroaching one upon the other and each one shall stay until his turn comes*'. And on 15th February 1574 a decree of the Rye assembly made attempt to stop the flow of illegal immigrants, mainly protestant refugees from France and the Netherlands, '*nor suffer to be put on land any of the Frenche or Flemishe nation (except marchantes, gentlemen, <u>common postes and messengers</u>)*'.[7]

The underlining is the authors. This passage is important as it is the earliest official reference to be found to indicate that Continental Couriers were accustomed to using the Rye route to London. Actual

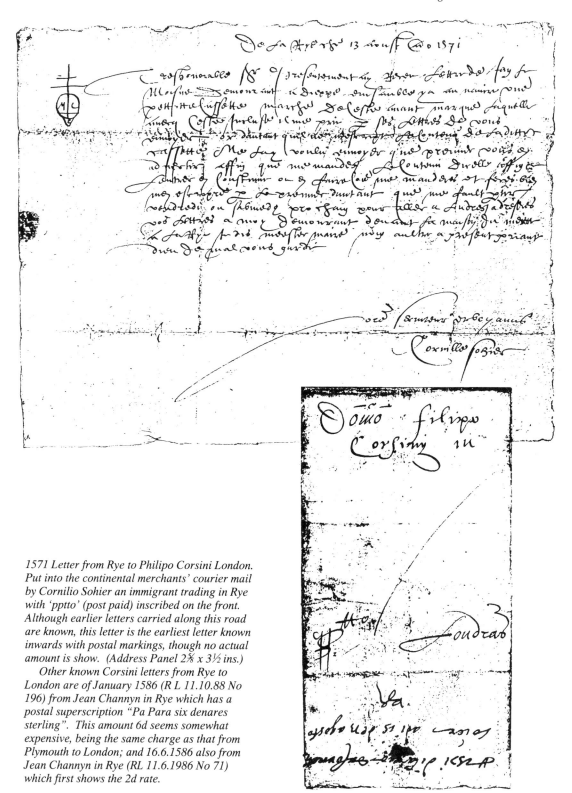

*1571 Letter from Rye to Philipo Corsini London.
Put into the continental merchants' courier mail
by Cornilio Sohier an immigrant trading in Rye
with 'pptto' (post paid) inscribed on the front.
Although earlier letters carried along this road
are known, this letter is the earliest letter known
inwards with postal markings, though no actual
amount is show. (Address Panel 2⅞ x 3½ ins.)*

*Other known Corsini letters from Rye to
London are of January 1586 (R L 11.10.88 No
196) from Jean Channyn in Rye which has a
postal superscription "Pa Para six denares
sterling". This amount 6d seems somewhat
expensive, being the same charge as that from
Plymouth to London; and 16.6.1586 also from
Jean Channyn in Rye (RL 11.6.1986 No 71)
which first shows the 2d rate.*

1571-1589 Examples of Continental transit mail along the Rye-Sevenoaks-London road with postal markings, from Lyons and Rouen, the capital of Normandy. (Address panels all 3 x 4 ins approx.)

To London via Rye and Chipstead in – (**a**) 1571. 34 days from Lyons 'pggto' Heirs of Gino Capponi to Fillipo Corsini. Thread still attached. (**b**) 1574. 35 days from Lyons 'pq' and 'd11' of Merchant Strangers Post in London. Niccolo Guilo Varenna and Cosse to F C. (**c**) 1575. 13 days from Lyons Guild mark Pier Antonia Bandini to F C. (**d**) 1575. 22 days from Lyons 'pqst7' and 'pin2' in second hand. Federello Spina to F C. (**e**) 1582. 30 days from Lyons Pailo Fr Manelli to Bartolomeo Corsini. (**f**) 1583. from Rouen 'Il porto p' with a '+' at top to B C. (**g**) 1585. from Lyons Luigi Capponi to B C. (**h**) 1588. 19 days from Lyons Lorenzo Ruberto Strozzi to B C. (**i**) 1589. 7 days from Rouen 'pptte' and 'd16½' of Merchant Strangers Post Hernandez de Miranda to B C. (**j**) 1579. from Rouen 'Il porto' to F C. A duplicate, in case the main letter miscarried. The two '2s' which disappeared under the flap when the letter was sealed were not postal markings but appeared to relate to the fact that it was a copy letter, a frequent procedure of the times.

letters with postal markings carried by these couriers along the Rye route through Chipstead to London exist from 1571 by which time their postal system was well established and had obviously been going for some years, probably decades. The 1571 letter referred to was sent by one Cornelius Sohier in Rye to London. He is a French Portestant refugee who set up in business as a merchant. By 1578 he was deemed an '*honest and creditable person*', but not before he had in 1573 tried to corner the market in candles to the disgust of the local townsfolk.[8]

By the 1580s the Italian merchants had a forwarding agent, Guillo Didsbury at Rye who later became Mayor of that Town. Commercial[9] letters that have recently become available show that in February 1583 he sent two cases from Rye to London by Richard Baker, the Ripier. Again in December the following year he had instructions that chest no. 14 arriving from Lyons via Dieppe and weighing 196 pounds Dieppe weight was to be sent '*par terre*' (overland) to Bartholomew Corsini a merchant in London. The previous year Didsbury was arranging to send a large chest by diligence but was thwarted in clearing the chest through customs as he had no list of the contents. Nevertheless this incident shows that there must have been some wheeled traffic on the road from Rye to London.

Italian Merchants had been established in London from the early 1400s. Henry VIII continued to encourage them and to allow them to use their own posts, the (Merchant) Strangers Post, with their own postmaster in London to link up with the postal and courier services of the continent; good communication being judged a necessary adjunct to international trade.

Merchant Strangers and Merchant Adventurers Posts

During the 1500s there was an efficient courier service linking the countries of the continent. On the inwards journey a merchant's courier might travel from the continent to London himself or possibly hand over his letters to the Merchant Strangers Post or, after 1584, the English Merchant Adventurers Post for the final lap to London. These two posts operated mainly, though by no means exclusively, from Dover. And if the courier landed at Rye and was not able to finish the journey himself he had the additional option to hand over the letters and packets to the ripiers.

There was also a messenger service from Rye itself to London and the names of messengers Solon Raisby, Tupper, Painter and John de Vigues are mentioned as travelling this road in the 1580s. Transit time was normally two to three days or longer when no unusual need for speed obtained, which appears to indicate that couriers were walking, although from a very early time posting houses were located at twenty mile intervals at Flimwell and Chipstead. These were the times when Drake was voyaging the world (1577-1580) and people had not yet learned to smoke.

English Couriers and Other State Matters

As well as Continental Business Couriers, the English Posts carrying H.M. Paquet and other State letters were from early times accustomed to using the Dieppe-Rye route to London as well as the more official but longer Dover route. In spite of regular exhortations not to use it, the Rye Road appeared to provide a needed second route of entry and is frequently mentioned from the mid-1500s until the port silted up. John Collard goes as far as to claim that '*Rye was selected as the transit port for the Royal Mail of Queen Elizabeth's Government*'.

Queen Elizabeth visited Rye for three days in 1573 passing through Sevenoaks on her way there. Her inclination was to dine at midday at the place where she was staying, then travel on and arrive to supper at the next place to be visited. Travelling from Orpington she arrived at Knole on Friday 24th July to supper leaving after dinner on Wednesday 29th July 1573 to supper at Birling, Lord Abergavenny's seat. And so through Northiam to arrive in Rye 11th August 1573. Staying three days she returned to Greenwich through Dover and Canterbury. In Rye she was presented with a purse containing one hundred pounds.[10]

In 1579 an English post, John le Roye carrying her Majesty's packet had an untoward experience after which he and various merchants came before the Mayor and Jurats to declare that on the previous day, August 18th thirty or forty Englishmen in a flyboat near the Ness by Rye boarded '*the passage wherein the merchants and post came from dieppe and spoiled them of their apparel and goods*'. But what was

'PRIVATE'. Gate across North end of the Early road through Chevening to London used in the 1500s, 1600s and part 1700s . (AGD)

happening to the Queen's Packet meanwhile? Had it been dropped overboard as were the instructions if attacked by foreigners? But these attackers were English. Had it been passed on to another messenger to avoid delay while evidence was being taken? Or had it simply been held up a day or so as seems likely? The records, however, are silent on the matter.[11]

Route North of Chipstead

Northwards the route from Chipstead to London went straight up over the North Downs rise following what today is now a footpath. According to the 1596 map of Symonds the road went to the west of the church past where now is Chevening House, along a road now closed since 1785 and up to Knockholt Pound emerging at The Three Horse Shoes. The footpath beside this old road is still open.

Another path up lies further to the east, next to the present Star Hill road. At first this path runs in the open then enters a wooded holloway to the top of the Downs. Once almost at the top the old way can be followed no more for the Fort at Halstead has recently acquired and enclosed this land and the way has been diverted.

At times, such as on Bromley Common, the road might broaden out and take several parallel paths depending on the state of the surface.

The Two Post Roads A few miles outside London at New Cross the Sevenoaks-Rye road branches off the London-Dover road. London-Dover was the 'official' route to the continent and there is no doubt that London-Dover-Calais was the senior route, well established during the first part of the 16th Century when

England still held Calais. It was the subject of a controlling Ordinance c1555 signed by '*King Phillipp and Quene Mary designating Poste Towns for Couriers and those riding post*'. This route has the shorter sea crossing to France,

	Land		Sea		Land				Total
London	72	Dover	19	Calais	179	Paris	251+19 =		270 miles via Amiens
London	63	Rye	60	Dieppe	109	Paris	172+60 =		232 miles

but runs to the 'expensive' port of Calais. Expensive in regard to port duties. Also the land part of the route is longer and land travel is more expensive.

The Rye road never attained the official status of the Dover route and indeed at one time Henry VII decreed that the Rye road was not to be used. Nevertheless it provided an alternative and probably much cheaper route to the continent. It was a very useful route opening into Rouen the then capital of Normandy, Paris the capital of France, Lyons and into Spain, Portugal and parts of Northern Italy. Rye was an important port and required[12] fortification against raiders. One of the earliest English letters along this route dated 25 May 1549 (but without postal markings) was from the Mayor of Rye to Somerset, Protector of the Boy King Edward VI detailing the scarcity of timber occasioned by its use as charcoal for the iron mills and requesting permission to use mortar and stone of Camber Castle for their (Rye's) fortification.

Much traffic, both persons and letters, passed along the Rye road, not all being in the best interests of the King of England. Indeed in 1524 a writ had been sent to the Warden of the Cinque ports requesting him to stop and search persons coming from abroad and '*to stop letters with sinister intention*'. Thus even in these early days postal censorship[13] was seen as a necessary fact of life, and postal emphasis is always on communication with the Continent not with the needs of the Towns through which the Road passes on its way to Rye.

Orders for Kent. Regulation of Movement

A proclamation in 1584, *Orders for Posts in Kent*[14] required that in Kent '*all strangers of what nation soever either coming into this Realme or going out . . . shall take their horses from stage to stage at the hands of the standing posts onely*', which meant that their particulars would be entered in the Posts Ledger; but this was not to infringe an Englishman's right to ride as he could, provided that '*they ride not with horne nor guide which markes are onely reserved for the Posts to use or allow of, for the more safetie in ryding, and better expedition*'. These 'Orders for Kent' proclaimed by Elizabeth I just four years before the Spanish Armarda came in 1588, were agreed upon by Sir William Brooke and others of the Cinque ports. By them '*Each Post . . . shall have always in his stable, or in readiness sixe good and sufficient Post Horses at the least . . . whereof two to serve for the packet, the rest to be ready at all occasions for such as either in her Maiesties affaires, or otherwise, for more speed shall run the Post*'. Not only postal censorship but some effort to control the movement of foreigners including the merchants' couriers is evident. This is Kent, the gateway to England, at a time when some sort of invasion from the Continent was felt to be quite likely.

Orders then proceeded to enumerate in some detail how these transport arrangements for both the King's mail and for personal transport were to be organised with the horses for messengers carrying the (King's) packet being expected to proceed at seven miles in the hour in summer, five miles an hour in winter '*more or lesse as the way shall fall out*'. Orders concluded with the admonition that if, in Kent, any Hackney-men, Ostlers, Capsters or others having horses to hire shall do so either to Englishmen or Strangers without the knowledge and agreement of the Standing Post that the Justice of the Peace shall commit the same person offending to prison, there to abide '*until he provide to the Post of the place a surety for observing the Orders*'.

Paul Hentzner, a travelling tutor to a young German nobleman, sets the contemporary scene in succinct manner at the start of his book 'A Journey into England' 1598:

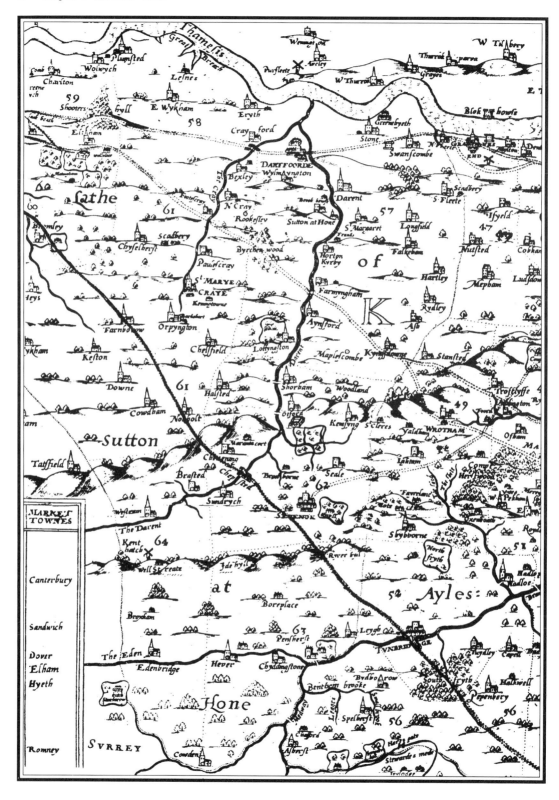

We arrived at Rye, a small English sea-port. Here, as soon as we came on shore, we gave in our names to the Notary of the place, but not till he had demanded our business; and being answered That we had none but to see England; we were conducted to an inn, where we were very well entertained; as one generally is in this country.

We took post horses for London: it is surprizing how swiftly they run, their bridles are very light and their saddles little more than a span over.

Flimwell, a village; here we returned our first horses and mounted fresh ones. We passed through Tunbridge, another village. Chepsted, another village; here for the second time we changed horses . . . London, the head and metropolis of England . . . On the south is a bridge of stone 800 feet in length . . . The whole is covered on each side with houses, so disposed as to have the appearance of a continued street, not at all of a bridge.

At 2d per mile for 65 miles plus half the guide 4d for each of three stages each traveller's single journey to London would have cost him 136d or 11s/4d and with an inflation factor of x 73 this amounts to £42 in 1987 money. More than going in a car or coach now-a-days, but it could well cost as much if attempting the journey on horseback.

Royal Messengers The early English posts were organised primarily for reasons of the King's messages and state business. Henry VIII saw the need for such organisation and the need for speedy transit. There are Treasury Warrants in existance for Royal Messengers to Kent and Sussex from 1516 onwards and the Wardrobe Accounts have payments at even earlier dates. The King's Posts were expensive to organise and to keep in full-scale operation, requiring numbers of horses to be '*at the ready*' at all times, day and night. The King's Posts were not at first organised for the benefit of local people. Hire of horses and messengers had to be paid for out of the King's personal estates or with customs duties, there being no parliament as yet to help the Government arrange its needs through taxation of the country's subjects.

And so we find the King's Posts running spasmodically. Even so, the messengers tended to remain unpaid for years at a time. There was a report of their unhappy situation in 1582 and in 1590 there is an actual reference to the payment of the London-Rye Posts

Calender of State Papers Domestic 1582 p83

Certificate of the state of the Posts in Kent remaining unpaid for want of money. Addressed to Walsingham with a request for payment. The charge for the posts amounts only to 300L (£28,000) for the whole realm.

CSPD 11th May 1590

Warrant to pay Thos. Randolph Master of the Posts the surplusage of 143 L.10s.4d (£12,000) for wages of the Posts between London and Rye with a yearly allowance of 1,250L (£103,750) for discharge of the Ordinary payments incident to the same office (Docquet).

The King's Posts

Paul Hentzner and his tutor, it may be noticed, followed in 1598 the laid down procedure for travelling the Rye Road. Being a road leading to a foreign port, the system was being tightened up at this time when danger from overseas was felt to be imminent. There had been the Orders of 1584 and a further proclamation to tighten things up in 1591. The Post Stages of Flimwell and Chipstead were by now well established and no doubt had been for some decades.

Post Stages As early as the latter part of the thirteenth century in the reign of Edward I fixed stations had been established at which horses were kept for hire and in 1482 when Edward IV was at war with Scotland

---

Opposite. 1586. Part of Philip Symondson's map of Kent showing the Road to Rye through Chipstead and to the south west of Sevenoaks. This is the earliest map with roads well marked.

he laid a special post to the North with stages every twenty miles rather than at the 'full days journey' apart of Roman Times. At the standard pace of six miles an hour, twenty miles represented about three and a half hours riding time perhaps a little less if the going was dry, but unless there were exceptional circumstances, galloping was not allowed. After Tuke had been put in charge of the King's Posts, the City of London Post Station for the King's Post had been established in 1526 at the Windmill in Old Jewry.[14] Innkeepers were to maintain there four horses always ready, the hackneymen another four making eight ready at all times.

In 1533, Sir Brian Tuke made an important report on the working of the posts and included a statement that the posts henceforth were to serve the convenience of travellers as well as to provide for the King's packet as '*there is no such usual conveyance in post for men in this realm as in the accustomed places of France and other parts*'.

Neither Chipstead nor Flimwell as might be expected was a town but two places at twenty mile intervals in a road of sixty or so miles, both stages located in villages where horses could conveniently be kept. No doubt the foreign post couriers when riding followed the same pattern as Hentzner when travelling the road, indeed they were expected to do so, though English messengers could well make their own arrangements if they turned out to be cheaper, providing the official Post knew what was going on.

Lack of Payment for Posts Even if unpaid the posts were kept busy. It is argued by some that the King's Posts tolerated this delay in payment because they were engaged in private mail carrying for profit. Articles drawn up by Randolph in 1584 show that there were so many private letters being delivered by the standing posts at this period as to interfere with the packet. Apparently the Posts were allowed as a perquisite to keep their fees for bye-letters, ie those letters originating and being delivered along their route and not touching London where the accounting took place, as long as the King's packet was delivered first. As the Posts official pay in the early 1600s fell steadily into arrears they came more and more to depend on money received from the general and business public for handling their letters, though ordinary folk would normally send messages and letters by members of their own household, friends or failing that by the carrier, though few carrier's letters have survived. The illustration shows a letter of 1597 from a member of the public that could well have been carried by such an unpaid Royal post.

Standing Posts

When there was a national need in a specific area, a greater state of readiness was called for, standing posts. A Standing Post meant that both men and horses were waiting on standby, ready to depart at a moment's notice, an expensive arrangement that would revert to the normal situation as soon as possible, a messenger and horse taken from their normal occupation occasioning a delay of half an hour or so. Standing Posts were laid on the Rye road in 1589 and 1597, but strangely not in 1588 when the Spanish Armada made its appearance.

In 1589 on the slaughter of the French King, Thomas Randolph Master and Controller of Her Majesty's Posts wrote from Maidstone to Mr Gaymer, Mayor of Rye,

"*Her Majesties pleasure is that for better expedition of such lettres as come to her Majestie's self or her Hignes Council out of France, post horses should be layde from your towne to London in places most convenient, and to that effecte hathe given me express commaundement to sea performed with all speede. Wherefore I praie you, Mr Maior of Rye, to make this choice in your towne of the most sufficient man either keapeth me an inne or comonlie servethe suche of horses as ordinarilie arrive out of Fraunce, and in her Majesty's name to require him to furnishe himself of thre [3] sufficient and hable post horses at the leste to carry her Majesty's lettres or such as to come from her Councell, so ofta as ether her Majestie herself or either of them please to send. And for that they shall knowe that this their service shall not be unconsidered, her Hygness is content to allow unto eyther of them 20d (£7) per diem from the daye of their placcing, duringe that service to be receaved quarterlie at my handes or so sone as I can have warrant for the same without faill. And to the intent they shall be the better hable to do her Majesty's service, they shall be allowed of everie man that rideth in poste 2d (70p) the mile for eche horse that he rideth with,*"

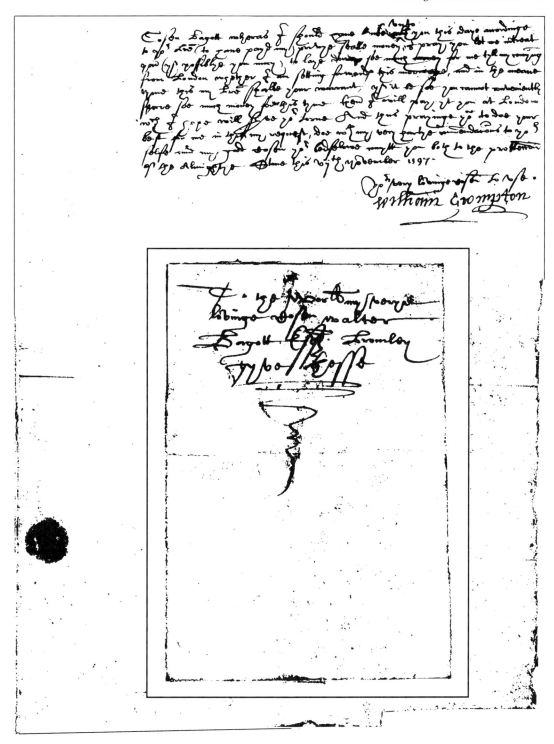

1597. English style Elizabethan Letter London to Bromley, addressed 'To the worthy my very lovinge cosen Walter Bagott Esq Bromley. Give thess'. (Address panel full size.)

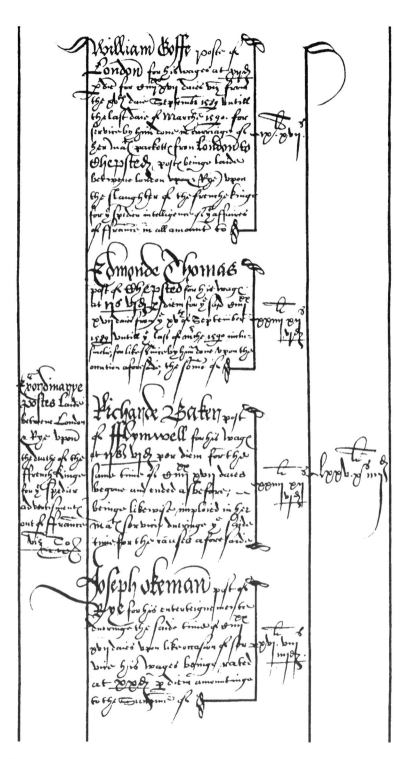

1589. *Post Office Declared Accounts. Audit Rolls for the Standing Post to Rye showing the charges for each post town, London, Chipstead, Flimwell and Rye, also total charge. (P.R.O. Kew. Ref. 17)*

and 4d (£1.40) for the guyde.

 This her Mast. serive beinge made known unto you, I doubt not but you will see performed accordinglie, for which purpose I have sent unto you this Bearer my servant to knowe the partie under your hande whome you name and what further you do this in. Not doubting of your diligence and care, I commit you to God at Maydston the 13th of September 1589.

 Your verie Lovinge Frende
 Tho. Randolph Mr and Con
 trowler of her Majestes Postes
Mr Gaynor I praye you gvye
your assistance herein.
Maior of Rye" [15]

This is the same Mr Gaymer, Mayor, who had in 1573 lent the Town the £100, £9,500 in to-day's money, to present to Queen Elizabeth on her visit on 11th August. He had received the money back on the 21st September as soon as the Town had received in the cess payments due then.

Good use of Standing Post in 1589

At this period many State letters ran through Dieppe to Rye and so to London. For example, taking a random sample, the Calendar of State Papers shows that a packet of letters was sent by this route during 1589 on August 16, 25, 26, 31, September 5, 10, 11, 14, 15, 20, 21, 26, 29, October 1, 4, 10, 14, 18, 21, 26, 31 and so on in the same quantities until 4th March 1590 the full eight month period previously mentioned. One letter of 29th May 1588 to Lord Seymour in London from the Mayor of Rye recounted that two pinnances off the French coast had intercepted Her Majesties packets between Rye and Dieppe and had taken one boat with passengers and the packet of mail. As has been previously mentioned, when there was likelihood of such an event occuring normal practice was to throw the mail overboard and sink it, though in at least one case in later years this only resulted in the mail being washed ashore, happily on a friendly beach.[16]

Standing Post Accouunts

The Accounting for the 1589 standing post provides the names of the postmasters along the Rye Road; Edmond Thomas at Chipstead, Richard Baker for fflymwell and John Okeman at Rye.[17] This standing post lasted eight months and subsequently there was a warrant of 11 May 1590 to pay wages of the posts between London and Rye.[18]

London to Rye Standing Post

From 15 September 1589 to last daie of March 1590. 197 daies.

L		s	d		£. s. d
ix	li[vres]	xvii s	- d	William Goffe post of London	9.17. -
xxiiii	li	xii s	vi d	Edmonde Thomas Post of Chepsted (197 daies at 2s/6d)	24.12.6
xxiiii	li	xii s	vi d	Richard Baker post of fflymwell	24.12.6
xvi	li	viii s	iiii d	Joseph Okeman post of Rye	16. 8.4
lxxv	li	x s	iiii d		75.10.4 [£6,430]

Richard Baker   There is little doubt that '*Richard Baker the post of fflymwell*' in 1589 is the same man as '*Richard Baker le rippier*' and '*Baker the waterman*' of the 1584/6 period previously mentioned as carrying Corsini letters and goods. The fact that he was accepted as a standing post by the Government in times of emergency tends to the view that he was not just a foot mesenger but, firstly that he had access to horses and secondly that probably he was a man of some standing in the transport and courier industry.

Of the Standing Posts laid along the Rye Road only that of 1589 is shown in the Pipe Rolls covering the Declared Accounts of the Post Office AD 1566-1637. This is not to say that other standing posts were not set up and their expenses treated in some other way, but their accounting has not yet been traced and may be subsumed under some other heading.

Standing Post of 1597   Again in 1597 Thomas Miller was required to carry out the same task. He chose Rye as a possible landing place with its connection past Sevenoaks to London.

1597. Thomas Miller, gent. sent in haste by special commandment of Sir Francis Walsingham throughout all the postes of Kent to warn and to order, both with the posts for an augmentation of the ordinary number of horses for the packet and with the countries* near them for a supply of twenty or thirty horses apiece for the 'through posts' during the service against the Spanish navy by sea and the continuance of the army by land.[19]

[* Right up to c1700 it was customary to refer to a county or even a smaller district as a man's 'country'.] and again

Extraordinary posts laid between London and Rye upon unwelcome news arriving from France and for more speedy advertisement of the same. Thomas Miller gent. sent at Easter 1597 to lay the posts and likest landing places either in Kent or Sussex upon intelligence given of some practices intended against the Queen's person. Judged Rye to be the likest landing place and on returning received £7 (£525) for his services.[20]

About this time one William Berdsworth who came from Sevenoaks and who had the Angel Inn at Milton was made Postmaster (1600-1608) of Gravesend.[21]

Use of the Rye Road for State letters begins to decline.

In 1603 July 9th the Mayor and Jurats of Rye petition Sir John Stanhope of his Majesty's Privy Council,

Whereas in times past the packets have usually been thought fit to be sent to this town as the nearest place of recourse for the service of the State, both by sea and land, until of late years the packets being sent by other ways the continuance thereof hath drawn with it from this poore town the postage and recourse of merchants and others travelling to the sea coast, the occasion whereof we can find to be and to have so long continued, by no other means but by the abuse of the rippiers, who finding the authority which the packet requires to be drawn other ways, have for their own particlar gain so exhausted upon all passengers that none at all have desired to come this way. Therefore for reformation thereof we pray that it would please you to erect a postage here and recommend unto you the bearer hereof, Jeames Apleton, to be the postmaster. Signed by Wm. Appleton.[22]

Their situation in Rye was becoming desperate with the silting up of the port and some measures were needed, particularly to make the post official. This move however seemed unproductive, perchance because the recomandee bore the same surname as the mayor, for Rye was not mentioned in the list of Post Towns of 1616. Nevertheless matters proceeded on an unofficial basis, and because of its organisation for quick movement, the road through Sevenoaks to Rye *was* used again and often state letters were still given to the Ripiers to carry to Rye and through their opposite numbers on to Rouen and Paris. In 1613 and even as late as 1638 at the time when Witherings was finally getting control of the inland post, the King was endeavouring to stop the Rye road's use, not because the organisation was indifferent, but because the French twitted him saying that his state letters were being carried by fishermen, as indeed they were even (in 1613) on the corresponding Dieppe-Paris stage of the route.

An Analysis of Organisation along a Road and its Development towards a Public Postal System carrying Letters

In early references the word '**post**' normally refers to 'travelling post', that is, a person riding along a road on posthorses obtained at the set stage points from the Post who organises the availability of horses and their maintenance, as distinct from someone using his own horse to travel the road. 'The Post' also referred to this person, usually an innkeeper, who officially looked after the stagepost and the provision of horses.

The word '**pacquet or packet**' is used to describe the bundle of letters that may be carried by either a special messenger or a regular rider. Sometimes a person might be both 'riding post' and 'carrying the packet'. So in course of time the word '*post*' comes to refer both to the person riding and eventually to the bundle of letters he carries.

Few people would travel for pleasure; it would be because some business had to be done and, whether it be by a written message in a letter or a person who on arrival speaks his message, 'information' travelled along a road on horseback. Apart from a rudimentary system of bonfire signals, beacons, to alert the country to invasion, there was no quicker way across the land. No semaphore, no telegraph nor telephone, no railways nor aeroplanes, few wheeled vehicles and the roads themselves were hardly able to support wheeled vehicles such as there were for in places the word 'road' was a courtesy title for a rutted muddy track full of deep holes. The horse reigned supreme.

Hackneymen were those who let out horses (later drive vehicles) to persons for their own conveyance along a road. To some extent they were controlled; even as early as the 1300s the prices per mile, or in the case of the Dover road per stage, being fixed.

Setting up a post entailed making arrangements for the availability of horses and ensuring their maintenance at set points along the route. Failing their availability at the posthouse it might be necessary to commandeer the nearest available horses by warrant. The stages might be permanent or merely temporary whilst an emergency existed. As to the rider, he might be a special messenger changing horses and travelling the whole distance or a 'stage' rider who might be on call when required and paid piece wages, or 'in post' and fully paid. In any case setting up a post was an expensive business.

A posthorse might be used simply to convey a person, or to convey a person carrying a pacquet (of letters), in which case it was the pacquet that became important, not the rider. Arrangements for the carrying of mail by the Posts went through several stages of development: each development stage might with hindsight seem an obvious development of the previous situation, but at the time the alterations that were achieved were the product of great effort and thought, particularly that from mode 4 to mode 5, a mode of working developed along the Bath road and subsequently taken up by Witherings who although at first in charge of foreign mail, later adapted this method throughout the inland service.

Mode 1

Post stages are set up on a Road, but no horses are kept immediately available. A through rider with a pacquet (of letters) picks up a horse at one stage and leaves it at the next. Horses are requitioned locally as required on a warrant at the King's price, an uneconomic rate so horses will often be hidden. The need for stages at which to exchange horses positioned at 20 mile (or less) intervals is because horses when ridden quickly soon tire and, if not changed, will, over long distances probably proceed more slowly than a trained footrunner. Pursuivants, through riders on state business, were experienced men who knew their rights demanding the '*hable and sufficient*' horses with which the law required the local inhabitants to provide them. Often they rode furiously and as often the local inhabitants felt their horses were misused, claiming compensation for damage to them.

Mode 2

Arrangements made to pay for some horses to be specifically kept available at the Post House. These would be used to satisfy demand. But requirements often came in sudden bursts of activity. If more horses were needed the keeper of the Post House would have to divert all his own horses from other work and this at the King's price, so the arrangement could still be unpopular, though less so than mode 1 above.

Mode 3

Riders also Guides available at the Post. The local rider knows his ground and knows his horse. He rides only over his own stage, handing on the pacquet to the next rider. Many high state officials considered it a lack of dignity to have the pacquet pass thus through so many different hands and not to be delivered personally by a single trusted messenger.

The local rider might be paid per pacquet carried or be '*in post*' at a weekly wage. Mounted guides with their horses and horns had also to be available to accompany persons who hired posthorses to travel from stage to stage and those who travelled on a warrant. The guide carried the luggage, knew the road, blew his horn to clear the way and brought back spare horses to their original starting point. All the above could be very costly, and so we find,

Mode 4

The Rider being allowed to carry private mail along with the official pacquet, but only to do so when the pacquet has to be taken. As the pacquet runs irregularly there is no knowing when private mail can go forward. So merchants and others still use carriers (very slow) or friends riding post or their own private messengers or sometimes employed municipal messengers (bodas) and the aforementioned Ripiers. At this time speeds of proceeding by horse were controlled but there was no letter-carrying monopoly before 1591 when Elizabeth proclaimed a monopoly of all mail to and from foreign ports. Once '*the Post*' employed servants to carry mail rather than doing the riding himself, he became a Post-master.

Mode 5

The great change. With Riders available, the new idea was to run the packet regularly for public mail and to take the Kings and the State Official mail as well whenever required. Public mail charges would pay the whole cost, instead of the service being a drain on the King's revenue. Once introduced it was not long before a profit was being made as well. With regularity and a speedy service being assured much, but by no means all, public mail switched to this Government Service. This change is the story of the next century.

Travellers Road Books

Early road books begin to record this road; Richard Grafton's booklet whilst only mentioning the Dover Road in his 1544 edition, shows in his 1571 edition of '*a little treatise conteyning many proper tables and rules*':

> *From Rye to London*
> From Rye to Plymwell (Flimwell) xv m   [15]
> From Plymwell to Tonbridge xi   [11]
> From Tonbridge to Chepstowe vii   [7]
> From Chepstowe to London xv   [15]
>   [48]

The '*Post*' a handbook for travellers by Richard Rowlands published in 1576 by Thomas East lists the Rye Road as,

'*From London to Rie . . . Chepstowe 15, Tonbridge 15, Plimwell 11, Rie 15. The Summe of myles 48.*'

Something is wrong with the summation which should be 56, though the present distance is 61 miles. It is more likely that the figures were copied incorrectly.

At this time there was no standard mile; it was not until 1593 that Parliament established the Statute Mile and as late at 1696 Morden's map of Kent shows three scales of miles: Great miles, Middle miles, small miles. The small mile is about 85% of the great mile.

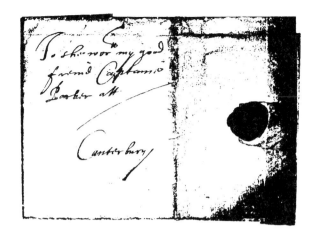

1623. *King James I. Letter from Evan Edwardes of the Earl of Dorset at Knoll, Sevenoaks, to Capt Parker at Canterbury requesting a warrant. Capt Parker was musket master of the Cinque Ports. Matthew Parker's house was at Canterbury but he was often away.*
(Address panel 2⅓ x 3 ins.)

The technique of measuring along the ground with a wheel had not yet developed; most mileages given in early lists are 'computed miles' which in most cases give an underestimate of the true distance in our statute miles.

Sevenoaks, Seven Oaks, Seven oke, Sennocke, Senoke, Sevnok, Sunnock, 7 Oakes

Now to the town of Sevenoaks itself.

The spelling of the town name varied greatly and the old spelling Sennocke or Senoke was always considered viable. Indeed in later years when the Inspector of Franks rejected items from the Bishop of London so superscribed, he was told off in no uncertain manner.

'Mr Stow begs the Presidents will inform the Inspector of Franks that Franks dated 'Senoke' from Seven Oaks are to pass free and that particular attention must be paid to those from the Bishop of London upon the charging of whose franks Mr Freeling wishes to see Mr Briggs early in the morning.' [23]

William Lambarde whose family was later resident in Sevenoaks at Sevenoaks Park and at Beechmont the house overlooking the escarpment by Riverhill and the then main feature when approaching the town from the South, writing in 1570 says of Sevenoaks in 'A Perambulation of Kent' [24]

The present estate of the Towne it selfe is good, and it seemeth to have been (for these many years together) in no woorse plight: And yet finde I not in all historie, any memorable thing concerning it . . . save only Jack Cade and his men in the time of Henry VI (1449) discomforted two Noble Gentlemen sent by the king to encounter them. [25]

and as to local districts (*parishes, townes and boroughes*) some idea of their comparative importance can be gained from the amount levied '*against eche of them . . . in the name of a tenth, and fifteenth . . .*'.

So from the same work the districts that relate to the present Sevenoaks postal district have been taken and put into order of fiscal magnitude,

Wrotham	*£ 10. 3. 4*	*Otteforde*	*£ 1. 2. 2*
Sevenocke	*4.15. 0*	*Rydley*	*17. 0*
Ashe	*3.19. 2½*	*Nokeholte*	*15. 0*
Towne of Shoreham	*3.18. 0*	*Halstead*	*14. 4*
Iteham	*3. 5. 3½*	*Sundridg*	*10. 8*
Seal	*2.19. 0*	*and for comparison*	
Kingsdowne	*2. 1. 3*	*Bromley*	*£ 8. 0. 0*
Westram	*2. 1. 2*	*Beckenham*	*5.19. 6*
Cheveninge	*1.19. 8*	*Orpington*	*4.13.10*
Kemsynge	*1. 9.10*	*Chellesfield*	*3. 6. 8*
Brasted Towne	*1. 7. 5½*	*Farneburghe*	*2. 5. 0*
Eatonbridge	*1. 4. 0*		

thus demonstrating the greater importance of the landed areas compared with the town itself.

The town was basically a centre of an agricultural area as indeed were many towns of the period. To the south there was still considerable tree felling and burning for charcoal required by the Tonbridge ironmasters and dragging heavy tree trunks did little to improve the state of the minor roads, at times virtually cutting off Penshurst.

Sevenoaks as a Town had by now, 1600, emerged from the earlier ecclesiastical organisation of Otford Palace with Knoll and to the south Penshurst.

A flashback . . .

Ecclesiastical Organisation based on Otford – *a flashback*

The other important route near Sevenoaks mentioned earlier is that from Otford Palace to London. In this much earlier period there were no posts provided for the general public, not so many persons were fully literate.

But as well as the King's need for messengers on State business there was also much need for the passing of messages for the purpose of regional administration and estate management.

In 791 AD Offa, King of Mercia, having fifteen years previously fought and beaten the King of Kent, granted the Manor of Otford (Shoreham to Tonbridge including Sevenoaks) to Christ Church Canterbury and so the manor came under the Archbishop of Canterbury.

Prior to the dissolution of the monasteries in 1536/40 under Henry VIII regional administration was to a considerable extent in church hands. In what is now the Sevenoaks area, this meant the see of Canterbury with the local centres of Penshurst and Otford/Knoll. Land tenure was dealt with through this administration.

Postal services a manorial duty. In 1085 the Manor of Otford covered Otford (Otta's Ford), Dunton (Dunna's Town), Shoreham (Ham by a steep slope), Sevenoaks, Sevenoaks Weald, Halstead, Chevening, Woodlands, Penshurst, except the last two all names that will recur when we consider Sevenoaks rural posts. The manor held some six to eight hundred people made up of villagers, smallholders, cottagers and slaves and was let out to farm, meaning it was controlled economically and in practice by a farmer who paid money dues for so doing, but who also had other manorial duties to perform in addition. Sir John Dunlop quoting from the *Custumole of Otford* refers to one of the carrying duties as that of carrying the Letters of the Lord Archbishop or his Steward and Clarke and Stoyel quoting from the same source list the manorial services required as the supply of food and fuel, money dues, carrying services, police and **postal duties**,[26] the last two of great importance to the Archbishop, this relating to 1284 but having been customary since 1100. An early example of a foreign letter of 1218 was the Papal letter (Bull) of Pope Honorius III sent in confirmation to Master Aaron, clerk, Chaplain of the Chapel of St Nicholas Sevenoaks.[27]

Edward I's Wardrobe account of 1299/1300 lists payments to Royal Messengers and Nuncio's, among them

'Garcionibus Dominorum Ri de Hastings et fratris sui 0.13.4' [28]

Early reference to Knole The first reference to Knole is found, 1281, in the Lambeth Palace documents, and a listing of the Archibishp's lands which later are to be met as the Sevenoaks Postal District are found written in Latin in AD 1316. This was just before English became the official language of Parliament and the Law Courts in 1362, though the changeover from Latin was not direct and during this period many of the Acts, eg one of the Sumptuary Acts controlling luxury in dress, are found written in French.

AD 1316

Hundredum de Westerham. *Archiepiscopus Cantuariensis et Abbas Westmonasterii sunt domini*
Villa de Westerham – Abbas Westmonasterii
Villata de Bradestede – Comes Gloucestrie
Hundredum de Coddeshethe. *Archiepiscopus est dominus*
Ville Otteford, Schoram   )
*   Sevenoke, Halstead   )   – Archipiscopus*
*   Chyvening, Sunderesshe)   Willelmus de Grandisono* [29]
*   Sele, Kemesinge   )*

Contact was maintained between Otford/Knoll and Penshurst with Canterbury and with London, the volume of message (postal) traffic and writs passing depending on where the King or the Archbishop was staying at the time. In 1348 for example, the time of the black death, the See of Canterbury being vacant, the King, Edward III, spent Christmas at Otford creating great activity there.

Early Letters. Ecclesiastical and Royal

Of this early period there are, luckily, many examples held in Canterbury Cathedral Archives.[30] These are the '*Christ Church Letters*' with many examples of the AD 1320 period, in particular one to this area concerning Westerham church and its transfer together with its chapel of Edenbridge from Rochester to Canterbury. The Letters are pasted into three large books and of the many letters these books contain perhaps the most interesting and distinct group are those of 1300-1350, written on a hard vellum or parchment. The sheets average about ten inches across. The writer wrote across this width to whatever depth he required and then cut off the piece leaving little space at top or bottom, using perhaps two or three inches.

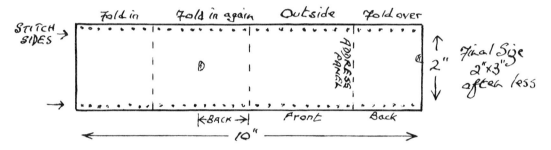

Letter written across width of roll of vellum. When finished a 2 inch piece cut off. Fold in, stitch sides and seal.

The letter was then folded in to give an address panel of perhaps 2" x 3". The sides being open were then stitched along to fasten down (as one would now gum down an envelope flap) with white thread the ends of which, no doubt, were then incorporated into the seal.

Where, say, a three inch depth was used, a small fold up was made before the folding in and stitching process began.

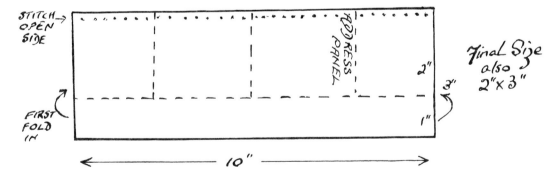

Longer letter, so extra depth. Fold up one inch, then fold as before, stitch (possibly only one side) and seal.

Throughout the whole period when many different types of parchment and paper were used, it is noticeable to what small size most letters were folded, particularly the paper ones, some only 1" x 2½" up to about 3" x 4" as a maximum. Few have any indication below the address as to who was the carrier and none have any monetary indication which is hardly to be expected if carried by the church's own messengers.

Two examples are taken from Volume Two:

Letter No 23. Outwards from Canterbury AD 1323 regarding tithes and the office of arbitrator, addressed to

> *Magistro Ric de Haut*
> *Rectori Ecclesiae de*
> > *Westerham*
> *per Epm Roff +*

stitched down the sides with white (? silk) thread and sealed. Address includes the superscription '*per Episcopum Roffensis*', 'through the Bishop of Roffensis'. Westerham was in the Roffensis diocese and the instructions to the church messenger would appear to indicate that the letter was not to go direct to Westerham but to follow normal line management channels through the bishop at Rochester, though as the letter was sealed one wonders whether the bishop did in fact read it to see what was going on and then reseal it.

AD1323   Kent letter on vellum, Canterbury to Westerham, sides stitched together with white thread. Superscribed 'Per Epm Roff +' By [the church messenger of] Roffensis diocese. (Full size). (Cant Cathedral Record office.)
   This was about fifty years before a child was found 'lying in the streetes at Sevenoke' and named William Sennocke.

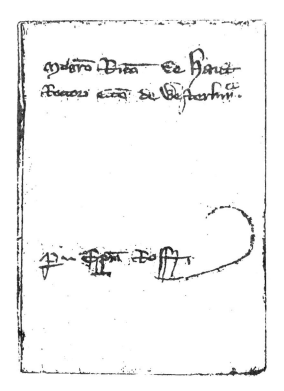

Letter No 86. AD1478 John Lambe Junior of Westerham regarding a lease taken of church lands and wrongful harvesting by the previous tenant. As John Lambe was not a cleric within the church management structure no doubt this letter went direct

> *To My Master Warden of Cryst*
> *Chyrch in Canterbury*
> *be this lre [letter] takyn*

Letters from Otford Letters of the time seen in archives are frequently addressed to a person rather than to an address as is done now-a-days. Being an important personage or official everyone would know where he was at the time and if he had moved on the messenger would follow on to wherever he might be in order to deliver the letter. The messenger's object being to deliver to the named personage or his secretary rather than to a fixed house address.

Archbishop William Wareham possessed Penshurst, Knoll and Otford and carried out a big building programme at Otford between 1514 and his death in 1532 when his place was taken over by Thomas Cranmer until in 1537 he surrendered Otford to the King, Henry VIII. Some of the more important letters sent from Otford are listed in the Calendar of State Papers Domestic and a small selection is listed here to give an appreciation of what letters passed at top level.

22	June	1516	*From Otford*	*Warham to Erasmus*
20	July	1516	*From Otford*	*Abp Warham to Erasmus*
16	Sept	1516	*From Otford*	*Warham to More*
22	June	1517	*From Otford*	*Thos Bedill to Erasmus*
22	May	1518	*From Otford*	*Warham to Oxford University*

....

5	Jan	1534	*From Otford*	*Cranmer to Cromwell*
9	July	1534	*From Otford*	*Cranmer to Sampson "desires an* *answer by the bearer"*
9	June	1534	*From Otford*	*John Lord Huse to Lord Lisle at Calais*
26	Aug	1534	*From Otford*	*Thos Bedyll to Cromwell*
28	Aug	1534	*From Otford*	*Thos Bedyll to Cromwell*
24	Oct	1534	*From Otford*	*Thos Bedyll to Cranmer*
5	Aug	1537	*From Otford*	*Thos Bedyll to Wriothesley in* *which he states Dr London's* *servant has just brought letters* *from Oxford which he encloses* *(ie they have been brought by* *private messenger).*[31]

Again in the same year, Cranmer writing to Cromwell, thanks him for his letters by his servant, showing that important personal letters were frequently carried by personal servants over long distances if one could afford to do so.

Development of Sevenoaks Town

Sevenoaks is situated on high ground, an outcrop of sandstone grit amongst the chalk. It is on a leyline that passes through Pulborough and Chichester to St. Catherine's Hill, the headland on the south coast of the Isle of Wight.[32]

The town gradually developed as a market centre greatly helped by the population explosion of 1284 when numbers more than doubled and this lead over Otford the Town maintained through the Black Death years of 1348, 1361 and 1368 when a third of the population in the country perished.

About 1370 at the time when Geoffrey, Lord de Say, took over Knole a boy baby was found near a tree in the town and given the name William Sennoke. He was apprenticed in London, prospered, and became Mayor of London in 1418 the year he founded Sevenoaks School, later endowing it in his will in 1432.

Mid-century saw rebellious times. In 1450 Jack Cade's rebellion against Henry VI was highlighted by a battle when Cade defeated the troops of the King at Solefields, hard by Sevenoaks School's contentious new covered lawn tennis courts, and, before perishing himself, went on to London to cut off the head of Lord Saye and Sele, Lord Lieutenant of Kent and a previous owner of the much-smaller-than-now Knole.

Knole House was expanded in the 1450s and the major part was built then by the next owner, Thomas Bouchier Archbishop of Canterbury. With the dissolution of the monasteries Otford was no longer a centre of power and as already mentioned Archbishop Cranmer had to hand over Knole to Henry VIII for his disposal.

The 1550 grant of the Manor of Sevenoaks created a powershift and from that time[33] Knole was taking precedence over Otford with Sevenoaks Town becoming the main centre of activity in the district. In 1554 Sir William Isley of Sundridge and Farmer Martell of Wrotham were hanged on Gallows Common Sevenoaks for treason; and in 1566 Queen Elizabeth gave Knole to Thomas Sackville her cousin whose descendents have lived there ever since. He was created '*Earl of Dorset*' in 1604, and Lionel Sackville the seventh Earl created Duke in 1720.

Roads Whilst there was constant complaint that the local roads around Penshurst were almost impassable in 1594 due to the local transport activities of the Tonbridge ironmasters, those between Otford and London were not so bad.

Maps of the time show a route from Otford going past the Saxon plegstow, the playing field at Twitton, up Sepham hill now called the '*old Polhill*' route, along Otford Lane to Halstead. Then along Church Lane and Stonehouse where there is a holloway, to join the road from Rye[34] at Pratts Bottom and so on to '*London and the Thames Crossings*', Lambeth Palace being near the River Thames, a little south of Waterloo station and nearly opposite the present Houses of Parliament. The 'Petley deed' 1588 mentions the '*Kings Highway*' from Otford to London.[35]

Maintenance of Roads For many years the Roman roads were the only roads in Britain that were actually built. Others just occurred through the passage of persons and horses. Concerning roads, the quotation from the Domesday Book AD 1086 states '*if anyone has made a fence or ditch whereby the King's public road is narrowed, or has felled into the road a tree that stood outside the road, and has carried off branches or foliage from it, for each of these offenses he shall pay 100s to the King*' and one might also add 'or has dug a hole in it to obtain clay or stones' underlines the early concept of '*road*' as a right of way and right of passage rather than the present concentration on goodness of surface that facilitates speedy travel.

Prior to their dissolution most monasteries had considered the upkeep of roads passing through their land as a necessary part of their work and this has been termed voluntary work for no law enforced it.

With the disappearance of ecclesiastical organisation some laws were necessary. The first came in 1555 (2&3 Philip & Mary c8) making parishes responsible for repairing the roads and bridges that ran through them and placing an obligation on parishoners to spend four days a year working on the roads under the supervision of highway surveyors elected by the churchwardens. Such surveyors were not qualified and served for only one year at a time. The Elizabethan Statute (5 Eliz c13) of 1563 increased the required work to six days a year. Parishes with a National Main Road running through them were in a bad position with high costs of upkeep.

SEVEN OAKS, KENT.

*This engraving by Dugdale in 1843 shows 'Beechmont' the house overlooking the
Southern Escarpment viewed from the road up from Riverhill to Sevenoaks.
It was built in 1796 and destroyed in 1944.*

Chapter II

1625-1695 Postboy on Horseback

The Route

Civil War and Commonwealth

Postmasters
    Political Situation, Salaries and Local Duties

Road Books

Farming of the Posts

1676 Sevenoaks becomes the Post Stage

Decline of Rye

Population and Volume of Letters

Monarchs	Charles I	(-1649)
	Interregnum	(1649-1660)
	Charles II	(1660-1685)
	James II	(1685-1689)
	William III and Mary II	(1689 both to 1694)

Chronologie

1626	Post Stages planned, to come into operation when required.
1629	Hutchings ran regular weekly post on Western Road to produce income.
1630	Queen Henrietta, queen of Charles I, visited Tunbridge Wells. Development of town started.
1635	Proclamation at Bagshot establishes official post open to the public.
1636	Longford Bridge over River Darenth built by public subscription.
1637	'Carriers Cosmography' by John Taylor.
	Witherings reorganises inland post once Stanhope's patent runs out. London to Rye post as part of Foreign Service.
1640	Parliament Dissolved.
1642	First Civil War.
1648	Second Civil War.
1652	During Commonwealth period, Members of the House of Commons and Ministers of State secured rights of Free Postage.
1653	Posts farmed by John Manley.
1657	First Postage Act takes place under the Interregnum.
	First public sale of Tea in Britain at Garways Coffee House.
1658	Edward Barlow, Postboy, on Chepstow ride.
1660	Restoration of Monarchy. First Postage Act confirming that of 1657.
1661	Introduction of London Bishopmark.
1662	Hearth or Chimney Tax. Abolished 1689.
1663	Certificate of Conformity of Church of England required of Deputy Postmasters.
1665	Plague year.
1666	Great Fire of London.
1667	Kentish Post Office in London removed to Grand Office in Bishopgate Street.
1666/7	Postmasters Salary Book available for Kent Road.
1668	Post Office contracted with Deputy Postmasters to deliver within ten miles of their stage at 2d per letter, collection free.
1669	P.O. Broadsheet - List of Post Towns.
1670	Riding half-post started (to Chester) ie, without guide.
1672	Tunbridge office opened.
1673	Test Act (Repealed 9 May 1828). Court of King Charles II at Rye to review fleet. Third Anglo-Dutch war.
1674	Customs search the mails (at Rochester) without warrant.
1675	Greenwich Observatory founded.
1676	Post Stage removed to Sevenoaks. Chipstead supressed.
1678	Bromley Office opened. Hastings postroad opened.
1686	The Red House in High Street built on a site first built on in 1631.
1689	Licencing and Regulating of Hackney Coaches and Stagecoaches (£8 yearly).
1693	National Debt started.
1694	Bank of England founded.
	Duty stamps required on Documents, sewn on (Cypher label on back and metal staple 1705).
1695	Freedom of the Press in England. Licencing abandoned.
1697	Act for licencing Hawkers and Pedlars (£4 plus £5 per horse or mule).
	Window Tax on houses having more than six windows (Repealed 1851).

Chapter II

1625-1695
Postboy on Horseback

Although letters of many private persons and also business letters had been carried by the King's Post, nevertheless, prior to 1635 it was the **King's** Post, not officially available to others. And so the large institutions such as Church and Universities, the Merchant Strangers and Merchant Adventurers had their own couriers who travelled the same roads; but naturally it was the King who controlled those roads, made the regulations and fixed the staging posts.

On 30th July 1626 Charles I sent a letter from Whitehall to the Earl of Montgomery[1] to say that the laying of posts in the county (Kent) was not to be put into execution, but that the deputy lieutenants should consider and assign the fittest places for the stages and how many horses to be in readiness, and fit persons to be postmasters, '*when there be occasion to use the service, the charge will be borne by the country*'.

Both Income and Profit Achieved

Then in 1629 Hutchins, a postmaster on the Western Road under control of Lord Stanhope finally achieved permission to run a regular weekly post along that road to a schedule instead of having to wait until the King's Packet was running; that is, in the analysis of the previous chapter he was allowed to move from mode 4 to mode 5. Such regularity of running greatly pleased the public; it also generated both income and profit, an unheard of situation up to now as the posts had always been a great expense on the King's purse. It was to be the major breakthrough! The post now producing income instead of being a charge as it had always been till now. Stanhope, in control of the Inland and Dominion Overseas Posts (but not the Dover Road Foreign [Continental] Posts) increased his charges to his Postmasters along the Western Road because of the profit they were now able to make, but made no further changes. For some reason he chose to ignore the great developments occuring under his aegis and it was left to Witherings to inaugurate the new method. Letters to the Continent were first carried officially in 1632 thus replacing the Merchant Adventurers own post, now to be supressed. Witherings, Postmaster for Foreign Parts and the Dover Road stepped into the domestic scene in 1634/5 with proposals for reorganising the inland post, based on the Western Road experiences. His proposals were accepted and when Stanhope's patent ran out in 1637, Witherings was able to carry out this reorganisation of the Inland Service. A Royal Proclamation of 1635 had given the Post Office the right to carry private letters instead of doing so unofficially. Common Carriers, personal servants and friends of the writer also shared that right. One view might be that throwing open the posts to the public by the Proclamation at Bagshot was doing little more than regularising and controlling an existing situation.

A Difficult Start   The situation existing locally at Chipstead in 1636 is well brought out by the Countess writing weekly each Wednesday to the Earl of Leicester whilst he is away. These are not State letters but have more importance than purely a private person's missives as they are to a State Official on duty. The comments give some idea of the difficulty in getting letters even as far as London. They also show that the Plague was not something that just happened in the one year 1665, but that it had bubbled on for some decades before finally erupting so seriously.[2]

'Fears some of her letters have gone astray for after the first one she sent to Chipstead has written weekly without fail. When Rochell went last to London he met her letter on the way and took it with him.'

'The Postmaster of Chipstead continually sent word back to her that her letters were gone but it troubles her much that the Postmaster finds such defect in passage and she does not know how to send frequently until it pleases God to withdraw the plague from London.' (25 Oct 1636 and 17 Nov 1636.)

The Route

The Post from London to Rye organised under Witherings was once again looked upon as part of the Foreign Service to France and beyond rather than to serve the local areas through which the road ran. On 11th February 1637 there was a proclamation to the Mayors of Rye, Dover and Canterbury to take care to help not hinder the posts in their town and handling of letters and packets by the ripiers was forbidden. Only those appointed by Witherings were to carry letters.

Later that year it was decided that all foreign (continental) mail should pass through Dover. A proclamation *'dated at Paris the 13th day of April, AD 1637, prohibits all the said posts and carriers accordingly: Now his Majesty, likewise, in pursuance of the said agreement, and taking into his princely consideration how much it imports the state and this whole realm, that the secrets thereof be not disclosed to foreign nations; which cannot be prevented if promiscuous use of transmitting or taking up of foreign letters by these private posts and carriers aforesaid should be suffered, which will also be no small prejudice to his merchants in their trading: And forasmuch as there hath lately been complaint made to his Majesty's ambassadors in France, that the said carriers or letter carriers do continually pass by the way of Rye and Diepe, as formerly they did, to the great prejudice of correspondences: his Majesty doth therefore straightly charge and command, and hereby declare his royal will and pleasure to be, that from henceforth no letters or pacquets whatsoever shall pass by the way of Rye and Diepe, but all shall be transmitted by the way of Dover, Calais, Bulleyne, Abbeville, and Amiens, according to the said agreement; and his Majesty doth hereby prohibit all the said messengers and French posts, and all other posts and letter carriers whatsoever, that have formerly gone by the way of Rye and Diepe, or any other posts, carriers, or messengers, except such as shall be appointed by the said Thomas Witherings, that they do not presume to take up, transmit, carry, or re-carry any letters or pacquets whatsoever into or from any foreign parts, by the said way of Rye and Diepe, or by any other way or road whatsoever, upon pain of his Majesty's high displeasure, and the pains and penalties which may ensue'* [3]
but this ruling can have had only temporary impact, for in 1640 there were again complaints that letters were passing through Rye. And in that year the Mayor of Rye, Robert Orwyn, wrote to Secretary of State Windebanks as Master of the Posts stating that George Edge ever since being Postmaster (at Rye) had been diligent in carrying the King's Packet and furnished good posthorses[4] but was hindered by one John Thrower. It seems that the London-Chipstead-Rye-Dieppe route to France could be both quicker and cheaper in certain aspects of communication. Certainly it was used a lot, and officials on both sides of the Channel must surely have been cognizant of and have been encouraging its use.

Local Roads   At the start of the period the local scene was that of slowly moving Carriers carts pulled by teams of six or more horses and of young boys on horseback as postboys carrying mail or riding as guide to gentlemen travellers. But they were soon to be joined by carriages of the gentry going to Tunbridge, following the discovery of health giving springs at 'The Wells'.

Carriers   In John Taylor's 'Carriers Cosmography' or 'a Briefe Relation of the Innes, Ordinaries, Hostelries and other lodgings in, and neere London, where the Carriers, Waggons, Foote-posts and Higglers doe usually come' printed by A.G. in 1637,
'The Carriers of Tunbridge, of Seavenoake, of Frant and Staplehurst in Kent doe lodge at the Katherine Wheele, they do come on thursdaies and go away on fridaies: also on the same dae come thither the

carriers of Marden, and Penbree, and from Warbleton in Sussex . . . Carriers from Westrum and Wrotham do lodge at the Kingshead in Southwarke. They doe come on thursdays, go fridayes'.

Those from Tenterden, Penshurst and Battle stayed at the Signe of the Spurre in Southwarke, '*come thursdays, go fridays'* and those from Tunbridge at the Greene Dragon in Fowle Lane in Southwarke. It can be seen that much passing on of messages and written notes could have taken place through the carrier network. No doubt much mail was carried to Sevenoaks for the carriers were legally entitled to carry messages and letters along their route. None such letters to Sevenoaks appear to have survived. John Taylor although writing about the carriers boldly states that letters should be sent to Thomas Witherings at his house in Sherburne Lane Abchurch London. Witherings was, of course, connected with the newly-organised official inland post.

No carriers names are mentioned anywhere in the text of this reference work and it is understood that, because of the delicacy of the legal position at that time of carriers and their liabilities, John Taylor's presence around the depots collecting Road Transport information was only tolerated on this understanding that no names would be named. And so to our loss no names are mentioned. Taylor was a poet, the famed 'water poet', so called because he spoke for the watermen and boatmen. He states he carried out this survey 'as a service to his readers'.

The Ford and the Bridge

The ford across the Darenth at Chipstead was shallow, normally but a few inches. The crossing lower down at Dunton Green next the mill at Longford was narrower but much deeper, as indeed it must have been, for it is said that the water-driven corn mill had been there since at least 1250 AD. The mill site was finally sold off and vacated in 1987 being then used to sell Japanese cars.

Requiring only a bridlepath of which there were many in this area it seems likely that the postboy and his horse were skirting Sevenoaks in early days, possibly like the Fish packtrains, taking the left fork at Riverhill across to Hubbards Hill, Cross Keys, Dibden and Salters Heath to Chipstead ford and staging post as mentioned by Marian Mills.[5] So avoiding part of the climb over the sandstone ridge to Sevenoaks Town, why else should Sevenoaks be on a Branch Post from Chipstead?

Eventually in 1636 a bridge was built at Longford, road repairs in the area being borne by the three parishes of Sevenoaks, Chevening and Otford, and the main road in to Sevenoaks carrying the coaches changed to that route as the bridged way was more suitable for wheeled traffic.

The Post Stage remains at Chipstead until 1676

The Post stage, however, remained at Chipstead for a further forty years after the bridge was built and only changed in 1676 when Chipstead was suppressed and Sevenoaks became the Post town. All this time the postboy rode on horseback as did other riders 'riding post'. In 1676 the Postboy obviously had to change his route to one through Sevenoaks Town, but whether he had skirted the Town right up to 1676 we shall probably never know, though certain it is that the stage point, which included also the provision of horses for those riding in post, remained at Chipstead until that date.

Postally a national scene begins to develop and what happened nationally was to have its considerable reflection into the local scene. No longer were communications along the Rye road to be considered as only a means to reach the seaboard and the continent. Slowly, emphasis begins to switch toward local needs.

Civil War and Interregnum

Although now open to the public, the Posts got off to a poor start, there were only six years before Parliament was dissolved in 1640 and the first Civil War began in 1642. The Official Post had not been used as much as it had been expected to be, possibly because Post Office mail was likely to be opened and the contents read. Even if this did not happen the Sender and Addressee names were recorded in a ledger in the case of foreign mails. Thus private enterprise posts were still encouraged to continue as also those run by the municipal authorities even though they might be doing so unofficially.

Civil War

From the Civil War period 1642-1648 there can be found little evidence of a post available to the public. Both sides in the dispute carried their own official letters but private persons may well have found it unwise to commit their thoughts or arrangements to paper. Kent was mainly in Parliamentary hands, but it is very difficult to find letters of the Civil War period that might have been carried by an official post open to the public and some examples to show the disturbed state of the County explain why.

The following recorded incident[6] epitomises the dangers of committing thought to paper. '*Early in August 1642 a packet of royalist correspondence fell into its (parliamentary) hands, revealing the imminence of a local Cavalier coup*'. Colonel Edwin Sandys, a member of a puritan family, was sent into Kent by parliament to suppress it. This was the first of his two forays into Kent. He arrived in Sevenoaks on Sunday 14th August 1642 and laid wait for Sir John Sackville who was leading a group with mild cavalier leanings and who was at church service. Sevenoaks townsmen went to the aid of Sir John but were outnumbered and he was captured, taken to London and subsequently committed to Fleet prison. Meanwhile Knole was ransacked and several wagonloads of arms removed together with money and other supplies, many storechests being forced open. The Earl of Dorset was absent at the time, being with the King's forces in York with a troop raised in Kent.

The following year, 1643, Sevenoaks became the focus for the countryside with up to four thousand Kentish rebels gathering in the surrounding unenclosed chartland forest with meetings on the open Vine commonland. Emissaries to the King at Oxford persuaded him to order the rebels to secure the crossings of the Thames and seize the ships at Rochester. There was much delay and many comings and going among leaders and many letters written but finally with no support from Oxford the rebel gatherings gradually dispersed encouraged to do so by the Parliamentary army with whom there local engagements.

Again in 1644 there were 4,000 disaffected troops at Sevenoaks nominally under Parliament. Sevenoaks was a key point being the way, through Westerham, that the King might enter the County to link up with sympathetic elements, skirting London from Oxford. Sevenoaks also guarded the entrance to Kent eastwards along the Holmesdale valley, the southern route along the Tonbridge road and also had access to the Thames Estuary and its shipping through the Darenth valley to the north.

Though business and farming must needs go on if at all possible the troubled state of the Sevenoaks area shown by the above examples must have precluded the continuance of an organised post, at least for the years 1642-1649 possibly on until 1654 as the county was in dissarray till then, many personages including the Duke of Dorset, being moderates and not really inclined to either extreme, Parliamentarian or Cavalier.[7]

Commonwealth

Cromwell took London in 1647 and with the Commonwealth established from 1649 to 1659, once peace returned, a reorganised post was opened. The 1654 Ordinance in Council farmed the Posts to John Manley for £10,000 p.a. (£420,000) and forbade unauthorized persons to set up postal services, keep horses for Posts or run a mailboat. As the Government of the times had taken money from Manley, they felt obliged to enforce his monopoly and help him put down pirate posts. For example, the Institutional Posts of the Cinque ports were running well and were old-established yet an attempt was made to suppress them.

Greenwood[8] quotes an entry of 24 July 1655 in the White and Black Books of the Cinque Ports showing a petition to the Cinque Ports Court held at New Romney made by John Edwards of Dover and others, messengers for the Ports to the City of London. They went weekly from the ports to London with letters, packets and small parcels but had now been prohibited by an order of the Commissioners for the Foreign and Inland Posts. The Cinque Ports Court decided that the messengers should continue to be used as before and that any fines that they might incur would be paid for them.

Whilst this was going on George Maplisden was visiting in 1651 many Kentish woods including Knole Park Sevenoaks and Chiddingstone looking for suitable timber for Naval Shipbuilding. Once found, it often took up to two years to get the wood from Kent countryside to the dockyards at Chatham.

During the Interregnum there were private instructions to Postmasters in 1653 [9], supposedly sent by Manley, cautioning them to choose discreet deputies or do the work themselves when handling '*all his Hns. packets*'. Nor were deputies to allow riders to accept private letters. All the letters on the road had to be put into the mail (i.e. handed in at post stages). Deputies had to record the names of all travellers by post and any found to be disaffected do their best to keep them in custody and inform the authorities. Deputies had also to have an eye on the disaffected who lived near them, observe their meetings and conversations and inform him. These instructions were not to be communicated to anyone else, but could be used as their authority for their actions. No wonder some members of the public were wary of using the posts in early days.

The Correspondence in Kent Archives of Sir John Heath of Brasted is a large one spanning before and after the Interregnum. Little is available for the war period 1642-48 but a letter of 10 March 1648/9 to Knolton in Kent is inscribed 'Post Paid' and four weeks later another dated 13 April 1649 at Maidstone addressed to Edward Heath at Brasted but with no postal markings contains '*my man being in London brought me 2 letters from you and from . . .*' which gives the impression that the older method of using personal servants to move messages about was still being used in preference to the post.

In 1656, after the Posts had been farmed to Manley in 1654, a letter is addressed to George Heath at Brasted. Though with no postal markings or charges, this letter could well have been carried by Edward Barlow or one of his fellow postboys on the London to Chipstead route (see later). After 1660 the flow of letters to Sir John Heath at Brasted starts up again.

The first Postage Act of 1657 under the Commonwealth set out the rights of the Postmaster-General to carry letters, to establish rates and to organise a supply of horses. The cost of a single sheet from Sevenoaks to London, being under 80 miles was again set at 2d. The Post Office monopoly position for letter carrying was confirmed. By 1658 the local post at Sevenoaks (Chipstead) was well established and running as the extract (see p.37) from Barlow's Journal shows; but first a spot of bother in 1659 running up to the restoration of the Monarchy.

The trouble occurred at Stonecrouch, but had the local militia at Sevenoaks standing by to help. It is also one of the first references to the posthouse now being at Stonecrouch, three miles to the north, rather than at the Flimwell of earlier days.

1 Aug 1659. Col. Robert Gibbon to President of Council of State. Finds all quiet at the Wells. Captain Lockyer will give an account of the prisoners. Has 2 troops in the town with Major Crooke's two troops and Capt. Browne's militia at Sevenoaks. The troop sent out last night took about 15 prisoners and at the posthouse at Stonecrouch near Flimwell took Arms and armour thus confirming Saturday's intelligence that Col. Culpepper appointed someone to receive a box at the posthouse.[10]

Restoration

1660 saw the Restoration of the Monarchy in the form of Charles II and also the inauguration of the Post Office as we know it today with the passing of the Post Office Act of 1660 (I Caroli II Cap XXXV) which in effect confirmed the Interregnum Postal Act of 1657. In this Act the Postmasters' monopoly of providing posters with guide and horn was renewed but he had to produce horses within half an hour of being so requested or the posters could go elsewhere. Charges were 2½d the mile besides the Guide Groat, 4d, for every Stage. The Post Office monopoly of letter-carrying was again confirmed. Expansion of postal services now takes place on the firm basis of this act.

Prior to 1660 the only postal markings likely to be seen on a letter is a manuscript numeral denoting the rate (eg 2d for Sevenoaks to London) but from now on postal markings begin to increase with the introduction of the London bishopmark (1661) to show date and month of receipt or transit. Henry Bishop who now farmed the Post Office included Rye in his list of posts.

WE the Minister and Church-Warden of the Parish and Parish Church of *nilton next Gravosend* in the County of *Kent* do hereby Certify, That *Nathaniel Kirk gent eldning master gunner of nilton Blockhouse in the said County of Kent* on Sunday the *nine Twentieth* Day of *March hereunder written* did receive the Sacrament of the Lord's Supper, in the Parish aforesaid immediately after Divine Service and Sermon, according to the Usage of the Church of England. In Witness whereof we have hereunto subscribed our Hands, the said *One and Thirtieth* — Day of *March* — 1730.

John Boys } Minister of the Parish and Parish Church aforesaid

[signature] } Church Warden of the said Parish and Parish Church

Anthony Ireland of nilton next Gravesend in the said County of Kent gent and William Harrison of Gravesend aforesaid gent Do severally make Oath, that they did see the said *Nathaniel Kirk gent* — — — — — in the above-written Certificate named, (and who now present hath delivered the same into this Court) receive the Sacrament of the Lord's-Supper in the Parish Church abovesaid; and that they did see the said Certificate subscribed by the said Minister and Church Warden.

A: Ireland

Wm Harrison

Postmasters

To stabilize the political situation oath-taking developed an importance and postmasters, like many other officials, became caught up with this requirement. Oaths of Allegiance and Supremacy were required in 1605 for senior officials of a county in a public position of trust, with an extension in 1609 to all professional and University men. This was part of the religious settlement of the times in the first few years of James I and continued under William and Mary in 1689 with a further act abrogating the oaths of Supremacy of Elizabeth I and James I and appointing new oaths to be sworn.

Oaths   The 1635 Proclamation on Posts, the 1654 Ordinance and 1657 Act contained within themselves nothing specific to oath-taking but the 1660 Postal Act required that a person '*having using or exercising the Office of Postmaster General or any other Imployment relating to the said Office must first take the Oaths of Allegiance and Supremacy*'[11] which also implied acceptance of the Established Church of England.

The changed climate of opinion that had led to the Restoration, together with the rules and regulations that subsequently flowed from the 1662 Act of Uniformity, caused many problems of conscience, not least, for example, that of the non-conformist John Bunyan who spent much of his life in Bedford Gaol, where during his second incarceration he seized the opportunity to write 'Pilgrim's Progress'. Postmasters were not to escape these regulations. From 25 May 1663 it was made a ruling within the Post Office[12] that all postmasters must produce a certificate of conformity to the Church of England, a document signed by the vicar and churchwarden and attested by two witnesses, as part of his conditions of service, on pain of dismissal.

An ensample of such a document is shown opposite. This one for a senior military official is on vellum dated 1730 and stamped with two 6d impressed stamps as a legal document. It states that the person attended divine service, heard the sermon and received the Lord's Supper. Hearing the sermon was an important aspect, for the Church being part of the Establishment, tended to reflect Government thinking.

Whether the lack of provision of the required document led to dismissal from postal service has not been established, but certainly Anthony Fuller and Richard Everest of Chipstead, also Robert Hockham of Sevenoaks would have been expected to provide such a document. Whether or not they did so we do not know. Nor do we know exactly when in later years the practice fell into desuetude, though the Test Act itself was not repealed until 1828. Ordinary citizens such as Mrs Watson of Otford who did not take the oath had (in 1702) to pay double tax on all six of her landholdings.[13]

Local Duties

Postmasters had to see that the letters on their road progressed from stage to stage on time and those they employed to do the riding work had to be at least 14 years of age and male. Edward Barlow was one such who was on the London-Chipstead stage prior to making a career at sea. He makes reference to the life of a postboy in his memoirs 'Barlow's Journal'[14] where he describes his life. At 13 he had tried harvesting and horsework at the coalpits and then went for a fortnight's stay '*a-liking with a whitester*' which he didn't like. And so then in 1658 he went a-liking at a tavern, his uncle Thomas Barlow's house in Southwarke, the Dog and Bear, which was also the post house for all Kent. '*I was employed by my uncle riding post to Kingston-upon-Thames and to Chipstow in Kent and to Dartford and Gravesend in Kent*'. The names of the Chipstead inns he visited are not recorded but four decades later they were The George, Flower de Lewes (Fleur de Lys), White Lyon and The Bull. Edward both carried the post and rode post as a guide. In his own words '*I was sent to the General posthouse at the stocks on Cornhill for the letters . . . late at night, found half a crown and kept it.*' '*Sometimes I had not gone into a bed for a week's time together for riding both night and day.*' '*I collected a little money which I had given me when I rode post with*

Opposite: Certificate of Conformity. An example dated 1730 of the type of signed and attested document that Postmasters were 'asked' to produce as a condition of service from 1663 on. (AGD)

gentlemen.' But he lost his last 2/- which he hid in a post in his chamber, *'to the maid or his fellow postboy found it'*. One might presume that the requirement to blow one's horn three times in every mile was not only to announce one's presence but sometimes also to keep the guide awake. Change too was scarce, the penny (worth almost 20p in 1987) was the smallest official coin and many public houses, in Sevenoaks The Grocers Arms, the Mercers Arms and the Merchant Tailors Arms, and also candlemakers had their own tokens as small change. In all there were twenty-seven different local tokens within our Sevenoaks locality.[15] The provision of local tokens fulfilled a need of the times and their minting was not finally prohibited until the Act of 29 July 1812.

London Office   'The Stocks' on Cornhill was the Stock Exchange of the times and opposite, at the west end of Threadneedle Street was the General Posthouse.   In 1663 on postnights which were Tuesday, Thursday and Saturday the office in London closed at midnight or later with despatches at 2am; so at 5mph Chipstead would be reached by 7am next morning, just as the office was opening.

But in 1661[16] and until 1666 Kent had its own letter office in Love Lane at the Round House 'nere Billingsgate'. During the Great Fire, 3rd/4th September 1666 both the main office and the Kent Office burned down. The main office moved temporarily for a few weeks to Two Black Pillars, Bridges Street, Covent Garden then to the end of Bishopsgate Street where it was joined by the Kent office finally both moving permanently to Lombard Street (20th Mar 1678) where they remained until the move to King Edward building. After burning down, the Kent Office had moved temporarily to 'to the House of Mr John Dyne in the passage to and from Tower Hill, near the pump in Crutchet Fryers'[17] before going to Bishopgate.[18]

Named Postmasters

Stonecrouch, a few miles to the north, had superseded Flimwell on the crossroad as the stagepoint by at least 1659 and in the Postal Survey of November 1666 just a year after the Great Plague of 1665 and two months after the Great Fire the stages were:

	Thomas Barlow	*Southwark (the uncle was still there)*
20 miles	*Anthony Fuller*	*Chipstead*
22 miles	*James Needler*	*Stonecrouch*
23 miles	*Michael Cadman*	*Rye*
————		
65 miles		

The Peover Papers of Col. Roger Whitley (Post 94) show Fuller as on-going Postmaster of the Chipstead stage in 1666 and this date can be taken back at least one year if not two to 1664 by the licencee records.[19] The earlier survey of 1660 covered only four of the six roads and not the Rye one. Mostly, as in the Salary Book following, the Rye Road and the Dover Road are considered as one, 'The Kentish Road' though they come together for a mere handful of miles, from London to Lewisham/Deptford; in this case the Rye section being given precedence.

Postmasters Salaries   A Salary List is given for 1666/7 for the six Great Roads.[20] Both the Dover Road section and the Rye Road section appear in one list under the heading 'The Kentish Road', the Rye stages being at the top of the list. Bromley does not yet appear as a stage, nor yet Tonbridge or 'The Wells'.

Opposite: Part of John Leake's Exact Surveigh of the Streets Lanes and Churches contained within the ruins of the City of London, Dec 1666. Shows the posthouse opposite the Stocks on Cornhill, Love Lane, Lombard Street. Bishopsgate Street was a continuation north of Gracechurch Street. The earlier location of the Corsini residence has been added to this map.

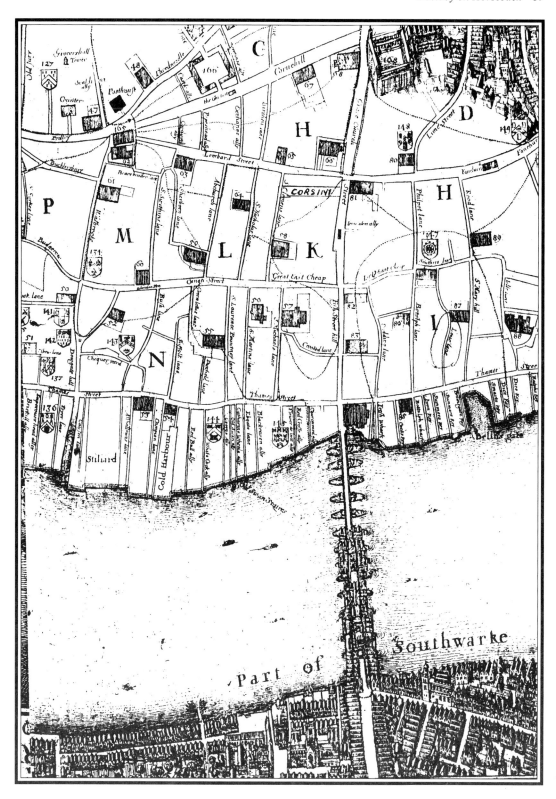

[mileage]			Old Sallary	Sallary according to Dir by Road	Sallary according to Judgement	Fines
14 + 14						
20 Single	Southwarke	Tho Barlow	80.00.00	96. 0. --	80. 0. -- Paid for	40.00.00
20 + 20	Chepstow	Antony fuller	-- -- --	40 -- --	riding ...	
20 + 20	Stonecrouch	James Maylor	-- -- --	40 -- --		
20 Single	Rye	Mirzoall Cadman	20.00.00	20 -- --	20. 0. --	20.00.00

But which column contains the salary actually paid? It has been said that postmasters were paid £1 per mile for riding work, both ways. Here the mileage distance appears to be computed miles, not actual ones, giving rise to the second salary column.

But more likely the salary paid was the third column 'according to (our) Judgment' and Chepstow got nothing, for Fuller was arguing with Col. Whitley in 1673 to obtain a salary. No salary shows in the accounts until after the Post Stage moved to Sevenoaks.

Post Towns

The post stages where horses were changed were the distribution points for the letters and became post towns. Later many more places for which separate bags were made up and places where the mail stopped to exchange bags were added as post towns, not necessarily where horses were changed also.

It has been mentioned that many postboys were very young. Mail at this time was still often given to persons travelling the road, particularly if the postmaster felt them to be more responsible than the postboys under his command. In September 1666 the King's Packet, including Court Mail, found its way to Stonecrouch where the Postmaster sent it on to Chipstead by a gentleman travelling that way. He would have been riding on a horse. The gentleman overtook a carrier and offloaded the bag onto him, presumably because it was an added burden when riding a horse. The carrier never got to Chipstead for once he reached Sevenoaks he heard about the Great Fire in London and turned back to Tunbridge. Finally the mailbag was located and after some days was sent on to London but not before it had been opened.[21] With the confusion in London following the fire no one was punished.

Travelling Half Post   The London Gazette of 7th April 1670 shows a new departure in posting arrangements, a first relaxing of the somewhat formal and expensive travelling arrangements. No doubt this occurs because of the improvements in roads and the less likelihood of becoming lost: '*a half post to be established to Chester to be horsed at the Post House to ride **without** guide at 3d (60p) per mile*'. Although this notice applies specifically to the Chester road, one can well believe that such arrangements would be applied to other roads, particularly one that was so well frequented at least as far as Tunbridge Wells if not Rye. Strangely little is written about this change of operation but that it must have quietly occurred throughout the whole land during the succeeding thirty years is obvious from later trouble over posting legislation. 'No guide' also means that at some stage a string of riderless horses may have to be brought back to their original stage and such a scene is occasionally depicted by artists.

Maintenance of the Roads   As mentioned before, parishes with a National road running through their area were heavily burdened with its maintenance and in 1663 Parliament was petitioned for the first time for permission to levy a toll on users of the road to help with its upkeep. Rather than ensuring that good roads were built, National laws at this time concentrated on controlling traffic; in 1663 wheels at least four inches wide to flatten the surface of the road were advocated and wheels sixteen inches wide were to pay

Opposite: Salary List for Postmasters on the Kentish Road 1666. Reduced (PO Archives Post 94/11)

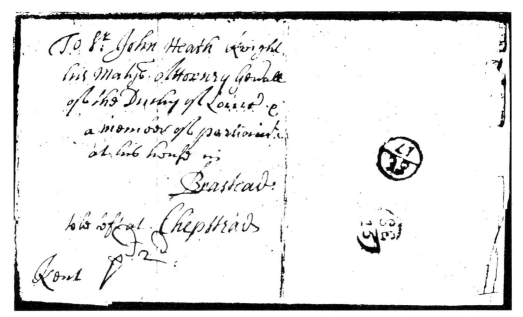

1669. Paid letter to Sir John Heath at Brasted inscribed 'To be left at Chipstead' and 'Pd 2d'.
The Rye Post went twice a week. This letter received bishopmarks of Se(pt) 15, a Wednesday, and
despatched Se 17, Friday. (Kent Archives U55 E100/87 with permission.)

half the toll of those only six inches wide. Traffic had a right to divert through unenclosed land bordering the highway and parts of some roads over rough ground became over a quarter of a mile (440 yards) wide. Waggons from Horsham were said to be obliged to go to London via Canterbury because the direct Sussex roads were so bad. One of the first toll roads was Reigate to Crawley (1693).

Branch Posts   From Chipstead a Branch Post was set up to Uckfield and Lewes in 1662 [22], which would have linked with the Sussex mail, but it was soon discontinued as it failed to make a profit. Most routes were individually costed. The Post Office Broadsheet of 1669 shows that Chipstead had bags for Sevenoaks, Otford, Reigate and Croydon. Lewes was by then connected to the Rye farm at Stonecrouch with the post only running 'as needed'. Later the Lewes connection was from the London–Chichester Road. The Broadsheet introduction makes interesting reading,

> *BROADSHEET OF 1669*
> *Whereas His Majesty taking notice of the daily infringement of the Act of Parliament (for establishing a Letter-Office) by common Carryers of Goods, &c. was pleased to issue forth His Proclamation to enforce the execution of the said Act; amongst other things injoyned the Poste Master-General to settle fit Correspondencies between the most considerable Market-Towns, and respective Post Stages in England and Wales, for Conveyance of Letters on Post, to supply the pretended Convenience by such common Carryers: The same is now accordingly done and the ensuing Table thereof made publike for general information.* [23]

The Broadsheet subscript apologises for any possible inaccuracies in this, the first essay of the Post Office into full scale advertising.
> *'This being the first essay in this matter, the practice thereof may perhaps require some amendments and alterations hereafter' (London Gazette Aug 9 1669).*

Hastings was shown on the Broadsheet as a market town under Rye and was still receiving its letters that way twice a week in 1675.[24] On 28 December 1678 [25] a new Branch post was set up from Stonecrouch three times a week to Robertsbridge, Battle and Hastings, but stopped in 1682 as the Postmaster ran into debt. The service was later started up again as part of the Rye Branch Farm. Offices at Coastal towns north of Rye, Lydd, Rumney, Hyth and Folkestone opened on 26th July 1697 [26] but were served from Dover, on a thrice weekly basis.

Local Distribution of Letters

Each postmaster was expected to make whatever arrangements he could for getting mail around to the surrounding villages as the Post Office undertook to deliver only to the nearest post town. In 1668 the local delivery requirement was put onto a firmer footing.

17 December 1668   Advertisement   London Gazette
Notice is hereby given that the Postmaster General has contracted for the ease and benefit of the people with all respective Deputy Post Masters to carry from time to time all letters directed to every particular person within Ten miles from their Stage-Towns, paying Two pence a time besides the London Post and to bring back their Answers to the said stage, Gratis.

The Kent County Archives at Maidstone hold a correspondance of letters to Sir John Heath at Brasted in Kent at this period with such superscriptions as:
    "These for Sir John Heath at Brasted in Kent to be left with the Postmaster at Chepsted to be sent above as directed."
The additional 2d due to the Postmaster does not appear to be marked on the early letters whereas in later years it sometimes is. Details are not known for Town delivery, if required. Fifty years later Town

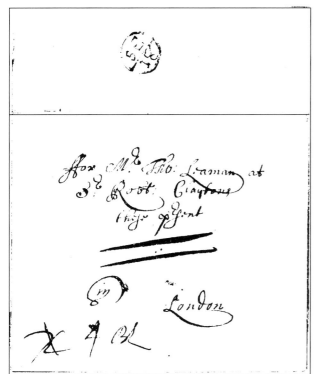

1672. Letter from Dan Sharpe in Westerham via Chipstead stage to London, with Bishopmark receiving stamp Se 18 (Wednesday). As there is only one sheet of paper it is not clear why the charge was increased from '2' to '4' by 'BL'. Normally at this time a local charge was made only for delivery. Letters collected and brought back to the posthouse for posting were collected 'free of charge'. Perhaps there was some enclosure that could be felt, if so the letter would be charged double.

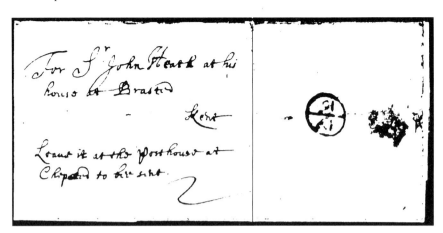

*1681. Letter from London to Sir John Heath at Brasted with bishopmark of July 15 and
inscription 'Leave it at the posthouse at Chipstead to be sent' and manuscript '2' to pay.
The instructions were wrong as by this date the posthouse had moved to Sevenoaks.
(Kent Archives U55 E100 with permission.)*

delivery was ½d and as there was effectively no inflation between 1670 and 1720, the chances are that it
was charged the same ½d at the earlier date. The 2d works out at 30p in 1987 money and contrasts well
with present private courier charges with which it might better be compared than with the free delivery
to the house now expected in this country.

Poor Addressing   Incorrect and incomplete addresses always cause a problem.
    2 Sept 1667   Advertisement   London Gazette
*Whereas divers Letters miscarry by not giving full Directions, whence blame is causelesly put upon the
Letter Office; All persons are desired hereafter to be more punctuall in mentioning the Shire, there being
severall Towns in England of the like Name, and also the Street and place adjacent of Note, if there be
not a Signe.*

    Blame was not always attributed to the public in all matters and in 2 July 1667 '*Complaints of
overcharging by Postmasters will be looked into*' was to be seen.

Benefit of Clergy   Few even in this age could write, and up to 1827 such as could could claim '*Benefit
of Clergy*'. Trial in the less stringent bishops' courts instead of the ordinary courts was at first available
only to clergymen offenders but in Tudor Times had been gradually extended to all who could read and
write, although Elizabeth had withdrawn most of the privileges.

Road Books

Ogilby's Britannia 1675   John Ogilby started life as a dancing teacher. After a leg injury he became
deputy Master and later Master of the Revels in Ireland and also opened a Theatre in Dublin. Losing all
his possessions in 1641 at the time of the civil war he later opened a publishing business in London, but
his possessions were all destroyed by the Great Fire in 1666. This happening was, however, to lead to
success: he became a '*sworn viewer*' of destroyed London.[27] Ogilby became Cosmographer Royal in
1671 and had 7,000 L of Charles II (1660-1685). He developed route maps, unknown in England at the
time although known in France for the past 100 years, which he subsequently published in his Britannia.

    Later by 1675 his assistants were using a *way-wiser* or perambulator measuring wheel to obtain
distances. His use of the statute mile of 1760 yards helped to establish it, seventy-eight years after the

passing of the Act in 1573. Most other 'miles' had been longer, varying between 1,600 to over 2,600 yards.

Of the New Posts he comments *"For the better information of all such as have occasion of conveyance of Letters into any part of England, which before made use of that tedious way by the Wagon, Carrier or Stagecoach . . . to be left with the said Postmaster to be sent as directed. For if the person be an inhabitant of any note he is known to the postmaster".*

Post houses were listed at:

Surrey	Kent	Sussex*
Croydon	Chipstead	Rye
Rygate	(Sevenoaks)	(Winchelsea)
Kingston	(Otford)	(Battle)
	Tunbridge	(Hastings)

*The list is prior to the opening of the direct link in 1678 from Battle to Hastings.

Mileage Map listing for Kent Towns showing Seve^nocke (sic) but only Knoll on the map. The Jacob van Langeren plates with new maps by Jenner, this being the final 1677 printing by John Garrett with maps redrawn. Cromwell's forces are said to have used the earlier version of these maps during the Civil War. Small wonder they never found Ightham Mote. (AGD)

Farming

In many respects farming is not unlike the modern concept of franchising. Exclusive permission is given to a farmer to carry out a particular task with the methods to be used and the prices to be charged laid down. The parameter that can be varied is volume.

In the farming of the Posts, the King who had claimed postal monopoly, contracted out the whole operation to a favourite or to the highest bidder for a fixed sum, laying down the rates to be charged and the overall method of working. The farmer then attempted to maximise his profits by efficient working and by increasing volume of traffic.

Not all national farmers managed the whole postal service. They would let out a whole road to another person to farm in exchange for a fixed sum per year. Or perhaps one end of a road, such as the Rye farm or the Tonbridge farm. At the smallest division, the bye letters (those arising along the way, and not routed through London) of Tonbridge and Sevenoaks were farmed out for a fixed sum to a separate person distinct from the General Post letters of that area. Sometime in the 1680's and right up to 1711 part of the Rye Road including Chipstead and Sevenoaks was let out to farm under Tonbridge. Whatever merits such financial arrangements might have at the overall level, farming appeared to cause some chaos at the operational level as will be seen in excerpts from Col. Whitley's letter books.

From 1670 till 1716 Chipstead and later Sevenoaks offices were involved in Tonbridge and Tonbridge Wells matters to a far greater extent than they ever were with their northern stage Bromley. Possibly this was because the Tonbridge/T. Wells mail was so seasonally intense and the then Post Office was quite unable to bring itself to implement an establishment suited to the requirements of the summer season. Nor was the main stage move from Chipstead to Sevenoaks in 1676 a particularly amicable arrangement.

Customs

Other problems basic to the postal service had to be met after trouble arose when Customs and Excise considered that many small dutiable articles were being passed through the post and persons were appointed to search. The customs searched the mail without warrant at Rochester in 1674 as they could see dutiable articles through holes in the mailsack but the next year 1675 it was agreed that they would only do so after acquainting the local Postmaster whom it was agreed was to help them. This arrangement was to apply throughout the Postal Service.

Col. Roger Whitley's Letter Books 1672-1677

Col. Whitley was Administrative Deputy under Henry Earl of Arlington, Lord Chamberlain of His Majesty's household. Arlington farmed the posts and was Postmaster General 1667-1685. The Letter Books, part of the Peover Papers, supply much detail. The following are some extracts.

King Charles II Visit to Rye   In May 1673 King Charles the Second and his Court removed to Rye where the fleet was to be reviewed at the time of the third Anglo-Dutch war. This move created great activity within the Post system of the Rye road. A letter of 11 May 1673 to Mr Welch of Rye was copied to Mr Fuller Postmaster at Chepstead:

> *Considering ye frequent occasion there may bee of Rideing Post betwixt London & Rye in this Conjunction, I doe herewth send you a war^t to presse horses for his Ma^{ts} Service, wch you are to vse prudently, as Necessity shall require - faile not to dispatch all Expresses, & Mailes y^t shall com to yor hands wth all possible speed & diligence soe rest &c*

and four days later,

> *Mr Needler May 15: 73. Stonecrouch*
> *These are to advertise you that ye Courte is remoueing to Rye, & his Ma^{ty} will bee there tomorrow Night;*

Wherefore you are required to haue still in Readiness, A Competent Number of Able horses wth Convenient Furniture, And bee Constantly in ye way yor selfe, dureing this occasion to Attend ye dutyes of yor Stage, in dispatching his Ma^{ts} Mailes & Expresses and to accomodate Gentlemen y^t shall Ride Post hereof I Pray & Advise you not faile.

yor &c.

Be sure to haue a sufficient numb^r of horses redy when his Ma^{ty} comes to yor stage to furnish all those y^t Attend him there will com a dayly post to & from Rye att ye usuall how^{rs} dureing ye King or Fleets stay there bee alwayes pvided to hast it Forward.

May 15th 73. Mr Fuller (Chepsted)
Another to ye the same Effect &c wth y^s addicon. There will come a dayly post to & from Rye at ye Vsuall houres dureing ye King or ye Fleets stay there be alwayes provided to hast it forwards, be sure you haue sufficient Number of horses redy when his Ma^{ty} comes to yor stage.

All must have gone to plan for there is nothing more until:

24 May 73
Now the Fleete is removed from you there will bee noe occasion for a dayly post, soe you need not send (unless with Expresses or upon Extraordinary occasion) But according to the usuall Course before the Fleete come Hither.

The Wells

Other changes had begun to gather momentum with the discovery of the springs at what was to become Tonbridge Wells. After the initial discovery of the spring in 1603, the Wells became firmly established when in 1630, following the birth of Prince Charles, Queen Henrietta visited and was restored to full health. Later in 1664 the amenities were improved in connection with the visit of Queen Katherine and in 1670 the Duke of York and his two daughters Princess Mary and Princess Anne also visited. The Wells became frequented by the Gentry in large numbers during the summer and their demands on the postal system stretched it to its limits and beyond for as mentioned the post office appeared quite unable to provide sufficient additional organisation and staff on a regular but seasonal basis. Whereas the general regulation was that the Post ran twice weekly, it ran more frequently during 'the season' from Midsummer June 24 to Michaelmas September 29.

The London Gazette of 22 June 1669 states that the post will run **daily** as far as Tonbridge where there was a footpost connection to Tonbridge Wells. Col. Whitley did his best to serve their needs as *'otherwise income was lost to the Revenue, they sending their letters by private means'*, which was not difficult as there was much coming and going between the Wells and London.

Mr Carter Tunbridge July 10th
I haue orderd the Mailes to goe from hence sooner then ordnary, y^t the Letters may be at Tunbridge, early in ye morning wherefore faile not to be there ready to receiue them, and then make all possible hast with them, to the Wells, y^t ye Gentry, may haue them before they goe to their Lodgings, allso be Sure to Call (every post day) on Mr Miles Confectioner on ye Walke who will deliver you what Letters he Receives, for London, or elsewhere, pray be verry Carefull herein, wch will oblige me to be:
Let me know what time you receiue the Bag every mourning
Yo^{rs} &c:

After their morning perambulations, the visitors liked to be able to collect their letters from the post office taking them back with them to their lodgings over lunchtime. The letters could then be answered and put in at the post office in the late afternoon when they again went out into the town. Whilst holidaying they still had to keep in touch with their business affairs.

> *Mr Fuller Cheapsted July 10th 73.*
> *I thincking it Convenient to haue ye Letters att Tunbridge early in ye morning, y^t they may be at the Wells before ye Gentry goe to their Lodging haue ordered the Maile to goe from hence sooner than accustomed, wherefore Lett me desire you, as soone as ye Maile Comes to your hands, to hast it forwards, with all possible expedicon wch is all at present, from*
> *Yo^{rs} &c:*
> *I pray haste ye Maile soe as to be at Tunbridge, by 5 or 6 in ye mourning at furthest, be sure not to faile, there being some of ye Lords of ye Councell there.*

Deputy Postmasters Salaries

Fuller at Chipstead was making great effort to obtain a salary for himself instead of relying on the benefit of the general activity that being a Postmaster created. He obviously was not receiving the riding distance, 20+20, salary shown in the 1666/7 salary list. But Col. Whitley was not greatly impressed and could not resist making the jibe that the mail was sent with the fishermen, whilst suggesting a face-to-face discussion rather than commit himself to writing.

> *Mr Fuller Chepsted 18th [Sept 1673].*
> *Yesterday I rec^d yours wthout date, I see you Continue your Resolucon to haue a Salary, but Could not Imagine, you would make soe vnreasonable a Demand, as you doe, something I am willing to doe; and haue a proposall or two to make to you; but being wee Cannott soe well treate by letters; as if you were personally here, I desire you to Come up in ye beginning of ye next weeke, and resolue to stay a day in towne, and I doubt not but wee shall Come to a faire agreement; I know you often send ye Maile by Fishermen, & such kinde of people, soe wonder att yor Extravagant demands: But I pray make hast hither; and I doubt not but to Giue you Content: Soe I rest*
> *Yo^r &c.*

Once again the Chipstead postmaster was being accused of sending his mail by the Ripiers instead of by postboy, regardless of the many prohibitions to do so, though the prohibitions were specifically directed to the carrying of state mail. Postboys would be employed by the postmaster and paid out of his own salary (if any) and they would not be crown servants as they were to be later on. Nevertheless the postmaster was expected to send reasonable persons in the capacity of his employees, male and over 14, and not any traveller that happened to be going in the right direction.

One wonders what took place at the meeting. No doubt they agreed to differ for Fuller remained at Chipstead for two more years until Everest took over in 1675 in the middle of the Lamberhurst incident. A branch postmaster whose name we do not know must have been appointed at Sevenoaks from at least 1669 on, probably from 1660, but the stage itself remained at Chipstead until 1676 in spite of the building of Longford bridge at Dunton Green as early as 1636. As the mail was carried on horseback and as the Darenth River is not particularly wide or deep at Chipstead, there might be no great pressure to change to a route with a bridge; in the event it took forty years to do so.

The Lamberhurst Incident 1675

It would appear that this incident had its roots in the farming system and the complexity of sub-letting it entailed. The Chipstead postmaster would not send letters on past Tunbridge where an office had opened in 1672, to Lamberhurst without a fee and had them brought back when this was not paid. So the situation remained when Richard Everest[28] took over from Fuller at Chipstead.

> *Mr Fuller Cheapstead Sep^t 4th. (1675)*
> *I need not tell you for you know very well, that you are obliged by yor Articles, & Bond, to deliuer the Lamberhurst Letters, But it seemes you haue Imployed a Sloathfull Ignorant fellow, who notwithstanding that he rides through the Town will not deliuer them, but returned them to the Office againe, wch doth not*

onely damnifie the office, but seuerall psons of Quality, suffer in theire Correspondence, by it, Sauerall Atturneys and others, Complaine of the Abuse, and particularly my Lady Hanbie, who had a Letter of L500 concerne, in the Bagge which was returned, you ought to haue giuen me an Accompt of this, or haue come up about it, which if you doe not upon Receipt hereof, I may phaps send a Messenger for you, neither shall that serue yor* turne, but I will alsoe sue your Bond and what you suffer, thank your selfe for, I am - Your Lou: &c:*

Mr *Everest Cheapstead 7*th *75. (Sept)*

You haue not onely damnifyed, and scandalized the office, by returneing the Lamberhurst Letters, but you haue Laid open y^e *way to Leade your self into trouble, the Complaintes, I haue recd against you are very odious, and you will be vndoubtedly prosecuted for your offence: and though, you pretend, noe person at Lamberhurst would take Charge of y*^e *Letters; I haue it from very good hands there that you refused to Leaue them (as formerly) w*th *Robert Crouche at y*^e *Chequer, who is the Person that did before, and would then haue recd them; I am further informed, that your Boy Carrying 5 Letters to my Lady Hanbyes and then refuseing to giue him 10d aboue the Port, he Ridd away, and would not deliver them, Judge you how Irregular a thing this was, and how you will be able Answer it, the like he Did w*th *Letters to m*^r *Dew, and severall other eminent persons, and this is not all, but he allsoe omitted to Call at y*^e *s*^d *Crouches, for the Letters, for London, W*^{ch} *hath bin very prejudiciall to the Partyes Concerned, you must answer for all, faile not, to send a speedy answer, to - yours &c.*

Col. Whitley, in London and therefore distanced from the scene of action, ever willing to think up and to try out new arrangements that might better fit in with local custom and requirement, a week later had quite changed his approach to Everest -

Mr *Everest Cheapstead Sep: 16*th *75.*

*I haue soe good an opinion of you, that I am Confident, you haue an honest meaneing, yet you may be wrongd, (& I suffer) by the neglects, And abuses of your servants, and if you thinke it troublesome, or Inconvenient to keepe an Accompt w*th *m*^r *Crouch, I haue it vnder Consideracon, whether I may not as good (if you desire it) send y*^e *Letters sealed vp in a Bagg to Lamberhurst, and Let y*^e *officer there, Accompt w*th *the office, and you to take noe further charge vpon you, then to deliver them allwayes safe to m*^r *Crouch, who is appointed to receiue them, pray order your Boys, to Call Constantly at y*^e *Chequer on m*^r *Crouch, and bring all Letters back, W*^{ch} *he, or any other in the Towne (from tyme to tyme) shall deliver to them, be allsoe very diligent, in the due performance of all other dutyes, relateing to your Imployment, and you shall finde me to be Yours &c -*

Whitley then makes Sevenoaks the Post Stage 1676

The Colonel's letter of June 1676 to Mr Everest is very definite–

This is to give you Notice y^t *I have appointed Mr Hockham, of Seaven Oakes to be Deputy Post M*^r *of y*^r *Stage, you are therefore to desist from acting any more in y*^r *Capacity; make haste to cleare y*^r *Accompt, to keep both you & me from Charge & trouble: I am -*
(undated but next to other letters of 24th June 1676.)

No doubt the Lamberhurst incident had had some bearing on the transfer of the stage from Chipstead to Sevenoaks as at the same time Lamberhurst becomes a Post Town, a sub-office under Sevenoaks, with Robert Crouch at the Chequers Inn as Postmaster.

Some time a little after June 1676 the post route changed to that through Dunton Green and over Longford Bridge. And so Chipstead passed into history and Sevenoaks itself, hitherto a branch office,

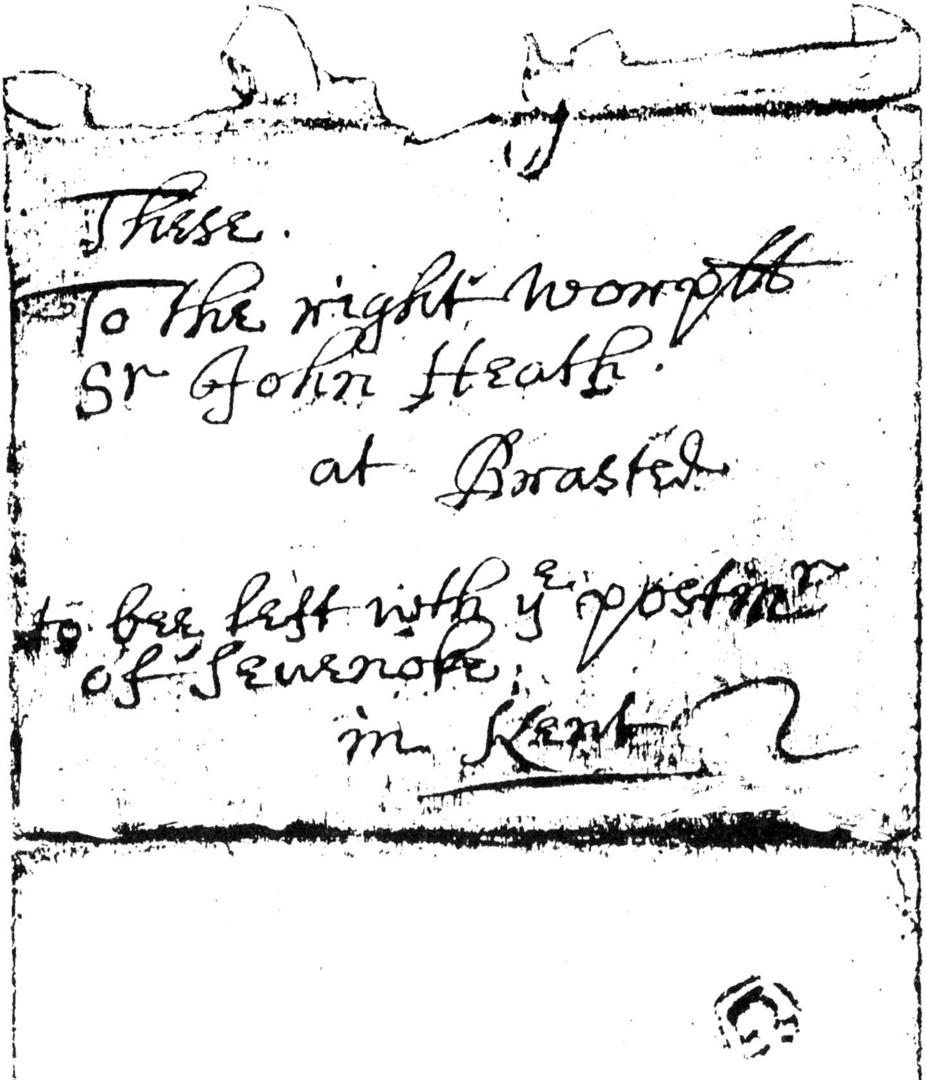

These.
To the right worpll
Sr John Heath.
    at Brasted

to bee left with ye postmr
of Sevenoke
        in Kent

becomes the main staging post. By now the Kent mail came three times a week outside the season, leaving London on Monday, Wednesday and Friday evenings. Bromley office opened in 1678.

The London Gazette of 3 July 1676 carries a repeat of the earlier seasonal advertisement of 1669,

'*There goes a post every day from London to Tunbridge, this will be continued during the Season at the Wells'*.

and then a footpost from Tunbridge to the Wells. This meant a daily post to Sevenoaks as well. The posts to Rye went twice a week. Such was to be the annual pattern.

Robert Hockham at Sevenoaks was soon in trouble and remained so over the years:

27 July 1676 Mr Hockham Seauenoakes
Your dispatches with the Tunbridg Baggs, backward and forward are so slow and negligent.

Mr Hockham Seuocke 10. August 1676
I haue dayly Complaints of the Late comeing of the Letters to the Wells, to the great dissatisfaccon of the Gentry there, and a shamefull Losse, and scandall to the office, they Leaueing the Post, and sending their Letters by the Coaches, and Carriers, Let me desire you (in one word) to make all possible dispatch that this may be amended, and you will oblige,
Yo^r Lou

In the same month, when the postboy travelling from Southwarke to Sevenoaks fell asleep, as well he might if he had repeated Barlow's experience of not being '*in a bed for a week*', Whitley was all praise for the Tunbridge and Sevenoaks postmasters and censure for Southwarke.

August: 76. Mr Whitley Southwark 11.
I haue dayly complaints from Merchants, and other persons of Quality, at Tunbridge, that they are commonly gone of the walkes, before theire letters come there, to their great dissatisfaction, and damage, they Leaueing the Post, and and sending their letters by the Coaches, and Carriers by your slow rideing, for I know, the Postmasters at Seuenoaks, and Tunbridge, doe their parts, but it is constantly very late, when your Boy comes to Seuocke, this day he was mett on the way asleepe, it being 8 of the Clock: I will only this once advise you to imploy such seruants, and Horses, as the businesse may be better done, for I will suffer these abuses, to the Gentry at the Wells, and allsoe to my selfe, no longer, for if these delays be any more committed, I will without more adoe, lay you aside, and Imploy another, vpon the next Just complaint, I receiue in this nature, I haue tould you what you must expect from
Yo^r Lou:

Yet soon the complaints of Tunbridge Wells arose again towards Sevenoaks.

Aug^t:1677. Mr Hockum
Now the time of your dayly rideing grows short, I pray make all possible dispatch wth the Mailes, for I haue greuious Complaints, from the Wells, of the late coming of them thither; I pray let me know, whether Mr Carter hath paid you my Bill, if he hath not, call on him for itt,
I am -

It was at this time that Hockham demanded £10 for carrying the Bye letters to Tunbridge Wells and got it.

Opposite: 1681 July 21 Thursday. Letter from London to Sir John Heath at Brasted inscribed 'to bee left with ye postmr of Sevenoke in Kent' with bishopmark and '2' to pay. (Kent Archives U55 E100/137 with permission.) Inset: The General Post Office 1678-1829 at Sir Robert Viner's house in Lombard street. Purchased by PO in 1705 after his death.

End of Post Office Farm on a National Scale

James, Duke of York, on whom the revenue from the post office had been settled by Act of Parliament in 1663 had granted the farm to Lords Arlington and Berkeley in 1667. When, ten years later the farm expired, the Duke decided not to grant another farm, but to manage the post office himself. In consequence of this decision, Col. Whitley who stayed on until Lady Day 1678 to see through the changes, issued the following circular in April 1677 to all 154 postmasters then employed.

"The ffarme of this Office expireing at Midsom'. and his R.H.
"the Duke of Yorke haveing declared his pleasure, to take it then
"into his owne Managem' Comands me to give you Notice of it,
"requireing you (if you intend to continue yo' Imploym' as Pos'mar.
"of ——————) to come yr. selfe, or Authorise some other to appeare
"for you, at this Office, before the 10th of May next ensueing, in
"order to yr. future Contract: & in the mean time to send me the
"names, quality and a bond of yr. Security that there may be time to
"enquire after theire sufficiency. If you faile herein, Care will be
"taken to provide another for yr. Stage, yt. the Publique may not
"suffer by yr. Neglect. I expect yr. Speedy Answer, and remaine
Yo' &c." [29]

No doubt the Postmaster of Sevenoaks, Robert Hockham, attended to look after his interests, or at least sent his representative. The following year, as can be seen from the accounts of 1678, he was receiving a 'sallary' of £12 (£565) per year paid quarterly £3.

The whole of the London Office in 1677 was managed by a deputy and 77 persons[30] and the London Administration of the Kent Road is shown in an undated manuscript circa 1678/80, with clerks of the Kent Road

Anthony Hafland	50 (£ per year)	(£2,350)
Anthony Markland	24 (£ per year)	(£1,130)

The book of Establishments 1682 shows the clerk of the Kent Road as
Mr Anthony Halford   050.00.0

presumably the same person with no increase in salary.

Postmasters and Local Farming   The 1685 account books show Hockham as Postmaster of Sevenoaks and Postmaster of Tonbridge[31], with William Crumps at Bromley near the Bell Inn. Then from 1686 on comes a somewhat mixed period when the local farming arrangements swing between Sevenoaks and Tonbridge. Robert Hockham, Edward Kent, Daniel Stephens, John Brett, Robert Vernon and Ann Vernon are all involved. Bye letters are farmed separately as may be seen from the list of postmasters at the front. The local farm continued until the 1711 act, but the pattern of organisation continued until 1716 at least with the farmers remaining as managers, matters to be dealt with in the next chapter.

Seven Day a Week Mail   In June 1687 the London Gazette carried an advertisement of a seven day a week post from Tunbridge during the season, previously it had been six days a week, '*it is ordered to come on Mondays as well as every other day of the week*'. But still it was to leave London only on six days a week. Whereas there may previously have been some Sunday working, this is probably the first example of seven day working in the area. But remember there were no telephones or any other means of communication. The experiment only lasted for three years and then reverted to six day working.

Opposite: 1678. Robert Hockham, Postmaster of Sevenoaks, quarterly accounts showing balance carried forward each quarter after deduction of salary £3 (£12 per annum) and other expenses giving an income to the Post Office of about £2 a month. (PO Arckives)

Warning Against Imposters   The London Gazette of 18 October of the same year 1686 also points out that '*several innkeepers and others have pretended to be postmasters*' when they are not so and that '*No Person is to be esteemed a Postmaster who has not a deputation under the hand and seal of the Rt. Hon. The Earl of Rochester, Lord High Treasurer of England and H.M. Postmaster General*'.

London Salaries   By 1694 for some reason the Clerks of all other Roads had had their salaries raised to 60L but not so the Clerk of the Kent Road.   Therefore a petition was made to have it raised.   In reply a warrant was raised dated 20 June 1694 allowing the Kent Road clerk's salary to be 60L the same as the others.[32]

Decline of Rye

The Anglo-French tariff war began in 1678 and greatly cut down the foreign trade passing through Rye; Rye being in competition with Dover for whatever continental trade existed.   At the same time the port became badly silted up.   So began the change in importance of the terminus of this road, Hastings beginning to gain ascendancy over Rye.

Hastings was still actively engaged in the fish trade and an order had recently been passed that the feeters or dossers, the large baskets in which the fish of the Town were carried on the backs of ten or twelve horses in a line under the charge of one man were to be made according to an assize, viz 12 inches wide in the yoke, between the bores 7 inches deep and 17 inches between bayle and bayle.[33]

1683. Letter from Lewes Oct 27th via London '2', to Sevenoaks '2' making 'in all 4d' to the Countess of Dorset at Knole, showing 'hot cross bun' mark of Robert Tayer Postmaster of Chichester and farmer of the Chichester Road, London bishopmark and inscribed 'Send this by the post from London to Sevenoaks'.   (Kent Archives U269c 98/8 (65) with permission.)

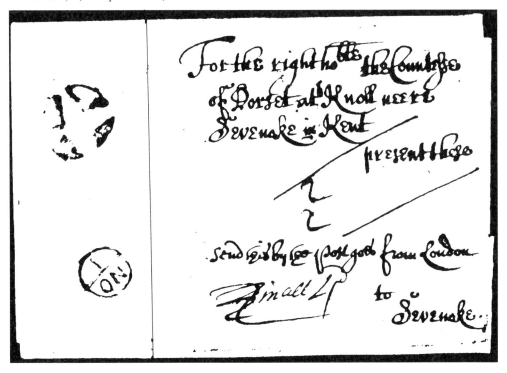

Coaches on the Road

The road was still pretty bad beyond Tonbridge. Lady Russell wrote in 1678 '*I do really think that if I could have imagined the illness of the journey it would have discouraged me: it is not to be expressed how bad the way is from Sevenoaks but our horses did very well and Spence very diligent, often off his horse to lay hold of the coach*'.[34]

Stagecoaches also began to appear. A 1680 copy of the Newsheet 'Mercurius Avlicus' gives a list of Stagecoaches including one for the Rose and Crown in Tonbridge from the 3 Tuns in Gracechurch Street, Blew Boars Head Fleet St, and Southwarke every Monday and Friday and return, presumably Tuesday and Saturday, but not stated. This coach would go through Sevenoaks and over Longford Bridge so they must have managed up and down 'Madam Scott's Hill' somehow.

The climb to the top of the Downs had always had several routes up it and it seems that with the building of Longford Bridge in 1636 the road up used by coaches must have shifted to one of the eastern tracks probably the extreme eastern route that has now been cut off by the expansion of RARDE at Fort Halstead, where the lower part only of the holloway is still open as a footpath. And that this shift happened even though the Chevening road remained open at the time.

Some of the owners of coaches are mentioned in de Laune. His 1681 edition has no mention of a stagecoach for Sunnock, Tunbridge or Bromley, but does mention Mr Varnham's coach from Maidstone to 'The Star' on Fish Street hill London. The 1690 edition again has no mention of a stagecoach originating from Sevenoaks or Bromley but says that Mr Varnham's coach from Maidstone (via Wrotham) came to The Star on Monday and Friday and left on Tuesday and Saturday.[35] A Stagecoach is also mentioned from Tunbridge, Mrs Foster and Mr Freckleton's coach which comes to the White Hart in Southwark on Tuesdays and Saturdays and leaves on Mondays and Fridays in Winter and in Summer, in and out every other day. These early coaches of the 1680s and 1690s were heavy lumbering vehicles very different to those to come in the 1830s.

Persons that travelled outside and on top had to hang on as best they could without any handrails, but the coaches of that period went slowly most of the time. The weather was not always kind and, too, there was always the possibility of being 'benighted', not managing to make the inn by nightfall through losing one's way or breaking down, and having to spend the night on the open road. During the 1684 storm just before Christmas the Tunbridge Wells carrier had to leave his son's body by the roadside after staggering on for miles with the dead child in his arms.[36] There were not so many people about to help or hinder; only a tenth of the present population.

Volume of Traffic

The volume of letters handled can be calculated in an approximate way by taking the yearly income and calculating the number of letters at 2d, the cost of postage up to 80 miles that this would represent. The number calculated would represent incoming letters to be paid for by the recipient and it might be assumed that there were as many outgoing. There are, of course, many assumptions in such a calculation: not all letters are 2d, some are more, so the volume may be overstated, no account can be taken of newspapers and 'frees', the number incoming may be less than the number outgoing and finally the number per delivery depends on the number of deliveries per week which changes with seasonal variations.

Notwithstanding the above caveats, the calculation gives an interesting insight into the amount of business and the rate of increase for charged letters.[37]

In the **Chipstead** days

							Delivery at	
							3 times	6 times
							per week	

£ 5. − .6 Income for year 1673 represents 628 incoming letters @ 2d averaging 4 | 2 per delivery

4.12.4	"	1674	"	554	"	@ 2d	"	3	1½
7.18.8	"	1675	"	952	"	@ 2d	"	6	3
10.16.-	"	1676	"	1296	"	@ 2d	"	8	4

After the move to **Sevenoaks** volume started to increase

| £ 20.12. 6 | " | 1677 | " | 2475 | " | @ 2d | " | 16 | 8 |
| 36.10.10 | " | 1678/9 | " | 4385 | " | @ 2d | " | 28 | 14 |

and, for comparison, a few later dates,

£ 55.4.4	"	1685	"	6626	"	@ 2d	"	43	22
193.4.7	"	1720	"	23187	"	@ 3d	"	—	50
159.9.0	"	1750	"	19128	"	@ 3d	"	—	41

Population

Some estimated population statistics put these letter volumes in perspective.

1660	*Sevenoaks*	*Westerham*	*Tonbridge*
	800	700	650

1695 Gregory King in 1695 collected statistics of the parishes of Sevenoaks in connection with his demographic work on static populations and small Kent families.[38]

	Sevenoaks Town	*Riverhead*	*Weald*	*Total*
Total Persons	891	371	310	1,572
Married Persons, Widows and Widowers	367	148	133	648
Unmarried Persons, Bachelors and Spinsters	51	5	6	62
Servants, Male & Female	110	71	41	222
Total Adults	528	224	180	932
Children	363	147	130	640
	891	371	310	1,572
Houses	206	80	79	365
Numbers per household	4.3	4.6	3.9	4.3

Chapter III

1695-1770
Post Office Surveyors, Cross Posts and Turnpikes

Monarchs	William III, alone	(1694-1702)
	Anne	(1702-1714)
	George I	(1714-1727)
	George II	(1727-1760)
	George III	(1760-1820)

Chronologie

1697   Celia Fiennes Tour of Kent.

     Parliament authorizes J.P.'s to erect guide posts or stoops at Cross Roads.

1706   About this time posting houses began to provide postchaises rather than horses to ride upon.

1704   Newcomen's steam engine.

1705   Some Towns had postal namestamps. Could there be an early undiscovered one for Sevenoaks?

1709   Turnpike Act 8 Anne c12 First in Kent.Sevenoaks to Woodsgate (Pembury) and Tunbridge Wells and on to Flimwell.

1710   Major Post Office Act 9 Anne c10.

     Lamberhurst casts and supplies the Heavy iron railings for use outside St Pauls Cathedral.

1711   Post Office Farming contracts ended. Many Farmers continued as Managers on Salary.

1712   Newspapers had to bear tax stamps.

1715   Treasury approval for Six Post Office Surveyors.

1719   Defoe wrote 'Robinson Crusoe'.

1720   Ralph Allen. First Bye and Cross Post Contract controlled from his own office near Bath.

1730   Francis Austen, solicitor, started practicing in Sevenoaks.

1733   Further authorisation to erect signposts.

1734   First recorded Cricket Match on the Vine 6 Sept.

1735   Act for building Maidstone Gaol.

1743   Aug 18, Postchaises for London–T.Wells road from Mr. Baldwin at George Inn, Southwarke

     Francis Austen bought 'The Red House'.

1745   Rebellion. Increased use of express messenger service by General Public.

1748   Turnpike Act. Farnboro' to Riverhill.

1752   Adoption by Britain of the Gregorian Calendar.

1753   British Museum begun.

1757   Post office notice. Additional Bye Road instructions.

1760-1828 Silk Mills at Greatness. Peter Nouaille employed 100

1761   Post Office notice. More cross-routes, more services.

     Earliest known Sevenoaks Townstamp.

1763   Sept 27, Notice in London Gazette on eight dates to confirm illegal carriers of mail would be prosecuted: Carriers, Coachmen, Watermen, Wherrymen, Dispersers of Country Newspapers, Higlers, and all other persons.

     Dec 31, Whole of Rye road and Hastings mail stolen from a horse 'parked' outside the front door of Horse and Groom, Kent Street.

1764   Bye and Cross Road Letter Office becomes part of GPO Inland Office on Allen's death.

     Highwayman at Sevenoaks.

1765   Cross-route Godstone–Westerham–Riverhead–Wrotham Heath turnpiked.

     Letter stealing made a capital felony.

     Several escaped prisoners from Maidstone Gaol shot and killed near Plaxtol by troops from the local barracks.

1766   American War of Independence.

1767   Byrom's Universal Shorthand book first published.

Chapter III

1695–1770
Post Office Surveyors, Cross Posts and Turnpikes

The Posts are now becoming more firmly established, yet the scene continues as that of postboy on horseback. Easily recognisable as such in spite of having no officially provided uniform, he would have a large 'portmantle' bag strapped to his back and resting on the horse's rump containing '*all the severall baggs of letters for his Roade*' from which each postmaster took the bag for his town and on the return journey placed in the bag for London; for all letters went into and out of London except for bye letters for places along his own road. These bye letters he separately carried in a satchel slung around his waist. His costume was completed with very heavy leather riding boots, a heavy coat and probably a large brimmed hat against the elements, for although the post went slowly by modern standards, it went forward in sunshine, rain, storm and snow, both by day and by night. And on a moonless night it was as well to be riding a horse that knew the road which now would take him across Bromley Common, up Rushmore Hill past 'The Porcupine' on the right going south with its nearby stabling for eighteen post-horses, past 'The Harrow' often a haunt for those up to no good, down Marams Court Hill (Star Hill) and into Dunton Green. Across the Darenth bridge at Longford against the mill and into Sevenoaks, since 1676 the Post town, blowing his horn as required by regulations.

Leaving the Town southwards by the High Street the road used to run almost straight as it went past Sevenoaks Park messuage, now Park Grange; the emphasised swing to the east was introduced when alterations, including diversions of the main road away from the house, were made some little time after Thomas Lambard first bought the property in 1654 from George Lone a Catholic whose family had for nearly a hundred years possessed large landholdings to the south and southeast of Sevenoaks until during the Interregnum he was forced to sell the land bit by bit to pay his 'fines' for remaining a Catholic, being considered almost an enemy by Parliament and 'sequestered for recusancy'.[1] And so the bend in the road has remained ever since, a continuing contemporary reminder of the penalty extracted by one's fellow men for following one's concience. But the postboy must press on, past where the battle of Solefields was fought in June 1450, then to descend the steep hill at Riverhill into the Weald and so to Tonbridge.

Quite apart from 'free' letters, the amount of 'dead' weight in the form of leather and gunny sacks with seals and brass fittings must have been enormous compared to the weight of the letters carried therein; it could well have been sixty percent or more of the total load. And this dead weight was moved day after day, day after day and probably weighed half as much again when it was sodden wet with rain.

The road itself was changing a little in character. Parliament in 1697 in the reign of William and Mary and again as the Georgian era progressed in 1733 had authorised the Justices of the Peace to order erection of guide posts or stoops at crossroads outside villages to point the way and the road was increasingly used by carriages.

The Farming Period for Local Posts
It is known that the whole section of the Rye road south of Chipstead was offered to Robert Hall of Rye

Above: Postmasters Accounts 1685 showing Hockham of Sevenoaks and of Tunbridge.
Opposite: Postmasters Salaries 1694 showing Sevenoaks and other Kent Towns. (Both PO Archives)

The Particulars of what Salaries have been paid to
the Several Post-Mast.ᵉ in the Year ending March 25, 1694.

23.	Lewis Stucley of Plymouth 2 q.ᵗ	95 00 0
23.	John Stucley of Plymouth 2 q.ᵗ	100 00 0
25.	Philip Hayman of Dartmouth	16 00 0
26.	James Buckley of Totney	20 00 0
27.	Solomon Tozer of Ashburton	72 00 0
28.	Joseph Quash of Exeter	100 00 0

	Brought over	647 00 3
29.	Thomas Web of Sittingbourn	20 00 0
230.	William Silvester of Sheerness	20 00 0
231.	John Cary of Maidstone	10 00 0
232.	Alexander Hart of Ashford	30 00 0
233.	Mary Bevis of Rochester	50 00 0
234.	Daniel Hall of Gravesend	5 00 0
235.	Barbara Ellince of Dartford	20 00 0
236.	Thomas Godwin of Bromley 1 q.ᵗ to June the 24	1 05 0
236.	Edmund Millington of Bromley 3 q.ᵗ to March the 25	3 15 0
237.	Robert Hall of Rye	18 00 0
238.	Edward Lloyd of Stonecrouch	2 00 0
239.	Robert Hockham of Sevenoaks	35 00 0
239.	Robert Hockham of Sevenoaks, for riding the Tunbridge Stage a Year, ending September the 29, 1692	00 00 0
241.	William Gardiner of Southwark	75 00 0
8.	John Westbrown of Harwich	00 00 0
9.	Daniel Gwin of Falmouth	10 00 0
250. 244.	Peter Vander Pool of the Briel	00 000 0
		677 00 3

in 1673 but whether it was taken up then is not certain. A southern section which included Sevenoaks at times was farmed under Tonbridge from 1686 until 1711 when all farming ceased.

As early as year ending 25 March 1686/7 Edward Kent was dealing with both the general Post Letters of Sevenoaks and the Bye letters which were accounted for separately. At March 1689 Robert Hockham had taken over at Sevenoaks and at midyear, 29 Sept 1689, the Tonbridge Farm started with Robert Verron coming onto the scene. Three years later Robert Verron had died and John Brett took over halfway through the year at Michaelmas 1692, sharing the farm with Ann Verron, probably Robert's widow, for the next four years, after which Brett operated on his own.

After a couple of years (1697/8 and 1698/9) with Daniel Stephens in charge of the Sevenoaks office, John Brett took over, again halfway through the year at Michaelmas, the whole of the Tonbridge Farm including Sevenoaks until the 1710 Postal Act stopped the farming system when from 29 Sept 1711 he continued as manager until 1716. As farmer he kept the money he collected and paid £360 (£16,250)per year plus £32, being one 4th part of the increase over £360, later reducing in 1704 to £330 pa. In year ending 25 Mar 1711/12 he paid for half a year's farm £165 to Michaelmas and picked up half a year's salary £83.15.0 thereafter getting a salary of £167.15.0 pa as manager until 1716. Until 1752, the year ended on March 25th of what now would be the following year and most changes were made on one of the quarter days, in this case Michaelmas, Sept 29th.

John Brett would be overseeing a largish area, and without doubt he had employees in charge of the various offices but their specific names are not known between 1699 and 1717. The continued mention of Anne Verron and Daniel Stephens in the accounts turns out to be the repetition of an outstanding debt from June 1696 and Jan 1703 respectively still being carried forward up to fifty three years later. Central Accounts of the Post Office had by then many thousands of pounds owing to it from Deputy Postmasters.[2]

The Year 1710 is to be remembered as the year when the Sussex iron foundries at Lamberhurst, long before development of the industry in the Midlands, supplied heavy iron railings for use outside St. Paul's Cathedral, used there for 200 years before replacement.

Post Office Surveyors

Once the concept of 'farming' as a method of controlling operations had been thrown out by the 1710 Act[3], the way was open for the Post Office to appoint a group of men controlling local operations and reporting back to London. The first six surveyors, covering between them the whole country, were appointed in 1715 and this body of men remained the motivating force ensuring detailed control from London until increasing complexity of operations drove the Post Office in 1933 to start a policy of decentralised regionalisation.[4] The 1710 Act had of itself allowed surveyors to be appointed but authorized no funds to pay them, until finally the Treasury was prevailed upon to allow the establishment on 13 June 1715.

The South East Region, later called the 'Home District', stretched from the Isle of Wight and took in most of Sussex, Kent and Essex. The appointed surveyor had to know his whole area in the most intimate detail and had many facts and a plethora of timings to absorb. Wilkinson had become very old and Barnabas Bartleet was dealing with Sevenoaks in 1793. Once the local surveys started up in 1801, the Surveyors reports remain intact, so much more about surveyors Mr Scott and Mr Aust in the next chapter.

Cross Posts

Yet although Farming was said to cease in 1711 and did so on the Main Post Roads, in effect Ralph Allen started 'farming' the cross posts in 1720, although such a word was not used. An enabling clause was inserted in the 1710 Act allowing cross-posts to be set up. Cross posts were routes joining main towns already on General Post Routes, which cross-routes did not pass through London. Prior to this Act, letters for major towns perhaps only 40 miles apart by direct route, had to be routed into and out of London and charged accordingly, possibly at the 70 mile rate. The purpose of routing through London was for accounting control.

In the Post Office at that time, Accounting Systems determined the method of handling; in many cases what might seem the most obvious way to handle mail expeditiously from an operational standpoint is not

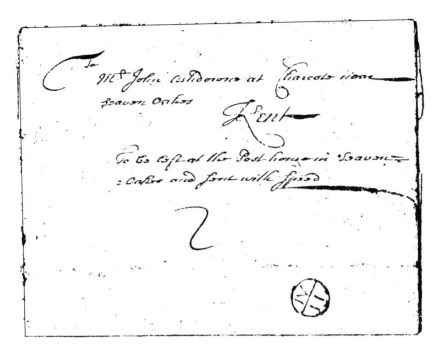

1709 Farmed Letter of Brett period. Letter from London with Bishopmark to 'Charcots' near Sevenoaks inscribed 'To be left at the Posthouse in Seaven-Oakes and gone with speed' Postmasters had authority to organise local delivery and charge 2d which was not marked on the letter at this time. Collection of letters when made was supposed to be free of charge.

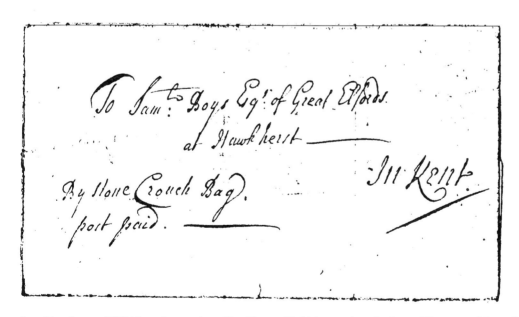

Local bye-letter of 1754 from Sevenoaks to Hawkhurst. No bishopmark as the letter did not travel through London and was accounted for separately. Prepaid, but no mention of the charge which in later years would have been put on in red ink. Marked 'By Stonecrouch Bag'. Until 1788 Stonecrouch was the stage at which the Rye and Hastings mail parted company; Hawkhurst was a post town on the Rye section.

observed as it would not allow the item to be properly accounted for. Always one must needs look for the underlying accounting procedure to understand why an item is dealt with in a particular way.

On 8 February 1719/20 the young Ralph Allen of Bath aged 27 but with a certain amount of Postal Deputy experience behind him was given a contract to farm the Bye and Cross Posts which he did from Offices over the stable block in his own home. This contract he maintained until his death at 71 in 1764 when the Bye and Cross Post Office was removed to London, later becoming part of the Inland Office, the accounts still being kept separately. In effect Ralph Allen operated a post within a post using his own method of checking and accounting, a method never fully disclosed and he operated his own team of Surveyors who at times worked side by side with the post office Surveyors.

Cross Post Accounting   Did Ralph Allen ever receive the money paid on the letter from Sevenoaks to Hawkhurst 1754 which, as it was a Bye Letter he was entitled to do under his contract? Or rather, it is surmised that he was entitled to do so, though it must be said that in Ralph Allen's book of instructions 1730-40 [5] no mention is made in the index of the towns of Sevenoaks, Tunbridge Wells, Battle, Hastings, Rye and Cranbrook; nor of Canterbury, Dartford and Maidstone. That he ever received money for Kent byeposts will never be proved, but it is possible that he did, for the one local fact that is available (but which relates to 1780 after his death) is that the Tunbridge Wells guidebook of Sprange requests letterwriters to put their letter in at the right window in his post office, distinguishing between 'Cross and Bye post' and 'General post', because separate accounts are made up. There appeared, however, to be no accounting division between Cross post and Bye post. Under the Ralph Allen contract this would not appear necessary from the viewpoint of the post office, though one might have thought that the distinction would have been necessary for Allen's control. However either description appears to be used on letters indiscriminately. Lord Stanhope's secretary at Chevening frequently used the superscription 'Cross Post' when sending a letter from Sevenoaks to Tonbridge, one which should surely have been designated a Bye letter, as it was along a General Post route but not touching London. Genuine **cross-posts** were not available in the area until after 1810 when bags were carried from the post towns of Godstone and of Dartford to Sevenoaks over 5th Clause and Penny Post routes but with full General Post mileage charges.

The Bye and Cross Letter office Reports 1757-1771 [6] relating to the period after Ralph Allen's death includes the following instruction:

> '*The Accomptant with the assistance of his Clerk is to open and keep a correct Account by Way of Debtor and Creditor with each Country Deputy concerned in the Bye & Cross Road Letters charging each Deputy according to the Receipt of Letters at his respective Office, as shall be verified by his Monthly vouchers and discharging each according to his respective Salary, Rebates, Allowances, Remittances and Payments; - and upon that foot to make out and transmit to each Country Deputy Quarterly Bills for the Ballances due from Him to the Office, or from the Office to Him, the latter voucht, checkt, and signed as below directed,*'

showing the completely separate accounting system from that of the General Post, also the intricate accounting methods that had to be worked, and disclosing the fact that a Postmaster's bye and cross post salary was still separate from his General Post one.

But there were bye-letters along the London-Rye/Hastings route and the one previously mentioned and shown on page 63 from Sevenoaks-Hawkhurst in 1754 has 'post paid' written on it, although the Post Office had put a notice in the London Gazette of 12th April 1720 (5842) to state that, starting 24 June 1720

> '*Places they are sent from cannot demand the Postage on Byeway or Cross Post Letters, unless the Parties putting them in desire it*'

ie they were allowed to pay at the receiving end in the same way as for General Post letters.

6 July 1761 saw a great increase in the number and frequency of cross posts routes, the subject of a notice in the London Gazette of 28 July 1761. There was also a general tightening up,

> '*all Carriers, Coachmen, Watermen, Wherrymen, Dispensers of County Newspapers and all other persons detected in illegal collecting, conveying and delivery will be prosecuted*'

with a fine of £5 per letter, £100 for every week the practice continues. But the practice was still going on openly, thirty years later.

Cross Routes   The major cross route on which Sevenoaks is situated is Guildford-Reigate-Godstone-Westerham-Sevenoaks-Wrotham-Maidstone. This route turnpiked in 1765 is shown as a major cross road in Cary's roadbook and later had a stagecoach service along it, but at no time has a mail route been set up along the whole distance nor even between Sevenoaks and Maidstone the county capital. Possibly there was only a small amount of mail to these places although one might have expected a large amount to be sent to the county town of Maidstone. This lack of direct communication appears most odd. Nevertheless there was no direct postal connection. Even at a later date letters to Maidstone were being carried 'by the Newsmen' who were responsible for distributing the newspapers printed in Maidstone and who travelled much of the area on a regular weekly basis. A letter in the possession of the writer still travelled Sevenoaks-London-Rochester-Maidstone carried by the post office as late as 1817 about when the cross route eventually became Sevenoaks-Tonbridge-Maidstone, never direct. No Cross Posts developed from Sevenoaks itself during the Ralph Allen era.

Sevenoaks Postmasters 'After the Farming Period'

Following the continued six year management period of John Brett, **Richard Adams** now at The Crowne and previously of The George comes in as Sevenoaks postmaster from Michaelmas 1716 picking up a year and a half's salary in his first payment; he may have understudied Brett for six months. The following year **William Bayley** joined him and so they continued, Adams drawing £45 pa (£2,025) and Bayley £40 (£1,800) until he left at Christmas 1726. Richard Adams continued on his own for fifteen months and for his last year in office was joined by (? his brother) **Thomas Adams**, until, again at Michaelmas, Jane Morley takes over at the same salary £45.[7]

Jane Morley, postmistress 1729-1738, was licencee at 'Ye old Crowne'; during which time one Thomas Barton became licencee at the 'New Crown' which obviously was a completely separate premises to Jane Morley's but possibly the same as Richard Adams'.

Thomas Harrison takes over in 1738 and **Thomas Barton** five years later in 1743, both these changes occurring at Michaelmas, September 29th. Little is known about Thomas Harrison and he does not appear to have been an inn-keeper. Thomas Barton, postmaster 1743-1748 occupied premises simply known as 'The Crowne' and he had been a Licenced Victualler for some years. The 'new' had been dropped from the title and it is thought that his premises was on the site of the later 'Royal Crown' and the present day main post office.

On 8th April 1748 Thomas Barton resigned and **Garnett Loving** was appointed. The Lovings, Garnett and Elizabeth, were licenced victuallers but during the period of their tenure of the postmastership it became the custom not to note the name of the inn on the licence forms they signed, so where their Post Office was cannot be known for certain. During Garnett's time the first recorded Sevenoaks postmark was used in 1761.

With Garnett's death in 1763 after fifteen years service, Elizabeth, his relict, took over until, after a further seven years, in 1770 she was dismissed with no reason given and a Mrs Elizabeth Dransfield appointed in her stead.[8]

Oath and Declaration

The requirement for oaths was continued with the 1710 Postal Act of Queen Anne. Needed from deputy postmasters were the Certificate of Confirmity, subscribing the Test and the Oaths of Allegiance, Supremacy and Abjuration.

Also introduced as from 1 June 1711 was an oath relating to conduct in postal affairs requiring staff not to meddle with the letters which oath all employees had to swear before a Justice of the Peace before starting work. Later this oath became a declaration and a more modern example of the wording is shown in the appendix.

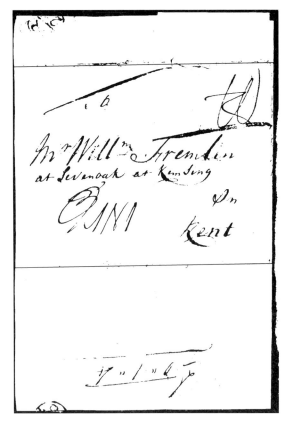

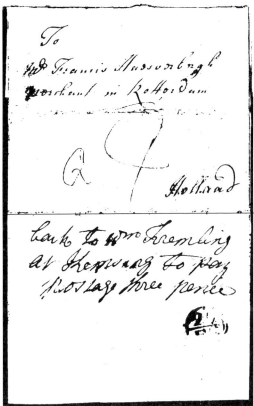

1751 Foreign mail with Local Delivery/Collection charges. Letter from Holland via London 10d plus London to Sevenoaks 3d, making 1N1, one shilling and one penny. Then 3d delivery charge to Kemsing to make £0=1=4 on back of the letter. Year of Calendar change: inside dated 2th of April 1751 N(ew) S(tyle), with bishopmark receiver of London on outside, March 25.
(Kent Archives U2133/c13.)

1748 Letter from Kemsing Sevenoaks to Holland via London with bishopmark, endorsed 'back to Wm Fremling at Kemsing to pay postage three pence'. This would not be the collection charge as this would have been paid direct to the private messenger, but the 3d General Post charge from Sevenoaks to London which at that time could not easily be collected from the foreign recipient. Had it been an inland letter it would have gone forward with the charge collected from the recipient.

Letter Stealing Becomes a Felony

The 1765 Postal Act was to make letter stealing a felony and this remained so until 1833, '*If any Deputy Clerk Agent Letter Carrier Postboy or Rider . . . should secrete embezzle or destroy any letter or letterpacket, he shall be deemed guilty of felony and suffer death as a Felon . . . without benefit of clergy.*' 'Benefit of Clergy' in this case relates to the manner in which commitment took place and the pardoning of sins after confession. Embezzlement of banknotes, but not of coin, became a capital offence. Only eighteen months previously a notice in the London Gazette had reported the whole of the Rye road and Hastings mail, including the Sevenoaks bag had been stolen between 4 and 5 o'clock on the morning of 31st December 1763 from a horse left outside the 'Horse and Groom' in Kent Street, now Tabard Street, whilst the Post Boy imprudently went inside to take some refreshment. The notice was repeated six times but there is no record of any of this mail being recovered.

Bond

A Bond was still required from the deputy postmaster signed by two guarantors to ensure financial reliability. Time to remit monies received for postage due on letters delivered was always given, but if in the end that money was not received the Post Office always sued on the Bond and the Guarantors had to pay up. Should a Guarantor die, another person of substance was immediately required. This was normal practice in any position of financial trust. Later the deposit of Government Stock was substituted for personal guarantors and later still insurance policies.

Earliest Town Stamps

Provincial Townstamps, inkmarks stamped onto each letter to show the Town of Origin, are known in Kent from about 1705 when there appears to have been a general issue. These were new and in 1718 Henry Harper at St Albans was convicted of counterfeiting and using a Town Stamp. He was not only fined but also *pilloried*. Why he should want to counterfeit a stamp, the London Gazette did not tell us.

Another issue appears to have been concentrated around 1720 relating to the time when Ralph Allen took over the Byeposts. Allen was keen to have all his bye and cross letters stamped as it helped his checking system. All the more odd perhaps that the 1754 Sevenoaks-Hawkhurst bye letter previously referred to had no townstamp of origin.

Although Bromley is known for 1721, Stonecrouch 1705 and Hurst Green as early as 1706, the earliest

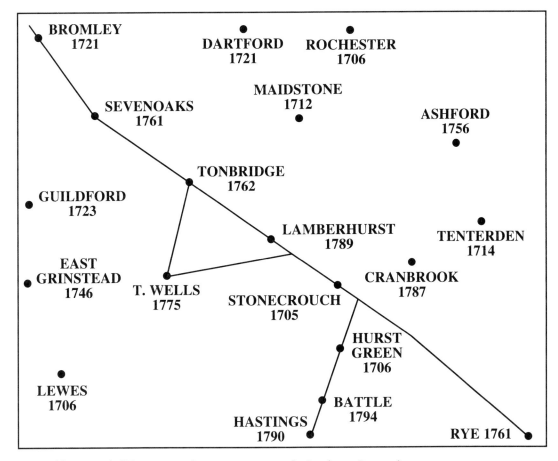

Dates of first recorded Town stamps for towns on or near the London to Rye road.

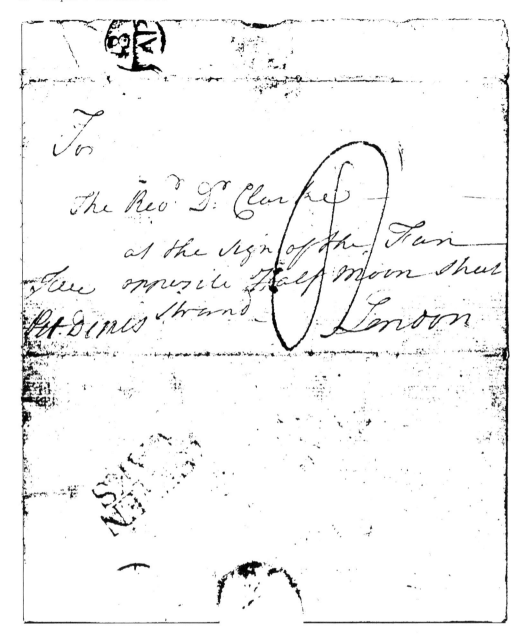

Earliest known Sevenoaks Townstamps. 17.4.1761.
Letter from Valence Westerham to London. A Free letter addressed to 'The Revd Dr Clarke at the sign of the
Fan opposite Half Moon Street Strand London'.

Sevenoaks townstamp at present known is 1761, the date when the Post Office greatly increased the number of cross routes. From searches in the Kent Archives many letters from Sevenoaks are seen for the period 1726-1759 without any townstamp, for example the Polhill Correspondance[9] 'primae facie' sent from Sevenoaks in the years 1726-1751 shows no sign of a townstamp of Sevenoaks or any other place. Nor do letters sent from Kemsing via Sevenoaks by William Fremlin[10] during the same period of

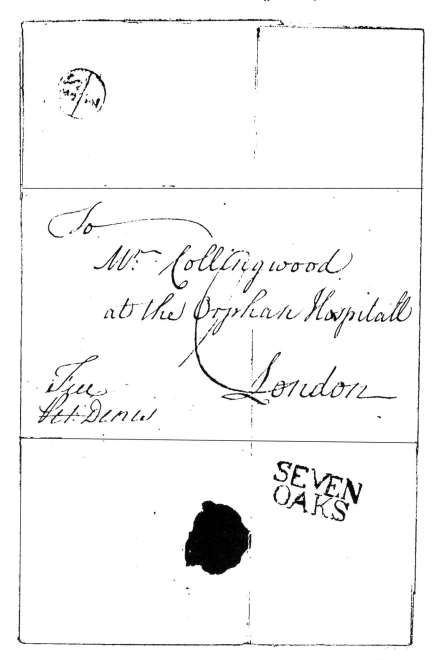

Letter of 1763 from Squerries Westerham 2 Sept. Another early Sevenoaks Townstamp. This letter is now in the Stevenson bequest. (Reproduced by kind permission of the Trustees.) (Reduced)

1748-52 as well as the bye letter of 1754 previously referred to.

Such is the nature of ephemera that no letters have so far been found to make it possible to check the period 1700-1726 in any conclusive way. Judging from the evidence of other towns along the route, Sevenoaks might well have had a townstamp in this early period. If so, the letter is likely to be in the archives of the county town relating to the person to whom it was sent.

Expresses   At this time there was increased use of express letters. Ogilby & Morgan's Travellers Pocket Book of 1755 shows[11] the cost of an express letter from London to Tonbridge as £1.0.3 that is about £45 in 1987 money; to Sevenoaks it would be a little less. For this amount a rider and horse would be provided and the letter could be sent out at any time of the day or night. The charge could well be equated with that of sending out a taxi and driver now. Sevenoaks has not been shown in this list as by 1755 and up to 1793 it was listed as a sub-post-town although still the stagepoint.

The Mail

Letters were charged according to distance to be travelled and the number of sheets which were checked by the 'feel' of the letter and by holding it to a strong light, normally a candle. The recipient normally paid the charge, although letters could be prepaid. When a letter was handed in the clerk checked the address to decide whether it was a bye letter or one to pass through London. These General Post Letters then had the charge to London placed on them. In London this charge was deleted and the total journey charge, the 'In All' charge, inserted. Prepaid letters would have the full charge calculated at the place of handing in and so the postmaster required to have tables of official distances routing in and out of London and measuring the official route the mailboy followed. 'To pay' letters were marked with black ink, 'prepaid' in red. There was no difference in the two charges. The numerals used assumed a style of their own, different in different decades in spite of official exhortations to avoid flourishes. Early numerals are small and usually easily legible, some of the later ones covered almost the whole face of the letter and are sometimes most difficult to decipher.

In London each 'Road' had a clerk in charge and a sorter. Queen Anne's Establishment book for 1702 gives. [12]

List of Salarys in the Post Office
Clerks of the 6 Roads and Assistants

Mr Da^{el} Bikerton of the Kent Road £60   (£2,650)
Mr Alex: Say Assistant and Sorter £50
Mr Geo: Colley of the Kent Road on By-nights £60

and from the Order Book 1737-74 [13]

Mr Sawtell Jnr. Appointed Clerk of the Kent Road

The Post Office still took responsibility to deliver only as far as the post town, after that the arrangements were between the local postmaster and the addressees. Some might call almost every day, others made arrangements for delivery. The General Post charge for incoming letters was collected by the local postmaster and checked to the debit voucher accompanying them from London. After deducting his Salary and other agreed expenses such as that for riding work, the balance and the 'dead' letters on which no money could be collected were returned to London where detailed accounts were kept.

Local Delivery Charge

The local delivery charge was not marked on the letters although in this area some have it marked on the back. Often this may have been put on by the recipient as part of his personal accounting. But however it has been placed there, it provides useful information. The 'country' delivery charge was beginning to go beyond the 2d negotiated in 1668 and was frequently 3d and might sometimes go as high as 6d additional to the General Post charge. Within the Town the Charge appears to have been ½d. This amount is confirmed from an impeccable source, Sevenoaks School. The Yearly accounts of Sevenoaks School are contained in the Sevenoaks Corporation Minute Book 1576-1719 and show receipts and disbursements. The disbursements are under general headings, but at times become more detailed, particularly for 'unusual' items. An item 'For own Riding Charges' appears by 1655 at £3.10.- pa increased to £4 in 1660 and down to £1.16.- by 1719. This heading probably includes the sending of local messages and

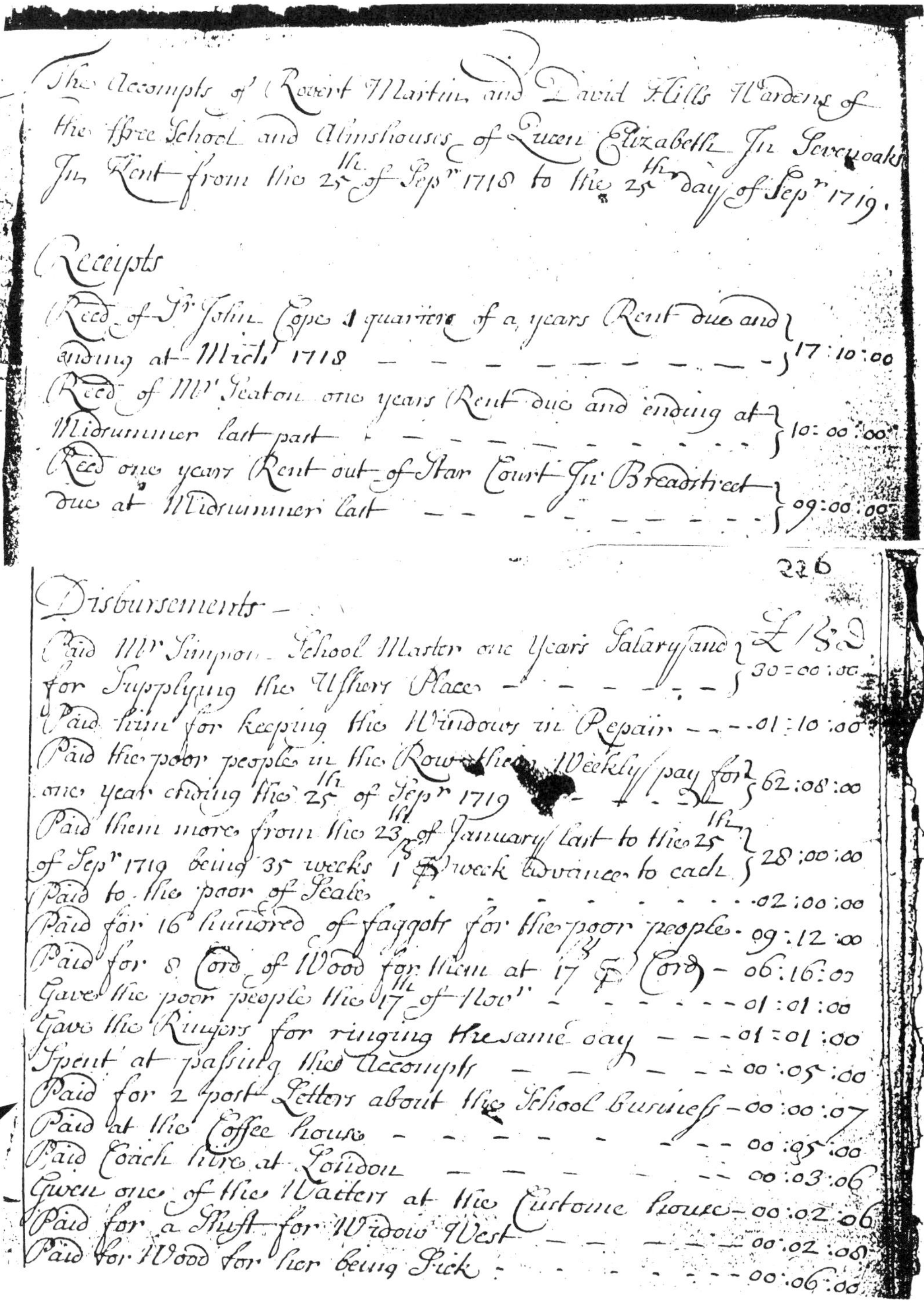

The Accompts of Robert Martin, and David Hills Wardens of the ffree School and Almshouses of Queen Elizabeth Jn Sevenoaks Jn Kent from the 25th of Sepr 1718 to the 25th day of Sepr 1719.

Receipts

Recd of Sr John Cope 1 quarters of a years Rent due and ending at Mich 1718	17:10:00
Recd of Mr Yeaton one years Rent due and ending at Midsummer last past	10:00:00
Recd one years Rent out of Star Court Jn Breadstreet due at Midsummer last	09:00:00

226

Disbursements —

Paid Mr Simpson School Master one Years Salary and for Supplying the Ushers Place	30:00:00
Paid him for keeping the Windows in Repair	01:10:00
Paid the poor people in the Row their Weekly pay for one year ending the 25 of Sepr 1719	62:08:00
Paid them more from the 23 of January last to the 25 of Sepr 1719 being 35 weeks 1 ₰ week advance to each	28:00:00
Paid to the poor of Seale	02:00:00
Paid for 16 hundred of faggots for the poor people	09:12:00
Paid for 8 Cord of Wood for them at 17 ₰ Cord	06:16:00
Gave the poor people the 17th of Novr	01:01:00
Gave the Ringers for ringing the same day	01:01:00
Spent at passing this Accompts	00:05:00
Paid for 2 post Letters about the School Business	00:00:07
Paid at the Coffee house	00:05:00
Paid Coach hire at London	00:03:06
Given one of the Waiters at the Custome house	00:02:06
Paid for a Shift for Widow West	00:02:00
Paid for Wood for her being Sick	00:06:00

Sevenoaks School Accounts 1719 from which a ½d local delivery charge can be inferred. (Sevenoaks Corporation Minute Book 1576-1719.)

letters, there being no official local posts then.

The sending or receiving of a letter by the official Post was a rare event and, as such, itemised separately. There are two such items:

> *Year to Sept 1718. Paid for a letter 3½d [The ½d delivery charge represented 10p in 1987]*
> *Year to Sept 1719. Paid for 2 Post Letters about the School Business 00:00:07*
> *[two at 3½d each]*

As the post charge to London was 3d at the time, there must have been a Town delivery charge never shown on the letter itself and accruing to the local postmaster of ½ d per item, as charged here, although the school was only just across the road if 'The Old Post Office' really was the old location.[14] But more likely these letters were sent up by Thomas Adams at The Crowne on the site where is today's Main Post Office. This would make the charge more reasonable.

The Wells at Tonbridge

Tonbridge Wells was now booming as a health resort. This activity required much wheeled traffic along the road from London and much letter writing during the season, May to October, which in the early days was an informal "season" attended by all classes of people, mixing and gaming.

Arrangements for a daily post through Sevenoaks to Tonbridge during the season continued and are reiterated in the London Gazette. Sevenoaks of course thus benefitted by having a daily post for five months of the year, a facility it would not have had on its own account. From Tonbridge the letters were taken by footpost to the Wells as described by Celia Fiennes when writing of her journey through Kent in 1697. In spite of the seven-days-a-week arrangements commenced in 1686 she is quite adamant that the present arrangements cover only six days, and she is right for after a few years the arrangements had reverted.

> *There are severall buildings just about y' Well where there are severall apothecary's shops, there is also a room for y' post house. The post Comes Every day and returns Every day all the while the season of drinking y' waters is, from London and to it; Except Mondays non comes down from London; so on Satturdayes non goes up to London. You pay a penny Extra-ordinary for being brought from Tunbridge town wch is 4 mile distance, that being a post town, you likewise have the Conveniency of Coaches every day from London for 8 shillings apiece dureing the whole season, and Carriers twice a weeke.*[15]

During the winter the post ran normally, that is, on three days a week only. Previously there had been a charge of 2d for bringing on the letters to the Wells, but this was considered excessive and by the time Fiennes wrote the extra charge had been reduced to a penny only.

The Routes

Celia Fiennes goes on to describe the trouble coaches had in ascending the North Downs escarpment north of Sevenoaks at Marams Court (now Star Hill). Whereas earlier foot travellers and horseriders attacked the rise directly and developed a holloway leading straight up the hill, coaches had to find a more circuitous route.

> '. . . in the Road from thence [T. Wells] to London you go either by Fairlane [Fairlawn near Plaxtol] or else you go by Sevenoake a sad deep clay way after wett; . . . you pass on to the River head as they call it, a fine spring of cleare water that runs thence in a little river; this is at the foote of a great hill . . . called Madam Scott Hill so steepe as seldome is either rode down or up, and few coaches but gaines the top of it by a compass round it, which is steep enough; thence to London.'

At the time Celia Fiennes wrote 1697 there must still have been some choice of route until the route came first to be turnpiked in 1748 when the direct route straight up the hill apparently came to be chosen (gY and then unmarked to rejoin just above W on the plan shown on p110). This is the direct eastern route through the holloway, now cut off by the extension to the grounds of Fort Halstead. Part of this old route can still be walked as a footpath. The plan calls this the *old* turnpike road.

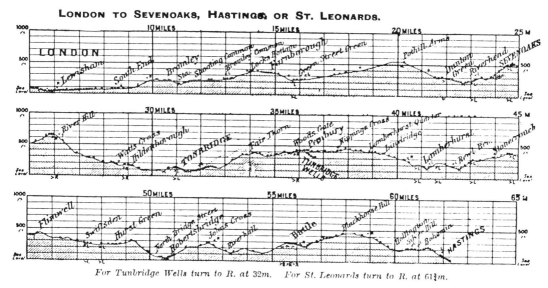

Gradient map for the London to Hastings Road via Sevenoaks and Tonbridge. (Gall and Inglis 1901.)

By 1783 the present road up Star Hill past the Star Inn, now residential houses, was in use (ebZYXWu) as the turnpike road. But even this new road, for the last third of the way involves a direct attack on the ascent.

The gradient map, actually an early motoring map gives a good idea of the hills then encountered by coach drivers, although it shows the Polhill route rather than the Star Hill (Marams Court Hill) one. Gradients become important once wheeled traffic abounds, particularly if horse-drawn.

Sevenoaks Matters   About 1724 Sevenoaks School's present day 'old buildings' had been designed by Lord Burlington and built.

The playing of cricket was coming into prominence. The first recorded local game was at the Vine on 6 September 1734 and during the next decades advertisements show cricket games being played between the Gentlemen of various localities often with as much as 500L on the outcome of the game. Duke's cricket ball manufacture started in Penshurst about 1762 later moving to Chiddingstone Causeway in 1848 and extending their range to bats, stumps, leg guards and gauntlets, the latter items necessary once roundarm and then overarm bowling became allowed.[16] Oral tradition has it that during the early 1820's John Willes of Sutton Valence uncovered the *mistery* of round arm bowling when for winter batting practice in his large barn he would get his sister to bowl to him and she in her crinoline must needs deliver the ball roundarm. His dog fielded. But when Willes tried out the method in 1822 when Kent played the M.C.C. the umpire declared *'No Ball'* each time and he was howled off the pitch by the crowd.

Cockfighting, too, was well advertised in the contemporary local newspapers, typically 4gns a fight with twenty or so battles to be fought at a meeting.

Maintenance of the Roads – Highway Overseers

Unskilled parish labour under overseers not necessarily trained in the work was not the most effective way to maintain roads and in 1691 vide *3 William & Mary c12* the system of parish labour was replaced by cash payments in lieu. The Highways overseers could then employ labour that in time became skilled in road making. Some idea of the condition of old roads can be guaged from the present day photograph of what is now a footpath at Oldbury near Ightham. The road past the Crown Inn is shown on Hasted's map of 1760 as the New Road, so this old road up Old Berry Hill at Seal Chart must have been out of main road use for 225 years. Now even the 'New Road' past the Crown is superseded.

In Sevenoaks as elsewhere the Justices had to nominate Highway Surveyors yearly[17] from amongst those qualified to be so appointed, ie those with a landholding to the value of £50 per annum. There were twenty three parish highway districts in the Sevenoaks area of the Lathe of Sutton-at-Hone and in most cases one man was elected for each district though for 'Sevenoaks Towne' there were two, Richard Adams and Thomas Everest for the year 1715. Some might serve for two or three years but frequent change ensured lack of continuity of repair policy and enforcement and of responsibility.

Richard Adams (Postmaster 1717-28) who was licenced Victualler at the Crowne Inn was a Surveyor in 1715 and 1716. Probably he ran the Post Office from his own inn which is shown by Sir John Dunlop[18] as located in London Road where now is standing the present main Post Office.

Thomas Everest, who might possibly be the son of Everest the Postmaster at the Chipstead stage 1675/6, was licenced victualler at the Royall Oake and Highways Surveyor in 1715 and again in 1721. The Royal Oak opposite the entrance to Sevenoaks school is still there. Once again he could have been involved when his father ran the post office in 1675/6 at Chipstead or he may have moved into Sevenoaks later. Once appointed, the Sevenoaks surveyors were not very good at attending before the Justices to report their position. Those who did, normally reported the '*ways pritty good*'.

Coming of the Turnpikes

The first turnpike act in Kent was that for the road south of Sevenoaks. This act of *1709 (8 Anne Cap 12)* concerned the section from Sevenoaks to Woodsgate [Pembury] and Tunbridge Wells, on to Kippings Cross, Lamberhurst and Flimwell. Much of this section had always been difficult to support as good stone necessary for road building was non-existant in the wealden clay and had to be transported many miles. Further acts in *1724 (11 George I)* and *1740 (14 George II)* increasingly developed this section.

The section from Farnborough to Riverhill just beyond Sevenoaks to the south was turnpiked in *1749 (21 George II)*.

Turnpiking meant that the road, instead of being repaired by the parishioners through whose parish the road ran or at their cost, was now to be supported by the tolls paid by those who used the road. The Turnpike acts laid down details of how wide the road was to be, the verges (no bonfires or unshielded fires within twenty yards), the drainage and the maintenance of the surface of the road itself. Tollbars and tollhouses were to be erected and the amount to be paid in tolls was laid down in the act. Altogether a great improvement, particularly for the wheeled traffic that was increasing. But not popular with local people. Trustees were appointed and in most cases money borrowed to effect the improvements, later to be repaid by the tolls taken. The Hastings (ex Rye) road was the first of the three Kent County roads out of London to be turnpiked. Tollhouses were erected at Pratts Bottom, Dunton Green and Riverhill; also later at Bessels Green, Seal Chart and Wrotham Heath when the main cross-route, Oxted-Westerham-Riverhead-Ightham-Wrotham Heath was turnpiked in *1765 (5 Geo III c68)*.

The Southwark to Rye road was controlled by six different turnpike trusts, the first having come into being in 1709, but it was 1781 before the whole length of the road was controlled. Some unexpected cross-routes came into being, for example Cowden-Penshurst-Watts Cross-Shipbourne-Hadlow in 1765. But not all appeared viable. The Shoreham-Chelsfield-Green Street Green proposed turnpike *(50 Geo III c18)* which in 1810 was to cut a new route, was cancelled the following year with a repealing act *(51 Geo III c205)*. The last local route to be turnpiked was Gravesend-Wrotham-Borough Green as late as *1825 (6 Geo IV c50)*.

Once again fish had special consideration, the year 1761 saw an Act *(2 Geo III c15)* dealing with vehicles carrying fish, which had only to pay tolls commensurate with a post chaise and nothing for carriages or horses when returning empty. Such vehicles could also travel on Sundays, full or empty. Fish

Present (1984) state of Cross Road through Oldbury near Ightham. A typical narrow 'holloway'. (AGD)

consigned to London had to arrive within the Bills of Mortality with load intact and was not to have bulk broken or any sales on the way. Nothing except fish and fish handling accoutrements were to be carried. Carrying game or passengers was illegal and incurred penalties.

Turnpike roads were to remain so organised until taken over by public authorities' Highway Boards in the period 1860-1880 when roads ceased to be financed through tolls and although there were to be attempts to enforce payment of tolls on Post Office vehicles, this idea was to be overthrown in England and Wales, though not so in Scotland from where many letters can be seen marked 'add ½d', the additional halfpenny being the contribution to the expense of the toll charges, when carried by mailcoach.

In 1765 John Metcalfe started his work on roads and bridges, mainly in the north of England and in the early 1800s Thomas Telford and John Macadam were working in Scotland. Thus began in Britain the first real effort to build roads since Roman times.

Postchaises for Hire

With improvements in the road surface came the desire on the part of the public, or rather that section of the public that could afford such things, to travel by carriage rather than on horseback. About 1706 the postmasters of stages within 100 miles of London received an order from the Postmaster General[19] '*to provide Post Chaises with an additional Number of Horses to furnish persons riding Post in the same manner as Post Horses*'.

To do so involved considerable outlay for Postmasters, but eventually over some years the provision was made and the travelling public educated to such good effect that, after some opposition at the beginning, it could be said '*the present method of travelling Post in all the great Roads is now in Chaises and very few persons call for Post Horses*'.

This method of posting was made more official with notices in the London Gazette eg. 18 Aug 1743; Mr Baldwin of the George Inn, Southwarke being nominated to provide post chaises for both the London-Dover and London-Rye roads, but the latter only as far as Tonbridge Wells.

The early information comes to light in 'the Case of the Deputy Post-Masters', a complaint written after the 1710 Act establishing a General Post Office was passed, which act again requiring Postmasters to keep Posthorses, not Postchaises, under penalty of a fine. One might be excused for thinking the legal draftsmen had merely updated the earlier act constitutionally but were not 'au fait' with the changed operational methods. Certainly the wording of *Para 9 of the Act of 1660* and *Para 22 of 1710* are similar. Both refer to '**Riding** in Post' and have similar penalties. Up to this time the Postmasters had had a monopoly of supplying the travelling public with horse at 3d per mile and guide with horn for 4d per stage and this monopoly should, they considered, be transferred to the hiring of postchaises. This matter was important to them for others were setting up in business to hire out carriages in competition but without the penalties for non-provision attached to the deputy postmasters' position and such persons were not being prosecuted for infringing the deputy postmasters' monopoly.

Clarification of the situation came in the *1749 Act (22 Geo II c25)* to explain and amend an Act for establishing a General Post Office 1710. This new Act was not to defeat any judgement prior to 25th March 1749 and now confirmed the Postmasters monopoly to hire out post**horses** for riding but stated that "*it shall and may be lawful for all Persons to lett out for Hire, as well upon Post Roads as elsewhere, **Chaises** duly licenced, with Horses to draw the same, and to furnish or exchange Horses for drawing any such Chaises or Calashes*" Persons accompanying the Chaise could also be horsed. This decision was not greatly to the deputy postmasters' liking.

And in Ogilby's Roadbook of 1755 the following information is still given to the public, with no mention of post chaises. That book, too, did not reflect the true situation.

'The Postmaster-General, or his Deputies, shall receive of every Person that they shall furnish with Horses and Furniture, or with Horses, Furniture and Guide, to ride Post in any of the Post-Roads of Great-Britain or Ireland, three pence British Money, for each Horse-hire for every English Mile, and four pence for the Guide of every Stage; but shall not charge any Person riding Post for the carrying any Bundle or Parcel along with him, so as the same exceed not the Weight of eighty Pounds Averdupois, to be laid on Horse rid by the Guide: and no Deputy is obliged to carry above that Weight for any Person riding Post.

That if any Deputy-Postmaster in any of His Majesty's Dominions, doth not or cannot furnish any Person riding Post with sufficient Horses within the Space of half an Hour after demand, such Person is at Liberty to provide himself as well as he can to the next Stage, and so at every Stage where he shall not be furnished; and the Person who shall furnish such Horses shall not be liable to any Penalty contained in the said Act, by reason thereof . . . But the offending Deputy Postmaster shall in every such case forfeit five pounds, one Moiety to the King and the other to the Person that shall sue for the same.'

Postmasters Loss of Monopoly   The eroded monopoly position of the Deputy Postmasters was dealt a final blow by a notice of the Stamp Office taken under a licencing Act of *1779 (19 Geo III)* whereby licences were to be taken out by all persons letting out horses for hire, "*from and after 5th July 1779 every Postmaster, Innkeeper or other person in Great Britain who shall let to hire any horse . . . shall pay annually the sum of five shillings for a licence for that purpose . . . No person whatsoever unless he or she be authorized by a licence shall let out any horse for hire*". The same applied to a four wheel chaise or other machine.

And so '*the monopoly of letting posthorses which the Post Office had enjoyed uninterruptedly since 1603 was (finally) taken away ! . .*'[20]

But worse was to come! The following year's act *(20 GIII c51)* added a duty of 1d per mile per horse or 1/6d if the mileage not known, as a duty on those travelling post and one half penny per mile for the carriage, increased to 1d per mile by the 1783 Act. The 1785 Act further increased the horse duty on those travelling post to 1½ d per mile, or 1/9d if the mileage not known. The Act also required the hirer to enter into a £50 bond and to add 'Licenced to let Post Horses' to his sign.

Present condition (1984) of the milestones. a. Mile stone 21. Opposite Rose and Crown Dunton Green. b. Mile stone 23. Tubs Hill Railway Bridge   c. Mile stone 24. Between High Street P.O. and Sevenoaks School. d. Mile stone 25. Opposite The White Hart, Riverhill. Centre inset. MS 22. Opposite Marley Tiles Ltd. (All AGD)

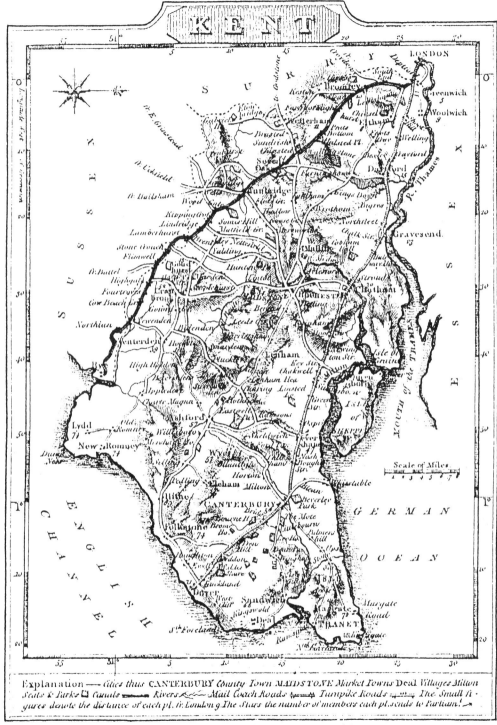

Kent by J. Walus c1810. London to Rye road at top is darkened.

The Postmaster or Innkeeper had to collect and record this duty with a system of tickets and special forms. The tickets were given to the person hiring the horse and handed by him to the Turnpike Gatekeeper who issued out their tickets in exchange. Loss of a ticket caused great concern, as much as losing a railway ticket to-day. Thus the Postmaster's recordings interlocked with the Turnpike recordings and movement along the road was pretty thoroughly controlled, at least in theory. Such tickets that have suvived till to-day are scarce and valuable.

Road Books

The Eighteenth century saw the rise to prominance of the travellers road book. At first these were very large ones with strip maps of the route. Later as the century progressed they were condensed into "handy" books for the travellers' pocket with much additional information added.

Stemming from the original Ogilby's Britannia of 1673, the best known ones are by Ogilby and Morgan, Paterson, Cary and Ogilvy Jnr.

Ogilby's 'Travellers Guide' of 1699 says of the Rye road *'Tis a well frequented road . . . but the way is not altogether so commendable, especially beyond Tunbridg'*.

It also lists road distances by Vulgar Computation and Dimensuration.

		Computation		Measure		
London to	*Lewisham*	*04*	*04*	*06,4*	*06,4*	*(The last*
	Bromley	*02*	*06*	*03,2*	*09,6*	*figure is*
	Farnboro	*03*	*09*	*04,0*	*13,6*	*furlongs,*
	Sevenoke	*06*	*15*	*09,2*	*29,0*	*8 to a mile)*
	Tunbridg	*05*	*20*	*06,5*	*29,5*	
	Rye		*46*		*64*	

The measurement to Sevenoaks 29,0 (which seems to be a printing mistake, as it should be 23,0) seems hardly more accurate than the reputed distance of Vulgar Computation 15. Both show the difficulties through which the agreeing of distances had to go.

John Ogilby and William Morgan's 'Pocket Book of the Roads' had a 4th edition in 1689 and by 1745 was in its 10th edition. The 'O & M *Travellers* Pocket Book' was brought out in 1755 and reached its 24th edition in 1794. In the 17th edition (1775) it states *'Distances according to the new erected Mile Stones'*.

Daniel Paterson's *'A new and Accurate Description of all the DIRECT and Principal CROSS Roads in Great-Britain'* is addressed to the Quarter-Master-General of His Majesty's Forces. It started in 1771 and reached a 15th edition by 1811. His rival John Cary's 'New Itinery' based on actual admeasurement and by Command of His Majesty's Postmaster General under the direction of Thomas Hasker Esq., Surveyor and Superintendant of Mail Coaches, from the initial edition of 1798 reached an 11th edition by 1828. John Cary used the measuring wheel and the statute mile and measured completely afresh for the Post Office.

Not to be outdone David Ogilvy Jnr. took the Road Book of Ogilby, added new information and rearranged it, publishing in 1804 his 'General Itinery'.

In 1799 Paterson shows the mileage from London, measuring from the Kent side of London Bridge through Kent street to Sevenoaks P.O. as 23½m, which seems accurate as the distance measured from the GPO has always been taken as 24 miles. Mogg's Pocket Itinery of Direct and Cross Roads did not have its first edition until 1826.

Calendar Change

In 1752 England finally adopted the Gregorian Calender promoted by the Pope as early as 1582. England was one of the last countries to do so, 170 years later.[21]

Almanack for 1752 of Tycho Wing, the philomath, showing September with but nineteen days, the other eleven having been 'stolen' by Act of Parliament from the lives of the populace, so some said. (AGD)

Until then the year end was March 25, not December 31, and therefore with a letter written in January, February or March there is some difficulty deciding in which year it was written. A letter written and dated 15 February 1745 is by our present reckoning really 15 February 1746. To overcome this difficulty records of such dates are usually written 15 February 1745/6. This double dating of the year is only necessary for the first three months, up to Quarter day March 25th.

On adopting the new calendar, eleven days were to be 'lost', to make up for the cumulative inaccuracies in the old Julian calendar. England lost 3-13 September 1752 inclusive and at the same time the year end was brought to December 31 in line with the Continent. The Financial Accounting year end continued in the old way in order to retain the full 366 days in 1752 for accounting and comparison purposes thus producing April 5th as the financial yearend.

No lasting fuss appears to have been made about the change, although there were some riots at the time by persons who thought their lives were being shortened. Tycho Wing's Almanack for the year leaves these days blank and states '*the Old Style ceases here and the New Style takes place; and consequently the next Day which in the Old Account would have been the 3d, is now to be called the 14th; so that all the intermediate nominal Days from 2d to the 14th are omitted, or rather, annihilated this year; and this month contains no more than 19 Days*'.[22]

It is interesting to examine a letter received from outside the country and written prior to 1752. One such is written to William Fremlin of Kemsing, it is dated by the writer in Rotterdam "30th of May 1749 N.S." and transit marked in London on the way to Kemsing, 22 May 1749. The various countries in Europe had long since gone onto the New Style of dating.

Postage Rates

Whatever the length of mile, postage along the Rye road had 'always' been twopence, the 'under 80 mile rate' from as early as 1586 when the first courier letter was so marked; the inflation factor (x 90) brought this amount to 75 pence in 1987 prices.

When the Post Office service commenced in 1635 the postage remained at 2d for a single letter up to 80 miles (x 49 giving 40p at 1987 prices) and so continued in 1660 when 2d represented (x 42) 35p.

With the passing of the Queen Anne Postage Act, the rates were raised on 1 June 1711; 2d would have meant a postage of 36p, but the act put the basic rate up to 3d (55p in 1987 prices). Presently, 10 October 1765, this somewhat high rate was reduced at the lower end with 2d (x 38 gives 32p) for two stages, Sevenoaks to London. Then back again on 31 August 1784 to 3d (x 33 gives 41p) for the two stages.

Further price rises were to come in January 1797 when a further change was also made in distance carried. Sevenoaks to London being 24 miles fell in the 15-30 mile bracket costing 4d (x 21 giving 35p). Very shortly after this in 1805 the 15-30 mile bracket was further raised to 5d but with inflation this still only represents (x 19) 40p. (For 'd' to 'p' conversion, divide by 2.4. Conversion factors are shown at the end of the Appendix. It may be necessary to interpolate for earlier years).

Summarising the Sevenoaks to London Charge

	contemporary rate	*1987 converted rate*
1585	*2d*	*75p*
1635	*2d*	*40p*
1660	*2d*	*35p*
1711	*3d*	*55p*
1765	*2d*	*32p*
1784	*3d*	*41p*
1797	*4d*	*35p*
1805	*5d*	*40p*

To finish with two cautionary tales . . .

Highwayman

Well after the road south of Sevenoaks had been turnpiked a highwayman turned up in 1764 near the 25th milestone at The White Hart Inn south of Sevenoaks. On a Saturday at 7pm Mr Childrens whilst riding over Sevenoaks Common was held up by a highwayman who demanded money. Mr Childrens decided to risk riding off and was hit by a ball in the thigh. A surgeon had to remove the ball. Two days earlier another rider from Pembury was held up at the same time and place. He also was fired at but the highwayman's gun *'flashed in the pan and the ball did not carry'*. The Highwayman made off towards Ightham.[23]

Finding a Mailbag. A Dangerous Pastime

Thomas Theobalds had been walking along the main road at Sevenoaks when he saw an object lying in the road. Not knowing exactly what it was he took it home, thinking to examine it later when he had time. This was October 1771.

Unwittingly he had committed a crime, for it was in fact the Tunbridge Bag that had fallen off the Kentish Mail and it contained a considerable amount of property in banknotes. Any property of the Royal Mail so found should have been handed in to the authorities *at once*, and as might be expected it was soon found to be missing.

Theobalds was apprehended and committed to Maidstone Gaol on suspicion, together with William Lasslot. On examination Theobalds said Lasslot was not with him at the time. *'Local Gentlemen and inhabitants were convinced of his innocence and were concerning themselves on his behalf and subscribing to the support of a wife and 11 children during **his** confinement.'*[24]

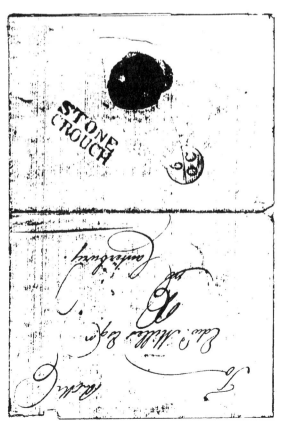

1774 A letter postmarked Stonecrouch in Kent, a hamlet where the roads from London to Rye and Hastings divided, back via Sevenoaks to London (transit bishopmark 6 October) then along the Dover road as far as Canterbury charged 'in all 6'd. There were no direct cross-posts at this date, Stonecrouch had had a Town Namestamp as early as 1705 with great postal activity there. Now it is remembranced only by the 'Post Boy Motel'.

However the London Gazette records a different aspect of the happening; the two men were not slow to put their apparent good fortune to use.

October 15, 1771   The Tunbridge Bag of Letters, which should have arrived at this Office on Monday Morning last, being lost or stolen out of the Mail somewhere between Seven-Oaks and Bromley, two of the Bank Notes sent in the said Bag were this Day put off in Rosemary Lane at two Cloaths Shops, by two Men.

The one about thirty-six or forty Years old, five Feet nine or ten Inches high, his own straight Hair, a Brown Complexion, long Nose and long Visage; had on a light coloured Coat, and a Scarlet Waistcoat, and dirty Leathern Breeches; and who bought, fitted for his own Size, a Salmon-coloured Suit of Cloaths, Lining and Basket Buttons of the same, with a plain Cuff, and fall-down Collar, a Cinnamon-coloured Surtout, and a Pair of new Buck-skin Breeches, marked on the Inside of the Waistband with the Shop Mark, E.I.

The other, stout set, about twenty-eight Years old, five Feet six or seven Inches high, his own straight Hair, swarthy Complexion, had on a round, dirty, or brown Linen Waggoner's Frock, Scarlet Jacket, with Cuffs, dirty Buck-skin Breeches, and who likewise bought, for his own Size, a Blue Cloth Coat, Scarlet Waistcoat, and a Chocolate-coloured Bath-coating Surtout.

Whoever shall apprehend and convict, or cause to be apprehended and convicted, both or either of the Persons above described, will be entitled to a Reward of FIFTY POUNDS.

October 19, 1771   William Laslett, one of the Persons concerned in stealing the Tunbridge Bag of Letters between Seven-Oaks and Bromley on Monday Morning last the 14th Instant, was Yesterday apprehended at Seale near Seven-Oaks, and committed to Maidstone Goal.

His Accomplice THOMAS THEOBALD found Means to escape from his House at Riverhead near Seven-Oaks Yesterday Morning. He is a stout set Man, about 36 Years of Age, 5 Feet 6 or 7 Inches high, brown Complexion, wears his own Hair of a light Brown Colour, had on when he escaped an Olive-coloured Coat, and a Red lapelled Waistcoat; about two Years and an half ago he lived as an Hostler at Witham in Essex, and has since lived in different Parts of Kent in the same Capacity.

Whoever shall apprehend and convict, or cause to be apprehended and convicted, the said THOMAS THEOBALD, will be entitled to a Reward of FIFTY POUNDS.

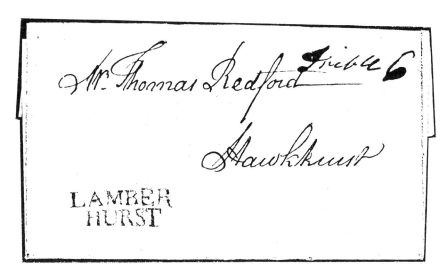

Newly discovered early bye-letter *Lamberhurst–Hawkhurst c1775 with m/s 'Trible 6' charge ie.*
6d=2dx3 because of enclosures referred to inside letter.

All the way London to Rye in 1775. Over 1oz was charged by weight as 4 singles regardless of how few or many sheets were used. So 1¼oz equals 5 singles at 3d = 1s/3d, written in contemporary style as 1N3. A good London bishopmark of 17 January is also shown.

Chapter IV

1770-1801 Mailcarts and Robberies

Monarch: George III   (1760-1820)

Chronology

1773	3rd Duke of Dorset gave Vine Cricket Ground to the Town.
1774	Court Case. Free Letter delivery to houses within Post Town area.
1776	Adam Smith wrote 'The Wealth of Nations'.
1778	Hasted begins to publish his 'History and Topographical Survey of the County of Kent' in 4 Vols. First (folio) edition 1778, 1782, 1790, 1799; Second (Octavo) edition in 12 Vols. 1797-1801.
	George III and Queen Charlotte tour Kent, visit Sevenoaks.
1780	Artillery encampment near Tonbridge.
	Galvani discovers electricity.
1781	Post to Sevenoaks and Tonbridge now daily thoughout the year.
1783	Early Balloon flights.
1784	Mailcoaches organised by John Palmer, but not on the Sevenoaks run.
	Bailey's British Directory. Lists Sevenoaks details.
1785	Closure of Roads through Chevening Estate.
	Stamp Duty on some medecines.
1788	Stonecrouch office suppressed, Lamberhurst took over.
	Jane Austen visits her uncle Francis Austen at The Red House Sevenoaks.
	'The Times' founded by John Walter.
1789-1815	Napoleonic Wars.
1788 &1790	Stagecoach Acts limiting numbers riding on top of coach.
1789	Bastille fell. French Revolution and War for next twenty five years.
1791	Porcupine Inn Rushmore Hill up for sale.
	Francis Austen died and his son Francis Motley Austen continued the law partnership with Claridge.
1792	Early Money Order arrangements by P.O. Officials.
1793	Forces encampment in Ashdown Forest 14,000 men.
1795	Hair Powder Duty Certificates.
1797	Government Tax on Watches.
1798	Sevenoaks Mail Robbery of 2 July and an attempt 21 September.
1801	Two further Sevenoaks Mail Robberies, January and March.
	The First Census in Britian.

Chapter IV

1770-1801
Mailcarts and Robberies

The whole of this period falls into the reign of George the Third (1760-1820).

Sevenoaks

Sevenoaks was governed by two wardens and four assistants. The district consisted of Town Borough, Riverhead, Weald. Sprange's 1780[1] guide tells that *'Assizes were held several times (in Sevenoaks) in the reign of Queen Elizabeth, in the year before the death of Charles I and once since. Gallows Common, at the North end of the town outside the inhabited area is used when the Assizes are held here.'* Gallows Common has now been built on.

About 1770 the town itself had a population of 1000-1500, being a small market town located between what is now Bligh's Hotel and Sevenoaks Park, now called Park Grange. Within the Town itself, Bailey's British Directory of 1784, the first available detailed directory covering Sevenoaks Town, shows the professional and tradesmen's occupations as,

3 Attorneys	2 Shoemakers	1 Miller	1 Coachmaster
5 Surgeons and	1 Hatter	1 Ironmonger	2 Wheelwrights
Apothecaries	1 Milliner	1 Brazier	2 Saddle and
1 Auctioneer	1 Fellmonger	2 Plumber and	Harness Makers
1 Coachmaster	and Glover	Glaziers	1 Currier
8 Innkeepers	3 Mercers and	1 Stonemason	1 Patternmaker
1 Brewer	Drapers	1 Cutler	2 Turners
2 Distillers	1 Watchmaker	1 Timber	1 Lath Cleaver
2 Wine Merchants	1 Silk Throwster	Merchant	
2 Maltsters	1 Gingerbread	2 Carpenters	
2 Coopers	Maker		
	1 Bookseller and		
	Stationer		
	1 Salesman		

These sixty persons would be the masters who employed others to help them in their occupations. Thomas Clout is shown as Bookseller and Stationer. Richard Dransfield is shown as an Inn Keeper but the Directory does not state the name of the Inn. Market day as before is still Saturday.

Sevenoaks Correspondance

Many of the early letters still extant come from legal sources and the names 'Austen' and 'Claridge' figure prominently about this period. Francis Austen was born in 1698 and died ninety three years later in 1791. His mother had married an Austen of Horsmonden, a branch of a substantial county family whose wealth was based on the cloth trade. On his father's death she moved house with her seven young children to Sevenoaks to look after boys and masters of Sevenoaks School. Here at Sevenoaks School her fifth child

Francis was educated, then articled as an attorney in Clifford's Inn. He subsequently returned to Sevenoaks to practice as an attorney. In 1743 he bought 'The Red House' having made money by buying and selling estates locally, becoming also general agent to the Duke of Dorset at Knole. He was a Governor of Sevenoaks School and became Clerk of the Peace for Kent in 1753 and remained so until at the age of 75 he passed this position to his son by his first marriage, Francis Motley Austen. Thus as a busy country solicitor holding many positions that also included the trusteeships of many Turnpikes, Francis' signature can be fouund on many letters and documents.

In 1785 Francis Austen, now 86, and the much younger solicitor John Fellows Claridge started off the partnership of solicitors whence Samuel Thomas Hills, clerk, was to come as Sevenoaks Postmaster in 1848. It was in 1864 that the first 'Knocker' joined the partnership now known as 'Knocker and Foskett'. The firm returned in 1936 to offices in 'The Red House' previously owned by Francis Austen who was visited there by Jane Austen his great niece who stayed for some weeks just before he died in 1791 at the age of ninety two. Francis Austen in his early years whilst practising in Sevenoaks had helped her father George Austen through Tonbridge School and purchased for him his living as a Rector in Hampshire. Many letters *to* Austen's partner Claridge are available, most are addressed simply, '*J Claridge Esq, Sevenoaks*'.

Francis Motley Austen the son of Francis Austen's first wife was also in the firm of solicitors though living in Lamberhurst until he moved to Kippington in 1796. He too was a Governor of Sevenoaks School and a Trustee of Turnpikes, as also in command of a company of local militia at a time when there was trouble with the French, though his men never saw service. He continued the work of Clerk of the Peace for Kent from 1753 until John Fellows Claridge took over the position in 1808.

Local Seats   Many, if not most, of the country seats to and from which large correspondances were likely, were situated outside the town. Those shown on Andrews and Dury's map, 1769, plus a few others, are,

Ash Grove	*John Smith (Army)*	*West Heath School.*
Beechmont	*Multon Lambarde*	*Later Boys school. Demolished by V-bomb 1944.*
Bradbourne	*Bosvilles 1555-1760 Sir Richard Betenson/Lambarde*	*Demolished 1926. Land for housing.*
Chipstead Place	*Polhills, Oppenheim*	
Chevening Place	*de Chevening, Lennard, Stanhopes*	*Used by the Government, currently Foreign Secretary.*
Coombe Bank	*Duke of Argyll*	*Now a School in the Independent Sector.*
Greatness House	*Peter Nouaille, Filmers*	*Blown up during WWI to make war propaganda film*
Halstead Place	*Robert Bagshaw Burnaby-Atkins*	*Demolished by 1950; Rebuilt as a school.*
Kippington	*Sir Charles Farnaby*	*Later Col Francis Motley Austen, Wm J. Thompson*
Knokholt House	*Vavasseur*	*Demolished. Land derelict*
Knole	*Duke of Dorset (Sackvilles)*	*Family still resident.*
Lullingstone	*Sir John Dixon Duke*	
Montreal	*Sir Jeffrey Amherst*	*Demolished.*
River Hill	*Francis Otway*	
Park Place/ Sevenoaks Park	*Lone, Lambard, Austen*	*Now Sevenoaks School as 'Park Grange'.*
Shoreham New House	*Thos Barnett*	
Wildernesse	*Jno Pratt, Camden Lord Hillingdon*	*Now a State Secondary School.*

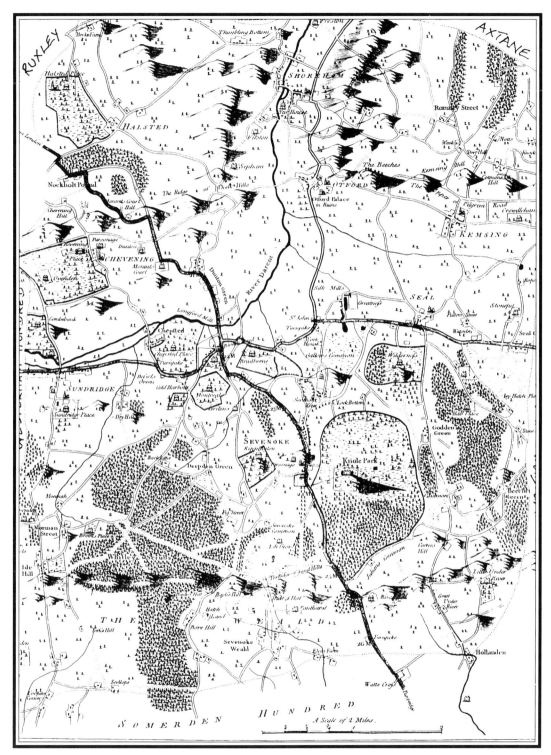

CODSHEATH Hundred in Hasted's History of Kent 1778. Boyle links the source of Hasted's maps as those of Andrews and Drury (sic) whose Atlas of Kent was published in 1769 (see bibliography).

The Road from London to Rye, strip map by C Bowles 1781.

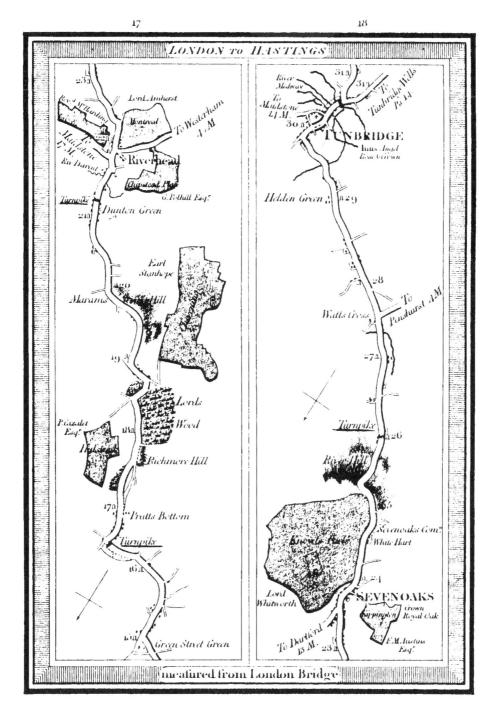

The Road to Hastings by E Mogg showing detail of the route, seats and main inns north and south of Sevenoaks and the Turnpike gate at Pratts Bottom m/s 16/17, Dunton Green m/s 21, and Riverhill m/s 26. (AGD)

An early well known small engraving by Dugdale (1843) with the title 'Sevenoaks' shows 'Beechmont' the house overlooking the Southern escarpment at Riverhill viewed from the road when ascending, a view that would be distinctive and well known to anyone entering the town from the South. But a view no longer to be seen. This engraving is reproduced on page 28.

Sevenoaks Town

In 1773 thirty nine years after the first recorded cricket match, the 3rd Duke of Dorset gave the Vine Cricket ground to the Town.

The London Gazette of 7 November reports that George III and Queen Charlotte made a tour of Kent and stayed at Sevenoaks overnight on 2 November 1778. They stayed at Montreal belonging to Lord Amherst, then next day drove past Sevenoaks school where they received a loyal welcome sitting in their carriage, then on to visit the military camp at Cock's Heath near Maidstone where Lord Amherst was in charge.

Torrington Viscount Byng who entered through the Sevenoaks Route when he made his tour of Sussex in 1788 was made of sterner stuff. He rode a horse, but appeared to spend much of his time walking to accompany his companion who was walking with his dog. Their route is described in detail but little comment made about the condition of it apart from the mention of good stabling and the stony condition of the road down the hill south of Sevenoaks. Much of their time was spent dodging rainstorms. August was a wet one that year, but their recompense was chicken pie at the Royal Oak in Sevenoaks.[2] So often was rain mentioned in their journey that it is as well to remember that the mail went forward to a fixed time schedule, and rain was of no account, was not to be dodged or fine weather waited for.

Postmasters

Elizabeth Dransfield was the wife of a Licenced Victualler Benjamin Dransfield of whom she had a son, Richard. Benjamin died and from 1770 the licenced victualler's registration was taken out in Elizabeth Dransfield's name.[3] In that same year she also became Postmistress at Sevenoaks when the incumbent Mrs Elizabeth Loving, relict of Garnett Loving, was dismissed her post.

19 Jan 1770. Ordered that Mrs Elizabeth Dransfield be appointed deputy of Sevenoaks in the stead of Mrs Loving, dismissed - to commence 24 Jan 1770.[4]

So Mrs **Elizabeth Dransfield** took over as postmistress at Sevenoaks, continuing to be a Licenced Victualler. There was also at that time living in Sevenoaks another Licenced Victualler called Philip Jones. Elizabeth Dransfield and **Philip Jones** married in 1774 and from then on only Philip Jones is shown as a Licenced Victualler. The Postmastership was also transferred into his name,

1 Dec 1773 Orders 1737-1771

Ordered that Mr Philip Jones be appointed Deputy of Sevenoaks in the stead of Mrs Dransfield whom he has married.

However it was Elizabeth who continued to do the postal work, and it was she who got into trouble when a letter to Lord Camden disappeared in 1795, later related. Philip Jones her husband must have taken ill in 1781, for the Licenced Victuallership is then transferred into Elizabeth's name, but, though inactive it did not appear that he died, as Postmaster salary payments continue to be made in his name and are not transferred to that of his wife.

Richard Dransfield her son by her first marriage who was a licenced victualler at 'The George' for 1793 and 1794 but not for 1795 or later and who had been helping her with postal duties since the time of the incident applied for the position in July 1797 at a time when the salary was £16 p.a. for the General Letters and £4 p.a. for the Bye Letters, quoting his experience of the work, and '*petitions to succeed his mother who he states has been upwards of 27 years in the office and is much advanced in life*'[5]

By December (1797) Richard's mother was dead and the need to fill the vacancy immediate. Freeling wrote to the PostMasters General[6] enclosing also a letter from a Mr Stone. The answer came back from

1775 Letter to Brighton with Seven/Oakes two line Town stamp. Charged 2d to London, then 3d to Brighton making 'In all 5d' London transit bishopmark. This letter would have been handled in Elizabeth Jones's (Elizabeth Dransfield that was) office. Possibly the '2' is her writing. This Sevenoakes mark is the only known example of that Townstamp.

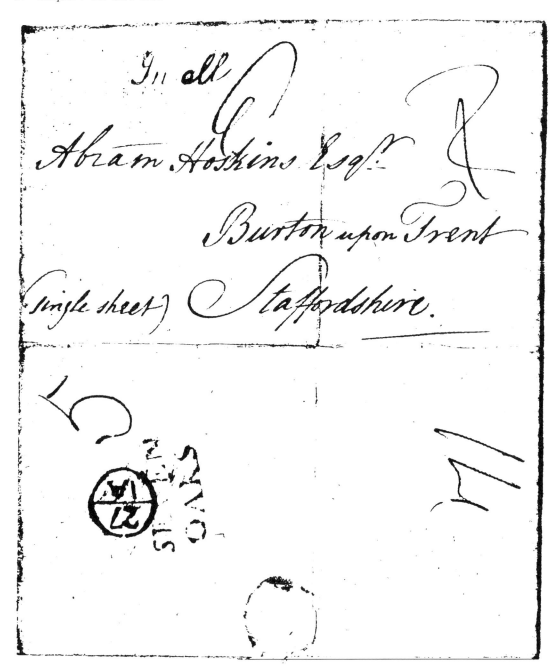

1780 Letter to Burton on Trent. Seven/Oaks two line Town stamp. Charged 2d to London, 4d to Burton for a single sheet making 'In all 6d'. Still Elizabeth Jones's office but a different sort of 2, probably the writing of a helper. The 5 & 14 probably refer to a bundle of letters for Abram Hoskins, not the individual letter.

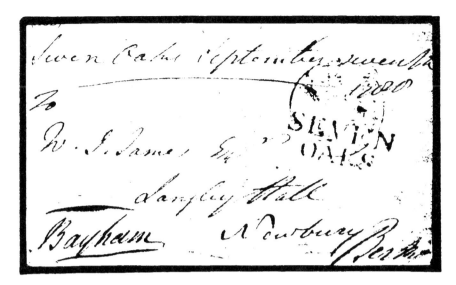

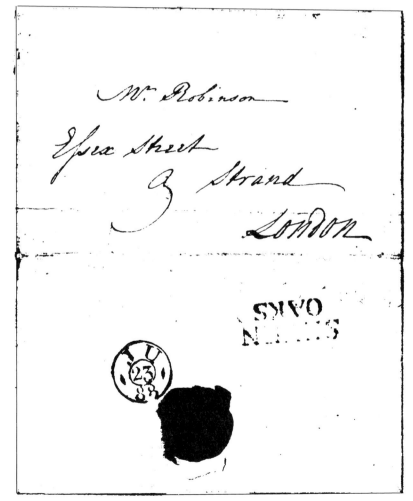

1788 Seven/oaks two line Town stamp on a Free letter of a member of parliament addressed to Newbury. A second example to London shows the manuscript long-looped 's' of Essex Street.

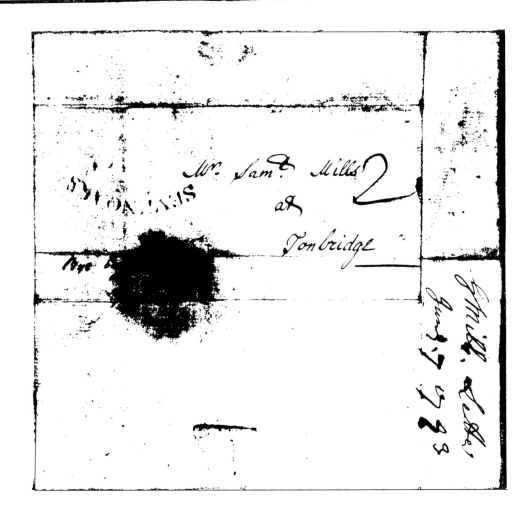

Sevenoaks, January first, 1786.

Countefs Dowager of Chatham

14 SXVP Burton Pynsent

JARS

Somerton

Free. Stanhope Somersetshire

Mr. Sam. Mills

at

Tonbridge

Above: 1792 The short lived single straight line townstamp, now to be impressed on the reverse of the letter.
Below: 1794 The larger curved Sevenoaks townstamp

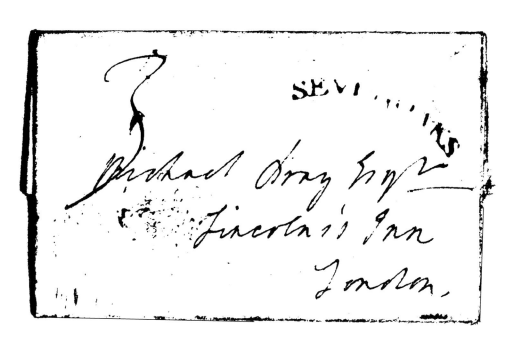

Opposite.
Above: 1786 The scarce '24 Seven/Oaks' Town Stamp on an early 'ffree' letter signed Stanhope. This stamp did not produce a clear impression.
Below: 1793 The curved Sevenoaks Townstamp on a single stage letter to Tonbridge when the charge had been reduced to 2d. The curved townstamps seldom give a full impression. This is still the Dransfield/Jones office four years before her death and the '2' looks not unlike the early one. (Reduced)

the Duke of Dorset via the PMsG to Freeling 'appoint James Hanson Postmaster of Sevenoaks'.[7] He was duly instructed in his office by Mr Aust the Surveyor.[8] Significantly Hanson was a licenced victualler at the Duke of Dorset Arms, a position he gave up on becoming postmaster.

Lord Camden's Complaint

Lord Camden's letter of early February 1795 vanished into thin air and was never seen, but Mr Pratt who also complained claimed that it had been suppressed in the post, a matter that was hotly denied by the Postmistress of Sevenoaks. Mr Pratt claimed that there were delays and that mail was sent back whence it came without the bags being opened, thus causing further delay. He claimed that there had been *'impardonable negligence and repeated blunders of the Postmistress of this place'*. So Mr Bartlett was sent to investigate. *'It appears that the Deputy is not so culpable as I at first thought her to be & your Lordships will find no difficulty in believing this as Mr Pratt is perfectly satisfied with what has been done & by no means wishes her to be dismissed'* wrote Freeling in his final report on the matter. Nevertheless she received a severe reprimand, which seemed a bit harsh in the circumstances. Mr Bartlett's report gives the details:

> [*Post 42 Minutes 75E & 91E*]
> > *Genl Post Office*
> > *March 5th 1795*
>
> *Dear Sir*
>
> *I have been to Sevenoaks and questioned the Postmistress about the neglect alledged by Mr Pratt. The Deputy is at a very advanced period of Life, and is not fully competent to the Duties: her son therefor has undertaken to assist her in transacting them - They acquaint me that the reason for the delay in the Letters arises from the negligence of the Postmasters on the lower part of the Road, whose bags do not come regularly, and the Riders, in not making the proper interchange. Of the truth of this, I was a witness. The Bag from Hastings of the 3rd March not arriving on the 4th and Postmaster of Bromley told me half the Bags upon the same line of Road never arrived on the 2nd Inst.*
>
> *At the time Mr Pratt mentions his letter being detained, the Postmistress' son acknowledges the interchange was not properly made - In regard to Lord Camden's letter missing, they have not the least recollection of its being put into the Sevenoaks Office, and if it was that it certainly went from thence.*
>
> *I however gave them a severe reprimand, and assured the Postmistress that the next complaint, however trivial, would ensure her dimissal. Her Son, who understands the Duties well, assures me he will take every precaution in future.*
>
> *I waited on Mr Pratt, and acquainted him with the result of my enquiries, and he is satisfied with what has been done, and by no means wishes the Postmistress to be now removed.*
>
> *The Deputies on the Hastings and Rye Roads are written to upon their own & their Servants shameful neglect, which will, I trust, prevent any more misconduct.*
> > *I am, Dear Sir*
> > *Your most obedt Servt*
>
> *F Freeling Esq   B Bartlett*

As he was still alive in 1795 at the time and officially in post, what one wonders was Philip Jones doing at the time of this incident and why is he never mentioned in the Surveyor's report when officially he was said to be in the position of deputy postmaster at Sevenoaks and thus should have taken full responsibility. Philip Jones was receiving both the General Post salary and the separate Cross Post salary at the time; not only those of Sevenoaks, but also Tunbridge.

Perhaps this incident has some bearing on the fact that the Dransfield son was not supported locally when he applied to become Postmaster on his step-father's death in 1797.

Cross and Bye Accounts

As has been mentioned the Bye and Cross Road accounts were operated separately and gave the deputy postmasters an additional small yearly salary.

Year 1791[9]

Battle	£4		
Hastings	£4		
Lamberhurst	£5		
Rye	£4		
• Seven Oaks	£4	(£120)	
* Tunbridge	£6	(£180)	
Dover	£9		
Canterbury	£12		

The receipts were also kept separate[10]
1793 Quarterly July 15
* • Jones of Sevenoaks £7.18. 2 (£212)
* * Jones of Tunbridge £5. 5. - (£138)

   According to the Bye and Cross Road Letter office list c1793 of '*Towns keeping vouchers with and places that each correspond with*'[11] **Sevenoaks** was in account with Tunbridge, Bromley to & from, Lamberhurst, Battle, Hastings, Rye. Other Post Towns mentioned were **Tunbridge** in account with Sevenoaks, Lamberhurst, Battle, Hastings, Rye (but not Maidstone), **Lamberhurst** with Tunbridge, Sevenoaks, Cranbrook, Tenterden, Battle, Hastings, Rye. **Battle** with Sevenoaks, Tunbridge, Lamberhurst, Hurst Green to & from, Boreham to & from, Hastings. **Rye** with Sevenoaks, Tunbridge, Lamberhurst, Tenterden, Cranbrook.

Local Posts   Cary's earliest lists of 1787 emphasise the fact that locally organised branch posts from the major towns were already a fact of life from an early date. Most of the arrangements were private and

The George Shoreham in early days. Branch P.O. 1765 to 1845. (DBC)

The Bull Wrotham today. The Branch P.O. 1786 to 1846. (AGD)

The Bell Kemsing today. Branch P.O. 1795 to 1867. (AGD)

involved an additional charge for delivery. Collection might be free but often was charged for. Mostly the places used were licenced Public Houses. At least the following were used -

Seal, The White Horse
Wrotham, The Bull Inn
Shoreham, The (Old) George
Kemsing, The Bell (by 1795)
Brasted, (no name recorded)
Westerham, (no name recorded)

Operational Difficulties   A few domestic items throw some light on day-to-day operations of the period.
P.O. 7 Oaks Aug 7 1789
[Post 14 Vol 246]
Sir,
This is to acquaint you that the Bill received this morning was but £2.10.5 instead of £3.11.5 therefor I imagine it must be entirely a mistake. I reckoned the letters up several times and am sure it was right & could make no more than the sum above mentioned.
I am Sir
Your most obedt Servt
(signed) James Hanson
F Freeling Esq   Post Mr
Mr Stone begs that the Clerks at the 8th Divn will be particularly careful to prevent such inaccuracies in future as above stated by the Postmr. of 7 Oaks.

But a similar type of mistake did occur twelve years later on 25 January 1801. These mistakes might be infrequent but they were looked on severely, and minuted.

[Post 14 Vol 241]
Rye Dec 10 1795
The Presidents will be pleased to order
stamps for Sevenoaks, Tunbridge Wells, Rye
and a Ship Letter Stamp for Rye.   *Ordered E.B.*
I am Sirs &c &c
B. Bartlett

[Vol 244/92 1797]
The President will inform the person at the 8th Div who tells up 7 Oaks that a letter for Bristol and that place is only 7d and not 8d which is the Charge they generally put on. The Box must be carefully looked in as the distance is as 149 miles.

[Vol 246 1798]
Post Office Sevenoaks
Sir, This is to acquaint you the letters which I charged to the Right Honble Edward Bouverie Squires Lodge Westerham - He is very much offended with me upon the account of his letters being charged. He sent me word he would write to you concerning it & he will not return any more Covers.
F Freeling Esq   James Hanson -
Postmr.
Sevenoaks
'President', here means the Presiding Officer of the day who is on duty.

Payment for Mail   It was felt by the public that payment in arrears avoided any chance of letters being destroyed as they were worth money on delivery. Whether this was true or not, strangely enough prepayment was not always popular. The recipient, if a private person, often said it cast doubts on his ability to be able to pay for his letters. Business firms had no such inhibitions, and a comment in the 'Maidstone Journal & Kentish Advertiser' of 12 January 1790 demonstrates ongoing practice,

'*If our Correspondant at Sevenoaks wishes to have his paragraph (of local news) inserted he will comply with our established rule of paying the postage of his letter*'.

That Correspondant and those to follow him from Sevenoaks evidently thought otherwise, for then and for decades later the said Newspaper denied itself any copy from 'Our Correspondant at Sevenoaks'.

Users Advisory Council

In 1782 Palmer had proposed local users advisory councils for the Post Office consisting of '*Gentlemen, merchants, commercial travellers*', in all districts as they knew the local needs.

What is not known is whether such councils ever came into existance locally, about that time. Nationally the users of Postal Services had to wait until 1921 before the national users advisory council came into being.

A reconstituted statutory body which is not part of the Post Office has been in operation since the 1969 Act, The Post Office Users National Council (POUNC). They claim that much of the contents of their reports, including matters relating to the local Sevenoaks/Tonbridge area are sensitive and cannot be made public. And so it remains to be seen, in AD 1999, whether any of their detailed information becomes available to the public under the thirty year rule and, for example that of the 1985 surveys in the Tonbridge MLO area, in AD 2015. Private bodies such as the Mail Users Association and the Association of Mail Order Publishers also came into being in the 1980's.

Vehicles

With improvements in the road surface following the Turnpike Acts and the increase in the number of social gatherings as compared to health visits at Tonbridge Wells, coaching along this road developed strongly.

Stagecoaches   On the London-Hastings road through Sevenoaks a card issued by the proprietors in 1745 had informed the travelling public that a Fast Coach left the Swan Inn Hastings at 4am Monday morning, arriving Robertsbridge the same day, Sevenoaks the next, London the next, returning to Hastings the following three days.

But by 1788 the various turnpikes had their intended effect and made considerable improvement to the road. Hastings, too, after having in 1768 two hundred dragoons billeted on the town to quieten the smuggling and piracy was becoming a fashionable resort and an advertisement for its charms states that coaches went up to London four times a week, still from the Swan Inn but now leaving at 6am. The stage coaches were now planned to arrive at Tonbridge at noon the same day where they met the coach that had left the Bolt-in-Tun inn London that morning and exchanged passengers *and parcels* (and some of the parcels may have contained bundles of letters to post locally and avoid full postal charges, rather in the way that mailings are sometimes sent from the continent now-a-days) and then returned back to their own bases in London and Hastings that same night. This method of horses and even vehicles keeping to their own 'ground' and so returning to their own base at the completion of their journey each day, passing on their payload, be it people, letters or parcels to the next vehicle appeared to have a certain vogue, for the same type of organisation appears again when considering the postal arrangements at Stonecrouch.

'The Sun' newspaper of 11th September 1797 carries a list of coaches that set out from Golden Cross Charing Cross. Although there are through stagecoaches to Brighton and Eastbourne, there is no through coach to Hastings, only as far as Sevenoaks, Tunbridge and Tunbridge Wells. As before, the Hastings Coach still came up and exchanged passengers even up at this late date.

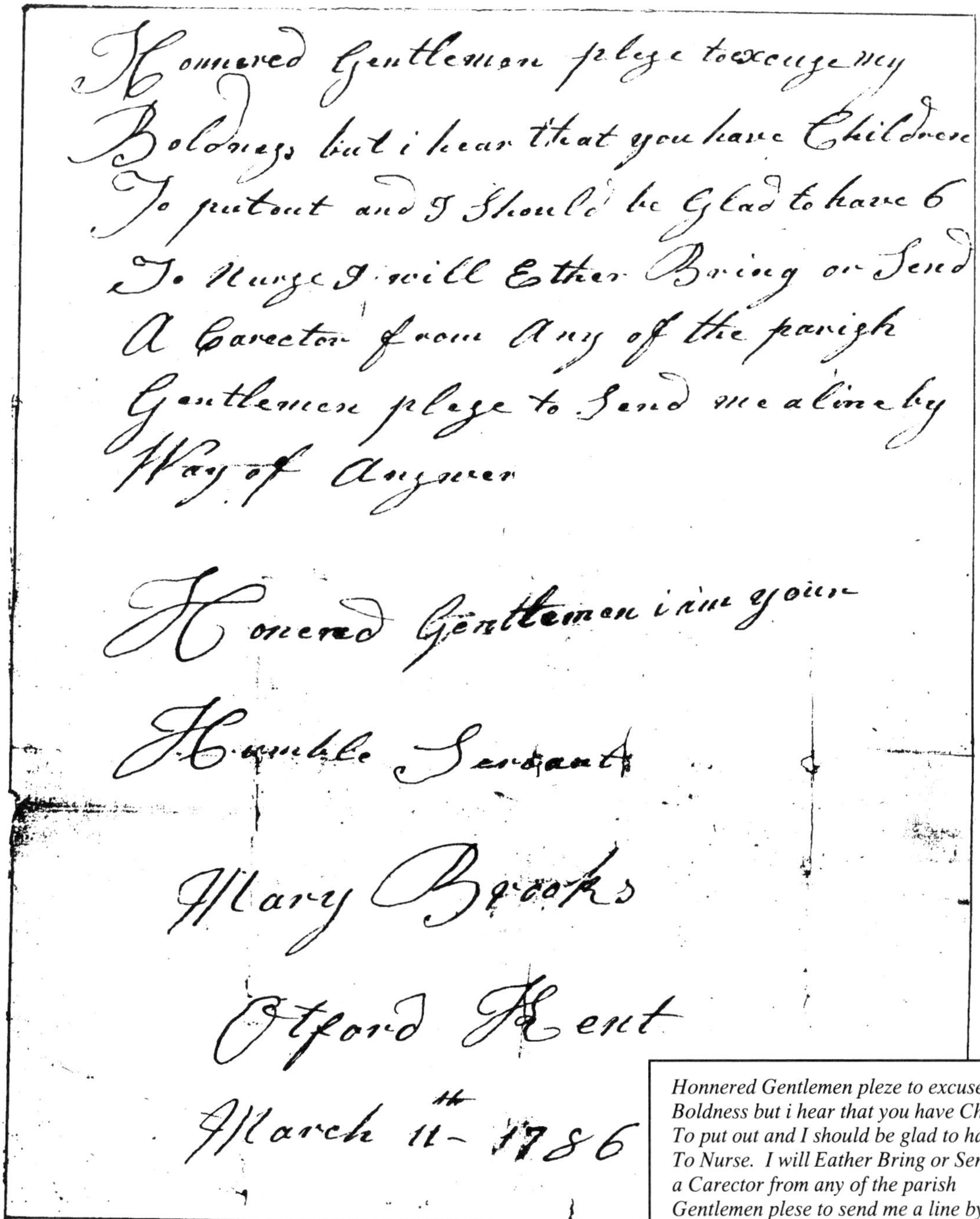

Honnered Gentlemen pleze to excuse my
Boldness but i hear that you have Children
To put out and I should be glad to have 6
To Nurse. I will Eather Bring or Send
a Carector from any of the parish
Gentlemen plese to send me a line by
way of Answer

Honered Gentlemen i am your
Humble Servant

Mary Brooks
Otford Kent
March 11th 1786

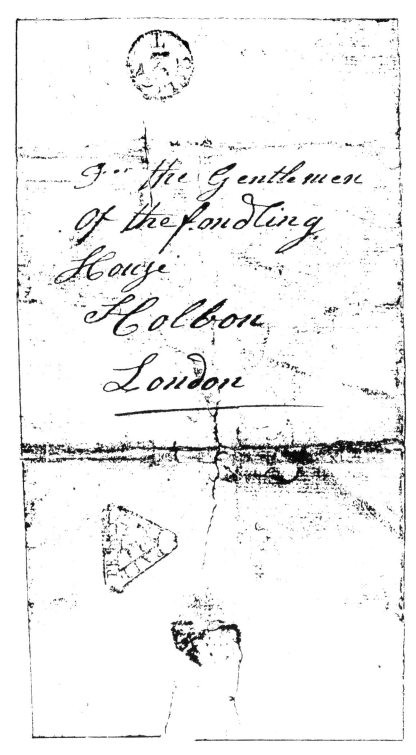

Letter from Otford 1786 taken to London and put into Penny Post there thus saving several pence. The triangle says 'Penny Post Paid'.

Number of Passengers allowed on Coaches

Acts were passed limiting the number of persons that could travel on the outside of a coach. The 1788 act stipulated only six passengers on the roof and two on the box. For exceeding this the driver was liable to a forty shilling fine and twice as much if he were the owner of the coach. Of the fines received, half went to the informer and half to the Highways Surveyor of the District where the incident occured. If not paid, the alternative was one month in a House of Correction. Two years later the number of persons allowed outside was reduced to four on the roof with four horses and only three (30 G III c36) outside with two. Taking up and setting down more within the limits of a tollgate was equally an offence and fines of 5/- had to be paid to the Tollgate keeper for each of these offences or again it was 14 days to one month in a House of Correction. Some additions to these numbers were allowed when operating within twenty five miles of London, which of course included the Sevenoaks run. This 1790 act also now required the name of the proprietor to be painted on the outside of the door; nor was anyone other than the official driver to drive without the consent of the inside passengers, of whom there were normally only four (even with twelve or more outside) though a few coaches were licenced for six inside.

Posting

By 1795 Posting had greatly changed. It now took three forms; hire of Post-chaises as often as not discarded private chariots with postboys on a mileage basis, the hire of horses to pull one's own carriage, and still the hire of riding horses but without guide. As well as the Post Office's Post Masters, these means of transport were provided by Innkeepers who on their trade cards might advertise "neat post chaises and able horses 1/- per mile".

In England, postboys, who could be any age, normally wore a bright yellow waistcoat, blue jacket, red in the north of England, white breeches, short top boots and a large beaver hat. Postboys would probably receive their keep from the innkeeper and depend on the customary tips for their cash income. An Innkeeper would always have one postboy ready for immediate duty and several more 'on call'. The 'post chaises' were referred to as '*yellow bounders*' to distinguish them from '*a bounder*', a gentleman's carriage. The Postchaises were, typically, a closed chariot carrying two passengers and a limited amount of luggage driven at a gallop by a postboy driving postillion on the nearside horse of the pair or four, with four horses probably having two postboys as postillions. Postboys tended to be indifferent drivers.[12]

In the Sevenoaks district at Wrotham there is an Inn, 'The Three Postboys'. Although the innsign sports a stagecoach, and a 'safety' one it seems at that for both front and rear sets of wheels are small, it is likely that the postboys were of the type just referred to and not persons concerned with handling mail officially, as no 'horsed' mailroute passed through Wrotham. However, it was indeed likely that they handled letters unofficially for it was well known to the Post Office that in this, to them, fringe area yet through which a main stagecoach road cut and where official postal services were so poor, the inhabitants along the stagecoach route were in the habit of passing over their letters to be posted in London (see p 133) when the coach arrived there, thus saving a day in time as well as a few pence.

Mail Coaches

Developments in the country as a whole saw John Palmer's new mailcoaches start in 1784. The following year they were exempted from paying tolls, thus giving rise to the traditional picture of the mailguard blowing his horn as the mailcoach approaches a turnpike tollgate, to warn the man in charge to have the gate open and let the mail through without delay. There was trouble when the gate was not open and the coachman had to slow up. This scene continued until the demise of the mailcoach in 1846, except in Scotland where in 1812 the bill to rescind the exemption was successful and mailcoaches once again paid tolls, though not individually. They were 'noted' as they passed through at speed. Being outside at all times in all weathers cannot have been easy for the mailguards and on the 18th of February 1795 the London papers reported '*a third of the mailguards ill either from the severe weather or colds they caught in the floods*'.[13] On the Hastings run, the Robertsbridge area was well known for its flooding.

After John Besant's early design for a specially built mailcoach used among other places on the Dover

The Three Post Boys at Wrotham. (AGD)

run, during most of this time specially designed and strongly built mailcoaches carrying four inside and only three outside were made and hired out to the post office by John Vidler who also serviced each one when it arrived back in London. In effect Vidler had a monopoly until his contract ran out in 1836 when he refused to re-tender.

Such 'Patent' mail coaches carrying four inside and only a few outside were used on the Dover nightmail which started on 31st October 1785 and on the Brighton nightmail starting on 5th April 1810, both of which coaches were classed as 'first class'. But no coach had yet appeared on the London-Sevenoaks-Hastings night mail run.

Development of Mailcoach design
a) Leather Strap Suspension 1790s (Besant)
b) Straight Perch 1820s (Vidler)
c) Bent Perch 1836 (design John Warde) Lower centre of gravity
(diagram adapted from postcards designed by Richard Blake, for National Postal Museum).

Stagecoaches

Stagecoach design was altering. Typical of the 1730-1790 period was the open top wickerwork basket or 'rumble-tumble' fitted on at the back of the coach for parcels or sometimes passengers as an alternative to riding on top though a ride in the basket was not to be recommended, particularly down hill when the coach gathered speed and the parcels bounced about. It was not till about 1800 that fixed front and rear boots became part of the stagecoach construction.

Mailcarts

Locally the Post Office eschewed such niceties as Mailcoaches which did not run in the Sevenoaks area for a full twenty-five, possibly forty years, after John Palmer started up. Complaints to postmasters about the slow transit of mail were frequent and not surprising as, after the journey to Sevenoaks, at first by horsed postboy as slowly as it ever had been, the letters then went on to Tonbridge Wells from Tunbridge by footpost. Many of the well-to-do became in the habit of sending their letters by the carriages of which there was a constant stream in summertime from Tonbridge Wells through Sevenoaks to London.

On the Sevenoaks route it was about 1775, but possibly even as late as 1788 at the time when the change of stage was made from Stonecrouch to Lamberhurst, that the Post Office switched its letter carrying facility from horsed postboy to mailcart with a single postboy driving it (and still called a rider) for the road was now well suited to wheeled traffic. Further towards the coast it is known for certain that the postboy was still riding a horse in the old style in 1771 for in November of that year, the Tonbridge bag was stolen from such a rider.

The Mailroute

Like the stagecoaches that exchanged passengers at Tonbridge, the London Mail went no further than Stonecrouch and was there met by others coming from the coast,

'on the great road leading to Rye, Hastings &c it [Stonecrouch] is likewise the centrical Post-office where the neighbouring branches (extending even to the coast) all meet and deliver their bags made up for and take their respective ones sent from the General Post-Office, London, which the Mail brings there on Wednesdays, Fridays and Sundays, and goes no farther; but returns on the same days.' [14]

The above is quoted in Sprange's guide for 1780, but the situation was not to last much longer. Stonecrouch, this very busy office, was suppressed in 1788 in favour of Lamberhurst, three miles to its north. All that now remains in Stonecrouch to remind us of its former glory is the *Post Boy Motel*, in this case 'Post Boy' referring to mail carrier. This quotation also provides the information that the post, south of Tunbridge Wells still went only three days a week, also that Sunday was worked as a normal day.

> [*Post 42*]   *Genl Post Office*
> *13th July 1792*

My Lords,
*   I have the honour to acquaint your lordships that the office at Stonecrouch was supressed on 20th Sept 1788 and an office established at Lamberhurst in its stead. Duties of Lamberhurst become more severe than those that were annexed to Stonecrouch by the establishment of a Daily post to Hastings and other very beneficient regulations, it was thought proper to recommend to the Treasury an increase of Salary of £1 per annum on the General Accouunt and £5 per annum on the Bye - the arrears of the former have been regularly settled and so have the Bye letter arrears, but the original salary of £7 per annum to Stonecrouch has not been transferred to Lamberhurst therefor the deputy of that place has a claim upon the Bye Letter Office of £7 per annum from 10th October 1788. The Arrears amount to £26.5.- up to 5th of July and I crave your lordships sanction to Mr Weaver to allow that sum in the account now making out*
*   I have the honour to be etc*
*   F. Freeling*

This letter is signed by Freeling. Freeling was a Bath man. He and Bonner were two of Palmer's senior men. Freeling was the 'inside' man carrying out overall supervision in London, who later became Secretary of the Post Office (1792-1836), dominating the scene during the period covered in the next chapter.

Hastings Road takes precedence

The 'Kalendar' of London states that the post to Sevenoaks and Tonbridge became daily *throughout* the year in 1781; but it did not go daily further along the route until sometime after 1787 but before 1791 by when there was a daily post to Hastings.[15]

Rye continued to silt up badly and as a last resort the inhabitants invested £60,000 (£2 million at 1987 prices) to develop a new harbour. John Smeaton began the works in 1769 but it was no good and in 1788 the work was abandoned, and that was the end of Rye's hopes of remaining a major port. All through the 1780s mail along the Rye section had decreased and that to Hastings increased, such that the dominant route now became London-Bromley- Sevenoaks -Tunbridge-Lamberhurst-Battle-Hastings (65 miles) and Stonecrouch had given place to Lamberhurst.

Closure of Route through Chevening

Because of the use of Longford Bridge the original western route down the downs from London through Knockholt Pound at 'The Three Horseshoes' to Chevening and on to Chipstead ford was little used and so in 1785, as previously mentioned, Earl Stanhope took advantage of an Order[16] to close that road and also a section of the east-west Pilgrims Way and so consolidate his estate. A footpath open to the public remains alongside the old London holloway up the hill. In effect, Earl Stanhope was closing the old London-Rye main road through Chevening that, although it might still be useful, had, as he says, '*ceased to be used as the main road some time since*'.

The Order stated that the main road part was closed on the basis that '*it is for the greatest part narrow and cannot be conveniently enlarged and made commodious for Travellers without diverting and turning the same*' and the map shows '*a course for the new Highway through the Lands and Grounds of Charles Polhill Esq*'. As regards the section of the East-West Pilgrims Way closed, the Justices found it and the other small sections of road closed '*are unnecessary, and may without inconvenience to the public be diverted*'. A somewhat naive statement; the writer has always found their closure a great inconvenience. The map of 1785 attached to the closure order talks of the *old* turnpike road and the *present* turnpike road up Star Hill. The old name '*Marams Court Hill*' was to give way to '*Star Hill*', this new name being linked to the Inn half way up. The earlier turnpike route of 1748 appears as a more or less direct attack on the hill whatever Celia Fiennes may previously have described.

An act of 1773 (13 Geo III) some twenty five years later continued the term of the Turnpike Trust and allowed for repairs and widening. It is probably at this time that the old eastern route up Star Hill was changed to the more circuitous route up Star Hill of to-day as there is no earlier Order or Act showing a change of route prior to 1773.

In 1791 the 'Porcupine' Inn situated towards the top of Rushmore Hill to the west where a loop of the old road meets the higher new road going north into Pratts Bottom was up for sale, and did not continue as an Inn. The 'New Stables' beside it was a posting house with stables as previously mentioned for eighteen horses. None of this now remains. The buildings have been demolished and Rushmore Hill House stands on the site which again in recent years has been rebuilt.

What does still remain along this old route is the 'Travellers Joy', the seed of the wild clematis remaining throughout the whole winter and draping itself in great profusion over both sides of the hedgerow at places like Star Hill in particular, to catch what little light there may be on a dark winter's night and delineate the way for both traveller and horses.

Operational Timings

Much of the work of the Sevenoaks Post Office took place at night. A preserved time bill of the 1790s shows the usual departure from the General Post Office in Lombard Street at 8pm, as was the case now for all night mails. A short stop at Bromley meant arrival at Sevenoaks at midnight. At the same time the Mail from Hastings arrived after leaving at 4pm in the afternoon and travelling 41 miles, an average in both cases of 6 mph. Then the work of sorting began and continued throughout the night. It was a 24 hour duty at Sevenoaks as at many other offices, receiving and giving out letters all day and at night attending to the arrival and departure of mailcarts and sorting the letters. The duty became even more onerous in later years with the later departure of the Hastings mail which then arrived at 3am.

The timebill shown does not appear to have been actually used, but is one of a batch of 36 covering the routes from London and the major cross routes made up for reference and showing the planned times of arrival and departure. The contractors who were responsible for providing the horses are named, Holding

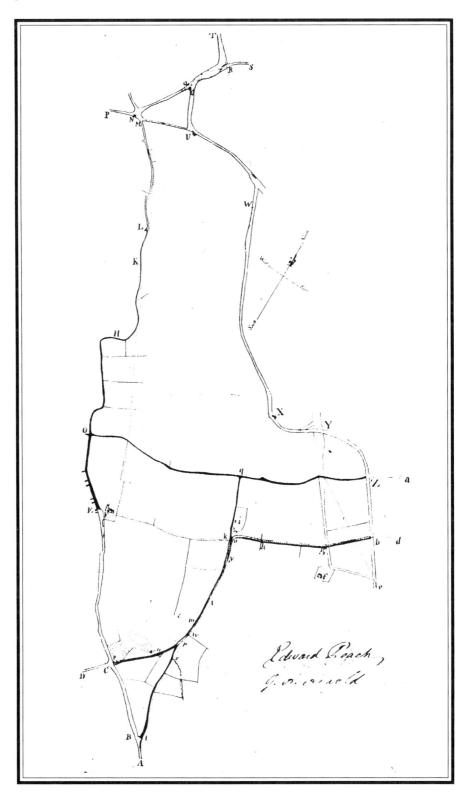

References

F	Chevening Church
E	Chevening Garden Gate
ECBA	Present high Road leading from Chevening to Chipstead
CD	New high Road leading to the high Road that joins Sundrish and Knockholt
EGHKLMN	Present high Road from Chevening to Knockholt Poun
L	Gate at the end of the private Road leading to Chevening Place called the Upper Gate of the old Road through Chevening Park
N	Knockholt Pound
NP	Present high Road leading from Knockholt Pound to Knockholt
Q	Guide Post upon the Turnpike Road leading to London
RS	Present High Road leading to Halstead
QRT	Present Turnpike Road leading to London
U	*'The Harrow'* Ale-House
W	The Nineteen Milestone from London
X	*'The Star'* on Morant's-Court Hill
QUWXYZbe	Part of the present Turnpike Road leading from London to Sevenoaks
Za	Present high Road leading to Otford
GqZ	Part of the present high Road (called Pilgrim's Lane) leading from Chevening to Otford
gY	Part of the old Turnpike Road up Morant's-Court Hill
qkmrst	Present high Road (called Water Lane) leading from Pilgrim's Lane to Chipstead
i	Farm House of Turvins Farm
f	Farm House of the Farm belonging to Mrs Mary Price
pnmkhgb	The new Proposed high Road
pn	Part of the new Proposed high Road through the Lands of Charles Polhill
nm	Part of the new Proposed high Road through the Lands of Philip Earl Stanhope
mkh	Part of the new Proposed high Road through the Farm called Turvins Farm
hgb	Part of the new Proposed high Road through the Lands of Mrs Mary Price
EGHKL	The part of the present high Road leading from Chevening to Knockholt Pound that is proposed to be diverted and turned
tsr and kq	The parts of Water Lane that are proposed to be stoped up
GqZ	The part of Pilgrim's Lane that is proposed to be stoped up

The dotted Lines:

Fkhgbd	The present Footpath leading from Chevening to Shoreham
tsrwxyohgb	The present Footpath from Chipstead to the Foot of Morant's Court Hill
wxy	Part of the present Footpath through the Lands of Mrs Mary Price proposed to be diverted and turned into the new Proposed high Road *pnmkhgb*
yoh	Part of the present Footpath through Turvins Farm proposed to be diverted and turned into the new Proposed high Road *pnmkhgb*

Opposite: Plan accompanying the Order for closing the Chevening to Knockholt and other roads, and shewing the old and new roads up Star Hill. (Kent Archives.)

196

General Poft-Office.

The Earl of CHESTERFIELD,   } Poftmafter-
AND
The Earl of LEICESTER,   } General.

London to Haftings Time Bill.

(Thro Bromley, Sevenoaks, Tunbridge, Lamberhurft and Battle)

	Miles.	Time allowed. H. M	
			Difpatched from the General Poft-Office, the of 179
			at *8* o'clock at Night
Holding Borough	10	1 4c	Received at Bromley at *9 . 40* o'Clock
			Poftmafter
	14	2 2	Received at Sevenoaks at *12* o'Clock
			And the Mail from Haftings at
			Poftmafter
Sprange, Tunbridge	17	2 5c	Received at Lamberhurft at *2 . 50* o'Clock
		1 0	One Hour allowed for Office Duty
			Difpatched at *3 . 50* o'Clock
			Poftmafter
Sharpe, Lamberhurft	16	2 4c	Received at Battle at *6 . 30* o'Clock
		10	Ten Minutes allowed for Office Duty
			Difpatched at *6 . 40* o'Clock
			Poftmafter
Lidwell, Battle	8	1 2c	Received at Haftings, the ot 179
	65	12 0	at *8* o'Clock in the Morning
			Poftmafter

This Time muft be punctually obferved, that the Mail may be at Haftings
at Eight o'Clock in the Morning

Returned

			Difpatched from the Poft-Office, Haftings, the of
			179 at *11* o'clock in the Afternoon
			Poftmafter
Lidwell, Battle	8	1 20	Received at Battle at *5 . 24* o'Clock
		10	Ten Minutes allowed for Office Duty
			Difpatched at *5 . 30* o'Clock
			Poftmafter
Sharpe, Lamberhurft	16	2 4c	Received at Lamberhurft at *8 . 10* o'Clock
			The Mail from Rye, at o'Clock
			The Mail from Tenterden at o'Clock
		1 0	One Hour allowed for Office Duty
			Difpatched at *9 . 10* o'Clock
			Poftmafter
Sprange, Tunbridge	17	2 5c	Received at Sevenoaks at *12* o'Clock
			The Down Mail from London at o'Clock
			Difpatched at o'Clock
			Poftmafter
Holding, Borough	14	2 20	Received at Bromley at *2 . 20* o'Clock
			Poftmafter
	10	1 4c	Received at the General Poft-Office, the of 179
	65	12 0	at o'Clock in the Morning

This Time muft be punctually obferved that the Mail may be delivered at
the General Poft-Office, at Four o'Clock in the Morning
By Command of the Poftmafter-General,

B. J. BARTLETT,
Surveyor, G.P.O.

GENERAL POST-OFFICE.

Earl of SANDWICH and Earl of CHICHESTER,
Postmaster-General.

London to Hastings
TIME BILL.
(Thro' Bromley, Sevenoaks, Tunbridge, Lamberhurst & Battle.)

Contractors.	Miles	Time allowed H. M.	
			Dispatched from the General Post-Office, the *17* of *Aug* 1816, at —— A o'Clock at Night. *WC*
			Delivered the Time-Piece safe. Letter to
Abraham Pitt of Lamberhurst			Received at Bromley, at *20 mints before 10* o'Clock. *John Acton* Postmr.
	11	6·50	Received at the Post-Office, Sevenoaks, at ... o'Clock ... Postmr.
			Received at the Post-Office, Tunbridge, at o'Clock.
			Postmr.
		1· 0	Received at the Post-Office, Lamberhurst, at o'Clock.
			Allowed for Office Duty.
			Dispatched at o'Clock.
			Delivered the Time-Piece safe. Letter to
	16	2·40	Postmr.
			Received at the Post-Office, Battle, at
			Dispatched at o'Clock.
			Postmr.
	8	1·20	
	65	11·50	Arrived at the Post-Office, Hastings, the *10* of *Aug* 1816, at —— *10* o'Clock in the Morning.
			Delivered the Time-Piece safe. Letter to
Mr. Wickham Stonecrouch			*no reason assigned* *J Norton* Postmr.

The Mail to be at Hastings at 50 Minutes past Seven
o'Clock in the Morning.

When any material Loss of Time occurs, the Deputy is to write the Cause of it upon the Time-Bill

The Time must be punctually observed, and the Bills correctly dated. On any particular irregularity happening, the Bill to be sent by the *first* Post, to the Surveyor of the District, the other by *every Monday's Post*, and One Month before they are expended, notice to be given and one enclosed to him. If these Bills are misapplied, and it should be necessary to re-print them before Twelve Months, it will be done at the Postmasters' expence.—August, 1815.———380.

A. SCOTT

Above: Time Bill London to Hastings 17/18 August 1816. A Saturday evening/Sunday morning trip.
Opposite: Time bill London to Hastings 1790s. The timings appear to be filled in on a 'pro forma' basis, for the record.   (Both PO Archives)

of the Borough having the local contract for two routes to East Grinstead on the Brighthelmstone (Brighton)/Steyning road as well as to Sevenoaks where Sprange of Tunbridge Wells took over the ground. Whilst the bill is undated, having Holding's name on it puts it as after 1793 as will be seen.

Jasper Sprange was a printer and bookseller in the Pantiles at Tunbridge Wells and as early as 1774 held the contract for horsing the Posts between Sevenoaks and Lamberhurst. On 10 August 1792 he asked for better arrangements of pay for the Sevenoaks to Lamberhurst ride. The ride was offered to Sevenoaks, Tonbridge and Lamberhurst and all refused to tender. Holding of the Borough subsequently took over. As may be surmised, contracts for horsing the Posts entailed fairly onerous duties for no great recompense and so they changed hands at not infrequent intervals.

The mail service from London to Hastings via Sevenoaks took 14 hours in 1787, the full length, and the same time in 1794. By 1804 the time had reduced to 13 hours.

The timebill illustrated of c1792 gives a time of only 12 hours. This appears to be filled out as a pro-forma timebill and, although the printed part shows the projected time as 12 hours, somehow this timing with its arrival at 4am in London does not fit into the general pattern. Later years show the arrival time back to the usual 6am with the time gradually reducing until by 1836 it was an 8½ hour run for the mail.

	1787			*1792*			*1802*	
	[Probably Mailcart]			[Mailcart]			[Mailcart]	
2000	London	0600	2000	London	0400	2000	London	0600
			2140	Bromley	0220			
	Sevenoaks		2400	Sevenoaks	0000		Sevenoaks	
			0250a	Lamberhurst	2110d			
			0350d	do	2010a			
			0630	Battle	1720			
			0640		1730			
1000	Hastings	1600	[0800]	Hastings	1600	0900	Hastings	1700
	14 hours each way			12 hours			13 hours	

No timepiece is mentioned as being carried as is the case on some later timebills on this route. Nor is any timed stop at Tunbridge shown.

Whilst from 1785 many mailcoaches were running, the conveyance to Sevenoaks was only a mail cart with a single lad driving it and he in ordinary clothes and no uniform or livery before 1794, contrasting with the Mail Coaches complete with guard in uniform, often armed, and with a sealed time piece to make sure the coach ran to schedule on the major post roads. But the coach driver's uniform, if he had any, was provided by the contractors. Normally this was not until late in the mailcoach era.

The Purported East Grinstead run

In 1793 what to the writer is a mystery appears in Post 35 - apparently a branch route from Sevenoaks to East Grinstead, or so it has been interpreted! East Grinstead was on the radial route through Godstone and Croydon to London and is hardly likely to have needed such a link, though later there was one between East Grinstead and Tunbridge Wells.

There had been difficulty over Mr Busby fulfilling his contract for horsing the ground,

[Post 35/11/85] 15 Dec 1793. East Grinstead and Sevenoaks Ride.
Mr Busby has no claim to favor. He is not to take the best part & leave the worst. He has done the business in such a manner as has given universal disgust & occasioned innumerable just & heavy complaints.
The PMG have no objection to Mr Holding's having the whole or Mr Boulton if he would serve it at the present price as it is now served but if the mail is once broken into it would soon be made a precedent

for further claims - otherwise a diligence or coach on that road would be a most desirable thing - Mr F may talk to Mr Hasker about it and see if they can get a Mail Coach or Diligence with a pair of horses at the Mail Coach price.

Certainly the duty must be well performed - that is an indispensible condition.

and once this situation became known, Mr Holding asked for the contract.

[*Post 35 Minute 175D*]

Mr Busby being taken off the contract for the Riding work to Sevenoaks and East Grinstead - want to keep at least the Sevenoaks (it pays better).

Sir,

Hearing that Mr Busby was about to be discontinued from the East Grinsted and SevenOaks Mails; I should be glad to exept the Work: upon the same Turm as what he had itt; should I succed to the appointment you may depend that everything shall be dunn; in my power to merritt your recomendation

    And I remain your

    humb. Sevt.   Dun Horse Livery Stables

De 10 1793   R. Holding   Boro

Mr Holding who was a Twopenny post contractor in the South London area did get the contract though very shortly afterwards the increased price of hay due to the Continental Wars was to make life difficult for him as for all Post Office Contractors.

Sevenoaks & East Grinstead riding work 1802   [Post 35]

Application for increases because of the price of hay by Mr Holding the contractor for riding work for the Twopenny post rides & the rides from London to Sevenoaks & East Grinstead.

The first letter above appears to show that there was a ride from Sevenoaks to East Grinstead, but this is most unlikely, and an example of a letter sent on such a route has never been seen.

If there was such a ride what route did it take? There are three possibilities:

i) Via Westerham **or**	If either of these ways were to have been the
ii) Via Edenbridge	route its existence was never subsequently mentioned when foot penny posts were being surveyed and introduced a few years later.
iii) Via Tonbridge & Tonbridge Wells	If so why did this ride not start from Tonbridge or T Wells. And how might it come about that there was a sufficient volume of mail to warrant a mailcart. Later in 1805 a 5th clause footpost connection between T Wells and East Grinstead was introduced at 5d for the whole route, 4d for part. As in the case of Westerham the detailed survey records do not mention any previous connection.

Mr Busby's letter refers to '*East Grinsted and SevenOaks Mails*', a reference which surely refers to contracting for the two separate routes from London to East Grinstead and London to Sevenoaks. Certainly this appears to be so when considering the next minute in 1793 concerning the livery proposed for the two drivers who, when they were up in London would see many others in uniformed livery at that period and might not only want a livery, but need one if they were to be treated properly.

Livery for Sevenoaks and for East Grinstead Mailcart Drivers

[*Post 42 Minute 157b*] *May 1794*
Penny Post Riders and all other persons employed in Carrying the Mails and Letters from hence [*Lombard St P.O. Main Building*] *are clothed at the expence of the Office excepting the two Boys who drive the East Grinstead and Sevenoaks carts hence there will be propriety in giving to each of them a suit of livery also, that is a Jacket, waistcoat and Hat . . . I can order the two suits to be made against the King's Birthday.*
They would have to provide their own trousers and boots.

[*Post 42 Vol 8 Minute 165b*] *June 1794*
The Chief Motives which induced me to request your Lordships to clothe the two Riders from London were . . . all the persons concerned in carrying the mails and letters in and about the Metropolis can be recognized as employed by Government with this solitary exception.

The reference to Penny Post Riders would be to the London Penny Posts whose carts would at that time be being driven around London by uniformed drivers. The other main mail routes at that time would be serviced by coaches with their royal insignia on the coach itself and the uniformed guard, even if the actual driver was not in uniform. The Dover mailcoach driving through the roads of the south east would look very important, though the other mailcoaches going west were serviced at their Inns by mailcarts also leaving the GPO at 8pm.

The two riders still so called although they now drove long distance mailcarts to Sevenoaks and to East Grinstead were probably not entitled to uniform as drivers but must have felt at a disadvantage in the streets of the capital and were probably called 'country bumpkins' or some equivalent endearment by their contemporaries and possibly jostled off the road at times. Uniform would be vital to them to enable them to keep their position among their peers. These boys would both be under the same contractor, Mr Holding, and from this incident and the following descriptions of hold-ups, it becomes obvious that there are two carts, one on the route from London to Sevenoaks and one from London to East Grinstead each driven by a boy without any guard at this time, and *not* a single cart from Sevenoaks to East Grinstead occupied by two persons, a driver and mate.

Post 35 also has some corresponding entries:
[*Post 35 157b*] *1 June 1794*
As the Postmaster General do not think the East Grinstead and Seven Oaks Carts are more entitled to an uniform than their common riders they are not disposed to give them a distinction which if granted to them will be claimed by others. The Postm. General has long wished to discountenance or get rid of these Carts - But if Mr Freeling has given them reason to expect it from himself they will not for such a trifle withhold an expectation which he may have engaged to them.

At this period the (singular) Post of Postmaster-General always had two occupants, normally Lords. Hence the phrase 'Their Lordships, the Postmaster-General . . .' with some confusion as to whether the following verb should be singular or plural.

Beginnings of Post Office Uniform and the authority it gave

It had been but two years previously in November 1792 that the Post Office had first started to negotiate with the Treasury to seek approval for expenditure on distinguishing uniform for letter carriers, coach guards and postboys as a way to instil good order into a large body of men.[17] This met with little opposition from the Post Office employees as the current vogue was to wear a uniform if one could find a way to become entitled to do so. But coachmen/drivers on general Post routes were employees of the horse contractors and so not provided with uniform by the Post Office, so this is an unusual case.

4 June 1794 Sevenoaks &c Boys [*Post 35*]
Uniform for the Mail Cart drivers - Yes

Perhaps more to be queried was why the Postmaster General had '*long wished to get rid of these Carts*'. Surely not to return to a Rider on a horse? But if not that, what was there to prevent the institution of a mailcoach, other than cost, if such prestige was considered necessary? Considering the amount of correspondance to Tunbridge Wells and the parties visiting there and considering the robberies that were to come and which might, with foresight, have been prognosticated, the lack of a mailcoach with guard seems most strange.

Loitering on duty

Next year, 1795, the rider on the Sevenoaks-Bromley stage, who remember was a mailcart driver in spite of being called a rider, was in trouble for loitering on the road three or four hours in a public house, presumably in his new livery, which seems a bit of a letdown for the post office. It was also an offence incurring on conviction one month in a House of Correction.

[Post 35 Minute 67G] 7 Aug 1795
My Lords
I have the honor to state to your Ldps that Mr Holding has very properly been with me this morning to represent the improper conduct of his Seven Oaks Rider who on the night before last delayed the Mail three or four hours by stopping on the Road to drink with some persons at a Public House.
The Postmaster of Bromley much alarmed at the non arrival of the mail very properly took a horse to go in search of the Rider whom he found in the situation I have described.
Your Lordships will no doubt recollect that Riders loitering with the Mail are liable to imprisonment, and I am of opinion that this Boy is a very proper person to be made an example of. I therefore hope your Lordships will approve of my having referred the matter to Mr Parkin and directed the Postmaster of Bromley to come up to Town to make an affidavit of the facts &c. I beg to recommend that when the Boy is examined & convicted the circumstances may be made known by paragraphs in the Newspapers and proper warning to all other persons employed in the Riding with the Mails not to be guilty of a like conduct.
All which &c
F.F.
Very right nothing could be more proper than to make an example of the Boy.
Ch
Lee.

Whether or not the rider was made an example of and whether or not he suffered for a month in a House of Correction and what he, or his mother thought of the whole affair is not recorded.

Military Mail '*A horse from Sevenoaks may not be sufficient*'

On 30 June 1793 Jasper Sprang wrote to London to mention that the Artillery were encamped near Tonbridge, a similar situation to the 5 Regts encamped there in 1780.

'*A horse to bring the bag from Sevenoaks is doubtful as 14 or 15 thousand men are in the neighborhood*' and added '*My £20 expenses from 1780 encampment not yet paid.*'

His £20 was sent and Freeling wrote to the PMG to discuss whether a messenger should be employed. By July 8th Mr Wilkinson, surveyor, had been down to investigate and reported '*that the Drum Majors come regularly to the office for and with the letters*' and no further action was needed for the present. It was normal army practice for the regimental bandsmen to handle a regiment's mail. In August the camp removed to Ashdown Forest. Letters were sent down from London in the usual way but the postmaster of Tunbridge received an allowance of 5/- per day for the additional sorting and taxing of letters and a messenger to ride to the camp was approved. After six days in the forest, the troops went on to Brighton.[18]

Princess Sophia visits Tunbridge Wells

The Royal Highness the Princess Sophia whose declining health was causing so much alarm in October 1793 stayed at Tunbridge Wells six weeks and made a rapid recovery. Her mail from Epsom, another spa, was brought through daily on a direct route through Croydon and Sevenoaks using the device of 'Expresses', previously alluded to. Some letters were thought to be delayed.

October 17th 1793
My Lord
I can readily explain the apparent delay in the enclosed waybill. The Postmistress of Croyden has written the date so imperfectly that it looks like 20 minutes past 10 whereas it means 20 minutes past 1 O'clock and this your Lordship will see must be the case for the Rider did not leave Seven Oaks till ½ past 9 and he had 20 miles to travel before he could get to Croydon.
Sprang tells me the arrival at the Wells is in most excellent time.
(Francis Freeling)

Their Lordships queries the wait and in reply,

My Lords,   G.P.O. Oct 24th 1793
I have seen the Tunbridge Way bill of the 22nd inst to which your Lordships allude in the Minutes of Yesterday.
I beg leave to observe that when I settled the Post between Staines and Tunbridge Wells I was aware that there would be a stoppage at Croydon, for in an arrangement for 50 miles, I was willing that there should be an hour or two more allowed than the strict discipline of the service would require, that in case of an accident no disappointment might be felt by their Majesties or the Princess and a waiting at some place became necessary unless I had agreed to pay for one of the Rides backward & forward.
Rt Honble the   All which & F.F.
P.M.G.[19]

My Lord   19 October 1793
Mr Church has handed to me your Lordship's Memorandum about the Wages to be allowed the Boys who take the Letters between Staines & Croydon.
I beg leave to inform your Lordships that I have settled with White of Staines to do the Ride to Kingston at 4½d p mile & s1/- the stage for the Boys and in like manner with the Deputy of Kingston for the Ride to Croydon.
I am therefore of the opinion that the Boys are fully entitled to their shilling per stage each journey.
If anything is necessary to be done in this matter I crave the favour of your Lordship's directions & as early an information as possible of the day the Princess intends to leave Tunbridge Wells that I may order the conveyance to cease when the purposes for which it was established shall have been fully answered.
Lord Walsingham I have the honour to be
&c &c F.F.

Three Robberies and an attempt at Robbery

Three years later on the night of 2 July 1798 at about 10.30pm came the first of the robberies, near Pratts Bottom. *The Postboy carrying the Mail* actually a young lad, hopefully in his uniform, driving one of Mr Holding's contracted carts which at that time were two wheelers, *from Bromley to Seven Oaks last night was stopt about Two Miles from Farnborough, between the Hours of Ten and Eleven o'Clock, by a single Highwayman, who presented a Horse Pistol and demanded the Mail, which the Boy gave him. He offered the Robber Half a Guinea, but he declined taking it.*

The First Robbery

The Robber is described to be a Young Man, Middle Size, had on a Drab coloured Great Coat, and rode a Horse with a White Face. The same Man, as supposed, passed through the Turnpike Gate at Pratt's Bottom, towards Riverhead, on Horseback about Three o'Clock in the Afternoon, returned about Seven in the Evening, and asked his Way to Croydon: He had a Pair of small Saddle Bags, and had the Appearance of a London Rider in the Opinion of the Turnpike-man.

The Bags taken away are,

Seven Oaks,	*Battle,*
Tunbridge,	*Rye,*
Lamberhurst,	*Hastings.*[20]

Without the clocks back an hour for 'Summer Time' which did not start until World War I, it would have been dark by this time and the postboy an easy target for any highwayman who was not to be deterred by the risks he ran; for robbing the mails, like sacrilege, was punishable by death prior to 1833. So the postboy was robbed in spite of offering half a guinea, about £10 in 1987 terms. The postboy had to attend the solicitors and make his statement and the matter was advertised in the papers for many a month, twice a week at first '*in most of the morning and evening papers*', later only once a week.

Whoever shall apprehend and convict, or cause to be apprehended and convicted, the Person who committed this Robbery, will be entitled to a Reward of TWO HUNDRED POUNDS, over and above the Reward of FORTY POUNDS given by Act of Parliament for apprehending Highwaymen: Or if any Person, whether an Accomplice in the Robbery, or knowing thereof, shall surrender himself and make Discovery, whereby the Person who committed the same may be apprehended and brought to Justice, such Discoverer will be entitled to the same Reward of TWO HUNDRED POUNDS, and will also receive His Majesty's most gracious Pardon.

Much of value carried through the mails and so,

[Post 42 Minute F70] 14 Aug 1798

- notified Exchange, Bank, Lloyds Coffee House & Post Office Yard so those who remitted bills by the Post last night may stop payment.

Attempt at a Robbery

Later that same year there is a letter relating to another incident at Farnborough on 21 Sept 1798 when the inhabitants saw two men disguised in smock frock acting suspiciously. The report by George Tibbs[21] as to what ensued with a covering letter by P Lawrie was sent in to the Postmaster General.

'In consequence of the late Robbery of the Mails near Farnborough, the Inhabitants observing two suspicious persons on Horseback lurking in the lanes between Farnborough and Grinstead Green armed themselves for the purpose of endeavouring to learn what might be their intention & proceeded by the different lanes to protect the Mail Cart in case of any attempt at it - at the bottom of the hill the mail had passed about 11 O'clock [pm] when the two men who had been lurking leapd their Horses from the field & followed at a quick pace & being called to and asked whence they were going they Immediately return in full Gallop & were Again desired to stop Or they would be fired at - without regarding anything they Galloped On & we fired at & a Considerable quantity of Blood was found in the lane leading past Holwood - from this circumstance we supposed the Horses were wounded the Men were disguised in Smock Frocks & it is hoped they may be traced from the foregoing description as it is probably they could reach town. Farnborough two o'clock 21st Morning.'

They were seen by various persons from [?] till eleven O'clock at night.

The Second Robbery

In spite of the furore no change was made in operation. No armed mailcoach, no drivers mate and so, three years later on, the scene is reenacted and the London 'Evening Mail' for January 9th to 12th 1801 carries this notice:

The Post-Boy conveying the Mail from Sevenoaks to London this morning, was stopped about half past 4 o'clock [am] within a mile and a half of Farnborough by two men on foot, who took from him the following bags of letters namely Hastings, Battle, Rye, Lamberhurst, Tunbridge, and Sevenoaks for London; and the Bye bags from those Towns for Bromley.

The Robbers appeared to be young men; one of them was dressed in a white jacket, the other in a dark coloured velveteen one, and round hats. After the robbery they proceeded towards Sevenoaks.

January 9th was a Friday morning and again it would be dark. The same rewards of two hundred and of forty pounds were offered as also a free pardon from His Majesty as well as the reward if one would 'discover' the other.

The letters were found. A gentleman, Mr Willoughby out with a shooting party in a wood near Farnboro' discovered some mailbags and letters and took charge of them. Some of the letters were opened and torn and all were wet. They were despatched to London and soon in the hands of the Supervising President; 'President' in this context taking the meaning of 'Presiding Officer' in charge of the current operations of the Post Office for that day.

> [*Post 15/9*]   *General Post Office*
> *10th January 1801*

Dear Sir,

The Mail I received from your office this morning was labeld (sic) Seven Oakes & contained the Bags, from Hastings, Lamberhurst, Seven Oakes, Tunbridge, Battle & Rye besides the Strap Bags from Battle, Lamberhurst, Rye, Hastings, Tunbridge, Seven Oakes.

The Letters had all been opened & not a dozen of them mutilated the enclosed paper exhibits the description of property found in the bags as also a list of such papers as appear to be of value.

I have directed the Clerks to be in waiting here tomorrow in order (if it should be so determined) to deliver the letters to such persons as may make application for them & to give any other information that may be required, upon reference to Mr Parkin's letter in Decr 1799 respecting the disposal of such letters as were then recovered that had not been opened, keeping back the payments Bills which come loose.

F. Freeling Esq   I am

> *Dear Sir Yours veye faithfully*
> *Don Stow*
> *Supv Presdt*[22]

The use of the description 'Strap Bags' for bye bags is interesting. 'Strap bags' contained bye letters between towns not very distant from each other. These bags were not stowed in the mailbox but hung outside on the 'strap irons'.[23] This reference is to mailcoaches, but no doubt mailcarts had such conveniences as well.

A further letter from Don Stow to Freeling on 23 January 1801 gives a list (not present) of '*those Letters selected from the General majority by the wish of the Solicitor towards producing as evidence . . . out of which it appears Bill and Notes have been stolen*'.

- and there's more!

The Third Robbery

There was a third Robbery near Farnbobo' between the 17th and 16th milestone on the 16 March of the same year 1801. About a quarter past five in the morning, a man on foot presented a pistol whilst the Postboy was going from Sevenoaks to Bromley. The robber was a young man dressed in smock frock with

A List of Letters without Property, opened by the Robbers. March 1801

Earl Camden	Arlington Street
F.I. Shellerson Esq	Foley House
Thos. Blackmore Esq	Brighens near Ware
Earl Shaftesbury	Portland Place
The Archbishop of Canterbury	Lambeth Palace
John Jeffry Esq	Devonshire Place

A List of Letters containing Property, opened by the Robbers

Edw & Robt Polhill, Borough	£184.19.0 in eleven bills	£20 Tunbridge Bk No B723 June 10 1799
		£10 Tunbridge Bk No B3207 Jan 6 1801
		£10 Bk of England 7350 July 10 1800
		£40 Not stolen
White Hume & Co Vinegar Merchants, Boro	£42 in eleven notes - All stolen	
Mrs Hume supposed to have been enclosed in the above	£5 Bank note No 3927 Dec 31 1801	
	£5 Bank note No 6975 Dec 5 1801	
	£10 - not stolen	
Mr Wm Saint No 25 Gracechurch St	Half notes - stolen	
Henry Peters Esq MP Lombard St	£330 a Draft and Notes - £250 supposed to be the Draft - not stolen	
	£100 Half Notes - stolen	
	£430	
Mr G. Tunnicliff 51 Gosmill St	£2 Note - stolen	
Messrs Mark & Co Berners Street	£170 Half Notes - stolen	
Thos. Everett Esq MP	£5 on Drummonds payable to Chapman - Half Notes - not stolen	
	£17.2.5 Cox & Greenwood - Half Notes - not stolen	
	£20 on Prescotts - Half Notes - not stolen	
	£70 Hastings Bill March 12 1801 in favour of Slade & Co - not stolen	
	£112.2.5	
R & S Bonsfield	£125.5.0 Half Notes - stolen	
Field & Reynolds Upper Thames St	£100 Half Notes - stolen	
Mr Wm Anderson Gracechurch St	£120.15.0 Sundry notes - stolen	

a round hat which had a light coloured hankerchief tied around it. This time the Hastings, Battle, Rye, Lamberhurst, Tenterden, Biddenden, Cranbrook, Tonbridge and Sevenoaks bags were taken.[24]

Nearly all the letters and bags were found, together with a handkerchief with the initials 'J.A.' on it. The notes that had been taken began to appear in all sorts of places, an alehouse in Wapping and another picked up in the street at Guildhall by a young boy. Two sailors had offered the note to the alehouse keeper in Wapping and when queried said they had obtained it from one James Austin. James Austin was traced and found to have a similar handkerchief on his person to the one found at the source of the crime. At his house a large quantity of banknotes and other notes was found. He was charged.

Then came the difficulties. The solicitor that handled G.P.O. business was out of Town and had left no deputy nor clerk on duty. This left the G.P.O. Officials in somewhat of a quandry. Francis Freeling was upset at the commotion and the Postmasters General insisted that in future the solicitor must leave someone on duty.

Advertisements were put in the newspapers and a subsequent summary shows losses of almost £700 in notes (£12,000 at 1987 prices) stolen. The resume gives insight into the business of the times. It was the large amount of cash and Bills of Exchange passing through the Post in support of commerce and other transactions that made any loss of mailbags so important.

How it all ended

Many of the notes taken appear to be those cut in half (the recommended method of transmission through the post, the second half being sent by the next post) and could not have been of much use to the robber.

Both Austins, James and his brother John, were examined before the Lord Mayor on the 8th April 1801. James was charged with both the January and the March robberies with his brother as an accessory after the fact.

James Austin is known to have been tried, convicted, executed and hung in chains for a note on the P.O. file says so.[25] Of the three robberies Austin appears to be the only person caught. Yet checking other contemporary records does not reveal his name. Horsburgh the historian of Bromley recalls a robber[26] hanging on a gibbet '*a little before the turn of the century*', yet all the evidence points to this occurance being 1801. The 'Scrapbook of Farnborough' compiled by the Womans Institute in 1955 contains some oral evidence.[27]

'*The old road from Farnborough to Polhill was by way of Church Road and the now disused Oldhill at Green St Green*', and of '*The Gibbet*' it '*. . . was fixed on the brow of the hill on the left hand side of the old coach road which ran between Lord Avebury's Estate and Mr Fox's. The site was just above the existing old chalk pit near the gate opening into Mr Fox's field from the old road going down to Green Street Green. Mr Fox states that this Gibbet was the last in England to be made use of. The firs near the site were planted to block out the view from their house*'.

Other than the note there appears no documentary evidence that the culprit was gibbeted at Farnboro', only a strong oral tradition which in the writer's view would be correct for certainly the P.O. pursued to the death a letter carrier in London[28] who was convicted and executed as late as February 1832. Next year the same crime was commuted to transportation for life. Letter stealing had been made a capital felony in 1765 and so it remained till 1833, although in later years juries were slow to prosecute, and looked for reasons to avoid the capital sentence.

Small Reward There was great dissension about the award of £200 which was split between eight persons, including the constables that made the arrest, in the proportions £50, 50, 50, 20, 14, 6, 5, 5. Mr William Anderson who made the first discovery of the letters and who received £50 was not at all pleased and wrote at length to show why he should have received the greater portion, if not all. But to no avail.

Chapter V
1801-1840 Mailcoaches and Balloons

Monarchs: George III   (-1820)
                  George IV (1820-1830)
                  William IV (1830-1837)
                  Victoria   (1837-   )

Chronology

1789 on	French Revolution.
1799	Jan 9 Income Tax Act.
1801	Westerham Local Survey. Abortive.
	Ordnance Survey beginning.
	First Population Census in Great Britain.
1803	War with France.
1804	Dartford and Wrotham Local Survey. 5th Clause Post established.
1804 - 07	Royal Military Canal between Rye and Hythe completed as a defence against French invasion under Napoleon.
1805	Battle of Trafalgar.
1807	Establishment of separate Rye division at London Main Office.
	Abolition of Slave Trade, Beginnings of.
1810	Burrells at The Wheatsheaf post office, probably since 1805.
	Second Westerham Local Survey. Penny Post established.
	Shoreham-Grinsted Green proposed new road.
	Early 1800's. First Rulebook for Postmasters.
1811	First London - Hastings Mailcoach may have started. (Short period only).
1812	Napoleon's Retreat from Moscow.
1813	Longford Bridge widened.
	An Act to Repeal the exemption from tolls (in Scotland). Additional ½d to cover costs.
1815	Battle of Waterloo.
	Sevenoaks-Lamberhurst an armed ride.
1821	London - Hastings Mailcoaches restarted.
1825	Balloon ascent at Seal Chart.
	Gravesend-Wrotham Turnpike.
1826	Sevenoaks - Wrotham 5th clause post converted to Penny Post,
	Wrotham - Dartford remains 5th clause.
1827	Boycott Breeds gets two GPO Patent mailcoaches on Hastings run.
1828	GPO in London moves from Lombard Street to St Martins le grand. Changes mileage distances by a half mile
1829	Watchmen superseded by Police Force in London. Extended by 1839 to Provinces also.
1832	Electric Telegraph invented by Morse.
1833	Letter stealing no longer punishable by death.
1834	Repeal of Stamp Duties on almanacks and directories (introduced 1711).
1835	Ogle and Summers Steam Coach.
	General Highways Act.
c1836	Introduction of bent perch on coaches.
1836	New main road through Polhill lands.
1837	Coach Route extended to St Leonards.
	Short stage (under 8 miles) 2d charge in General Post. November.
1838	Sept, Charging by distance along nearest public road instead of route actually taken.
1839	4d General Post. 5th December.
1840	Universal Penny Post 10th January.
1841	Fatal accident on night mailcoach at Polhill.

Chapter V

1801-1840
Mailcoaches and Balloons

These were the times of the French Revolution which began in 1789. Disturbances lasted until Napoleon's retreat from Moscow in 1812, the battle of Waterloo in 1815 and beyond. There were fears that the French disturbances would spread to England. A series of Martello tower forts were erected in Kent, also a system of semaphore telegraph signalling, the idea developed from a paper found on a French POW, and operational in 1796, which was said to be able to transmit a coded message from the coast to London through relay stations in two minutes. Trade was disrupted and we were at war with France by 1803. The Military Canal between Rye and Hythe was completed in 1804, to prevent invasion across the marsh. Prices rose and in particular the price of hay for horsefeed rose to a point where post office contracts had to be adjusted.

Mailcarts, Coaches and Routes

Contractors appeared frequently to change and in 1806 there was a new contract on the London-Lamberhurst ride including the repairing of carts and again in 1810 another contract when Boorman of Lamberhurst took the London to Lamberhurst contract at £550 per annum[1] taking over from Sprange of Tonbridge Wells who had horsed the Sevenoaks-Lamberhurst ground since 1793.

1811: A Coach for the mails to be started

By 1811 mention is made of a Coach to be started on this route. One factor might have been their Lordships the Postmaster General's complaint that the London-Lamberhurst section only averaged 5mph overall when 6mph was expected.

> *[Post 42] 28 Feb 1811*
>
> *An agreement being made, as has already been reported to yr. h. with certain coachmaster for a coach to Hastings to commence on 5th June next which will be a considerable annual saving it becomes necessary to provide for the conveyance of mails by Horse between the 25th March when your present contracts expire to the 5th day of June, I enclose Mr Scott's report by which it appears that the present contractors will continue to 5 June on their allowances provided they are indemnified against the Taxes they must incur for their Horses* for the whole year by continuing their employment beyond 5 April. The Taxes will amount to a less sum than sending the mails by express or making any other agreement & therefor I recommend y. h. to Mr Scotts proposal.*
>
> *All which . . .   F. Freeling*

(* Scott's letter to Freeling of the previous day mentions "*Taxes upon the horses <u>and carts</u> employed in the performance of that service*".)

Coaches, Mail and Stage

One might be forgiven for thinking that the mail**coach** service from London through Sevenoaks to Hastings did start in June of 1811 as planned, for there is no note of the arrangements being altered. But if it did start it cannot have lasted above a short time for there is no record in the Incidents (payments) Books (Post 6/15) which books clearly show regular quarterly payments for both the Dover and the Brighthelmstone mailcoaches but none for Hastings. Being a contractor's coach and not a GPO Patent Coach it might be argued that the payments are recorded elsewhere. But no London to Hastings mailcoach service is recorded in the contemporary yearbooks and another proof that the service, if started, cannot have lasted long is that it is not shown in the Post Office list of c.1812/14 giving routes of First class, Second class, Third class and Fourth class (Penny Post) mailcoaches. Also in the Surveyors circulation map of 1813 the route is shown in purple denoting a mailcart and not in the red of a mailcoach route. The 1816 time bill also appears to relate to a single horse that fell and was injured. That, too, would indicate a mailcart.

Running a coach was an expensive business and needed constant income from passengers to make the proposition viable. Perhaps the late night hours at which mailcoaches must needs run, made them unpopular with passengers, compared with scheduled daytime stagecoaches, on what was a comparatively short journey of only seventy miles the whole distance, and this general view is supported by Austen.[2]

The daytime coaches were frequent. From the George Inn Borough in 1813 there were morning stagecoaches four days a week and one every afternoon except Sunday. By 1815 this service had become a stagecoach daily, except Sunday, at 6am to Sevenoaks, Lamberhurst, Battle and on to Hastings with a stagecoach every afternoon at 2.15pm again except Sunday to Farnboro', Riverhead and Sevenoaks.

Mailcarts

After the two robberies in the early part of 1801, a trial was carried out on the Sevenoaks-Hastings mailcart of the 'Wigan Box', a contrivance developed after the robbery of the Warrington to Wigan mail at '*230am on Sunday 9th November 1800 when a man on foot pulled the Rider off his horse, mounted it and rode off with the mailbags*' in spite of the penalty of hanging and gibbeting if caught. Times were hard and there was a spate of robberies. The 'Wigan Box' was a heavy iron box bolted to the floor of the mailcart into which the mailbags were locked for their greater protection.

With the reversion to mailcarts on the Sevenoaks run if indeed there ever had been a mailcoach and with the continually increasing volume of mail to be carried, the design of available carts became progressively larger and stronger: four wheels instead of two, two horses instead of one, and by 1807 (see later) a second man as well as the driver, and with a closed-in section to the cart the better to protect the mail.

In 1815/17 the Sevenoaks-Lamberhurst section was authorised to carry an *armed* guard, but a list of armed/unarmed rides and walks in 1823 shows only the following as armed:

Rides:	Croydon & Lewes via Uckfield	Rochester & Maidstone
	Lamberhurst & Rye	Maidstone & Tunbridge
Footposts:	Hawkhurst & Benenden	Newenden & Tenterden

so presumably by 1823 the Sevenoaks-Lamberhurst section was no longer armed.

While the Contractors did not have to use a standard type of provided cart, the cart they did use had to be approved by the Surveyor of the District as of appropriate construction. Such required approval meant that the Post Office through its Surveyors had control over the type of cart actually used. Judging by the fuss over the use of a fourwheeled cart described in the following report, it could be a fair assumption that on this route it contiued to be the habit to use two wheelers most of the time.

Mailcoaches: the 1821 start

In 1821 came the arrangements for a Mailcoach, one with two horses, a Contractor's coach. The introduction of the coach has its story, with a hark-back to the independent action of the Ripiers of old following this route.

Sevenoaks 24 boxed handstamp, the second mileage stamp.

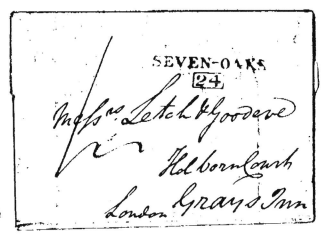

1804 4d charge to London with early 'Sevenoaks 24'

1805 5d charge to London.

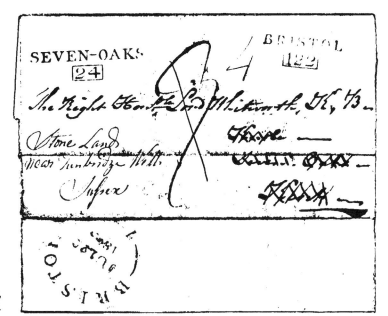

1805, Item from Bristol to Sevenoaks 9d paid on receipt, Readdressed to Tunbridge Wells, charged further 4d (all reduced).

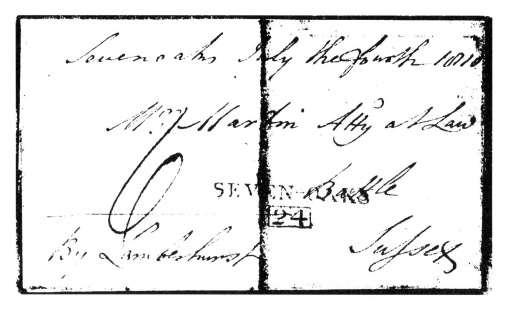

1810 There was no other way that a letter could be sent from Sevenoaks to Battle except 'By Lamberhurst' and so the inscription is redundant. But that and the place and date written along the top make it appear that the sender was trying to make the letter look like a 'free'. If so, he failed. The letter was charged the usual 6d to the recipient.

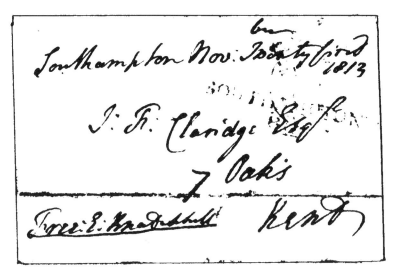

1813 'Free' from Southampton through London addressed to '7 Oaks'.

[Post 42] Minute 146
To A Scott Esq   *General Post Office*
                                               32rd May 1821 (sic)
Sir,
    Mr Johnson has entered into an agreement for establishing a Mailcoach between London & Hastings.
I therefor beg you will immediately give the requisite notice to the Contractors on that road to quit, and
put an end to the existing agreement.
    It is with no little surprise I learn that the Contractor has set up a four wheeled Carriage to convey the
Hastings Mail from thence - unless he has done so with your consent and approbation I beg you will put
an immediate stop to it.
(signed)   *F. Freeling*

Scott's reply came the following day.

    To Francis Freeling Esq   *Romney 24th May 1821*
Sir,
    Agreeably to your directions and the Agreements entered into, I have this day given notice to the
Contractors for the London and Lamberhurst and the Lamberhurst and Rye & Hastings Rides, to quit the
conveyance of His Majesty's Mails at the expiration of three Calendar Months from the date hereof.
    I was not aware until last week when I was at Lamberhurst that Mr Hammond conveyed the Bags from
London in a four wheeled Carriage, which appeared to me constructed to take a Passenger. I then
informed him I would not permit it to be used, and I have written to him to-day to say that if he continues
it, I shall consider his Contract at an end, it being particularly expressed that the Carts for the conveyance
of the Mails are to be approved by the Surveyor of the District.
    I am, Sir
    Your most obedient servant
    Anthony Scott

Freeling then passed on the information to the Postmaster General,

My Lords,   *25th May 1821*
    By the enclosed Correspondance Your Lordships will see that notice to quit has been given to the
Contractors for conveying the Mails between London & Hastings in consequence of the agreement for
covering that Ground with a Pair Horse Mail Coach. Lord Chichester will recollect a recent conversation
in which I stated to His Lordship the gross impropriety of the Contractor conveying Fish & parcels of every
description by his Mail Cart and will be surprised to find that the Man has thought it proper to set up a
four wheeled Carriage, so constructed as to take a Passenger. To this I lost no time in calling the attention
of the Surveyor that an immediate stop may be put to such Irregularity, which I have no doubt will be
approved of by your Lordships.
    All which is humbly submitted by
    F. Freeling

In approving Freeling's actions, their Lordships the Postmaster General (Lord Chichester and Lord
Salisbury) commented:

    'The above must have been known to the Deputies at Hastings and Lamberhurst and ought to have been
reported to the Surveyor - an enquiry should be made into the Date of its commencement.'

So for Sevenoaks, after the possible experiment of one or two years from mid-1811, the true mailcoach
era, as opposed to the stagecoach era, lasted at most twenty three years, from 1821 until the mail came up

1827 Letter from Edinburgh to Hastings 1/2½ for 420 miles including the 'additional ½d' for Scottish tolls.

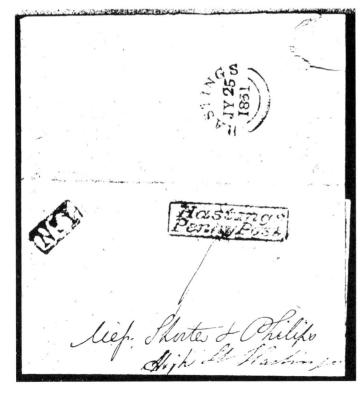

St. Leonards - Hastings Penny Post

1831 After St. Leonards started to build in 1828, there was a penny post connection between the two, much used until the mailcoach route was extended to St. Leonards in 1836. (Reduced)

from Tonbridge Railway Station in 1844, by mailcart again and later by omnibus.

Whether the mailcoach was in continuous use from 1821 to 1844 is in fact in some doubt for at least one temporary hiatus is mentioned:

[*Post 42 Vol 44/308*] *28 May 1827 and 15 June 1827*
re London-Hastings mailcoach
Changing from mailcoach to Ride (ie Mailcart)

Mailcoaches: the 1827 change

It would seem from local newspaper reports[3] that the operators of the Old (1821) Coach gave up in 1827 when the two Coaches, which must have been local ones and not the standard GPO pattern, after six years continuous use wore out. It was presumed that they would not be continuing and it should be noticed that the GPO appeared quite happy to make the replacement a mailcart, so there cannot have been great profit in the passenger-carrying side.

But they reckoned without Mr Boycott Breeds, a businessman of Hastings who finally persuaded the GPO to allot to this route two of the Royal Patent Mailcoaches contracted and serviced by Vidler. On 20 June 1827 *"a dinner was served up by Mr Edwards at the Kings Head (Hastings) in honour of the spirited exertions of Mr Boycott Breeds in getting mailcoaches to run"*. Brett relates that there were two coaches each night, one starting from London and one from Hastings, *"two of them were put on between London (via Sevenoaks) and Hastings in the year 1827 about ten months before the town of St Leonards was commenced. Their complement of horses was four, but I have seen them in wintertime, when travelling was impeded by snow or other causes, come in and go out with six. By the new arrangement the time for travelling the 64 miles was at once reduced from fifteen hours to nine"*.[4]

These comments of Brett highlight the difficulty encountered when delving into historical data: from official records the complement of horses for the mailcoach on this route has never been other than two, to use more would have required special approval for payment and this would only be forthcoming if special and unusual conditions prevailed. The old coach timing, too, was ten hours for the trip, so the new timings were not quite so dramatic in reduction of hours. The new coach working stop for PO Business (15/20 mins) was at Woodsgate just before Lamberhurst.

Hastings was a go-ahead town in those days. In July 1825 the Commissioners had passed a resolution to have houses numbered and the resolution was quickly put into effect. Sevenoaks numbered houses sometime between 1871 and 1881; it is on this latter date that numbering is first recorded in census data.

Brett also gives the only known contemporary eye-witness account of the coach, though it must be remembered he was writing in his old age about forty years after the events took place. He was writing towards the end of his life, about 1880/85, as he recalled watching the mailcoach from Sevenoaks approaching Hastings before going on to St Leonards which dates the observation between 1837 and 1844. *"Having risen at 4.15am at the start of a nineteen hour day Sundays not excepted"*, and early breakfasted on 'David's Elixir', a quarter pint of very old ale, *"I start out to meet the Mail. I usually come up with it at the top of the town, just about the time the skid-pans are being removed from the wheels,"* but this time the Mail is overdue and Brett gets to the Hare and Hounds at Ore *"before the red coach and the red-coated guard begin to show up"*. In this part of the description there is no reference to the number of horses; the PO returns to the House of Commons for these years consistently list this mail as a 'Pair Horse' mail. The standard Mailcoach was black and maroon probably with red lettering and wheels and underside to the driver's footboard seen from the front, with the guard's coat a military red.

The Post Office at Hastings from which Brett worked was in the Old High Street on the east side almost opposite the old Town Hall, now a museum. The mail to London closed at 7pm in the evening with a penny late fee for the next half hour and a rather expensive 6d late fee between 7.30 and 8pm when the bags were sealed and sent off.[5]

Steam driven carriages

Later by 1835, steam traction was experimented with. One of the earlier events recorded was of a steam carriage being built to carry stone for road building from the Ightham quarries.[6]

Before the high tolls and bankruptcies put an end to such frivolities, Ogle and Summers Steam Coach was travelling the Sevenoaks-Tonbridge Turnpike giving demonstration runs at speeds up to 30mph and frightening both horses and people.[7] Frank Hills of Deptford c1840 running from Deptford to Sevenoaks reached over 23mph before '*the pumps got out of order*' and The Sevenoaks Advertiser (22.10.1841) reported that '*the furnace wagon paid another visit to the Town*'. Refuelling at The Crown Hotel in Sevenoaks there were difficulties on the way back when it reached Southend Pond.

Day Mails   There is no record of post office contractor's horses being frightened, but, of course, these demonstrations were by day, whereas the mails travelled by night. There was never a day mail coach on the Hastings road, although both the Dover road (between 26 August 1839 and 1 May 1845) and the Brighton road (from 23 July 1838 to end of 1841) had them.[8] These two daymails were not in mailcoaches but in normal yellow painted stagecoaches already running that obtained a Post Office mail contract and were provided with a post office guard. A public meeting in Hastings to petition the P.M.G. to establish a daymail coach London-Sevenoaks-Hastings is reported but the proposal was rejected as inexpedient.[9]

It was the Dover Day Mailcoach where the Mailguard insisted on the '*Queen's right of precedence for the Royal Mail*', quoted in Vale's 'Mailcoachmen' (p58) and went through the marching soldiers. This was at Chatham where the Military Road along which the soldiers were marching crossed the General Post Road. Normally, traffic stopped for the soldiers, but the mailcoach pushed through. Being the daymail there would be no royal insignia on the coach, nevertheless the mailguard told the driver to press on, his only visible authority his posthorn and mailguard's uniform. The soldiers' officers were very annoyed.

The Route north of the Town

Further in, Longford bridge at Dunton Green had been widened by the Turnpike Trust in 1813. The work was completed in March and to this a stone on the bridge is said to testify, though by now it has flaked badly and is quite unreadable.

Changes at Star Hill   During the twenty three year coaching period, for the first seventeen years from 1821 to 1838 the Star Hill (Marams Court Hill) route was in use, and for the last six or seven the new route down Polhil hill, Polhil being the name of the man through whose land the new route mainly ran, sometimes spelt with one 'l' at the end, sometimes with two.

Before the building of the new Polhill route north of Sevenoaks was authorised a traffic census was undertaken in 1835 on the Star Hill Road. The following figures are analysed from those given in Sir John Dunlop's book 'The Pleasant Town of Sevenoaks':

Figures provided by Earl Stanhope of Chevening
Average for the two days (Sat) 25th and (Thur) 30th July 1835
Star Hill Both north and southbound

Carriages	*61 per day*			
Gigs	*62 per day*			
Carts	*70 per day*	*Horses*	*65 per day*	
Wagons	*42 per day*	*Bullocks*	*49 per day*	
Vans	*57 per day*		*114*	
Stage Coaches	*36 per day*		*328*	
	328	*Total*	*442*	*passages*

The bullocks were probably on their way to Smithfield Market. Before the Railways were built all meat arrived in London 'on the hoof', even geese and ducks.

The proposed new road was detailed in
An 5 Guliemi IV Regis Cap xx 12 June 1835
with an additional act
An 6 Guliemi IV Regis Cap ii 18 March 1836
the following year 1836, the year in which Sir Francis Freeling the Secretary of the Post Office died.

The new road at Polhill 1836   A route north of Sevenoaks up onto the Downs was never easy. As early as 1810 evidence[10] had been taken for a proposed new cut from Shoreham up to Grinstead Green (Green Street Green) and a Turnpike Act passed (50 Geo III c18) but a year later the act was repealed, and the road was never built. The new Polhil hill route was of equally bold conception striking out from Dunton Green six miles along an entirely new route to join the old road again at Pratts Bottom. According to the schedule at the end of the first Act land occupied by no less than fifty persons was to be affected. The gradient up on to the north downs was well engineered, this time in one straight line past the chalkpit and

1837 Letter from Town Malling to London given to stagecoach guard and posted at Cornhill, London Two Penny Post (3 - T.P. Cornhill) saving some cost but more importantly TIME.

inadvertently exposing many of the graves of the early AD700 settlement. At the top, the new road cut across the Halstead to Otford lane where the Polhil Arms now stands. George Polhil owned the land in this area and the family name of Polhil has been attached both to the inn and to the hill itself. The purpose of the second act so soon after the main one was because, to put the matter in modern parlance, the drafters of the first Act had forgotten to include a slip road from the villages of Brasted, Sundridge and Chevening to connect with the main bypass and this matter had to be remedied although there was no difficulty in acquiring the necessary land which was all occupied by William Tongue Esq and much of it owned by George Polhil. The Acts also allowed for the turnpiking of the new roads.

Cross-route   Whilst considering routes passing to the north of Sevenoaks, the lack of a post along the third great Kent road that from London-Eltham-Farningham-Wrotham-West Malling-Maidstone and on to Hythe has been mentioned. There was no direct postal link either from Sevenoaks to Maidstone, the route taken being into London and out via Rochester and later via Tonbridge, and that county town, Maidstone, felt the lack of such links. Evidence of the strength of feeling about the lack of a communication route has been unearthed in the Kentish Gazette of 3 May 1816 by John Dann of the Kent Postal History Group;

'The grand Jury at the Maidstone Quarter Sessions resolved to petition the General Post Office for the establishment of a Mail Coach through Foots Cray, Farningham, Wrotham & Malling to Maidstone, Ashford, Hythe and Folkestone.'

There were many stagecoaches on this route but, a mailcoach route it was not destined to be. And so it became common practice for letters from West Malling and Wrotham and probably elsewhere along the route to be passed to the stagecoaches for posting in London (p133). The P O knew well of this practice, which was illegal, but felt their own services in this area, the Wrotham 5th clause and Malling via Maidstone, so poor and round-about that they were embarrassed and did nothing to stop the malpractice.

This part of the Sevenoaks district also had one of the very last turnpikes to be enacted, that from Gravesend to Wrotham and on to Borough Green 2 May 1825.[11]

Routes South   South of Sevenoaks the route ran through Tunbridge and then sometimes direct through Pembury to Lamberhurst and sometimes through Tonbridge Wells.

At first the route taken was the direct one through Pembury and mail was sent on from Tunbridge to Tonbridge Wells by footpost and, after about 1805 by mailcart, an armed ride.

Scott's report details that the Tunbridge-Tonbridge Wells walk ceased on the 23rd February 1824 when the coach started to run through Tonbridge Wells in spite of the great difficulty in entering the Sussex Hotel yard there. The Lamberhurst stop was cut out of the schedule, the coach running through to Robertsbridge ten miles further south. On the 13 June 1827 the Tunbridge-Pembury route with stop at Lamberhurst (Woodsgate) was again brought into use and the armed Tunbridge-Tonbridge Wells walk reinstated. As the original pistols were found still to be in good shape, the same ones were used. Robertsbridge became an additional Post Town when the new horse contractor in 1827 complained about the hour's wait at Lamberhurst (Officially 20 mins at Woodsgate) whilst letters were being sorted to and from the branches. He disliked his horses having to wait so long at night in the middle of their journey, saying that more than half an hour's wait chilled them off and made them ill. So he refused to carry out his contract as laid down, and a chaise had to be hired to carry the mail. With Robertsbridge made a post town it was found the sorting work could be more evenly distributed along the road and waiting at any one point cut to a shorter and acceptable length.

Again by 1834 the Tonbridge Wells route was in use with 'a person' meeting the coach, receiving the bags and conveying them to Tonbridge Wells Post Office for 1/- a day. At some later date there must have been another reversion to the direct Pembury route for on 29 Jan 1841 there are *'arrangements for the mailcoach to pass in future through the town (Tunbridge Wells) leaving bags at the Receiving House'*, extra pay to the contractor for longer distance covered, walk discontinued, all having been approved by Lord Chichester on 25 February 1841.

Road Surface

The road still suffered from lack of availability of stone in the area. As late as 1799 Mr Bartlet, the surveyor, had had prepared three indictments at the last assizes at Maidstone against parishes on the road from Lamberhurst to Tenterden for not repairing the road.[12] But, as usual, the Grand Jury returned them as '*not true bills*', to which The Postmaster-General's comment was '*carry on with more indictments*'.

Nationwide, the road system began to improve in the 1820s on. Telford had advocated an expensive hard stone base and stone was scarce in the Weald. Macadam, later on, advocated small top stones that welded together as iron tyres on the coaches filled in the interstices with grit, an effective solution until the use of pneumatic tyres sucked out the grit and made tarring to obtain a smooth surface, necessary.

In 1835 there was a General Highways Act when every parish obtained power to levy a rate to be spent on roads other than turnpike roads and Statute Labour was abolished; in 1841 some of the Highways money was allowed to be used to repair Turnpike roads as well.

The Horse reigns Supreme In these decades between 1810 and 1840 the horse rose to its zenith of use. With a human population of 20 million persons of whom 1 million were in the horse trade in various ways, by the 1830s there were 1 million horses on the road, 20% of them coachhorses. Horses ate about one third of the total amount that people ate. Being away from the fields whilst working, horses had to be fed with oats and grain.

Their pattern of use had also changed now that most were pulling a vehicle on reasonably good roads rather than being ridden upon. With stages now down to ten miles rather than the previous twenty, a working horse might have a working life of three or four years. His task might be two trotting trips of 10 miles per day helping to pull a vehicle weighing up to two tons and working three days out of four. The coach horse had to trot, not gallop, or rather at least one horse of the team of four must do so, and he, the *parliamentary* horse, had to be able to trot as fast as the other three galloped.[13]

Coaches along the Road

The Star Hill survey of 1835 already mentioned lists 36 stagecoaches per day in July. Many of these are listed in Robson (see appendix) and Bates. Few of them completed their journey in Seven Oakes, other than the 'United Friends', but went through to Tunbridge Wells, Hastings and Rye.

In 1831 Robson's lists of licenced coaches show that, not counting the Royal Mail coaches that passed through at night and that were seen probably by few local residents of Sevenoaks, there were seven stagecoaches on the Hastings run and two on the Rye run making single journeys each day with one to Sevenoaks and three to Tunbridge Wells making return journeys, a total of 17 passings, both ways, by day.

The road to London through Wrotham was almost as busy with nine coaches (including two vans) but five of these were doing a return journey and so there were 14 passings.

By 1837 public Transport had increased to ten single journeys between London and Hastings, two to Rye, and return journeys, five to Tunbridge Wells, one to Seven Oaks and an omnibus to Southboro', making 26 passings both ways by day. This is considerably lower than the figure recorded in the survey, but does not appear to include vans, eg Shepherd & Co's Royal Blue Coach van for Seven-Oaks and Tonbridge Wells at 4pm daily carrying 6/6 passengers and Luggage, and no doubt some adjustment should be made for additional transport during the summer season at the Wells, the survey being taken during summertime.

An analysis of the seating capacity gives twenty one coaches of the standard 4 inside/11 outside, one 4/8, and three smaller ones 4/2, 3/3, 3/1, plus the omnibus with 9 inside and none outside. So it is not to be wondered that the standard pattern in everydoby's mind, including artists, was the 4/11. Taking this into account, if all the places were filled it means that in 1837 before the railways came only 2,500 people per month could be taken through Sevenoaks by coach to the seaside at Hastings.

About this time 1836, Wrotham had many named coaches passing through, 'The British Queen', 'The Favourite', 'The Balloon', 'The Reliance', Martin's Omnibus to Maidstone and 'The Tally-Ho' to Tenterden.[14]

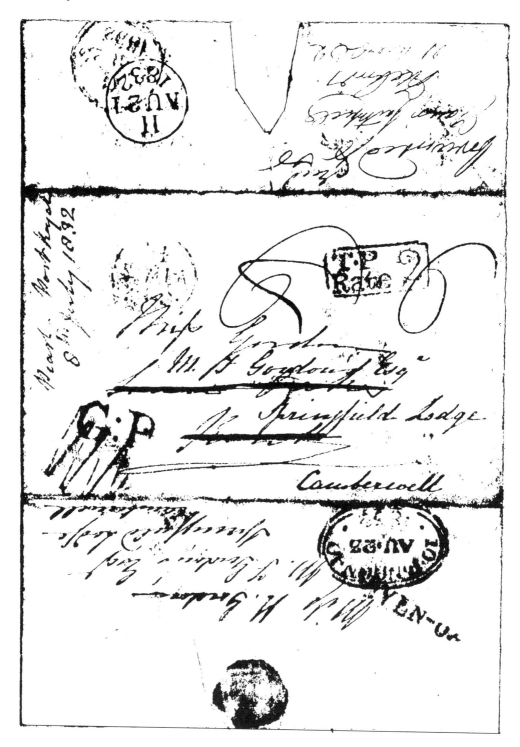

1832 Letter from Port Royal Jamaica carried privately to avoid Ship Letter charges and put into the General Post in London to Sevenoaks, charge 6d. Readdressed to Camberwell so returned to London in General Post 6d and then transferred to the London T.P. (Two Penny Post) 2d and G.P. cancelled.

Bolt-in-Tun Fleet Street   From the appendix it will be noted that many of the coaches to Hastings were operated by Robert Gray and Co. This same company also ran coaches from the Bolt-in-Tun to Bath and Bristol in conjunction with Moses Pickwick and Co. This personage was the original of Charles Dickens' famous character.

Licencing Acts (Operations)

The 1806 act allowed five persons on the outside with two horses, and if four horses were being used, up to ten persons in the winter (29 Sept to 1 Apl) and twelve in the summer. These were in addition to the coachman (driver) and guard, so there could be 4 inside and 14 outside, in total.

The 1810 act, with four horses allowed ten outside excluding Coachman but including the Guard and these ten had to be distributed one on the box, three at the front and six at the back. If, however, the lower boot for luggage was incorporated in the design of the coach there could be twelve outside (inc the guard) and so arriving at the standard coach capacity of 4/11 that is 4 passengers inside 11 outside plus the two 'crewmen'. The 4/11 became a standard capacity for stagecoaches and many were built to this pattern.

The 1833 Act changed the basis of calculation somewhat. For a coach such as to:

be licenced to carry up to 9 passengers then 4 inside 5 outside
be licenced to carry up to 12 passengers then 4 inside 8 outside
be licenced to carry up to 15 passengers then 4 inside 11 outside
be licenced to carry up to 18 passengers then 6 inside 12 outside

and for every additional three, two may be carried outside. The Driver and Guard not to be counted nor babes in arms. Under 7's counted as a half.

Austen[15] mentions that as early as 1810 stagecoaches were carrying as many as 10 outside. They did so of course because the acts allowed them to do so, but which came first, the permission of the acts or the greater safety of the coach? It is interesting that right up to 1836/7 **mail**coaches were limited to three or at most four outside.

Under 3 Geo IV Licencing Act for Stagecoaches (1822) number plates were given gratis in exchange for the licencing fee. 7 Geo IV c33 (1826) gives more detail about how the plates were to be affixed.

Sevenoaks Mailcoach details

Early Sevenoaks mailcoaches to Hastings would have left from the Post Office at the Western end of Lombard Street about 7.30pm. At Lombard Street mailcoaches could only load one at a time because of the narrow road, and the situation became very cramped before the move to the St Martins-le-Grand site on 23rd September 1829, which remained in use until demolished in 1912. Even here there was not much room; only eight of the coaches loaded here and many others, the Western ones, stayed at their inns and their guards with the mailbags journeyed to them by mailcart as soon as ready. The move to St Martins altered the milage distances by three quarters of a mile or so and led to removal of the mileage on the provincial town-stamps.

1810/1813 (Cart)	*1822 (Contractors Coach)*
2000 London 0600	1930 London GPO 0630
0030 Sevenoaks 0230	Sevenoaks
0800 Hastings 1700	0600 Hastings 2030
12 hours[16] via Pembury	10 Hours via Pembury (T'Wells in 1824)

From St Martins-le-Grand all coaches left at 8pm. The Hastings coach left by the gate next Cheapside its earlier schedule having been–

Golden Cross Inn Charing Cross	
(owned by Mr Horne)	7.00pm
Bolt-in-Tun Inn Fleet Street	7.30pm
General Post Office	8.00pm

Then once over the river, handbills c1837 show the Royal Mailcoach stopping at the George Inn Borough on its way south to Hastings. Before the by-passes were built, Woodsgate on theA21 route is midway between Tonbridge and Lamberhurst but now signposted 'Pembury', the main inn being The Camden Arms.

For the **1827 Contract** with the new GPO mailcoaches, *Messrs Horne and Gray horsed the double (there and back) 14 miles 6 furlongs of ground between the GPO London and Farnboro' being allowed one hour 54 minutes; Stephens the double 9m 4f on to Sevenoaks via Star Hill (Marams Court Hill) in 1hr 15 mins; Hart and Harris the double 11m 2f to Woodsgate (Pembury) in 1hr 35mins where there was a stop for postal business of 20 mins on the outward journey and 15mins on the return. Woodsgate to Flimwell 9m 6f was horsed by Pawley and Walker taking 1hr 16mins and finally on to Hastings 19m 6f, rather a long distance but a road fairly clear of traffic, in 2hr 40mins horsed by Breeds, Wood and Emary.* Sixty five miles in all in a total of nine hours, all in the dark of night with very poor carriage lights judged by today's standards. Deducting the 20 mins business stop this made an overall average speed of 7½ mph. with not a great difference between stages.

1827 (New GPO Coach)			*1836*			*1841 to cessation*
2000 GPO	London	0600	2000 GPO London	0605		
2145	Farnborough	0410	2305 Sevenoaks	0300		
2309	Sevenoaks	0246	0034 Tunbridge Wells	0135		as 1836
0044	Woodsgate	0111	0229 Robertsbridge	2338		
0104	Woodsgate	0056	0311 Battle	2256		0311 Battle
0220	Flimwell	2340	0415 Hastings	2142		0438 Hastings
0500	Hastings	2100	0437 St Leonards	2130		0500 St Leonards
9 Hours via Pembury			*8 Hrs 37 Mins via T'Wells not L'hurst*			*9 Hours*

At first the Route terminated at Hastings. St Leonards started building in 1828 and the route was extended in 1836. In 1836 for a passenger who had to join at an Inn, the schedule gives 9 hours 7 minutes overall for a night time journey at a time when the stagecoach direct to St Leonards took only 7 hours during the day.[17]

The driver and the horses were normally hired by the GPO from a private contractor. Mail Coaches out of London were normally hired from Vidler until his contract ran out in 1836; tho' apparently not so the London-Sevenoaks-Hastings Coaches of 1821 but those of 1827 probably were. When the coaches arrived in London each morning at the end of a double run Vidler serviced every one, then brought each

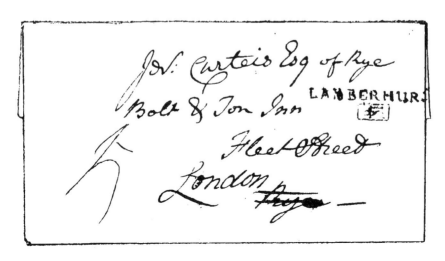

Letter to John Curteis, solicitor of Rye when staying at the Bolt-in-Tun Inn during 1804.

GEORGE INN, BOROUGH.

COACHES.

Maidstone, *(Favorite)* through Malling and Wrotham, every Morning, at half-past 9.

Maidstone, *(Reliance)* through Wateringbury and Mereworth, every Day, at half-past 1. (Sunday excepted.)

Maidstone, *(Balloon)* through Malling and Wrotham, every Day, at half-past 2, (Sunday excepted.)

Maidstone, *(Royal Sovereign)* through Malling and Wrotham, every Day, at half-past 4, (Sunday excepted.)

Folkstone, *(Times)* through Sandgate, Hythe, and Ashford, every Morning at 8,

Tenterden, through Biddenden, Headcorn, and Rolvenden, daily, at half-past 1.

Faversham, through Sittingbourne and Rainham, every Day at 12.

Orpington, through St. Mary Cray, Chislehurst, and Eltham, every Afternoon, at 4, (Sunday excepted.)

Brighton, every Morning at 8 and 10, and Afternoon at 1 and 3, (Sunday excepted.)

Hastings & Rye *(Royal Mail)* through Battle, Robertsbridge, Lamberhurst, Tunbridge, Sevenoaks, Beckley, Northiam, and Hawkhurst, every Evening, at 8.

Hastings, through Battle, Robertsbridge, Tunbridge, and Sevenoaks, every Morning, at 9, (Sunday excepted.)

Rye, through Beckley, Northiam, Lamberhurst, and Hawkhurst, every Morning, at 11, (Sunday excepted).

Brighton, *(Royal Mail,)* every evening, at 8.

Tunbridge Wells, through Tunbridge, and Sevenoaks, every Morning at half-past 8, and Afternoon at 4, (Sunday excepted.)

Dover *(Union)* through Canterbury, Ramsgate, Margate and Deal, every Morning at half-past 8, and Evening at 7.

Worthing, Horsham, and Dorking, every Morning at half-past 8.

Dartford, Crayford, and Welling VANS, every Afternoon at half-past 3.

WAGGONS.

To Ashford, Brighton, Cobham, Dorking, Emsworth, Epsom, Guildford, Goudhurst, Havant, Horsham, Hawkhurst, Hythe, Ightham, Lewis, Lingfield, Maidstone, Petersfield, Pulborough, Rye, Riegate, Storrington, Tunbridge, Tunbridge Wells, Tenterden, and all Towns and Villages adjoining the above—For Particulars, see Waggon Bills.

Mr.................   *................£. s. d.*

Carriage········

Paid out········

Porterage ······

JOHN SMART, } Porters.
JOHN RAYNER, }

N. B. The Proprietor of this Office, will not be accountable for the Loss of any Parcel or Luggage above the Value of £5, unless Insurance is paid above the Carriage at the time of delivery.

FRANCES SCHOLEFIELD.

(Above) 1837 George Inn, Borough. Advertising and Porters Hand bill showing Royal Mail via Sevenoaks to Hastings.
(Over page) 1839 Bolt-in-Tun Fleet Street Advertising Handbill showing the St Leonards mailcoach via Sevenoaks, organised by Robert Gray & Co .

BOLT-IN-TUN

ROYAL MAIL & COACH ESTABLISHMENT,

Sussex Tavern and Family Hotel,

FLEET STREET, LONDON.

Royal Mails.

PORTSMOUTH & ISLE of WIGHT, With a Branch to Chichester, Bognor, & Petworth.

HASTINGS & TUNBRIDGE WELLS, With a Branch to Rye and Hawkhurst.

Every Evening .... at Half-past Seven o'Clock.

Fast Coaches.

	Morning	Afternoon
ABERYSTWITH, Kington, Penybont, and Rhayader	7	½ past 5
ALRESFORD, Alton, and Farnham	½ past 8	......
BATH, Melksham, Devizes, Marlborough, and Hungerford	7	¼ to 7
BIRMINGHAM and Stratford-on-Avon,	7	......
BLACKWATER, Sandhurst (Royal Military College,) Egham, and Staines	......	3
BRISTOL, Clifton, Bath, Devizes, and Newbury	7	¼ to 7
BRIGHTON, Reigate, and Crawley	½ past 8 ½ past 10	......
CHELTENHAM, Witney, and Oxford	7 & ¼ to 8	¼ to 6
CHICHESTER, Midhurst, Hazlemere Petworth, and Godalming	9	½ past 7
CHIPPING NORTON, Enstone, Woodstock	10	......
CHERTSEY, Shepperton, Halliford, Sunbury, and Hampton	......	½ past 3
CAERMARTHEN, Llandilo, Llandovery, Brecon, and Crickowell	7	½ past 5
DOVER, Deal, Canterbury, Sittingbourne, and Rochester	9	½ past 6
ESHER, Claremont, Ditton, and Kingston	8 & 9	½ past 3
EXETER, Collumpton, Wellington, Bridgewater, Taunton, and Wells	7	¼ to 7
FROME, Trowbridge, and Devizes	7	......
GLOUCESTER, Cheltenham, Northleach, Burford, Witney, and Oxford *(In direct communication with Coaches for all parts of South Wales.)*	7 & ¼ to 8	¼ to 6
GODALMING, Guildford, Ripley, Cobham, and Esher	8 & 9	½ past 3
HAMPTON COURT, Hampton, Twickenham, and Richmond	8 & ½ p.10	½ past 3 ½ past 6
HEREFORD, Ross, Gloucester, Cheltenham, and Oxford	¼ to 7	¼ to 6
HASTINGS, Battle, Robertsbridge, Flimwell, and Tunbridge	10	½ past 7
MARGATE and Ramsgate	9	½ past 6
MONMOUTH, Whitchurch, and Ross	7	½ past 5
OXFORD	7, 8 & 10	¼ to 6
PORTSMOUTH, Horndean, Petersfield, Liphook, and Godalming	½ past 11	½ past 7
READING, Wokingham, Bracknell, and Virginia Water	½ past 11	4
RYE, Northiam, Sandhurst, Hawkhurst, and Lamberhurst	11	½ past 7
SHREWSBURY, Bridgenorth, and Kidderminster	7	½ past 5
SOUTHAMPTON, Winchester, Alton, Farnham, and Guildford	½ past 8	......
St. LEONARDS and Hastings	10	½ past 7
SEVEN OAKS and Riverhead	10 & 11	½ past 3 ½ past 7
SWANSEA, Neath, Cowbridge, Cardiff, Newport, and Chepstow	7	½ past 5
TUNBRIDGE WELLS, Tunbridge, and Seven Oaks	10	½ past 2 ½ past 7
TROWBRIDGE and Devizes	7	¼ to 7
WEYBRIDGE, Oatlands, Walton, Mosley, and Hampton Court	......	4
WINCHESTER and Farnham	½ past 8	......
WINDSOR, Eton, and Slough (Patronized by Her Majesty.)	½ past 9	½ past 2 4
WORCESTER and Tewkesbury	7	¼ to 6
WANTAGE, Wallingford, and Henley	8	......

ROBERT GRAY & CO. Proprietors.

Every information relative to the different **STEAM PACKETS** from

BRISTOL .... to Cork, Waterford, Swansea, Ilfracomb, Haverfordwest, and Tenby.
PORTSMOUTH .... to the Isle of Wight, Torquay, Plymouth, and Falmouth.
SOUTHAMPTON .... to the Isle of Wight, Guernsey, Jersey, St. Maloes, Havre de Grace, France, and Italy.

☞ **NOTICE**—No Parcel, or Passenger's Luggage, will be accounted for above the Value of **Ten Pounds** unless entered as such, and Insurance paid accordingly.

one back ready to start its evening run. Vidler's mailcoaches were painted black and maroon with scarlet wheels and like all mailcoaches carried the Royal Insignia and Coat of Arms, not the licencing plate of the passenger carrying stagecoach. They were strongly constructed and normally carried four inside and three passengers outside. Prior to the mid-30s all coaches including Vidler's were constructed on a 'straight perch' a timber across the two sets of wheels with the carriage part above, which method of construction resulted in a high centre of gravity. The introduction of the 'bent perch' made possible the lowering of the passenger carrying part, so lowering the centre of gravity and making the coach less likely to overturn when fully loaded.

Procession of mailcoaches   There was much pride in the turnout of the mailcoaches and a yearly procession through London to show them off, starting at 4pm from Lincoln's Inn Fields, up Pall Mall, Piccadilly, Hyde Park and back to the GPO in time to start work at the usual time. Not every coach took part each year. In 1824 there were twenty coaches in the procession including the Dover coach. In 1838 there were twenty seven coaches including the Dover, Hastings and Brighton Coaches.

Some Statistics on Horsing Contractors. Taken from the 7th Report on the Post Office 1837 and the Select Committee on Postage 1837/8.

The 1836 coach to Hastings and the 1837 coach to St Leonards compared: the figures for the 1837 coach are in brackets.[18]

London to Hastings via Sevenoaks Coach 1836		67 miles 2 furlong
London to St Leonards via Sevenoaks Coach 1837 accelerated and extended		68 miles 7 furlong

Hours taken, inc changing horses	8h59m (8h17m)	Rate of travel 7m2f (8m2f)
Stoppages-meals & office duties	15m (20m)	
Total	9h14m (8h37m)	Rate of travel 7m0f (7m7f)

Mileage paid to horsing contractors 1⅜d (1⅜d) per single mile 2¾d (2¾d) double ie there & back.
Mileage paid for supply of mailcoach 1¹⁄₁₆d (1¹⁄₁₆d) per single mile 2⅛d (2⅛d) double
Total mileage for Horsing and coach 2⁷⁄₁₆dd (2¹⁄₁₆d)* per single mile 4⅞d (4⅛d) double
* sic ? printing error.

Horsing Contractors for the 1836 Coach, With Stevens now a longer Polhill mileage, and Hart via T. Wells

				Cumulative	
From London	Horne & Gray	14 miles	6 fur	14m	6f
	Stevens	8	0	22	6
	Hart	15	1	37	7
	Breedes	29	3	67	2

(Coaching Contractors, see later.)

On this route a 'Sunday only' toll of 6d each trip was payable.

The details given in the appendix to the Select Committee report 1837/8 appear to be a mixture of new route details and old average speed and cost per mile, though the additions look a trifle suspect. The Sunday Tolls exacted by the Turnpike Trusts of London were shown on a map published by John Cary in 1790. South of the river, on the Kent Road there were the following gates: Kent Street RSC under Surrey New Turnpike Trust; Green Man Gate, New Cross Gate, Deptford Gate under New Cross, under New Cross TP Trust.

'A ticket for the Sunday Toll rec'd from either Gate will pass any other described under the same colour'. Judging by the report, these Sunday tolls did apply to mailcoaches but how the toll was collected is not gone into.

The average rate of 7m2f and then 8m2f per hour was toward the bottom end of the speed scale for 'first class' routes, some were as high as 10m4f. But this coach only had two horses which probably helped to account for the slower speed and on a short route there would be no great advantage in arriving at the coast at 3.30am instead of 5.30am. But two horses should be reflected in lower total costs per mile and so they were at 4⅛d (or 4 ⅞d) at the lower end of a scale that showed considerable variation from 2d to 11⅛d per double mile.

From 5th April 1843, the London-St Leonards mail Contractor was to be paid 8¾d per double mile, twice the 1838 rate.

London & St Leonards Coach
Builders Wright, Williams and Co

A Standard Mailcoach - internal dimensions
Roof to floor   4ft 8ins
Roof to top of cushion   3ft 4ins
Cushion to floor   1ft 4ins
Back to front   4ft 10ins
Side to side   3ft 7ins
Between seats   1ft 8ins
4 inside 4 outside

Operations on the Route

Artists of the period almost without exception depict Mailcoaches and Stagecoaches being drawn by four horses, but the Hastings Mailcoach that served Sevenoaks and quite a few other Mailcoaches officially had only a pair of horses to draw them. All *official* reports without exception point to the London via Sevenoaks to Hastings and later St Leonards mail coaches as having a pair of horses only, at least until the end of 1841 which leaves only two and a half years before the coaches ceased running, yet accounts in newspapers and other contemporary writings speak otherwise. Perhaps it is because most mailcoaches out of London did have four horses, the only exceptions in the later years being the St Leonards and the Brighton evening mailcoach which had a pair only. That this is so is shown by a report from the Secretary of the GPO to the House of Commons dated 2 June 1841, no doubt a written reply to a question, giving for the years 1837 to 1841 inclusive *'the Names of the Mail or other Coaches carrying Letters ... showing number of Horses by which drawn, the Number of Outside Passengers &c ...'*[19]

Number of coaches with		Outisde Passengers								
Two Horse	Nil	3	4	5	6	7	8	9	*Total*	
1837	-	1	60	-	-	-	-	-	61	
1838	-	1	58	-	-	-	1	-	60	
1839	-	1	57	2	-	-	4	-	64	
1840	-	1	54	3	-	-	10	-	68	
1841	-	2	40	3	-	-	21	-	66	
Four Horse	Nil	3	4	5	6	7	8	9	*Total*	*GT*
1837	-	24	26	-	1	1	-	-	52	113
1838	1	23	28	2	1	1	-	-	56	116
1839	1	13	31	4	1	1	7	-	58	122
1840	1	6	29	4	1	1	18	-	62	130
1841	-	5	21	4	2	1	21	1	55	121

This report, covering five years, shows the trend. The Hastings (via Sevenoaks) coach, whilst drawn by two horses, had in 1835[20] a licence to carry only three outside; in 1837 and 1838 increased to take four outside passengers, reduced to three in 1839, 40, 41, which indicates they might well have been the old straight perch coaches in those years. The Brighton coach continued to carry four. Other Mailcoaches out of London with four horses also carried three passengers outside. An interesting analysis of the figures can be made and the two tables opposite show the effect of the new springing and 'bent perch' on the carrying capacity for outside passengers, on **Mailcoaches**, with an increasing number of coaches carrying eight outside even when drawn by only two horses.

Mailcoach Contractors   'Vidler' had the contract to supply mailcoaches for many years. After the early mailcoaches built by John Besant, John Vidler was on the scene before 1800, John Vidler Junior circa 1815 and Finch Vidler in 1830. The year Vidler's contract to supply mailcoaches ran out at the end of 1835 and he refused to retender was the year that the *'Commissioners appointed to inquire into the mode of conducting the business of the Post Office Department'* were investigating. Their 5th Report of 13 August 1835 was on Mailcoach Contracts and included obtaining *'the supply of mailcoaches for 7 years from 5th January 1836'*. For the Southern district the tender of Messrs Wright and Horne was accepted. (Other accepted tenders were Williams for the Midland district, Croall and Wallace the Northern.) Rates were reduced in the Southern district from 3d to 2⅛d per double mile to include cleaning, oiling and greasing. This amount was for the coach only. Up to now coach contractors had been paid through the horsing contractors and not direct by the PO. The present proposal was to pay direct, and would give a saving for the whole country of £12,000pa on mailcoach contracts, possibly more.

The new batch of coaches were built to new specifications, no doubt specifically to allow larger numbers to be carried and these additional passengers would be outside rather than inside. The coach built by John Waude in 1836 certainly had a 'bent perch', the main frame that went the length of the vehicle underneath, but still carried only four outside: the great increase in numbers carried outside had to wait until 1839/40. But the coaches on the London Sevenoaks Hastings and St Leonards run never had more than four outside and in most cases only three, until perhaps the years 1842 to mid-1844 at most.

The Post Office Mail Guard

The Mailguard who travelled outside at the back of the coach, generally in uniform of scarlet and blue with gold braid, was a post office employee, a minor civil servant. He was responsible for the safety of the mails and that the coach was operating within the general laid down pattern. A return to Parliament covering 1840 names the two guards on the London-Sevenoaks-St Leonards run as J Maule and G Thorne. Each was paid £100pa (£1.18.4¼ a week) and they were prohibited from taking Fees from the Public. This was the standard rate for the job, although others in this category might be paid as high as £130pa down to £70pa. On the Dover run two of the guards were also paid at the £100 rate but four others received only £27.7.6pa in wages from Post Office money, the rest of their emoluments coming from Fees paid by Passengers.[21]

The guard was often armed with blunderbus and pistols and was provided with a horn which he blew when necessary to clear the road as Mails have precedence over all other road traffic including marching soldiers. As in 1785 an act had been passed exempting carriages carrying mails from paying tolls, he blew as an advance warning to the turnpike man to have the gates open so that the coach could pass through without delay. At times he might drop off mailbags and collect others held up to him on a long pole, without the coach stopping though no doubt it slowed down. At Bromley where the coach passed through to London at 4am the Postmaster stayed asleep and the mailbag was given to Charley who lived near the Swan Inn. On hearing the blast on the horn of the approaching mailcoach, Charley opened his top window, threw out the mailbag and received one in. Then off went the mailcoach.[22]

Occasionally there were muddles with the bags and then there was great trouble for the mailguard for the letters might contain bills of exchange and their delay would hold up commerce. Fines or suspension

1826 'Free' Letter originating in Penny Post and so liable to pay that penny.

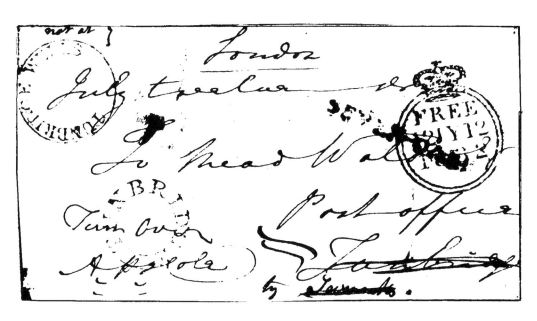

1832 'Free' Letter from London addressed to Post Office at Tonbridge and readdressed twice, Tunbridge Wells and Sevenoaks. As all these offices are on the General Post Route and the letter was franked there was no charge.

might then occur or transfer to another route of more lowly status. A loss of several mailbags by the Hastings guard at Tonbridge in November 1838 including the bag for Sevenoaks resulted in a reward of £5.5.- being offered for their return unopened and the guard had to pay 12/- towards the cost of the search.

On many routes the guard carried a Post Office timepiece, sealed so that it could not be altered and times of arrival and departure were noted by the Postmaster on the Timebill which was in the Guard's charge, sometimes detailing both as to local time and time shown by the time piece. Prior to 1852 when Greenwich Mean Time or 'Railway Time' as it was often called spread across the land by means of the telegraph, such a travelling timepiece could be needed if progress along the route was to be rigorously controlled. For each main town set its time by the sun and there could be as much as a quarter of an hour's difference in time in a long east-west journey. The difference in sun time between London and Rye is only 3½ minutes on the clock and although some mention is printed on timebills still existing for this route of a timepiece being carried, detail is never filled in.

The Guard had to check that the driver, who would be an employee of the contractor who horsed the coach over a length of ground, acted in the correct manner to ensure the delivery of the mails on time and it was the Guard's duty to report on any wrong or poorly conceived acts of the driver. This could easily lead to friction between the two, but they had to get along together as they needed to work as a team to get the job done. The guard, for instance, carried the 'spares kit' so that he could effect running repairs to the coach if it broke down on the journey, and it was his job to fit the skid pans to the wheels at the top of steep hills and remove them at the bottom.

The Guard was responsible at all times for the mail and had to attempt its onward transmission if the coach broke down or was delayed, say a wheel broke or it could not proceed for snow or flood or fallen trees. In such a situation his instructions were to take the mailbags, press one or more of the contractor's horses as necessary and ride to the next post town on their route.

Mailguards Rulebook A set of '*Rules for Mail Coach Guards*' dated November 1829 is still in existance. As well as covering the points already noted, the rules specifically mention that the guard may not carry parcels and that he must permit the Coach Contractors and the Post Master to examine his mailbox in which only official bags may be placed and which must be kept locked. (The coachdriver controlled the front box) He must not remove his lock until the next mailguard is ready to put on his. Nor must he collect or deliver letters or packets. He must behave with civility to passengers, not allow too many passengers on the coach and no extra ones inside without the permission of those already inside. Passengers' luggage had to go into the boot before being placed on top of the coach. Three articles, portmanteaus or carpet bags, the largest 2'4" long by 1'6" high, and no baskets or bundles were all that were allowed per passenger. A portmanteau was '*an article made of or covered with hair*', its use being as its name suggests, to carry clothes.

When going for his weekly pay, the Post Master through whom he was paid was expected to examine his firearms also the tool and spares kit to see it was complete, clean and in good order.

Probably one of the guard's most difficult tasks was to get the passengers back on the coach after a mealbreak of only twenty minutes or so. If the meal had not been quite ready for their arrival or had the soup been very hot they might well have been not much more than half way through when he sounded his horn to remount and somewhat reluctant to leave their repast or to pay for it if they did.

Mailguard Wages and Fines

The London and Hastings mailguards Maule and Thorne were placed on the Treasury scale from 11 October 1840 with wages of £100pa. On the 23rd of that same month, Thorne, the mailguard, was '*suspended from pay 3 days*' but no reason is noted.[23] Some of the recorded incidents make one wonder whether the training of mail guards was up to the standard of that of postmasters where considerable care was taken. G Moore another of the guards officially on the London-Sevenoaks-Hastings run appointed April 1840 had his name in '*The Blackbook of Errors*' four times and only one occasion related to his own official ground. (There was a specially printed form on which errors committed by one Deputy Postmaster and observed by another were to be recorded.)

May 1840 Left London Bag at Tunbridge Wells. Fined half the cost of the Express to bring it up £4.8.6.

Nov 1840 Left a box of Ship Letters at Poole. Suspended from pay one week.

Jan 1841 Neglected to leave the Petworth and Esher bags at Kiphook. Suspended for a fortnight and seriously cautioned.

Nov 1841 Caused the non-arrival of the Wheatley bag, on the Worcester run. [24]

Writing his letters of explanation for this last demeanour from his address at 12 Cross Keys Square, still there midway between St Pauls and Barbican, Moore says

'*the moment the Bags are thrown from the window, the Coachman drives off, consequently I had no time to perceive the error until it was too late to rectify it*' and '*. . . not being sufficiently acquainted with the road as to know that the two mails met near there and would be likely to cause such a mistake*'.

It was decided that he should have satisfied himself that he had the right bag. It was recommended that he be suspended from pay for three days and the Acct Genl saw that he was. There is no record that the person that threw out the wrong bag got into trouble. The onus was on the Mailguard whether he knew the route or not and he could hardly ask the Coachman for he was a contractor's man whose only concern was driving to time. Poor Moore appeared to lose over 10% of his wages in fines within one year.

Weather

The year 1836 was the heyday of coaching and although now 150 years ago, the scene is still a favourite one for Christmas cards, showing the coach getting through the snow to the town or the guard riding off on horseback with the mailbags whilst the coach passengers and driver all stand around disconsolately.

On Christmas day of that year 1836 there was a great snowstorm and the London mail through Sevenoaks was overturned at Ore just before it reached Hastings, and needed forty men to dig it out. No mails got through either way for five days. Later the snow melted causing much flooding along the route.

Being a mailguard and having an active outdoor job, yet one that was sedentary and in wet weather for long spells, was taxing to health. Once again in 1837 one third of the mailcoach guards were off with heavy colds and chills, a serious matter at a time before there was even aspirin to combat high temperatures.

A Fatal Incident on the new road down Polhill

The new road had been built without much delay and the mailcoach switched to this route as the more convenient one. It was just a few years after it had been brought into use that a coaching incident occurred which it is convenient to relate here, vividly described by Charles G Harper in his book 'The Road to Hastings' 1906 and now reproduced in full by kind permission of Messrs Chapman and Hall.[25]

It was here, on the night of August 27th, 1841, that the down Hastings Mail met with the first of the two misadventures that befell it on this occasion. The coach had passed through the toll-gate that then stood here[Pratts Bottom], *and was going at about eight miles an hour, when it ran over an old woman seated in the middle of the road, helplessly drunk. The apparent truth of the old saying that Providence especially looks after fools, drunkards, and children lost none of its point here, for the coach and horses, in some marvellous way, passed over her without doing her any injury except a slight bruise on the forehead, supposed to have been caused by the drag-chain. By some almost miraculous interposition, the horses seem to have dashed past on either side of her. The coach was stopped, and the passengers and guard, naturally thinking her days were ended by her being run over or kicked to death, got nervously down to remove what they thought was at least a dying, if not an already dead, creature, when they were assailed by a vigorous torrent of abuse. Somewhat relieved by this evidence that she could not be very seriously hurt, they picked her up, and, as she was much too drunk to walk, placed her on the grass by the roadside, out of the way of the traffic. Then the coach started again; but they had not gone beyond two miles when, through the clear air of a very beautiful night, the coachman saw a number of waggons ahead, approaching. He called to the guard to blow his horn, which the guard accordingly did, when the waggons drew off to one side. Unfortunately they were drawn to their off-side, directly into the path of the on-coming mail, which dashed into Barnett's Tunbridge van, at the head of them. The van was hurled violently into the hedge, and the coach, going off at an angle from this terrific impact, then went full tilt into a hay-wain and so, happily for the passengers, kept the coach from crashing over; but the shock of the encounter flung the coachman from his seat and the wheels went over his body. He rolled over and moaned piteously, but never spoke again. Carried into the 'Polhill Arms', he shortly expired there.*

Rough-and-ready roadside repairs were effected and the coach went on to Riverhead, but the passengers, thoroughly unnerved by the chances and disasters of this ominous night, preferred to walk on to that village, three and a half miles away where at the 'White Hart', they rested. [With road widening, the White Hart Riverhead is now memorialised by the so-named parade of shops there].

The Times account of the incident on Monday 30th August 1841 *'Fatal Accident on Hastings Mail'* continues the story but says the waggons drew off to their *nearside*. The driver was Joseph Meppone. The mailcoach was full inside and out. The night was clear and fine. When the guard blew his horn *'the waggons drew quite on their own side of the road, but whether from pulling the wrong rein from nervousness at the late accident or a sudden shying of the horses, the mail dashed against the hind wheel of the first waggon, Burnetts Tunbridge waggon which it hurled against the hedge, then ran full tilt into a wain of hay belonging to Mr Cheesman'*. This kept it upright and so there was no great hurt to the passengers, but the Coachman was hurled off at the first encounter and the wheels ran over him. Johnson, the guard sprang down and had his fingers run over and his leg grazed but got to the horses heads. A Medical gentleman Mr Duke of Hastings was in the coach and looked after the driver and Johnson *'got one pair of the horses once more put to the coach with what broken harness remained and tied the splinter bar to the pole and so to Riverhead, the passengers walking, whence letterbags and passengers were forwarded in a postchaise'*.

This incident shows vividly the work a guard was expected to do in an emergency, and notice too that the report speaks of Johnson getting *one pair* of the horses put to the coach, which surely indicates that the coach had four horses. Once again on-the-spot accounts speak of four horses whilst official records speak of two.

Balloons

The first well-recorded ascent of a balloon, a hot-air balloon, was in France in 1783, but for Sevenoaks the aerial era commenced in 1825 when at the end of August there was a successful gas-filled balloon ascent from a field on a small farm at Seal Chart. Preparations for the ascent took over a week and towards the end of this time when news of the preparations had spread locally many people arrived from Sevenoaks to gawp and generally make a nuisance of themselves by touching everything. The local constable was unable to protect the equipment and it was necessary to engage watchers to avoid damage to the balloon. Many of these were ruffianly men warding off their same kind. One of the watchers engaged had watched in Seal churchyard a few months previously for thirty three nights running to the great hindrance of the Resurrection men, who were trying to dig up the coffins to sell the bodies for medical research.

The balloon was filled with hydrogen produced by the reaction of water brought with difficulty by horse and cart from Riverhead and the Sulphuric Acid and Iron Filings brought by the Organiser. The preparations had commenced on Saturday 22nd August 1825 and were somewhat held up by the difficulty of obtaining sufficient quantities of water. After a week inflation began. This took nearly three days but was followed by a successful flight round the area by Messieurs Cornillot and Joliffe, Frenchmen. The balloon went up at 5pm, travelled South West and then circled back finally landing in a field about three hours later, M Joliffe being slightly hurt by a beanpole during the landing.[26]

The opportunity was there to transport commemorative mail, but was not apparently taken. No mail was carried, or dropped!

After the landing, Joliffe and Cornillot saw that everything was safely attended to and then went into Sevenoaks where, as Anckorn records in By-Gone Kent for September 1987, they saw the horses for the mailcoach being changed and so took passage for London in the 'old coach' which evidently was not fully booked that night.

Head Office Administration

After the first few years of the century, which for Sevenoaks were important ones under the Postmastership of James Hanson prior to his dismissal as they saw the first local post surveys and the inception of the official Dartford route, came the Burrells, Joseph and Elizabeth of the Wheatsheaf Inn, where the post office now became located. Both Hanson, who was dismissed, and Burrell had the patronage of the Duke of Dorset at Knole. Burrell's nomination came from Charles Lord Whitworth who also supported his Bond of £400, the second supporter being George King, shipowner of London. James Hanson had become unable to cope with the official regulation for the local posts to Westerham and Wrotham which previously had been privately organised and failed to show sufficient interest in them to satisfy the surveyor. The surveyor complained that he was lax in controlling and organising the letter carriers. And so he left the job, nor did he go back to being a licencee. Perhaps he was wise to leave for the reorganisation of the local posts thoroughly upset the new man Burrell's finances and might even have contributed to his early death in the service.

Post Office at 'The Wheatsheaf'

The Burrells took over the Postmastership at Sevenoaks in 1805[27] and from 1810, if not a few years earlier, it is known that the post office was in 'The Wheatsheaf' yard. The Wheatsheaf is the last office associated with a public house before the office began the move to the High Street and became in effect 'a shop'. At

Entrance to The Wheatsheaf yard London Road; the smaller arch, where the P.O. was 1810-37, the larger arch leads to Coffee House Yard. The cinema is on the site of the Royal Crown Hotel, and earlier Crown Inns. Taken in 1985. (AGD)

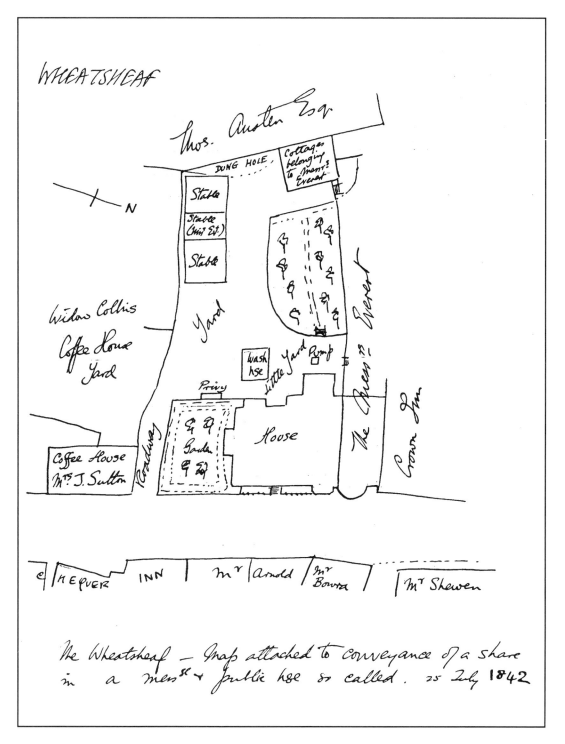

Plan of Wheatsheaf Inn Sevenoaks shown in Dr Ward's note books 1842. Reproduced here with permission of Kent County Libraries Sevenoaks Branch. It was at the Wheatsheaf Inn that the Sevenoaks Post Office was located 1810-1837.

that time 'The Wheatsheaf' was situated in London Road on the West side at the centre of Sevenoaks communications, but little now remains to show it was once a public house.

It is, however, recorded in Dr Ward's note books where there is a diagram of the house and yard as it was in 1842, just five years after it had ceased to be the post office.[28]

It was situated 'higher up' (south) of what was to be the 'Royal' Crown Hotel which occupied the site now taken by the present post office at the south corner of South Park and London Road. The Royal Crown, sold off in 1932 and demolished in 1939 had a theatre within its purlieu in 1806 and was becoming the social centre of the area. The Wheatsheaf was almost next door.

E G Box, a retired Master of the High Court, writing in 1926/7 says '*The Wheatsheaf Inn ... was above the Royal Crown Hotel and is now Messrs Knocker & Foskett's offices. The Sevenoaks Coaches changed here at one time*'.[29] The Inn was between the hotel and Coffee House Yard and had behind it '*tea Gardens & a skittle ground*'.[30] At the time of Box's quotation, 1927, Knockers offices were not then in the Red House but at 9 London Road (they moved to the White House in 1929 and the Red House in 1936) which still (1987) has an arched entrance to the rear, the other arched entrance beside it to the south is the entrance to Coffee House Yard, the yard behind what was the Sevenoaks Book Company's shop at No 7 London Road. The Coffee House was also called the 'Old Assembly Rooms' where County Balls were held.[31] It was known to be in existance in 1820 and concerts were held here in 1840-43.

The Sevenoaks Book Shop at No 7 has lately been a garden shop and is now occupied by Sevenoaks Tool Room, a tool shop. At present there are two separate but contiguous arched entrances between No 7 and No 9 giving access to large back areas but with a high dividing wall between the two. Particularly is the area behind No 7, Coffee House Yard, large and it is occupied by several work buildings. The rear is at present up for sale and will no doubt be developed. The arch at No 9 opens out on to a smaller area, but it is here that the Wheatsheaf post office was said to be located. Together the two arches open on to a good large sized flat area and it is easy to imagine this being a compact centre of activity more convenient than the present day spread out town, but serving much smaller numbers.

In 1811 Joseph Burrell was sharing his premises here with John Poulter who had rented two thirds of it from him.[32] So young Thomas Poulter who was to succeed the Burrells as postmaster in 1837 must have grown up knowing all about the postal business going on next door. No doubt his services were called on at times to help, so that when he took over as postmaster he would not be without firsthand knowledge of the way the business worked.

Postmasters Rulebook

There is extant an early postmasters rule book, '*General Regulations relating to Postmasters and the Management of their offices*'.[33] It is the prototype in layout for the many similar ones that were issued at intervals throughout the 1800s, the next known issue being dated 1845. This first booklet is undated but from its content can be placed in the early 1800s and so be the one that regulated the Burrells' era at Sevenoaks and their activities at the Wheatsheaf. They were required to

Provide '*a separate and distinct office or apartment ... for conducting the public business ... furnished with the following lists conveniently arranged for reference:*

English, Irish, Scotch & Foreign Postage List

List of the House of Peers, of Commons, of persons who frank by virtue of their office.

(If the lists were lost or defaced the Postmaster had to pay for the new ones.)

Exhibit the words '*Post Office*' in bold and conspicious characters to attract public attention.

Provide a securely constructed box with the words '*Post Office Letter Box*' written over it.

The office was not to be removed without the consent of the Postmaster General. It was to be open from 7am in summer and 8am in winter, closing time was not mentioned, but it was late, being 10pm in 1846. But remember the public had no other public means of sending messages. No unauthorised persons were to enter the premises, no persons under 16 were to be employed and all had to make the Official Declaration before a Justice of the Peace before commencing work. Additionally employees were exhorted to conduct themselves with civility to the public.

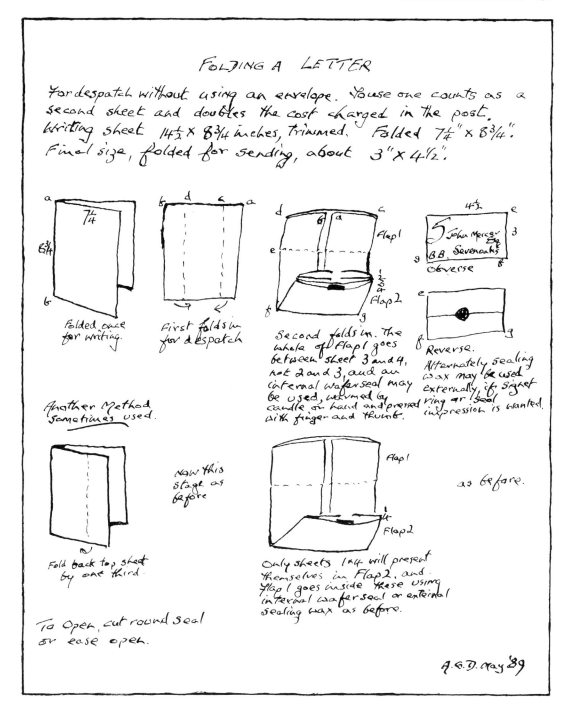

FOLDING A LETTER

For despatch without using an envelope. You use one counts as a second sheet and doubles the cost charged in the post. Writing sheet 14½ × 8¾ inches, trimmed. Folded 7¼" × 8¾". Final size, folded for sending, about 3" × 4½".

Folded once for writing.

First folds in for despatch

Second folds in. The whole of Flap 1 goes between sheet 3 and 4, not 2 and 3, and an internal wafer seal may be used, warmed by candle or hand and pressed with finger and thumb.

Obverse

Reverse.
Alternately sealing wax may be used externally, if signet ring or seal impression is wanted.

Another Method sometimes used.

Now this stage as before

Fold back top sheet by one third.

To open, cut round seal or ease open.

Only sheets 1 & 4 will present themselves in Flap 2, and Flap 1 goes inside these using internal wafer seal or external sealing wax as before.

as before.

A.E.D. May '89

Letters once posted became the property of the recipient. Letter Carriers were not permitted to commence sorting until the letters had been checked and told (the amounts on them added up and totals tallied with the way-bill) by the Deputy or Clerk. All letter bags had to be correctly exchanged with the Different Guards and Riders. Mailcarts must be built according to Official Regulations and any iregularities including loss of time reported to the Surveyor.

The Postmaster was not to quit his Town without leave first being obtained of the Surveyor of the District. In the case of Death or Bankruptcy of either of his two sureties, he must give immediate notice to the Secretary and name a new surety. Failure to do so held the Postmaster, by Act of Parliament, as having forfeited his office.

Postmasters had to transmit to the Secretary for information of the Postmaster-General an immediate account of all remarkable occurances within their district, to be passed on to the Secretary of State if necessary.

The Postmaster and all others employed including Clerks and Letter Carriers could not vote or take part in any way in the Elections for Members of Parliament, under penalty of instant dismissal.

The remaining sixteen pages dealt with the various rates of letter postage, newspapers and Franks, soldier and sailor's letters, sample post, prices current and commercial lists, all of which were quite complex.

Also applying, although not printed as a rule until the 1846 issue was the requirement to close the box by the Town clock (local time) but to despatch the Mail by the Guard's clock (London time, later Greenwich mean time).

Establishment of a separate Rye Division at London[34]

The story of what happened is best told in the words of the participants.

[*Post 14*] *26 February 1807*

As Mr Stow intends in the following week to take the Brighton and Rye mails from the 8th Division and make separate Divisions of each, he requests Messrs Carter, Field, Langstaff and Beale will in the interim inform themselves of the Deliveries of all places belonging there to, so that on the first Night the Bags are so made up, there may be no impediment to the Duty being completely and well performed. (Initialled by all of them.)

[*Post 14*] *27 February 1807 The following arrangements to take place on Monday Morning next, viz*

8 Div	*Ede*	)	*Mr Beale to tax all the letters*
Rye Mail	*Field, Carter alternately*	)	*for these places and to lay*
Brighton Mail,	*Langstaff every evening*	)	*them out in three parts.*
	Beale in the morning	)	

Rye Mail *Battle, Bromley, Cranbrook, Footscray, Hastings, Lamberhurst, Rye, Seven Oaks, Tenterden, Tunbridge, Tunbridge Wells.*
Brighton Mail *Brighton, Croydon, East Grinstead, Eastbourne, Godstone, Lewes, Steyning, Shoreham, Uckfield, Wrothing.*
8th Div (remainder) Appleby, Alnwick . . . Darlington, Durham . . . Ripon, Sunderland.

Strange bedfellows indeed and ripe for separation, one wonders how Rye and Brighton mail came to be in the 8th Division in the first place. Evidently this separation was a success for in January the following year, '*the Rye & Brighton divisions to be sorted in one parcel . . . for which Purpose Boxes will be placed at each sorting Table to receive them*' (12 Sorters initialled).

Whilst this changed method of sorting was going on, the separate bags for each post town were being grouped together in sacks before being put into the locked mailcart as a further protection against robbery, or such was the intention.

[*Post 14*] *Nov 23 1807*

'*This evening and until further notice, a sack ticketted Rye will be laid out in which Mr Stow requests all the Bags for that Division may be enclosed instead of their being sent loose as here to fore.*' Then comes this entry, '*The Cart not being big enough to receive the bag, this order could not be carried into effect.*'

Interesting to note that Mr Stow "requests" and this is considered an "order". The local surveyor, Mr Aust, was notified and he came to London as soon as possible to attend the dispatch of mail.

[*Post 14*] *Dec 11 1807*

'it did appear that the whole of the Bags being packed in one sack, could not be put into the cart without difficulty. I therefore directed another pack to be provided and divided them when they were easily packed.' But the Gentlemen on Duty said even this wouldn't work on Saturdays and Mondays, so after further inspections '. . . directing that three leather Sacks be provided for the Hastings road, the first ticketted <u>Bromley</u> to contain the Bags for that place and Seven-Oaks, the next ticketted <u>Tunbridge</u> to contain the bags for that place and Tunbridge Wells - and a larger sack ticketted <u>Lamberhurst</u> to contain the Bags for that place, Tenterden and Cranbrook, Rye, Battle & Hastings, and as the Guards have received my directions how to place them no further difficulty can occur.

I am &c L. Aust.'

This is the first definite reference to the Seven Oaks mailcart carrying a guard, something which it did not do at the time of the robberies of 1801.

Local Operations

A Summertime day's duty at Sevenoaks Post Office, Wheatsheaf Inn c1810,

0030	Mailcart arrives from London
	Bags exchanged, probably by the nightclerk and cart sent on to Hastings/Rye after change of Horse.
0230	Mailcart arrives from Hastings/Rye
	Bags exchanged, probably by the nightclerk and cart sent on to London after change of Horse.
0400	Postmaster rises to open, tell (check numbers and money amounts to waybill lists) and sort bags.
	Once told, letter carriers sort letters for their walks.
0500	Westerham Local Delivery despatched. Letters/Newspapers/Franks.
0530	Wrotham Local Delivery despatched. Letters/Newspapers/Franks.
0700	Town Deliveries commence (most letters require money for postage on them collecting as well as Town delivery charge).
0700-2100	Public Office open
	Giving out letters to Callers
	Receiving of letters. Checking Franks
	Taking in the soldiers letters and other letters 'paid with'
	General Business and Queries
	Dealing with Private Bags
	Taxing of Letters (calculating the postage required and writing it on the front) and stamping with the Town Stamp
2100	Public Office closes. Westerham and Wrotham Letter Carriers return.
	Dockets and cash to be checked.
	Letters taxed
	General Post and Cross post bags made up and sealed.
2200	Day's work completed

There is a lull for six hours from 10pm to 4am, broken only by the arrival and despatch of the main route mailcart, on two separate occasions, at intervals, attended to by the nightclerk though sometimes by the Postmaster himself.

The night-time arrival of the mail from London and from the coast varied over the years. At one time the arrivals coincided, at another the times moved up to three hours apart. But in all cases they could be said to be thoroughly inconvenient if they had to be attended to by someone who also had to do a full day's work.

Burrell's Finances

Official postal salary at Sevenoaks was but £28 per annum (£750), akin to that of a small sub office now-a-days, or rather less. Whether this £28 included the Cross Post salary of a few pounds per annum as well

---

PROPERTY TAX
For the Year commencing 6th April, 1809, ending 5th April, 1810.

To the Postmaster of *Sevenoaks*

BY Virtue of Acts passed in the 43d, 45th, and 46th Years of His present Majesty's Reign, for granting to His Majesty Rates and Duties on Profits arising from PROPERTY, PROFESSIONS, TRADES, and OFFICES, you are required to prepare and transmit to me, within TWENTY ONE Days from the Date hereof, an Account in Writing, of the annual Amount of the Emoluments of your Office, under the Postmaster-General, and arising from any of the following Heads :—

INCOME.	£.	s.	d.	DISBURSEMENTS.	£.	s.	d.
Salaries	28	0	0	Payments to Clerks	8	–	
Allowance for Clerks	–	–	–	Ditto Letter Carriers, whether allowed	10	0	0
Ditto for Letter Carriers	–	–	–	for by the Office, or paid from the	40	2	0
Perquisites, (being gross Amount of	138	0	0	Postmasters Profits			
Pence, on Deliveries, Pence for	6	0	0	Rent of Office	10	0	0
Letters after Time, and any other				Coals, Candles, String, Wax, &c.	15	0	0
Emoluments)							
Pensions or Compensations	–	–	–	Total Disbursements £	83	2	0
Total Income	172	0	0				
Total Disbursements	83	2	0				
Net Income £	88	18	0				

I do declare that the above is a true Statement, calculated on the whole of the annual Profits I have derived from the Department of the General Post-Office.

Dated this *22 nd* Day of *April*.   18*09*

(SIGNED)   *Jos Burrell*

The following Declaration may be made by a Person in Office, or intitled to any Annuity or Pension payable by His Majesty, or out of the Public Revenue, where the WHOLE of the Income arises therefrom, as having an Income under £150. per Annum, on the 6th Day of April, 1809 ; but this Declaration is not applicable to Persons who have any Income, besides what is derived from the General Post-Office.

I do declare, that on the 6th Day of April, 1809, the *whole* of my Income was derived from my Appointment under the Postmaster-General, and did not exceed

Dated this   *22*   Day of *April*   1809.

(SIGNED)   *Jos Burrell*

Property Tax (and Income Tax) 1809. The special form for Postmasters filled in by Mr Burrell, Postmaster of Sevenoaks. (P.O. Archives.)

one cannot be sure, but probably so. This salary was supplemented by other postal income, late fees and delivery charges but the cost of running the office, employing a clerk for some of the night work and local letter carriers on the Westerham route was the concern of the postmaster and postmistress. That in effect the postmaster was running a business can be seen from the printed part of the Tax return that was specific to Postmasters and which had to be returned by all those whose gross income, not profit, was in excess of £150 per annum (£2,500 in 1987 terms).

This was a new tax and probably genuinely not fully understood or accepted. Income Tax had been inaugurated by the Act of 9 Jan 1799 to raise funds for the French Wars. Incomes over £200 pa were then taxed at 10%. Later by 1860 this had dropped to 7d in the £ (2.85%).

There is no doubt that the official takeover of the Westerham route upset the Burrells' finances. Matters were going along smoothly when the Post Office took over a major part of their business. Of course, compensation was offerred and eventually received, but the question was how much was it to be? Different analyses of the business operation appeared to have been offerred to the Inland Revenue and to the Post Office and so it is difficult even now to reconcile the overall position. The Burrells themselves had difficulty, the Surveyor had difficulty, and really the true situation is not much clearer with the lapse of time. A possible analysis might show that Burrell lost £88 of gross income on the Westerham walk but he also loses his costs so his net loss is only £50 or so. He attempts to recover the full £88 but finally only achieves a salary rise from £28 to £50, an increase of £22 rather than the £88 he claimed or the £50 by the above calculation.

The situation is described to Francis Freeling by the surveyor in documentation supporting Post 42

Sevenoaks April 13 1810
To Francis Freeling
Dear Sir
    . . . The Salary of this office (Sevenoaks) being only p annum £28, I have been earnestly applied to by Mr Burrell to represent to you that the emoluments derived from this source constituted his principal remuneration and that as this is now taken from him he is obliged to pay a Letter Carrier to be up the greater part of the night for the purpose of attending the mails up & down, the latter arriving at about½ past 12 & the former at ½ past 2 for the very small recompense of p annum £28. He states that he used to derive from the Westerham walk about £90 p annum & although I have ventured to assure him that a suitable remuneration will be granted to him for the advantage of which he has been deprived yet he is anxious to be assured upon this point by yourself. .

And well might he have worried, for nothing at all was being done about it.

    To Francis Freeling 7 Oaks 21 August 1810
Sir
    It is with great difidence that I take the liberty of troubling you but trusting to your goodness I hope you will pardon the freedom I am taking - when Mr Aust took the Westerham walk from me he assured me that I should have a compensation equal to my loss and promised to make the necessary application to you. I have received the Quarterly Account and find that no allowance is made the salary as it now stands will not pay for more than House rent and Taxes. Rents being very high at 7Oaks which leaves me and my Family destitute of a maintenance having nothing else to depend upon - I need not state to you the constant attendance the office requires both by day and night for which my sallary will only be twenty eight pounds per year - I humbly beg you will take my case under consideration and inform me what steps I must take to obtain relief.
    your Obedient Servant
    Jop Burrell

Francis Freeling got in touch with the surveyor who replied speedily.

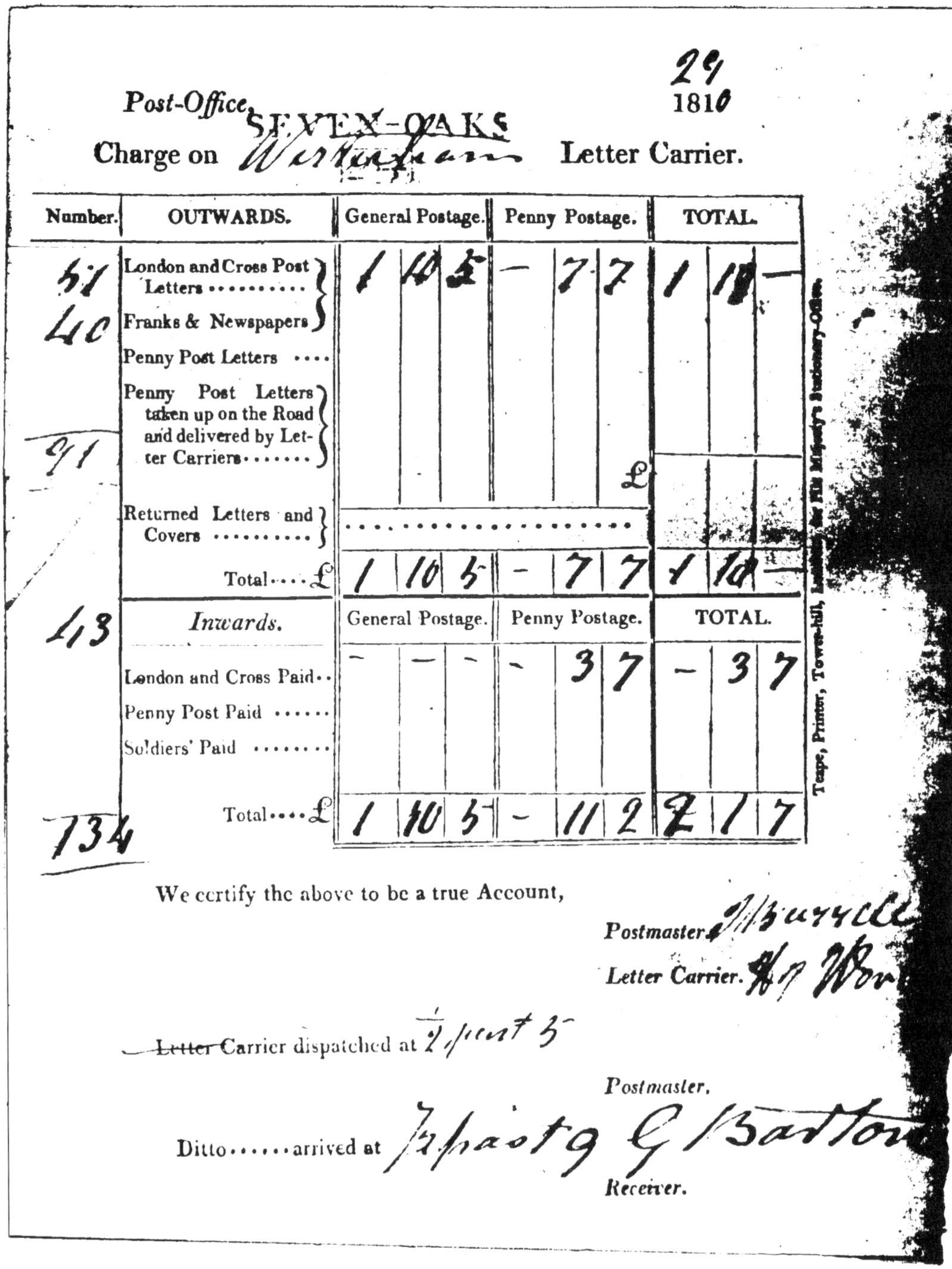

Post-Office, SEVEN-OAKS — 29 1810

Charge on Westerham Letter Carrier.

Number.	OUTWARDS.	General Postage.			Penny Postage.			TOTAL.		
51	London and Cross Post Letters	1	10	5	–	7	7	1	18	–
40	Franks & Newspapers									
	Penny Post Letters									
91	Penny Post Letters taken up on the Road and delivered by Letter Carriers									
	Returned Letters and Covers									
	Total £	1	10	5	–	7	7	1	18	–
43	*Inwards.*	General Postage.			Penny Postage.			TOTAL.		
	London and Cross Paid	–	–	–	–	3	7	–	3	7
	Penny Post Paid									
	Soldiers' Paid									
134	Total £	1	10	5	–	11	2	2	1	7

Tegg, Printer, Tower-hill, Law Stationer to His Majesty's Stationary-Office.

We certify the above to be a true Account,

Postmaster. J Burrell

Letter Carrier. H Wor

~~Letter~~ Carrier dispatched at ½ past 5

Postmaster.

Ditto……arrived at ½ past 9 G Barton

Receiver.

1810 Local Letter Carriers form filled in for Sevenoaks-Westerham delivery. Signed by J Burrell. (P.O. Archives.)

Dear Sir   August 31 1810

I return to you a variety of papers relating to the Seven Oaks office and the Penny Post to Westerham, forwarded to me previous to my taking a review of the Duties the Postmaster at Seven Oaks has to perform and which might tend to assist my judgment in ascertaining the real amount of his loss occasioned by our taking the conveyance of the Westerham Letters into our own Hand. It appears the Penny Post has produced since its establishment £13 a month which is at the rate of £156 a year, from this is to be deducted 19/- a week paid to the Messenger, leaving a profit of £106.12.0. I am therefor led to believe the Postmaster's statement is not erronous when he calculates his loss at 90L per annum. It is true in making a Return of his income for the year ending 5th of April 1807 he estimates his perquisites at £60 only - the year following he made no return at all, and was charged with the Property Tax as in the preceding year - In that ending 5th April 1809 he made no return and was charged on £100 as the net amount of his income / instead of 70 as before / which he paid -

In 1810 he returns the gross amount of the Westerham letters at £138 and the Disbursements attending the delivery of them at £48.2.0. He observes the low return made by him in 1807, arose from him not understanding how to make out the Account. The Salary allowed as the Postmaster of Sevenoaks has been for a length of time £28 a year only out of which he has paid £10 a year to a Letter Carrier.

I beg to offer it as my opinion that a clear salary of £50 a year is hardly commensurate with the duties of the Seven Oaks Office.

The London Letters down amount to about £3.10.0 a day/Bye Accounts are kept with Bromley, Dartford, Tunbridge, Lamberhurst, Battle, Rye and Hastings//The Office shuts at 9pm and it takes an Hour to make up the Bags - the Mail Cart in its way down arrives at half past Twelve, and the one up, at ½ past 2. The Postmaster must rise at 4 in the morning from the 6th April to the 5th October, and at 5 the remaining months, to open his bags, and sort those out for the Westerham Messenger who I have ordered to be despatched at 5 in Summer, and at 6 in Winter and for the Dartford 5th Clause Postman who departs half an Hour after the Westerham Man - most of the Gentlemen in Seven Oaks and its vicinity are in the habit of sending for their Letters and it affords almost constant employment to one person to deliver them out, and to take in the Soldiers, and such other Letters as are to be paid with. The Westerham Man did not formerly depart until seven o'clock in the morning and the 5th Clause Post has been established without any additional allowance being made for it.

The salary was raised to £50 (£850) per annum. Eventually in 1822 Joseph gave up his efforts and left his wife to carry on for the next fifteen years or so on her own, a determined woman as no doubt life had taught her to be, until in 1837 she too died.

Allowing her to remain in office was in line with normal Post Office practice of continuity; as employers the Post Office were loath to disturb an ongoing situation as long as it worked, and even longer. Her Bond was £500, later £600, still supported by Lord Whitworth and when he died, the Earl of Plymouth as also John Jenkin Maclean gent of Sevenoaks and Thomas Blackman of Sevenoaks, farmer.

The surveys relating to district deliveries commenced in 1801 and the projected alterations struck at the heart of the manner in which offices throughout all the country were financed.

In 1804 the Wrotham/Dartford area had become a 5th clause post and any delivery income that might have accrued to the postmaster was lost, although it was stated at the time that there was no such income and so no adjustments to salary was made. The Westerham area was different. The inhabitants may have had their own messenger in early times, but from at least 1805 and probably well before until the route became a Penny Post route in 1809, the delivery was arranged by the Sevenoaks postmaster as a private venture and much of his total income was derived from it.

Promises were made by the Surveyor that the postmaster would be recompensed for the official take over of the Westerham route and so eventually he was, but not without having to struggle first.

Mrs Burrell was connected with, or proprietress of, 'The Wheatsheaf' and no doubt further family income arose from this source. Mr Burrell says in his letter that the Post Office was **his** only source of income, not theirs.

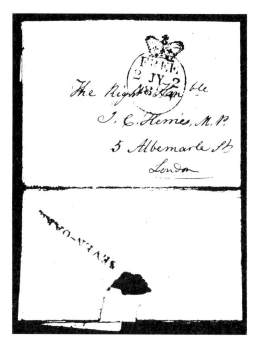

1834 Sevenoaks 'mileage removed' Town Stamp. Letters addressed <u>to</u> a Member of Parliament could also travel free, after the Post Office had checked that he was a sitting member. Such letters bore no superscription nor signature.

1834 Prepaid letter from Sevenoaks through London to Louth, paid 10d. The letter was prepaid and by now the sending office marked the charge for the full route, not just to London. There must have be an alteration to the route making it longer, but Sevenoaks cannot yet have been notified of the change. Hence the penny extra charge. As from 31 August 1784, amount taxed was based on total distance between Post Towns and not the total of a rate into London and a rate out.

1838 Single Stage Sevenoaks-Tonbridge now reduced to 2d, with further 1d to Leigh.
(All reduced)

Letter sorting changes

The introduction of the Mailcoach in 1821 did not greatly disturb arrangements at Sevenoaks. Timings varied but slightly. The instructions at Lamberhurst were

> [*Post 42 Minute 223*]   *15 June 1821*
> "... *the whole of the Letters on the Rye Road, including those for Stonecrouch, Flimwell, Ticehurst and Wadhurst will be sent from Lamberhurst by the Rye Cart, so that there will be no detention on their account. The Postmaster however, will have to sort from the Bromley, Sevenoaks, Tunbridge & London Bags, the Letters for Hurst Green, including those for Etchingham and the Letters enclosed in the Robertsbridge Bag containing those for Dallington, Brightling and Whatlington, which duty may be performed in 15 minutes. But if in result it unavoidably occupies more time, Mr Scott will propose another Arrangement which in such case must occasion an augmentation to the Allowance to the Burwash messenger in proportion to the increased distance he would have to travel.*

On the 3rd August[35] 1821 there was however an order to stamp the Town namestamp on the **back** of letters and this order Sevenoaks complied with. The office had at that time been stamping on the front, as had many other offices, but this practice it was felt could deface the address. The order exhorted offices to stamp legibly and to mark the rate of postage in the plainest manner with as little flourish as possible.

The Penny Post number continued to be put on the **front**.

Free Town Delivery for G.P. Letters: A Further Salary Disturbance

But not long afterwards a further disturbance of the Postmistresses salary occurred when the Town delivery was taken over officially, following objections to the delivery charge.

> [*Post 42 Minute 158*]   *31 Mar 1827*
> *My Lord, The greater part of the inhabitants of the post town of Sevenoaks having objected to the payment of the gratuity of a halfpenny on the delivery of their letters it will be necessary as in numerous similar cases to abolish the extra charge & and to grant a free delivery throughout the town.*
> *The surveyor proposes an allowance of 5/6 a week . . . if a fit person for the service can be procured.*

Sevenoaks Town delivery charge ceased during April 1827. The basis of the charge which had always been ½d was expressed as,

> '*custom, from time immemorial; and the payment is not compulsory if the parties choose to object*'.[36]

Along the Road, Tunbridge Town delivery charge ceased in January 1829, but Bromley, Tunbridge Wells and Rye were still paying at the end of 1829.

What continued to remain under Post Office control was the delineation of the Town delivery boundary. Outside this, charges might still be made if delivery took place, as also for delivery to houses outside villages and more than 50 yards from the line of walk. For the next ninety years free delivery areas were being gradually extended, every yard of ground being fiercely contested. Much information about the extensions is given in the appendix under each village.

Late fees   No mention is made yet of lifting the 'late fees'. The Pigot Directory of that date (1829) gives an entry for Sevenoaks;

> *One penny on letters by the Tonbridge mail at 8.30 at night. One penny on letters by the London mail from 9 to 9.30 at night and twopence from 9.30 to 10.*

The fees were paid on handing in the letters and accrued to the Postmaster although they had to be shown in the Property Tax return and so any profit made through them had to suffer income tax. The late fees were not shown on the letters themselves, only the distance charge to be paid by the recipient, or in red the fact that it had been paid where that was so.

Assistance   By now the Sevenoaks office was taking in upwards of £1,900 (£50,000) a year with much work at night. £30 per annum was allowed for Post Master's Assistance.[37]

Salaries by 1840   As these additional fees, originally accruing to the Postmaster, were gradually abolished or brought into account, some compensation might be given, but the compensation ceased with the tenure of office of the postmaster to whom it was granted though it might, it seems, be renewed.

Salaries and emoluments for Postmasters along the Road in 1840 were:[38]

	1840	*1835 (where known)*
Bromley	£ 58	
Sevenoaks	50 + £6.10.-	50 + £6.10.-
Tunbridge	80	80 + 5
T Wells	56 + 16	
Lamberhurst	78	78 + 3.8.-
Battle	50	50 + 5
Hastings	100 + 12.10.-	62 + 81.11.7
St Leonards	50	
Rye	44	
(Brighton	200 + 200	200 + 381)

Thus Sevenoaks office can be seen still to attract the same £50 salary in 1840 as that agreed with Burrell in 1810, thirty years earlier. But a glance at the inflation tables in the appendix will show that the fifty pounds in 1840 was worth some 25% more in purchasing power than Burrells, just the opposite to our present inflation.

Two unrelated incidents

Youth has his fling   There was a bit of excitement just before Christmas 1824. On 6th December word got back to the Postmaster of Tonbridge that the young letter carrier of Southborough, Frederick Martin, had probably stolen a letter containing money, one sovereign and three one pound county banknotes, and a patrol was sent out. Martin must have been convincing for he bragged of having money and took the constables for a drink. Evading them he took a Hastings carrier's horse and van and set off for London at 11pm sending back the keys of the place where his bag was kept. The Tonbridge postmaster sent an express after him and he was caught '*ten miles north of Tonbridge*' which is somewhere near Sevenoaks.

Martin appeared at Maidstone Assizes and was found guilty but young, being only eighteen. He did not have to forfeit his life as he might well have had to do had he been over twenty one at the time.

Food at the Wheatsheaf   John Thomas Pocock gave his views on vittles at 'The Wheatsheaf' in 1829. His father was ill and had gone to the coast at Hastings to recuperate whilst his mother stayed in London with the family. John Thomas at fifteen years old decided to walk to Hastings to see his father and cheer him up.[39]

On his way out "*I rested at 'The Wheatsheaf' (29 July 1829) and was obliged to partake of some bread and cheese, the latter bad dutch, as they had no meat in the house and I could not wait their cooking any*". He also had some fine Kentish blackheart cherries and managed to obtain a lift to Tonbridge.

On the way back on September 6th he "*put up at the Wheatsheaf intending to wait for a meal but as there was a party of young rascals swearing and gambling, he went on to a neat little inn in Riverhead*". Might this have been the White Hart?

The 8d complaint of 1828 or when is a letter a parcel?

The opening query came from Lord Camden of Wilderness Park Sevenoaks regarding the carrying charge on the Calendar of the Assizes at Maidstone Goal giving the list of prisoners which he received at regular intervals and on which 8d was charged.

[*Post 42 Minute 973*]   *31.12.1828*

Wilderness Park
near Sevenoaks Dec 15th 1828

Sir

I enclose to you a letter which is charged Eightpence to me - The reason of my troubling you upon this particular subject is, that these Papers, which contain the Calendar of the Prisoners in the Goal, for trial, at the Assizes at Maidstone, have been for a considerable time always so charged to me & Lord Brecknock, myself being Custos Populorum of the County & He generally, foreman of the Grand Jury.

If it is a regulation of the Post Office I have no observation to make, but if it an irregular Charge, of one of their Offices, It should be corrected - as I am writing to you, would you give me leave to ask you, how far Country Post Offices are permitted to charge 1d per letter if sent for before the usual Hour of Delivery and the same sum if sent, after the usual Hour of receiving letters. If such Charges are usual & permitted, I beg to repeat, in this Instance as in the other, I have no objection to urge, but if this Tax is imposed by the Country Post Master, It ought be resisted

I have the Honor to remain
The Weight of the   Your most obedt hble Sevt
letter is under   Camden
1 ounce

A query by Freeling to the Postmistress of Sevenoaks to explain what was going on produced a by no means uncertain reply:

Sir

In answer to your application respecting the Calendar directed to the Marquiss Camden I beg to state that it was sent to Tunbridge from Maidstone as a parcel and 4d was charged for its conveyance which is expressed on the cover - 2 pence was charged from Tonbridge to 7Oaks and 2 pence I charged for taking it in.

In further explanation I have to add that my Office is now open from 8 in the morning 'till 9 in the Evening and from 7 'till 9 in the summer.

His Lordship frequently sends for his letters before the hours of delivery sometimes an hour or more and when he does 6d is charged and not a penny per letter for sometimes there is more than twenty, but a penny each letter is charged after nine in the evening - I have always complyed with his Lordship's request when he has wanted his letters before time and I have now kept his Lordships Bag and account 23 years without emolument for so doing

I am, Sir
7Oaks   Your Most Obdt Servt
Dec 17th 1828   Elizth Burrell

Having received this explanation, Freeling thought it wise to have his local surveyor investigate the matter and sent the papers on to Scott

General Post Office
18 Dec 1828

Sir

I enclose a letter from Lord Camden together with the reply of the Deputy at Sevenoaks to my enquiry from which I am led to infer that the sealed Packet in question was first conveyed by the Post Boy from

Maidstone to Tunbridge, who made a charge of 4d, afterwards by the Rider from Tunbridge to Sevenoaks, whose demand was 2d and lastly that the Postmistress charged 2d for taking it in and putting the Official Mark upon it.

The whole of this appears to me so extraordinary and open to observation that I must request you will investigate it and explain the circumstances.

I shall also be glad of your observations upon the other points of his Lordship's letter -

                            I am &c

A Scott Esq   signed/F Freeling

Anthony Scott's report came back ten days later - a quick response considering the large area for which he was responsible in detail, and the intervention of Christmas.

                    Lewes 28 December 1828

Sir

With the papers relating to Lord Camden's complaint I enclose to you a Letter from the Postmaster at Maidstone in reply to me. I wrote to him desiring to know if the Packet addressed to His Lordship had been put into his Office or brought to it to be conveyed by the Tunbridge Rider. The Postmaster states it was delivered to the Driver as a Parcel at the Goal with several others of a similar nature as has been customary for many years. The Driver charged 4d for his trouble and gave it to a person for conveyance to Seven Oaks who charged 2d more and the Postmr at 7Oaks 2d for its care and custody as she has been in the habit of doing upon all parcels left at her House the whole constituting the charge of 8d. The Postmaster at Maidstone properly observed had the parcel been brought to his Office he should have forwarded it in the Bag to Tunbridge with other letters untaxed its weight being under one ounce.

In reply to Lord Camdens questions respecting the delivery of Letters before the time prescribed by the Postmaster General viz. 7 in summer and 8 in the winter it has been customary to make some remuneration to our deputies if required to afford particular accomodation to Individuals, and they have also the sanction of the Postmaster General to receive a Penny each upon all Letters brought to their Offices after the closing of their Boxes preparatory to the making up of their Mails, it should seem by the Postmr at 7Oaks Letter that this last charge has not been made by her but that she has Kept a Bag and Account for his Lordship for 23 years without receiving any remuneration whatever for having done so.

                    I am
                    Sir
Sir Francis   Your most Obedient Servant
Freeling Bart   Anthony Scott

The whole matter was referred to the very top, to the Postmaster General, who was the Duke of Manchester at that time, for a decision.

                    General Post Office
                    31st Dec 1828

The Postmaster General
My Lord

Having received from Lord Camden the enclosed letter desiring to be informed whether the charge of 8d which was made for the "Calendar of Prisoners" in Maidstone Goal addressed to his Lordship in a sealed cover at the Wilderness near Sevenoaks was correct, I at first corresponded with the Postmistress of the latter Town and elicited that these Packets were delivered to the Driver of the Tunbridge Mail Cart at Maidstone to be carried as Parcels, and by him consigned to the MailCoach to Sevenoaks, where they were received as Parcels by the Postmistress each party making a charge which altogether amounts to 8d. This practice appeared to me so extraordinary and irregular that I addressed a pointer Letter (No

2) to the Surveyor, whose Report (No 3) merely confirmed the information I had previously received. In the interim Lord Camden sent to me the enclosed Packet addressed to Lord Brecknock which had been delivered at Wilderness without charge. I transmitted it in a further Letter (No 4) to Mr Scott who states in No 5 that it was put into the Post Office at Tunbridge by the Rider from Maidstone and from there sent in the Letter Bag to Sevenoaaks.

I am rather surprised that it appears to have escaped the surveyors that the practice in regard to these Packets has been decidedly irregular. They have no appearance of being Parcels, but are in the form of Sealed Letters, and I question whether our own Servants who have been in the habit of conveying them and receiving a consideration for their trouble, have not rendered themselves amenable to the Laws - I presume there can be no doubt that they ought to have been refused in the first instance by the Mail Driver, and the Parties at the Goal referred to the Post Office, and I submit that the Surveyor be instructed to apprize the Parties of the situation in which they have placed themselves, and to order that the practice may be immediately discontinued.

All which is humbly submitted by
F Freeling

Nothing further appears to be recorded on the matter. It does show, however, that there has for long been difficulty in distinguishing between letters, packets and parcels.

Lord Plymouth's Complaint

The nature of Lord Plymouth's complaint against Sevenoaks is not to be discovered. The minute has a number, no 56 of 25 January 1830, but the pages allotted to it remain blank, intriguingly so and most out of character. But it must have been a serious complaint for the result is minuted *'withdraws his suretyship'* and what type of suretyship might it have been? Probably the signing of the required Bond for the Postmistress, which he had done when Lord Whitworth died.

Volume of Traffic[40]

The closing years of the Wheatsheaf era saw the collection of a great number of different statistics which, unlike the present day statistics of the Post Office, were related to specific towns in the public reports.

The Appendix of the 7th Report of the Post Office in 1836 gave

Number of Letters and amount of postage on them, which have arrived in London by the Morning Mails and been despatched at night for six successive days ending 23 July 1836

1836		Sevenoaks		Tonbridge		Tunbridge Wells	
18 July	Monday	42	£1. 3.11	38	£1. 6. 0	74	£2. 7.6
19 July	Tuesday	39	1. 7. 0	16	0.10. 2	59	1.14.1
20 July	Wednesday	27	0.17. 5	28	0.16.10	51	1.12.4
21 July	Thursday	34	1.10. 7	34	0.17.10	64	2. 2.4
22 July	Friday	33	1. 2. 8	27	0.17.10	35	0.18.7
23 July	Saturday	29	0.17. 2	24	0.17. 2	52	1.14.9
		204	£6.18. 9	167	£5. 5.10	335	£10. 9.7

'*A return of the number of Letters which have arrived* [*at London*] *by the Morning Mails and have been despatched at night*' *ending Dec 3 1836* [*Transit Mail*]

	Sevenoaks		Tunbridge		Tunbridge Wells	
	Town	*Rural*	*Town*	*Rural*	*Town*	*Rural*
Monday	23	26	22	18	53	8
Tuesday	13	21	6	15	25	4
Wednesday	8	21	7	17	27	14
Thursday	12	21	4	18	29	11
Friday	7	24	7	20	32	3
Saturday	6	36	8	14	33	5
	69	149	54	102	199	45
	Total 218		Total 156		Total 244	

Rye had an overall total of 81 to London but Hastings had 430.

What these data show is how small still is the total number of letters sent. It shows also that the letter writers, the well-to-do in Sevenoaks and Tonbridge lived at their country seats outside the town, although one might expect this number to be offset by the town businesses, such as solicitors. It also means that one might expect the still existing 'penny post' letters to be twice as numerous as the 'general post' letters, which however is not the case.

The 1st and 2nd Select Committees on Postage both reported in 1838. Here are some of the financial data for Sevenoaks together with that of other local towns for comparison.

Bromley, Sevenoaks, Tunbridge and Tunbridge Wells are all listed as **Post towns**. Edenbridge, Bletchingly, Biddenden, Northiam, Rolvenden, Farnboro' are shown as **Sub Post Towns**. Westerham and Wrotham are shown under **Penny Posts** only.

	Sevenoaks	*Bromley*	*Tunbridge*	*Tunbridge Wells*
Total Annual Expense	£131.3.0	80.-.-	103.15.-	114.19.-
Gross Income	61.-.-	89.19.-	88.4.6	81.17.1
Net Income	39.-.-	44.19.-	57.8.-	31.12.7
Salary	50.-.-	58.-.-	80.-.-	56.-.-
	(*2nd duty*)	20.-.-		
Private delivery		6.-.-		
Fee on late letters	2.12.0	-.5.-	2.12.-	15.12.-
Pence upon letters put into the office for del'y in the Town;				
Profits arising from Delivery of letters	3.-.-	4.3.-	-.17.-	8.-.-
beyond the Fixed Boundary				
Gratuities for Private Bags;				
Xmas boxes	4.-.-	-.-.-	4.10.-	1.1.-
Profit on Money Orders	1.4.-	1.5.-	-.5.6	1.4.7
Office Rents	10.-.-	10.-.-	15.-.-	25.-.-
Salaries to Clerks paid by Postmasters	-.-.-	25.-.-	6.-.-	20.-.-
Other Outlays	12.-.-	10.-.-	8.17.6	5.5.-
<u>*Number of Clerks*</u>				
Paid by Crown	1	-	-	-
Paid by Postmaster	-	1	1	1
Paid by fixed Salary	1	1	1	1

*The **Sevenoaks Penny Post** figures for an earlier year to 5 July 1836 are also given:*

Revenue			
	Wrotham	£116.8.-	
	Sundridge	35.18.-	
	Riverhead	39.3.1	
	Brasted	43.2.10	} 274.19.9
	Chipstead	23.17.8	
	Westerham	132.18.2	
		391.7.9	
	Expense	150.14.-	
	Net Income	£240.13.9	

Also in the same reports a considerable amount of data on volumes of traffic is given. Figures below relate to the week commencing 15th January 1838 with those for the week commencing 29th January 1838 in brackets.

Letters sent from Sevenoaks

	Total	Sent to London	Sent Elsewhere
Letters	1304 (1377)	959 (909)	345 (468)
Newspapers	174 (159)	117 (110)	57 (49)
	1478 (1536)	1076 (1019)	402 (517)

If a percentage calculation is made from the figures given, a comparison with some other towns gives:

	To London*	Singles**	Franks**
Bromley	71%	94¼%	22½%
Sevenoaks	66%	95%	17%
Tonbridge	60%	95½%	8½%
Tunbridge Wells	68%	95%	13½%

* w/c 29 January 1838
** w/c 5 March 1838

Items sent to London
W/c 15.1.1838, with w/c 29.1.38 in brackets.

	Number of letters inc Priv Letters and packets	Number of Privilege Letters and packets	Number of Newspapers
Bromley	243 (206)	27 (28)	29 (22)
Sevenoaks	959 (909)	209 (236)	117 (110)
Tonbridge	624 (642)	114 (127)	79 (109)
Tunbridge Wells	819 (799)	77 (73)	137 (126)

Number of Letters posted, by type of letter
Dates as above.

	General Post		Penny Post		Priveleged	Total	
	Letters	Letters			Letters &	All	News
	Paid	Unpaid	Paid	Unpaid	Packets	Letters	Papers
Bromley	50 (56)	209 (201)	1 (6)	44 (22)	35 (40)	339 (325)	70 (41)
Sevenoaks	125 (151)	809 (791)	12 (7)	108 (148)	250 (280)	1304 (1377)	174 (159)
Tonbridge	157 (125)	617 (728)	30 (13)	89 (74)	120 (137)	1013 (1077)	121 (151)
T' Wells	174 (209)	873 (867)	- (24)	49 (90)	94 (95)	1109 (1285)	203 (201)

Letters by number of sheets *Week 5-11 March 1838*

General and Bye Letters (excluding Franks)						Penny Post Letters				
					Above					Above
	Single	Double	Treble	Oz	Oz	Franks	Single	Double	Treble	Oz	Oz
Bromley	230	9	2	-	1	82	36	2	1	1	-
Sevenoaks	945	35	5	-	1	224	138	11	4	-	-
Tonbridge	979	31	7	1	-	108	134	9	1	-	-
T'Wells	1071	56	6	-	-	188	72	6	1	-	-

Number of Letters by Postage charged *Weeks 14 and 21 May 1838*

Charge	Bromley	Sevenoaks	Tonbridge	Tunbridge Wells
1d	22 (8)	153 (125)	147 (127)	84 (77)
2d	8 (1)	60 (65)	106 (111)	67 (49)
3d	-	5 (9)	39 (33)	21 (27)
4d	*108 (88)	52 (56)	41 (61)	29 (14)
5d	17 (31)	10 (6)	33 (30)	48 (64)
6d	30 (27)	*525 (661)	53 (53)	53 (28)
7d	16 (26)	89 (81)	*443 (441)	*676 (668)
8d	10 (19)	124 (120)	49 (59)	63 (55)
9d	- (2)	51 (33)	89 (72)	121 (151)
10d	2 (4)	30 (43)	35 (35)	47 (46)
11d	- (1)	23 (24)	23 (20)	33 (29)
1/-	-	27 (21)	16 (13)	18 (23)
1/1	-	5 (2)	4 (10)	4 (7)
1/2	-	- (6)	21 (21)	9 (7)
1/3	-	1 (1)	2 (2)	3 (5)
1/4	-	-	-	4 (8)
1/5	-	1 (1)	2 (-)	- (5)
1/6	-	1 (-)	3 (4)	- (3)
1/7	-	-	-	1 (1)
1/8	-	-	-	1 (1)

[*Rate to London]

*1838 **Volume of Letters**   from 2nd Report. Week 29.1.1838*
Sevenoaks is the seventh largest town in Kent for volume of Mail.

Maidstone	4095
Canterbury	3268
Chatham	2580
Dover	2552
Gravesend	1720
Ramsgate	1477
*Sevenoaks	1377
Rochester	1351
T Wells	1285
Lamberhurst	1141
Tonbridge	1077
Sheerness	921

Taxing according to nominal distance

Towards the end of 1838 a very important but little noticed change occurred in the method of taxing letters. An explanation is given in The Times of 19th September 1838. Instead of taxing a letter according to the mileage of the route it actually took, the distance between the two post towns along the nearest public road was to be charged.

Some 1,200 rates had to be recalculated for each post town, a mammoth task expected to take some time. An example for Kent is the charge from London to Lydd, 8d for the actual route of 92 miles through Dover and along the coast changed to 5d for a nominal 65 miles through Maidstone and Ashford.

The public had long demanded this change as they considered this original method of charging unjust

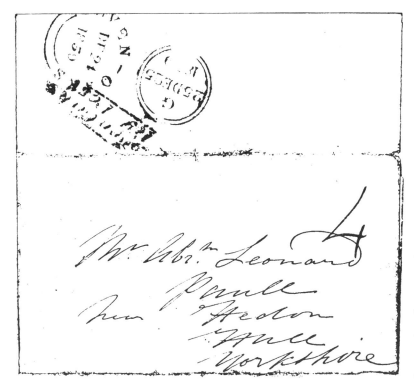

1839 General Fourpenny Post. Ightham to Hull maximum charge 4d including Penny Post charge, for one month from 9 December 1839 to 9 January 1940. Ightham Receiving House had no number allocated to it, but later received an 'Ightham Penny Post' stamp.

and were infuriated at having to pay for what they regarded sometimes as a very circuitous and time-consuming route, particularly for cross mail through London, and the Post Office itself had long been in favour of the change. It was Treasury approval for the change that was so long delayed. The Treasury felt that there would be considerable loss of revenue.[41]

None of the operational charge sheets showing the full list of charges between a particular post town and all the others have come down to us (except possibly one relating to a different area). It would be of great interest if one for the south-east were to be discovered.

Distorted pattern of charges   Nationally, during the 1836-1839 era it was calculated that paying letters made up only 10% **by weight** of the total 'payload' carried. Franks which travelled free by act of Parliament made up a further 10% by weight and Newspapers that also travelled free by virtue of the tax stamp already on them, made up the remaining weight 75%, together with PO sundry supplies 5%.

Ship Letters landed at Rye and Hastings

In the days of sailing ships it was the practice to touch land as soon as possible before proceding on to the final port of call for unloading. Many letters were landed at Rye and Hastings as indeed they were in many other ports around England. These ships letters were stamped (postmarked) at the port of entry and then travelled along the route to London. Such letters landed from ships came in sudden bursts as the ships arrived, this was particulary so over the sailing period 1765 - 1850. So sometimes at very short notice this meant the filling up of all travelling space in the mailcoach to London with letter bags and no space for passengers and at times the quantity of letters even necessitated the hiring of an extra diligence.

Measuring Mileages

In 1952 the Ministry of Transport announced that henceforth the Official London Mileages would no longer be measured from the seven traditional points: Whitechapel Chuch, Shoreditch Church, Hick's Hill (St John St EC1), Tyburn Turnepike (Marble Arch), Hyde Park Corner and the two Bridges but that all would be measured from Charing Cross. The Post Office always measured from the GPO which means that about ¾ mile needs to be added to the southern points, the south ends of Westminster and London Bridges. Consequently GPO milages do not always correspond with mileage posts.

Passing oncoming traffic

Until coaches took to the road the need for rules hardly arose although there could be problems when large numbers of animals being driven approached each other to pass.

As can be noticed British coaches from say 1785 were driven by coachmen/drivers sitting on the coach using reins as contrasted with, say, the French continued predeliction for postillion driven coaches. The coachmen normally held his whip in his right hand and so sat on the right side of the coach to use it unobstructedly. He thus liked to pass other oncoming traffic by keeping to the left so that he could clearly see how close he was to the other vehicle. Continental postillions for reasons best known to themselves rode the lefthand horse and so preferred to pass on the right so they could see their situation better.

Up to the early nineteenth century, traffic had to give right of way to allow oncomers to pass, but how was not laid down and it is said that this could be either side, left or right, as convenient at the point of passing. The Highways Act of 1835 section 78 favoured keeping to the left when 'passing' and imposed a fine of £5 (£135) or up to six months in a House of Correction if this fine was not paid. Twice the fine if the offender was the owner. This in addition to any civil action. The offender may be apprehended without warrant by any person who sees the offence and brought before the JP. If the offender would not discover his name to the JP he could be committed to the House of Correction by description only. Section 78 is a long one and lists many interesting misdemeanours; it also appears to prohibit postillion driving. There is no mention of overtaking as such, unless it can be said 'passing' includes 'overtaking'

ENTRANCE TO HASTINGS, FROM THE LONDON ROAD.

Published by Geo. Wooll Printseller Highst Hastings Nov.r 1823.

Road down into Hastings, 1823.

ENGLISH INLAND LETTER RATES
UP TO 100 MILES

Single Sheet under 1oz.   1839 ½oz

1635 – 1653
A. Under 80 miles 2^d
   80 miles up to 140 4^d

1653 – 1711
B. Under 80 miles 2^d
   Above 80miles 3^d

c.6. 1711 – 1765
c. Up to 80 miles 3^d
   Above 80 miles 4^d

D. 10.10.1765 – 1784
One Stage 1^d
Two Stages 2^d
Over 2 stages up to 80m. 3^d
Above 80 miles 4^d

E. 31.8.1784 – 1796
One Stage 2^d
Two Stages 3^d
Over 2 stages up to 80 m. 4^d
Above 80 miles to 150m 5^d

F. 5.1.1797 – 1801
Not above 15 miles 3^d
above 15 up to 30 miles 4^d
above 30 up to 60 miles 5^d
above 60 up to 100 miles 6^d

G. 5.4.1801 – 1805
Not above 15 miles 3^d
above 15 up to 30 4^d
   " 30 " 50 5^d
   " 50 " 80 6^d
   " 80 " 120 7^d

H. 12.3.1805 – 1812
Not above 15 miles 4^d
above 15 up to 30 5^d
   " 30 " 50 6^d
   " 50 " 80 7^d
   " 80 " 120 8^d

I. 9.7.1812 – 1839
Not above 15 miles 4^d
above 15 to 20 miles 5^d
   " 20 " 30 " 6^d
   " 30 " 50 " 7^d
   " 50 " 80 " 8^d
   " 80 " 120 " 9^d

MILES	A 1635–1653	B 1653–1711	C 1711–1765	D 1765–1784	E 1784–1796	F 1797–1801	G 1801–1805	H 1805–1812	I 1812–1837	J 1837–1839	K 1839	L 1840
Not Above 15m	2^d	2^d	3^d	ONE STAGE 1^d	2^d	3^d	3^d	4^d	4^d	2/4^d	4^d	1^d
Above 15, under 20	2^d	2^d	3^d	TWO STAGES 2^d	3^d	4^d	4^d	5^d	5^d	5^d	4^d	1^d
" 20 30	2^d	2^d	3^d	3^d	4^d	4^d	4^d	5^d	6^d	6^d	4^d	1^d
" 30 50	2^d	2^d	3^d	3^d	4^d	5^d	5^d	6^d	7^d	7^d	4^d	1^d
" 50 80	2^d	2^d	3^d	3^d	4^d	5^d	6^d	7^d	8^d	8^d	4^d	1^d
" 60 80	2^d	2^d	3^d	3^d	4^d	6^d	6^d	7^d	8^d	8^d	4^d	1^d
" 80 +	4^d	3^d	4^d	4^d	5^d	6^d	7^d	8^d	9^d	9^d	4^d	1^d

J. NOV. 1837
Short Distance 7 miles, later 8 miles 2^d

SEPTEMBER 1838
Rate charged according to direct distance by public road, not route travelled

K. 5.12.1839 No rate above 4^d (but only half ounce)

L. 10.1.1840 1^d per half ounce if prepaid otherwise 2^d for all distances.

CALCULATING THE CHARGE: Letters were taxed according to mileage. Along the Sevenoaks road these were, to LONDON 24m. to Bromley 13m, Battle 33m, Hastings 41m, Rye 39m, Lamberhurst 17½.

CROSS LETTERS: At first charged a rate into London then a second rate out — Lewes to London 2^d London to Sevenoaks 2^d, Total 4^d. Later in 1700s the in and out mileages were added and a single rate charged. After 1804 cross routes developed and over the next two decades the cross route mileage became the basis of the charge. In September 1838 the direct mileage between two post towns became the basis of the charge irrespective of the route taken.

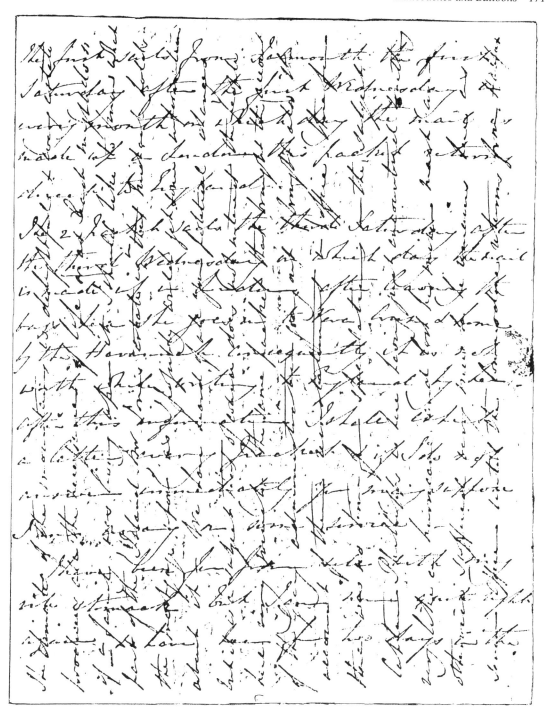

Cross-Writing is sometimes employed in a family letter where there is much news to send and the rate for a single sheet is high, such that a second sheet would give an air of extragavance. But the gaps necessarily left between the lines both ways to make the letter legible means that one could probably write as many lines in a straight forward manner when written closely together. Cross-writing can be considered a conceit of the times demonstrating the writer is prolix in his effusions and has not planned his letter in advance.

WINCHELSEA TO LONDON,

THROUGH RYE, TUNBRIDGE, SEVEN OAKS, AND BROMLEY.

Winchelsea			
Rye	4	4	Inns—*George, Red Lion.*
....			*Mountsfield.*
Pease Marsh....	3¼	7¼	
Beckley	2	9¼	
Northiam	2¼	11½	
A new T. R. to Rye, R.			
Cross the Rother.			
Newenden T. G. .	2	13½	
A T. R. to Tenterden, R.			
Sandhurst Green.	2½	16	
Meagrim's Hill. .	¾	16¾	
Field Green.....	¾	17½	
Four Thoroughs .	¼	17¾	*At Hawkhurst, Elford*, L. *and Fowlers.*
....			
Highgate	1	18¾	
Philpot Cross ...	1	19¾	
A T. R. to Cranbrook, R. *on* L. *to Goudhurst.*			
Seacock Heath . .	1	20¾	
Flimwell...	1	21¾	
A T. R. to Battle and Hastings, R. *on* L. *to Gouldstone.*			
Pillory	¾	22½	
Stone Crouch ...	1	23½	Inn—*Post Boy.* *Bedsbury*, R.
....			*Combwell*, R. *Scotney*, R.
Lamberhurst....	2¾	26¼	Inn—*Chequers.*
Lamberhurst Quarter. .	1½	27¾	*Bayham Abbey. Earl Camden*, L.
A T. R. to Maidstone.			
Kipping's Cross..	2	29¾	
Copingcrouch Green	1½	31¼	
A T. R. to Tunbridge Wells L. *to Maidstone* R.			
Woodsgate	½	31¾	Inn—*Royal Oak.*
Pembury Green. .	1¾	33½	
Cross the Medway, on L. *a T. R. to Tunbridge, on* R. *to Maidstone.*			
Tunbridge	3	36½	Inns—*Angel, Rose and Crown.*
Hildon Green ...	1½	38	
Watt's Cross....	1½	39½	
At Watt's Cross a T. R. to Tunbridge Wells, L.			
Seven Oaks Common. .	2½	42	
....			*Ash Grove*, L.
Seven Oaks....	1	43	Inns—*Crown, Royal Oak.* *At Seven Oaks, A white house, & Knowle Park, Duke of Dorset*, R. *Kiplington*, R.
At Seven Oaks, a T. R. to Farningham, R.			
Riverhead	1½	44½	Inn—*White Hart.* *Montreal, Lord Amherst.*
At Riverhead a T. R. to Dartford and Maidstone R. *to Westerham* L.			
Dunton Green...	1	45½	
Madam's, or Maram's Court Hill	1¼	46¾	Inn—*Star. From Maram's Court Hill, see Chevening Place, Earl Stanhope; Coombank; Chepsted Place; Ovendon; and Wilderness, Earl Camden.*
Knockholt......	1¼	48	Inn—*Harrow.*
Rushmore Hill . .	1	49	
....			*Halstead Place.*
Pratt's Bottom T. G.	1	50	
Greenstr. Green .	1½	51½	
Farnborough....	1	52	Inn—*George. Wickham Court.*
Lock's Bottom. .	1	53½	Inn—*Lion.*
Mason's Hill....	2¾	56¼	*Hayes.*
....			*Eden Farm, Lord Auckland; Langley Park; and Kelsey Park.*
Bromley	½	56¾	Inns—*Bell, White Hart.*
Holloway	1¼	58	*A Palace of the Bishop of Rochester.*
A T. R. to Croydon.			
South End... ...	1	59	*Beckingham Place.*
Lewisham	1¾	60¾	*Brockley House*, L. *and Lee Place.*
A T. R. to Eltham and Maidstone R. *a little further to Deptford* R. *Cross the river Ravensbourne.*			
Loompit Hill	1¼	62	
A T. R. to Dover, R.			
New Cross, T. G.	1	63¼	
Kent Street	2¾	66	
London	1	67	

RYEGATE TO MAIDSTONE,

THROUGH WESTERHAM.

Ryegate to			
Water Street....	1¾	1¾	
Nutfield........	2¼	4	
Bletchingley	1¼	5½	
At Godstone Green on L. *a T. R. through Croydon to London, on* R. *to East Grinstead.*			
Godstone Green. .	1¾	7¼	Inn—*White Hart.*
Rooksnest..	1¼	7½	
Oxstead Street . .	1½	9	
At Limpsfield on R. *a T. R. through Croydon to London, on* L *to Lewes.*			
Limpsfield	1½	10½	
Moorhouse	2	12½	
At Westerham, on R. *a T. R through Bromley to London, on* L. *to Lewes.*			
Westerham	1	13½	*Squirries.* Inn—*King's Arms.*
....			*Hill Park.*
Brasted	1¾	1	
Sundrish........	¾	16	*Chevening Place, Earl Stanhope. Orendon, Lady Stanhope.*
At Riverhead on L. *a T. R. through Farnborough to London, on* R. *to Seal.*			
Riverhead	2	18	Inn—*White Hart.* *Montreal, Lord Amherst*, R. *Chepstead Place*, L.
Within two miles of Seal a T. R. on L. *to Dartford, on* R. *to Seven Oaks.*			
....			*The Wilderness, Earl Camden.*
Seal	3	21	
Waterden	½	21½	
Seal Charte......	1	22½	
Ightam	1½	24	
Borough Green...	1	25	
At Wrotham Heath on R. *a T. R through Eltham to London.*			
Wrotham Heath..	1½	26½	Inn—*Royal Oak.*
Larkfield	4¼	30¾	*Leybourn Grange*, L. *Malling Abbey, and Bradborn House*, R.
Ditton..........	¾	31½	
Maidstone	4	35½	Inns—*Bell, Bull, Star, Swan.*

Distance Tables *from Cooke's British Travellers Guide c1830's showing the main route London to Rye and Winchelsea along which the General Post letters travelled and the main Cross Route Godstone - Sevenoaks - Maidstone along which local letters from Sevenoaks only travelled to Westerham.*

Chapter VI

1801-1839
Local Surveys 5th Clause and Penny Posts

Post Office Surveyors working at Sevenoaks
    Illegal local Posts, 'The Newsmen'

1801 Survey covering Westerham and Wrotham
    Abortive attempt to put into operation

1803/4 Survey. Start of Sevenoaks-Wrotham-Dartford 5th Clause Post

1809/10 Survey. Start of Sevenoaks-Westerham and Edenbridge Penny Post

1820/1827 Surveys. Extension to Godstone and beyond

1826 Survey. Change of Sevenoaks-Wrotham 5th Clause to Penny Post
    Halstead and Chelsfield

Synopsis of local arrangements

Monarchs: George III   (-1820)
               George IV   (1820-1830)
               William IV   (1830-1837)
               Victoria   (1837-   )

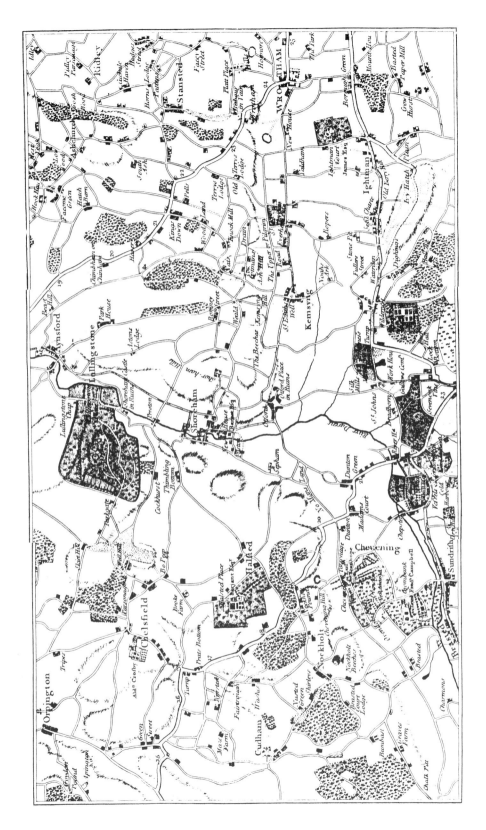

*Cary's '**15 miles around London**' map shows Sevenoaks villages to the North and East.*

Chapter VI

1801-1839
Local Surveys
5th Clause and Penny Posts

Originally the Post Office catered for transmission of letters between towns designated as 'post towns'. Post towns occurred very approximately at about twenty mile intervals along a post road. There was therefore a wide area of country between the various post towns and between the postroads. Beyond the post towns it was up to private citizens to organise their own receipt of incoming mail and despatch of outgoing mail. Small towns and larger villages might have their own official town letter carrier, large country houses used private messengers whose services were probably not available to others living in the locality, and in widespread areas the messenger might simply be someone who supplemented his other work by carrying messages and letters for anything from ½d to 4d a time. Sometimes the local postmaster organised the distribution in his private capacity, as he had authority, indeed encouragement, to do this under the 1668 order. Before the age of the telephone such a messenger service fulfilled a most necessary function.

During the period 1801-1839 many of these local routes were taken over by the post office, and very often they had considerable difficulty before doing so. The Post Office was interjecting officialdom into what was an ongoing situation, a privately organised system that had grown up over time to suit the idiosyncracies of the particular place and people. The post office had to please all parties, an impossible task, by running more frequently at less cost and with added authority. What tended to please the recipients of letters probably went against the existing interests of the messengers and they frequently rebelled.

Penny Posts and 5th Clause Posts

Although London had had a local post since 1682, it was 1793 before even the large cities like Manchester had a local service, authorised under the Penny Post provisions of the enabling act of 1765. The delay appeared due to the Post Office concern that each such local service should support itself financially once taken over. For under these regulations once a Penny Post was established no other person might operate a private collection and delivery service without a licence. In effect the Post Office took over full responsibility at once.

A more competitive style of local service could be initiated under the *Fifth clause* of 41 George III Cap 7 1801 where local service arrangements could be agreed with local inhabitants, but the services then offered were not exclusive and the local inhabitants could still make their own supplementary arrangements. However the great benefit of this act from the point of view of the Post Office was that a local person of wealth could underwrite any losses that might occur in the operation and many were persuaded to do so. It was always hoped that once a route was made official, that fact in itself would greatly increase the amount of correspondance along it and that the need to make good any loss would only apply to the first few years at most. And so, many local routes started as fifth clause posts later converting to Penny Posts once more firmly established.

In the Sevenoaks area private arrangements were gradually taken over and the period 1801-1839 is dominated by the large number of local surveys in which H M Surveyors reported on whether or not, in their view, the time was yet ripe to take over officially the local arrangements and in so doing what alterations, retimings and additional payments were necessary. These re-arrangements covered not only the messenger's route which could at times be up to twenty six miles every day on foot regardless of weather and walking to a set time, but also the arrangements for his points of contact. Whereas the existing messenger might be in the habit of leaving letters at an inn for collection by other messengers, this inn might be replaced by an official Receiving House with someone in charge at a yearly wage, responsible, in addition to other occupation they might have such as a shop, for the safekeeping of the mail and later (August 1811) for the positioning of an open box for the depositing of mail when, under the Penny Post regulations it became no longer necessary to prepay the outgoing local charge as it was allowed to be added to and collected with the General Post charge payable by the recipient. Such was not the case under the 5th clause post where the outgoing local charge from Receiving House to Post Town had always to be paid in advance by the sender on handing in the letter, thus necessitating face to face contact.

Under the 5th Clause Post, Newspapers and Free Franks (letters to and from members of parliament and others which were carried without charge) which came to be a large proportion of the physical bulk of the mail to be carried, travelled free (although at first the Post Office did charge until the charge was found to be legally unsound) which was not the case under the Penny Post legislation where from the beginning the legislation required both Papers and Free Franks to be paid for on their local journey. In later years the Postal Surveyors continually wished to convert well established 5th Clause Posts to Penny Posts, a move often strongly resisted by local inhabitants, particularly the larger landowners who were also MPs and who might become subject to considerable increased charges thereby.

What is considered here then is the distribution of mail from a post town to the surrounding villages. At the start of our period this distribution was carried out legally by private messengers as indeed it could still be under the 5th Clause Posts, but not so under the Penny Posts which were exclusive.

Illegal Local Mail: 'Newsmen' Services between Post Towns

But it was not legal for these messengers to carry letters between *post towns* even if their route was more direct and quicker than the official one, and the report of the surveyor for 10 December 1797 complains

An abuse exists in this neighbourhood which it is highly necessary not only to prevent, but punish. There is in the Town a letter box for letters from Sevenoaks to Canterbury, Maidstone and Ashford which are conveyed by the newsmen, this practice has been carried on for some years.

No mention is made of the charge made by the Newsmen. No doubt it would be less than the official charge based on a mileage into and out of London, and the journey performed more expeditiously. On the other hand, as will be seen in a later surveyor's report the practice of sending letters from Town Malling and Wrotham by their local stagecoach into London there to be put into the General or the Twopenny post appeared to be condoned.

Sevenoaks Local Messenger Services

In the Sevenoaks area the local messenger services fell into two distinct groups:
Those to the West: Westerham, with subsequently a through connection via Godstone Penny Post to the London-East Grinstead-Eastbourne route, and Edenbridge;
Those to the North and East: A connection to the Dover road at Dartford and a local service to Wrotham (with no connection through to Maidstone). These two routes were often interconnected.

PO Surveyors and the Local Surveys

Surveys were carried out by Mr Aust (to 1812) and then by Mr Scott. These were the two men concerned with the setting up of Penny Posts in the Sevenoaks area. **Leonard Aust** was appointed on 11th October 1795 and in 1809 had a salary of £150pa. On his transfer from the South East in 1813 to the Bristol area he was earning £350 + £30 for the Penny Post there, and responsible for Somerset, Devon and Cornwall. **Anthony Scott** was appointed 6 January 1809 and he by 1813 was on £240pa rising to £300 in 1816 &

1820. He held office twenty four years till 1833 but had a serious illness in August 1832.

These were quite large salaries for the times, but Post Office work was onerous and there was much working away from home. Additional out-of-pocket expenses were paid but the awkward hours and the frequent wet weather were not conducive to good health. The long hours took their toll of all Post Office employees and the frequent requirement of seven day working not infrequently led to death '*on the job*'. The job at all levels needed stamina and the will to keep going whilst working against the clock. As long as you could do that you were alright.

Each surveyor had a considerable geographical area to cover, in this case the whole South East corner of England, from the Isle of Wight, Sussex, Kent and extending north of London into Essex was covered by one man. He was expected to know his area intimately, to hold conversations with persons of standing who might underwrite costs and with local inhabitants to ascertain their wants and needs together with views of the local postmasters, to weld into a single decision of what might best be done, to advocate this plan and, once approved by Their Lordships the Postmaster General, to find persons to carry it out and engage them, again subject to approval, to be present both at the start of the new scheme and to return later to see how the matters of change turned out. The surveyors spent much of their working life away from home spending a few days at a time in each area, with always the need constantly to appreciate the passage of time. For the Post Office is a most time-sensitive institution always on the alert to save half an hour here, ten minutes there in order to make a connection more expeditiously, much of the journeying being in the middle of the night, although *local* post workings were daytime operations albeit necessitating very early rising. The local letter carrier, not officially called a postman until the introduction of parcel post in 1883 in spite of frequently burdening himself with parcels unofficially, must often have had his boots wet with dew.

Now to the actual Sevenoaks surveys. In Post Office Archives each survey is filed in date order with supporting documents under reference Post 40, giving original letters and representations relevant to that survey together with the surveyors' handwritten report. The bulk of the report is also hand copied into the bound ledger of the Postmaster General's Minute Book (Post 42) occupying a half page, each page being divided into two vertically. In the other half page are given comments, often by (Sir) Francis Freeling the Secretary to the Post Office and the final decision by their Lordships the Postmaster General. Until 1823 it was the custom to appoint two Lords to the single appointment of Postmaster General. Normally both endorsed any decision and even minor points such as the approval of changes in a route or the increase in a Receiver's pay had to be referred to them both for authorisation and in the case of money, for Treasury approval also, costs being borne by 'Incidents Account' until Treasury Approval came through. Normally their Lordships fell in with the advice of the Secretary who in most cases endorsed the recommendation of the man on the ground, in this case Mr Aust and Mr Scott. The local surveyors appear as very shrewd persons, working within the given constraints of that time period and their recommendations appear always as sound and firm, but with the ability to relax when equity and necessity demand it, for example, not enforcing a fixed payment for mileage but recommending it be increased when the cost of oats for horsefeed increased alarmingly in the early 1800s when wars were being fought with the French and before the repeal of the Corn Laws in 1846.

In most cases the Post Office paid a reasonable sum for the work of messenger, of rider, for mailcoach hire, for Receiver, postmaster and others but not a penny more, perhaps they could best be described as a 'frugal' employer.

1801 Survey. Mr Aust (Post 42 1801 Minute 90E)

The first Sevenoaks survey under the Act of 5th April 1801 took place almost immediately, that is in the same year just three months after the passing of the Act and being one of the early surveys it is important and is treated in full as regards Sevenoaks area.

At this time all local services were private. No change came of this survey but it is important as being

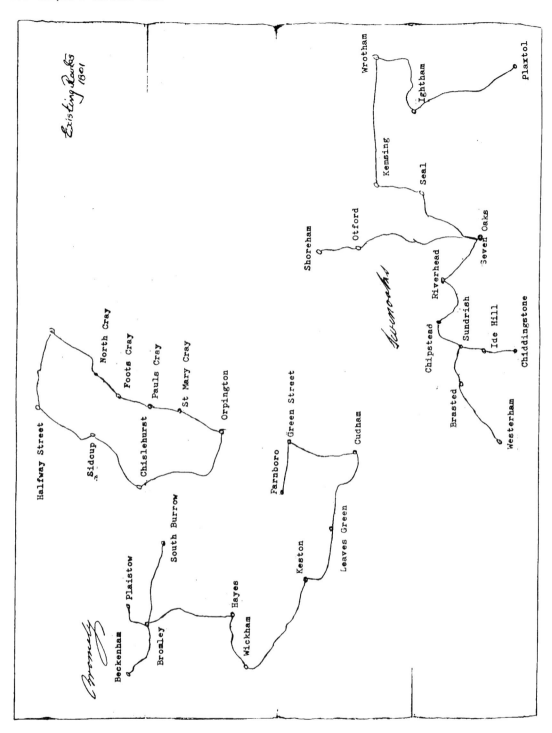

1801 Existing Routes. *These were covered by private arrangements either of the Sevenoaks Postmaster or the village inhabitants. The map, hand-drawn by the Surveyor in his report (Post 40), is greatly reduced and the village names have been typed in to make them legible.*

the first one that could have initiated change in the area and for the information it gives on the then current scene. Statistics were collected.

Letters delivered outside Town 23/24 June 1801

	June 23			June 24		
	Letters	*Newspapers*		*Letters*	*Newspapers*	
Riverhead	Not shown	Not shown		8	1	
Chipstead/Chevening	12	3		5	2	
Sundridge	8	3		6	2	
Brasted	6	3		4	3	
Westerham	<u>20</u>	<u>9</u>		<u>21</u>	<u>12</u>	
	<u>46</u>	<u>18</u>	64	<u>44</u>	<u>20</u>	64
Seal	3			4	2	
Ightham				5	2	
Wrotham				<u>25</u>	<u>6</u>	
				<u>34</u>	<u>10</u>	44
Shoreham				7	5	
Otford				5	-	
Chiddingstone				9	2	
Plastow [Plaxtol]				19	7	
East Camden				<u>4</u>	<u>-</u>	
				<u>44</u>	<u>14</u>	<u>58</u>

As well as Sevenoaks this survey covers the Bromley and Chislehurst local deliveries coming down as far as Cudham for which, including Farnborough, there were 3 letters and 2 papers. The report is a lengthy one and it is treated only in so far as it relates to Sevenoaks. As this is the start of the survey period Lord Charles Spencer's reply is also given in full.

Extracts from Mr Aust's report of June 1801
To Francis Freeling Esq
Dear Sir,
   I returned to London yesterday having surveyed the deliveries of the Bromley, Chislehurst and Sevenoaks offices . . .
   Enclosed you have an accurate account of the numbers of letters and papers delivered from the office at Sevenoaks on the 23rd & 24th inst. I have to observe that the delivery to the villages of Riverhead, Chipstead, Sundridge, Brasted and Westerham is completed by ten o'clock; the messenger waits till four and then returns. The fee is one penny per letter and, taking the returns as in the instance of Chislehurst at one half, may amount to about £1.17.- per week. The messenger is paid fifteen shillings per week and I have reason to think would continue the duties for the same allowance. I beg to add this delivery includes the letters for Marams Court Hill, Nockholt & Halsted, the letters for which places are generally left at Brasted the letters also for Ide Hill, [at] Sundrish, but I am of opinion the messenger might employ himself in delivering the letters for this latter village as well as Chiddingstone the letters for which place are now fetched by the messenger appointed by the inhabitants. I have also to inform you that the letters for Greatness, Seal, Kemsing, Ightham, Wrotham, Plaxtol, Otford & Shoreham are all fetched by messengers appointed by the inhabitants, on <u>three</u> days in the week. I have exhibited in one of the enclosed papers the number of letters and Newspapers delivered for these places on the 24th instant.
   It is certainly a most desirable thing to establish an everyday's Post to these villages, I have therefor proceeded to Wrotham & had a conversation with the principal inhabitants upon the Subject and I am

happy to state, they will readily concur in any arrangments that may be made for their better accomodation.

I am of the opinion that the fees at this time on three days in the week may be averaged at about £18.2.- but as in the event of an everydays communication being established, My Lord Camden, by whose seat the messenger would pass at an early hour, as well as Mr Evelyn & others would most likely avail themselves of the convenience when it is understood [th]at Wrotham now very generally send their letters by the Maidstone Coach for want of a better conveyance and that we can if necessary avail ourselves of that part or clause of the act which authorises the Postmaster General to receive an indemnification from the inhabitants and so demand a fee of 2d (the present fee) upon letters delivered at Wrotham and that in all probability the inhabitants at Plaxtol may be desirous of availing themselves of this arrangment, I am induced to recommend that an agreement may be made with the messenger, now employed by the inhabitants on three days in the week, to travel every day to take the same Route as at present, to include Plaxtol and Basted if the inhabitants are desirous of being so accomodated the messenger might be paid 15s and 16sh per week and a receiving house might be established at Wrotham.

I am also of opinion that the village of Farningham which gets its letters at present from Dartford can be as well served from Sevenoaks. It is nearly midway between the two offices, across the contry, and as the inhabitants of Otford & Shoreham fetch their letters from Sevenoaks & as I am aware that the letters for Lullingstone, the seat of Sir Jn Dyke the villages of Eynsford & Farningham are considerable both in number and amount, I am greatly inclined to think that it may be advisable to send a messenger from Sevenoaks to Farningham by the route pointed out on the map. [note that Shoreham has been put in twice]. A receiving house might be established at Farningham and letters for the numerous farmhouses in the neighborhood could be left there, added to which the inhabitants would have a daily post and could not object to pay the sum of 2d upon a delivery as I am informed they now pay 3d & 4d.

I beg to assure you sir that I have used every means in my power to obtain the best information upon the different heads of this report and that should be Lords be pleased to direct that the propositions contained in it, be carried into effect, I have the best reason to believe they will eventually prove a very great accomodation to the public, and a benefit to the Revenue.

I am dear sir
Your faithful and most -
L Aust
Surveyor

Francis Freeling then writes a six page letter to the Postmaster General, commenting on and supporting the proposals and enclosing the report. An extract:

30th June 1801

. . . the salary of this [Sevenoaks post town] office has been purposely kept so low in consequence of the emoluments arising from the delivery in question, and this observation will apply to other offices, where we meditate similar arrangments. It may be essentially necessary that the deputies in such cases should have for "their Continuance in Office" a compensation bearing due proportion to the loss they may sustain and the increased duties they will have to perform; and these compensations must for a time be heavy on the Revenue especially in the instances of such places as Southall, Isleworth, Chisleworth, Sevenoaks etc etc etc.

The description of the present mode of delivery and the proposed arrangments for Sevenoaks is interesting - Material conveniencies may be given to some part of that district, although a considerable part cannot derive other than the advantage of an official and recognized Messenger.

The report is accompanied by two sketches one exhibiting the present and the other the route proposed and I have reason to believe that, informed as the surveyor is, the mode he has pointed out will be the most generally useful and accomodating.

There is a matter upon which your Lordships will decide, and that is, whether the sum of 2d in addition

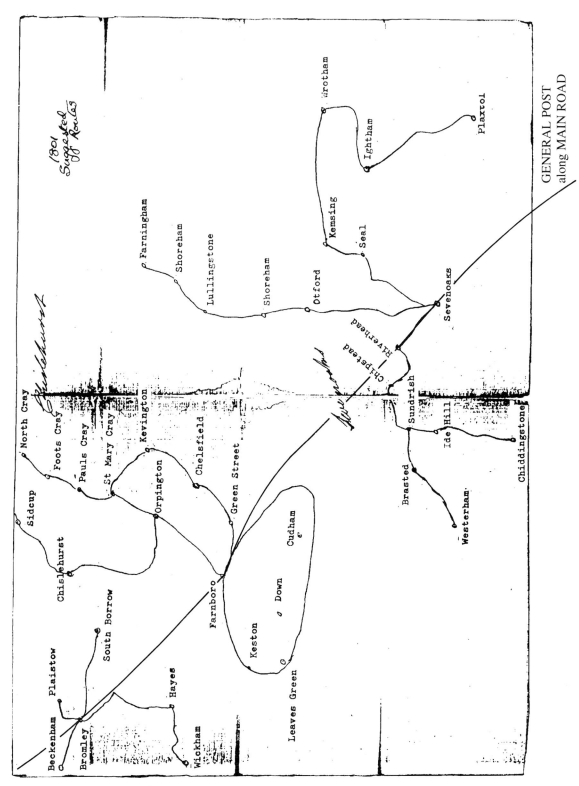

1803/4 Routes suggested by the Surveyor *in his report (Post 40) to be adopted as Official Routes. Again the map is greatly reduced and so the village names are typed in to render them legible. (Main Road Added)*

to the postage should be charged on the delivery of letters at Wrotham and a few other places where that sum is now paid and even 3d; and where the inhabitants have their letters only three times a week.

It should seem that the payment of 1d might not amount to a sum to justify the expence of accomodating Wrotham with a daily Post, and if the Inhabitants do not object to pay their usual fee, it may be demanded. It must be a great accomodation to receive their letters six days with time to answer them, instead of three days only, and with all the regularity of an established Post.

All which is humbly submitted (for your Lordship's approval)
by
F Freeling

To which proposal Lord Charles Spencer replies:

From Lord Chas. Spencer
July 16 (1801)
I have perused this report and its inclosures repeatedly & attentively; & I think with Mr Freeling that Mr Aust's statements are given with ability & clearness; and also with a due anxiety to promote both the accomodation of the Public and the interests of our Revenue. I am willing to believe that both those objects may be essentially advanced by the new powers entrusted to us: but it must be a work of time. We must proceed with great caution: the several neighbourhoods must be led to understand & to seek the quick safe and convenient circulation which we are authorized to give to their correspondance. There can be no doubt that a ready & regular delivery of Letters will produce an increased Return.

A great step will be made towards the system in question if we can put this new accomodation into activity in two or three places in such manner as may make its advantages plain and perceptible. Other districts will become eager for the same benefit and will facilitate our endeavours by suggestions . . . for each particular neighbourhood.

With respect to the offices to which this report more particularly refers I am satisfied that the consideration of Bromley must stand adjourned - I concieve however that Chislehurst and Sevenoaks will gladly adopt the arrangments proposed by Mr Aust & further improvements will occur in the course of the experiment - Mr Freeling will consider how the proposed deliveries may now be instituted & to what extent. Individuals now in our service must of course be compensated for any resulting loss - similar enquiries might be made as to other principal and populous districts; and when the Revenue shall be sufficiently related Ld Charles Spencer will probably wish to call a Board upon it.
Al
C.S.

It must be remembered that the Post Office is now about to enter a completely new field, that of local deliveries, under powers given to it under the recent act. This request is one of the first, if not the very first, for a local service and Lord Charles Spencer is at pains to ensure that any start made into this new venture is a successful one. In the event, for Sevenoaks, it was not to be so.

Abortive attempt to put the 1801 Sevenoaks recommendations into operation

Mr Aust proceeded to put the plan into effect but on the 26th of July 1801 he reported difficulties and by mid-August the proposed arrangments had been abandoned. Mr Ward the principal gentleman at Westerham at that time would not agree to the plan unless the charges were reduced to ½d per letter: On the Wrotham route rather than pay at a rate of so much per letter and newspaper, Col Evelyn of St Clere wanted to continue to pay a standard yearly charge (£2.10.-) which arrangement did not appear to be allowable under the regulations.

Efforts that disturb the 'status quo' are never greatly appreciated by those already 'in post', such that in the event the co-operation of existing messengers was not forthcoming. When Mr Aust started to implement the plan both messengers adopted defensive tactics, but of a different nature. The existing

Westerham messenger dropped his private charge to ½d per letter. The Wrotham messenger agreed at first, but later changed his mind and demanded all the pence due on the letters for himself and obtained some support for his actions. Other opposition mounted. Post Office officials were not impressed by these reactions.

The Act under which the Post Office was enabled to start 5th Clause Posts required the agreement of all the existing parties and it was not in the nature of the Post Office to force itself in against opposition. And so the scheme to give Sevenoaks rural areas a local 5th clause post fell through on this occasion. A full account for the discontinuance of the proposals is given in Mr Aust's report of 1 & 2 August 1801 (Post 40/42). An alternative proposal to make both Westerham and Wrotham post towns, which because of the extra distance would have made certain of a further penny to the post office on all letters carried, was also dropped.

On the 11th August 1801 Lord Charles Spencer comments '*I do not feel any resentment for the perversity of any of the individuals concerned in opposing the Sevenoaks arrangment, nor if I did do I desire any other Direction Measure than the negative result of remaining without the convenience which was offerred to them*'.

Lord Charles Spencer's previous minutes leading up to this final comment had been:

[*Post 35 vol 21 260 1801 Minute 427*]
30th July 1801 Sevenoaks District Mr Aust's Letter
Mr Freeling I can only refer to my report of yesterday. When Mr Aust shall have finally completed his enquiry respecting this business (the details of which are become somewhat embarrasing) two questions will arise
1st whether to try the experiment by appointing a proper person for twelve months to make the deliveries as proposed
2nd whether to seperate Wrotham & its vicinity from the too extensive delivery of Sevenoaks.
   Signed p Auckland
   Charles Spencer

[*and Minute 429*]
Mr Freeling As the inhabitants of Wrotham as well as those of Westerham and their districts do not seem to favour these establishments, I fear nothing remains for the present but for Mr Aust to return to Town and to proceed to Haslemere where he is much wanted to instruct the New Deputy.
It is not however a good example that the messenger should carry his point in his own way.
   Signed p Auckland
   Charles Spencer

1803/4 Survey

But matters were not left idle for long. A further report by Mr Aust of 8th September 1803 was finally successful in part and saw the introduction in 1804 of a 5th Clause post to Wrotham and Kemsing at 1d per letter, paid by the sender. The route finally chosen was a little different to that proposed in 1801 (see map).

[Extract from Post 35 Vol 22/255] Proposed new communication. Mr Aust's report of 8th September 1803.

Mr Freeling! I have long been anxious again to ascertain whether some creditable arrangments of the Posts about Sevenoaks &cc &cc was not practicable. I begin to flatter myself we shall now succeed. The Postmaster General will recollect how much we were thwarted on a former occasion by the Persons whom we intended to benefit.
We must wait for Mr Aust's further report.
   Signed p. Auckland

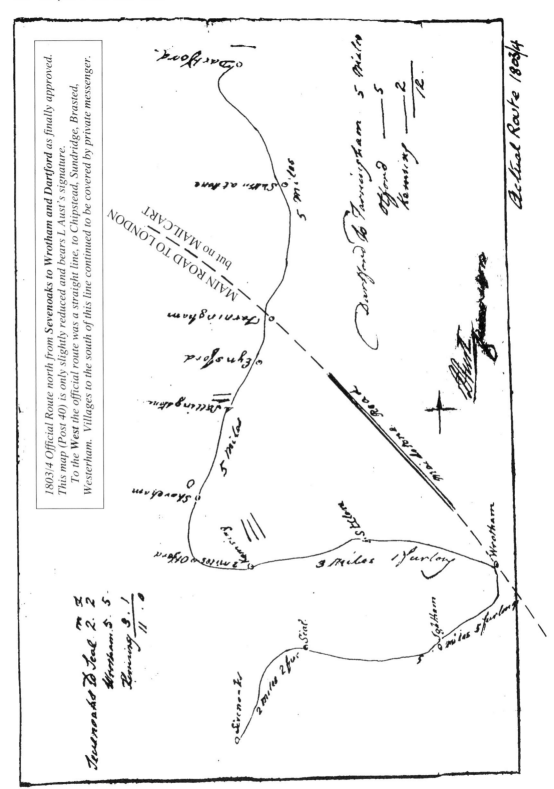

1803/4 Official Route north from **Sevenoaks to Wrotham and Dartford** as finally approved. This map (Post 40) is only slightly reduced and bears L Aust's signature. To the **West** the official route was a straight line, to Chipstead, Sundridge, Brasted, Westerham. Villages to the south of this line continued to be covered by private messenger.

The 8th September 1803 report in effect stated that the climate of opinion had changed, possibly because of the successful operation of similar posts around Tonbridge and Maidstone. The operative report was dated 8th July 1804 (Post 42/95/2S).

Sir William Geary had put forward a proposal for a local post from Dartford to Sevenoaks via Farningham and Wrotham, to be performed on horseback. The Post Office Surveyor, Mr Aust, having conferred with the Rev Moore of Wrotham and others at Shoreham proposed that the journey be covered by two messengers on foot under the 5th Clause Provisions.

Some of the inhabitants of the Dartford end of the route had been paying a subscription of 1 guinea per annum for delivery but others were charged 3, 4, 5, & 6d upon delivery of every letter in addition to the General Post fee. Those at the Sevenoaks end fared a little better; Shoreham & Otford were served from Sevenoaks on three days a week by a messenger who charged 3d per letter. Seal, Ightham, Wrotham and Kemsing also had a messenger whose charge was an additional 2d per letter. Their time of delivery also made it very difficult to write and post an answer on the same day as the receipt of a letter, '*driving the correspondance of the District into other [See p.104] and illegal channels by which the Revenue is a considerable loser. This official post would however open both the Hastings and Dover roads to the inhabitants of the district*'.

1804 Proposals

The proposal that was put into effect was: One man from Sevenoaks at 6am Summer 7am Winter and one from Dartford, '*to meet at Kemsing and exchange bags, severally made up at Dartford and Sevenoaks as well as any letters they may have collected for the Circulation of these offices*'. The charge was to be 1d for each letter and paper. The 1d charge covered the villages in both sections, for example a letter from Sevenoaks through the whole of the first section to the Dartford section at Farningham was charged a single penny. Mail between post towns as between Sevenoaks and Dartford although not strictly travelling in the General Post were taxed the full mileage, being charged as if in the General Post. For this the Postmasters Salaries and Expenses books frequently use the somewhat quaint technique of negative description calling the route for the sealed bag carried between post towns as '*not 5th Clause, not Penny Post*'. This charge in 1810 was 4d. Had a letter been put in at the first village receiving house, it would have been only 1d. The charges were put into effect but the charge for papers was contested almost immediately and found by the courts to be illegal under the 5th clause legislation.

The charge of 1d per letter compares favourably with the East Grinstead-Tunbridge Wells 5th Clause route of September 1805 underwritten by Lord Whitworth and Mr Beale where the charge for the whole route between Post Towns was 5d per letter, '*because it was over 15 mile*s' and 4d for part of the route. Sevenoaks to Dartford was 23 miles as walked via Wrotham, 14 miles direct.

Costs of the Sevenoaks-Dartford Route (estimated)

Two Messengers @ 19/- per week   £98.16.-

Receivers:	Wrotham per annum	£5	
	Farningham	5	
	Sutton at Hone	2	
	Otford	3	
	Shoreham	3	
	Kemsing	2	
		20	£20.-.-
			£118.16.-

Estimated income on a most modest calculation was £120 per annum.

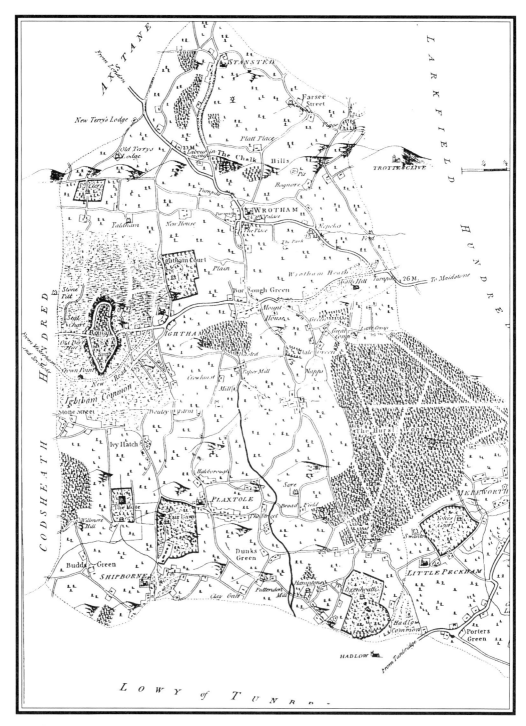

Wrotham hundred. Hasted c1780

Inauguration of 5th Clause Route Sevenoaks to Dartford
And so the Route was started.

Post 14 minute 259 July 18 1804   L Aust to Freeling
   Sir, As it is my intention to commence the new regulation on Thursday (July 19) I have to require you will direct the letters for Otford and Shoreham to be sent to Dartford instead of Sevenoaks on and from tomorrow evening - L Aust.

Charges for Newspapers Mr Lockley complained immediately of the 5th Clause local charge for the delivery of newspapers (as each paper already bore a Government tax stamp and travelled free in the General Post) which was then reduced to ½d by the Surveyor and shortly after was cancelled. Lord Charles Spencer's note of 27th August 1804 states *'From the reasons assigned, Newspapers need not be charged'.*

Report on operations
On the 5th March 1805 a report [Post 40/96/53V] was made on the working of this post.
   ... I reported upon the produce of the Extra Charge between Dartford and Farningham for one month in consequence of a stipulation entered into with Mr Lockley when my Lords the Postmaster General were induced to consent that the Extra charge upon the Newspapers should be taken off.
   And as in that Report I have promised to watch the progress of the Regulation, I have caused the exact amount of the produce to be made up for six months from August 6th to February 5th which is as follows:

Amount of the extra charge under the 5th clause of 41 Geo.3 upon Letters
sent to and from Dartford, Farningham & Kemsing from August 6th to Feb 6th

£29.12. 6

Amount of Bye Letters between Dartford and Sevenoaks for the same period,
as per voucher

1.10. 7

Amount of the Extra charge under the 5th clause upon Letters between
Sevenoaks, Wrotham & Kemsing for the same period

14.13. 6

Amount of Bye Letters between Sevenoaks and Dartford for the same period,
as per voucher

2. 3. 6

£48. 0. 1

The Expence of this arrangment attached to the Dartford office is £62.8.- pr annum
and the produce at the rate of £62.6.2   [almost balances]
While the Establishment [charge] from Sevenoaks is   £56. 8. -
and the Produce   33.14. -

[Deficiency] £22.14. -

   From this statement it will be seen, that although the Revenue is very nearly recompensed by what has been produced, between Dartford, Farningham & Kemsing, that there is a deficiency in what has been derived between Sevenoaks, Wrotham & Kemsing at the rate of £22.14.- pr annum which it is not at all difficult to account for, as notwithstanding the messenger who has been employed has performed the duty in an exemplary way, yet there persons who still support the former messenger notwithstanding the delivery from the new Regulation is much earlier, and the extra charge considerably less.
   It is worthy of remark that the amount produced in this walk in the month of August was £1.18.11

September to Oct 10th	*2.14. 0*
October	*1. 7. 0*
November	*2.19. 0*
December to Jan 5th	*3. 3. 9*
January to February 5	*2.10.10*
Total	*£14.13. 6*

  The very material increase in November I can justly attribute to my being at that period at Sevenoaks, and rendering the necessary assistance to the Regulation, whereas Mr Hanson who was Postmaster

1811. Letter from Kingsdown via Farningham to Leybourne about 6 miles direct. Put in 5th clause post to Dartford, local 1d paid no markings, then General Post Dartford via Rochester to Maidstone 5d, for 24 miles. On delivery to Leybourne the charge is increased to 8d, an additional 3d, making 9d in all for 36 miles travelled.

previous to that time, I have a strong impression had little or no inclination to assist it, the amount in December and January it will be seen is also much improved arising I have no doubt from the present Deputy (Mr Burrell took over on Hanson's resignation) paying strict attention to my orders.

The sum produced by the Voucher between the offices is certainly much less than the gentleman who projected the Regulation expected, it does appear that the sum produced has been materially dificient. I should not consider myself justified if I omitted to lay before you the foregoing statement, altho' My Lords have directed that the Arrangment shall be continued for twelve months by way of experiment.

The circumstances of the former Messenger opposing the regulation and being supported by Colonels Evelyn and James are fully stated in my reports in July (actually the August report) and it will be in your recollection that it was through this Mans means, that the arrangment to Wrotham attempted some years since was given up:- from a letter however which I received last week from the messenger employed by the office, I have strong reason to believe that this man might be induced once more to come into the service, if a small addition were given to the present allowance by which means the opposition would be done away and the Regulation become productive, and if this suggestion should meet with the approbation of my Lords the Postmaster General I will see him or write to him on the subject and in that case the messenger at present employed can perform the duty between Dartford and Kemsing, where his services I find are much wanted.

I avail myself of this opportunity to notice an application from Mr Ward of Westerham, referred to me by you as long ago as the month of September but as I was then aware that Mr Hanson would resign in October, I put the papers by untill I went into that neighbourhood and before I quitted Sevenoaks in the month of November I had an interview with Mr Warde on the subject.

You will no doubt recollect Sir, that it was this gentleman as well as Lord Campbell, and other of his neighbours who rejected a similar arrangement which I was directed to offer them some years since.

The number of letters to Riverhead, Chipstead, Brasted and Westerham is very considerable, as I have ascertained, and Mr Warde's application is produced from his receiving his Letters late, and which arises

1811. Letter from London to Sevenoaks 5d and along the then 5th clause route to Wrotham making 6d. But wrongly addressed as the route stops short and there is no connection from Wrotham on to Leybourne (nor yet is). So letter sent back to Sevenoaks and on via Maidstone. Extra penny for official Maidstone-Leybourne delivery charge, making 7d. The Maidstone-Leybourne charge depended on which day of the week the letter travelled; three days a week it was an official post at 1d, the other days the local post was privately organised and made a higher charge.

from his Residence being at the greatest distance from the Post town, but as my Lord Campbell, the Bishop of London, Dr Heath, Mr Polhill and most respectable residents are served in good time and are perfectly satisfied with the messenger, I have a thorough conviction that a most decided opposition would be the consequence of any attempt the office might make to take the delivery into their hands, Mr Warde admits that he can only engage that the inhabitants of Westerham will support an Official interference.

As Mr Warde was leaving his Residence for some time on the day I saw him and as most of the other Gentlemen were then in London on account of the season of the year, it was not possible for me at that time to take the sense of the Inhabitants, the circumstances of an opposition on the Wrotham Walk has also operated very much on my mind, to the prejudice of attempting any Arrangement to Westerham under similar circumstances. As however the Principal Residents will now be very shortly returning to the Neighbourhood I will take an opportunity of seeing them on the business, and will report further.

I am dear sir
Your faithful and most obedient servant
L Aust. Surveyor

Under this arrangement, Shoreham and Otford Receiving Houses both came under Dartford. Otford was subsequently placed on the Halstead walk in 1839, yet both offices received their first circular handstamps through Dartford office in 1841. Shortly after that, on 5th March 1847, both offices returned to Sevenoaks.

1809-1810 Survey

The first two surveys have been quoted in some detail to discover the manner in which the Post Office approached the problems involved. The volume of available papers increases for the period now being considered and a greater selection of material has perforce to be made.

"Sevenoaks-Westerham with the possibility of extending to Godstone and/or Edenbridge."

Mr Aust was busy in other parts of his area and could not attend to this matter. So an assistant Augustus Godby was to be trained at Tonbridge office before carrying out the Sevenoaks survey under Aust. But Godby, after training, had to continue to help Tonbridge office where he was also needed. Eventually a new surveyor Mr Scott arrived to work with Aust for a short time until Austs' transfer, when Scott was to take over the south east area. And so Scott it was that carried out this survey.

Sevenoaks - Westerham Survey

A survey of the Sevenoaks-Westerham route was made by Anthony Scott reporting 31 March 1809.

Francis Freeling Esq & & &   *Sevenoaks*
                                  March 31st 1809
Dear Sir,
*   I have made particular enquiry respecting the letters sent and received between this Town and the Villages of Riverhead, Sundridge, Brasted, Westerham and Eaton Bridge and I find that during the last four days the amount has been as follows sent on the*

Tues 28th	*89*
Wed 29	*81*
Thur 30	*72*
Fri 31	*73*

and the returned Letters on the

28th were	*26*
29	*30*
39	*32*

so that it appears that an average [of] the Number sent has been 78 per diem and the Number returned

26 the produce of which at 1d each would be 8s/8d a day or £3.0.8 a week; and this the Postmaster of Sevenoaks considers as somewhat below the general amount.

He pays the Letter Carrier 20/- per week, so that it should seem the Nett Profit remaining to himself is upwards of £2 within the same period.

The Letter Carrier leaves Seven Oaks at ½ past 6 in the Summer and an Hour later in the Winter and proceeds according to the sketch herewith enclosed which embraces a distance of 8 miles out allowing for detours and 8 miles back - Westerham is his boundary to which Village the Gentlemen of Eaton Bridge send a Messenger of their own for their Letters. He leaves Westerham at 3 and Riverhead at 8 and returns to 7 Oaks before nine pm.

Looking to the amount of this correspondance I feel myself fully justified in proposing the establishment of a Penny Post at Sevenoaks which should comprehend exactly the same line of Country that the man now travels over.

In adopting this plan it will be necessary to establish a Receiving House at Westerham to which place the Gentlemen of Eaton Bridge, and beyond may still send their Letters, and I see no reason why another hour should not be given at Westerham; Four o'Clock being quite early enough for our Messenger to depart on his way back to Sevenoaks.

All which I beg to submit and am
Dear Sir
Your very faithful and Obedient Servant
Anthony Scott

P.S. I beg to add that the Postmaster of Seven Oaks charges a Penny on Franks and Newspapers and that they are included in this account. No objection therefore on the ground of a new Impost can possibly be made by the Inhabitants.

and Mr Aust enclosed Scott's findings when he (Aust) reported on the 16th April 1809 on the possibility of taking over the Sevenoaks-Westerham route as a Penny Post (as authorised under the 1765 Postal Act) and by 30th March 1810 he was able to produce costs.

Village Problems and the Eaton Bridge Messenger

The problems of a messenger at Eaton Bridge highlights the difficulties that villages had. Where letters had to be taken to and collected from a Receiving House say six miles distant, what more natural than to employ a local village man who is trusted and on whom an eye can be kept as to how well he does the job as he lives locally? The locally based man goes to the Receiving House in the morning and comes back in the afternoon with the letters. They cannot then be answered the same day. Little advancement in the service can be made until the village can bring itself to accept a 'foreigner' as their lettercarrier based at the distant Receiving House. He can then leave the Receiving House at, say, eight am and arrives by at least 11am. The inhabitants then have until about 4pm to answer letters before the letter carrier then returns to his base, thus saving a whole day in reply. This ability to reply the same day is of great importance in an age with no telephones. So much emphasis is placed on the trustworthiness and timing and timekeeping and method of working of the local letter carriers that no 'foreign' man was likely to be accepted unless he was working under the regulation of Post Office employment.

Long distance walks were normally considered to be man's work and the novel '*Larkrise to Candleford*' by Flora Thompson in which a detailed description is given of the life of a young girl who did the deliveries for her aunt who was postmistress, belongs to a later age, the early 1900s, also it describes the local deliveries, not the main walk between Receiving Houses.

In Eaton Bridge there had always been the possibility of taking letters either to Westerham which was still some distance from the post town Sevenoaks, or to have one's servant walk two or three miles further each way and put the letters directly into the General Post at Godstone. The Eatonbridge messenger appears in early days to have gone to the General Post at Godstone (8½ miles each way) and the writer

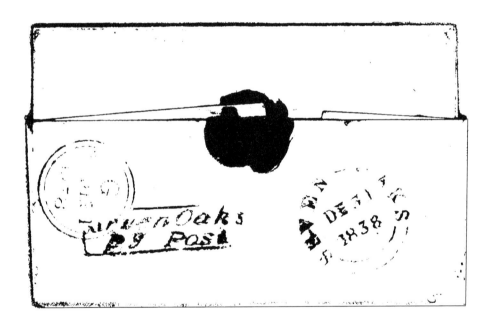

1829-1839. The early unboxed 'Seven Oakes Penny Post' handstamp and the later 1837/9 boxed 'Seven Oaks Py Post' as normally applied on the reverse. Earliest handstamp 1811.

has seen letters of the 1775-1790 period headed 'Eaton Bridge' and posted at Godstone which was a post town on the London to East Grinstead Route which then carried on to Eastbourne and Brighthelmstone (Brighton). By 1800 or at least by 1804 the Eaton bridge messenger had diverted to Westerham (5 miles each way).

For Eaton Bridge the Postmaster at Sevenoaks Mr Burrell by 1808 was in the habit of sending a sealed bag to Mr Parsons, a shopkeeper, who agreed to handle it, containing the letters of Thos Hayton, minister of Eaton Bridge, and his friends. Mr Parsons also returned their letters to Sevenoaks in a sealed bag. This was a private arrangment between the minister and the postmaster of Sevenoaks. Not every letter for Eaton Bridge appeared to be placed within the bag and some were sent loose to Westerham via the messenger employed by Mr Burrell the postmaster of Sevenoaks and taken on to Eaton Bridge by the man the Westerham messenger was said to have employed himself and in at least one case there was delay when that messenger left the letters at an inn in Eaton Bridge for collection without making arrangements and they were only noticed lying there by chance, though these facts are disputed by Mr Burrell:

Sir,   *7 Oaks March 13 1809*

. . . I am surprised at Mr Hayton's complaint as it was not intentionally the case in that Mr Hayton's letter was sent with the letters to Westerham instead of putting in the bag with which I have accomodated Mr Hayton & his Friends with it was carried by the man whom is employed by the operate party which caused the delay. I am sorry for the mistake & will endeavour to prevent complaint in future. With respect the Letter Carrier deputising another person to do his Businefs is a mistake as the letters were never carried further then Westerham by the 7 Oaks letter Carrier, the distance from 7 Oaks to Edenbridge being to far for him to make his delivery in time., he has no power in delivering the letters as my Orders are to deliver the letters for Edenbridge as requested by the Parties.

Your Obedient Servant
J M Burrell

Although the survey had been made in 1809 the decision to implement had to be set aside for some months as Mr Aust was so busy and Mr Scott not yet fully trained. It was 1813 before Scott was able to take over the district fully on his own.

After some difficulties the route was finally inaugurated on the 13th April 1810 with additionally a Receiving House at Eaton Bridge with a Receiver paid 3gns per annum which inadvertently was not officially approved until 1811. The connection from Westerham to Edenbridge was by private messenger and 1d, presumably additional to the Sevenoaks-Westerham penny post charge, was paid to the Westerham receiver when the service was finally established after much difficulty.

Inauguration of the Sevenoaks to Westerham/Edenbridge Penny Post

A letter from Mr Aust on March 30th 1810 again brought up the matter of implementation:

. . . with reference to my report dated April 16 1809 I have to observe that I consider the Penny Post regulation can be carried into effect to & from Westerham upon the following terms:
To pay the messenger for carrying the letters

from Sevenoaks & Westerham	*£46.16.*	*-*
To pay Receiver at Riverhead	*3. 3.*	*-*
Sundridge	*2. 2.*	*-*
Brasted	*2. 2.*	*-*
Westerham	*5. 5.*	*-*
	£59. 8.	*-*

As I have already provided a proper messenger I shall be prepared to commence the arrangments as soon as I receive your directions.

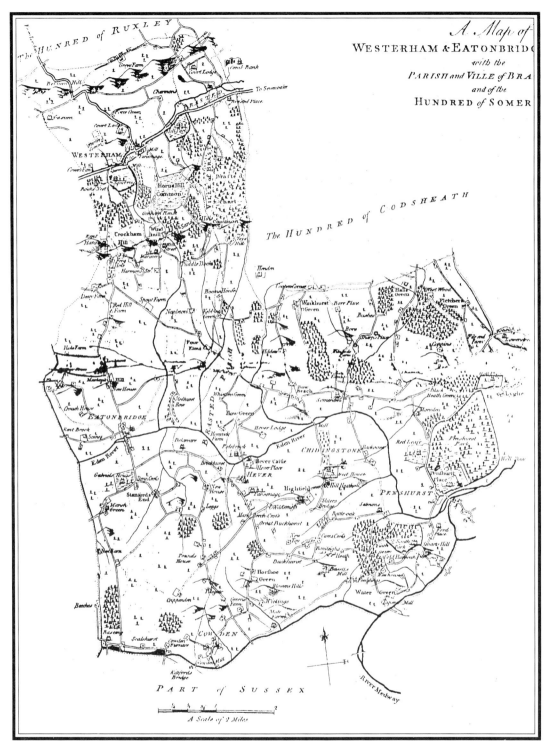

Westerham Hundred. *Hasted c1780.*

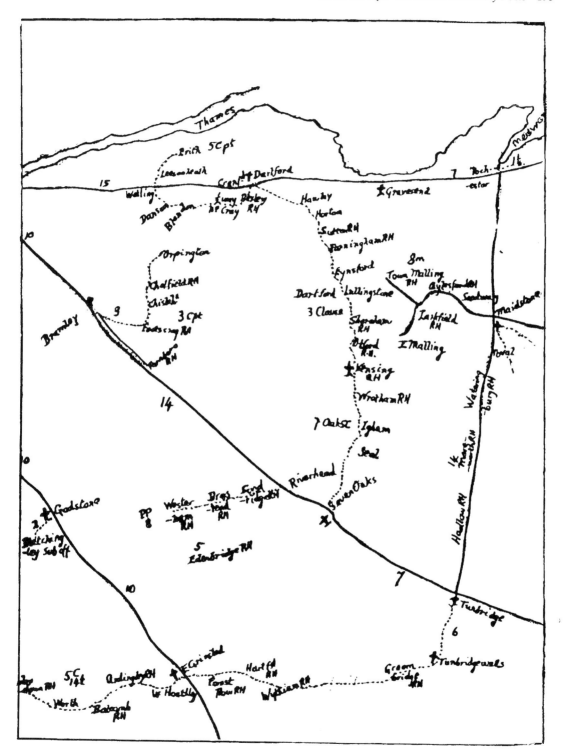

1813. **Local Deliveries around Sevenoaks** *from the Post Office Official Circulation Map (Post 10a). There is an absence of connection to Edenbridge.*

But on the 13th April 1810 a letter from Aust to Freeling states:

Dear Sir, In consequence of the messenger I had originally intended should undertake the duty of conveying the letters to & from Westerham having disappointed me I have been prevented from commencing the Penny Post Regulation until this day.

The Number of Letters and Papers was 91 sent out but as the messenger is not returned I cannot say what number may be brought up . . .

A letter carrier's return of that year shows 91 outwards and 43 inwards. In a further letter of 11 May 1811 concerned with the carrying out of the inauguration, an official charge for the Receiver at Eaton Bridge is recommended, 3gns to be backdated to 13 April 1810 the start of the service:

[Post 30 11 May 1811] I am sorry to see by the enclosed report of Mr Scott that Mr Aust to whose last district he has succeeded seems to have omitted to enable me to procure your Lordships regular consent to a salary of three guineas per annum intended for the Receiver at Edinbridge when the Westerham Penny Post was established in April 1810.

Your Lordships will no doubt authorize the same to be allowed on incidents until the consent of the Treasury can be obtained.

All which etc

F. Freeling

No late request was made for a Westerham-Edenbridge messenger's salary nor had a request previously been authorised.

Thus occurs the odd situation, substantiated by the district map of 1813, where there is an official Receiving House '*on its own*', not connected by an official messenger but by a private one. It was 1839 before an officially paid messenger trod this route. The situation was unusual but not apparently unique, Seahouses R. H. also is so shown on the same map which covers the area I.O.W. to Essex.

Day to Day Operations

So much for the authorisation of the Westerham route; now about its day-to-day operation. There were the expected teething troubles. Within three weeks Thomas Hayton the Minister at Edinbridge was again writing that the mail had not been sent to them on market day because Mr Barton in the Westerham Receiving House had been busy.

Another interesting letter of complaint was received from the Rev Mr Gibbons at Brasted written on Sunday 22nd July 1810

Sir, In the month of April last Boreman the Postman was displaced and another Man whose name I cannot learn, appointed to deliver the letters and receive them for the Office at Seven-Oaks. He said he was not to call at the houses in the Evening for Letters as Boreman had done, but that every person must send their Letters to the house fixed on by Mr Burrell where he was to take them up and where there was to be a Locked Box of which he was to have the Key, into which the letters were to be put with the penny that is paid with every letter sent to their office. - The place where the letters are sent is to Reginald Nortons a Butcher who also keeps a Shop which is attended by his daughter Mrs James and a Grand-daughter - In the Shop is a Nest of drawers as usual for pins thread &c &c &c - into one of these drawers the letters are thrown and are at the mercy and within the ready reach of anyone in the Shop - As the Postman thought proper not to bring my letters to this House in the morning, but to leave them at the Ale-House to be sent up by any Child or person that the Landlord could find I wrote to complain of him to Mr Burrell, and at same time told him he had not provided the Box he promised for the Letters and that an open drawer in a Shop was not a secure deposit for them.

This is full five weeks ago and the letters are still thrown into that open drawer - I have desired my servant repeatedly to ask if the Box is there, the answer has always been "a lock is to be put on the drawer next week" - A Lock of which Mrs James is to have the key is no more security than an open drawer - The reason the Postman gave for not bringing the Letters up in the morning was that it delayed his going on to Westerham - The Parsonage is not two minutes walk from the road, but the man retards himself by being so heavily laden with parcels and Banboxes which he carries for extra profit - For some little time (a Fortnight) he has delivered the letters regularly till this morning, when he left the paper at the Ale-House for the Landlord to send up. I called to desire that they never would take in any of my Letters or papers as I would not have them delivered out of the regular mode. The Landlord told me the Postman said an order had been received last Night from you that he was not to deliver letters in future at the respective houses but leave them at Mrs James's where they are to be sent for by each person - I shall be greatly obliged if you will inform me whether these are your orders, and whether the open drawer is in your opinion a proper secure place for Letters - A Stiff Leather Box, with a slit in the top might be left for the receipt of Letters and taken to Sevenoaks in the Evening for Burrell to open - or a Box fixed on the Counter the key kept by the Postman & the same key to open the Boxes that were promised to be at Sundridge and Westerham as well as this place - There is full time for the Man to go to every House if he did not so encumber himself with parcels - I am sorry to give you so much trouble and hope you will pardon me. I am Sir

> *your obedient humble servant*
> *John Gibbons*

I send this to be put in the 2d post as it may otherwise not reach you.

The twopenny post referred to was presumably somewhere on the Farnborough walk based on Bromley the furthermost south point of the London Posts (? Cudham, Leaves Green). Interesting too is the way in which the Letter Carrier is referred to as a Postman as it is generally understood that that term did not come into official parlance until 1883 when in addition to letters he had to carry parcels as well as part of his official duties, not as a private venture as here demonstrated, thus outdating the term letter carrier. Yet here the description 'postman' is being used colloquially almost seventy five years before the official change.

In time matters settled down. In August 1811 Penny Post Receiving Houses had to provide an open box into which letters could be put without paying the penny at the time. In this case it was added to the General Post charge for the recipient to pay.

Description of the Westerham Walk

In a long report of 31.8.1810 Anthony Scott describes his walk over the ground accompanying the letter carrier from Sevenoaks to Westerham:

Mr Wade of Squerries having complained of the late arrival of the Messenger with his letters I thought it advisable to go over his walk that I might make such alterations as appeared to be necessary . . . He first leaves letters at Lord Amhurst's Lodge, then goes down to Riverhead where he delivers a great many letters, leaves at the Receiving House there those for Green Lane, Bessels Green, Marams Court, Longford, part of Chevening parish and Dunton Green. He then goes on to Mr Polhill's Lodge, afterwards to Chipstead where he leaves the letters as he goes along, those for the village of Chevening, Dry Hill and two or three small houses at the George public House - thence to Sundridge, leaves at the Receiving Ho. there Lord Fredk. Campbell's those for Nockholt, Hide Hill & To Brasted - leaves the Rev. Mr Gibbons (whose house is a quarter of a mile out of the road) at the Receiving House. thence to Hill Park (Mr Barrows) leaves the letters at the lodge and on to Westerham where he delivers the letters leaving those for Eaton Bridge at the Receiving House to be conveyed by a private messenger. His time of arrival at Westerham has been ½ past nine in summer, it is now to be at 9 and at 10 in winter (having left Sevenoaks at 5 in summer and 6 in winter). It will appear he takes much time to go over a walk of 7 miles but it must be recollected he is greatly detained in the early part of it from servants and others not being up, to take in, and pay for the letters . . .

This report was a major one covering also The Dartford route and the possibility of an extension from Westerham on to Godstone and beyond, both of which subjects will be treated later, as also the claims of the Postmaster at Sevenoaks for compensation for loss of his privately organised deliveries to Westerham and Edenbridge already covered in the previous chapter. The report was sent to the Postmaster General under cover of a long letter from Freeling.

Westerham Local Deliveries

Freeling's covering letter of 6 Sept 1810 states:

Mr Scott has fully described the Letter Carriers route as now fixed and his hour of arrival at Westerham is to be 9 of Clk in summer which cannot fail to be greatly convenient to the whole district - Mr Ward of Squerries who had expressed particular anxiety about his Letters cannot have them so soon as 9 o'clock unless he sends for them to the Receiving House for Mr Scott has very properly explained that Mr Ward's House being some Distance from the village, the Inhabitants must be served first.

To treat first of all of the Established Westerham route:

Chipstead   Chipstead was again given some recognition if not restored to its former glory when a receiving house was added in December 1824 on recommendation from Mr Scott '*for a Receiving House at Chipstead, a village served by the Sevenoaks Penny Post & where letters are now left at a Public House*'. This was also to give accomodation to parts of Chevening and to Mr Polhill, the Rev John Austin & others.

Edenbridge   The Penny Post was finally fully established to Edenbridge on 2nd March 1839 with the Receivers salary increased from 3gns to 8gns per annum and an official messenger from Westerham to Edenbridge, Hever and Chiddingstone. No mention is made yet of Receiving Houses at these latter two places; Hever's first Receiver was appointed on 14th June 1843 at £4 p.a. With the 1839 change, presumably the additional 'Westerham' penny now ceased. But this reorganisation was not to last long. By 1841 the railway had passed through Edenbridge and by 1848 Edenbridge was itself to be a Post Town in its own right with a large delivery area.

Connection to Godstone

Mr Scott also had to consider the possibility of a through route on from Westerham to Godstone, bringing in Oxted and Limpsfield. The distance was little more than six miles and it was felt that a similar arrangement to that on the Dartford walk where messengers met and exchanged bags might provide a workable solution. In the end no such recommendation was to be made for

It appears that the removal of Lady Rupert from Limpsfield has materially decreased the number of letters in the district between Westerham & Godstone & Mr Scott cannot recommend yr Lordships to incur the Expence of a Foot messenger at present. [*Probably he means Lady Russel*]

The Extension to Godstone and Beyond

The post from Sevenoaks to Dartford connecting the Hastings and the Dover roads was achieved as early as 1804; the route through Wrotham to Maidstone was never achieved as a Penny Post, the Godstone route out was finally achieved on the 30th January 1827 but not without difficulty.

Once the idea of Local Posts was established in the area in 1804 the gentlefolk of substance at both the Sevenoaks and Godstone ends often discussed the need for such a connection between the two roads, saving the need for letters to go into and out of London. The first examination of the route was, as has been seen, in 1810 when Mr Scott was in process of establishing the Sevenoaks-Westerham Penny Post. In one month he found 910 letters passing between Westerham and Godstone, which would generate an amount of £3.15.10 per month at 1d per item. At that time a private messenger took the letters daily from

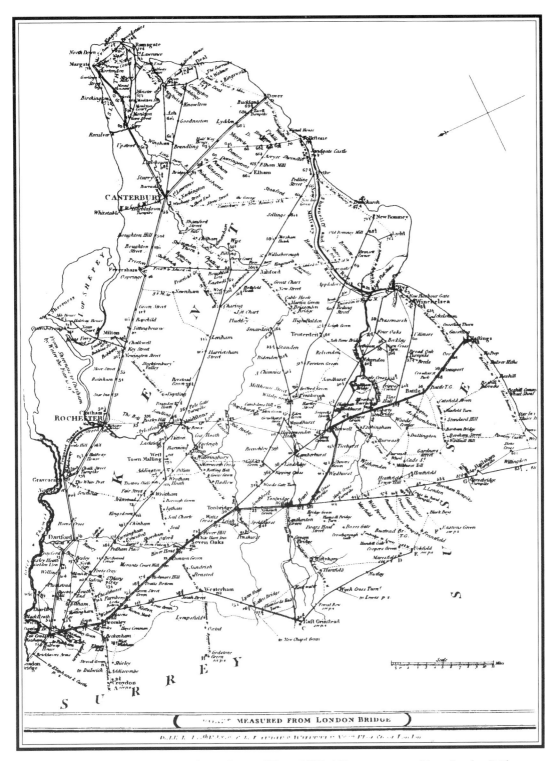

Laurie and Whittle's Distinctive straight-road map of Kent c1807. Mileages measured from London Bridge.

Godstone to Limpsfield '*they are charged 1d to Oxted and 1½d to Limpsfield & upon all Newspapers and 1d upon the return letters; [messenger] employed by the postmaster and paid by him*'. There was the suggestion that the two footposts could meet and exchange bags but it came to naught. '*owing to Lady Russel having quitted Limpsfield; the number (of letters) now passing would not cover the costs of an official messenger*'. Letters passing along the whole route from Sevenoaks to Godstone were few. The next survey was not until 1820.

1820 Survey

In October 1820 Mr Scott again tackled the problem at the instance of a letter to Mr Freeling from W Levison Gower Esq of Titsey who suggested a post from Reigate to Sevenoaks thro' Nutfield, Bletchingley, Godstone, Oxted, Lympsfield and Westerham to connect with the Sevenoaks and Hastings road, with a possibility that such a route might even extend back as far as Guildford. Such a route from Guildford via Westerham and Seal and on to Maidstone (A25) was shown as a cross route in all the guide books of the period, such as Cary's and Patterson's, but the route never attained post office favour. Mr Scott objected that it would not be possible to arrange a timetable that would provide earlier delivery than that which occurred when letters passed through London, and as the distance would be less, the lower charge would mean less revenue. As the full distance Reigate-Sevenoaks involved, 22½ miles, was about the same as the Sevenoaks-Dartford connection one may wonder why in this case the superficially similar data now supports a negative decision. It seems it was so because of the established position. There would be three post towns involved and the inhabitants of Bletchingley area were used to free letter and newspaper local delivery, being a sub-post town attached to Godstone. However the section between Godstone and Titsey presented no such disturbance of existing arrangements and it is recommended to be taken over as a penny post. Over this route there were 202 outgoing and 91 inwards making 293 letters in a week. Quoting from Anthony Scott's report of 9th October 1820:

> *I object to it on the ground that the correspondance would not be accelerated it must pafs thro various hands and the letters would come within reduced rates of postage. The Messengers must leave Seven Oaks and Reigate early in the morning, the letters therefore conveyed by them must be written overnight; they would not arrive at each end until the following night and consequently could not be delivered until the second morning and at present the same would be the case for Letters sent from Reigate and Godstone to Seven Oaks and its delivery and vice versa. Bletchingley and Nutfield must in such a case be put under Reigate, and if a Penny Post were established to join the one from Seven Oaks to Westerham the Letters and Papers for Bletchingley would become chargeable which I presume would be strongly objected to by the Inhabitants after the free receipt of them for so many years: the Nutfield Letters are obtained from the Receiving House at Bletchingley where £10 per annum is paid to a sub-deputy who has a further allowance of £10 a year for conveying the Letters between Bletchingley and Godstone. Independent of this the Daily walk from Reigate to Westerham would be too much for a foot messenger to perform.*
>
> *It appears by the accompanying account which I desired might be kept at Godstone that the Letters and Newspapers sent to Oxted, Lympsfield and Titsey, amounted to 202 in a week and there were 91 returned which at a Penny each wd have produced 24s/5d, they are now conveyed by a Person employed by the Postmaster of Godstone who charges 1d to Oxted 1½ d to Lympsfield and Titsey and a Penny each on the Newspapers and Letters returned; and the Man has from 12 to 14 Miles of ground to go over daily with detours.*
>
> *As it appears that this Post would yield a profit to the Revenue; and the Inhabitants of Lympsfield and Titsey would be relieved from the charge of ½ d upon each Letter outwards if it were taken into our Hands and converted into a Penny Post I beg to recommend that such an establishment may take place accordingly.*
>
> *I am Sir*
> *Your most Obedient Servant*
> *Sgd. Anthony Scott*

Costs Messenger 15/- per week   *£39. pa*
Oxted RH   *3.*
Lympsfield RH   <u>*3.*</u>
     <u>*£45.*</u>

Estimated Profit £20 pa.

The route was put into effect in January 1821 and the report on working for the first year showed good results:

Sir,   *20 May 1822*

   The Penny Post from Godstone to Oxted, Lympsfield and Titsey having produced 73.16.6 between the 6 January 1821 and 5th January 1822 and its expences being £45 per annum leaving a gain of £28.16.6 to the Office, I beg to recommend that it may be made permanent.
Francis Freeling Esq   *Sgd Anthony Scott*

Closing the Westerham-Titsey Gap 1827

But it was 1827 before direct communication was opened from Sevenoaks through Westerham to Godstone with the closing of the Titsey-Westerham gap, six years later. In January 1827 the subject was again opened following a petition signed by 24 inhabitants, all of standing such as Wm Manning of Coombe Bank; Austen & Claridge Solicitors Sevenoaks; J Warde, Squerries Westerham; Mathias Wilkes Tandridge Court - persons the whole length of the route had been asked to sign so as to have full representation. Without the connection it was taking letters two days to travel via London when the actual distance between correspondents was only a few miles. Lady Harriet Neville and the other Ladies signed a '*Round Robin*' in support. The overriding factor in deciding for the Post appeared to be that communications were already going along this road and that under the Penny Post regulations they were illegal and needed to be brought to account. The solution achieved on 30 January 1827 was that the Godstone messenger was to continue from Limpsfield Receiving House to Westerham Receiving House (he already went as far as Titsey) at an additional wage of 4/- per week and there to exchange bags with the Sevenoaks man. The Westerham receiver would get a further 3gns pa for checking the accounts.

   The Residents of 'Rooks Nest' (see Hasted map) about half a mile west of Westerham just beyond 'Squerreys Court' but within Kent appeared to give their mail to the Godstone Penny Postman as he went past on his return with the result that it was put into the General Post at Godstone not Sevenoaks. And to complicate matters there is a 'Rooks Nest House' at the other end of this Penny Post walk, between Oxted and Godstone. Usage of these local routes gradually increased over the years and in March 1839 it was agreed '*that the Sevenoaks-Westerham messenger's salary be increased from 18/- to 27/- a week as in consequence of the number of bags he cannot carry them on horseback but will be under necessity of using a cart*'.

1822. A folded letter-sheet passed through the Penny Post and General Post by a Member of Parliament from Brasted to London. It pays only the penny of the local penny post and is so marked. Unlike the General Post, the Penny Post was not free to Members of Parliament. (Reduced.)

1833. The Penny Post basic unit was 'under 4oz' without relating to the number of sheets used and so envelopes did not necessarily incur an extra charge, unless also entering the General Post. (G.F. Oxley p.17)

Here an envelope from Sevenoaks to Sundridge is inscribed as would be a Member of Parliament's 'Free' letter in the General Post, but a charge is made, because the free facility did not extend to the Penny Post.

An MP could have sent a letter in a wrapper (early envelope) free of charge in the GP, but a member of the public would be charged double, as for two sheets.

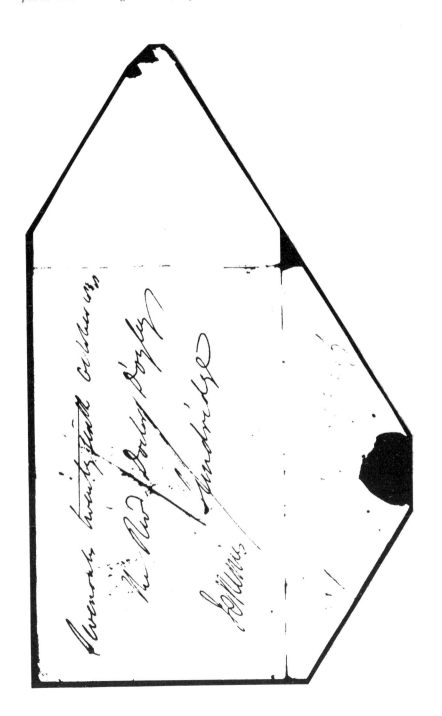

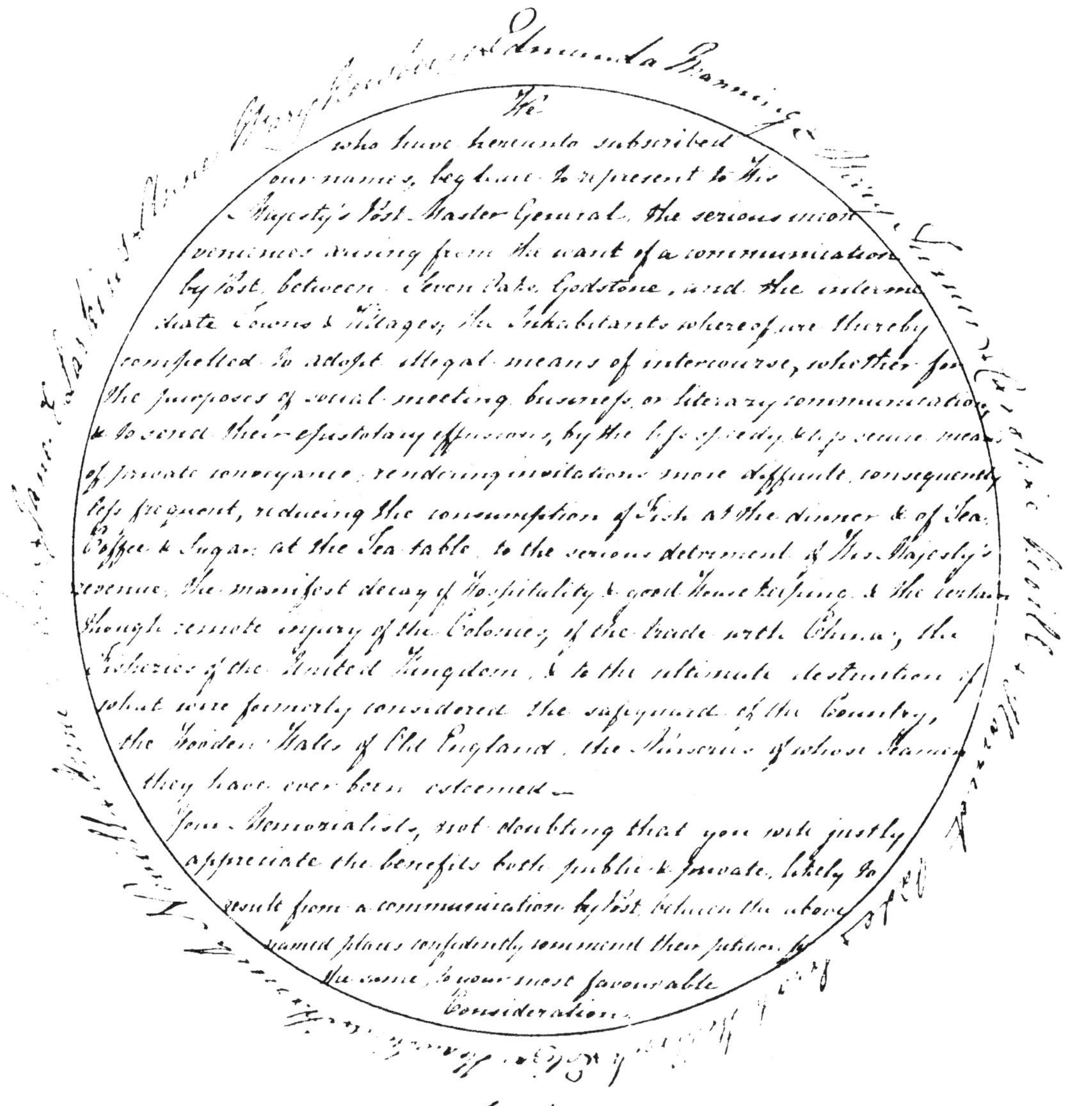

Round Robin

Jan 7 1827

Reduced frm 6" diameter

We who have hereunto subscribed our names, beg leave to represent to His Majesty's Post Master General, the serious inconveniences arising from the want of a communication by Post, between Seven Oaks, Godstone and the intermediate Towns and Villages, the Inhabitants whereof are thereby compelled to adopt illegal means of intercourse, whether for the purposes of social meeting, business, or literary communication & to send their epistolary effusions by the less speedy & less secure means of private conveyance, rendering invitations more difficult, consequently less frequent, reducing the consumption of Fish at the dinner, & of Tea, Coffee & Sugar at the Tea table, to the serious detriment of His Majesty's revenue, the manifest decay of Hospitality & good Housekeeping & the certain though remote injury of the Colonies, of the trade with China, the Fisheries of the United Kingdom & to the ultimate destruction of what was formerly considered the safeguard of the Country, the Wooden Walls of Old England, the

Nurseries of whose Seamen they have ever been esteemed - Your Memorialists, not doubting that you will justly appreciate the benefits both public and private, likely to result from a communication by Post between the above named places confidently commend their petition for the same to your most favourable Consideration
Janry 1827

Edmunda Manning, Mary Turner, Caroline Neville, Harriet Vade, Sarah Welbank, Eliza Hawkins, Harriet Neville, Anne Newbery, Jane E Larkins, Anne Mary Newbery

Transcript of the 'Round Robin' organised by Lady Caroline Neville in support of closing the Titsey-Westerham gap. A circle was drawn around the writing and all the names signed on the outside of this line, thus creating the Round Robin.

Letter between post towns after the Titsey gap closed,1837. GP bags carried between post towns over PP routes. Letter picked up by PP at Rooks Nest and taken to Godstone 1d, put into GP at Godstone and carried over PP route between post towns as GP, Godstone to Tonbridge 6d, makes 7d in all. If picked up when going the other way and put in at Westerham, might have been charged only 1d and 4d, makes 5d. (Reduced.)

c1835 Westerham to Sevenoaks over PP route 1d, then GP Sevenoaks to T Wells 4d makes 5d in all. (Reduced.)

*St Valentines Day
llustrated London News 1871.*

*The Village Postman by J M
Carrick reproduced in Illustrated
London News 9 August 1856.*

Village Postmen. *Somewhat romanticised engravings of village postmen showing the type of clothing worn before
the issue of uniform.*

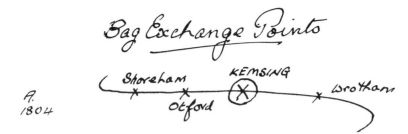

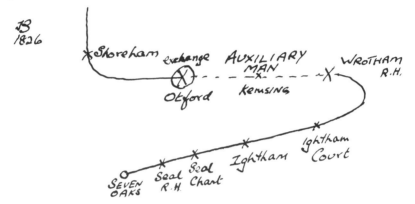

1804 Bag Exchange Point between Sevenoaks and Dartford. Original arrangement at Kemsing. (Redrawn from original map.)

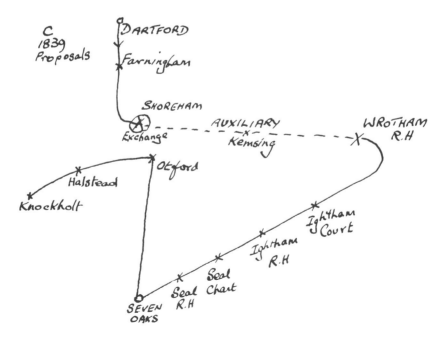

1826 New arrangements with an Auxiliary between Otford and Wrotham. (Redrawn from original map.)

1839 Proposals for new routes. No certainty these proposals were implemented.

Change of Sevenoaks-Wrotham 5th Clause Post to Penny Post 28 December 1826

The new survey started with the complaint of '*the Kentish Postman, named Heron, residing at Dartford*' who had a daily round from Dartford to Kemsing of 30 miles, on foot, six days a week and who was now '*much worn from fatigue*' but who could not give up as he had a family to support. A suggestion was made to shorten the distance and to finish at Otford; but at the same time the Sevenoaks-Kemsing man's walk could not be increased as it also was a long one. The suggestion was made

that the Wrotham bag be forwarded to Dartford & by him (Heron) left at Farningham where there is a coach would take it on to Wrotham, & bring back the bag which would meet him at Farningham on his return from his round - if this could be done the Postman from Sevenoaks being relieved of going to Wrotham, could easily come on from Kemsing to Otford to meet Heron.

But this was not to be the answer.

The 5th clause post had not paid its way. The Dartford section had costs of £61 and income of £63 and so a trifling profit. The Sevenoaks section income of £30 and costs of £56 making a loss of £26 pa due mainly to Mr Evelyn of St Clere, and others of Croodeham, Wrotham, Kemsing and Seal sending privately for their mail. Newspapers and 'frees' were also not charged for. There is no indication that the guarantors had been asked to make up the loss. The impression gained is that they had not, and so they were not in a position to object when the Post Office decided to convert to a Penny Post, thus being able to charge for newspapers and frees and prohibiting the use of private messengers so that letters would be delivered by the letter carrier and charged for.

The conversion involved employing an auxiliary between Wrotham and Otford. A man could not be found for 6/- per week and the wage had to be raised to 9/-, an additional 3/- a week, so 1/- was taken from the Sevenoaks man whose round had been reduced. Being a Penny Post, Newspapers and Frees now were subject to the local 1d charge, but the inhabitants could deposit their letters without need of prepayment of the outgoing 1d local charge which under Penny Post regulations could be collected from the recipient. Thus was paved the way for '*open letterboxes*'. Such a change to 'Penny Post' organisation did not, it seems, relate to the Dartford section as well. There is no mention of such an occurance in the detailed papers still available relating to the change. It is true that occasionally the '*Dartford P.P.*' stamp is seen on letters that have travelled this section, but then more frequently is seen the Dartford Circular stamp which is the correct one if the section remained 5th Clause. Dartford did have other Penny Post routes and so administratively it would have been an easy matter for the wrong handstamp to have been used on occasion.

1838 Criticism and 1839 Changes

Criticism of the Wrotham service was still rife in 1838 at which time only a five day a week service appeared to be operative from Wrotham, although officially still six days a week. Saturday and Monday were the difficult days and the post left for Sevenoaks at 3pm on Sundays. No wonder there were great unofficial dealings with the stagecoach guards who transported 'parcels' along the London-Farningham-Wrotham-Town Malling-Maidstone route.

The March 1839 changes extended the auxiliaries walk to Shoreham, putting his pay up 3/- to 12/- per week; and establishing a receiver at Ightham at £5 pa to include delivery of the letters. Whether the auxiliary still called at Otford as well as Kemsing on his way back from Shoreham to Wrotham is not known; for under the 1839 changes, Otford was placed on the new Halstead walk.

Halstead and Chelsfield

Whereas letters for Knockholt and sometimes those for Halstead too came via Sevenoaks and were left at Sundridge for collection, Halstead inhabitants always felt that this was a long way round and craved more direct communication with London. No doubt this feeling was engendered in all geographical areas

1836. Wrotham (No 8) but via Sevenoaks to London 6d plus 1d, make 7d. Checked by inspector (Crown mark) and charged double 1/- and 1d, makes 1/1.

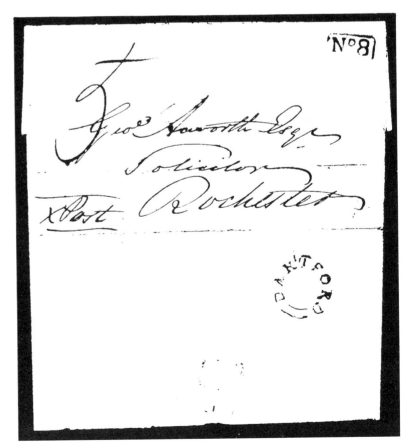

1834. Cross Post Letter from Basted, Wrotham (No 8) out through Dartford 1d in the Penny Post and so on to Rochester in the General Post 4d, making 5d in all. As this letter went out through Dartfod it does not bear 'Seven Oakes Penny Post'. Dartford, being the 5th clause end of the route uses its ordinary handstamp. (Reduced.)

situated just beyond the boundaries of the London posts. In 1825 letters were coming to Halstead through Chislehurst and Chelsfield, at an additional messenger cost of 1½ d per letter, by the 5th Clause post started in 1803. The Rev. I Williams, Minister of Chelsfield, writes to Sir John Lubbock on the 14th June 1825 concerning the posts to Chelsfield mentioning the plight of the inhabitants of Halstead and asking him to petition Francis Freeling about the matter:

Dear Sir John,

As you have given me reason to hope that Mr Freeling would be disposed to attend to a representation respecting our Post office, I beg leave to make the following statement with a request that you would have the kindness to submit it to his consideration. The Post office at Chelsfield is connected with that at Chislehurst, a Village about 7 miles distant from us. The letters of this place and also of Halstead an adjoining Parish, are conveyed here daily by a postman who leaves the Halstead letters at the office and in a few instances delivers them here - Having to pass thro' five villages or more on his way hither, he never arrives at Chelsfield before twelve at noon, tho' we are but 17 miles from London, and as his stay is limited to one hour it is impossible in a Parish so extensive and widely scattered as this, to answer the letters by return of post. In consequence of this, the inhabitants are obliged either to forward their letters to Farnboro', or to send them by private hand to London. The Parishoners of Halstead are still more inconvenienced, as they have no letter carrier, and therefore have no opportunity of answering their letters the same day. Now I would beg most respectfully to suggest that the Post office here is affiliated to that at Farnboro' which is only three miles distant, and if a postman were appointed to convey the letters from thence to Chelsfield and then proceed to Halstead, charging the present rate of 1½ d per letter he would thereby be repaid for his time, our letters might arrive three hours earlier, and ample time would be afforded for answering them. This is the general wish of the neighbourhood, and if by any arrangment it could be complied with, Mr Freeling would confer on us a particular obligation. If I have not been sufficiently explicit in this statement, your personal knowledge of our local situation and relative connection with Farnboro' will enable you to add any further particulars. With much respect, I have the honor to remain, Dear Sir John,

Your obedt humble servt
(Sgd) I Williams
Minister of Chelsfield
Rectory House
June 14 1825

But his plea was unsuccessful, not because the idea was not a good one, but because on Anthony Scott's survey he found only 24 letters a week were passing which were not enough to pay the expense of a messenger from Farnboro'. Scott did however suggest that they had their letters addressed to Farnborough which was a Post Town and to send their own messenger to collect, so getting the letters early enough in the day to allow an answer the same day. Scott was not too happy about this possible solution as the pence of the Chislehurst 5th Clause Post (the 1½d per letter) would be lost to the Revenue.

When discussing the travels of letter carriers in these times, it is perhaps pertinent to remember that 1830 was the year of the Farm Labourers Revolt with poor labour conditions and high prices. Mechanisation was being introduced on farms and farmhands only employed as casual labour, instead of by the year. Gangs of twenty to fifty men were roaming the countryside with blacksmiths as skilled machine-breakers and in the Bromley, Orpington, Sevenoaks area twenty hayrick fires were reported between June and September of that year. 'Swing', one of the gang leaders, demanded '*the maried men give tow and sixpence a day, the singel tow shillings or we will burn down your barns and you in them*'[1]

In March 1839 Halstead had a Receiving House established, based on Sevenoaks,

The last proposition submitted by the surveyor is to appoint a new penny post messenger to serve the villages of Otford, Halstead & Knockholt at an allowance of 14/- a week whose duty it will be to deliver the letters in the parish of Knockholt, that a receiver may be appointed at Halstead with a salary of £4 pa to include delivery of letters and that the salary of the receiver at Otford may be increased from £3 to

£4 per annum to remunerate him for the additional duty of delivering the letters.

Fourteen shilling a week is *'tow shillings a day'* so perchance the post office was looking to employ a single man. The post office rates were always just, frugal perhaps, but always sufficient for the job.

That Halstead letters were indeed being handled through Chelsfield rather than being taken down to Sundridge on the Westerham route a considerably further distance, is evidenced by a *'Free Front'* superscribed,

"Sevenoaks 23 March 1838 (Signed) Leveson (Lord)"

which has been postmarked "Footscray", the office under which Chelsfield operated and has passed through the post to London without comment. The Frank office in London was 'hot' on the slightest irregularity.

Lastly for this period there is a complaint in Post 14

13 January 1841

Halstead Kent is in the delivery of Sevenoaks but letters for this place are continually sent to Bromley & Footscray when the word 'Sevenoaks' is omitted. The officers at the Hastings division will distinctly understand that Halstead Kent must in future be sent to Seven Oaks and it is hoped no further complaint will be made upon the subject, great inconvenience having arisen from these errors.

But perhaps correspondents were being deliberately asked to omit 'Sevenoaks' from the address, by their friends in Halstead.

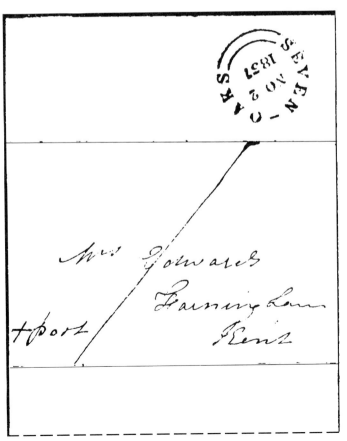

Cross Post. *Penny Post past the Sevenoaks-Kemsing section into the Dartford 5th Clause section at Farningham. But still only a penny for **both** sections.*

Though it must be said that there is nothing here to prove that a further '5th clause penny' was not also demanded without being marked, quite apart from any possible 'off-walk' delivery charge.

Synopsis

Local Arrangements East and North

1668/9	**The 1668 Contract** allowed Postmasters to supply Market Towns within ten miles of a Stage Town with their letters at an additional charge of 2d per letter, with free collection of outward mail. Wrotham was a market town, but so far there is no evidence of a Postmasters 2d delivery existing in the area.

The 1669 broadsheet mentions Branch Bag arrangements for Otford and Sevenoaks from the local Stage Town, Chipstead.

1740-51	Archive correspondance (Fremlin U2133) of Kemsing shows a local charge of 3d from Sevenoaks.
1787/1793	**John Cary lists**. Shoreham and Wrotham shown as Receiving Houses.
1801	Position at the time of the **1801 Survey** was that all mail was collected by private messengers.

2d per letter   Greatness   )   3 days   Collected by messengers
     Seal   )   per week   appointed by the
     Kemsing   )   inhabitants
     Ightham   )
     Wrotham   )
     Plaxtol   )

3d per letter   Otford   )   3 days   Private messenger
     Shoreham   )   per week

Further up towards Farningham they might be charged a 3d, 4d, 5d, or 6d delivery charge.

1804 end July	**5th clause post**. Six day a week service.

1d per letter   Dartford
     Sutton at Hone R.H. (£2)
     Farningham R.H. (£5)
(Newspapers   (Eynesford)   Dartford 5th Clause
charged for but   (Lullingstone)   Footpost
soon made free)   Shoreham R.H. (£3)
     Otford R.H. (£3)
     Kemsing R.H. (£3)   Exchange of bags
     (St Clere)
1d per letter   Wrotham R.H. (£5)
     (Ightham)   Sevenoaks 5th Clause
     (Seal)   Footpost
     Sevenoaks

1826 Dec 28	**Sevenoaks, but not Dartford, Fifth Clause Post converted to a Penny Post** both with a six day service.

     Dartford
     (Hawley)
     (South Darenth)   Dartford 5th Clause
     Sutton at Hone R.H. (£2)   Post remains
1d per letter   (Horton)
(Newspapers   Farningham R.H. (£5)
and Frees as   (Eynesford)
before - not   (Lullingstone)
charged)   Shoreham R.H. (£3)
     Otford R.H. (£3)

	1826	1839
	Auxiliary	Auxiliary
	Wrotham-	Wrotham-
	Otford	Shoreham
Kemsing R.H. (£2)		
(St Clere)		

1826 *continued*

Sevenoaks Penny Post

1826   1839

1d per letter (Newspapers and Frees charged for)	Wrotham R.H. (£5) (Borough Green) (Ightham Court) Ightham (Seal Chart) Seal Sevenoaks	R.H. (£2 1826)	R.H. (£5 March 10 1839)

1839

Otford goes to Halstead walk (but according to Post 9/132 remains a 5th Clause R.H. under Dartford).

Notes:

The linking of a Penny Post to a 5th clause route in the middle of a long walk may possibly be unique.

The Otford Receiver's wages were raised to £4 pa as recommended by the Surveyor when proposing the Sevenoaks, Otford, Halstead, Knockholt walk but his wages continued to be paid by Dartford.

Ightham salary increased to £6 about 1841 to include delivery in the village.

Between Post Towns situate at the terminals of 5th Clause and Penny Post routes the full General Post mileage rate was payable; thus from 1812-1839 the Dartford-Sevenoaks charge was 4d. Such letters were considered General Post Cross-Post letters and put into a separate bag. Such letters did not appear to be brought into the calculations when assessing the viability of a village route.

Local Arrangements West

1669   The broadsheet mentions Branch Bag arrangements for Croydon and Reigate. Both these towns have been queried by other writers as somewhat unlikely to have been operative, at any rate for any length of time.

Croydon is not so certain as that town appears near to London by a more direct route than that through Sevenoaks, but a branch through *Westerham to Reigate* makes good sense in the early days. Going west from Sevenoaks it is seven miles to Westerham, another eight to Godstone, and ten miles on to Reigate. Beyond Reigate another ten to Dorking and finally fifteen miles to Guildford which was on the next radial road out of London, that to Arundel in the 1600s. Even as late as the 1760s the nearest radial road to Sevenoaks was that through Dorking to East Grinstead, so Reigate still required a connection. From examining letters in archives this valley route appeared to have considerable activity, with Sir John Heath at Brasted and Dan Sharp at Westerham, although so far correspondance from Reigate to Sevenoaks has not been found.

1787/1793   Brasted and Westerham shown as Receiving Houses on John Cary lists. The Survey describes the Pre 1801 route, all done by a private messenger at 1d per letter. Although it is not stated at this date that the delivery is organised by the Sevenoaks Postmaster it is stated that he must be compensated for any loss, which seems evidence enough. Certainly by 1805 the delivery service was being organised by Mr Burrell as a private venture.

	Riverhead	)	Messenger organised by the Sevenoaks Postmaster as a private
	Chipstead	)	venture, but under direction of the office.
	*Sundridge	)	
1d per letter	**Brasted	)	Daily delivery - completed by 10am; Return Journey starts 4pm
	***Westerham	)	All mail charged 1d inc Newspapers and Frees

* inc Ide Hill, Chiddingstone	)	these then collected by other Messengers
** inc Marams Court, Nockholt, Halstead	)	appointed by the inhabitants
*** inc Edenbridge	)	

Note that by this time the Post was charging 1d and not the 2d authorised under the 1668 Ordinance.

1810 April 13   Penny Post started
          Receiving Houses at
             Riverhead (3gns)
             Sundridge (2gns)   1d charge on all letters inc Newspapers
             Brasted (2gns)   and Frees
             Westerham (5gns)
             Edenbridge (3gns)
          Additional to above, a further 1d to Receiver at Westerham - private arrangement - so 2d in all. And from 1805 approx a sealed bag also sent by the Sevenoaks Postmaster to Mr Parsons of Edenbridge as a private arrangement with Mr Thos Hayton, minister, and his friends.

1812 Nov*   Riverhead R.H. 3gns increased to £5.10.-) These Receivers would not continue on low salaries.
               Sundridge R.H. 2gns increased to £4.8.-) They were not innkeepers and their actual salary
               Brasted R.H. 2gns increased to £4.8.-   ) was important to them.

1824 Dec 18   Chipstead R.H. Previously letters left at a Public House

1827 Jan 30   Through Route to Godstone
               Westerham R.H. 5gns increased to 8gns

1839 March   Edinbridge Sub-deputy increased to 8gns Also an official messenger via Hever and Chiddingstone
                                              (so presumably the additional 'Westerham penny' creased).
               Riverhead R.H. £5.10.- to £7; Chipstead R.H. £2 to £4; Sundridge R.H. £4.8.- to £5.10.0; Brasted R.H. £4.8.- to £5.10.-

1840   About 1840 there was a Receiver at Horns Cross (£3.3.-). Horns Cross is three quarters of a mile south of Cudham on the road to Brasted.

* Post 9/132 (1838-43) lists this post as 'daily', whereas most six day posts are noted as such, so presumably it was now 7 days/week.
Westerham to Sevenoaks messenger converted from footpost to mailcart in March 1839.

Halstead
Pre 1803   Halstead letters sent via Sevenoaks and collected privately from Brasted.
1803   Chislehurst 5th clause post started (Chislehurst-Footscray-St Mary Cray-Chelsfield)
               1½d per letter to Chelsfield. (1802 Chelsfield 5CI under Footscray).
               Halstead letters collected from Chelsfield by inhabitants, no village letter messenger.
1839 March   Sevenoaks Penny Post. 1d per letter
               Knockholt
               Halstead R.H. (£4 to include delivery in the village)
               Otford R.H. (£3 to £4)**
               Sevenoaks

** The Otford receiver continued to be paid by Dartford. Otford came under Sevenoaks administratively in 1847.

Through Route West
Once a radial route came out of London to East Grinstead via Godstone, any possibility of a through cross-route was finished.

1810 Reported situation, which was not changed –
    Godstone: Private deliveries by Godstone Postmaster
                  to Oxted 1d in and 1d out including Newspapers (Frees not mentioned);
                  to Lympsfield/Titsey 1½d out and 1d in inc Newspapers (Frees not mentioned)

1820 The reported situation over the whole route was
Reigate post town ➤ Nutfield ➤ Bletchingley sub-PT ➤ Godstone PT ➤ Oxted R.H. ➤ Limpsfield R.H. ➤Titsey

Nutfield had a private messenger to Bletchingley. Bletchingley was paid £10 per annum and received its letters from Godstone. Godstone postmaster delivered privately to Oxted, Limpsfield, Titsey.

1821 Jan	**Godstone Penny Post**	1d per letter inc N'papers
		to Oxted R.H. (£3)
		to Limpsfield R.H. (£3)
		with delivery at Titsey
1827 Jan 30		Through route Godstone to Westerham R.H. 'Daily'.

Note: Once the connection has been made in 1827, as well as the letters for the villages on the route, there was also a separate Cross Post Bye Bag to Tunbridge Wells from Godstone, described as '*not P.P., not 5th clause*' (Post 9/132), and charged on a mileage basis between the post towns, as in the General Post.

Town-Letters Although Sevenoaks Town had a free delivery for General Post letters by 1827, letters put in locally for local town delivery would be charged 1d as in the Penny Post.

Tradecard for Shrubsoles Hotel Wrotham. (Probably about 1860)

Chapter VII

1839-1920
Railways, Local Growth and Expansion, World War I

Monarchs   Victoria   (1837-1901)
              Edward VII (1901-1910)
              George V   (1910-   )

Chronology

1837	Queen Victoria ascended the throne.
1838	Money Order business taken over by G.P.O. from Clerks of the Roads.
1840	Jan.10 Universal Penny Post. 5 May Adhesive labels (stamps) available for prepayment.
1841	Railway from London to Tonbridge completed.
	Jan 6. Registration as we know it started.
1844	Mail to Sevenoaks by Railway via Tonbridge.
1851	Great Exhibition. Crystal Palace in Hyde Park.
1852	Greenwich Mean Time (Railway Time). Pillar Boxes.
1855	General Post and London Post merged.
1857	Indian Mutiny.
1859	Superannuation Act. Gas lighting introduced in Sevenoaks.
1860-1900	Campaign against Sunday working.
1860's	Campaign for letter boxes in front doors.
1861	Post Office Savings Bank started (September 16th).
1862	Railway to St. Johns (Bat and Ball).
	Act for the better Management of Highways
1865	Government Insurance and Annuities sold at P.Os.
1868	Japan starts Westernization. Railway to Tubs Hill, Sevenoaks. First class commuting to London commenced.
1869/70	Issue of Dog Licences and other licences at all Money Order Offices.
1870	Post Office takes over Telegraphs. Postcards introduced.
	Married Woman's Property Act. Amended 1874.
1871	Local Boards instead of old Highways Boards.
1871-81	Numbering of Houses in Sevenoaks.
1872	Ballot introduced in Britain. Post Office Good Conduct Stripes introduced.
1876	Penny Farthing Bicycle.
1881	Postal Orders obtainable from MOSB's. Sevenoaks Chronicle started.
1883	Parcel Post.
1885	Start of 6d Telegram (previously 1/-). Boy Messengers.
1887	Queen Victoria's Golden Jubilee.
1889	Standard safety bicycle.
1890	P.O. compulsory retirement at 65.
1891	Extension of Express Delivery Service.
1892	Double peaked shako, previously one peak at front. Free reposting within 24 hours.
1894	Delivery Postman's weekly Half-day off introduced locally.
	Opening of Tower Bridge.
1896	Sevenoaks connected with the National Telephone Exchange.
1897	Queen Victoria's Diamond Jubilee.
1898-1902	Boer War.
1900	Electric Lighting Order. Bicycles at Sevenoaks and Westerham P.Os. Third (Second) Class commuting to London commenced.
1903	Aeroplanes commence to fly.
1906	Sevenoaks a Crown Office. Whitley Committees.
1907	Sevenoaks and District Mutual Building Society established.
1908	Telephones develop locally.
1909	Payment of Old Age Pensions through Post Offices.
	Movement of Brigade of Guards from London through Sevenoaks to Hastings by motor car.
1911	Compulsory National Insurance.
1912	GPO Takeover of business of National Telephone Company. Coronation. Airmail.
1913	Sevenoaks Electricity Company founded.
1914	Electricity Generating Station at Sundridge.
1914-18	World War I
1916	First Daylight Saving Bill.
1917	Biggin Hill Wireless Research Establishment founded.

Chapter VII

1839-1920
Railways, Local Growth and
Expansion, World War I

Queen Victoria ascended the throne in June 1837; the same year Freeling died. At this time many rural postmen were walking their twenty or so miles every day of the week including Sundays, in all weathers. The lack of a day's rest proved most taxing even to the strongest of constitutions and there were many breakdowns in health. But one must always remember that the post was the only available means of communication and that telegraph, after 1871, and telephone, after 1912 locally, when they did become established were organised by the post office itself.

Once again it was to be a period of agitation with pressure for reduced postal rates. About November, in 1837, a short run 2d rate was introduced between post towns not more than seven miles apart, subsequently raised to eight miles. Lewes to Brighton, almost ten miles, dropped to 2d and there is evidence of this lower rate being applied to the Sevenoaks to Tonbridge stage, a distance of about seven miles only.

The following year about September 1838 the method of calculating mileage for the mileage charge was altered from the distance of the route actually taken however circuitous that might be and charged as such, to a nominal direct mileage by the nearest public road which in many cases effectively meant a 'crow flies' distance. Again there was no great change in the rates applying in the Sevenoaks district.

Then came the main changes, first to the overall fourpenny charge on 5th December 1839 when all rates higher than 4d were reduced to a standard 4d per *half* ounce in the General Post and, a month later on January 10th the introduction of the Universal Penny Post, when rates were reduced to a prepaid one penny, twopence if the recipient still paid, to cover both General Post and the operating Penny and 5th clause routes, though those routes with private deliveries continued for a time with their local charges. Special one penny and twopenny labels and similar stamped stationery were introduced as from 6th May to make prepayment easier and facilitate the use of open collecting boxes, but these novelties were optional right up to 1853 and the penny could be handed in in cash with the letter. Habits die hard. Even as late as 1877 the heading of 'Situations Vacant' in the South Eastern Gazette said 'Letters to be post paid'.

The New Labels and Prepaid Stationery
Advertisement in the 'Sevenoaks General Advertiser' 1st June 1840.

James Payne, Bookseller, Stationer, Printer &c being the appointed Sub-distributor of Stamps for the district of Sevenoaks and its neighbourhood has a supply of the Stamped labels, Covers and Envelopes now in use under the new Postage Act, which may be obtained of him at the following prices:-

Labels 1d and 2d each; Covers 1¼d and 2¼d each   *(1.25d and 2.25d ea)*
Half ream, or 240 Penny Covers   £1.2.4   *(1.117 ea)*
    do   *Envelopes*   £1.1.9   *(1.0875 ea)*
Quarter ream, or 120 Twopenny Covers   £1.1.4   *(2.133 ea)*
    do   *Envelopes*   £1.1.1   *(2.108 ea)*
The Penny Stamp carries half an ounce (inland); the Twopenny Stamp, one ounce.

   James Payne
    Bank Place
    Sevenoaks

1840 Universal Penny Postage.   Mulready Envelope Sevenoaks to London. The Maltese Cross impressed over the figure of Britannia in the centre acted as the cancellation.

A penny, which is 9p by today's reckoning covered only half an ounce whereas the charge is now 17p for 60gms, about two ounces. The basic first step charge for a letter was held through the inflationary period[1] (although the first step weight was varied) in line with the equivalent of one penny from 1840 until 1975 when the rate was suddenly almost doubled. There must have been some policy change behind this great rate change but it was never made fully public, unless it be that of the Government's insistence that the Post Office generate its own funds for expansion.

The Coming of the Railways

First introduced to the public in 1825, Railways were becoming well established by 1835.

At first Sevenoaks saw little change but within a few years the railways came into Kent, taking of necessity very different routes to the mail coach routes they supplanted because of the difficulty of tunnelling through the North Downs as at Polhill.

The first main Kent route from London left the London-Brighton line at what is now called Redhill and travelled past Edenbridge and Tonbridge; completed by 1842 from the Tonbridge end, the materials being brought up the Medway by water to Tonbridge; then the railway continued on to Ashford and Folkestone completed by 1843, Dover 1844. Branches from this line extended to Maidstone 1844, Tunbridge Wells 1845 and by 1846 the rail connected to Canterbury, Ramsgate and Broadstairs.

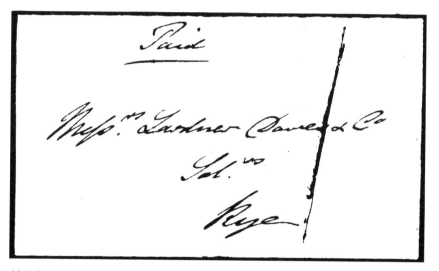

1840 Sevenoaks to Rye with single stroke '1' handstamp in red to denote the penny paid.

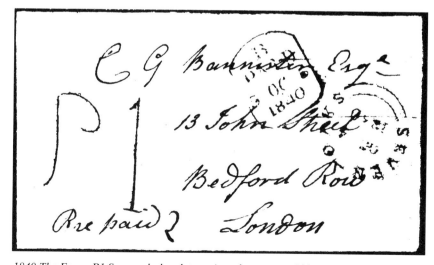

1840 The Fancy P1 Sevenoaks handstamp in red on a prepaid letter.

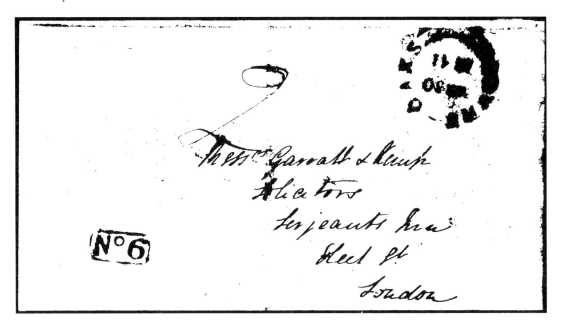

1841 Universal Penny Post. Posted unpaid, so double fee charged, 2d in black manuscript, No 6 denotes Edenbridge Receiving House. This letter went by foot to Westerham, mailcart to Sevenoaks, then mailcoach to London.

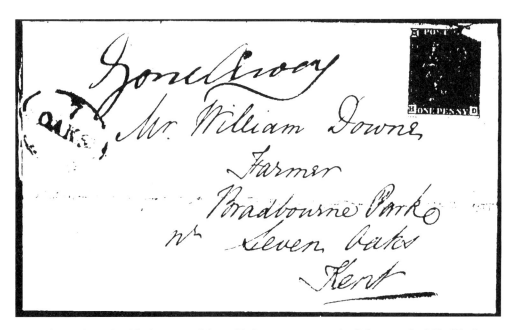

1840 The 7Oaks oval in black on an undeliverable letter concerning the dishonour of a Bill of Exchange.

Up to 1843 matters along the mail coach route on the Hastings Road produced the usual complaints.

Dec 18 1840 Post 14

The President* will please to direct the Sevenoaks Box to be strictly examined to prevent letters addressed to Viscount Sydney, Frognal, Footscray being missent there.
(*The Presiding Officer on duty)

Aug 1841 Sevenoaks Advertiser

After complaints to the PMG by members of the public that the evening closure of the Sevenoaks letter box was too early, the last collection was altered from 8.30 to 9 pm. After that time letters pay 2d if required to catch the night post. This late fee was twice as much as the Universal Penny Post Rate of 1d started the previous year, and was not marked on the letters but accrued to the Postmaster, although recorded.

13 Sept 1843 Post 14

Great complaint has been made that letters addressed to Westerham Kent which is well known to be in the delivery of Sevenoaks are constantly missent to Lamberhurst. The officers of the division are specially cautioned against a repetition of these mistakes as serious notice will be taken of any future cases of missent.

The Main Route Change from Road to Railway

The first few years of the 1840's were to be only a pause while the Post Office judged the reliability of this new form of locomotion and then made contracts for the carrying of the mails. Though the Railway charged the Post Office heavily for their services, speed of transit was judged essential and the contracts were in due course made.

Suddenly the road used for four hundred years was used no longer, at least for letters, and from 10th May 1844 Sevenoaks mail was sent via Tunbridge and up by mailcart along the old coach road, thus reversing the direction of the normal flow.

9 May 1844 [Post 14]

On and from friday evening (tomorrow) Brighton, Hastings and part of the Dover Mail including the foreign mails and Deal Ship Letters will be sent by the Dover or South Eastern Rail Road - in consequence of this arrangement there will be many changes in the deliveries and at the Hastings division, Staplehurst and Hurst Green will be made post Towns and Foots Cray & Lamberhurst will be discontinued as such, the former with its delivery will be sent to Bromley and the latter town will be under Hurst Green, part of the extensive delivery of Lamberhurst will be transferred to Hurst Green, Cranbrook and Staplehurst - also at the Brighton division, Godstone will be discontinued as a post Town and transferred with its delivery to Reigate.

The President is informed that the various alterations have been entered in the Hastings, Brighton & Dover division Order Books - and new making up cards written out for the respective officers, who have attended the Superintending President's office for that purpose, they are therefore fully acquainted with the various changes, all the officers will nevertheless sign this order and the President will be good enough at the same time to direct them carefully to examine every night (and morning) where it appears the Letters for Maidstone, Tunbridge, East Grinstead & Uckfield (the towns chiefly affected by the alterations in delivery) until the changes are thoroughly known as in the event of errors, the delays will be most serious - to this end had better summons an officer on Friday, Saturday and Monday evenings.

The <u>Night Dover Mail</u> will continue to run as usual but will only convey the bags the line of Road as far as Canterbury & Wingham inclusive - also the <u>Dover Day mail</u> and the <u>Brighton-Day mail</u> will be despatched as usual and made up as at present. Also on the same evening (Friday) in addition to the changes alluded to Walmer is to be sent to Dover instead of Deal.

Despatch Bills similar to those in use for the Northern and other Rail Roads will be printed containing the list of Bags and Sacks and Foreign Mails which must be ticked off & signed by Mr. Walton, assisted by W. Hibbard - the <u>number</u> of Foreign Mails and Deal Ship Letter Bags must be stated on the bill.

1843 Edenbridge to Westerham, then Sevenoaks to Tonbridge and on to Penshurst. About 25 miles, whilst only 5 miles direct.

The Truncated Mailcoach Route   The London-Hastings mailcoach now ran only between Hastings and the Post Office at the Railway Station at Staplehurst, and a mailcart ran from Staplehurst to Rye.

Start of Railway Day Mails
Next year there were some important changes, bringing in day mails,
24th January 1845 [Post 14]

> *On and from Monday 27th January, <u>Day</u> bags are to be sent to and received*
from   Tunbridge.
>   *Tunbridge Wells*
>   *Sevenoaks*
>   *Ashford*
>   *Folkestone*
>   *Dover, to be enclosed in a sack*
>   *labelled 'Reigate and Dover' -*
also   Staplehurst

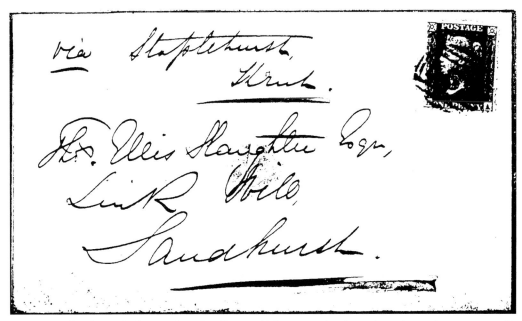

1844 Start of Railway. So Sevenoaks to Sandhurst, which was previously on the main road route, now mailcart to Tonbridge, train to Staplehurst, then mailcart again.

> *Cranbrook*
> *Hurst Green*
> *Battle*
> *St. Leonards*
> *Hastings, to be enclosed in a sack*
labelled 'Staplehurst and Hastings' -
the above two Sacks to be sent and received by the <u>Brighton Day Mail.</u> Also on and after the same morning the letters for Hawkhurst & delivery are to be sent to Cranbrook by the Day Mail only - to Staplehurst as usual by the Night Mail. The Hawkhurst delivery is in the Hastings Order Book.

4 Mar 47. As from morning of 15 inst [15.3.47] letters for Shoreham Kent to be sent to Sevenoaks instead of Dartford.

Edenbridge becomes a Post Town

Then came a big change in the Sevenoaks district. Edenbridge, having a station on the new railway line then became a Post Town in its own right on 1st September 1848, never to return fully to the Sevenoaks fold (its circulation was later with Tunbridge Wells and now since 1984 with Tonbridge) although the Westerham group that was part of Edenbridge for a while subsequently returned to Sevenoaks.

[Post 14] 31 Aug 48. As from tomorrow morning [1 Sep 1848] Edenbridge will be a post town & bags must be made up for it both night and day mails and given to the guard of the Dover mail. Annexed is the delivery of Edenbridge.

There was a surveyors report covering this split but it appears no longer to be extant. The greatly detailed books of the Freeling era have come to an end with his death in 1837 and the tale is taken up in Post 30, but after following the Edenbridge saga through many references (the habit of the times was to file earlier documentation within later references to the same subject) the trail becomes circular. One finally realises that much of the supporting documentation of Post 30 has been destroyed, as also for Post

A LIST

OF

Places, Gentlemen's Seats, and Principal Houses

IN THE

Delivery of Edenbridge.

Bassett's Mill	Hole Farm
Boons	Hoath
Boar Place	Hobb's Hill
Bow Beach	Ivy House
Bower Farm	Larkin's Farm
Brook Street	Lewins
Braxham	Lydens
Causeway	Lindhurst
Camp Hill	Lock Skinners
Chiddingstone Castle	Little Warren
Chiddingstone	Little Browns
Charcot	Marsh Green
Chippings	Marlpit Hill
Chisel Hall	Medhurst Row
Cooper's Corner	New House
Crockham Hill	Pootings
Crouch House	Sharp's Place
Dairy Farm	Skeynes
Dencross	Skinner's Farm
Finch Green	Somerden
Four Elms	Spout Farm
Fringdon	Starboro' Castle
Gabriels	Stone Wall
Greyberries	Stanford's End
Hever	Treavereux
Hever Castle	Trow Town
Hever Lodge	Vex Hour
Hilders	Weller's Tower
Holdfast	Westerham Lodge

50.—July, 1848.

14, and that would appear to have been the fate of the Edenbridge report.

There is one small reference:

[Post 35] 28 Ap 48. As it appears that the present Receiver at Edenbridge is qualified to fill the office of P.M. I presume your dept will allow him to take this situation & that the penalty of his bond may be fixed at £300 as the Surveyor proposes.

I presume also as the present messenger between Westerham & Hever will be thrown out of employment when Edenbridge is established as a Post Town your dept will allow this man to take one of the two new walks which you have already estab in connection with this measure.

   N.M.L.

  28 April 48 "Approved".

A list of the delivery of Edenbridge as at July 1848 is shown.

Railway Time Bills

The early railway days are shown on a group of time bills for 1852, 1860, 1862 and 1864 kept in the Post Office Archives. The general pattern of the bills follows that of the mailcoach timebills with the Post Office relying for time upon its own timepiece which was carried, rather than any other.

The London and Dover Railway were not allowed to build their own line into London via Norwood as previously authorised and had to take a longer route, sharing track with the Brighton Railway and others after joining at Warwick Town, now named Redhill, but at that time just a few houses so the junction took its name from Reigate, the nearest town two miles away.

This way the distance to Tonbridge was forty one miles with an additional six miles by mailcart up to Sevenoaks, forty seven miles in all; but the time taken to travel it was less than the mailcoach took for the twenty four miles direct.

Mailbag Exchange Apparatus was approved for Edenbridge as early as April 1848 after the successful trials at Croydon, and Tonbridge too obtained the apparatus for exchanging mailbags whilst the train was in motion, although it is not so mentioned in the first few timebills shown here. Times were varied over the years to suit local needs and to make connections. The greatly speeded up Night Mail started on 1st May 1860 and had a Railway Post Office incorporated, although some sorting had been carried out since April 1850. From the time bills it can be seen that the Night Mail reached Tunbridge in 55 minutes instead of the more usual one and a quarter to two and a half hours. Nor did it stop, for on the down run apparatus was used at both Edenbridge and Tunbridge, achieving the 41 miles in 55 minutes giving an average of 44 miles per hour. On the up journey a stop was made at Tunbridge with apparatus again used at Edenbridge.

At this time some small changes occurred:

[Post 14] 30 April 1862. On and from tomorrow the 1st May the Day Mail bags for Battle
Sevenoaks
Tunbridge
& Tunbridge Wells
will be despatched single for conveyance by the 9.30 am train. A cart will be provided for their conveyance to the station.*

The station at this time was London Bridge. Cannon Street did not come into use until 1866. Three days later, on the 3rd May, 1862, the time was put back to 9.05am, but the times for posting letters remained unaltered.

Opposite: *Edenbridge Delivery July 1848*
Over page: *Some Railway Time bills:-*
     Day Mail 1852 London/Dover and Dover/London
     Night Mail 1852 London/Dover and Dover/London
     Night Mail 1862 London/Dover
     Night Mail 1862 Dover/London   *(All PO Archives)*

DAY MAIL

London and Dover Railway TIME BILL.

Despatched from the General Post-Office, the *1 of April*

185 *3* at *9. 30 r...* | 9. 30 **A.M.** by Time-Piece | **P.M.** by Clock

at | With a Time-Piece safe No. to

M. F. Yds.	Time allowed H. M.		
		10	Arrived at the *Railway Station*, at
		10	*10.0 a.m* Ten Minutes allowed. Off at *10*
2.7.100			*New Cross*
7.3.13.			*Croydon*
10.3. 15	30		Arrived at *Reigate*, at *10.35 12. 4*
	1 34		*One Hour and Thirty-four Minutes allowed.* Off at *12. 8*
5.4.180			*Godstone*
4.7. 20			*Eden Bridge*
4.7.195			*Penshurst*
4.3. 35	32		Arrived at *Tunbridge*, at *12. 30 12. 45*
5.0. 20			*Maidstone Road*
4.4.190			*Marden*
2.4. 30	19		Arrived at *Staplehurst*, at *1. 1 1. 10*
3.2.110			*Headcorn*
5.2. 10			*Pluckley*
5.5. 30	28		Arrived at *Ashford*, at *1. 23 1. 35*
8.0.100			*Hythe*
6.6. 70	18		Arrived at *Folkstone*, at *1. 57 2. 2*
5.5.140	19		Arrived at the *Railway Station, Dover*, at *2. 2*
	5		*2. 0 r...* Five Minutes allowed.
		10	Arrived at the *Post-Office, Dover*, the of
			185 , at *2. 15 p...* 2. 35 **P.M.** by Time-Piece
87.4. 60	4 35		at . **P.M.** by Clock
			Delivered the Time-Piece safe No. to

Express

RETURNED.

Despatched from the Post-Office, *Dover*, the *1 of April*

185 *3*, at *5. 5 a.m*   5. 5 **A.M.** by Time-Piece

at | **A.M.** by Clock | With a Time-Piece safe No. to

M. F. Yds.	Time allowed		
		10	Arrived at the *Railway Station*, at
		5	*5.20* Five Minutes allowed. Off at *5.20*
5.5.140	10		Arrived at *Folkstone*, at *5. 30 5. 30*
6.6. 70			*Hythe*
8.0.100	25		Arrived at *Ashford*, at *5. 55 5. 56*
5.5. 30			*Pluckley*
5.2. 10			*Headcorn*
3.2.110			*Staplehurst*
2.4. 30			*Marden*
4.4.190			*Maidstone Road*
5.0. 20	45		Arrived at *Tunbridge*, at *6. 40 6. 42*
4.3. 35			*Penshurst*
4.7.195			*Eden Bridge*
4.7. 20			*Godstone*
5.4.180	30		Arrived at *Reigate*, at *7. 10 7. 23*
10.3. 15			*Croydon*
7.3.135			*New Cross*
2.7.100	40		Arrived at the *Railway Station, London Bridge*, at *8. 5 a.m*
		10	*7.50 a.m* Ten Minutes allowed.
		10	Arrived at the General Post-Office, the of
			185 , at *8. 10 a.m* 8. 26 **A.M.** by Time-Piece
87.4. 60	3 5		at **A.M.** by Clock
			Delivered the Time-Piece safe No. to

The Postmaster to give a Fortnight's Notice when a further supply is required

By Command of the Postmaster-General.
GEORGE STOW,
Surveyor and Superintendent.

(9 –52)

NIGHT MAIL

London and Dover Railway TIME BILL.

Despatched from the General Post-Office, the *1 of April*

185*3*, at   *6. 0 p.m*   P.M. by Time-Piece

at   P.M. by Clock

{ With a Time-Piece safe

{ No.   to

M. F. Yds.	Time allowed H. M.		
	20	Arrived at the *Railway Station*, at	
	10	*8.30* Ten Minutes allowed. Off at *8.30 p.m*	
2.7.100		*New Cross*	
7.3.135		*Croydon*	
10.3. 15	34	Arrived at *Reigate*, at *9.4* *9.8* Off at	
5.4.180		*Godstone*	
4.7. 20		*Eden Bridge*	
4.7.195		*Penshurst*	
4.3. 35	32	Arrived at *Tunbridge*, at *9.36* *9.45*	
5.0. 20		*Maidstone Road*	
4.4.190		*Marden*	
2.4. 30	19	Arrived at *Staplehurst*, at *10.1* *10.10*	
3.2.110		*Headcorn*	
5.2. 10		*Pluckley*	
5.5. 30	28	Arrived at *Ashford*, at *10.23* *10.35*	
8.0.100		*Hythe*	
6.6. 70	18	Arrived at *Folkstone*, at *10.50* *11.2*	
5.5.140	19	Arrived at the *Railway Station, Dover*, at *11.20 p.m*	
	5	*11.0 p.m* Five Minutes allowed.	
	10	Arrived at the Post-Office, *Dover*, the of	
		185 , at *11.15 p* *11.35* P.M. by Time-Piece	
87.4. 60	3 15	at P.M. by Clock	
		{ Delivered the Time-Piece safe	
		{ No. to	

London and Dover Railway Company

RETURNED.

Despatched from the Post-Office, *Dover*, the *1 of April*

185*3*, at *1.45 a.m*   *1.45* A.M. by Time-Piece

at   A.M. by Clock

{ With a Time-Piece safe

{ No.   to

M. F. Yds.	Time allowed		
	10	Arrived at the *Railway Station*, at	
	5	*2.0* Five Minutes allowed. Off at *2.0 a.m*	
5.5.140	10	Arrived at *Folkstone*, at *2.10* *2.10*	
6.6. 70		*Hythe*	
8.0.100	25	Arrived at *Ashford*, at *2.35* *2.36*	
5.5. 30		*Pluckley*	
5.2. 10		*Headcorn*	
3.2.110	22	Arrived at *Staplehurst*, at *2.57* *3.4*	
2.4. 30		*Marden*	
4.4.190		*Maidstone Road*	
5.0. 20	23	Arrived at *Tunbridge*, at *3.20* *3.25*	
4.3. 35		*Penshurst*	
4.7.195		*Eden Bridge*	
4.7. 20		*Godstone*	
5.4.180	30	Arrived at *Reigate*, at *3.50* *4.7*	
10.3. 15		*Croydon*	
7.3.135		*New Cross*	
2.7.100	40	Arrived at the *Railway Station, London Bridge*, at *4.50 a.m*	
	10	*4.30* Ten Minutes allowed.	
	20	Arrived at the General Post-Office, the of	
		185 , at *5.0 a.m* *5.20* A.M. by Time-Piece	
87.4. 60	3 15	at M. by Clock	
		{ Delivered the Time-Piece safe	
		{ No. to	

London and Dover Railway Company.

By Command of the Postmaster-General.

GEORGE STOW,

Surveyor and Superintendent.

200 (9—52)

98.

London Night Mail.

GENERAL POST OFFICE.

London and Dover TIME BILL.

Guard's Remarks as to Delays, &c.	Distance from London M. F. Yds.	Time allowed H. M.		Proper Times H. M.	Actual Times, by P.O. Watch H. M.	Actual Times, by Ry. Clock H. M.	P.O. work completed at (by P.O. Watch) H. M.	This Column to be left blank
			To be despatched from the General Post-Office. the of 186 ....at	P.M. 8 15				
			Time-Piece, No. Received safe by					
		10	To arrive at **Railway Station** ...at	8 25				
		15	Off at	8 40				
	10.2.154		Croydon (Apparatus) ....(8 55)					
	21.0. 0		Red Hill (Apparatus) ....(9 10)					
	32.0. 0		Eden Bridge (Apparatus).........(9 22)					
	41.0. 0		Tunbridge Junction (Apparatus) (9 35)					
	53.0. 0	1 10	To arrive at **Staplehurst** ....at	9 50				
	67.0. 0		Ashford (Apparatus) ....(10 6)					
	82.0. 0		Folkestone Junction (Appar.) (10 28)					
	88.0. 0	45	To arrive at the New Platform, **Dover** ....at	10 35				
			To arrive at the Admiralty Pier ......at	10 40				
		2 25	Last Bag on board Packet ....at					
			Packet started from *					
			* Pier or Harbour, as the case may be, to be written in this blank.	P.M.				

The Mail Guards are to state on this Time Bill any failure of a Junction which may occur; and they * are* to be exceedingly particular not to omit giving the cause of every delay which may take place. The *number* of Carriages in the Train, *over each line*, is also to be stated. Care must be taken that all Remarks *entered* on the Time Bill, in the proper Column, and *opposite the Stations to which they refer*. The Column *showing* the Actual Times of Arrival by Railway Clock, only requires to be filled up at the commencement *and* termination of each Company's Line.

By Command of the Postmaster-General,

EDWARD J. PAGE, Inspector-General of Mails.

200 3/62

Dover and London TIME BILL.

Sorter's Remarks as to Delays, &c.		Proper Times		Actual Times, by P.O. Watch		Actual Times by By. Clock		P.O. work completed at (by P.O. Watch)		This Column &c.
		H.	M.	H.	M.	H.	M	H.	M.	
Belgian Packet.	To be despatched from the Post-Office, **Dover,** the of 186 , ...at	A.M. 1	45							
	{ Watch, No. { Received safe by									Received tl following Fo eign Mails the Station
Packet came alongside the* at A.M.	To arrive at **Railway Station** ...at Five Minutes allowed. Off at	1 2	55 0							viz.—
Mails arrived at Station, at A.M.	To arrive at **Folkstone Junc.** ...at	2	10							_____
Last Bag in Train, at A.M.	To arrive at **Ashford** ....at	2	35							_____
	To arrive at **Staplehurst** ....at	2	57							_____
* Pier or Harbour, as the case may be, to be written in this blank.	To arrive at **Tunbridge Junction** at	3	20							_____
	Eden Bridge (Apparatus) ......(3 34) To arrive at **Reigate Junction** ...at Off at	3	50							_____
	Croydon (Apparatus) ....(4 10) To arrive at the Railway Station, **London Bridge** ....at	4	30							_____
	The Bags to be transferred as quickly as possible, and to arrive at the **General Post-Office** not later than	4	50							_____
	The of 186	A.M.								
	{ Watch, No. { safe to									

EDWARD J. PAGE, Esq.,

Inspector General of Mails,

General Post Office,

LONDON.

LONDON and DOVER. Night Mail.

TIME BILL.

Spur Line to St. Johns Station 1862, used for Daymail only 1866

Next came a spur line leaving the London and Chatham line at Swanley and with a terminus within Sevenoaks though right at the bottom of the hill to the north of the town. St. John's station, now called Bat and Ball after the pub which is near to it, opened in 1862.

Three years passed and then there was an enquiry into possible savings if the new Sevenoaks station at St. Johns were to be used (for Day mail only).

1869 Double Franking. A letter from Austria to Sevenoaks dated 26 April 1869 is readdressed to London. The new address required a further 1d stamp which has been added and was cancelled in Tonbridge on the way back to London. It was not until later in that same year that the contract to handle Sevenoaks mail through the new Tubs Hill station was signed with the railway and came into effect.

[Post 30] 45/5396 1865

The Present Day Mail Service is performed by Omnibus to & from Tunbridge on the South Eastern Rly & involves the receipt of a despatch as early as 9.30 am with arrival at 12.30.

If London Chatham and Dover railway were used however, there being a branch line to Sevenoaks, an arrival at 10.30 with a despatch at 11.35 might be effected.

Present Omnibus Sevenoaks-Tunbridge	*£ 26*
Return fare, London & Chatham Rly	*31.6.0*
Omnibus Post Office, Railway Station	*10*
at Sevenoaks	
	£ 41.6.0

With the increased traffic from Sevenoaks to Tunbridge to join the railway as the years passed, it appears that the original GPO mailcart service became no longer necessary as there were now sufficient other scheduled services, coaches and omnibuses, making the journey for the GPO to be able to rely on them. In spite of the opening of the new spur into Sevenoaks the GPO appeared satisfied with the Tonbridge service and it was four years before any change was made, and then only for the daymail service.

[Post 14] 19th February 1866. On and from Wednesday next, the 21st instant, the <u>day mail bag</u> for Sevenoaks will be conveyed by the London, Chatham & Dover instead of the South Eastern Railway. It shall be despatched with the bags for Chatham etc. at 9.15 am for conveyance by the 9.35 am train.

Day Mail Bag for Sevenoaks will on and after the same date, arrive by the L, C&D line at Ludgate Hill Station at 1.28 pm - it will be conveyed to this office by an officer attached to the ECDO.

Some months later there was a change in timing:

[Post 14] 1 Jan 1867. On and from tomorrow morning the Day Mail bag for Sevenoaks must be despatched at 8.45 by a messenger on foot who should deliver it to the Cab inspector at the door of Ludgate Hill station in time for the 9.5 am train.

3 Apl 1867. In future the Day Mail bag to Sevenoaks will be despatched from this office at 9.15 am by Cart to Ludgate Hill Station with the Chatham, Sheerness and other bags to be despatched by the 10.25 train.

The day mail bags would constitute a later delivery, those received by the night mail going out as first delivery and throughout this period no entries are found for alterations to the night mail; presumably it continued to come via Tunbridge and up by omnibus until Tubs Hill station was in use a few years later. The fact that the nightmail did so continue can be confirmed from actual used envelopes of the period.

A Direct Railway Line through Tubs Hill 1868, used by GPO 1869

At last the railway engineers tunnelled successfully the North Downs and the main through line arrived at the north west of the town, though still at the bottom of the hill. Tubs Hill station of the South Eastern Railway opened on 2nd March 1868. The line went through to Tonbridge Junction by 1st of May of the same year in spite of trouble with water in the tunnel which bankrupted the contractors but provided a good supply of water for the Town.

Obviously this direct line was to be the main railway route into Sevenoaks and so the Post Office lost little time in coming to arrangements for mail carrying. On 30th July 1869 an Indenture was signed between the Postmaster General and the South Eastern Railway Company [3] outlining the arrangements for mailcarrying to come into effect on 1st August 1869; letters only at this time for parcel post did not come into being until 1883. Arrangements were made for Sorting Carriages as well as for pickup apparatus which as well as at the other places mentioned was also installed at Sevenoaks and remained in use until July 1904 when it was dismantled and a stop scheduled. Whilst one mail train continued to run through Redhill the schedules of mail trains through Sevenoaks listed in the Indenture of 1869 were:-

*London to Dover **via Sevenoaks***

	Daily	Daily ex Sun
*Cannon Street	8.55pm	7.48am (*Cannon Street had
Dover Town	10.35pm	9.26am come into use in 1866)
Dover Admiralty		
Pier	10.40pm	9.30am

	Daily ex Sun	Daily ex Sun
Dover Town	4.15am	3.45pm
Cannon Street	6.00am	5.30pm

with each train to be provided with two sorting carriages and as many ordinary vans as necessary.

Tubs Hill Station Working [Post 35]

As might be expected there was in 1869 an allowance for station service and a late despatch to London. Disruptions to the service schedules occurred in 1873 when there was a discontinuance of the midnight despatch to Folkestone and Dover; then the same year its subsequent reestablishment.

Two years later the '*despatch to London by the 9.46am train was established*'; this would seem to imply that 1875 was the date when contracts ran out and the daymail to London was switched from St. John's station to Tubs Hill in the new contract.

1876 gives the first actual reference to mail exchange and pickup apparatus at Sevenoaks when '*Provision for station and apparatus duties were made*'. Subsequent to this date there is mention of apparatus at regular intervals. Apparatus messenger allowances were approved in 1878 and a year later, 10 March 1879, there was a failure when the Apparatus messenger was late for the Mail Train and was censured for misconduct. Yet in general the mechanism which allowed trains to drop off and to pick up mailbags at speed without stopping or even slowing down must have worked excellently for it was 1890 before the next recorded failure.

Station handling duties increased considerably and in 1885 it was necessary to institute a horse and cart service between the station and the Main Post Office in the High Street at the top of the hill, with a new contract for the mailcart service in 1894, the Station allowances being converted into the wages of an auxiliary rural postman in 1893.

On the main line, Post 35 states -

1898 SETPO (South Eastern Travelling Post Office) Bag established.

1899 Ashford Kent bag (from) established by 1.15am train.

1899 Newspaper bag at 5.50 from London established.

1904 SETPO bag 3.17am established.

1904 Dover 1.45 (from) & Ashford 2.20am bags established.

In 1904 the pick-up apparatus at Sevenoaks station was removed and a two minute stop introduced into the schedule.[4]

Other Connecting Railway Lines

Further lines were being built and in due course the Post Office made use of them.

The spur line to St. John's was driven through to connect with the Southern Railway at Tubs Hill in 1869 and the line to Otford and Maidstone was completed and opened 1st June 1874.

A branch line from Dunton Green to Westerham was opened in 1881 and closed in 1961; by 1967 the track had been lifted.[5]

Use of such lines is recorded in Post 35, though sparsely:-

1895 Ightham Rural Postman to assist in station duties at Wrotham allowance for horse raised.

1897 Maidstone and Tonbridge bags established, station service raised.

1899 to Boro Green and Wrotham. Evening delivery established and bags by 4.14pm train.

In 1896 a new mail cart service to Westerham was contracted but by –

1899 Brasted (from) Bag by 12.16 train
1905 Ex Westerham Bag at 5.33pm established.

General Effects of the Railways

The effect of the Railway on 'the Road' had been sudden and disastrous. Trade fell away overnight in many places along the road route but in the new runs trade picked up as coaches and omnibuses were organised from major centres of population to 'the station' which was often three miles or more away. New houses were built near to the station with shops and services. Whole new centres of activity developed.

Long distance traffic left the main roads and the bulk of road traffic became local to the station. By 1860 the 'walking' craze of the empty roads became popular. In Sevenoaks coaches were organised in 1841 from Riverhead to Tonbridge station, about nine miles, when that line was opened; other coaches

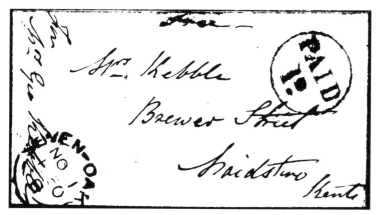

1850 The later Sevenoaks circular 1d handstamp in red. Instead of purchasing a stamp the sender has paid over cash in the post office and the later 'Paid 1d' handstamp has been applied. The envelope has also been inscribed 'Free' at the top to let the recipient know the money has been paid and no further amount is due. It is not a free letter.

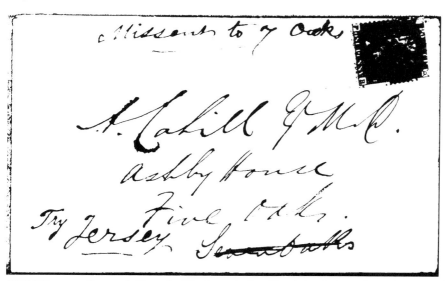

1853 'Missent to Sevenoaks' but why 'Try Jersey' when Five Ashes is just a few miles south of Mayfield and Five Oaks near Horsham?

going to Penshurst station, about the same distance. For Sevenoaks that need was passed by 1862 and certainly by 1868 when both Sevenoaks stations were open and in use.

Parishes had been combined into Highway Districts in 1862 when an act for the Better Management of Highways was passed. But Toll Gates became abandoned as there were few tolls to collect, the Gate at Pratts Bottom being discontinued about 1865 and by 1870 the road network was in a bad condition for want of repair.

Horsed Coaches   Yet throughout all these changes there continued to run a **coach** during the daytime from London to Sevenoaks and back. A trade card dated 1854 informs the public that an omnibus from the *Wheatsheaf Sevenoaks for the Spread Eagle Regent Circus* leaves at 8am returning at 5pm, taking 2½ hours each way, charging 4/- inside, 3/- outside and at the Polhill Arms and Pratts Bottom stops 3/- and 2/6. A similar trade card of 1856 in Maidstone Carriage Museum advertises the London and Sevenoaks Coach, H. Thorpe Proprietor, from *The Spread Eagle Regent Circus at 10am to The Crown Hotel Sevenoaks,* returning at 5.30pm, 4pm in winter.

Such a coach was still running in the late 1880's and was the subject of an article in the Illustrated London News[6], 'The Excelsior to Sevenoaks'. The coach was now used more in the nature of a 'day-trip' into the country and could be said to be the forerunner of the motor bus routes.

When Mr. Blyth in the year 1880 ran the Defiance from London to Brighton, he took the long route through Sevenoaks, Tunbridge Wells and Lewes. Four horses were used and between Tunbridge Wells and Lewes five horses, the three leaders abreast.[7] Again in 1880 Mr. Welling ran a horsed coach from London to Tunbridge Wells via Sevenoaks.

1843 Sevenoaks and Germany, unpaid letter from Dresden to Sevenoaks with standard charge of 10d (in black) for continental letters to be paid by the recipient (not a double charge).

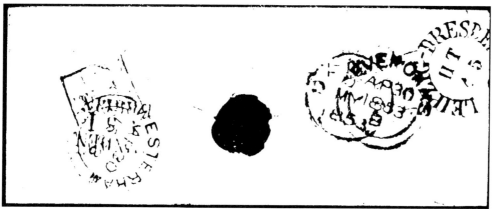

1853 Westerham via Sevenoaks to Dresden. Prepaid 4 x 2d = 8d.

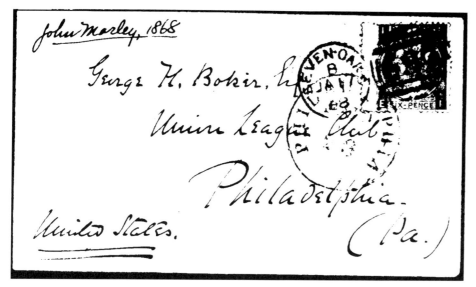

1868 Cancelled Sevenoaks Round Duplex 6d to Philadelphia USA.

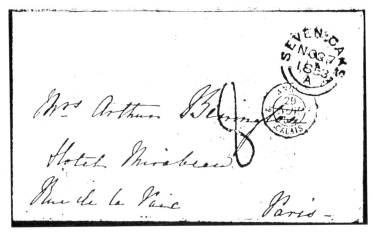

1853 Unpaid letter Sevenoaks to Paris 8d. Journeyed Sevenoaks to Tonbridge by omnibus, put onto the Continental Mail Train at Tonbridge to Dover where sorted and the '8' applied. Crossed Dover to Calais then on to Paris by train.

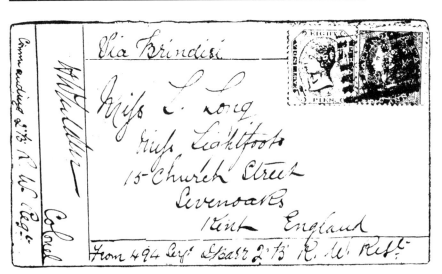

1881 Letter sent by Sergeant in India to Sevenoaks at private soldier's concession rate of 1½ annas. To obtain this rate the letter had to be signed by the Colonel of the Regiment. Stamps had date of posting inked in to prevent removal prior to being postmarked.

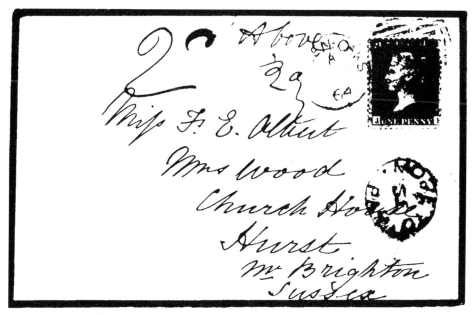

1864 Letter above ½ oz but under 1oz so charged double the extra 1d needed, ie 2d to pay. After 9 Feb 1859 inland letters had to be prepaid with adhesive stamps (at least partly). Unstamped letters were to be returned to the recipient.

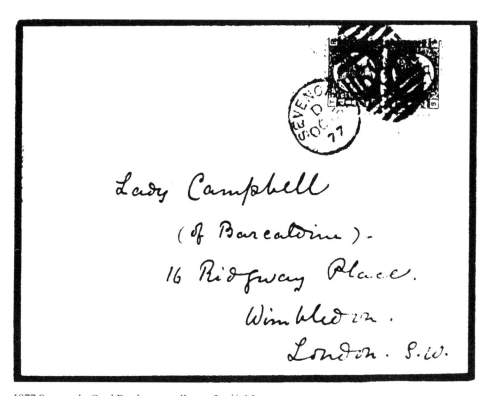

1877 Sevenoaks Oval Duplex canceller on 2 x ½ d for penny rate.

South Eastern Travelling Post Office (SETPO)

Originally the Railway Post Office ran through Redhill, Edenbridge and Tonbridge to Dover, but as soon as the line through Sevenoaks was in 1869 contracted for postal business the route through Sevenoaks was taken until the end of 1919. Pickup Apparatus was in use at Sevenoaks until July 1904 when apparatus working stopped and the UP Night left five minutes earlier; with a two minute stop at Sevenoaks, the other three minutes were absorbed in slowing down and starting up again.

In 1903 working via Sevenoaks the timetable was –

Cannon Street	*10pm (Sun 9.37pm)*	*3.51am*
Dover	*12.30am*	*1.45am*

By 1917 the Schedule for the Dover Night Mail was –

	Depart Daily	Depart Sunday	Arrive
Cannon Street	*10.00pm*	*9.26pm*	*3.51am (Sun 3.53)*
London Bridge	*10.03 (5min stop)*	*9.29 (3min stop)*	*-*
New Cross	*- -*	*9.38 (1min)*	*-*
Hither Green	*- -*	*9.44 (1min)*	*-*
Grove Park	*- -*	*9.50 (1min)*	*-*
Elmstead Woods	*- -*	*9.55 (1min)*	*-*
Chislehurst	*10.26 (1min)*	*10.00 (1min)*	*3.35 (1min) Sun only*
Orpington	*10.32 (1min)*	*10.07 (1min)*	*-*
Knockholt	*-*	*10.15 (2min)*	*-*
SEVENOAKS	*10.48 (2min)*	*10.25 (2min)*	*3.17 (2min)*
Tonbridge	*11.01 (3min)*	*10.39 (5min)*	*3.07 (5min)*
Staplehurst	*11.22 (3min)*	*11.00 (2min)*	*2.42 (1min)*
Ashford	*11.44 (5min)*	*11.23 (5min)*	*2.20 (3min)*
Shorncliffe	*12.11 (3min)*	*11.48 (1min)*	*-*
Folkestone	*12.20 (4min)*	*11.53 (2min)*	*1.55 (4min)*
Dover	*12.30am*	*12.05am*	*1.45am*

One letter sorting carriage and as many vans as required for stowing letter bags.[8]

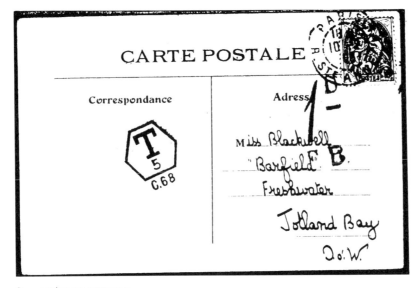

See caption on next page.

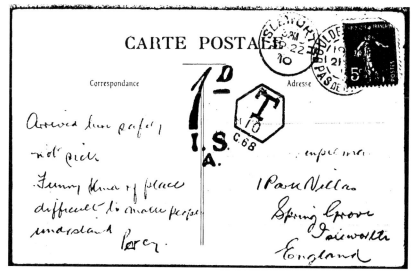

Postage due mark 'C68' applied to underpaid continental mail during sorting on the mail trains. 1905 and 1910.

In addition to South Eastern RPO and TPO postmarks the railway sorting carriages also used the taxing mark 'C68' (night) and 'C72' (day) which may be found on unpaid and underpaid letters and postcards from the Continent.

In January 1916 there had been a landslide onto the track between Folkestone and Dover, so the train had to finish at Folkestone. This was repaired by October 1919 and the train ran through to Dover again.

From 1 January 1920 the Up Night ran via Redhill; the Down Mail also ran through Sevenoaks on Sunday night only until 7th June 1929. Cannon Street was used.

From mid-1929 SETPO ran through Redhill, not Sevenoaks. With a suspension during the war years, 1940-1946, the service finally ceased at the end of February 1977.

Summarising, the SETPO route was through Sevenoaks
1869 - 1919
1920 - 1929 (Sun Down Train)

How the Mail came in – a Synopsis

Railway via Tunbridge Station
Railway completed 1841/2 to Tunbridge
Mail Contract commenced night of May 9/10 1844
Mail brought up to Sevenoaks by mailcart, later by 1860 by omnibus.
Edenbridge becomes a Post Town 1 September 1848 and serviced Westerham 1857 to 1896

Railway to Sevenoaks, St. Johns
Railway completed 1862
Mail Contract Daymail only 21 Feb 1866 probably till 1875

Railway to Sevenoaks Tubs Hill
Railway completed 1868
Mail Contract Nightmail 1 August 1869, Daymail probably 1875.

Locomotives on Roads

What meanwhile has been happening to locomotives on roads? The early experiments with steam on roads faded out with the difficulties of operation and high tolls producing bankruptcies. Yet it was recognised that locomotives would eventually come on roads and when the second phase started it was controlled.[9]

The 1861 Act (24, 25 Vict c70) concerning the Use of Locomotives on Turnpikes and other roads required two persons to be in charge of the vehicle and limited speed to 10 m.p.h. on the Highway, 5 m.p.h. in Towns. For Toll purposes 2 Tons of machine (unladen) represented 1 horse. Four years later and operational 1 September 1865 came a punitive act (28, 29 Vict c83). A third person was now necessary to operate the locomotive on the Highway and he had to walk at least 60 yards ahead with a red flag and assist other traffic to pass. Speed was limited to 4 m.p.h. and 2 m.p.h. in Towns with a weight restriction of 14 tons and 9 foot width maximum, thus effectively strangling the development of steam on roads, and this at a time when steam was developing mightily and, one might almost say, unchecked on rail. The 1878 Act abolished the red flag but still required that an attendant walk in front twenty yards ahead.

Light Locomotives (Motor Cars)   'Freedom' did not come until 14 November 1896, a Saturday, the date when the Act of 14 August 1896 (59, 60 Vict c36) came into effect. This Act created a new category of vehicle, a 'light locomotive' under 3 tons to be treated as 'a carriage' and allowed to proceed at 14 m.p.h. with of course no man in front. The Act had come about after pressure from drivers already experienced on the continent where such freedom was already extant and helped by such individuals as Sir David Salomons well to the fore in promoting demonstrations of the new means of locomotion within his private grounds. A local man, Sir David Lionel Goldsmid-Stern-Salomons of Broomhill, Southborough, Kent, Baronet (1851-1925), had 62 early cars of 19 different makes in his garage and in addition the electrical one he made himself in 1874. In 1895 he formed the Self Propelled Traffic Association, the first motoring organisation in Britain, which later merged with the Automobile Club of Great Britain and Ireland and in 1907 became the Royal Automobile Club. That same year, 1895, he organised the Horseless Carriage Exhibition in Tunbridge Wells, the first Motor Show in the Country.[10]

On the day the 1896 Act came into force a run from London to Brighton was organised by the Motor Car Club,[11] with many vehicles and experienced drivers coming over from the Continent specifically to take part.

The way was open for change; steamers, electrical and internal combustion engines took part in the early days. The 1898 Act relieved 'heavy locomotives' from the need to have a man in front. There had to be two to attend to the locomotive and an assistant who did not now need to walk in front and a further assistant if in addition to the water wagon more than three wagons were being towed.

The Various Propulsion Methods developed for Road Locomotives

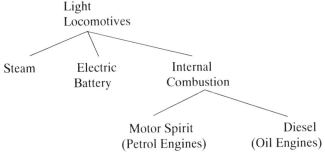

Petrol 'motors' eventually achieved ascendancy, and 'light locomotives' became 'motor cars'. The 1903 Motor Car Act, effective 1 Jan 1904, allowed speeds of 20 mph and brought in all the current requirement of car licences, driver licences which had to be produced on demand, number plates, trade plates and the need to stop after an accident.

Highway authorities began to put up signs, dangerous corner, etc. As to responsibility for the roads themselves, after the 1858 Local Government Act, the parishes within counties were in 1862 combined into Highway Districts and in 1888 under the new Local Government Act responsibility for main roads went to County Councils. Thus there were roads under the responsibility of County Councils, Town Councils and Rural District Councils.

The Post Office were not slow to adopt the new form of transport, not only for short range deliveries but also for such long run trips as the London - Hastings - St. Leonards parcel coach which was motorised about 1905.

The Local Situation 1839-1920

The great changes in the main distribution of mail into and out of the area have been shown; now to see the local effect.

Matters on the local ground did not alter magically with the coming of cheaper rates, the 4d Post in December 1839 when 4d became the maximum charge for a single letter, and subsequently with Uniform Penny Postage in January 1840. Existing *official* local delivery route charges were said to be subsumed in the penny charge, but these routes did not cover all areas and some local charges continued to exist for many years to come. Those householders not on a delivery route or just beyond the end of an agreed route still had to send in for their mail or make private arrangements with a neighbour or the postmaster himself to have letters sent out to them. It would be doubtful, for instance, that the Ide Hill local delivery charge disappeared at once with the coming of the 1d post. Where the date of an extension to a delivery route is known, then prior to that date private arrangements had to be made and most likely delivery charges paid. Some charges probably did not cease until after the turn of the century, though great effort was made to clear them in time for Queen Victoria's Diamond Jubilee.

Just what did happen during this early period of change is difficult to discover from official records. Freeling's hand-written minute books and supporting documentation (Post 40,42) come to an end with his death and contain very little detail after 1837/8. Post 35 and subsequently Post 38 continue, but only the supporting documentation of **national** importance has been kept; nearly all documentation of local importance has been destroyed. This principle has been adhered to so strictly that it must have been the basis of the comb through, possibly to obtain scrap paper in wartime. Printed reports and guidebooks mostly start their runs from 1853 or so, and even making a visit to libraries throughout London and the whole of Kent does not, surprisingly, produce a complete run of all possible items. And so for fifteen years when change was at its height records are sparse and patchy.

With the lower charges, the volume of traffic built up and so did the coverage of local areas; the network of routes expanded and in Sevenoaks expansion was still going on in 1922 although some of this expansion would relate to new house building. Officially, full delivery to the door of all houses was achieved by 1890, Queen Victoria's Diamond Jubilee, but it was probably nearer 97/98%.

This period was one of great expansion of small offices, the struggle was on to bring postal services within walking distance of every inhabitant of these islands. Even such places as Lundy Island in the Bristol Channel had its own Post Office, since closed.

Increased Services
Locally the developments split into two categories:-
    1 An intensification and upgrading of existing services
    2 The introduction of new types of services
  Thus there are the
    Opening of many new smaller offices
    Extension of delivery to whole new areas

Extension of Daymail (second) deliveries
Extension of delivery to single houses positioned at a distance
Extension of 3 days/week deliveries to 6 days/week and also Sundays
More postboxes for easier collection
Slits in front doors for easier delivery of prepaid mail
New services:-
Telegraphs, Telephones, Money Orders, Savings Banks, Insurance & Annuities, Parcel Post
And better facilities for Postmen:-
Shelter Huts, whilst waiting between deliveries
Bicycle posts where helpful
Sunday relief where Sunday working continued
Half-days off

Much of the detail relating to this expansion is shown in the Appendix under Village Headings.

Registration as it is known today was introduced on 6th January 1841, although it seems obvious that some early system must have operated and indeed some of the early Italian merchants' letters of the 1500's previously mentioned were 'Registered'.

In structure the biggest change was the designation in 1848 of Edenbridge as a post town and with the growth in volume of letters its subsequent taking over of the 'Westerham' group of offices. What was then left for Sevenoaks can be seen from the hand-written delivery sheet of 1864. In 1896 the Westerham group returned to Sevenoaks.

In 1855 the London Post merged in with the General Post and in 1857/8 London was split into ten Postal Districts classed as ten Post Towns. Once the system was established Sevenoaks (and Edenbridge in 1867 21 Dec)[12] had to make up bags for each separate London District. This overcame the bottleneck of all mail having to pass through one London office. They were also able to exchange mail with each other. In 1917 the ten postal districts were further split down by number, eg SW7.

Postcards were introduced in 1870, to be sent at a cheaper rate. They had strictly controlled limits of size. The service started with a maximum size of 5½ x 3½ ins and no minimum size.

In 1901 a minimum 4" x 2¾" was imposed with no change in the maximum and in 1925 the sizes allowed became 5⅞" x 4⅛" maximum, 4" x 2¾" minimum.

Reposting of full-rate letters where an addressee was not at home was allowed free if to another address within the same district. The position was changed as from 1st June 1892 when free reposting to all inland districts was allowed if carried out within 24 hours. Labels denoting postage due where the sender left that to the recipient to pay were introduced in 1914; twice the normal rate was again the charge.

1850 Changes often occur at the boundaries. Here Kingsdown is under Farningham which came under Dartford. Later Kingsdown was under Wrotham which came under Sevenoaks.

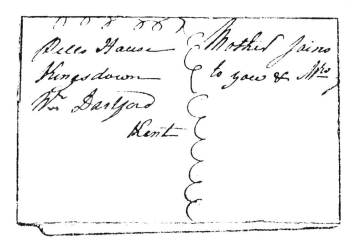

Inside address panel relating to envelope on opposite page showing Kingsdown near Dartford.

Expansion of Local Offices (Sevenoaks and Westerham)

Prior to 1840, there were 13 local offices. Between 1841 and 1920 as many as 27 new offices were opened, many of them small. Ten of these are now closed. That this was the main local expansion period is evidenced by the fact that in the sixty-five years from 1920 to 1985 only a further 7 new offices were opened and of these one is closed.

1841 Hever (to
     Edenbridge 1848)
1844 Plaxtol
1845 Ash 1980
1844 Knockholt
1845 Chiddingstone
1847 Borough Green
1850 Ide Hill
1857 Underriver 1944
1857 Weald
1870 Stone Street 1929

1871 Fairseat
1873 Godden Green 1934
1885 Ivy Hatch
1889 Dunton Green
1890 Kingsdown 1975
1890 Hodsall Street 1973
1891 Tatsfield
1891 Wrotham Heath
1892 Westerham Hill 1973
1897 Cudham tfr from Orpington
1897 Bessels Green 1899

1897 St. Mary's Platt 1989
1897 Stanstead
1898 Brasted Chart
1899 Biggin Hill
1902 Chevening 1946
1906 Toy's Hill 1973
1920 East Hill

and since then

1935 Knatt's Valley
1937 Badgers Mount
1939 Bessels Green
     reopened
1951 Berry's Green 1974

1959 Dynes Road Kemsing
1967 The Valley Biggin Hill
1973 Hever Road West Kingsdown

Postmasters, their Staff and the Location of the Post Office

Thomas Poulter (1837-1844) who at fifty-one years of age took over the Sevenoaks Main Office on Elizabeth Burrell's death in February 1837 was no stranger to Post Office activities. Born in Camberwell, his family had lived in Sevenoaks for many years, next to the Burrell's in Wheatsheaf Yard. As early as 1811 James Poulter rented property from Joseph Burrell[13] and no doubt at times young Poulter helped with some of the work or at least watched it closely.

Thomas Poulter's move from Wheatsheaf Yard to the High Street did not appear to be direct for in 1838[14] he occupied **two** fairly large rented houses in the Shambles area with an assessment of £11.5.- each (whereas a cottage normally was rated at about £3.15.- p.a.)

Rural Sub-Office Hodsall Street Pre-WW1, opened 1890 closed 1973. (Unknown)

Town Sub-Office. Vine PO c1910 in Mr J H Lorimer the Postmaster's shop with bicycle and delivery trailer painted 'The Vine Post Office Sevenoaks' outside. (J Salmon)

It would appear likely that one was for postal business and one for living in. Here he was for a few years before taking up premises in the High Street. By 1841 Poulter, his wife Jane and daughter Elizabeth lived in the High Street. His salary was still £50 p.a. plus the £6.10.- emoluments. But by 1843 just before his death, Thomas Poulter's salary had risen to £102 p.a. with his assistant, his daughter Elizabeth Poulter, on £35 per annum. His bond was £600.

A record of Thomas Poulter's staff remains in the 1841 Census. This shows the employees at the main office but does not include contractors or employees on the 'penny post' local network except to mention James Poulter whom one might surmise to be the Postmaster's younger boy learning the business and living in lodgings in Otford and who ten years later was back in Sevenoaks, married and living in the High Street as Postman and Tea Dealer.

Staff in 1841[15]

Thomas Poulter	55 Postmaster	M 1 child at home	High Street. Not born in Kent
William Nall	40 Postman	M 3 Children	Black Boy Lane. Not born in Kent
William Bennett	60 Postman	Widower	West Town
			(Black Boy Lane is now Bank Street and' The Black Boy Inn' changed to the 'Evergreen')

Poulter did not long survive the coming of mail by railway. He died in August 1844. Many changes occurred during his short seven year occupation of the post. There were rate changes, the 4d post followed by the 1d Universal Post, the fatal accident on Polhill, the move to the High Street where the office was to be located for the next fifty years or more, and greatest of all the cessation of the mailcoach and the regular arrival of the Sevenoaks mail from Tonbridge Railway station starting on 10th May 1844.

Before that last event, but perhaps in anticipation of it, for here there is the break between the old type 'horsing' postmaster based on an inn and the new style postmaster, on 7 July 1843[16] is seen '*Postmaster allowed to remove his office as recommended by the Surveyor*' '*Approved*'. Thus came the first of several moves in the High Street; further moves within the High Street occurred in 1857 and 1865.

Henry Morris (1844-1848) who had been an Assistant clerk in a Lawyers Office, took over as Postmaster in September 1844 probably occupying the same office in the High Street as Poulter. Morris remained Postmaster for four years only before his death. During his short time there were no further High Street moves and against the background of Railway development already described, he started to establish new village offices; Plaxtol, Ash, Knockholt, Chiddingstone and Borough Green were opened under his aegis.

In 1846 a further edition of the 'Instructions for the Guidance of Postmasters' was issued. Morris was instructed to open to the public between seven and eight in the morning, the exact time being agreed with the Surveyor of the district, and close at 10 pm - this, of course, was still at a time when there were no telegrams or telephone and letters were the only way of sending messages. No one was to be employed under 16 and an employee must first subscribe to the 'declaration' before starting work. Once in the service neither postmaster nor other employee may vote, nor need he serve as Mayor or in other public office, nor even serve on any Jury or Inquest or in the Militia.

During all this time, from the Burrells in the 1830s to the Hills in the 1850s, the required security bond remained constant at £600.

In 1847 an item of news about James Poulter the Otford postman was printed in the Maidstone Journal[17] relating how, when he was going back to his home near Hartsland '*he says he was attacked by two men who tried to get his watch*'. James Poulter was a large man, then about 26 and it was known that he often carried P.O. money on him. He fought back and took out his large deer knife and stabbed one of them in the shoulder. From the wound it ought to be easy to trace his assailants but so far they had not been.

The report ended by stating that a Correspondent, having considered all the details, remarked '*Master Poulter .... was dreaming at the time*'.

In 1848 the year of Henry Morris's death, Edenbridge being on the Railway line and so able to receive mailbags direct from London, became a Post Town in its own right and together with its village offices then Chiddingstone and Hever, left the 'Sevenoaks fold'.

Samuel Thomas Hills   December 1848 saw the arrival of Samuel Thomas Hills as postmaster, in his earlier years holding also the office of managing clerk at Austen and Holcroft solicitors and later being Secretary to the Sevenoaks Water Company and also in 1881 declaring an interest in the new local newspaper being started up, The Sevenoaks Chronicle. Together with his son, Frank, who succeeded him, the Hills dynasty lasted in office for sixty-one years. In 1848 when he took over, Samuel was forty years of age, he too had been born in Camberwell and was married with a young family of four; Agnes, who later taught music, Frank, who was to train as a telegraphist, Charles, one day to be a solicitor's clerk and Alfred the eldest.[18] His Penalty of Bond was then £600.

No mention is made of change in location of office when he took up the position, so once again the same premises were probably occupied. By this time also had come to live in the High Street a retired gentleman of over seventy, Thomas Hooker, with his two daughters, Hester and Agnes and grandson William. Hester soon became Sevenoaks' 'assistant to the Postmaster' and so served for well over thirty years, yet when she retired she was to be refused a pension.

It was during the Hills period that the main rural expansion took place. Early in 1848 just before Hills arrival, Edenbridge had become a post town in its own right. But that loss was soon offset. Twenty new offices were opened (of which eight are since closed) on the basis that *all places the letters for which exceed 100 per week are entitled to a receiving office and free delivery.* (June 1843)[19] and within the service he developed the main new ancillary services to become so well-known: Postal Orders (1881/5), money orders developed, telegraph (1870) and parcels (1883) became firmly established, together with the introduction of many pillar and wall letter-boxes.

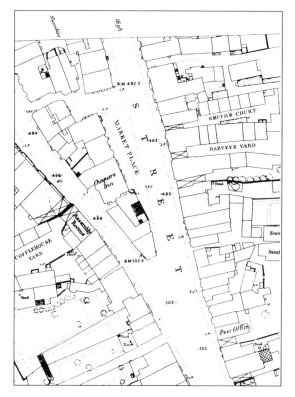

Left
Part of OS 10" map of Sevenoaks 1867 showing location of Post Office. (HMSO)

Opposite Page Above
Sevenoaks Main Post Office in the High Street about 1890. (Gordon Anckorn Colln)

Opposite Page Below
Entrance to Old Post Office Yard High Street with painted stripes across the entrance and contemporary mailvan by the Edwardian pillar box outside The Red House. Taken by Gordon Anckorn from the roof of the National Westminster Bank opposite during the 1950's after the PO had transferred to South Park. (Gordon Anckorn)

In 1850 the basis of opening a new office altered to

A post office established anywhere where it would pay its way

and in 1851 to

A Post Office opened where it would pay the messenger wages, counting ½d per letter and no more walking than 16 miles a day. [20]

Often this was every day including Sundays.

Local staff are shown in the **Census return of 1851**, with the description Postman well established

			Lives	Born
Samuel Thomas Hills	*43 Postmaster*	*M 4 Children*	*High Street*	*Camberwell*
Hester Hooker	*34 Asst to PM*	*S Lives with Father*	*High Street*	*Sevenoaks*
William Bennett	*70 Postman*	*Widower*	*West Town*	*Kemsing*
Jonathan Lee	*64 Postman*	*M*	*Brans Lane*	*Seal*
Thomas Longhurst	*53 Postman*	*M 2 Children*	*Taylors Cottages*	*Sevenoaks*
John Smeed	*21 Postman*	*S With family*	*Hoopers Yard*	*Sevenoaks*
Charles Stamford	*45 Post Office Keeper*			
	St. Johns Hill	*M 6 Children*	*St. Johns Hill*	*Newington Surrey*

In **1861** Samuel Hills and Hester Hooker are still there but the others have changed

George Heare	*39 Letter Carrier*	*M 4 Children*	*Tubbs Hill*	*Sevenoaks*
Thomas Clout	*57 Post Messenger*	*M 3 Children*	*Riverhead*	*Sevenoaks*
William Thompson	*54 P.O. Messenger*	*Live on own*	*Riverhead*	*Broughton N'hants*

Charles Stamford was still at St. Johns Hill.

Movement of Post Office in High Street   Then came a move along the High Street for a second time, recorded by the bald statement

10 July 1857 [Post 35 Vol 182 p427]

'Post Office, removal approved'

and this removal no doubt took place. Sevenoaks Preservation Society records give the location 1860 as *'where now stand Nos 60-62'*.[21]

The third and final move along the High Street took place in 1865, **after** the writing of Jane Edwards' Diary in 1863[22], and yet Hyde Turner,[23] as also Dr. Gordon Ward commenting on Jane Edwards' positioning of the Post Office in the High Street appear to relate their remarks to the post-1865 situation, as shown in the photograph and neither to have noticed that in the pre-1865 situation described by Jane Edwards the Post Office was possibly two shops along the road (south). But if this were so, the distance is not great.

The records of this final move in the High Street are

30 May 1865 [Post 35 Vol 141 Min 2668]

I submit that the Postmaster of Sevenoaks should, as proposed by Mr. Newman, be required to move to another house and to provide a really good office and in consideration of his so doing some addition should be made to his salary and allowance for assistance.

£102 to £110 (and not £120 as proposed by Mr. Newman)

Assistance from £25 to £40 (instead of £30 as proposed)

The increase that has taken place in the work of the Post Office at Sevenoaks since the Postmaster was appointed in 1849 would justify a far larger addition to the cost than that now proposed. 'Approved'.

Jas. Hy. Newman was S. Eastern District Surveyor stationed at Dorking for at least the years 1863-74.

Hester Hooker's contribution to the working of the office was apparently given full recognition, but

High Street Sub-PO c1900 with St Nicholas in background. Opposite Sevenoaks School. (Unknown)

High Street Sub-PO c1900 Close up.

little addition to the Post Master's salary, which was £102 twenty years earlier, is being proposed though the volume of traffic must have increased greatly. The office return of 1865 still showed S.T. Hills as '*He is a Solicitors' Clerk*'.[24] By 1869 this part of the return showed '*nil*'; it would appear that Mr. S. T. Hills retained his second position for twenty years and only gave it up when he attained 60 years of age.

The **1871 Census** showed S. T. Hills, Hester Hooker and Thomas Clout still working at the office, but changes in the others

				Born
Edward Hever	*Age 60 Postman*		*Oak Lane*	*Sevenoaks*
Richard Langridge	*21 Postman*	*Single*	*Riverhead*	*Riverhead*
Albert Bennett	*Postman*		*London Road*	*Sevenoaks*
John Albany	*40 Postmaster at St.Johns Hill and grocer*	*M 7 Children*		*Hoxton Middlesex*

and George Ashdown of Wrotham had taken over from George Bennett as Carrier and Mail Contractor.

As mentioned, Pickup Apparatus was introduced at Sevenoaks station about 1876 and this involved arranging special station duties that had to be done exactly to time.

Frank Hills   A few years later in June 1879, his father having died at 71, Frank Hills took over. *As he is qualified - and his appointment would seem to be acceptable to the inhabitants your Lordships will perhaps appoint him without notifying the vacancy and calling for Candidates in the usual course.*[25] This was approved by P. M. G. at Salary of £170 p.a. and he remained in charge for thirty years.

The First Crown Office in South Park 1907-1974. (Gordon Anckorn)

Perhaps the highlight of his career was the move in 1905 from the High Street to Sevenoaks' first purpose built Post Office, a specially planned new building on the north side of South Park opposite the present telephone exchange. This became a Class II Crown Office maintained by the Department (Class I were maintained by the Ministry of Works) and later Class I. It appeared to be part of the financing to sell and leaseback and in December 1906 this Sevenoaks office was rented at £275 p.a. from Mrs. Tosh of Solly Hill, Birmingham. Meanwhile the Telephone exchange remained on the top floor of the old building in the High Street in its first position at 58 High Street. This was the shop to the north of the entrance to Postman's Yard (shown in the photograph) wherein was also the mineral water works, R. White's. In **1881** the occupants in that part of High Street were

Red House

	No	52	*Surgeon Dentist/Pharmacist*
		54	*Edward Bevan. Carpenter and his two daughters with Hester Hooker, the P.O. Assistant, now 64, as a Lodger.*
		56	*James Nash, manager of the Mineral Water Works, his wife, two sons and one daughter*

Entrance to Postman's Yard

	58	*Frank Hills (33), his wife, Susannah, their children, Mable, Charles and Margaret and one domestic servant, a young girl.*

Subsequently there was a violin shop in the vacated Post Office ground floor and by 1905 the list of occupants had become[26]

Red House
Pain Chemist
Wickham, Sevenoaks Press
    Archway to R. White's Ginger Beer Factory
Franklin Philip, Violins. Telephone Exchange on top floor
Lowe, Baker
Horncastles
Rush
Butcher
    Passage to Slaughter House
Kent Messenger Office
Warren, Jeweller

At a later date when the lines had been relaid the telephone exchange moved to new premises in South Park. Later still No 58 High Street the old P.O. and the whole Post Office Yard complex disappeared when Waitrose's new store, opened in 1983, was built on the site. At that time the old Post Office Yard street nameplate was affixed to the wall by Waitrose's carpark.

Returning to the **1881 Census**, the employees showed a mixture of youth and old age:

William Bonner	17	*Postman.*	*Born in Sevenoaks and living with parents*
Frederick Law	17	*Postman.*	*Son of a Bootmaker of Bromley Marsh living with parents in Cleveland Place, St. Johns.*
Henry Reynolds		*P.O. Letter Carrier*	*Born Westerhan, living at 5 Cromwell Cottages Sevenoaks.*
William T. Reynolds	67	*Letter Carrier*	*Born Sevenoaks and living in Bradbourne Road, Sevenoaks.*
Charles Kingsland	18	*Civil Service Post Office*	*Born Sevenoaks and living at home with his parents in Cobden Road, St. Johns.*
and James Bradlaugh	59	*Postmaster*	*St Johns Hill, Born Essex*

Officially they were letter carriers not postmen until 1883 when parcels were introduced but this use of the word '*postman*' on an official document shows how the word was gaining currency.

For the first time too in 1881 the designation *P.O. Pensioner* also shows up:

William Herbert   73   Pensioned London Letter Carrier with his wife and daughter living in St. Johns.
Edward Hever   70   Post Office Pensioner. A widower living in Oak Lane Sevenoaks who in 1871 had
*   been shown as a Sevenoaks postman at the same address.*

Mr. Hever, according to his 1877 Pension Application, had been working as a Rural Messenger from Sevenoaks to Underriver on pay of 17/- a week, £37.16.1 a year. He had been taken on on 18th October 1858 nineteen years earlier, when 48 years of age and had had no absences from duty whatsoever according to the record (But does this statement really mean that if he had a bad cold and could not report for duty he always supplied and paid for himself a substitute who was a suitable person and who arrived in his place on time?). Hever had become ill at 67 and as he was over 60 and had an exemplary character and work reference was granted under the regulations which by 1877 had been somewhat extended to include lower-paid employees, a pension of 'half pay', 8s/6d a week. Being a widower he could probably support himself on this amount, £11 in today's money.

Late in 1884 the Postmaster General stayed at Ightham and special postal arrangements had to be made. The details of what arrangements were necessary have been lost in the mists of time, as all references have been destroyed. This was, however, a changeover year when Henry Fawcett, the blind PostMaster General (1880-84) gave way to George J. Shaw-Lefevre, later Lord Eversley (PMG 1884-5), in November 1884.

Postman outside 'Beechmont'. Uniform with single peak shako should date this photograph pre-1896, but the new issue appeared to come late to Sevenoaks. (Gordon Anckorn Colln)

Henry Fawcett had been blinded in a shooting incident when only 25 yet became a Cambridge University Professor at 32 and later a Liberal M.P. Under his aegis were introduced the Parcel Post, Postal Orders, the P.O. Savings Bank. He had the P.O. Vans painted a bright scarlet as well as introducing the slogan 'Post early for Christmas' when Christmas Cards were introduced in 1880.

Fawcett had been ill in 1882 with a cold, though both diptheria and typhoid were mentioned. He recovered well and for the next year or so carried on his busy life, lecturing at Cambridge and travelling to many places in Southern England on Postal duty which could well have included Ightham , though his biographer does not mention such a visit. In November 1884 Fawcett took ill again at Cambridge. Pleurisy developed and he died within the week at 54.[27] Lefevre, his deputy who previously had stood in for him when he was ill, took over the post.

In 1894 there were defalcations at Sevenoaks P.O. attributed to the first clerk who was reported as absconding with the office cash £348 and who was arrested and charged with embezzlement. The Postmaster was required to make good the loss but in 1895 was relieved of a portion of the amount.

About the same time there was a fire in the office.

With Frank Hills, who remember was trained as a telegraphist, comes the age of the professional service manager who has expertise in his equipment rather than a local person appointed for his local knowledge or inn keepers appointed for their ability to provide horses. From now on appointments are for this technical ability and managerial capability.

In 1.1.1899 the first clerk at Sevenoaks is shown as Thomas Pearch, age 31, whose first appointment had been as a clerk at Tonbridge office in 1885.

Sunday Working

In the absence of the general use of the telegraph until 1870 and of the widespread use of the telephone until about 1910, letters were the only form of communication for both private and business purposes and the amount of Sunday working must be viewed against this background, for it accounts for the pressure to retain Sunday working and Sunday deliveries even if the post offices themselves were to be shut to the public. Even Queen Victoria cautioned that stopping public means of communication entirely might cause individual hardship that outdid the general benefit occasioned by the reduction of Sunday duties.

Locally a first hint of this pressure can be seen in 1839 when the link between Kent and the Sussex Coast mail which had been established in 1805 with the Tunbridge Wells-East Grinstead connection was increasingly used at weekends. There then appeared in the Sevenoaks Almanack[28] '*Letters for West Sussex, Havant, Portsmouth and Southampton sent daily via Tunbridge Wells and on Saturday night all letters for the West of England are despatched by the same route*', thus keeping down the number of letters passing through London on a Sunday, although the mailcoach still went through to London on Sunday morning after leaving Sevenoaks at 3 am. For it was in London where Sunday working was most apparent and where agitation against it was strongest.

Agitation was also taking place in provincial cities for Post Offices to be shut on Sundays between 10 am and 5 pm with petitions being signed by businessmen. To shut between these times would still allow early incoming mail to be sorted and delivered and for outgoing mail to be handled in the evening; effectively the normal midday lull between delivery and collection would be extended to some seven hours.

By 1845 Sevenoaks Main Office was so closed between 10 am and 5 pm.[29] The Illustrated London News of 20th October 1849 reports an important meeting of Clergy who expressed concern over the new P.O. Regulations and the expected increase of [mail] traffic on Sundays. 1850 saw the official ending of Sunday working, or rather might it be better said the official ending to any further extension of the existing Sunday working and the start of an effort to curtail the large amount of Sunday duty that was being worked.

There are two main aspects to the situation:

i)The objection that an employee cannot attend divine service on a Sunday morning if he is on duty working at the time of the service regardless of time off in lieu, i.e. inability to attend the service is the key matter.

ii)Unrelieved seven day working that gradually wears down the constitution. Here the need is to work only six days and to have a 'Sunday Substitute', as long as the substitute is not already working six days elsewhere, would meet the case.

The National Campaign against Sunday Working attempted to cover both points and some say its weakness was that it did not distinguish clearly between the two objectives, also at first the concept of substitute working on a Sunday appeared unthought of, possibly because most available substitutes were already working six days elsewhere.

Sunday work affected differently:

a)   The Main Post Offices and the General Post coaches
b)   The Village offices and the rural letter carriers.

Rural Sunday Working   For example, a village rural office might open for a couple of hours early Sunday morning to sort mail then close so that the staff could go to church or chapel, then open again for an hour in the evening, yet the poor letter-carrier be plodding his round all Sunday long. Whilst doing his delivery he was also officially prevented from distributing leaflets[30] in official time presenting his case for a day off. Recipients of letters[31] who felt strongly about the situation were allowed to sign a request at the office that they required their mail **not** to be delivered to them on a Sunday. If they did so, they were not allowed to collect it themselves. On the Continent the matter became so heated that postage stamps were printed with an extra tab at the bottom 'This letter may be delivered on a Sunday'. If the sender objected he tore off the tab and the letter was held back.

Tramping eighteen or more miles a day in all weathers and to a time schedule eventually wore down the strongest constitution and many a letter carrier died in service. Though it must be said that with no pensions or Social Security people tended to work as long as they were able. The Sevenoaks Union Workhouse (now a hospital) still standing on the road to Ide Hill was not considered a viable alternative except as a last resort.

Sevenoaks 'Union' (of parishes) acting as a Local Authority covered Sevenoaks, Sundridge, Brasted, Westerham, Leigh, Penshurst, Chiddingstone, Cowden, Edenbridge, Hever, Kemsing, Otford, Shoreham, Halstead, Chevening. Although the Local Government Board was instituted in 1871, remnants of the Sevenoaks Union persisted until 1930 when the final Sevenoaks Union meeting was held.

Other parts of the postal district were in other unions. Knockholt, Cudham in Bromley Union; Ash, Kingsdown in Dartford Union; Tatsfield in Godstone Union; Boro Green, Ightham, Plaxtol, Stansted, Wrotham in Malling Union.

In one local walk in a nearby district, the evidence of seven day working appears clear:

15th Dec 1831 [Post 35]
East Grinstead - Tunbridge Wells 24 miles
'cannot do it without resting one day in 7 - so recommend a six day post'.
'Only to Groombridge then an auxiliary for 6 miles' so 18 miles for the main letter carrier, six the
auxiliary , 'and do daily'.   *Approved Richmond*

This example appears to relate to unrelieved seven day working, but it would not appear that use of the word 'daily' in the case of Sevenoaks relates to anything other than six day working of the local posts, in most cases six day working is actually stated.

In the rural posts the early private arrangements were for 3 days/week and 6 days/week working and the Wrotham Post up to 1840 distinctly refers to 6 day working both as a 5th clause post and later as a Penny Post. The Westerham route makes no mention, but there is no evidence in other supporting papers that the Westerham route up to 1840 incurred unrelieved seven-day working. For rural posts in general where 7 day posts had been instituted, the rules in 1867 were that the Rural Postman could only be relieved from his Sunday walk on the petition of the persons in his district who received six-sevenths of the Sunday Correspondence, the proportion being reduced to two-thirds in 1894. Unfortunately the number of letters of the period still extant are far too few to allow their dates to build up a case.

After 1840 there is evidence, shown under villages in the Appendix, of Sunday deliveries but in most cases the arrangements for relief are also mentioned. By 1890, where specific relief was not obtaining, there was a general alternate Sunday relief and in 1894 a half holiday for all postmen on Wednesdays when one afternoon delivery was suspended.

Main Route Seven Day Working   Sevenoaks Main Office does not appear to come off too badly. On the **General Post** route there was seven-day working, from London to Tunbridge Wells 'during the season'. This of course meant manning the Sevenoaks office seven days a week. Such seasonal seven day working appeared to continue for only a few years. Sprang in 1780 mentions the winter three day working and one of these three days was a Sunday. The 1815 Hastings Guide shows only six day working so obviously there was no Sunday mailcart between Tunbridge Wells and Hastings. But this does not mean there was no Sunday working from London to Sevenoaks and Tunbridge Wells. Brett in 1836-8 refers to seven day working at Hastings, the end of the route. Many statistics gathered locally by the surveyor show only for six successive days and Sunday is not one of these; Monday is double in all cases. Perhaps Brett is right and this is a piece of surveyor's window-dressing.

The campaign was intense in London more so than in the provinces and at times weekend coach schedules were arranged to work as far as could be and keep a low profile in London. In any case the posts and mailcoaches arrived early morning and left at night so they were not visible on the streets at the time people were going to church. In June 1850 Lord Ashley carried a resolution forbidding the Sunday delivery of letters. Queen Victoria felt that having no communication available could cause hardship to private persons and she was not in favour of the vote *but would not withhold her consent to a compliance.* A committee of inquiry was appointed and reported against the proposed change which was then abandoned. Nevertheless the P.O. took steps to cut down on Sunday working and began to give relief where possible. The 1850 Report following shows relief given and obviously there must have been Sunday working in the first place to give relief from.[32]

1850 Sunday Labour in the Post Office. Relief given

Main Offices	*Sevenoaks*	*Tonbridge*	*Tunbridge Wells*
Relief from Money Order Business			
commencing 7 Jan 1849	*4 hrs*	*2 hrs*	*3 hrs*
Hours between 7 am & 10 pm during which			
the office was closed on the Sunday			
previous to 28 Oct 1849	*7*	*7*	*7*
ditto 28 Oct 1849 to 6 Jan 1850	*7*	*7*	*7*
ditto since 13 Jan 1850	*12*	*12*	*12*
Number of deliveries discontinued by			
Letter Carriers on the Sunday at			
the Post Town	*-*	*-*	*-*
Postmasters Clerks and others engaged in			
the office	*1*	*2*	*3*
Average relief in hours to each	*2½*	*2½*	*2½*
Letter Carriers exclusive of Rural Post			
Messengers	*-*	*2*	*3*
Average relief in hours to each	*-*	*-*	*-*
Rural Area			
Sub-Posts and Rural receiving offices			
Number of persons employed exclusive			
of Rural Post Messengers	*15*	*6*	*8*
Average Relief to each	*7*	*10½*	*8*
Total Personal Relief in Hours	*107½*	*68*	*71½*

No mention here of any relief to the rural letter carriers which could be said to support the thesis that both routes, Westerham and Wrotham, had six-day working from the start.

Later came the concept that there could be relief. At first this was for alternate Sundays only.

Nationally the situation developed to -

1867 25,902 employees of whom 80%, that is 20,961, worked on Sundays.

1894 136,447 employees of whom 30%, that is 41,274, worked on Sundays.

Was this success? The percentage working on Sunday has more than halved, but the actual numbers denied their Sunday has doubled, and the Lord's Rest Day Society was still campaigning strongly in 1907.

From these efforts came the limiting of the opening of the Sevenoaks main office to three hours on a Sunday from 7 to 10 am, as the evening opening was curtailed. Morning opening continued until 1959.

By 1908 in Sevenoaks, Town postmen had a Sunday duty of 10½ hours a fortnight and Boy Messengers a Sunday Duty of 1½ hours. At Westerham there was already an allowance to the Office for relief to Town Postmen for Sunday duty. In 1921 Sunday Duty was abolished.

The 1911 Instructions laid down that a Surveyor or Independant Postmaster might abolish but not initiate Sunday Services in Town Districts, subject to satisfactory evidence of the wishes of the inhabitants supported by a resolution of the Local Authority.

Conditions of Service

This work has concentrated mainly on the local operational aspects of the postal service. Conditions of Service do affect operations, but 'conditions' is a wide ranging heading and only some aspects can be brought to consideration here.

Postmasters' Pensions   Postmasters and Sub-postmasters appointed on or before the Superannuation Act of 19 April 1859 who had been earning £120 or more per annum were recommended for pension whether or not they carried on another trade.[33] Samuel Hills was on only £102 at the time, so he and for that matter all the other Sevenoaks Sub-postmasters, were on too low a point on the scale to qualify. When Samuel Hills salary was increased in 1865, notice that it was limited to £110 and not the recommended £120 which would have carried an automatic recommendation for a pension. No doubt this was why Samuel did not retire, but continued his Post Office occupation until his death in 1879 at 71 years of age, although his son Frank was well-trained and ready to take over at any time.

In 1871 the rules were tightened[34] and those appointed Postmaster from outside the department could not obtain a pension unless they had a Civil Service Certificate and this they could not obtain if they had another trade or occupation and did not give the whole of their time to the duty of postmaster. Pension availability was being extended to lower salaries and as Samuel Hills had given up his solicitors clerk work by 60, he might have qualified for a pension but it would at most have been 'half pay'.

Job Restrictions on Postmasters   In 1860 the Prohibition on Postmasters being Newsagents was rescinded. In 1885[35] Postmasters and all Post Office servants were prohibited from being appointed Collectors of Parish, Water or other Rates, Vaccination Officers or School Attendance Officers. And a circular of 1893[36] prohibited postmasters and sub-postmasters from undertaking as agent or principal any Banking, Life Insurance, Money Lending business or Building Society business. The Post Office itself was beginning to enter some of these fields, some successfully, others such as Life Insurance and Annuities less so.

Appointments by Postmasters   'Patronage' came to be abandoned in the selection of Letter Carriers about 1855 and in a P.O. Circular of 1859 Postmasters were entrusted with appointing their own Letter Carriers where wages were less than 10/- a week, his Lordship the PMG reserving to himself the appointment of Messengers with weekly wages above that sum as they were required to pass an examination of the Civil Service Commission and receive a certificate of qualification. New entrants to the appointment of Clerk or Letter Carrier who hitherto had to be between 17 and 28, now had to be under

Christmas Cards started in 1880. This one sent by PO staff in 1887 evocative of an earlier era recalls the mailcart deliveries of the early 1800's that went forward whatever the elements. (Raphael Tuck & Sons/Fine Art Graphics Bedford. PO Archives Colln)

24, in good health and the Letter Carriers at least 5ft. 3ins. But this top limit of 24 could be extended to 40 for applicants who had previous service, civil or military, and were in receipt of a pension from the Crown. A much centrally controlled situation compared with the Burrell era of fifty years or less ago. The contents of the 1874 exam which was non-competitive was laid down -

> **Postmaster** *(21-50): Clerks (16-20); Boy Clerks (14-16)*
> > *Handwriting, writing from dictation, elementary arithmetic*
>
> **Sorters** *(16-30); Boy Sorters (14-16); Letter Carriers (16-30) Rural Post Messengers (16-35);*
> **Porters and Watchmen** *(16-35) with some grades extended to 45 if receiving a Crown Pension.*
> > *Writing tolerably a few lines, reading, addition*
>
> (Somewhat similar, but modern, tests are given to postmen and postal cadet entrants today)
>
> **Telegraph Learners** *(14-18)*
> > *More detailed examination of the above subjects, Geography*
> > *Medical examination with special reference to eyesight[37]*

Establishment   During this expansion period the movement was
  i) to convert 'allowances' to Auxiliary Rural Postmen ('Auxiliary' meant an established post with less than eight hours work a day, i.e. part-time, but nevertheless pensionable).
  ii) to convert auxiliary posts where possible to established Rural Posts which were full-time.
  1881 Reclassification of indoor establishment at Sevenoaks.
  1885 Boy Messengers engaged
  1885 Parcel Post delivery allowance converted to Auxiliary Postmen's wages.
  1889 Postman Force increased.
  1889 Additional Town Postmen.

Numbers employed at Sevenoaks [38]

	1897				1899		
	M	F			M	F	
Sevenoaks Head Office	40	6			45	7	
Town Sub-offices	4	5			4	4	
Other Sub-offices	91	31			107	22	
	135	+ 42			156	+ 33	
Overall Total			177				189
Unestablished	69	32	101		77	24	101
Established	66	10	76		79	9	88
Established % of Total	49%	31%	43%		51%	27%	46%

The full-time established posts show as a rather small fraction of the whole, showing the difficulty of organising full eight hour shifts in an occupation subject to peaks and troughs of activity.

Pay   Rural Letter Carriers by 1883 were on a flat rate of 16/- a week. They normally walked 16 miles a day with a starting out load of 30 to 35 lbs. They often provided their own horse and cart or a pony only on hilly routes for which they received an allowance for keep. Sometimes help was given with a loan for the original purchase. Bicycles began to replace horses about 1903; the daily distances became 26 to 28 miles if the roads were good and the load increased to 50 lbs. By 1908 the pay of a Rural Postman on maximum was 21/- a week, probably with a bicycle allowance of 1/- a week.

In the 8th July 1908 List of Provincial Offices Sevenoaks comes under Class III for Rates of Pay, with maximum rates for
Sorting Clerks & Telephonists: 48/- a week Male   32/- Female
Postmen: 25/- a week

Westerham was Class IV with a maximum outdoor rate for Postmen of 23/-
Edenbridge was Class V with indoor rates of 40/- and 28/-; 21/- for postmen.
     By 1920 the 1st January Revision gave
Sevenoaks now Class II   Males 17/- to 55/- a week; Females 17/- to 37/-
Westerham S.O. now Class III M 16/- to 49/- a week; Females 16/- to 34/-[39]

Pay in relation to available accommodation   In Sevenoaks there had always been a limited number of small housing units in the Shambles area and in the courts and alleys off the High Street. These were gradually rebuilt offering better but more expensive accommodation. From 1870 on, when the large estates were released for building, it was quite usual for a clause to be inserted in the agreement stopping builders from providing smaller houses for tradesmen; only large houses were to be built on the land released. Many letters were written to local newspapers at the time such as The South Eastern Gazette pointing out that Sevenoaks was creating its own problem about services, as many persons working in the town would not be able to afford to live in it and would have to travel in from a distance. This was being pointed out in the 1870's.

Sickness and Leave   Sickness half-pay was organised in 1872. Previously to that the man off-duty was expected to arrange and pay for his own substitute making the best private arrangement he could, perhaps being able to retain only a third or a quarter of his usual pay but the arrangement was not complicated by Income Tax. Entitlement to Annual leave was recast as from January 1887 and in 1890 Compulsory Retirement at 65 was brought in, or if one's Head of Department called for it, at 60.
     Medical Officers were appointed the same year. The first name to appear in the Sevenoaks records is that of Dr. O. Stedman in 1890 and three years later Mr.(?) O. D. Marriott. In 1904 when the area was extended, Dr. F. Osmond was appointed in addition. Another three years later Dr. P. A. Mansfield was associated as Medical Officer with Dr. Marriott. Dr. Mansfield assumed full duties in Sevenoaks in 1911. He served with the Forces and in 1918 is shown on the Post Office Roll of Honour in the main Sevenoaks Post Office.
     The outlying districts had separate Medical Officer appointments by the early 1900s: J. Cunningham, Boro Green; H. H. Dunmere, Brasted Cudham Knockholt; J. Sterry, Riverhead Chipstead Dunton Green; H. S. Desprez, Shoreham Halstead Kemsing; A. Maude, Westerham Tatsfield; A. A. Lipscomb, Wrotham Ash, W. L. Hubbard, Edenbridge, W. C. Woods, Bough Beech. The list of qualifications of these doctors is so great, the writer trusts he may be excused from detailing them here.[40]

Some Attacks and Mishaps   In 1883 a burglary is recorded at Upper St. John's Hill and the following year some boys were convicted of throwing burning matches into a letterbox. A more serious event occurred in 1885, when Driver Cook was attacked whilst driving the mailcart at Seal Chart. His assailant was fined. In 1888 a dog bit F. Whitehead, Rural Postman; and again in 1908 Thomas Johnson, Rural Auxiliary, was bitten by a dog but his claim for compensation was not allowed. In 1889 the Ightham postman was sick and there was much delay of letters.

Shelter Huts   Having completed a morning delivery/collection rural postmen often had several hours to put in before the evening part of their split shift commenced. The lucky ones had paid work to do at the local office; others found paid local work such as shoe repairing and others just had to sit out the wait. These last needed somewhere to go and some protection from the elements. Shelter huts were an answer where other already-existing accommodation could not be hired. In 1895 Huts to accommodate three Rural Postmen were erected in the Cudham-Biggin Hill area and 1904 Sundridge and Ide Hill were given shelter huts and the one at Weald was removed to the village green.

Clothing   Whilst Mailguards, some mailcart drivers and London Letter Carriers had some uniform from 1793 on, it was 1856 before uniform was worn in the provinces, at first in the big towns. By 1859 this facility was extended first to towns that had as few as four letter carriers including auxiliaries and very shortly afterwards to all.

Sevenoaks could well have had uniform by 1860 when the issue was a scarlet coat but the next year, 1861, this style was replaced with a blue coat with scarlet stand-up collar and cuffs and scarlet piping, blue winter trousers with a broad scarlet stripe and summer trousers in grey with a similar stripe. The records simply call the colour blue but it is thought to be dark or navy blue and not the sky blue of the early London Letter Carriers. In 1872 uniform was extended to Rural Letter Carriers both established and auxiliaries. Uniform was now becoming thought of as part of wages. The Town Letter Carriers had both Summer suits and Winter suits. Boy Messengers for Telegrams, etc. when the grade was first commenced in 1870 also had a uniform as some of the private companies taken over already provided it.

The early headgear was the single-peaked shako but this let water down the back of the neck and as a postman cannot stop his walk for a little rain, the double peaked, front and rear, shako introduced in 1896 was warmly received but it was not immediately issued in the provinces as Sevenoaks photographs of 1910 and later show. That same year there was an order to say '*Postmen may wear white straw hats and a black band in hot weather*'.[41] The period set great store by uniform and the wearing of same.

In 1910 a complete overhaul of uniform took place. Gone was the military-style tunic. The summer civilian 'lounge suit' style was retained all year, but still blue with red piping. The Local Post Office Archive Books show issue of the following items in 1917 -

Tunic, Blouse or Coat	Leggings or Gaiters	Apron
Waistcoat	Belt	Lamp
Trousers or Knickers	Pouch	Plate, Knife and Fork
Cap or Shako	Boots	
Overcoat	Knee-Guards	
Waterproof Cape	Puttees	

Knickerbockers and puttees were issued for those on cycle duty but these were not popular; puttees take an abominably long time to wind on straight, and were withdrawn in 1920. The 1915 uniform issued to postwomen in wartime included a blue cap or blue straw hat. The blue 'girl guide' felt hat came next.

Good Conduct Stripes   These bars, up to six in all, were awarded and worn on the lefthand side of the tunic for the forty two years from 1872 in London, 1882 in the Provinces until 1914. They were introduced for regularity, diligence and fidelity in performance of duty, carried 6d per week per stripe and could be lost. It took at least 10 years to gain the first, 15 years to gain two and 20 years to gain three. In 1874 the money attached to gaining them was raised to 1/- per stripe and it was emphasised that the gaining of the them was not automatic but that there was an element of selection. In 1882 when the system was extended to the whole of the country their gaining was to be based on certainty of acquisition after the requisite number of years service and the Treasury who had to foot the bill insisted on an element of superiority (seniority).

In 1897 the number was increased to a maximum of six after 30 years and they were considered to be good conduct stripes. The system ended in 1914 with the allowances being incorporated into the pay scale. The system was always contentious as to the exact meaning to be attached to the award, long service or faithful service and as to whether the stripes did in fact denote superiority in the service. Yet the scheme appeared to satisfy some basic need for recognition of good work done and echoes of it may be found in the current 'safe driving' awards often formally presented by the Chairman of the Sevenoaks Urban District Council.

Opposite: **Uniform** *- these may not be local personnel*
a) 1910 style uniform with double-peaked shako. b) 1910 style uniform worn with puttees for cycle duty. c) Post-woman's uniform worn with 'girl guide' hat, d) Boy Messenger in uniform c1910. This uniform with stand-up collar and single peaked cap is based on the earlier postman's uniform (All unknown photographers)

a

b

c

d

Sevenoaks Post Office Staff 1910. (Sevenoaks PO Official Photo with permission)
T E Miles, Head Postmaster.

Unions   A regulation of 1866 forbade postal workers to meet outside the Post Office for discussion of official questions. This prohibition somewhat inhibited the formation of unions and in the early 1880's the Letter Carriers aired their disaffection through the medium of petitions. Wages improved and some provision was made for annual holidays. With the introduction of parcel post their work became more difficult and a Postman's Association was formed later in the 1880's. In 1890 hundreds of postmen were sacked or suspended for trying to set up a postman's union and striking.

Meanwhile the Telegraphists struck in 1871 and their leaders were 'exiled' to other offices. In 1897 there was a Deputation of Provincial telegraphists. The PMG of 1905-1910 Sidney Buxton listened to the unions and in effect gave them official recognition.

In 1920 the various sectional unions united together to form the Union of Post Office Workers, and in 1980 this same union changed its name to The Union of Communication Workers. Unions, of course, as well as being involved with pay and conditions treat with management over changes in methods of operation.[42]

Sub-postmasters are not employees but enter into a contract with the Post Office. They have different pressures on them, their work being undertaken generally in a shop carrying on some completely different but allied trade. They have their own quite separate 'Association of Sub-Postmasters' to look after their interests.

Little is recorded in public records concerning the early Union activities in Sevenoaks.

Whitley Councils   From 1918 it was decided to implement Whitleyism and the Post Office had a departmental council within the National Council responsible for the Civil Service. Arrangements ceased in 1928 but restarted in 1932.

Social Clubs   No doubt there were and still are several Post Office social clubs over the years but the one that has left its record is the Sevenoaks Postal Athletic Club of the 1909-1914 period that played Cricket on the Vine and Football. It was quite successful at these activities and it's Hon. Secretary, Mr. E. J. Boyce, reports that for Cricket 1909 saw eleven games played with seven wins: 1910 twelve games played again with seven wins and in 1913/14 eleven wins out of sixteen games played. The Clowns Comic Cricket match played on the Vine on 9th July 1913 and a concert afterwards raised £40 for the local Cottage Hospital, a tidy sum in those days. Fifteen wins were reported for Football with three games abandoned. No mention of how many lost nor how many played in total, presumably eighteen![43]

Delivery and Collection

Having completed their 'long-distance' journey and arrived at the post-town, the letters still have to be distributed to individual localities, in the United Kingdom these are the house doors and business premises.

The recipient is concerned with the frequency and the timings of these distributions and also of the charges that may be levied on him if the delivery charge is not already included in the general post charge, even if such charge is classed as a gratuity.

The November 1864 list shows the delivery of Sevenoaks during most of this period; from 1848 when Edenbridge was hived off as a separate post-town until 1895 when the Westerham area returned to Sevenoaks. But how many houses within this area received free delivery? The situation is complex.

Free Delivery after 1840   In the Town area there was free delivery after 1827. But how far did the Town boundary extend for postal purposes? The Court case requiring the post office to give free delivery also allowed them to set their own boundary within which it would be given. Exact details will never be known, for the delivery charge was now considered as a 'gratuity' given to the postman and never marked on the letter, not that it ever had been in the past. St. Johns was 'without' the Town boundary up to 1866 and after that 'within'; and there was another extension of the Town boundary a decade later. The decision on where to place the Town boundary was entirely the province of the Post Office as it still is today.

Free delivery took place in the villages and fifty yards either side of the route a walking letter carrier took to get there. Again what of the house seventy yards from the route or the one just fifty yards beyond the termination of the route? Officially a charge could be made, or shall it be said a gratuity could be demanded. Up to 1853 the letter carriers mixed up their official and unofficial duties, delivering on their official route then in the middle making a detour and charging. This practice delayed the completion of the main walk and spread some confusion into the public's mind and so the practice was stopped in 1853. Only letters on the official route could be delivered in official time. Others for which a charge could be made could only be delivered afterwards. This would probably not be convenient for the letter carrier who would probably be well away from the area when he had free time.[44]

Later when delivery arrangements had settled down some limited use of the former practice was allowed after 1862. As has already been mentioned the continued extension of official delivery routes can be read in the Appendix. As part of the drive for free delivery nationwide, reports were called for, for example the second report of the PMG in 1856. Sevenoaks is not one of the Towns in the sample but the Report does mention that in Tunbridge Wells 1,420 [more] letters per week are now delivered *for which it would formerly have been necessary [for the addressee] either to send a messenger [to collect] or to pay a gratuity to the postmaster[to deliver]*.[45]

Receptacles for Letters   After the first few returns, the reports of the PMG become entirely statistical and it is not possible to identify specific towns. Nevertheless these statistical reports contain interesting general information that can be extrapolated to apply to Sevenoaks and which otherwise would not be

Nov 1864 Delivery of Sevenoaks (*Handwritten*)

Ash S.O.
Ashgrove
  do Cottage
Ash North
Basted
Beeching Wood
Beechmont
Belle Vue
Bessels Green
Boro Green S.O.
Brasted
  do Place Lodge
do Court
  do Hill Farm
Broke House
Broughton House
Burlyns
Castle House
Chevening
  do Lane
  do Place
Chipstead S.O.
  do Lane
  do Place
Claygates Cross
Colegates
Coombe Bank
Cotmans Ash
Crouch Lower
Crowhurst
Dunton Green
Emmetts Lodge
Everlands
Fair Seat
Ford Hill
Fullers Street
Godden Green

Godden Farm
Great Comp
Greatness
Halfway House
Halstead S.O.
Hanging Bank
Heaversham
Hodsall Street
Hubbard Hill
Idehill S.O.
Ightham S.O.
Ivy Hatch
Kemsing S.O.
Kippington Lodge
Knockholt S.O.
  do Wood
Long Barn Farm
Lords Wood Farm
Lower Crouch
Lower St. Clere
Luffs Green
Manor Farm
Morants Court
Mount House
Neppicar
North Ash
Park Farm
Plaxtol S.O.
  do Villa
Pollacks Cottages
Portland Farm
Prestons
  do Farm
Ridley
Riverhead
Riverhill

Royal Oak
St. Johns Hill S.O.
St. Juliens
St. Mary's Platt
Scots Lodge
Seal S.O.
  do Chart
Sepham
Shelleys Farm
Shoreham S.O.
  do Castle
  do Place
Singles Cross
Stansted
Stone Street
Stonnings Farm
Sundridge
  do Hill Farm
Tebbs Farm
The Billet
  do Grove
  do Horseshoe
  do Harrow
  do Mill Crouch
Tubbs Hill
Twitton
Underriver
Upper St. Clere
Warren House
  do Farm
West Yoke
Woodlands
Wrotham S.O.
  do Heath
  do Nap
Yaldham East
Yaldham West

S.O's in 1864
  Ash
  Halstead
  Kemsing
  St. Johns Hill
  Wrotham

Boro' Green
Ide Hill
Knockholt
Seal

Chipstead
Ightham
Plaxtol
Shoreham

known at all. Such is the information in the 8th Report of the PMG. With the advent of adhesive stamps, there was now seldom need to collect postage money from the recipient but there was still need to ring the bell to have the door opened to hand in letters. A movement took place to encourage householders to make a slit in their front door through which letters might be pushed. Not the sort of thing a householder liked to do, for other things might be pushed through as well and anyway there was the draught to consider. But persuasion was afoot and change came, if slowly.

	Proportion of Receptacles for Letters to inhabited houses (whole of England and Wales)	Number of Letters per year to each inhabited house
1863	1 to 327	137
1864	1 to 321	144
1865	1 to 309	151
1866	1 to 300	157
1867	1 to 296	159
1868	-	168
1869	-	170

Progress was slow but steady. Now everyone has a letterbox in the front door, though many are very small and not the right height for easy access.

Although several persons would be living in each house, probably more than at present, the number of letters seems quite high.

The numbering of houses in Sevenoaks between 1871 and 1881 also helped to attain accuracy of delivery.

Mr Atkins at Otford Lane, Halstead. He and his horse-drawn mailcart served Sevenoaks to Halstead, Knockholt and Cudham from 1890 to 1922. (Gordon Anckorn Colln)

a

b

c

d

Above: **Edwardian VII Boxes.** *1904 Type C wallbox at Kippington. (left) Box at Fawke Common. (right)*
Opposite: **Four Victorian Wall Boxes.**
a 1861 Type. 2 Opposite Rose and Crown Dunton Green.
b 1871 Type. B Knockholt Village (West of church).
c 1871 Type. C Yaldham St Clere.
d 1881 Type. Largest wallbox. At entrance to Brewery, A25 west end of Westerham. (All AGD, taken 1983)

Letter Boxes   Similarly came a revolution in the collection of letters. Once it had become a requirement in 1853 to use stamps and it was no longer possible to hand in a single letter with the cash, the Treasury authorised Pillar Boxes in 1854. If one were willing to purchase a few of the new adhesive labels in advance to have by one against the writing of a letter, there was no need to walk all the way to the nearest Receiving House with letter and cash each time a letter was to be sent. With the label paying the postage the letter could be put into a letter box at any convenient time.

At first boxes were green: after 1875, or when the next repainting took place which could be up to 10 years later in the provinces, red. Apart from those located at Post Offices, Letter Boxes did not come quickly in Sevenoaks. In 1863 a wallbox near St. John's Station was refused and as late as 1869 no mention is made of letter boxes other than those at post offices. The first Town box mentioned is that at the bottom of Tubbs Hill by 1870, located near the new Railway Station and presumably green in colour. Three years later there are several more boxes at Upper Tubbs Hill, St. John's Hill, Vine and Common and by 1881 Granville Road is added making six in all. Each box makes considerable extra work and cost, for instead of the public walking to the office, a postman has to walk round all the boxes several times a day emptying them. Stoneville Park is added in 1882: by 1886 Bayham Road and Lower High Street have been added. In 1892 they were all repainted; definitely red by now.

The 1901 list in the Sevenoaks Telegraph Directory shows 19 Town boxes, with only one a free-standing 'pillar' box, others were wall boxes and 'lamp' boxes attached to lamp standards or telegraph

Pillar Boxes: Edwardian Pillar Box outside the Red House, New 'K2' box at Kemsing (AGD)

poles. Many boxes appear to be still there from their original placing. New ones were added and some of the older ones discontinued until in 1938 there were 31 Town boxes. Most famous of these is the Victorian 'Ludlow' box at High Street Office opposite Sevenoaks School; it is said to be one of only ten exactly similar now in use. The enamel plate has been changed from the original Victorian one, otherwise it is still as it was when placed there in 1898. An example of interesting street furniture is the row of seven free-standing pillar boxes down the High Street, starting with the old King Edward VII box at Knocker & Fosketts outside the Red House, then at Market Place in the High Street, besides Tesco's opposite Blighs, in Pembroke Road at John Colliers by the traffic lights, at Upper St. Johns outside the Post Office and finally at St. Johns similarly located. There are other pillar boxes but mostly wall boxes and lamp boxes are used.

In the villages can be seen many different examples of 'Ludlow' boxes with their various types of enamel plates at post offices including Stone Street now closed (see photos). Rural boxes of note are the lamp box built into the wall at Ightham Mote, the large type box let into the wall at Westerham Brewery, the roof tiled box at Heaverham next the St. Clere estate and oldest of all the 1861 type wallboxes at Dunton Green opposite the Rose and Crown with a similar one at Chevening. A most recent 'vandal-proof' K2 type is at Kemsing. At Cowden Pound an old box has an internal flap to keep out rain.

The Timing of Deliveries and Collections[46]

Town Town letter deliveries in Sevenoaks in 1891 were three, commencing at 7 am, 11 am and 6 pm with one only on Sundays at 7 am, timed to finish before 10 am. By 1901 the Town had four deliveries,

*Opposite: **Four 'Ludlow' type Posting Boxes in 1983** (All AGD)*
Top left: High Street Sevenoaks. Top right: London Road Sevenoaks. Bottom left: Stone Street. Bottom right: Halstead.

at 7 am, 10.30 am, 4pm and 7.30 pm, with the Main Post Office open from 7.30 am to 10 pm, particularly for telegraph business. Remember this was still a time when telephones were not generally available. Collections from letterboxes were at least three times a day, sometimes four.

Rural   At first one 'daily' delivery was given, arriving in the village early, before 8 am. The lists opposite show the effect of boundary changes and the increase in number of places delivered to and intensity of delivery.

Letters received in the villages had to be checked and sorted before delivery commenced.

A place such as Ash not shown separately in 1862 would have its mail taken daily to Wrotham and delivered on from there.

1902 Delivery Times   By 1902 deliveries were more frequent than one per day. The times shown are those from Sevenoaks Main Office. Before a letter was actually delivered there would be the journey time to the village and the time within the delivery postman's round.

Leaving Sevenoaks at:-

First despatches were made to Villages between 0455 and 0600.

0455	Wrotham, Borough Green, Ash, Fairseat, Hodsall Street, Stansted.
	Seal, Ightham, St. Mary Platt, Wrotham.
	Chipstead, Sundridge, Ide Hill, Brasted, Westerham, Westerham Hill, Tatsfield.
0500	Riverhead, Halstead, Knockholt.
0545	Kemsing, Kingsdown, Stone Street, Ivy Hatch.
0555	Dunton Green, Cudham.
0600	Godden Green, Underriver, Otford, Shoreham.
0915	Riverhead, Chipstead, Sundridge, Brasted, Cudham, Dunton Green, Knockholt, Halstead.
1025	Seal, Ightham, Kemsing, Kingsdown, Stone Street, Ivy Hatch, Plaxtol, Weald, Godden Green, Underriver, Shoreham, Otford.
1130	Ide Hill
1525	Westerham, Westerham Hill.
1540	Borough Green, Wrotham, Wrotham Heath.
1600	Seal, Ightham, Shoreham, Plaxtol, Weald, Chipstead, Riverhead, Dunton Green, Brasted.
1925	Godden Green

Ightham, Seal and Shoreham; Riverhead, Dunton Green, Chipstead and Brasted, also Godden Green, all received three deliveries a day. Most other villages received two deliveries except the northern ones beyond Wrotham which had to make do with a single daily delivery.

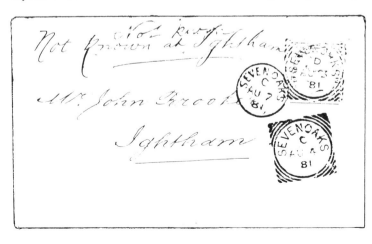

*1881 Sevenoaks Square
Circle Postmark, only in use
for a few years.*

1840

Daily to
Shoreham R.H.
Otford R.H.
Halstead R.H.
Knockholt
Chipstead R.H.
Sundridge R.H.
Brasted R.H.
Westerham R.H.
Edenbridge R.H.
Hever R.H. (to 1841)
Chiddingstone R.H. (to 1841)
Seal R.H.
Kemsing R.H.
Ightham R.H.
Wrotham R.H.

1845

Daily to
Shoreham
Otford
Halstead
Knockholt
Chipstead
Sundridge
Brasted
Westerham (to 1857)
Edenbridge (to 1848)
-
-
-
Kemsing
Ightham
Wrotham

also Stone St
Ivy Hatch
Shipbourne (by 1846 under Tonbridge)
Plaxtol R.H.

3 times/a week
(Sun, Wed, Fri) to
Basted
Godden Green
Weald
Ash

1849

Miles from Sevenoaks		Delivery Starts in village	Box Closes
6	Westerham	7.15 am	5.45 pm
4½	Brasted	7.30	6.15
4	Sundridge	7.30	6.15
2½	Chipstead	7.00	6.30
1½	Riverhead	7.00	6.30
0	Sevenoaks	7.00	7.30
6	Halstead	9.00 am	4.20 pm
5	Shoreham	8.00	5.00
3	Otford	7.15	5.30
0	Sevenoaks	7.00	7.00
10	Ash	8.30 am	3.30 pm
7	Wrotham	8.00	5.30
7	Borough Green	7.15	5.45
6	Ightham	7.30	5.45
2	Seal	7.00	6.30
0	Sevenoaks	7.00	7.30
6	Plaxtole	9.00 am	4.00 pm
3	Kemsing	7.30	5.30

1862

Daily to

Shoreham
Otford
Halstead
Knockholt
Chipstead
Sundridge
Brasted
-
-
-
-
Kemsing
Ightham
Wrotham
Stone St
Ivy Hatch
-
Plaxtol

Weald (every day)

Letters received in the villages had to be checked and sorted before delivery commenced. A place such as Ash not shown separately in 1862 would have its mail taken daily to Wrotham and delivered on from there.

Rural deliveries 1840–1862

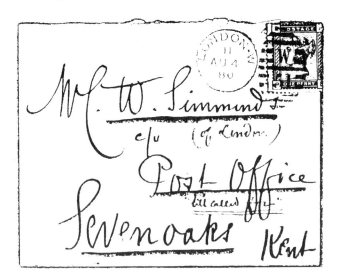

1880 Letter addressed to Sevenoaks Post Office 'to be called for'.

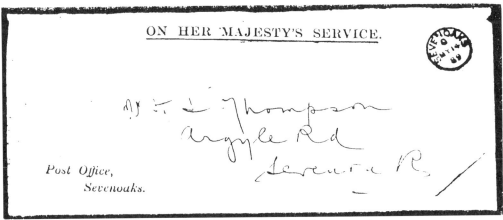

1889 OHMS evenlope used from Sevenoaks Post Office for Official correspondence.

1897 Official tender envelope to Sevenoaks UDC with early type adhesive Registration label.

1891/94/1902 Two Edenbridge Duplex cancels and an OHMS Statistical Dept unpaid letter. The first shows the error 697 which should be 967 for Edenbridge. (J Weston)

Rural Delivery Postmen[47]   The main villages now had delivery postmen attached to them and living in the area.

In 1908 as well as 16 Town Postmen, Sevenoaks itself had 5 Rural Postmen and 5 Rural Auxiliaries plus 2 under Allowances, taking mail to village areas. Postmen attached to rural offices for delivery were constantly changing in detail with pressure constantly on to convert 'auxiliaries' and 'delivery allowances' into established full-time posts. By 1920 the 'delivery allowances' had all been so converted.

	1908				*Early 1920's*		
	Rural Postmen	Aux. R.P.	Del'y Allce	Bicycle Clng. Allce.	R.P.	Aux. R.P.	Bicycle Allce
Biggin Hill	1	3	-	-	1	-	-
Boro' Green	1	1	-	-	1	-	-
Brasted	1	2	1	-	1	-	-
Chipstead	1	-	-	-	1	-	-
Dunton Green	1	-	-	-	1	-	-
Fairseat	-	1	-	-	-	-	-
Halstead	1	1	-	1	1	1	1
Ide Hill	-	1	1	-	-	1	-
Ightham	1	2	-	2	2	-	2
Kemsing	1	1	-	-	1	-	-
Knockholt	-	1	2	1	-	3	1
Otford	-	2	-	-	-	1	-
Plaxtol	-	1	1	-	-	1	-
Riverhead	1	-	1	-	1	1	-
Seal	1	3	-	3	3	-	3
Shoreham	2	-	4	1	1	-	1
Sundridge	1	2	2	2	2	-	2
Tatsfield	1	3	-	1	1	1	1
Weald	-	1	2	1	-	1	1
Westerham	3	-	-	-	3+3	-	-
W'ham Hill	1	2	-	1	-	1	1
Wrotham	2	2	1	4	4	1	4
	20	29	15	17	27	12	17

As can be seen, in 1920 the full-time Rural Postman posts have increased, the part-time auxiliary posts have decreased and delivery allowances disappeared.

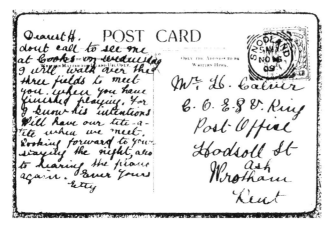

1909 Rural delivery. A card to Hodsoll St, Mr King was the postmaster.

Collections   were organised from the villages to leave as late as possible. The object was to leave as large a time-gap as possible between the receipt of a letter and the collection of the reply to it, at least several hours.

1902 Last Collection Times[48]

350 pm	Ash	630 pm	Cudham	700 pm	Stone Street
500	Hodsall St.	635	Wrotham		Ightham
530	Fairseat	640	St Mary Platt	710	Chipstead
	Wrotham Heath	645	Brasted	715	Westerham Hill
	Kingsdown		Ivy Hatch		Otford
555	Halstead	650	Boro' Green	720	Riverhead
615	Ide Hill		Knockholt	730	Dunton Green
625	Stansted		Kemsing	735	Seal
	Plaxtol	655	Sundridge	750	Godden Green
	Underriver		Shoreham		

On *Sundays* the collection was straight away after the first delivery and very much earlier than weekdays. In passing it may be noted that the Sunday collections are thus mostly between 10 am and noon coinciding with the usual Sunday morning time of Divine Service.

955 am	Plaxtol	1045 am	Otford	1135 am	Kemsing
1015	Shoreham	1050	Knockholt	1200	Brasted
	Kingsdown		Weald	1210 pm	Sundridge
	Ivy Hatch	1055	Ash	1215	St. Mary Platt
1020	Fairseat	1105	Halstead	1225	Chipstead
	Hodsall St	1130	Ide Hill	1235	Riverhead
1030	Cudham		Godden Green	155	Wrotham
	Underriver		Dunton Green		Westerham Hill
	Stone Street		Wrotham Heath	215	Ightham
				250	Seal

The norm for rural boxes was two collections a day, but Town boxes had three collections, often more. In September 1886 Private Posting Boxes were introduced on private premises from which the post made a collection, normally for a fee.

Expresses and Express Delivery

By 1846 Expresses involving a special horse and rider were 9½d per mile (7½d for horse, 2d for rider) and were only accepted upon Public Service. If bulky, a post chaise was hired as had always been the case.

With the advent of most mails being sent by Railway which was the quickest and only method for a long journey, the concept of a special journey became outdated and emphasis was now put on quick delivery as soon as the item was received at the office, to be called the Express Delivery Service for which an additional but relatively small fee of 2d the first mile, 3d each succeeding mile was to be charged. The new service was tried out in London from 25 March 1891 and after its great success there was extended to the country areas in August 1891.[49] Delivery was by Telegraph boys as well as postmen. A new scale of fees was introduced in January 1892.

All offices to which sufficient delivery staff were attached would deliver express letters and parcels as soon as they arrived at the office instead of waiting for the next delivery round. Local messages could be sent Express throughout their entire journey, and if a special conveyance had to be hired then additional charges above the usual postage and express fee were incurred. On Sundays letters only were so treated, not parcels. Other types of special arrangements could be made and the local Postmasters were exhorted to fit in with customer requirements.

By 1895 the following 16 offices were classed as EDO, Express Delivery Offices: Sevenoaks, Brasted, Sundridge, Ide Hill, Westerham, Knockholt, Halstead, Riverhead, Weald, Otford, Shoreham, Seal,

1895 Registered letter to Holland with Time in Asterisk Code MAXP = 12.05pm. The public had long asked for 'time' in the postmark instead of A, B, C, but the code introduced by the Post Office was a failure as the public soon cracked the code and it was stopped mid-1895 or used until a new stamp was required. Thereafter 'time in clear' was used.

Clock Code: Code   A B C D E F G H I K L M
                 Hour   1 2 3 4 5 6 7 8 9 10 11 12
                 Min   5 10 15 20 25 30 35 40 45 50 55 60
                 also   A = AM, P = PM. *So 9.15am is* ICxA, *6.30pm is* FFxP

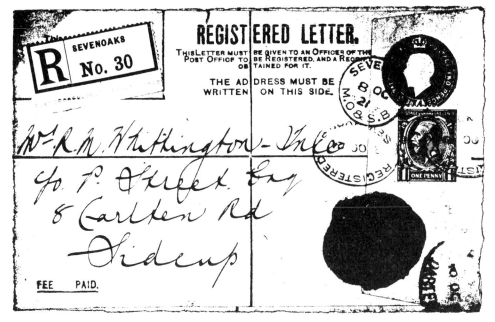

1921 Registered Letter with early Registration label and MO&SB Counter cancel. Also oval cancellation of sorting office, registration section.

POST CARD

THE ADDRESS TO BE WRITTEN ON THIS SIDE

1900 Victorian 'Court' size correspondence postcard with the new double ring postmark canceller incorporating the date. Inset 1908 Picture Post Card with Double Ring Sevenoaks cancel showing the broken 'V'.

View looking south of the London Road through Riverhead c1905 showing the road before widening on both sides and the now non-existant White Hart Inn (W.J. Upton) on the left. (Sennoke Press)

Ightham, Plaxtol, Platt, Wrotham; and the service further extended; by 1899 Wrotham Heath, by 1909 Fairseat, by 1911 Ash, by 1913 Biggin Hill and Kemsing, by 1918 Boro' Green and Chevening.

As time progressed the pattern altered; by 1907 Halstead and Otford and by 1918 Shoreham, Ightham and Platt were no longer designated as EDO's.

Local Transport – Bicycles   Once the main route coaches had given way to the railways and the roads were rather empty, it appeared to be a suitable time for the bicycle to develop. By 1860 there was only local traffic on the roads and by 1870 the condition of the roads had become very bad. Perhaps that was the real reason for calling the first cycles of 1869 'boneshakers'. By 1876 came the 'ordinary' cycle, the bicycle as it is known today. Bicycles developed in comparative quiet, motor cars did not come onto the roads till about 1895, although there were always some experimental ones about. The Post Office tried out the use of various types of cycles from their inception.

There were official bicycles at Sevenoaks (two) and Westerham (one) in 1900 and this method for rural delivery developed strongly between 1904 and 1910 (details are listed in the village appendix) for shorter runs. Bicycle cleaning allowances mostly of 1/- a week were given.

Horses and Motor Vehicles   Horses were used right up to the early 1920's. For example, George Harry Atkins on the Cudham walk was not dismounted until September 1923.[50] In 1905, E. Bates at Brasted was granted a loan of £20 to buy a horse and in 1907 there was a mounted service between Westerham and Tatsfield. The normal carrying load weight for a single horse mailcart, excluding short run station service, was 4½ to 6½ cwt. according to the nature of the route, The weight of a mailbag is usually 2lbs, but sacks can be up to 4lbs., when empty.

The story of the conversion to motor transport to the villages belongs to the next chapter. On the main road the London - Hastings parcel coach, which had by 1909 been motorised, stopped both at Sevenoaks main P.O. and the station thus saving two separate trips to the station each day having to be organised by Sevenoaks P.O.[51]

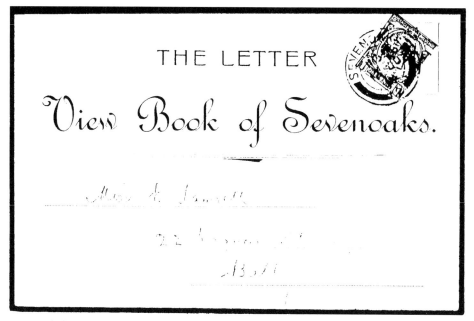

1914 Only known Sevenoaks local 'Perfin'; the piercing of the sheets of unused stamps with small holes so that ownership could be established and their appropriation discouraged. 'S P C^O L^D' Salmons Printers.

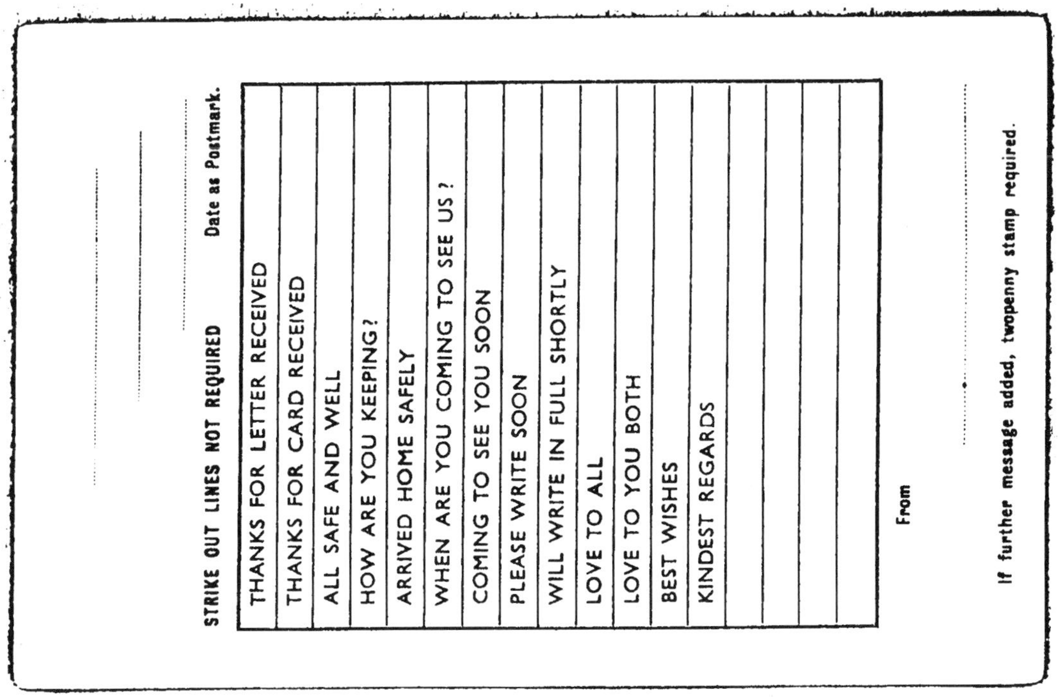

STRIKE OUT LINES NOT REQUIRED   Date as Postmark.

THANKS FOR LETTER RECEIVED

THANKS FOR CARD RECEIVED

ALL SAFE AND WELL

HOW ARE YOU KEEPING?

ARRIVED HOME SAFELY

WHEN ARE YOU COMING TO SEE US ?

COMING TO SEE YOU SOON

PLEASE WRITE SOON

WILL WRITE IN FULL SHORTLY

LOVE TO ALL

LOVE TO YOU BOTH

BEST WISHES

KINDEST REGARDS

From

If further message added, twopenny stamp required.

PRINTED PAPER RATE

THE ECONOMY SAVE-TIME POST CARD

POSTAGE
ONE
PENNY

COPYRIGHT. J. SALMON LTD . SEVENOAKS.

4846

The Economy Post Card by J Salmon Ltd, Sevenoaks, printed paper penny rate applies to 1921.

Postal Stationery   Reply Postcards were introduced in 1882 and immediately several efforts were made to improve the idea. One such improvement was the 'Sevenoaks' Reply Postcard, an invention of H. Lebas, about 1889/91, which he was trying to patent and have accepted by the G.P.O. for the '*benefit of correspondents*'. He would, of course, expect an honorarium upon its acceptance and this expectation increased over the years from £100 to £1,000. The Post Office were swamped by such offers and did not respond, much to Le Bas' chagrin.

The postcard consisted of two pieces and was inscribed at the bottom:
'H. LEBAS SEVENOAKS ENGLAND, INVENTOR   WATERLOW & SONS LTD., LONDON. PRINTERS'

According to Kelly's there were George Lebas at the Blackboy Inn and Robert Lebas at the Greyhound Inn at St. John's Hill in the early 1860's; by 1887 Robert and Henry Lebas were auctioneers at The Vine and in 1890 a H. Lebas of Les Bas & Co., who were House & Estate Agents, was at 5 Camden Villas in London Road.

In the 1920's an 'Economy' Postcard, the civilian equivalent of a field service Postcard with set phrases to tick and that travelled at Printed Paper rates was produced by Salmon's, the Sevenoaks printers.

Traffic Volumes - Some Statistics

Sevenoaks Growth 1860-1869 and comparison with Edenbridge[52]

	Sevenoaks 1860	Sevenoaks 1865	Sevenoaks 1869	Edenbridge 1869
Average items delivered	9,690	12,760	13,593	6,350
in one week. Newspapers	2,085	1,014	-	-
Letters	7,605	11,746	-	-
Letters delivered from				
Town Office	1,450 (19%)	2,203 (19%)	3,266 (24%)	904 (14%)
Sub-offices	6,155 (81%)	9,543 (81%)	10,327 (76%)	5,446 (86%)
Letters Registered				
in 4 week period	28	64	76	37
Sealed bags Rec'd daily	not	not	27	15
Despatched do.	given	given	26	31
Money Order Transactions				
per year	6,637	9,543	10,131	2,339
Savings Bank Transactions				
per year	-	511	1,116	406
Costs per annum				
Postmaster salary	£ 102	£ 102	£ 110	£ 90
Clerks	25	25	40	35
Sorters/Letter				
Carriers/Stampers	267	305	47	23
Rural Messengers	-	-	271	125
Sub-Office and				
Town RH Costs	240	270	346	243
Total Cost	£ 634	£ 702	£ 814	£ 516
Night duty - period office	Not	No one	No one	No one
unmanned	given	10 pm to	8.40 pm to	11 pm to
		5 am (7 hrs)	5 am (8¼ hrs)	2.30 am (3½ hrs)

Note the large number, mostly 4 out of 5, 'out-of-town' letters both for Sevenoaks and Edenbridge.

From 1844 when the railway contract started, mostly there were two separate rides, from Tunbridge to Sevenoaks and from Tunbridge Station to Sevenoaks until 1869. With the opening of Tubs Hill Station only the Tunbridge to Sevenoaks mailcart persisted.

The mailcart ride between Edenbridge and East Grinstead was not in operation before 1856 but started about 1860 and continued on from that date.

At about the same time, 1860, there was a mailcart from Tunbridge Station through Leigh to Penshurst where the Receiving House had been for some time at the Leicester Arms. This mailcart had superseded the long established walk from Tunbridge to Leigh and on to Stonewall, later served by Edenbridge.

Letters delivered in <u>One Week</u> (during the quarter to March 31)

1870		1871					
Letters		Letters	Books Packets Circulars	Pattern & Sample Packets	News Papers	Post Cards	Total[53]
11,620	Sevenoaks	12,051	1,972	89	1,472	565	16,149
14,958	Tunbridge	15,191	2,394	437	2,613	2,060	22,695
26,709	T. Wells	30,409	2,799	526	3,190	1,375	38,299
10,463	Bromley	11,049	578	541	651	569	13,388
32,254	Maidstone	30,846	3,694	240	4,596	2,224	41,600

Making an average of daily items in Sevenoaks of 2,307.

Number of Registered 12 months to 21st March 1899[54]

Total of Letters Registered 10,245

	Fee Paid	2d	10,120		Fee Paid	7d	7
		3d	74			8d	1
		4d	24			9d	1
		5d	9			11d	1
		6d	4			1/-	4

Postal Return, One Week 20 May 1905

	Letters	½d open Letters	News Papers	P.O. Cards Official	Private	Total
Rural	3,846	305	253	182	942	5,528
Town	50,140	4,829	2,557	2,753	10,024	70,303
	53,986	5,134	2,810	2,935	10,966	75,831

Costing   Much costing information as detailed in the current Postmasters Manual had to be collected to support the existing situation and any proposed changes in delivery and collection arrangements. In a combined collection one parcel was calculated equivalent to 25 letters.

Agency Services and Non-Postal Work: Telegraph and Telephones

Strictly speaking these services are outside the scope of this survey. But an overall precis of what happened needs to be included as these new services were of great impact on the total G.P.O. Service and in the case of telegraph and telephone siphoned off many messages that hitherto had been sent by letter.

Money Orders   The 'Clerks of the Road' who ran the six divisions from London were allowed to meet a pressing demand from the Public and in 1792 they set up a money order business for the transfer of money around the country. Demand for this very necessary service was kept by them deliberately low to a minimum that they were able to handle themselves. However, demand by the public was so great that in December 1838 the Post Office took over the service officially. No mention of availability at Sevenoaks is made in the 1840 editions of Local Directories, but as early as March 1839 an extant letter from I.L. Wallace of Sevenoaks to cousins near Aberdeen mentions Bank Post Bills of £48.1.1, one of which was received safely, the other not so. *The two letters were posted at the same time and ought to have been delivered in the usual manner on the same day .... I shall immediately communicate with the Post Office authorities in London that the matter may be righted, and stop the payment of the Bank Post Bill.* The letters were registered when they were posted in Sevenoaks, but the 'stop payment' appears to be something done direct with London. Certainly by 1845 Sevenoaks is listed as providing the service and the facility gradually became available at many village offices (see appendix for dates). Additional forms and staff training in their use then became necessary.

Postal Orders   In 1881 Postal Orders were made available for smaller amounts at offices that transacted Money Order and Savings Bank business. By 1885 many other small offices sold and encashed them and by 1904 postal orders were sold, but not necessarily encashed, by all offices.

Savings Bank   In 1861 the Post Office Savings Bank commenced; again many new forms and the need for staff training in their use. No doubt but that Hester Hooker soon became competent in filling up the forms. Interesting, too, that the original Sevenoaks Savings Bank office had been in London Road at the entrance to Wheatsheaf Yard next to the Post Office way back in 1838 so they would not be complete strangers to the work.[55] The Trustees of the Sevenoaks Savings Bank gave notice in May 1888 of their intention to close that bank.

Annuity and Insurance work started in the Post Office in 1865, and after the Government Annuity and Insurance Act became effective June 3 1884 the service was carried out in all Savings Bank Offices. The concept was a good one and the service needed, but it was found to be better carried out on a commercial competitive basis and, after staggering along for some decades, the service was considered a failure and ceased.

Licences   The selling of many types of licences, gun, dog, servant, carriage and later motorcar, began in 1869/70 at those larger offices that sold money orders. Again many more forms to cope with, and in 1874 the sale of 1d receipt stamps.

Pensions   The handling of Old Age Pensions began in 1909. This work involved making regular cash payments out and eventually the selling of many types of special stamps, many of quite high individual value once compulsory National Insurance began in 1911.

Ordnance Maps were sold at the Post Office from 1897.

The Telegraph and Telephone

The Telegraph was invented in 1833 and the Private Telegraph Companies started between 1840 and 1860, many of the long distance lines being laid alongside railway tracks. As an immediate by-product a master clock was built at Greenwich to control the railway station clocks and Railway Time, which was Greenwich Mean Time, spread across the land with the trackside telegraph lines to help, pushing out local Sundial time which had a difference of 4 minutes for each degree of longitude, about 67 miles of east-west travel.

The Telegraph Acts of 1868 and 1869, which latter Act reserved to the P.O. the exclusive privilege of transmitting telegrams within the UK, paved the way for the GPO take-over of 1870 and that in turn produced Telegraph Sub-offices and the Telegram as a means of sending messages that formerly might have gone by post. For he first time information could be sent otherwise than along the ground by foot, horse or train, particularly once the rate was reduced to 6d in 1885. The next year 50 million inland telegrams were sent and by 1895 79 million, each representing a message that previously would have needed to have gone by letter.

Local dates in the development of the telegraph by GPO after takeover are 1869 Telegraph Assistants engaged and trained; 1870 (5 February) Telegraph open for public messages; 1875 Riverhead and Sundridge Telegraph extension under guarantee; 1875 Rating of Telegraph wires within the Sevenoaks Union; 1877 Telegram delivery allowances; 1877 Wm. (whoever that may be) proposes to lay wires passing over his property underground; 1880 Renewal of Submarine Co. wires through tunnel; 1882 Telegraph wires underground; 1885 Boy Messengers engaged; Thompson, clerk and telegraphist commencing day; 1901 Telegraph Messenger Boniface P.J. summoned for riding a bicycle after sunset without a light; 1903 (Further) Bicycle for Telegrams. In the private era 1850-1870 before the G.P.O. take-over, messages could be sent from some Railway stations and Company offices. Local information about these services is patchy (but see appendix).

Boy Telegraph Messengers   An analysis of 24 Telegraph Messengers employed at Sevenoaks Town, on pay of 6/- a week, revealed that the actual age of engagement was between thirteen and fourteen years of age, mostly tending to the lower end of that scale with three of them only twelve years ten months old and one lad had to leave employment as he was '*not qualified to leave school*'.

Normally the youths worked as Telegraph Messengers for about two years with four years as the maximum, before promotion or leaving. Promotion at 19 was to postman. Local reasons given for ceasing to be boy messengers are :-   3 promoted to Rural Auxiliary Postman, 7 still working as Messenger, 10 Resigned, 2 Dismissed, 1 Absconded, 1 Not Qualified.

With rural pay at only 5/- a week, the pattern at Westerham, Seal, Ightham, Knockholt was otherwise not dissimilar.

Many a Postmaster started working life as a boy messenger and such was the case with Mr. Clancy.

Telephones   Graham Bell, a Scotsman in America and teacher of deaf and dumb children, conceived the idea of the telephone in 1874. Its development required a microphone and here Edison was concerned. As with the Telegraph in the first years of development, the decade of the 1880s, many private companies were set up covering local areas, and later many of these merged in 'The National Telephone Company'.

Sevenoaks Town had the first exchange in the district, on the top floor of the High Street Post Office and on 4 April 1896 this Exchange was connected with the National Telephone Exchange, thus giving the possibility of long distance trunk calls. In 1911/12 the G.P.O. took over from the National Telephone Company. Expansion of the Sevenoaks District network then took place right up to the end of the 1920's.

By 1903 Sevenoaks had 120 subscribers, in 1905 180; 1907 208; 1912 272; 1914 305. The growth was steady but not spectacular.[56]

In 1909 a young lady, Miss M. Malraison, joined the telephone service and some five years later became supervisor of the Sevenoaks exchange. She retired in 1952 after forty-three years service, thirty-eight of them as Supervisor, and having received the British Empire Medal for WWII wartime service in that capacity.

Outside the town, at first a series of small manually operated inter-connected local exchanges sprang up. *Riverhead was operating by 1899. By 1907 Westerham exchange opened with 25 subscribers and Brasted with 18; by 1908 Boro' Green with 10 subscribers; by 1911 Knockholt which opened with 11 subscribers*[57] *had structural alterations for a new replacement exchange; by 1932 Otford, and Biggin Hill.*

The first automatic exchange in the country was at Epsom in 1912 and as soon as the small manual exchanges that had to be constantly manned by an operator on duty were opened, the move was on to concentrate them into larger units and to automate them, although it must be said that there were many small exchanges still in use in 1939 when war broke out.

At the outbreak of war, 1939, the exchanges were at Badgers Mount, Boro Green, Biggin Hill, Brasted, Dunton Green, Ide Hill, Knockholt, Otford, Plaxtol, Pratts Bottom, Seal, Shoreham, Tatsfield, Weald, Westerham and Edenbridge.   And in addition to Edenbridge there were Chiddingstone, Cowden, Crockham Hill, Four Elms and Mark Beech exchanges.

In 1985 there were exchanges at Sevenoaks, Westerham, Knockholt, Dunton Green, Ide Hill, Otford, Boro' Green, Fairseat, Plaxtol, West Kingsdown, Weald, Biggin Hill, Tatsfield, Edenbridge, Four Elms, Cowden all automatic and with a greatly increased number of subscribers, and all carrying messages that previously would have had to go by post.

Public Call Boxes   But perhaps more important to the general public who could not afford a separate telephone in their own home was the availability of public call boxes. By 1905 Brasted, Westerham; 1909 Ash; by 1910 Biggin Hill, Boro' Green, Kemsing, Kingsdown, Knockholt and Tatsfield; by 1913 Seal and Wrotham; by 1914 St. Botolph's, St. Johns, Upper St. Johns, Chevening, Dunton Green, Ide Hill, Weald; by 1915 Plaxtol, Sundridge; by 1917 London Road, Halstead, Otford, Riverhead and Shoreham.

In February 1928 the Police in Westerham were still not on the telephone. The Westerham Telephone Exchange had to accept messages and run across the road with them.[58]

The Start of Airmail and World War I

Balloons   Many of the very early balloon flights carried a few private letters written by the balloonist or his passenger. Earliest records of such mail are those of Dr. Jeffries, who in Blanchards' hot air balloon, went in 1784 from London to Stone in Kent and an unmanned magnesium balloon in 1870 from Crystal Palace that dropped a bag of post cards posted at Hythe.[59] The S.E. Gazette of 26th May 1861 reported that on Whit Monday a balloon which had ascended from Crystal Palace with four gentlemen had landed at a farm of Earl Amherst's near the town of Sevenoaks and '*they went back to London by conveyance*'.

The turn of the century saw a renewal of local interest in ballooning. This took place from Knole Paddock where the Sevenoaks Gas Co. had installed a gas main specifically for the purpose of inflating balloons. Among others, Capt. Percival Spencer, with his balloons Vivienne I, II, III, was well-known,[60] but there is no record of his carrying souvenir mail or dropping leaflets.

Balloons that did carry souvenir postcards that were dropped for mailing were those that left Beckenham at Coronation time, 9th August 1902, passing over Knockholt and Wrotham and dropping bags at Leeds (Kent), Godmersham and Dover and the 12 July trip in 1905 from the Beckenham Flower Show of a motorised balloon that also passed near Halstead and dropped mail for posting at Chislehurst, coming down at Romford. One balloon that was carrying souvenir mail and did land was that of 10th June 1978 commemorating the 25th Anniversary of the Coronation. The envelopes were handstamped at Sevenoaks as proof of landing.

Early Aeroplanes   Although aeroplanes had been flying since 1903 no very early flights originated from this district, probably the earliest being the Polish aviators that built planes before the first world war and flew them from the field at Sundridge.[61] None of the early aviator publicity flights originated here although some of the pioneers made unexpected stops in the area as when John Moisant in August 1910 crashed at Wrotham and at Heaverham and again at St. Clere and landed near Shoreham after his Channel crossing in his vain attempt to reach Crystal Palace in time to claim a prize.[62]

The well-documented London-Windsor airmail flights in 1912 from Hendon Aerodrome attracted much philatelic mail and some is addressed to Sevenoaks and at the end of the war in 1919, some mail from France and from occupying troops in Germany was brought back by air, but as it may not be so marked it is difficult to distinguish. Also on 10th November of that same year 1919 the Post Office official

Aerial Post. *The 1911
Coronation flight
envelope and enclosure
addressed to Sevenoaks.*

air mail service London-Paris was inaugurated, flying over Kent, but with fog on that day, completion did not take place till the 11th. Air fee was 2/6 per ounce.

Airfields   As well as the small field at Sundridge, there was 'Biggin Hill', originally part of Earl Stanhope's Cudham Lodge farm but handed over to the War Office in 1915 as an emergency night landing field. It became an operational field in 1917 on 13th February when the 'Wireless Testing Park' of the Royal Flying Corps completed transfer to the South End having come from Joyce Green Airfield near Dartford, which was often waterlogged and misty although conveniently near the Army Signals Establishment of the Royal Engineers at Woolwich which prepared the sets they tested. Their brief was to perfect 'ground to air' and 'air to air' wireless *telephony*, that is speech in clear rather than wireless telegraphy, the morse code then used by air observers. Later that year on 1st December 1917 the airfield also became operational when 39 Squadron charged with the air defence of South London moved into the North End.

'Ground to Air' and 'Air to Ground' wireless telephony had been successfully demonstrated to Lord Kitchener in Autumn 1915 but was not accepted until 1918. 'Air to Air' was first established in July 1917 when an airborne plane near Sevenoaks and another flying near Edenbridge transmitted and received clear speech.[63]

To take over the responsibility for military flying from the Royal Engineers, the Royal Flying Corps had been created on 13th April 1912, with a Naval Wing and a Military Wing. The Navy appeared to have difficulty in accepting that it was a part of the R.F.C. and on the 6th April 1914 they were separated and each attempted to expand on its own. But co-ordination was considered paramount and on 1st April 1918 the Royal Naval Air Service and the Royal Flying Corps[64] were merged and became the Royal Air Force. The 'Wireless Experimental Station' renamed 'Instrument Design Establishment' remained at Biggin Hill until 1922 when it removed to Farnborough, Hants.

Wartime

Early days in Sevenoaks, 1659, had seen the keeping of a militia, required service from each parish often chosen by lot, mainly for ensuring civil peace. The nineteenth century saw war with France and later in South Africa, with therefore a need to be prepared. The need was understood by the general populace and hence the establishment of Volunteer Forces.

In 1859, during the war with France, Lord Amherst had an open public meeting in Sevenoaks to put the situation; a hundred men turned up and of these fifty put their names forward. There was to be no money from the Government for payment; recruits paid 10/- to join and got a uniform. Thus was formed the 33rd (Sevenoaks) Coy of The Kent Rifles, Tonbridge formed the 14th Coy, Tunbridge Wells the 17th, Penshurst the 23rd, Westerham the 27th. In 1870 they had a dark green uniform but were uncertain about headgear and that went from Cap to Shako to Busby to Round Forage Cap.[65]

The Post Office being nationally a very large crown employer of men had a co-operative attitude with the Forces, giving special employment conditions to ex-forces men and acknowledging service in the Forces of their own staff both in general terms such as Riflemen or in the Navy and as specialists, e.g. Army Signals and members of Army Post Offices.

In 1899 when P.O. employees went as Army Reservists to South Africa their families received half pay as well as separation allowance. By 15 May 1901 service with the Army Post Office available to those between twenty and thirty years of age gave full P.O. pay plus Army pay.[66]

Between the Boer War and World War I there were many Territorial camps and Army manoeuvres but only one is recorded in this district. In 1904 the West Kent Light Yeomanry camped in Knole Park. Unlike other camps of the period they did not appear to have a special Camp postmark, probably because the camp was so near permanent town postal facilities.

W.W.I. Local effects   *There being no wireless or Sunday newspaper, the P.O. staff used to copy out the news telegrams that came in and put them, written in a large hand, in the window. To walk to the Post*

Office on a Sunday afternoon or evening to get the news was a regular habit of many.[67]

Soon after the outbreak of war, by 11th December, when there were 5,000 Territorial troops quartered in the town, the Churches organised a Christmas fund for them.[68] As the war progressed many of the local halls became hospitals: the Cornwall Hall to which Dr. Mansfield the P.O. doctor was attached, St. Johns Hall Dr. Stenning, Congregational Hall and Wildernesse. There were large hutted camps at Knole, Parkfield and Woodlands Rise and tented camps at Solefields Rise and Blighs Meadow. The Vine Cricket Pavilion became a YMCA Canteen. In 1915 the YMCA rooms in Mount Harry Road were for the use of soldiers and an application was made for a telegraph sub-post office there. This was refused but the sale of stamps was authorised together with a posting box. The following year a fighter 'plane landed on the Vine during 'Help the Soldier Week'

When a postman left to join the Forces and a replacement was deemed necessary his place might be taken by a woman, a less able-bodied 'exempt' man, or a youth awaiting his call-up. In effect, the understanding was that when (and if) he returned and was able to take up his work again as a postman, it would be made available to him.

By 1916 the Sevenoaks to Otford trains were discontinued and the summer-time experiment of advancing the clocks by one hour took place, this act being made permanent in 1925.

Some of the camps had their own army post offices and the following Home Defence camps are known:

10.6.1916 - 7.1916	Army Post Office (HD)3 3/10 Middlesex 201 Bde (67 Div)	at	Dunstall Camp Shoreham
6.1916 - 10.1916	Army Post Office (HD)35 202 Bde (67 Div)	at	Wildernesse Camp Sevenoaks
7.1917 - 9.1917	Army Post Office (HD)M11 3 Mtd Bde (13 Cycle Bde)	at	Wildernesse Camp

Wartime in Sevenoaks.
Wrotham YMCA.

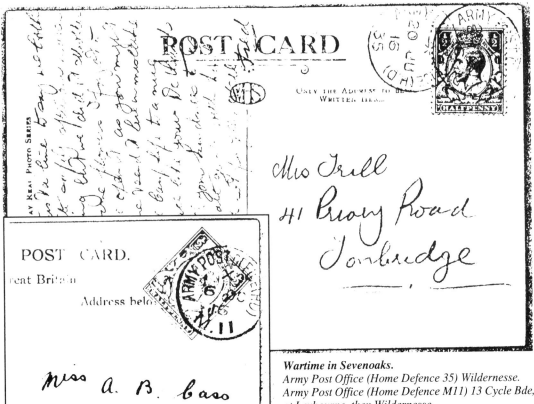

Wartime in Sevenoaks.
Army Post Office (Home Defence 35) Wildernesse.
Army Post Office (Home Defence M11) 13 Cycle Bde,
at Leybourne, then Wildernesse.

The Roll of Honor   The Roll of Honour for the two World Wars carved in wood for the Edwardian office on the North side of South Park has been moved across to the new functional office on the South side where it now dominates the East wall.

Sevenoaks Postal District
Roll of Honour

1914	1915		1916	1917
Ashdown G.A.	Boyle E.J.	Ashdown H.	Allen T.W.	Anderson A.G.
Best W.A.	Buckmaster W.T.	Baldwin J.	Bateman F.C.	Callow H.
Camber G.	Cosgrove J.	Cox F.	Bevan T.H.	Clark J.
Dewbery J.S.F.	Cross H.T.	Cross E.W.	Boniface P.J.	Elphick E.G.
Donaldson J.E.	Cull F.W.	Deering J.	Brown C.M.	Fennell B.W.
Dutnall F.T.	Fuller A.G.	Dunn T.J.J.	Buley F.A.	Letchford G.S.
Griffin F.	Green A.R.H.	M.M. bar	Burr H.G.	Lorimer J.L.
Hayward W.	Hartnup W.G.	Emery J.W.	Callow F.	Lynch J.
Hider G.A.	Holland P.	Marchant J.	Cheeseman F.F.	Osbon C.J.
Mills W.G.	Pankhurst A.A.	Palmer A.W.	Day A.H.	Sawyer A.T.
Mitcham H.	Thompson A.W.	Shepherd C.A.	Eastwood C.H.	Shepherd P.J.
Mitchell G.A.	Thompson H.J.	Tidy D.E.	Ellis G.	Walkling F.J.
Payne G.M.	Yates S.J.	White D.U.A.H.	Greenway E.R.	Whale G.A.F.
Phillips A.E.		Heath H.J.	Henshaw G.W.	**1918**
Pocock C.H.		Hollman F.A.	Hollands T.E.	Bassett W.J.H.
Pryer F.			Lock W.	Frayne H.T.
Shaw W.G.		**1939 - 1945**	Nicholas A.J.	Russell C.S.
Warren H. (M.C.)		Allen T.A.	Orpin G.A.J.	Mansfield P.A.
Webb W.R.		Booker C.W.	Pellin C.H.	Medical
Wenban T.C.		Pottenden A.A.	Spring F.S.	Officer
		Rowe P.F.	Taylor D.C.	Rowe R.L.
		D.F.C.	Walkling C.H.	
			West E.W.	

1914   Who Stands if freedom fall Who dies if England Live   1918

Many of those who joined the Forces had been in the postal service for fifteen years or more. There was a wide spread of enrolment throughout the district. For example, the following names can be found in the village data section in the appendix: G.A. Ashdown Ivy Hatch, T.W. Allen Sevenoaks, J. Baldwin St. Mary Platt, P.J. Boniface Westerham, C.M. Brown Biggin Hill, F. Callow Boro' Green, F.W. Cull Westerham, J. Deering Plaxtol, T.J.J. Dunn possibly the T. Dunn of Ightham, C.H. Eastwood Kingsdown, A.G. Fuller Westerham and Cudham, H.J. Heath Riverhead, J. Marchant Chipstead, C.H. Pellin Bessels Green, W.G. Shaw Kingsdown, C.H. Walkling Ightham.

Those names listed in the centre column all appear in the weekly P.O. Circulars of WWI as 'Killed in Action' or 'Died on Active Service'. The names of those for WWII were later added to the centre column.

History of the Post Office and the Army

It would be interesting to trace those that served in line regiments and those that served in the Army P.Os but to do this does not appear at all easy to achieve and so here a very compacted history must suffice.

Being a large employer of men the P.O. tended to have an interest in the Army, another large employer of men and some regiments have been formed almost exclusively of volunteer P.O. staff, both from a view of defence and of communications; there were Rifle Regiments and the Army Postal Corps.

To take defence first   In 1796 The Clerks and Letter Carrier Volunteers prepared to form an Association to repel expected French invaders. Then in 1859 a note from Roland Hill asking for volunteers led to the formation of the Civil Service Corps of Rifle Volunteers (21 Middlesex). With the Irish Fenian riots and bombings of 1867/8, 1600 London P.O. staff paraded and were inspected by the Lord Mayor and P.M.G. at Guildhall and that year the 49th Middlesex Volunteers were formed. They had to attend 30 drills a year, pay for their uniform and for their substitute if needed when put down for duty. Having renumbered, when the 21st became the 12th Middx and the 49th the 24th Middx, the 24th (P.O. Riffles) adopted full Rifle Brigade uniform and traditions, yet contributing 450 Officers and men to the Royal Engineers Telegraph Reserve over the period 1899-1902 of the South African conflict and 600 to the Army Postal Corps.

Change of name and type of duty is endemic to army life, but these Regiments continued as rifle regiments and went to France as such in W.W.I., the 1/8 Bn. P.O. Rifles with 47 Div in March 1915 and the 2/8 Bn also to France in 1917 with 58 Div. 1,836 men were killed, 3,700 wounded gaining 1 VC, 5 DSO, 24 DCM.

After demobilisation these Regiments reformed as territorial P.O. Rifles converting in 1935 to RE Searchlights for the defence of London. In 1940 all Searchlights converted to Royal Artillery. After WWII these batteries reformed as Light AA, Royal Artillery.

Army Postal Services   In 1816 Volunteers from the GPO went to Paris to deal with letters of the British Army of Occupation after the defeat of Napoleon. With the Crimea War of 1854 six officers and some sorters with military rank sorted letters in Constantinople, Scutari and Balaclava on civilian pay plus £2 per week. There was also a small postal unit with the Abyssinian Campaign at that time.

In 1877 the Army Postal Corps enlisted men to deal with Army Correspondence in time of war and in 1892 the Army Post Office Corps was sanctioned by the War Office. In 1899 the Officers and Men transferred from 24 Middx went to the Boer War in South Africa to man the Army P.O. Corps and the R.E. Telegraph Reserve.[69]

One of those who did go to South Africa was 'Old John', Mr. Warrior, who subsequently became Postmaster at Sevenoaks in 1933. He was employed in the Post Office in Manchester and as a young man of barely twenty, no doubt before he became known as 'Old John', served from April 1900 to July 1902 as an N.C.O. in the Army Post Office Corps in many locations in South Africa during the Boer War. He was then chosen to represent the Army Post Office Corps at the Coronation of King Edward VII but this ceremony was suspended owing to the illness of the King.

1914 and the start of WWI saw the R.E. Postal Section taking over postal duties from 24 Middx. All were P.O. men including, later in WWI, many of the wounded from the P.O. Rifles.

Chapter VIII

1920-1985/6
Motorisation, Wartime, New Organisation

Interwar Years 1920-1938
    General Strike. Motor Vehicles

World War II 1939-1947
    Post Office and Defence
    Local POW Mail. Airfields and other Service Stations

Post War Years 1947-1984
    New Services
    Sorting Offices and Circulation of Mail
    Sevenoaks and the switch to Tonbridge Mechanised Letter Office

1984-1985/6
    New Policies and Administrative Organisation
    'Royal Mail' and 'Post Office Counters Ltd'

Monarchs: George V   (1910-1936)

               Edward VIII (1936)

               George VI   (1936-1952)

               Elizabeth II (1952-   )

Chronology

1920-30	Tarring of Local Roads. Motorisation of Local Delivery Services.
1921	Users Advisory Council; now Post Office Users National Council POUNC.
	5 June. Sunday duty 'abolished'. Sevenoaks Main P.O. still open Sunday morning.
1922	Franking machines in use. No need for adhesive stamps.
1923	January 1. Railway grouping effective. GWR, LMS, LNER, SR.
1925	Summertime Act becomes permanent.
1926	General Strike.
1927	Lindberg flies the Atlantic.
1932	Business Reply Service starts. Peaked cap replaces shako.
1934	Bridgeman Report of Committee of Enquiry on the Post Office 1932 starts policy of Regionalisation. End of the system of P.O. Surveyors, Administration decentralised. School of A.A. Defence at Biggin Hill.
1935	Automatic Transorma sorting of letters at Brighton.
1936	Sunday afternoon/evening collection facilities reinstated to catch night mails.
1939-1945	World War II.
1948	Railways nationalised. British Railways.
1950	Sunday working officially stopped (i.e. no extensions).
1952	Queen Elizabeth II ascends throne.
1953	Post Office Act. 1, 2, Eliz II c36. Sugar rationing ends.
1955	City of London a Smokeless Zone. First Atomic Power Station, Calder Hall.
1961	Post Office Act. 9, 10 Eliz II c15. Recorded Delivery Started. Betting Shops opened.
1962	Go-slow. Pay pause. People League Post for parcels.
1963	23 June. Reorganisation of Parcel Mails. PCO's - Parcel Concentration Offices. Philatelic Bureau opened.
1966	National Postal Museum opened.
1967	20 February. Postbuses started. Colour Television Broadcasts commenced. Post Office Preferred (POP) sizes of stationery to fit in with mechanisation.
1968	16 September. Two-tier Post started. All inland envelopes may be sealed. National Girobank Service started.
1969	1 October. Post Office Act. P.O. gets National Corporation status - no longer a Government department.
1970	April. Sevenoaks new functional Post Office and Sorting Office opens.
1971	Postal Strike. 15 February Decimalisation of coinage.
1972	Registration of Parcels ceased, compensation fee instead. Unsolicited advertising. "Household Delivery".
1973	Administration of Sevenoaks P.O. under Tunbridge Wells.
1976	7 May. Sunday afternoon collections abolished by the Board. No consultation.
1980	Expresspost.
1981	P.O. Vesting day. British Telecom hived off.
1982	Christmas private delivery services allowed under licence.
1983	Administration now at Tonbridge above new mechanised Letter Office. Local Parcels speeded service. 'Sheep pen' queueing device put into Sevenoaks main office. Datapost. Local mailbombs. 'Book Post' service.
1983/4	Mechanised Letter Office. Sevenoaks TN13, TN14 Wrotham TN15, Westerham TN16, Edenbridge TN8.
1984	June 8 Railway Letter Service ceased. Closure of some rural sub-offices. Report of National Federation of Sub-Postmasters. July. Letters now taken to Tonbridge MLO for postmarking, coding, sorting and despatch.
1986	January. New Delivery Schedules. Post office New Structural organisation.
1990	March 31. Electricity Vesting day

Chapter VIII

1920-1985/6
Motorisation, Wartime, Mechanisation

Much of the detailed information now comes from Post 38 which starts at 1920; effectively it is a continuation of Post 35. Supporting papers relating to *local* matters, as opposed to national matters, are mostly destroyed having been kept at first for three years, later extended to ten years and lastly destroyed under the Public Records Act 1958, the papers involved being first notified to the Public Records Office to see if they were interested. Unfortunately they did not appear to be at the time. Therefore information on factual decisions and occurrences may still be available, but not on the detailed situation that led up to the decision.

The Post Office Archives are a part of the National Archives and as such subject to the 30 year rule, such that after 1957 only that information made available to the public is available to the writer; this, however, is a considerable amount, much more than might be expected.

Changes in Sevenoaks
The Royal Crown Hotel was sold-up on the 29th April 1932, the Rose and Crown was pulled down in 1936 and later became Youngs Department Store, now Bejam Freezer Foods. Electrification of the Main Railway line to London took place during 1934, the first electric train coming into Tubs Hill on 6th January 1935.

The Inter-war Years 1920-1938

The inter-war years saw a succession of professionally qualified postmasters at Sevenoaks as everywhere else, rather than local men. These were managers who came to Sevenoaks for five to eight years as part of their career structure, many moving on to larger offices.

Postmaster **A.H. Trinder** (1929-1933) expanded the motorisation of local deliveries and this work was continued by **John Warrior** (1933-37) who tackled the problem of changing contract mail services into official post office ones. **Mr. Wigger** (1937-1944) saw his staff change from permanent employees to temporary wartime personnel.

Need to Live Near Place of Work
In those days Postmasters and Postmistresses in common with all such staff were expected to live near their work as a condition of employment. On 12 January 1937 Miss Lambourne, at Westerham, now a Crown office, asked for and was given permission to live in Sevenoaks, but '*must attend on time at Westerham*'[1]. Now-a-days the situation is quite different and employees of all types of companies live where they can and often at long distances from work; yet it can be argued that weather and transport difficulties do delay arrival on occasion and there is something to be said in favour of the older approach.

Regionalisation

At the peak of the Surveyor system, there were fifteen districts in all, Sevenoaks in 1938 still coming under the South-East district based at Croydon with Mr P.W. McIntyre in charge and A.S. Langlands OBE and H.D.Wooster as assistants first class, also three assistants second class.

But under the Bridgeman Report, the Report of the Committee of Enquiry on the Post Office 1932, a policy of Regionalisation was started in 1934. Whilst the Main Post Office Board framed policy, the Regions were empowered to make day-to-day decisions on routine affairs without the need to refer to London. This new policy was a complete reversal of early Post Office practice where even the smallest detail required approval of London and ofttimes of the Treasury if money was involved. But Regionalisation was to prove invaluable during the coming war. There were ten Regions: Sevenoaks came under the South Eastern Region at Milton House, 39 Churchill Square, Brighton. The Regional method of organisation was to last fifty years until a new approach was introduced in 1984.

General Strike   1926 saw labour relations worsening and the General Strike. The Sevenoaks Chronicle reported[2] *'Special wireless apparatus at the Town Hall is receiving the broadcast bulletins which are being displayed for information. The public are earnestly requested not to use the post or telephone services more than is essential.'* Newspapers were dropped from the air in some rural areas in East Sussex, but not as far as is known anywhere near Sevenoaks.

Sunday Working   The end of full Sunday working came on 5th June 1921, although the Head Office Counters at Sevenoaks still were open for business for an hour and a half on Sunday Mornings and this facility remained until the late 1950's. In 1936 a Sunday afternoon/evening collection to connect with the night mail T.P.Os was started up as part of the overall national network.

Double peaked shako and uniform of 1920's (pre-1932). Thought to be local, but who are they? (Gordon Anckorn Colln)

Uniform Clothing and Mishaps   Normally postmen bought their footwear;   that this was so is emphasised by the many advertisements for boots in *'The Post. The Organ of the Union of Post-Office Workers'* in the 1920's.

Most prominent of all was the disappearance of the double-peaked shako in 1932 to be replaced with a peaked cap. The uniform became a dark blue heavy worsted suit, lounge style, with thin red piping worn with a collar and tie.

There were the usual mishaps, for example, the fire at Tatsfield premises in 1926 when Mrs. Parker was commended for removing documents and the attempted robbery at Biggin Hill in January of that same year.

More Telephone Call Boxes   For those relying on public telephones, and there were many such persons, kiosks and inside call-boxes were spreading to the outlying areas. Wrotham Heath and Ightham by 1922; Fairseat, Stone Street and Chipstead by 1923; Ivy Hatch by 1928; Brasted Chart, Cudham, Hodsall Street, Stansted and Toys Hill by 1930; Godden Green, St. Mary Platt, Underriver and Westerham Hill by 1931 and, one of the last, East Hill by 1932.

Clubs   The Cricket Club already mentioned still played on the Vine. A description of one match may serve as an example and bring to mind some of the old players. In June 1937 a single innings match played on a Tuesday took place between Sevenoaks Post Office (152 runs) and Rochester & Chatham Post Office (37 runs) in a competition match for the S.E. District P.O. Surveyors Shield. Sevenoaks' scorers were A. Boyce bowled 13, J. Marshall b 2, W.H. Hodge b 1, G. Orton b 1, C.S. Vincent run out 39, C.W. French run out 69, F. Walkling b 0, B. May b 8, R. Green b 9, C. Hodge not out 1, Extras 2. Vincent bowled three wickets, Marshall three and Green one. Webb stumped one b. Vincent, Hodge caught and bowled one, one run out, one not out. Sevenoaks went forward in the competition.

Transport - Motorisation

Once World War I was over the Post Office was able to restart its motorised transport development. In 1920 it possessed 60 vans and 4 motor cycle combinations; by 1926, 1002 vans of various descriptions, 176 motor cycle combinations and 48 motor cycles. Many of these were to replace contracted vehicles, also to speed up the work, for a postman can carry out work a contractor may not do. It was found that the 'motorisation' of two footposts required one footpost, one part-timer and one van at the same time giving some acceleration in the carrying out of the work. The change was effected where there was a saving of £20 per week, later this level of required saving was reduced to £5 per week.[3]

But pneumatic tyres, and motors were now having pneumatic tyres not solid ones, required 'tarmacadam' roads or else the tyres sucked out the grit in the interstices between the roadstones that the iron tyred coach wheels had impacted into the road surface, and so produced clouds of dust in the wake of the travelling motor vehicle. Main roads were, of course, tarmaced first, work starting about 1906 and then during the 1920's and early 1930's the process extended bit by bit to the minor roads, aided by the steamroller and tar machines, heating up the tar so that it would pour. Such tarmaced roads tended to become sticky in very hot weather. Playing 'tarsticks' became a favourite game for children, with a hot bath afterwards to try to remove the tar, or the more effective remedy of being 'buttered'.

Local Post Office change and development towards mechanisation is recorded in small items but with little supporting detail[4]: *1922 Borough Green and Wrotham post revision; 1923 Mounted Post converted to motor mail service; 1925 New contract for Sevenoaks Mail Contract services; 1928 Sevenoaks-Weald, Underriver Official motor cycle combination working - introduction; 1929 Wrotham-Garage Accommodation at the Three Post Boys Inn for m/c combination (ceased Dec 1935); 1929 M/cycle combination garage at Ightham; 1933 also at Ivy Hatch (ceased 1936).* The period 1923-1936 was to be the decade of motor cycle combinations for village collection and delivery.

Bligh's Meadow began to be used as a Public Car Park in 1930.

From   **PHONE 38 BORO' GREEN.**

PIERCE,

Builder and Decorator,

PLATT, BORO' GREEN, KENT.

BRANCHES:
HIGH STREET, WEST MALLING &
SEVENOAKS ROAD, BORO GREEN.

Sept 21st. *192* 3

Messrs. Winch,

Greensted & Winch.

Sittingbourne.

681

Dear Sirs,

Replying to your letter of the 19th. inst.

re account due from us to Messrs. Smeed Dean & Co

1920's letter showing early Boro' Green Telephone Number, Sevenoaks double ring handstamp prior to machine cancelling, Sevenoaks skeleton with whole of outer rim missing on postcard from France.

Motor Vans By 1935 the move was toward motor **vans**. As a general statement the Post Office always bought and maintained its own fleet of vans rather than hiring from a contractor. The Post Office was also its own insurer, having deposited a large sum of money for that purpose, and introduced solid rubber front wings to many of its smaller vehicles to cut down damage repairs.

1935 saw the rent of many garages, Old Post Office Yard; 86a High Street (1937) for three 1 ton vans; Ightham; Westerham at the George and Dragon and Wrotham. By 1940 Wrotham had two motor vehicles and Ightham one. After WWII in 1947 garages were being rented at Durlings in Ightham, George and Dragon at Westerham, Burgess Service Station at Wrotham, Borough Green, 86a High Street and The Old Post Office Yard.

Motorised Omnibuses As well as their own vehicles and the railways, the Post Office made use of local bus services to carry mail bags. Standard practice was for the bag to be padlocked to a stanchion inside the bus and to travel unaccompanied, the post office at the receiving end having the only other key to unlock it. This sometimes caused problems en route when a bus had to be taken out of service for some defect.

The Westerham Diary[5] gives more detailed information on how motorisation progressed and the various problems encountered. It also shows that bus transport was regularly used to transport mailbags between Westerham and Redhill and between Westerham and Biggin Hill.

Mon. 12 Sept 1928 *A combined despatch containing all letters and parcels at present due for delivery from Biggin Hill S.O. should be made up and despatched by bus leaving Westerham at 11.00 am (prepaid by labels).'*

6 July 1936 *Outdoor and Motor Post to Toys Hill commenced.*

31 August 1936 *Non-arrival of Redhill mail. Bus broke down at Redhill.*

30 November 1936 *Punctured tyre on Mail Van - missed collection.*

25 September 1937 *Bag for Redhill not locked on bus because of accident. Conductor states he may have to change buses.*

28 March 1938 *Motor van Service started for Rural deliveries.*

14 Feb 1939 *Breakdown of Toys Hill Motor at French St. 7 am. Mechanics arrived 9 am.*

These are all the road items considered worthy of noting in the Westerham diary in the pre-war years. There must surely have been more happenings, but on the whole the motorisation programme seems to have worked well.

The current numbering of bus routes took place in 1924. Controlled entry to routes started in 1931 not to be loosened until 1987, by which time buses had long ceased to be used for regular mailbag carrying.

Despatches to Villages and Collections
1924

0430	First despatch to villages, *then further despatches from Sevenoaks sorting office at*
0915	Dunton Green, Halstead, Knockholt
1110	Ide Hill
1330	Ash, Boro' Green, Fairseat, Hodsall St., Ightham, Ivy Hatch, Kemsing, Kingsdown, Plaxtol, St. Mary Platt, Stone Street, Wrotham, Wrotham Heath.
1350	Otford
1430	Underriver, Weald
1445	Brasted, Brasted Chart, Chevening, Chipstead, Dunton Green, Riverhead, Sundridge, Toys Hill, Westerham
1600	Godden Green

Lamp Posting Boxes 1983: Georgian box in wall opposite to Ightham Mote. (AGD)
Georgian box attached to sawn-off Telegraph Pole Wrotham Road, Borough Green. (AGD)

Last Collections were mostly between 6 pm and 730 pm.

Ash	4.50 pm	Hodsall St.	4.50 pm	St. Mary Platt	6.05 pm
Biggin Hill	6.00	Ide Hill	6.25	Stansted	5.00
Boro' Green	7.15	Ightham	7.20	Stone Street	6.20
Brasted	7.20	Ivy Hatch	6.10	Sundridge	7.25
Brasted Chart	6.25	Kemsing	6.35	Tatsfield	6.00
Chipstead	7.35	Kingsdown	6.20	Toys Hill	6.10
Chevening	5.45	Knockholt	7.10	Underriver	6.00
Cudham	6.20	Otford	6.30	Weald	6.00
Dunton Green	7.35	Plaxtol	6.10	Westerham	7.00
Fairseat	5.10	Riverhead	7.40	Wrotham	7.05
Godden Green	6.00	Seal	7.40	Wrotham Heath	4.50
Halstead	7.20	Shoreham	6.10	Westerham Hill	6.15

By **1935**, as transport improved and became motorised, the first despatch now left Sevenoaks for the villages at 0500; there were no despatches at 0915 and 1110. Then came –

1330	A similar round to that of 1924.
1400	Cudham, Halstead, Knockholt, Otford, Shoreham.
1500	Brasted, Brasted Chart, Chevening, Riverhead, Sundridge, Toys Hill, Tatsfield, Biggin Hill, Dunton Green, Kemsing, East Hill, Kingsdown.
1515	Godden Green, Seal, Underriver, Weald, Westerham.
1545	Ide Hill

With last collections mostly between 5pm and 730pm.

Some village Sub-offices: Toys Hill cross-road and post office (inset) c1907. (Unknown)

Knockholt Post Office 1984. Now closed. (AGD)

In **1940** despatches to all villages were at 0500 and 1300, with last collections much earlier, between 4pm and 6pm. Later during the war, second deliveries in rural areas ceased.

Afterwards the policy in rural areas became to give a second delivery where this had been given pre-war, but not to extend the second delivery.

Stansted street furniture and wallbox in brick pillar 1984. (AGD)

Halstead Sub Office at Jessamine Cottage 1985, now demolished. (AGD)

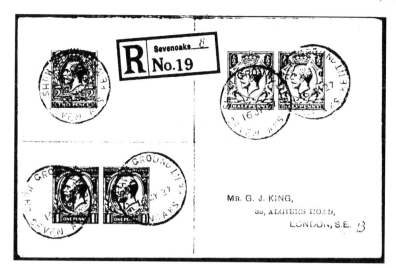

*Mail of 1920-30's:
Sevenoaks' first
commemorative handstamp,
for the Agricultural show July
1927.*

*1932 On inspection, turned
out not to be 'Printed Paper'
which went at a cheap rate
and so, 'Liable to letter rate
697' and '1d to pay 697'
with the new Krag machine
cancel, first used in 1928.*

Some Statistics 1921-1939[6]

Letters and Parcels Posted and Delivered. Sevenoaks. (One week)

	Letters posted	Letters delivered	Parcels posted	Parcels delivered
1921	62,702	88,707	1,864	2,863
1922	68,179	102,732	1,817	3,186
1923	72,207	108,836	1,969	3,604
1924	75,030	114,327	2,037	3,632
1925	79,188	123,238	1,955	4,012
1926	83,536	129,674	1,985	3,971
1927	88,461	142,756	2,110	4,268
1928	88,592	144,522	2,123	4,313

Missorting outwards 1932/1939

Random items (Letters, short and long, packets, parcels) examined, not total sent -

Feb 1932	32/13488	(0.24%)		Jan 1939	264/48920	(0.53%)
Mar	26/11403	(0.22%)		Feb	341/64268	(0.53%)
Apl	44/16940	(0.25%)		Mar	446/81555	(0.55%)
May	39/13663	(0.28%)		Apl	539/102951	(0.52%)
June	37/11114	(0.33%)		May	653/125719	(0.52%)
July	33/ 7328	(0.45%)		June	804/149739	(0.43%)
Sept	24/10122	(0.23%)		July	900/166008	(0.54%)
Oct	20/ 5540	(0.36%)		Aug	981/185636	(0.53%)
Nov	21/ 9016	(0.23%)				
Dec	17/ 8334	(0.20%)				

Airmail

Airmail progressed, at first to Europe then to the Empire overseas. At first there was a large additional charge but by 1938 came the 'all up' Empire airmail scheme with no additional charge above the normal 1½d rate.

A local incident occurred in 1927[7]. On Saturday afternoon 10th July 1927 Capt. McIntosh, piloting the Imperial Airways Airliner from Paris to London, was forced to land at Hundred Acres, Brasted, through poor visibility and shortage of petrol. There was no damage. He was carrying twelve passengers, mostly Americans and a mechanic. The passengers went to Bonds' Garage whence they were picked up by a tender from Imperial Airways and taken to Croydon. Although no mention is made in the report, it is more than likely that the aeroplane was carrying mail.

World War II 1939-1947

Once the Second World War started, it was soon to have its effect on Postal working. As early as 14 September 1939 the Sevenoaks News was informing the public that owing to lighting restrictions the 8 pm to 9.30 pm late collections in the rural areas were to be suspended in Biggin Hill, Westerham, Brasted, Sundridge, Chipstead, Riverhead, Otford and Kemsing. The Town collections were also to be earlier, the last being between 8 pm and 8.30 pm with 10 pm at the Head Office Box.

By 30 October 1939 Sevenoaks main office opening was restricted to 8.30 am to 6.30 pm (not 8-7.30) and Westerham the same with all sub-offices open 9 am to 6 pm instead of the usual inter-war hours of 9-7. However, these restricted hours were relaxed and longer ones worked in the week's run-up to Christmas that year.

11 July 1940 the second delivery became restricted due to staff call-up for service with the Forces. Villages with now only one delivery were Chevening, Godden Green, Ide Hill, Ivy Hatch, Knatts Valley, Otford Hills, Shoreham, Underriver, Weald and outlying parts of Chipstead, Dunton Green, Riverhead and Seal. Areas that previously had three deliveries now had only two, but *'Correspondence will be available for callers as notified in the sub-post office windows'*.[8]

Trouble was ahead for the 'Sevenoaks News'. It was bombed out with a direct hit during the late evening of 11 October 1940, a Thursday.[9] Happily Mr. and Mrs. Hooper, who were there working at the time, were not badly hurt and happily too they were soon rescued before any escaping gas exploded. They had almost the full week to organise before the paper had to be on the streets again for Wednesday 17th October 1940, which it was, carrying a report of its own misfortune in unidentified third person terms as required in wartime and another item from the Postmaster of Sevenoaks, Mr. S.D.W. Wigger to say that as from Sunday 20th October 1940 last collections, both town and rural, would be at least one hour earlier because of difficulties of travel in the blackout; Town boxes to be closed at 5.30 pm instead of 6.30 pm and Head Office box closing at 6.45 pm.

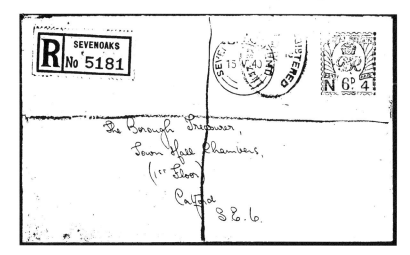

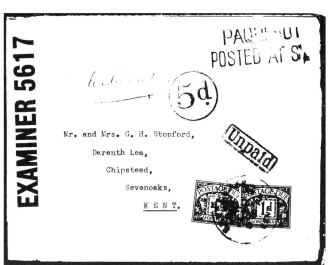

World War II mail.
Top: 1940 Registered Letter with early meter mark.

Middle: 1941 Paquetbot. Posted at sea. Presumably no stamps available, but still charged double as from a civilian.

Bottom: 1944 Local letter to Dr Gordon Ward the well-known medical doctor and writer on local historical matters, in his wartime position as a Lieutenant-Colonel.

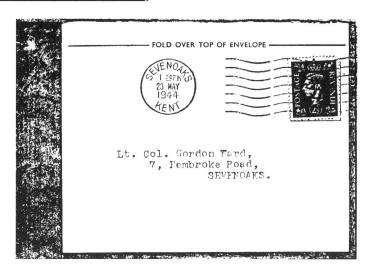

Following the invasion scare, signposts were taken down and milestones uprooted under the Removal of Direction Signs Order, as from 31 May 1940. These signs subsequently began to be replaced, in towns from October 1942 and in rural districts from May 1943, the restrictions finally being fully lifted in October 1944.[10]

Double summertime with its long daylight evenings came into effect during the summer of 1941 to save fuel, with single summertime continuing through the winter. But these arrangements were not made permanent and reverted in 1946 (but not 1947) and then from 1948 onwards to the single hour summertime arrangements enjoyed today. In April of that same year, 1941, Riverhead Parish Council observed to the Head Postmaster of Sevenoaks that it was reasonable to have a collection in the village later than 5.15 pm now the nights were lighter as the early collection left so little time to answer correspondence.

Sevenoaks Town in 1942 adopted H.M.S. Gallant and later H.M.S. Zenith. In October 1945 a Petty Officer and two ratings of H.M.S. Zenith travelled to the town with four bunches of that unknown fruit, bananas, which were given to children in local hospitals, some of whom had never seen one.

The impact of World War II is also recorded in the Westerham Postal diary.

18 January 1939	*880 Circulars, the Air Raid Precautions Evacuation scheme leaflets were received for delivery within the next two days.*
15 June 1939	*The Rural motor van service having started in March 1938, the Postman driver Mr. A.J.F. Sherry was now called up for military training for an 'uncertain' length of time.*
8 July 1939	*Blackout practice started.*
3 September 1939	*War declared 11.30 am and leave suspended.*
11 September 1939	*Air Raid Precaution equipment received.*
6 November 1939	*New duties for Wartime arrangements of mails*
22 April 1940	*Anti-Gas equipment received.*

After 31 August 1940 Westerham office will be reduced to dependent status and no mails will be despatched or received except through Sevenoaks H.O.
Second Rural deliveries cancelled.

As might be expected there are wartime records of women on outside staff, often classed as *'Temporary Auxiliary Postwoman'*. The temporary nature was due to the wartime regulation that a person joining the forces had his civilian job kept open to return to on cessation of hostilities.

A.F.Davis, to become postmaster 1959-62, spent the whole of the war in the Royal Corps of Signals, having joined from Post Office employment. P.A. Mansfield, Medical Officer in 1918, is again recorded in that position.

Home Defence

The H.Q. of the 8th (Home Defence) Bn of the Queens Own Royal West Kent Regt was at 'Moorcocks' Brasted as letters of the time show, with one of its more important detachments at Penshurst aerodrome. The Commander Royal Engineers was at Beechmont, Gracious Lane; Beechmont was not hit by a V-bomb until 1944.

Then the creation of Local Defence Volunteer Units was announced over the wireless by Anthony Eden on 14th May 1940. By the 18th May 1940 there were armed LDV men on patrol in Kent. By 24th June the County Territorial Association became responsible for their finance and administration, records and rations. On 3rd August the companies were affiliated to local infantry Regiments which meant among other things that they could wear the Regiment's cap badge, in the case of Sevenoaks area, the Queens Own Royal West Kent Regiment.

Winston Churchill insisted that the volunteers' name be changed and on 23rd August 1940 the Companies became known as 'Home Guard'. In November of the same year the Battalions were numbered. Sevenoaks became the 20th Bn of The Royal West Kents and had 1,500 men in 9 Companies.

The 20th Bn was a 'General Service' Battalion commanded by Lt. Col. G. Shaw, MC, with H.Q. based at Knole Park Golf Club. The Bn was also responsible for the defence of the Fighter Station at Biggin Hill. Tonbridge was the 21st Bn and Tunbridge Wells the 22nd, all General Service Home Guard Battalions.

At first there was some doubt as to whether Post Office employees, being civil servants, should be allowed to join, although some did. This doubt was finally dispelled by a letter of 22 May 1940, sent to all employees of the Post Office, saying they could join. At the same time special 'Utility' Battalions were formed, the 25th (Post Office) Kent Home Guard, the 26th (Kent Buses) Bn, the 27th (Kent Electric Power) Bn, the 28th (Southern Railway) Bn. These were designated for specific tasks and their Companies, four in the Post Office Bn at first, later six, were split across the whole county of Kent. By June, the 25th (Post Office) Bn commanded by G. Casemore, Esq., had enrolled 1,628 volunteers.

In April 1941 Home Guard Officers were finally given commissions. Eventually the 20th Sevenoaks General Service Bn became very large and split to form the 32nd Edenbridge Bn as well. Edenbridge was a Nodal defence point. In the event of invasion the civilian population would be evacuated and the town had to be held locally for at least three days until reinforcements arrived. In February 1942 there was compulsory direction into the Home Guard for war work and its fully volunteer character changed. The Home Guard units 'stood down' on Sunday 3rd September 1944.[11]

J. Dewsbury of Sevenoaks won the Darts Cup in 1944 and was presented with it by Lieut French of the Post Office Home Guard[12], the one who was run out in the 1937 Cricket match previously recorded.

In the troubled times of 1952-1957, the Home Guard Battalions of the Royal West Kent Regiments reformed, more or less as before, but Edenbridge was with Tonbridge: 20th Bn Sevenoaks, 21/32 Bn Tonbridge, 22nd Bn Tunbridge Wells.

Prisoner of War Mail

As the war progressed Prisoners of War arrived into the area, Italians and Germans. There was no main camp located actually within the Sevenoaks Postal District, but there were three main camps just outside:

Camp 40   at Tonbridge, Somerhill Camp

Camp 267 at Mereworth Castle, Wateringbury.

Camp 154 at Dartford, Swanscombe Ministry of Works Camp.[13]

At Tonbridge there were two camps each holding about 250 prisoners. Under the War Agricultural Committee arrangements were made for POW's to work on farms and one of these camps at the corner of the road leading to Capel from Pembury Road opposite the Vauxhall Inn supplied labour for farms as far as Seal, Sevenoaks, Weald but not Wrotham[14], firstly Italians and latterly Germans. The men were brought out by transport in the mornings carrying midday rations and collected in the evenings. These camps were for rank and file soldiers, not Officers or S.S.

The camp at Somerhill Park, Tonbridge, prefabricated huts,[15] was taken over for the homeless families when the last prisoners went home and is now the site of the Weald of Kent Girls School.[16]

For the Wrotham area there was a POW camp for Italians on the right of the road to Wrotham just outside Borough Green.[17] As this camp is not listed, it was no doubt a sub-camp, probably coming under Mereworth.

As with all POW camps, the prisoners in these local camps were allowed limited mail facilities, normally on the standard printed POW postcard of which each man received a rationed number each week. These were always censored and despatched through the main camp. An example of one such from Camp 40 is illustrated.

There is a mystery entry in Post 38 '1949 Wrotham Camp - Postal Arrangements - Boundary'. There are no further details or supporting documentation. This entry could refer to the OCTU camps that had been there, or the old POW camp, by 1949 probably put to some different use.

Airfields Inter-wars and WWII

Once the Wireless Experimental Station had departed Biggin Hill Airfield this gave an opportunity during the inter-war years for the AA School of Defence under Col. Sinclair and Capt. Sims, the R.A.F. Anti-

World War II mail. Paid stamp and cachet in red from Chief Superintendent of Design, The Grange Knockholt; Letter to OC Defences Penshurt Aerodrome; DRLS cachet from Biggin Hill; Prisoner of War postcard (Italian) from Camp 40 Tonbridge.

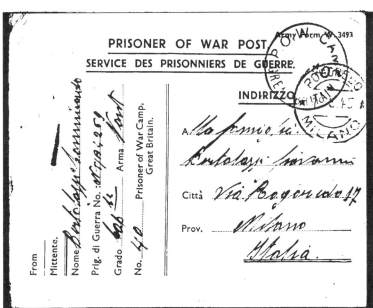

Opposite page.
Wartime re-use of envelopes.

Top: 1941 War Office London posted to O C 8th Home Defence Battalion, West Kent Regiment at Moorcocks, Rectory Lane, Brasted. Re-used to Redhill carried by Army Signals Dorking and subsequently to Penshurst detachment of 8th Bn West Kents guarding Penshurst aerodrome.

Bottom: Before Beechmont was destroyed by a V1 flying bomb. Letter to the Commander Royal Engineers by Army Signals Despatch Rider Letter Service (DRLS).

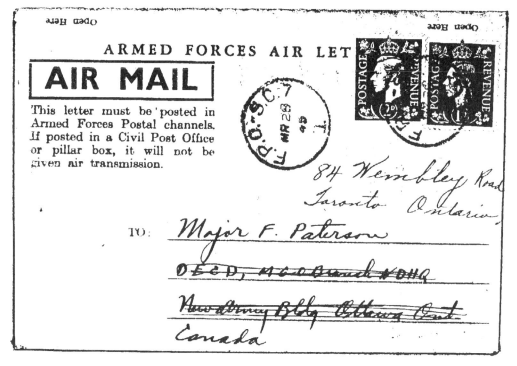

World War II Transit mail. *Mail to and from Canada, bags routed through Biggin Hill on 'mail can' run.*
SC7 was the postmark of Canadian Military HQ London.

Aircraft Corps under Sq. Leader Venn, the Search light Experimental Station and Acoustical Section Royal Engineers, to be concentrated and then expanded and developed. At most times there was also a night flying squadron and a fighter squadron in residence.

There are no specific postal services on the airfield known during the inter-war period, though obviously each unit would have its handstamps of an official (non-postal) character. During the 1926 General Strike Avros stationed at Biggin Hill were used to drop copies of 'The British Gazette' over South Coast villages, the year before parachutes became standard equipment in 1927.

During the run-up to WWII, 1936-39, interception techniques in conjunction with Radar and Radio Telephony (R/T) to a ground operations room were developed from their WWI beginnings.

RAF Post Office

Wartime saw Biggin Hill become the home of many fighter squadrons with many hundreds of personnel on the site, at times a thousand or more. During this period a Class B RAF Post Office with double ring steel date stamp was opened on the airfield, coming under Westerham P.O. Eventually by 1946 this post office was downgraded to an RAF postroom. The opening and closing dates of the class B office are not exactly known. Like all other airfields, Biggin Hill also had a Despatch Rider (Don R.) letter service during wartime and examples are shown.

At times, Royal Canadian Air Force Squadrons as opposed to individual Canadian pilots serving with the RAF, were stationed at Biggin Hill, 401 Squadron in 1941/2 and 1943/4, also in this latter period 411 and 412 Squadrons. The Squadron P.O. at Biggin Hill, MC71, handling Canadian mail used a British FPO 492 handstamp. The Main Canadian Post Office for Biggin Hill also used a British handstamp allotted to it FPO 847.

During 1945 control of the airfield passed from 11 Group Fighter Command to 46 Group Transport Command.[18] The Canadian 'Mailcan' run ceased to terminate at Prestwick and transferred to Biggin Hill, when in June 168 (Heavy Transport) Squadron of the Royal Canadian Airforce was based on the airfield. The Flying Fortresses and later Liberators carried Canadian mail from their base in Rockville Ontario to Biggin Hill for the UK and for transfer to Dakota aircraft for distribution to Canadian personnel in France, Belgium, Holland and Germany.[19] Mail was also carried in the reverse direction to Canada. 314 Squadron of the USAAF also arrived. In December 1945, 168 Sqn. went back to Canada and 436 Sqn. of the RCAF came till June 1946 by which time the 'Mailcan' service had ceased. Although there was mailbag transfer, according to US records,[20] there was no USAPO on the station; there could have been a Canadian post office at the later date but the records are rather vague on this point.[21]

After the war regular yearly commemoration celebrations started up. Rather a special one was that of 1955 at the end of September when the 'At Home' was opened by Jack Hawkins on the Saturday and on

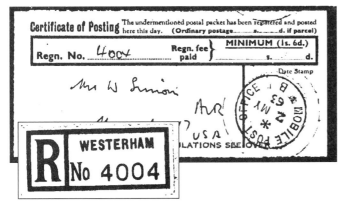

Biggin Hill Commemorative mail. *Civilian. Mobile Post Office B at annual Air Show using Westerham labels 1963. Military. FPO 999 The Royal Engineers Field Post Office visits Biggin Hill 1983.*

the Sunday there was a Drumhead Memorial Service when the memorial windows commemorating the Battle of Britain were dedicated, followed by a fly-past. At these meetings the Mobile Post Office often attended. From 1965, the 25th Anniversary, there have been a series of special covers with British Forces Post Office cancels, as well as the frequent attendance of the Royal Engineers Army Field Post Office using FPO 999 cancel on mail posted there.

Other Stations   The airfield situated just to the north of Penshurst at the edge of the Postal District area, like Biggin Hill, started in 1917 as a Wireless School (No 2) co-operating with AA and Coast Artillery[22]. In the interwar period it became a civil landing ground and reopened again in 1942-45 for Air Observation Post Squadrons (653, 658, 664), part of the Army Co-operation Command.

During WWI the airfield at Sundridge was used as a Royal Air Force Recovery Unit for crashed aircraft.

RAF Kingsdown was the house at Hollywood Manor in (West) Kingsdown where many WAAF were stationed, it being a Signals Intelligence Station for the RAF 'Y' Service.[23] Now a home for boys, Kingsdown Hall

In July 1941 the Country Club at Wilderness became **Guy's Hospital's U.S.A. Hospital** sponsored by the Hollywood Branch of 'Bundles for Britain'. It was felt there was a need for Hospital Patients to gain some relaxation away from the rigours of London. Correspondence between the US givers and UK recipients was encouraged.

Fort Halstead situated on the A21 at the top of Polhill Hill is the home of the Royal Armament Research and Defence Establishment. Received wisdom has it that Halstead Fort together with Westerham Fort were built to defend London against French invasion during the Napoleonic Wars. However, in fact, Halstead Fort came into being when in 1888 the Government accepted General Sir Edward Hamley's plan to establish a series of lightly fortified assembly points along the North Downs around which Volunteer units could mobilise and the site was acquired in 1890 for £2,939 with the works costing £22,254. Interest flagged with Hamley's death but the site was used to store ammunition in WWI after which the site was sold in 1921 when it was used as a camp site for local Territorials, Scouts, Guides and destitute refugees. The site was bought back by the War Office in 1937. Atomic weapons work carried out here was transferred to Aldermaston in 1955.[24]

In the 1960's, the Fort ordered from the Post Office its own double ring steel date stamp, but no-one now can recall the use to which it was put. In 1962 the Fort became 'Royal' at the time of a visit by the Queen and in 1984 expanded its boundary westward to overlie the top half of the earliest turnpike road up Star Hill (connecting the open junctions WY on map p.110), which had by then become a footpath and which was diverted.

The Post-War Years 1947-1984

Mr. Ottaway (1944-1948) had the task of welcoming back and settling in those employees that returned from wartime service in the Forces. **J.R.Henderson** (1948-1959) had one of the longest spells in the position here, nearly twelve years before retiring to his native Scotland.

Postal Acts

After the Second World War came the Postal Acts of 1953, 1961, 1969 and lastly the 1981 Act to be deal with later.

Up to **1961** the Post Office had to plan with the knowledge that its forecasts had to gain Treasury acceptance. The 1961 Post Office Act began the change in status. The Post Office would no longer receive a vote of expenditure from Parliament and this differentiated it from other Government Departments.

The **1969** Postal Act continued the change in status. The Post Office became a Public Corporation with complete separation from the Civil Service. The Act transferred power from the Post Master General and the Ministry to the Post Office and its Board, defined the objectives of the Post Office, set limits on its

Sevenoaks Post Office staff 1965 outside the Crown Office. D E Middleton, Head Postmaster. (Sevenoaks Post Office Official Photo. Permission W Clancy)

powers and ensured it discharged its functions in the national interest.[25] It was no longer a Government Department but still came under the jurisdiction of a government department, the Ministry of Posts and Telecommunications, later the Ministry of Industry, now Trade and Industry.[26] In effect the Post Office now became a commercial concern able to compete with other commercial concerns. It did, however, retain the monopoly of letter-carrying, challenged unsuccessfully by 'Post Haste' company in 1971, but most of its other services are open to competition.

Sunday Working   On 23rd June 1950 Sunday Working was said to be officially stopped. Perhaps the best way to interpret this would be to say that there was to be no further extension of existing Sunday work. Sunday evening collections continued until 1976 when they too stopped, by a management decision. No business correspondence was carried on a Sunday night and the cessation meant one less batch of Travelling Post Office operation to pay for.

Transport   Whilst giving out the safe driving awards for 1954/55 it was recorded that at Sevenoaks there were 40 vehicles in use, 55 drivers and the yearly mileage 411,800. There had been nine accidents with the P.O. at fault.

General Working   January 1962 saw a 'Work-to-Rule' go-slow occasioned by Government insistence on a pay-pause and refusal of pay arbitration for the P.O. The 'Peoples Post' handled parcels but were prohibited from dealing with letters. 1971 saw the full scale shut-down for the strike which occurred in February when the weather was poor and at a time when the country was converting to decimal currency. Local posts were licenced to ameliorate the situation. There did not appear to be a local post in Sevenoaks, although in theory the Culverstone Local Post, with a ten mile radius, would cover all of Sevenoaks but come short of Brasted and Cudham. There was a post from Hadlow to Tonbridge and an unlicenced Free Post in Biggin Hill.

This was a period of rising labour costs per unit of mail, from an index value of 100 in 1965/6 to 390 in 1975/6 and hence wages stayed low. Productivity and mechanisation were being held-up by the union.[27] Advertisements in local papers for postmen in Sevenoaks during 1961 gave wages at 24 years of age and over of £11.1.6 per week after one year's service plus 12/6 if driving, and in 1970 '£18.8.- basic at 22 plus overtime, Sundays and night work'. These were wages before the strike. Part of the increased wages after the strike were passed on in higher charges and this resulted in lower traffic volume nationally. Taking into account inflation, the first step letter-rate which had remained static at 1840 levels was suddenly jacked up by almost two-thirds, and has remained at that level ever since.[28] At this time the 'Union of Postal Workers' changed its name to the 'Union of Communication Workers'.

Uniforms are altered every twenty years or so now so that they do not become too out of line with current needs and fashion. In 1955 a new style summer uniform was introduced, again dark blue, and the following year single-breasted jackets were replaced by double-breasted and again, three years later in 1958, a new style of peaked cap and badge.

1969 (men) and 1970 (women) saw perhaps the biggest change, quite a dramatic one to a lighter weight suit in grey with a red metal badge. Some of the jackets had darker collars and cuffs. These have now changed back (1984) to the familiar dark blue with red piping.

Christmas Rush   The local Territorial Army drill hall in Sevenoaks is in Argyle Road, used by the 'West Kents', but after several amalgamations of infantry regiments since WWII, this name, as also that of 'The Buffs' in east Kent, has been dropped in favour of '5th (Volunteer) Bn The Queens Regiment'.

'Traditionally' at Christmas time this Drill Hall is used to sort parcels and contractor vans are engaged, five in 1954. In 1958 there were nine, six of which were S. Bowen of Knockholt's cattle trucks used for carrying Odham's of Borough Green's many books in their heyday. Part-time staff, many of them students, were engaged over the Christmas period to help with sorting and delivery and as some of these

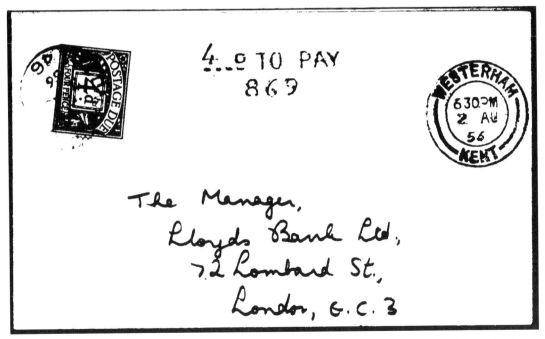

1956 Unpaid Westerham letter showing the 869 office number and double charge. Also the early type double ring thin arc handstamp.

carried out the work year after year they brought their expertise with them. 135 temporary staff were engaged in 1956, 190 in 1961 and down to 150 in 1963.

At the same time the Post Office was exhorting customers to 'post early'. In 1954 'All the staff came in on Christmas Day but got things cleared by lunchtime'. The peak posting day in 1960 was December 20th and by the following year this had been taken back to December 18th. Now customers have been persuaded to post earlier and earlier. The rush period now starts by December 10th or even a few days earlier and Christmas Eve postwise has become an anti-climax as most letters and parcels have been received several days earlier.

Closure of Westerham Railway Branch Line   Under Ernest Marples, the last run on the Westerham line was on 28th October 1961 and the track was lifted in 1967. Possibly it was a small item but actions like this made it obvious to the Post Office that in future its short, and possibly even medium distance runs would have to be by road.

New Building   The Post Office owned land on the south side of South Park, which had been part of the land of 'The Royal Crown' and where now a new P.O. complex was to be built. In the early 1960's there was a collection of huts used by the P.O. Engineers and where also van maintenance took place. In 1963 about 80/90 vans and 29 motor cycles parked there but this number would include P.O. Telephones and P.O. Engineers, not just GPO delivery vans.

In planning the current Post Office, Sevenoaks Council insisted on space for pedestrian access from the High Street to the public car park at the rear.

The new functional building at the south corner of South Park and London Road was occupied in 1970. The Counter Building and the Sorting Office which was still in full use were contiguous, with administrative offices above.

Opening of the present South Park Office 1970. Mr Ottaway, Mr Middleton, Mr Henderson.
(Sevenoaks Chronicle)

Major Offices of the District 1984.   Top: Edenbridge Crown Office; sorting office at rear. Counter shut 1990. Bottom: Westerham Crown Office, with sorting office at side.   Opposite Top: Wrotham Office with sorting office inside at back and parking for delivery vans at rear.   Opposite Bottom: Biggin Hill (Westerham) Sorting Office London Road, previously the telephone exchange. (All AGD)

Subscriber Trunk Dialing, STD, came to Sevenoaks in March 1963, and on the same site but separate and further west was the Telephone building, the telephone services at that time still being part of the Post Office. This large telephone building, now part of British Telecom, effectively prevents any expansion of the Post Office site which is somewhat limited in van parking facilities. Van maintenance is now organised from the Tonbridge MLO site.

Administration   In 1973 Sevenoaks, whilst still remaining a Post Town, came under Tunbridge Wells administratively. Then in 1980, when the administration offices had been built on top of the MLO at Vestry estate in Tonbridge, the local administration moved out of central Tunbridge Wells to Tonbridge.

Post WWII Developments in Army Postal Services.

From the 1950s the Royal Engineers Postal Section became increasingly involved with handling the mail of the other two armed services. The name changed to Royal Engineers Postal and Courier Communication Service. Service here is, of course, full-time but Territorial Army units attached to REPCCS consist of GPO personnel thus ensuring current expertise to call on and interfertilisation of methods and techniques. Additionally, there has been some limited exchange of personnel at top level.

Courier Services   Having taken over much of the handling of the 'written communication' work from the Royal Corps of Signals and after several trials, by 1958 the Security Courier Service was fully formed as part of REPS. By 1974, renamed the Forces Courier Service, it was carrying classified and time-sensitive material for the Ministry of Defence covering the three Armed Services and other approved organisations such as Commonwealth Defence Forces and NATO. In 1985 this organisation was again expanded, reorganised and renamed 'Defence Courier Service'.[29]

New Postal Services

From 1961 on many new services have been introduced. In 1961 Recorded Delivery was introduced for a relatively cheap fee, the more expensive Registration Service being retained. 1963 saw the introduction of PCOs, Parcel Concentration Offices, and the gradual complete reorganisation of parcel handling with new depots dedicated to parcel handling only, fully mechanised and with good road access serving with specialised transport an area that included many post towns.

In 1967 POP sizes of stationery were designated. These were Post Office Preferred sizes that would fit the machines soon to be installed in the new Mechanised Letter Offices. That same year, the Postbus service started in some rural areas. Instead of a small van, the postman is provided with a passenger-carrying vehicle that will transport up to a dozen or so persons who, for payment, are able to treat the vehicle as a bus as the postman carries out his rounds. Although there are postbus services starting from Tunbridge Wells, there has never been any such service in the Sevenoaks district, although one might have thought that the Ash-Wrotham area was suitable Postbus territory, but it was not to be. However, an out of service postbus was used from Sevenoaks in the 1980s to take town postmen to the start of their delivery rounds in the same way as the Shillibeers did in London in the 1840s and during the rest of the day the old postbus filled in with Datapost deliveries. In the 1960s and 70s Landrovers had to be used in the Biggin Hill/Tatsfield areas on the steep unmade roads.

Two-Tier Post   In 1968 the letter rate and the cheaper printed paper rate, one sealed and the other requiring to be left open, gave way to the two-tier post for inland mail, first class and second class, both of which could be sealed. Second class took longer but was considerably cheaper than first class though little cheaper than the old printed paper rate. What came to happen was that instead of working in the sorting office at night until all outward mail was cleared, thus incurring extra payments for late working, the first class was extracted and dealt with that day and the second class left for outwards sorting next morning thus ensuring a more even flow of work through-out the day.

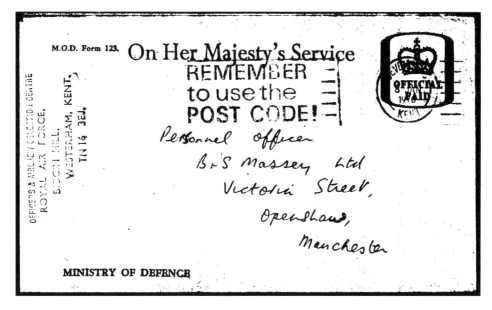

Above: c1970 Earliest Postage Paid Indicator (PPI) Sevenoaks Serial 1. There is no mention of first or second class which means it was used pre-1971. Mail with PPIs is not postmarked, consequently one has no means of knowing when it was despatched. Below: 1976 OHMS letter sent from Officers and Aircrew Selection Centre at Biggin Hill.

A New Marketing Concept

A Postal Marketing Department was set up in 1971 and a more aggressive marketing policy ensued, competitive and in line with the new status under the Act. From this, further new services began to flow.

In 1972 was started 'Household Delivery', the delivery of leaflets, often loose, not in envelopes and on an unsolicited basis. Persons not wishing to have such deliveries could say so. In similar vein, the Post Office in 1983 gained the commercial contract from British Telecom to distribute Yellow Pages and did so within 14 days of their receipt.[30]

Datapost   is available at Sevenoaks and some of the village offices. The service started in the 1970's at the time of the large first generation computers when firms would not own their own computer but rent a fixed period time, e.g. Tuesday 2 pm to 2.20 pm. The data to be put through had to be collected and delivered on time to the computer firm and the results brought back. From these beginnings an inland, subsequently world wide, document timed-delivery service has developed. Datapost resources include (in 1982) a fleet of seven chartered 'planes based at Luton airport. A second 'hub' is soon to be developed (1987) based on Manchester. Data post is now grouped with 'Parcels'.

Express Post 1980   A courier-type timed service. The 'express' of an earlier era now returns in the form of a motorcyclist, or rather now because of quantity a specialised van. Within the district there is a morning collection at set times to reach London and Heathrow (and on to other cities) by 1.30 with a return run back to deliver about 3.30 to 4 pm.   The morning run is -

9.30 Cranbrook			
9.45 Goudhurst			
9.45 Pembury		10.00 Crowborough	
	10.30 Tunbridge Wells		
	10.45 Tonbridge		
	Hildenborough		
11.00 Otford	11.15 Sevenoaks	10.20 Westerham	10.10 Biggin Hill
11.00 Dunton Green			
11.00 Riverhead			
	1.30/2.00 London and		
	Heathrow		

Charges for packages
to London	up to 10 kg -	1980 £6.50;	1981 £8.50
to Heathrow	up to 5 kg -	1980 £10;	1981 £12.50.

Intelpost   Started in 1980, Intelpost gives the instant transmission of facsimile representation be it letters or diagrams from one station to another either for single copy or multiples but is not yet available (1985) in the Sevenoaks area, the nearest Post Offices providing the service being, Dartford, Chatham, Croydon and Maidstone.

Electronic Post   Starting a year later in 1981, Electronic Post is a computer based laser printing service for bulk mailings. At the time of its inception all addresses in the Sevenoaks area were sent a long explanatory 'typed' letter produced by this service. No doubt few of these now remain. Both Intelpost and Electronic Post use what are now British Telecom lines.

Bulk Posting and Contract Mail   Now that the Post Office is a business corporation it is in a position to bargain with companies large and small concerning its charges and to make contracts tailored to suit individual companies within the district, covering the outgoing mail to be collected from the company's premises and carried. Both letters and parcels are involved and can often be spotted by the 'PPI' and 'C' printed where the stamp would normally be.

Bulk mail can now be pre-sorted based on post towns and postcode areas and bundled by the sending firm. This really is a help to the local MLO and qualifies for formal rebates, which also increase according to quantity, for example a pre-sorted second class mailing of between 5,000 and 23,529 should qualify for a discount of 15% and a mailing of over 1 million a discount of as much as 30%. Bulk mailing at first developed in conjunction with Football Pools, Mail Order Stores and dividend payments of large companies, is greatly expanded now the postcode directories are available. It is under this heading that the large circulations of what has come to be called 'junk mail' is handled, much of it unsolicited and based on purchased address lists. Much presorted mail now carries the 'M' for 'Mailsort' in place of the Postage Paid Indicator (PPI).

1970's Airmail Commemorative Covers
1972 Daily Express Trophy Shoreham
Sussex to Biggin Hill.
1972 Sheila Scott Biggin Hill Air Fair
via Iceland to Washington DC USA
1978 Balloon landing at Sevenoaks.

also
1971 Culverstone Strike post
(6d and 1/-)

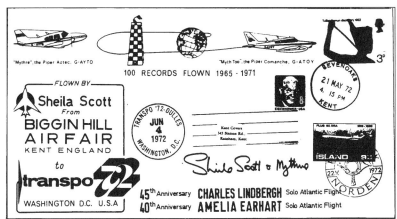

Some Town Sub-Offices in 1983:
Upper St John's Hill. (As it looked then.) Top
St Botolph's Road. (Now closed.) Bottom
South End Edenbridge. Opposite top
St John's Hill. Opposite bottom   (All AGD)

Sorting Offices and Circulation of Mail

Sevenoaks Sorting Office, in mid 1984; *(that is immediately prior to transfer of main sorting to Tonbridge MLO where sorting to first and second class, postmarking, coding and machine destination sorting now takes place)*[31]

Sevenoaks sorting office is adjacent to the main Post Office in South Park, situated between the public counters and the new Telephone Building. Sorting starts in earnest about 4.30 to 5 pm as the afternoon collections begin to come in. This is hand sorting to class, postmarking on a 'Universal' machine, then hand sorting to main destination. Bags are then made-up, sealed and labelled and sent off by train from Sevenoaks Tubs Hill Station, the first class mail leaving for London between 3.30 pm and 9 pm. The vans drive through the Car Park on the Down side and underneath the station to the unloading area where bags can directly enter the station or be taken across to the Up side by the goods lift.

Second class mail is no longer sorted the same evening as it used to be but is now sorted next morning as this avoids working after 7 pm when time plus one third is paid. It is then taken to Tonbridge MLO.

As from July 1984, all letters (except first class local ones posted in the special local box) are sent to Tonbridge MLO. There was a short interim period of a few weeks when letters were postmarked in Sevenoaks before sending to Tonbridge, for coding and machine sorting to be carried out there. Only local letters, some batch mailing and some parcels continued to be dealt with at Sevenoaks. Consequently the sorting staff is much reduced which incidentally is said to solve Sevenoaks' continual problem of finding sufficient suitable staff to employ at the nationally agreed level of wages that could be offered, a situation said to have been brought about by the 1880's town building policy already referred to and never fully solved by council house building.

Each Christmas from about December 10th for a fortnight such offices as Sevenoaks are fully opened up for sorting to handle the rush.

The new functional Post Office and Sorting Office at South Park Sevenoaks with Telephone Exchange showing to rear of the lighted sorting office. Taken 1985. Main Office now back on the site of the Crown Inn. (AGD)

Current Sevenoaks PO Ephemera1985.
Top: Instructions for local posting
Lower right: The Sponsored wastebin showing the council logo
Lower left: Portico as subsequently reconstructed for Girobank machine. (All AGD)

If this card can reach you - so can our Gas ~

2

KENT GARDEN & LEISURE CENTRE LTD.
FREEPOST
SEVENOAKS
KENT, TN14 6BR

SECOND CLASS

No Postage Stamp required if posted in Great Britain or Northern Ireland

BUSINESS REPLY SERVICE
LICENCE NO SV153.
Dept. AKL, The Hamlyn History of
The World in Colour,
Odhams Books, Basted,
SEVENOAKS, Kent.

R POSTAGE
PAID
SEVENOAKS
SERIAL No.4

DEV. ENGR.

AIRPORT WORKS,
ROCHESTER,
KENT.

Jermyn
Manufacturing Sevenoaks Kent

*Freepost. By arrangement, the recipient pays the
postage.*
*Business Reply Service, with Sevenoaks licence
number SV153. Not available from abroad so
stamps used. (1972)*
*Postage Paid Indicator where large quantities
mailed. In this case 'R' means 'Rebate' not
'Registered'.*
*A 'Sevenoaks Chronicle' wrapper with final 's'
missing in the cancel.*

Woodvale,

HALSTEAD, NR Sevenoaks
If undelivered, please return. Kent.

SEVENOAKS CHRONICLE
54 HIGH STREET, SEVENOAKS

*Mainly 1980's
A selection of*
Sevenoaks Meter Marks.

Mr Clancy, Head Postmaster of Sevenoaks, presents Mr Frank Woods with his retiring present. Sevenoaks sorting office. 16.3.84. (Sevenoaks Chronicle)

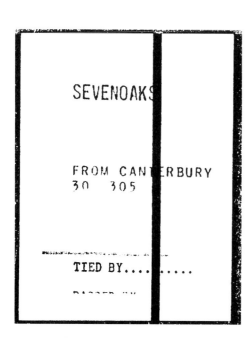

Pre-Sorted Bundle label for despatch.

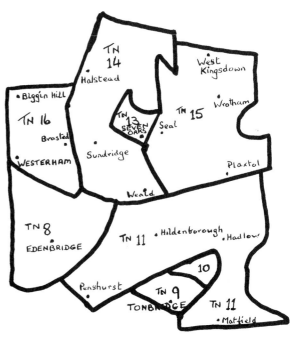

Post Code Districts near Sevenoaks.

Mechanised Letter Office at Tonbridge

The Country is now covered with a network of some eighty or so MLOs. The local office at Tonbridge is a functional building on the Vestry Estate, with top floor administration offices transferred from the Tunbridge Wells Headquarters, thus the building serves two distinct purposes. The MLO handles both letters and parcels and the TN area extends from Biggin Hill to Hastings, Westerham to Ashford.[32]

As with other S. East MLOs access is entirely by road. Some of these local roads can become very congested in the evenings. There have been a considerable number of roadworks recently. The railway bridge adjacent to the MLO is narrow and only permits one lane of traffic. A considerable amount of mail is routed via Tonbridge Station which is not far distant.

Official opening day was 4th November 1983 with a gradual take-over. Sevenoaks started to send in mail in August and by September 1984 the Sevenoaks machine postmark had all but disappeared, being subsumed in the Tonbridge one.

At Tonbridge the outwards mail from Sevenoaks (except for the local mail and some bulk postings) is hand sorted to first and second class, postmarked, coded and sorted to destination automatically on the basis of the coding of "the dots of the bottom line'. Then it is labelled and bundled up with the ubiquitous post office rubber band, often to be found growing along front garden paths now-a-days and bagged for onwards transmission, much by rail. Non-POP items, those awkward shapes not of the 'post office preferred' sizes, are extracted by hand and do not go through 'the system'. Most difficult of all are the items that appear regular and so are not extracted, but contain some inflexible enclosure that will not bend as it travels along the belts of the postmarking machine.

Postcoding   The essential factor on which MLOs are based is the postcode, enabling automatic sorting to take place. Automatic sorting has developed from the early machines at Brighton in the 1930's.

Postcodes cover the whole of the country and consist of two sections -

A A N (N or A)   (N) N A A

(A = alphabet letter   N = decimal number)

It took several years to develop the British system which unlike those of most other countries (e.g. the American Zip code) employs both letters and numbers. This combination gives it great flexibility but seemingly experiments have found that a mixture of numbers and letters is more difficult to memorise than all numbers. The coding system was then related to the whole of the United Kingdom. The bottom line relates to the Post Town and its district, the top line, which is not at present, 1985, fully in use at Tonbridge, relates to a road or small area within the district.

Thus for the Sevenoaks area there is

TN (Tonbridge)	13 Sevenoaks Town	TN 15 Wrotham	
TN	14 North West	TN 16 Westerham/Biggin Hill	

Relating to Sevenoaks				Relating to Tonbridge	
TN13	TN14	TN15	TN16	TN11	TN8
Sevenoaks	Halstead	Ash	Brasted	Chiddingstone	Bow Beech
Town	Ide Hill	Boro' Green	Biggin Hill	Causeway	Chiddingstone
Chipstead	Knockholt	Fairseat	Cudham	Hildenboro	Cowden
Riverhead	Otford	Ightham	Tatsfield	Leigh	Crockham Hill
	Shoreham	Kemsing	Westerham	Penshurst	Edenbridge
	Sundridge	Platt	Westerham	Shipbourne	Four Elms
	Weald	Plaxtol	Hill		Hever
	Chevening	Seal			Mark Beech
	Badgers Mount	Wrotham			Marlpit Hill
		Wr. Heath			Marsh Green
		Knatts Valley			
		Riverhill			
		Kingsdown			
		Stone Street			
		Stanstead			
		Underriver			

Post Office Boundaries do not follow Local Administration Boundaries; Tatsfield is in Surrey and Biggin Hill in the London Borough of Bromley.

Letters are coded to the **post code** if there is one (e.g. TN13 1AA), the Post Town **extract code** if there is no postcode (e.g. SEVKS = Sevenoaks), or the **local area short code / local delivery code** when dealing with letters travelling locally. This is why addressing to a village and county, e.g. Halstead Kent in many cases will send the letter off to Halstead Essex which is a post town, if coded by an operator in, say, the north of England, who does not know this area intimately. After the postcode, the post town is more important than the county.

	32	16	8	4	2	1	32	16	8	4	2	1	Start	
Parity														
*	*	*	*	*	*	*	*	*	*	*	*	*	■	←
TN13					*	*			*		*	*	■	11/3
TN14				*					*		*	*	■	11/4
TN15					*	*			*		*	*	■	11/3
TN16					*				*	*			■	12/2
Local area short code					*	*	*	*	*	*		*	■	61/3
Sevenoaks SEVKS	*	*	*		*			*	*				■	24/58
Wrotham WROAM					*	*			*		*	*	■	11/3
Westerham WESAM	*		*		*			*	*	*			■	28/42
- do -	*	*	*	*	*		*	*	*			*	■	57/62
Edenbridge	*	*		*	*			*			*	*	■	19/54
Edenbridge	*	*	*	*	*				*				■	8/62

The dots read on a binary scale from right to left after the square start dot, giving a maximum of 63/63. A parity dot is included as a check so that the number of dots is always even. The allocation of a code number to a specific area is normative and has no special significance other than that it is so recorded in the current code key book. The allocation of a code number can be altered, thus at the moment TN13 and TN15 are not differentiated both being brought up by the computer program as 11/3. When the need arises to differentiate between TN13 and TN15 a separate number will be allocated, all computer programs altered accordingly and so the sorting will be split without any changes being made by the public.

Occasional cases can be ambiguous. For example, Biggin Hill under Westerham gives an extract code 'Wesam' (28/42): West Wickham also gives 'Wesam'. To overcome this at Tonbridge, Westerham receives the local delivery code 61/23 and West Wickham the Semi-National Forward Code 57/62. A local delivery code is specific to the office using it, whereas a Semi-National Forward Code can be used by a number of MLOs and the binary code printed will be the same for each office although the short code keyed by the operator may differ, eg, for West Wickham Tonbridge MLO keys WKM and Redhill WWM but both print dots representing 57/61.[33]

Position at Tonbridge January 1984 In January 1984, a little prior to Sevenoaks sending to Tonbridge MLO, only 47% (50,000) of letters that might have been coded bore a full postcode. About 160,000 items per day were being handled at Tonbridge of which 105,000 (65%) went through the coding desks. To make mechanisation viable 71,000 (68%) of these possibles needed to be coded.[34]

Inland Transmission

Once sorted the letters are bagged, labelled and sealed so that once on its main journey what is being handled and sorted is a labelled bag, possibly full of loose letters but more likely in rubber-banded bundles of fifty or more to one town or district. For the main journey the bag labels are in effect the addresses.

Sir Ronald Deering, the Post Office Chairman, has said the most effective method of transmission are

      1 - 100 miles - by road
   100 - 200 miles - by rail
    over 200 miles - by air [35]

The leaflet 'latest recommended posting times for first class mail', issued at Sevenoaks in May 1985, gives 1845 hrs at the main office for all places other than local to achieve next day delivery for first class mail (excepting Powys, Northern Ireland outside Belfast and some northern parts of Scotland).

Inland Transmission By Air   With the experiences of the early pioneering days among the Scottish Islands in the 1930's and the flights between main towns, London, Glasgow, Edinburgh and Belfast starting in 1961 behind them, the GPO set up the Liverpool Speke spoke system in 1979 using chartered aircraft of several companies. Thirty six chartered services were involved, some with planes in Royal Mail Livery. Using several separate private companies gives some insurance against rail strikes. From Speke there are flights to fourteen centres and 5,000 mailbags are handled within a two hour period at night. Some of the chartered flights are using normal passenger aircraft from which the seats are taken out four nights a week to make room for the mailbags. At different times Sevenoaks has sent mail through both Lydd and Gatwick. The mail leaves late evening, arrives at Speke at midnight, is sorted and the 'planes leave on their way back between 1 am and 3 am.

The Kent routes Lydd-Speke were by Skyways Ltd. from 10 September 1979 to 6th November 1980, Dan-Air carried on till 15th January 1983. The Lydd air route was then no longer used for Liverpool mail which went through Gatwick.

The Speke spokes were so successful that a second radial service started on 4th October 1982 from East Midlands Airport (EMA) Castle Donnington, Derby. This is an integrated Road, Rail and Air Centre; the air connections are listed and additionally there are

Rail   Derby to Nottingham and Lincoln; to Leicester and Peterboro';
            to Birmingham, Gloucester, Bristol; to Crewe
Road   Derby to Nottingham, Coventry, Leicester, Peterboro'

There is also a connection Speke-EMA and one from EMA to the Datapost distribution centre at Luton.

Lydd airport was used from October 1983 and when it went into liquidation in August 1986 the terminal was switched to Manston near Ramsgate. Not all first class letters are sent the whole way by air as EMA is integrated, giving great flexibility, bags can be sent on the Travelling Post Offices (TPOs) and then switched to air at EMA, depending on the needs of a particular day/night.

Bag label.. Sevenoaks-Lydd-East Midlands Airport-Speke, Liverpool.

Circulation - Air

Liverpool	Derby,Castle Donnington
<u>Speke Airport</u>	<u>East Midlands Airport</u>
(starting 1979)	(starting 1982)

	(Lydd (1983-1986)
Lydd (to 1982)	Manston (1986-)
Gatwick	Gatwick
Southend	Southend
Stansted	Stansted
Bournemouth	Lyneham
Exeter	Exeter
	Newquay
Bristol	Southampton
	(Luton - Datapost Centre)
Norwich	Speke <—> EMA Norwich
	Liverpool Derby
Belfast	Belfast
Glasgow	Glasgow
Aberdeen	Aberdeen
Edinburgh	Edinburgh
(EMA Derby)	(Speke Liverpool)
Newcastle	Inverness

Circulation - Railway

The Post Office's first contracts with the Railways for mail letter carrying was signed in the late 1830's, and over many years a complex network of routes has been built up. The contract arrangements have always involved hard bargaining. At first the PO was rather in the hands of the railways as they were the only means of fast transport but now with good alternatives in road and air the percentage of the total mails moved by the railways has dropped, although in actual terms it has risen.

Travelling Post Offices now run four nights a week only, Monday to Thursday. As few business offices are open on Saturday there is not the pressure for Friday night services; and as mostly private letters are posted on Saturdays and Sundays there is said to be no call for a Sunday night service and that it would be uneconomic to have staff to collect on a Sunday afternoon to run TPOs on a Sunday night for mainly private mail.

Travelling Post Offices based on London that are still running (1985) are:

		Bag Label Colour Code at Tonbridge
North West TPO and Down Special TPO	Euston	Yellow
East Anglian TPO	Liverpool Street	Grey
Great Western TPO	Paddington	Green
North Eastern TPO	St. Pancras	Red
South Western TPO	Waterloo	Orange.

The Colour-coding helps visual sorting. Euston, for example, is said to handle 10,000 bags a night.

Much mail from London and the South East can be sent on the first leg of its journey by train to Derby EMA and then continue by air. Having a road/rail/air central link gives a certain amount of flexibility in routing. In December 1983 there was a new five year contract with British Rail, the first fundamental review for fifty years. The five years will be up at the end of 1988.

TPO Avoiding London 1988   With the Dover TPO's reinstatement on Monday 16th May 1988 providing a Monday to Friday service in the new Royal Mail Letters TPO network, the new route starts from Dover and stops at Folkestone, Ashford, Tonbridge and Redhill as before.   Then, avoiding London, it goes through Guildford to Reading and on via Oxford and Birmingham to Manchester.   Sevenoaks main evening collection to connect with this TPO was put forward to 630 pm.

Bag Labels.

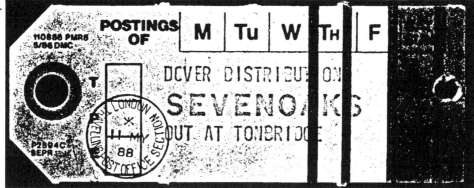

Dover-Sevenoaks, out at Tonbridge.

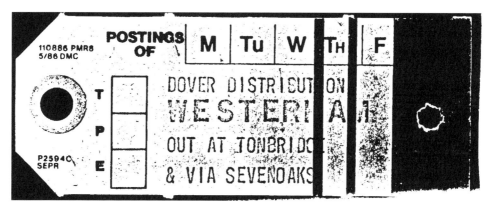

Dover-Westerham, out at Tonbridge and via Sevenoaks.

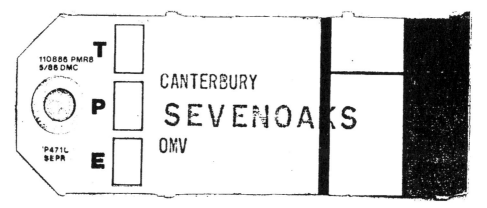

Canterbury to Sevenoaks. Own Motor Vehicle OMV.

Circulation - Road

The Post Office has concentrated on road haulage for medium distance in most cases tending to own its own vehicles.

Many vehicles seen on the road locally are parcel lorries on their way to Salfords Reigate sorting centre (see next chapter) and on the M2 the Road Trains take the European Mail to Spain, Italy, France, Switzerland from London via Dover to the Continent. Contract vehicles are also used.

Other P.O. vehicles seen are those taking letters to the South East Road Postal Network sorting centre at Goldsworthy Road Woking where bags are exchanged covering Hampshire, Wiltshire, Sussex, Surrey, Kent, Essex and beyond. It is said that road exchange makes good saving per bag exchanged over use of rail and that it is both quicker and more flexible for these shorter runs. Of course, it also produces more road traffic.

Charity Local Posts at Christmastime

For the next twenty-five years, that is until 2007, organisations with charitable status may be sanctioned to allow delivery locally below the £1 minimum. This is at Christmastime and normally applies to Christmas Cards delivered locally as a service to the Community and giving a small input to Society funds charging prices below the second class post rate. The delivery area is often just a few miles, few Christmas Posts go more than ten miles.

In the majority of the country Boy Scout Posts monopolise the scene, but locally it is The Girl Guides of Otford and of Shoreham that have been first off the mark. There is also the Welsh Society's Dragon Post at Tunbridge Wells.

At first the charge was 5p. Both Otford and Shoreham posts started as separate posts in December 1982. By 1984 links had been forged between the two posts and mail posted in one village could be delivered in the other. Mail collecting poimts were set up at various points in the villages including the library or mail could be handed in at specified houses. Shoreham's stamp was a peelable label that was not cancelled. Otford had no stamp but used an undated handstamp 'delivered by the Girl Guides', the wording varying slightly each year. At Tunbridge Wells both an adhesive 'stamp' value 5p and a dated canceller were used by the Welsh Society's Dragon Post. The Culverstone and Vigo Boy Scout Christmas Post extends to the village of Fairseat. In 1984 the charge was 10p but this was not shown on the stamp used which depicted a snowman.

1984–1985/6 New Policies

The 1981 British Telecommunications Act hived off the Telephone and Telegraph side of the Post Office and made it a separate national corporation. This corporation has now, in 1986, been sold off to the public in the form of shares in British Telecom PLC. British Telecom retains the monopoly in the transmission and switching of electronic signals on which the Post Office's Intelpost and Electronic Post will depend until 'Mercury' develops as an alternative carrier.

But the 1981 Act also contained provisions relating to the operation of the Post Office. The Minister was given the power to grant licences and under this power allowed the private Courier services to carry time sensitive mail at a minimum charge of £1, allowed the Christmas posts and, in 1982, allowed the private document exchange system to operate. The Act also clarified the 1953 Act and developed powers in the 1969 Act to the point where the Minister can suspend the exclusive monopoly privilege conferred on the Post Office for such time as may be specified in the order. He can, in effect, demonopolise the British Post Office by Order and without recourse to legislation.[36]

One may well ask: 'How free, then, is the Post Office to operate?' Certainly it has been freed in day-to-day operations such that it can deal competitively with customers without fear of a detailed question being asked next day in Parliament as it used to be. No longer do its officials, as they had to under the 1711 legislation of 9 Anne, attend the Treasury every Tuesday with £700 to be paid into the Exchequer

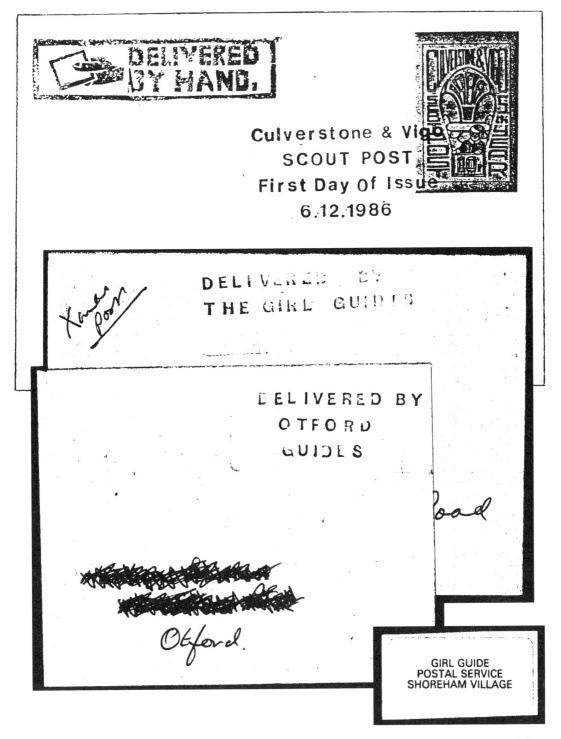

Local Christmas deliveries were authorised from 1982. Otford village handstamps shown for 1984, 85 and also the Shoreham peelable label. After the first year the two services covered the joint area. Culverstone and Vigo Boy Scout delivery touches the area by covering Fairseat, using both label and cachet in later years.

'for carrying on the War and other Her Majesty's most necessary occasions', but there is still a policy supervision by a Minister and Government does not shirk its task of imposing its will even though at 'arm's' length. At present Government is concerned with the organisation structure of the Post Office and its Girobank, with the suggestion that it be reorganised into four businesses and what was suggested becomes fact forthwith!

Supplies   After the Telecom hive off, the Post Office central supply warehouse at Swindon was faced with a massive task of removing B.T. items and centralising Post Office stores from all other depots. All items except such things as postage stamps are now stored there, using a microcomputer control system to handle about 9 million items.

Strikes   In 1985 there was a possibility of a strike over the acceptance of the Optical Character Recognition machines at Mount Pleasant as well as other matters. Employees were told that the Government might take away the P.O.'s monopoly on mail delivery if the strike went ahead. Such is now this Government's standard response to any threat of a strike and such action could be a possibility, though it is reported in the national press that possible competitors, including TNT, have admitted the difficulty posed by the scale of operation if to be taken over wholly and could probably only attack piecemeal. Eventually the matter was settled.

1980's Local Changes

Local Offices   Under the rationalisation of offices programme London Road, Sevenoaks and The Vine were not renewed when the occupants ceased. Ightham village closed for lack of another to take it on, St. Mary Platt became uneconomic and closed, Brasted Chart ceased to function postally.

It had become difficult to make a living in the villages. At the end of 1983 the sub-post office minimum salary was £1,700.[37] *'So much per transaction'* at that time meant 3p to cash a pension; a busy office could increase the minimum salary but it was hard effort.

Many of the sub-offices, and including Westerham Crown Office, now shut two afternoons per week, Saturday afternoon and early closing day for the locality, and thus achieve the regular five-day week. Westerham Crown office, a salaried sub-office was investigated in an effort to make the Counter Service more cost-effective. There was talk of the office being regraded an agency office, but the counter argument that if this was carried out counter staff would not be so well trained as they would be employees of the sub-postmaster not the Post Office, appeared to hold the day and no change has yet been made. The Post Office no longer, since 1983, sells a book listing the Crown and Village offices and so changes can now go unnoticed except to persons living in the immediate area.

The crop of mishaps continues with recent raids on Knockholt, Cudham and Fairseat among others. During the letter bomb scares of recent years a parcel was received at Ightham by the lady of the house who subsequently died. The matter appeared, however, not to be politically motivated.

Counter Staff training was inaugurated at Sevenoaks Head Office and from 15th July 1983 a notice, *'Regular Staff Training Office will not open till 9.30 on Friday for Staff Training. W. Clancy, S.W. Thake'* appeared on the door.

Gradually delivery postmen based on Sevenoaks Main Office took over from local sub-office based delivery postmen. Some of the last to undergo this change being Boro' Green in 1977 and Wrotham as late as November 1985. Westerham and Biggin Hill Sorting Offices still function.

In July 1984 Sevenoaks became a delivery office only with mail being sent to Tonbridge for sorting and postmarking. A special box was opened 'For Sevenoaks mail only', some of which was handled locally rather than being sent to Tonbridge. This left about 115 to 120 staff at Sevenoaks[38] but with further cuts to come. With the increasing need for the use of Postcodes, the Sevenoaks Chronicle was running a 'Bottle of Champagne' spot the postcode competition in 1986. As part of the Post Office Users National Council the Tunbridge Wells and Tonbridge Post and Telecom's advisory Committee now hold a consultative meeting quarterly.

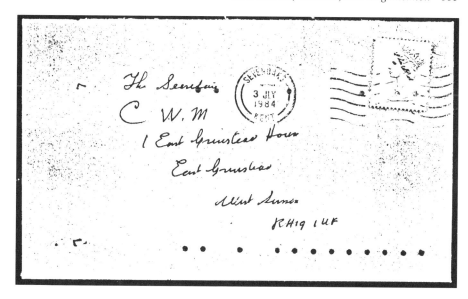

Above: The Transition period July 1984 when letters were cancelled at Sevenoaks, then postcoded at Tonbridge.

Side: The new 'frama' labels of 1984, on sale in London. Now discontinued.

Below: A wrongly dated meter posting from Sevenoaks, corrected and stamped at Tonbridge so as not to be picked for quality assurance sampling for time taken in transit.

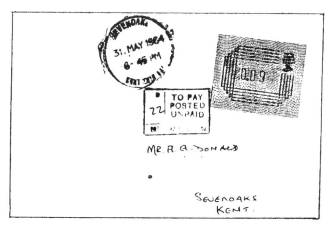

Current 1980 mail. *Some recent Sevenoaks machine cancels. Things are not always what they seem, 'Tonbridge M' has been used at Sevenoaks (1985) and 'J' at Edenbridge both at Christmas time.*

Revision of Deliveries

The Report and Accounts of 1985/6, page 8, says of the new organisation '*the immediate point of contact is the local postman or post office and this will remain unchanged*'. Unfortunately for many this has not been the case. There has been change at the outset, in fact, to judge by the outcry in the local press, it would not be an overstatement to say that the Post Office started off its '*new look*' with the public by scoring a gratuitous '*own goal*'.

As part of the 1985/6 revision there was a national requirement to revise delivery walks. There was an internal investigation in the latter part of 1985. As with the cessation of Sunday evening collections, an internal decision was to come to without effective external consultation. Towards the end of January 1986, as the snow lay on the ground and many people were abed with 'flu as usual now-a-days a new type of virus was around, small notices appeared on letterboxes. At first no-one really understood their import. Even when the new delivery and collections came in, for the first few weeks many persons believed the delay was due to snow or staff sickness, an acceptable situation. Then it dawned on the residents and business people of Sevenoaks and District that the whole operation had been planned and was no accident. More so, it was to be permanent. Great was the outcry and many letters were written to the local papers but no great changes were promised nor were they made, and mostly the situation remains as it was. Many rural delivery walks, for example, continued till noon or later with collections half an hour or so earlier, say 4.15 instead of 4.45pm. Very often a person toward the end of a rural delivery walk had only three or so hours in which to answer his letters and to get the answers in the post. A situation more akin to the 1870's than what is to be hoped for in the 1980's; strange, too, to be called a rural area when only twenty miles from London and the more so when Government has encouraged the idea of persons working from their own homes.

Difficulty appears to centre around what parameters should be agreed as those which are useful in assessing the provision of a 'good' service. The views of the Post Office and the Public do not appear to coincide and there appears to be no Ombudsman to whom specific matters or, more importantly, matters of principle can be referred. Consultative Committees and Users Committees do not appear to fulfil this role entirely, being mainly business oriented. The Post Office regards an item delivered before noon as 'next day' delivery in their statistics, but private persons who have to leave for work by 8.45 am at the very latest do not, for they do not see the letter until evening, nor do smaller businesses that expect to have their day's mail opened and ready to be dealt with by 8.30 am. (Large businesses may be able to collect.) It would appear that the real area of dialogue between user and the post office might be the changing of the delivery parameter to pre-10 am as constituting 'next day' delivery. Certainly this type of 'tightening up' might be more acceptable to the customer than the promised large increase in junk-mail deliveries.

From the point of view of the Post Office there are also problems and two of these in the local area would appear to be:

a) A Workload Assessment scheme for the delivery postman that requires the sorting of all items on hand before starting on the first delivery instead of "nearly all" and leaving the rest for second delivery, thus making a later start to the walk.

b) The altering of walks such that a full days work load is achieved for a full-time employee. This alteration tends to make the walks longer and so more deliveries are at a later hour.

The longer walks are said to be more suitable for full-time employees and better than split-shift working or the employment of many part-timers. This may be so, but deliveries late in the day in so-called 'country' areas do not endear the Post Office to the General Public. As a rule-of-thumb unofficial method, the Town area is often equated with the 30 mph built-up area of a town.

Sevenoaks Town deliveries improved again after the curtailment of early 1986, by two additional walks in late '86 and four more in '87, the criterion being completion of first delivery by 9.30am. But there was no rural improvement the first delivery still being allowed until noon for completion.

Apart from the management and unions both of which are obviously watching the situation closely, there has recently been a local survey (first half 1987) by POUNC, the Post Office User's National Committee, into the time taken for test letters posted in the Tonbridge district to be delivered. Some

The Swiftair service, in this case registered as well, but the intended recipient had moved.

information has been released but overall the report is confidential, presumably subject to the thirty year rule and not available until 2117.

The difficulties to customers of morning first deliveries at a late hour appear at last to be appreciated by the P.O. for in June 1987 there was a national announcement reported on T.V. News that money resources were being set aside so that '*everyone would receive their first delivery by 9.30 am*'. But again it seems that this relates to Town areas. The results await to be seen.

New Administrative Organisations

Following 215 years of Surveyors and the 50 year period of Regionalisation, the Post Office is currently restructuring itself after various studies and following the orders of Mr. Pattis, Minister of Information and Technology in June 1985, to meet present day needs and pressures with a new system of administration to start late 1986.[39]

At present there are 10 Post Office Regions with 142 Head Post Offices. For Sevenoaks, Tonbridge is the Head Post Office and Brighton the Regional Office and these offices used to cover all aspects of Post Office work. This is to change and will be the first change since regionalisation was introduced in the late 1930's.

As from October 1986, there will be three distinct businesses as well as the Girobank which will continue to be treated separately.

The Postal work will be separated to **Royal Mail** and **Counters**, and the 'Royal Mail' operation itself will be split to **Letters** and **Parcels, including Datapost the Courier Service**. A new start, as is often the way, involves a new vocabulary.

It is said that this organisation will allow the development of specialist expertise whilst each business will continue to be a mutually reinforcing element within the Corporation. Relationship between the three postal businesses '*will be conducted on a business-like basis with contracts drawn up between them*' at District level.[40]

'Letters' and 'Parcels' appear self-explanatory. 'P.O. Counters, as well as selling stamps and other postal business such as Postal Orders and Money Orders, will conduct much Agency business, e.g. for the Department of Health and Social Security, selling T.V. licences for the B.B.C., Vehicle licences and also operate one end of the Girobank business.

For '**Letters**' there will be 64 District Offices split into Territories: Sevenoaks coming under Tonbridge District Office with London as H.Q. of East Territory.

For '**Parcels**' there are 12 District Offices, Sevenoaks coming via Tonbridge MLO under Salfords at Redhill.

For '**Counters**' there are to be 32 District Offices, Sevenoaks coming under Hastings, then Colchester as H.Q. of East Territory.

Strong support from the 'Counters' management team will also be available to Sub-Postmasters/Mistresses, they being Contractors to the Post Office. Locally this means all sub-post offices in village and suburban locations, that is, all offices except Salaried Offices at Sevenoaks, Westerham and Edenbridge.

Advertisements For **Counter Staff at Sevenoaks Main Office.** In January 1987 an advertisement appeared on the public side of the Crown Office for Full-time Counter Staff. Postal Officer, permanent and pensionable with three weeks holiday in summer one week in winter, with application to the District Office in Hastings. A 42-hour week, age limits 16-45 years, and salary £6,304 to £8,193. Also for part-time work normally of 21 or 32 hours a week with application to Area Office, Tonbridge. Age limits preferably under 40 but up to 55 considered with experience in Crown or Sub-Office preferred. Pay £2.87 per hour at 19 years rising to £3.74 per hour in 4 increments.

Royal Mail Delivery Staff are still subject to turnover and require replacement. The current advertisement in 1989 at Sevenoaks stresses that the Post Office is an equal opportunities employer and advertises '*Be a Postman or Postwoman now - Ring Peter Cox at Tonbridge*'. Other advertisements for the Tonbridge area have been seen advertising for 'a postperson'.

Certainly there appear now to be more local delivery Postwomen than heretofore. But it is interesting to examine the position in 1844 at the Higher Managerial Level when in England and Wales 20½% (126 out of 615) of the Post Town offices, not the sub-offices, were under the management of women. How many of these were married it is hard to say as in the return only the Christian name and surname of the office holder is given.[41]

Road As foreshadowed on p332 Royal Mail continues its switch from Rail to Road for the medium length journey up to 80 miles, with an extended network of direct road links from October 1990. In the South East the Road base is now at Nine Elms SW8 and mail handling at London Bridge and Waterloo stations has ceased.

Canteen When evening sorting outwards took place at Sevenoaks the Canteen provided meals in the early evening before staff commenced sorting duty. Now this evening sorting duty takes place at Tonbridge, the Sevenoaks Canteen concentrates on early breakfast provision before morning delivery starts.

New Uniforms

In the early 1970's the Post Office uniform was based on a light grey lightweight terylene and worsted suit, the jacket with darker collar and cuffs plus a metal badge more suited to indoor work and travelling in a van than the heavier blue serge it displaced.

The current new uniform of the mid-eighties shows a return to navy blue bearing a thin horizontal red stripe motif with a wide range of available items from which the bearer can choose on a mix'n'match basis according to the conditions under which (s)he is working, indoors or outdoors, moving or sitting, and according to personal preference.

One problem is getting a good personal fit from issue sizes of which there are no less than 46 sizes plus made-to-measure for those outside the range.

The issue of the many different items to everyone poses problems but overall this issue appears to have met with approval. For uniformed staff the issue comprises shirts, blouses, tie, hat, belt, trousers, skirts or slacks, jacket, jumper, thermal coat, outdoor waterproof and leggings. The 'cheesecutter' stiff peaked cap is retained with a new badge 'Royal Mail' instead of the Crown and Posthorn device, but a soft cap is also available. Footwear of a suitable type is available but has to be bought. For some reason footwear was not included in the deal as is the case with the police.[42] Some now like to wear 'trainers'.

From personal observation it would seem this uniform can be the least distinguishable so far issued. It depends on which of the items are being worn, but often one can now recognise a postman only from the front and by the narrow horizontal red stripe at chest level. If the cap and badge is worn this makes recognition much easier as does the red and navy blue letter-bag if being carried. Winter protective clothing is also very colourful in red and navy. But whatever items of uniform are worn it seems from a report in the Sevenoaks Chronicle in 1987 that dogs guarding houses have no difficulty in distinguishing postmen and postwomen and bite them without discrimination just as much they did a hundred and fifty years ago.

So far uniform has not been supplied to counter staff, but the possibility is said to be being looked into. Outdoor staff began to be seen in Sevenoaks area fully kitted out in the new uniforms in October 1986.

Way Ahead

The Post Office hopes that its grouping into four businesses is not to be the prelude to being sold off and privatised.

The Pamphlet championing that cause issued through the Centre for Policy Studies is somewhat lightweight and free of detailed argument, uncluttered by appendices and invokes the name of economist Martin Friedman, as might perhaps have been expected. One awaits with further expectation the more detailed arguments that will undoubtedly flow from it. Perhaps by its very success Girobank may be a candidate to be hived off (*and so it will be 1990*) but the postal business, although split into three can be shown to be largely inter-dependent, and hardly a candidate for individual privatisation.

Now that the Post Office has this new organisation and now that the unions appear more amenable to the acceptance of New Technology, such as Optical Character Recognition, the Post Office really does appear to be '*geared for growth*' and to have a bright future. But it does still seem to be dogged by political argument and still considerably dependent on which government is in power. It has been told by this government to try and attract private capital into the business.[43]

Development of '**Counters**' is next on the list. The local office in Sevenoaks was adorned with a '*Sheep-pen*' queueing system in 1983. Approved by the unions, it certainly took the pressure off counter clerks from close-up encounters with irate queuers and greatly added to privacy. According to mathematical queueing theory such a '*device for letting out the next available client to the next available service station*' is the most efficient method of servicing a queue, but it does limit customer choice and is anathema to some sheep who may still find solace in the hurdle-less greener pastures provided in the villages by sub-postmasters. In the future counters may well be automated on the French pattern but, with the multiplicity of agency work now in hand, it would be a relief to find a few of the positions, as once they were, reserved for postal business. One doesn't go into the Gas Board to buy an oven-ready chicken.

More recently still 'Counters' has reorganised itself into a limited liability company 'Post Office

Letters are sorted by machine,
so please
Pass on your Postcode

Out-of-Service Postbus being used for Datapost delivery. Seen outside Woodvale Halstead 1985.

Counters Ltd.' and great changes are on the horizon, the full marketing concept including counter automation. But, being a newly built office, Sevenoaks Main P.O. is not on the first list of 400 main offices due for renovation in 1988. The initial developments are in the Thames Valley area.

Last in the line of Sevenoaks Postmasters

William (Bill) Clancy will be the thirty second and last to be designated as Postmaster at Sevenoaks. The position is now to be split to a Local Branch Manager of Post Office Counters Ltd. (Mr. R. Griffiths) and an Area Delivery Manager of Royal Mail (Mr. Clancy) as from 12 October 1987. The latter position embraces Sevenoaks, Westerham, Biggin Hill and also Edenbridge, although Edenbridge circulation will continue to entail a main delivery from Redhill and a secondary one from Tonbridge rather than any direct circulation contact with Sevenoaks. So once again we have the two managers of what are now separate companies, 'Royal Mail' and Post Office Counters Ltd. needing to work together in close proximity on one location as did the driver/coachman and mailguard in the mailcoach era.

Chapter IX
Parcels and Other Services

Non-GPO: Letter and Packet Carrying, both legal and illegal
　　Carriers, Tradesmen, Newsmen, Stagecoaches, Servants, Friends, Railway Letters, Documents and Cheques, Couriers, Electronic Mailbox, Fax.

Non-GPO: Parcel and Goods Carrying
　　Carriers, Coaches, The Sevenoaks Stagecoach Robbery, Smuggled Goods, Railway Parcels, Motor Bus Parcels, Road Delivery.

Official GPO non-letter Services
　　Prices Current, Book and Sample Post, Newspapers, Bankers Parcels, Parcel Post, Articles for the Blind, London-Hastings Parcel Coach.

GPO Salfords Redhill Parcel Concentration Office
　　Local Parcels, Heavy 'Parcels', Trackback, Barcodes.

Chronology

1455-1475	War of Roses. Long distance carting pattern developed.
1660-1720	Smuggling Wool out, 'owling'.
1677	Wm. Loquer, a carrier on Sevenoaks route, brings into London 60/70 letters a week.
1711	Govt. Tax on Newspapers, allows free passage in post.
1720-1820	Smuggling in, spirits, tea and tobacco.
c1750	Bankers Parcels and Registered Post.
1763	Sept 27. London Gazette warns against illegal carrying of letters
1788	Message and letter service to other post towns by 'Newsmen' declared illegal.
1800s	Stagecoaches carry many parcels as Government monopoly applies only to letters.
1841	Railways begin to develop in South East. Engaged in Parcel Carrying. February 21. Book Post.
1842	Sevenoaks Stagecoach Robbery.
1855	June 22. Last date for Newspaper Tax. Then on, optional for postage.
1856	Carts drawn by dogs became illegal.
1863	Pattern Post.
1883	August 1. GPO Parcels service starts.
1891	February 1. Railway Letter Service began. End of 'String' letters.
c1895	London-Hastings Parcel Coach (Horse) via Sevenoaks and Tunbridge Wells.
1905	Motorisation of Hastings Parcel Coach.
1906	September 1. Blind Post.
1919 on.	Motor Omnibuses develop and carry indiviual parcels. Road Parcel Delivery service begins to develop.
1960s	Parcel Concentration Offices organised.
1970	Datapost.
1972	Compensation Fee for Parcels. Registration ceased.
1981	British Telecommunication Act allows Private Courier Services with item charge of at least £1.
1982	GPO Summer Sale, 30% off County Parcels for two months. Book Post returns in conjunction with bookseller 'Post-a-Book'.
1984	Railway Letter service ceased. Parcels now up to 25 kg (55½ lbs).
1985	GPO Direct Pallet Service up to ½ ton on negotiated contract.
1986	Trackback using barcodes for GPO parcels. Receipted parcels ceased.
1990	February 27. Royal Mail Parcels separated from RM Letters and designated 'Parcel Force'.

Chapter IX

Parcels and Other Services

Letter and Packet Carrying; Non-GPO

Caravans have travelled the trade routes since pre-history bringing goods and news. It has been said that the English carting network developed about the time of the Wars of the Roses (1455-75). Certainly the carting network was well developed by the time John Taylor wrote the Carriers Cosmographie in 1637. Although there would be some short distance and cross-route carting, the main carting routes by then were into and out of London, and the extent of this network can be judged from Taylor's work. His guide gives the routes and the days and explains how letters may be forwarded on from one route to another; though he does not explain how payment is made when three carrier routes are involved. Did the carriers act as agent for one another or might they have had a financial clearing system? It is thought that the carters may have had some exchange in London through which letters could be sent to other towns. But little is known of their organisation which was legal at the time.

Carriers, Carters and the King's Post

In the Postal Act of 1635 which opened the King's Post to the general public, Carriers had been given the right to carry letters, as distinct from the documentation they had always needed to carry relating to the goods they were transporting. They had always carried letters and they continued to operate in the way they had always done and to good effect. When the trade routes were running again after the Civil War, that same right continued with the 1657 Commonwealth and 1660 King's Postal Act, the main difference was that now more effort was being put into making the official postal system work.

There is a complaint in the Calendar of State papers (21 August 1667) that *'a carrier on the route through Sevenoaks, William Loquer (Lockyer), was bringing into London 60 to 70 letters a week by cart, six times as many as the official post was handling at that time'*. And not a single carter's letter from this area appears to have survived although some have from Norfolk. Loquer bringing in 70 letters a week means a rate of carrying that could have amounted to 35,000 over ten years, yet none now remain that have been recorded so far, although one can never be certain what may turn up in the future.

The King's Post was new and the populace was used to sending any messages that they did send by cart, which may have been slower but was probably cheaper and was the way it had always been done. Besides, they probably thought, and not without reason though it was probably not now true, that letters sent by the official post might be opened to see what had been written.

Once the King's Posts had been set up, the official attitude to the Carter and Carriers' right to carry letters became ambivalent. After the arrest of Carrier Grover of Norwich, 15 December 1637, and the subsequent concession of 24 January 1638 *'shall be permitted to take letters provided they arrive not more than 8 hours before the main cart'*, the Parliamentary Committee of 1642 enquiring into the use and misuse of private carriers by the public gave compensation to Grover and the private service was allowed to continue alongside the official letter service but only on their own carrier route, a partial curb of the carrier's letter-carrying activity. The Government did not feel sufficiently confident of their own service completely to prohibit the carriers in the 1657 and 1660 Acts, but in 1684 Gilbert Staunton Carrier and Coachman of Kettering was fined £380 (£18,000) for carrying great quantities of letters and by 1687 the 'Vade Mecum' reported an order of the Post Master General, the preamble of which begins -

'Whereas by an Order from the Post Master General, bearing Date the 11th of March, 1684/5; all Carriers, Stage Coaches, Higlers, and Drivers of Pack-horses, are forbidden to Carry, or re-carry any Letter, or Pacquets of Letters, except what concern their Packs, upon the Penalties therein exprest; Therefore ...'

The Carriers letter-handling so continued until the 1711 Act. By this Act they were restricted to carrying letters only on their own goods route and only to send on a horseman with letters ahead of their vans to arrive in the next town half-an-hour before their carts and vans were due to arrive. It was normal carrying procedure where possible to send ahead the goods documentation so that it could be dealt with and preparations made to receive the goods with a minimum of delay. By limiting the carrying of letters to

1817 Letter asking for a parcel of documents to be sent to Sevenoaks by stagecoach. (AGD)

this procedure, it hampered the carriers in any attempt to organise a separate letter-carrying service unconnected with their goods carrying service. Yet after 1711 many letters must still have been carried, perhaps illegally, and at a lower cost than that of the official mail, particularly in the large areas of the country where the official mail did not penetrate. For example the notice in the London Gazette of 27 September 1763 warned 'Carriers, Coachmen, Watermen, Wherrymen, Dispersers of Country News-Papers, Higlers and all other persons whatsoever against the illegal conveying and delivering of Letters and Packets, promising prosecution of the utmost severity.

What then is known of Carriers letters and packages in the Sevenoaks area of a later date? Even in later years ephemera related to Carriers is very much scarcer than letters carried in the Royal Mail, but occasionally a letter is to be found marked 'With a Parcel' or just plain 'Parcel' to show the letter accompanied a parcel and to give it that special status. This almost amounts to documentation, depending on what is written in the letter, and is distinct from a letter travelling by carrier in its own right.

A letter (p.356) of 1829 so inscribed 'Parcel' with no postal markings sent by Messrs. Austen & Claridge of Sevenoaks is part of a large correspondence to Cradock, a solicitor in Loughborough, all the others of which have been sent to Loughborough by post. It probably accompanied documents.

Some carriers letters (outside Kent) have been found with £.s.d. markings on them denoting carrying charges and some researchers consider that large operators used adhesive labels to denote charges paid many years before the penny black was introduced in 1840. If so, then none remains; strange, when one sees the reasonably large quantity of official post that is still extant.

Tradesmen

Tradesmen mostly operated within say a twenty mile radius of a Town, and were often used for taking letters and messages within their purlieus, even to a late time and they were often used to take GPO mail on to its final destination when the recipient lived some way off the official walk. This latter arrangement would be a private one between recipient and tradesman, but if the tradesman already went weekly to a house to obtain a grocery order there would be little extra work to bring out the letters and any parcels and the charge, if any, might not have been high, rather in the nature of general goodwill in trading relations. Nevertheless a vital service and one that was respected on both sides and efficiently carried out. The post office left the letters either at the nearest sub-office or at an accommodation address by arrangement with the addressee.

Position in 1839

Illegally carried letters, mostly charged at only 1d each, exceeded in number those carried by the Post Office in some parts of the country, mostly the manufacturing towns, according to evidence given to the Postal Reform Movement.[1] In one firm for 2,068 letters put into the post, 5,861 others were sent by private means. Mostly these were to places within 20 miles (5,000) or within the 60-100 mile band (600). Old women and young children would call and collect the letters on 'carrier's nights' three times a week and there was no depot to which the letters might be sent. The actual carriers were of varied occupation, stagecoach owners, waggoners, tradesmen, single individuals who travelled on stage coaches. Some had carts, others travelled on foot. They made their own deliveries and seldom did a letter miscarry for their livelihood depended on their service and all were in competition with each other. Other letters were brought back. Foreign mail was sent in parcels to the ports to avoid internal costs. Such was the position in the larger industrial towns, but probably not so in the smaller agricultural towns such a Sevenoaks, where there was not the quantity of correspondence to make such arrangements worthwhile. Here the possibilities were tradesmen to carry local mail and the newsmen and coachmen for longer distances. Such carrying was not felt to be illegal.

A PO cautionary notice about illegal collecting and delivery appeared in Northern newspapers as late as 1843, some years after the universal penny post had commenced.

Newsmen

The Maidstone Journal and Kentish Advertiser (established 1788 every Tuesday 3d, by 1802 6d) had newsmen who covered the whole of Kent and East Sussex. There were also twenty-six agents including those in Sevenoaks (Mr. Clout, who also did Hair Powder Certificates to show the tax had been paid), Tunbridge Wells (Mr. Sprang), Tonbridge, Hastings, Lewes, Canterbury and the London Coffee Houses. As a service to the public the Newsmen ran an (illegal) letter service, even to the extent of having their own letter box in Sevenoaks. The circumstances are well chronicled in Post Office Records so it is again strange that so few of these 'By the Newsman' letters ever turn up and some letters concerning payment for newspapers that might usefully have been transmitted by this system have in fact been sent through normal postal channels at considerable cost.

Stagecoaches

During the 1800's stagecoaches carried letters, packets, parcels and Bankers' Parcels, sometimes legally sometimes illegally, sometimes with the knowledge of the coach operator and sometimes as a private arrangement with the coachman.

An example of illegal conduct was in 1800 when the Post Office successfully prosecuted John Weeks, coachmaster of Bristol, for illegally carrying a letter from Bristol to Gloucester in his stagecoach. After the prosecution, Francis Freeling published his usual caution in the newspapers.

Because stagecoaches ran to a tight advertised schedule, they were to be preferred to carriers, for a stagecoach could always be met without much inconvenience and the items it might be carrying, collected. Nearly all legal documents were transferred in this way (see p.346), for with their heavy weight it would have been of prohibitive cost to send them by mail classed as a letter. Where a stagecoach was carrying mail, the charge in the coachman's front boot might be 1s.6d for 192 ounces (up to 14 lbs). If carried in the rear Royal Mail guard's boot the charge would be 1s.6d for 1 ounce if marked 'Sample, of no value'. So it was stated in evidence given in 1839.[2]

But such parcels of documents are not letters and the Post Office's monopoly of letter carrying did not extend to parcels and documents. What was not legal was for a country office to bundle up say thirty or more letters into a parcel and make arrangements with the guard for them to be posted in London, thus saving money. Brett, writing about this matter regarding Hastings in 1839, says that the mailcoach guard was prone to indulge in this practice. But returning to stagecoaches, the practice, at least of carrying single letters, was common on the Wrotham run. A letter written in Malling in 1837 to an address in London has been seen posted in London, Cornhill. This letter is probably one given to a stagecoach guard to post, thereby saving a few pence but also in this case saving at least one day in the post if not two. As previously mentioned, the Post Office well knew this practice went on but was so ashamed of its own service that it let matters ride. What would be cracked down on if spotted was the letter parcelling from Hastings which was on a main route and showed no saving in time.

Servants and Friends, also Travellers

Barring letters with subversive contents, writers have always been allowed to send letters by their personal servants, indeed in early days this was one of the few ways in which letters could be sent. Those without the means to employ servants would send letters by their friends; and those without friends travelling in the right direction might well entrust their letter to a complete stranger. To do this was quite legal until the stranger might start to accept several or many letters and demand payment, then he became a messenger. Messengers might then be flouting the Post monopoly of letter carrying (but see Couriers).

Railway Letters

The Railway Letter scheme for the carriage of single letters as opposed to the carriage of sealed bags of letters commenced 1 February 1891 at a Railway cost of 2d plus postage. Paying this Railway Fee allowed a letter to be taken to a railway station and put on a specific train. At the other end it was either collected by someone who knew it was coming or posted, at a time when there were many deliveries a day. The

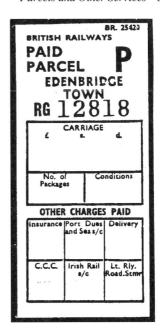

Railway Letter: part of an envelope enclosing a letter sent by railway from Bat and Ball station Sevenoaks to London by SE & C Rly and then posted at 12.15pm 4 May 1912 on arrival there. Bears 2d Railway stamp and 1d postage. Ordinary Parcel labels, such as this British Railways one for Edenbridge Town, were used on Railway letters in later years when the Railway stamps ceased to be issued.

object was to save time. Prior to 1891 letters sent by train had to be disguised as parcels generally by tying string round them, and were called 'string letters'. After 1984 the Railway Letter service ceased. The Railway 'Red Star' service remains, (see later) which does not involve paying any postage. When the Railway Letter Service ceased in 1984 only Tubs Hill and Wrotham stations accepted letters and parcels.

Private Message Systems

Probably one of the most efficient private message systems operating in this area was the smugglers one between Wrotham and the Coast operating in the second phase of smuggling around 1800.

Messages were sent between the main storage depots in Great Hurst Wood, Mereworth Woods, Ightham Sandpits and Oldbury Camp, and the landing beaches at Romney Marsh and around the coast to Hastings, by dog, rather in the same way that pigeons have been used. At least one dog was kept at each end belonging to the other, and sent off with messages as needed.[3] Often dogs travelled alone but 'Old Sobers' recalled that at 13 he would be sent off by dogcart from Wrotham at midnight with a message for some one in the Marsh. This was about 1813. In passing, such carts drawn by dogs became illegal in 1856. At other points messages could be passed by tethering animals in the fields in pre-arranged patterns, the patterns of windmill sails or the tunes coach guards played on their trumpets.[4]

Documents and Cheques

The London Document Exchange for legal mail started up in 1975 in Chancery Lane as a specialist postal service for the legal profession. The Post Office Act 1981 allowed the various legal exchanges to interlink and there are 80 offices in London and 480 in the rest of the country. Now the British Document Exchange, BritDoc Ltd. (Hays), claims to be '*the only licenced and private postal and mail operation in the UK*'. It handles items for Banks, Retail Groups, Estate Agents, Newspapers, Publishers and Printers and Advertising Agencies, as well as business in general. The various annual charges are based on two-thirds Royal Mail first class rate.

Bankers clearing of cheques has always required a considerable movement of paper. The Bankers Clearing System has a clearing house almost opposite Cannon Street Station where cheques and other vouchers are taken daily by Private Security Companies for sorting, then out again to their respective banks and branches.[5] Now the clearing house is automated, computer tapes are involved, but the cheques still move physically. The writer still receives back (in 1988) his paid cheques every month with his statement, by post.

Couriers

Perhaps the most well-known service of the couriers now is the Diplomatic Bag, letters sent thus being inscribed 'By Bag' and the Foreign Service Couriers. Often items are sent over the foreign stage 'By Bag' and posted internally in the UK.

In 1843, a Return to the House of Commons covering Queen's Messengers [6] shows that there were ten messengers employed on the Home Service of whom two died during the year. Their salary was £60 p.a. plus expenses, which '*at home were 7/6d a day with 3d a mile in the UK*'. The Military, too, has its Forces Courier Service, now Defence Courier Service, for time-sensitive letters and documents.

Most obvious of all on our streets are the multifarious motor-cyclists often seen stopped by the side of the road in London, their communications radio going whilst endeavouring to consult an A-Z without taking off their crash helmets. No easy feat: the writer never achieved it, one's glasses steam up!

Such cyclists are delivering individual letters and packets as 'immediates'. The Post Office monopoly of collection and delivery of letters has been suspended until 2006 under the British Telecommunications Act 1981 which permitted individual delivery by private messenger companies as long as the fee was £1 or over for each item. But the PO retained its monopoly of the issue of postage stamps. As well as motor cycles, vans are used and many of the security companies run van courier services. The highish fee is crucial. It is said that there would be much private development if the fee allowed were dropped to 50p.

In the Sevenoaks area several firms advertise courier services. The locally based ones are shown as

A.C. Cars, Sevenoaks.	Deadline Despatch, Sevenoaks, Biggin Hill, Edenbridge.
Allways Couriers, Sevenoaks.	Sunningvale Couriers, Biggin Hill.
A.D. Brett, Sevenoaks, West Kingsdown, Dartford.	C.W.G. Hawken, Biggin Hill.

Electronic Mailboxing

This book is about information symbols transmitted on a paper or similar carrying-medium, letters. But a few lines on other information carrying media should not go amiss. A good example of this is the electronic mailboxing system of British Telecom, called Telecom Gold. Equipment needed is an intelligent keyboard with modem (telephone interface), a visual display unit, possibly a printer for hard copy print-out on paper and of course the rental of a mailbox with its specific address number.

Other users of the system can then address a person using his mailbox number and leave messages. Then the recipient using his keyboard via a modem to connect to a telephone in any part of the world can key in to his mailbox and extract any messages left there. These messages can be answered straight away using the keyboard and addressing to the sender's mailbox number, stored in his personal computer short-term to be dealt with later or printed out as hard copy (on paper) for retention.

Business visiting cards now often have an electronic mailbox address on them as well as a physical house address. The system tends to be for business use, for the cost is a little more expensive than the cost of an 18p stamp. But then messages can be passed more quickly.

Fax

The world-wide reproduction system both sending and receiving and using the telephone network came to Sevenoaks for public use in mid-1987 at Floss Copy Shop in London Road. Charges were per A4 page £1 UK, £2 EEC, £3 USA and rest of the world, all plus VAT 15%. Receiving 50p per page. Fax sprang to prominence and many users, both private and companies soon bought their own equipment, leaving the GPO Intelpost little used.

Parcel and Goods Carrying, Non-GPO

Until 1883 the Post Office had no parcel service and so from earlier times Carriers and Stagecoaches were the ones that carried all parcels.

The Post Office had a monopoly of letter carrying. Limited in 1840 to 1 lb weight, this restriction was lifted in 1847, but no such monopoly applied to parcel carrying when the service did start in 1883 and so the Post Office was in direct competition with other road users, carriers and tradesmen and also the Railway.

Carriers

The 1637 list of John Taylor is the first overall list to include Carriers of the South East and gives an idea of how well the area was covered. The rest of the country was covered in like manner. In general a trip to London and back was made each week.

Carriers to London (Southwarke) 1637

KatherineWheel Tunbridge, Seavenoake, Frant, Staplehurst, Marden, Pembree,Warbleton.
Spur S'warke Tenterden, Penshurst, Battell.
Green Dragon S'warke Tunbridge
King's Head S'warke Chillington, Westrum, Penborough, Slenge, Wrotham.
Greyhound S'warke Hawkhurst, Darking, etc.
George S'warke   Wannish, Goudhurst, Chiddington, Battle, Sindrich,Hastings.
Tabbard or Talbot S'warke Cranbroke, Lewis, Petworth, Uckfield,Cuckfield.
White Hart S'warke Dover, Sandwich, Canterbury, Biddenden, Mayfield,Eaton Bridge, Horsham, etc.
Queens S'warke Portsmouth, etc., Rye, Lamberhurst, Wadhurst, Godstone, etc.
Falcon S'warke Reygate, Surry.

Carrier Ticket:
1833 Shepherd & Co. Van for Passengers and Luggage to Sevenoaks and Tonbridge Wells 4pm daily. (AGD)

SHEPHERD & Co.
CARRIERS TO THEIR MAJESTIES.

HASTINGS AND BATTLE
ROYAL BLUE COACH VANS
For Passengers and Luggage, Daily,
at 4 o'Clock, Afternoon.

TONBRIDGE-WELLS & SEVEN-OAKS
VAN for Passengers and Luggage, at 4 o'Clock, Daily.

BRIGHTON ROYAL BLUE VANS, for the safe conveyance of Goods only, every Afternoon at 5 o'Clock.

From 35, CAMOMILE STREET, CITY.

Mr.

Carriage of	Articles	
Cartage	ditto	
Warehouse	ditto	
Porterage	ditto	
	Charges paid out	

William Byfield } Porters
D. Clements

Some Carriers Serving Sevenoaks to London

In an advertisement of 12th February 1788 William Wheatley states that his '*Balloon Waggon with a guard sets out from Swan Inn Maidstone every Mon, Thur morn 8am goes through Larkfield, E. Malling, T. Malling, Wrotham, Farningham, St. Mary Cray and Eltham to White Hart Inn in Borough. Goods and Parcels carefully delivered at 2/- per cwt.*'.

The Carrier's life was not all the time as idyllic as it might appear on woodcuts. On 1st December 1834, James Wright, Carrier of Rye, was alleged to have committed a misdemeanour whilst passing through Sevenoaks in that he '*passed through Riverhill Tollgate with a broadwheeled waggon drawn by 4 horses and after passed through added another three to such waggon up to the town of Sevenoaks*'. He would probably have saved a toll of 3d on each of three horses but was liable to a fine not exceeding £5 on appearing before the Justices of the Peace. He had to appear at Court Hall in Tonbridge. This manner of adding on horses after passing through a tollgate was a common happening particularly where a steep hill over a short distance was involved. Perhaps James Wright was just unlucky that day, more likely he had ignored several previous warnings and a trap had been set for him.[7]

Parcels by Stagecoach and Mailcoach

In the early accounts of stagecoach travelling it is frequently mentioned that parcels went in the basket at the back of the coach. It is also mentioned that outside passengers tired of trying to hang on on the roof with no rail to grip, sometimes transferred themselves to the basket. This gave a more comfortable ride uphill or along the flat if the speed did not exceed five miles an hour, but was murder down hill on a rough road and they all were rough, if the speed got up. The parcels came alive and hit one in every part of the body and could not be fended off for one needed to hang on with both hands to avoid being thrown out.

By 1780 it is mentioned that the stage coaches from London and Hastings met half way at Tonbridge and exchanged Passengers and Parcels.

In recalling 1836, Brett says '*I gain two or three minutes by running off with the crosspost while the (mail) guard is getting out the London sack and **his parcels***'. And again and on the return journey to London '*the (letter) bags are sealed in readiness for the mail guard when he comes in at eight minutes to ten. But what about the letters in the shape of parcels which the said guard carries in a private and clandestine manner?*' Parcels were legal on stage coaches but probably not so on mailcoaches, certainly not in the mail guard's box.[8]

In 1843 a stage coach advertisement for parcels quotes the rate from Sevenoaks to Tunbridge as 'under 24 lbs 1/-, every additional 1 lb at ½d., delivery included'.[9]

Parcel wrappings are just about extinct as well they may be from an era that heated with open fires which needed kindling to light them. So the picture of what happened has to be built up from snippets of information widely scattered, although a single item sent 'by Hastings coach' has come to light.

The Great Sevenoaks Stage Coach Robbery

In 1842 on the 22nd June Messrs. Palmer & Co. as agents in Sevenoaks of the London and County Bank sent, as was usual, a parcel of gold to the value of £249 (£10,500) to London by the Sevenoaks Coach. Presumably it was declared what was in the package or **I Gulielmi IV Cap 48 of 23 July 1830**, an Act that protected '*Stage Coach Proprietors and other Common Carriers ...... against loss or Injury to Parcels delivered to them for Conveyance ...... the value and contents of which shall not be declared to them*', might have applied.

The parcel, presumed stolen, disappeared from the Coach and William Peacock, the Sevenoaks Coach guard, was held responsible. Peacock was a man of good character and of long service and it was not within his capability to repay such a large amount (his pay likely was between £50 and £100 a year). A subscription list was opened on his behalf which eventually settled the matter,[10] and for which he duly expressed his heartfelt thanks in print.

The interesting point is that it was the Coach Guard himself that had to meet the loss, not his employers. The Coach name is not mentioned in the report of the matter. It could have been the 'United Friends' that

Some Carriers Serving Sevenoaks to London
(by no means complete)

	Name	Inn used as terminus	Days
1637	Not named	Katherine Wheel	Come Thur go Fri
1667	? Wm Locquer	via Sevenoaks	
1681-1690	Richard Cockett	Spur Southwarke	Mon, Thur
1681	-	White Hart Southwarke	Wed from Tonbridge
	Nathaniel Field	Queens Head Southwarke	Tues from Tonbridge
1690	Wm Reeves	George Southwarke	Mon, Thur (Winter Tues)
	R. Roofs	George Southwarke	Mon, Thur (Winter Tues)
1745	Not named	Spur Southwarke	Mon, Thur, Fri
	Not named	Bell & Bear, St. Margarets Hill	Tues, Fri
1788	Wm Wheatley later Sarah Wheatley	Ex Maidstone to White Hart Boro via Wrotham	Mon, Thur. Passengers 2/6 Parcels 2/- cwt.
1800	Morphew	Queen's Head Boro	from T Wells
	Thos. Smith	Spur Boro	from Battle
	Messrs Tuty & Co	White Hart S' Warke	from Hastings
	John Hunter	Queen's Head Boro	from Rye
1800-22	Barnett (Bennett)	George Inn Borough	M, T (T. Wells, Ton., Sev.)
	Evenden	George Inn Borough	Mon (Ightham, Wrotham, Kingsdown)
1814	Quinnell	established at Bradbourne	
1831	Baines, Stenning	Spur Borough	Mon, Thur
1833	Shepherd & Co Van	35 Camomile St. City	T. Wells & Sevenoaks daily van for psgr & l'gage.
1836	Stenning	Spur Borough	Mon, Thur
1838-41	James Reynolds	Kings Head Borough	Mon, Thur
1839	Barnett's Vans and Waggons	Lewis Arms Van & Waggons Inn, Great Dover Road Borough (Removed from White Hart)	Daily (T. Wells, Ton, Sev.)
1840	Thos. Bird	Talbot Inn Borough	Mon, Thur return Tu, Fri
	(Thos Stenning)	Spur Inn Borough	Mon, Thur
	(Jesse Langridge)		
	Wm Franks	Nags Head Borough	Mon, Thur
1841	John Reeves	Catharine Wheel Boro	Mon, Thur return Tu, Fri
1845	Stenning Thos	Spur Inn Borough	Mon, Thur
	Reynolds James	Kings Head Borough	
	Franks Wm	Nags Head Borough	
	Wm Lisney	Half Moon Inn Borough	
	Whitehouse, John	Queens Head Borough	
	Quinnell		
	Barnett's	George Inn Borough	
	Marchant		
1847	Thos Skinner		Tues, Thur
1855	Reynolds, Lisney, Thos Quinnell		
1886	Quinnell		
1891	Mrs Fanny Quinnell	Queens and Nags Head Borough	Mon, Thur

SPUR INN, YARD, BOROUGH,

DREWETT'S
ORIGINAL WAGGON AND VAN OFFICE.

Mr.

	£.	s.	d.
Carriage			
Warehouse			
Cartage			
Porterage			
Paid out			

J. EAST & T. SKINNER, Porters.

J. D. respectfully informs the Public, that, all Goods, entrusted to his care will be forwarded with the utmost dispatch to the following Places.—

Hastings, Rye, Battle, Brede, Sedlescomb, West Field, Ewhurst, Brookland, Ore, Bexhill, Lydd, Udimore, Catsfield, Robertsbridge, Hurst Green, Lamberhurst, Flimwell, &c. Daily. T. RICHARDSON

Worthing, Arundel, Littlehampton, Tarring, Lancing, Goring, Augmering West Grinstead, and Horsham, Daily. —

Brighton, Shoreham, Hove, Rottingdean, Cuckfield, Crawley, &c. Daily } GANDER & Co.

Petworth Chichester, Midhurst, Pulborough, Fittleworth, Stopham Tillington, Graffham, Lavington, North Chapel, and Godalming Thursday Noon } COLLINS

Lewes, Newhaven, Seaford, Bletchington, Rodmell, Newick, Alfriston, Wilmington Firle, Glynde, Ringmer, Falmer, Stanmer, Offham Fletching Dane Hill, Chailey, Cooksbridge, West Hoathley and Forest Row. Wednesday and Saturday Noon............ CORK.

Tunbridge Wells, Tunbridge, Southboro' , Penshurst, Pembury, Speldhurst, Bidborough, &c. Tuesday, Thursday, and Saturday Mornings. — ROOTS & Co.

Town Malling, East Malling, Hunton Birling, Addington, Ryash, Leyborn, Snodland, Wateringbury, Mereworth Teston, Barming, East and West Farleigh, East and West Peckham, Yalding, Hadlow, and Wrotham. T sday and Friday Noon. G. LARKIN.

Henfield, Cowfold, Bolney, Ditchling Hurstperpoint, — — — { KING.
Slaugham Handcross, Crawley and Horley. — — —

Maidstone, Lenham, Leeds, Hollingbourn, Loose, Linton, Boughton, Aylsford, Boxley, Torell, and Larkfield. Tuesday and Friday Noon. — GOREHAM.

Tenderden, Bolvenden, Benenden, Biddenden, Bithersden, Fritenden, Newingden, Smarden, Iden, Standen, Highalden, Appledore, Wittersham, Headcorn, Peasmarsh, and New Romney, Monday Noon. — HOLLAND

Headly, Liphook Milford, Bramshot and Godalming Thursday Noon. MILLS.

Sheire, Dorking, Albury, Cranley, Ewhurst, Westcott, &c. Tues. Day and Friday Noon. — D. TIDY.

Waldron, Maresfield, Framfield, Crossinhand, Uckfield, and East Hoathley. Tuesday and Friday Noon. — FARRANT late SUSANS.

Sevenoaks, Riverhead, Farnboro' and Bromley Monday and Thursday, Evening. — late BAINS and now STENNING

Farningham, Eynsford, Horton Kirby, Sutton at Hone, Grinstead Green, Southdarn, and Foots Cray. Tues. and Friday Morn. DRAY.

East Grinstead, Godstone, Forest Row, &c. Tuesd. and Friday Even. CORK.

Rotherfield, Groombridge Crowborough, Eridge Green, Boarshead Street, Dangate, and Speldhurst. Wednesday Morning JESSE CORK.

Worth Copthorn, Burstow, Blindly, Heath, &c. Tues. & Fri. Morn. COLLINS.

Dartford, Crayford Wilmington, Bexley Heath and Welling, Daily. CLARK.

Ardingly, Hapstead Green, West Hoathly, Turners Hill, Lindfield and Godstone, Tuesday and Friday Noon. — CRONK

Pulborough, Wisborough Green, Billinghurst and Storington, Tuesday and Friday Noon. — STRINGER.

Croydon, Streatham, Brixton, &c. Daily. — GRANTHAM

Tooting, Balham and Clapham, Errand Carts, Daily. — FRANCIS.

Carts kept for the conveyance of Goods.

N. B. No Package or Parcel, above the value of £5, will be accounted for unless entered as such, and Insurance paid on Delivery.

Please to observe the —Office is down the Yard, on the Right Hand,

Robinett, Printer, 7 & 18, White St Borough.

J. JARRATT's
Lewes Arms Van & Waggon Inn,
GREAT DOVER ROAD,
NEAR ST. GEORGE'S CHURCH, BOROUGH.

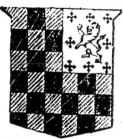

Vans and Waggons to Uckfield, Lewes, Brighton, East Bourne, Hailsham, Newhaven, and Dieppe, *daily*; for the express conveyance of Gentlemen's Goods, Wines, Glass, Furniture, Plate, & all kinds of Merchandise in general.

Please to take Notice, that the Original Lewes Waggons, late Mr. J. Shelley's, are removed from the George and White Hart Inns to Jarratt's Office.

N. B. Also his Original East Bourne and Hailsham Vans and Waggons, late Martin's, are removed from the White Hart and Catherine Wheel, to Jarratt's Office, Great Dover Road, Borough.—Load Daily.

[handwritten carrier ticket]
Carriage of
Porterage do.
Cartage do.
Paid out
Warehousing

SPRING VANS DAILY AT 3 O'CLOCK LIGHTED AND GUARDED, TO THE FOLLOWING PLACES :—

Eastbourne	Hailsham	Lewes	Brighton	Newhaven and	Uckfield	Buxted	Heathfield	E. Grinstead
Southbourne	Willingdon	Southover	Rottingdean	Dieppe	Maresfield	Hadlow down	Mayfield	Godstone
Pevensey	Hellingly	Malling	Stanmore	Seaford	Isfield	Crowborough	Warbleton	Kidbrooke
Westham	Horsebridge	Firle	Patcham	Alfriston	Little Horsted	Rotherfield	Rushlake-grn.	Forest Row
Wartling	Dicker	Glynde	Falmer	Alciston	Barcombe	Fletching	Cross-in-hand	&c. &c.
Herstmonceux	Chiddingly	Beddingham	Street	Bishopstone	Ringmer	Newick	Brightling	
Gardner Street	East Hothley	Iford	Plumpton	Blatchington	Framfield	Offham	Dallington	
Boreham Street	Laughton	Rodmill	Ditchling	Wilmington	Waldron	Chailey	Burwash	

Tunbridge Wells, Maidstone and Brighton Luggage Vans, from J. Barnett's Office, Tunbridge Wells, every Tuesday and Friday, to Blue Van Office, East Street, Brighton, and return the following day.

BENTON'S VANS every TUESDAY, THURSDAY, & SATURDAY at 8 o'Clock.

Ashford	Folkstone	Hythe	Sandgate	Canterbury	Dover	Maidstone
Lenham	New Romney	Chart	Smeeth	Wye	Deal	Malling
Charing	Old Romney	Egerton	Sellinge	Eastwell	Sandwich	and
Dymchurch	Hastingly	Pluckley	Lympne	Boughton	Wingham	Neighbourhood
Aldington	Hothfield	Sutton	Willesborough	Harietsham	Ash	

MOORE and Co's. VANS DAILY at 5 O'CLOCK, for PASSENGERS and LUGGAGE, to HASTINGS, ROBERTS BRIDGE, BATTLE, BEXHILL, and all adjacent places.

BARNETT'S VANS, and WAGGONS, DAILY at 4 O'CLOCK, to TONBRIDGE WELLS, TONBRIDGE SEVENOAKS, and all adjacent places.

Extra Vans or Waggons for the removal of Gentlemen's Furniture, Wines, &c. to any part of England, on the shortest notice.
Letters addressed to J. JARRATT, Van Office, Uckfield, Sussex, or to his Book-keeper, Lewes Arms, Dover Road, Boro', will be duly attended to.
N. B. Manufacturer of, and Wholesale Dealer in, Charcoal.

Goods Carted in and from all parts of the Town on liberal Terms, by addressing a line to the Book-keeper, Lewes Arms, Dover Road, Borough.
All Goods which shall be delivered for the purpose of being carried, will be considered as general Liens, and subject not only for the carriage of such particular Goods, but also to the general Balance due from their respective owners, to the Proprietor of the said conveyance.
Senders of Oil, Vitriol, Aqua-fortis, or any ardent Spirits, packed up with other goods without proper notice, and leakage of Casks, or Bottles of Oil, or Ink, will be holden responsible for any damage that may arise therefrom.

Errand Carts daily at 3 o'Clock 10 Miles round Town.

J. JARRATT gives Public Notice, that he will not be accountable for any article, unless it be entered and signed for as received by him or his agents; neither for the loss or damage of any Goods put into returned wrappers or boxes, nor of any goods left until called for, or to order, or warehoused for the convenience of the parties to whom they are consigned. No claim for damage. Dogs and all other Live Animals, and Carriages, will be taken the greatest care of, but at the sole risk of the owner if any accident occurs to them.—Dogs will not be taken without proper chains, &c.

Barnes, Printer, Southwark.

Carrier Tickets:
Opposite: 1831 Drewetts Spur Inn Yard Borough. Sevenoaks Waggon Monday and Thursday evening.
Above: 1839 Jarratt Lewes Arms Van and Waggon Inn Barnetts van and waggons daily to Sevenoaks, Tonbridge, T Wells.

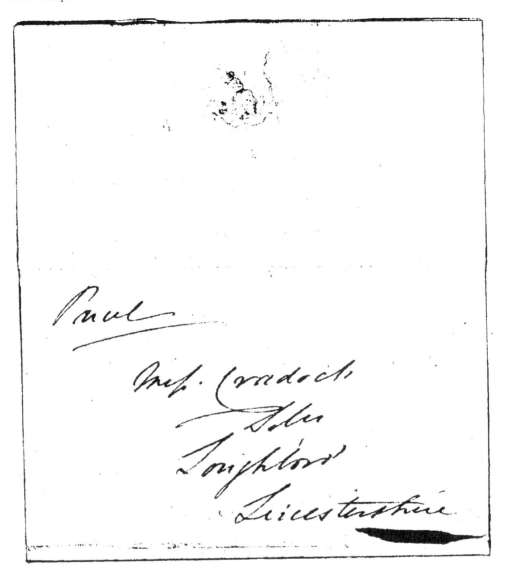

1830 Letter from Austen & Claridge Sevenoaks to Loughboro' accompanying a parcel of documents sent by stagecoach and so inscribed 'Parcel'. The contents of such a letter could only refer to the goods being sent or it infringed the PO's monopoly of letter-carrying, as Freeling was wont to explain in frequent notices in newspapers as early as 1806, warning merchants against enclosing letters in parcels sent by stagecoach.

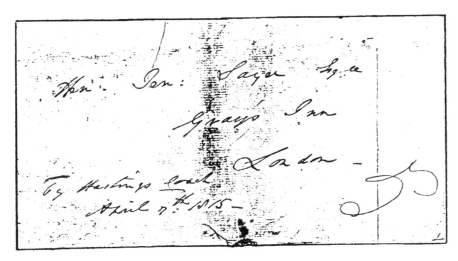

*1815 Part of such a parcel wrapping that **was** saved; the only one known to exist on this coach run. 'By Hastings Coach' April 7th 1815. 2/- charge. (Richard Blake of Caterham)*

left the 'Rose & Crown' (later Youngs Department Store, later still Bejam) at 8 am every morning for London.

Smuggled Goods

Smuggling was rife around the whole coast, but nowhere were there more goods to transport than in the Kent/Sussex area. Smuggling went through two phases. The first phase about 1660-1720, the 'owling' period, so-called because the participants alerted each other by hooting like owls, was based on the prohibition of the export of wool except through controlled channels. Wool went out from the Coastal regions and lace and brandy came in. The 'trade' was controlled by the Hugenots who, when they fled religious persecution in the mid-1500's, had kept up their contacts with the Continental clothiers who liked the English wool and could not get enough of it.

The second phase was about 1720-1820 and was based on the high duty placed on tea, spirits and tobacco. Tea duty was as high as 129%. After a landing from[11] small boats at Romney Marsh or along the coast at Hastings, the goods would be brought by packhorse sometimes up to 200 at a time and some carts drawn by two strong dogs through the woods to Battle or Groombridge or the storage areas at Mereworth, Wrotham and Ightham. Most of the goods were destined for London, some for what they would fetch, others to a definite order. The smugglers brought the goods inland as far as they could and then the Chapmen came down from London to meet them. As the goods got nearer to London they were forced onto or near to the turnpike roads. The Groombridge smugglers carried their goods as far as Rushmore Hill and in 1740 a captured exciseman was held by smugglers at Pratts Bottom.

In 1784 in a bid to undermine the 'trade', the tea duty was cut from 129% to 12½ % (and the Window tax increased to offset the loss in revenue), but the turnpike roads continued to support the movement of much contraband.

As late as 1839, R. Butler, the mailguard, was prosecuted when contraband was seized from the London-Dover Mailcoach.[12]

Railway Parcels

As well as carrying passengers and heavy goods the railways early on (1830's) became entrenched in carrying parcels with the local post office letter carriers taking parcels from the houses to the railway station pre-1883 as a private venture. Parcels up to 1 cwt (hundredweight - 112 lbs) could normally be sent quite quickly by passenger train. It was this already existing position that was the cause of the delay and difficulty in the commencement of the Post Office Parcels Service. The Railways were strong on main line transportation but weak on collection and delivery to individual addresses. The Post Office had a strong collection and delivery service, but were weak on main line transportation, which they usually contracted for.

Once established in the mid-1830's on, the Railways drained the roads of their traffic, the mail coaches, the stage coaches, the carriers; even the drove roads became empty as by 1845/6 instead of being driven by road to market beasts were slaughtered first then the carcasses sent by train. The busy roads were the short distance ones to the local Railway station.

Unlike Postal Parcel Services when they came, Railway Parcel Rates were linked to distance travelled. Rates from Sevenoaks, Bat and Ball or Tubbs Hill, to London in 1920 were:

For Rate B (Under 30 miles)   South Eastern & Chatham Railway

2 lbs	9d. *	7-8 lbs	1/3 *	20 lbs	2/1 - 4/1
3 lbs	1/- *	11 lbs	1/6 *	40 lbs	2/8 - 7/7
5 lbs	1/- *	15 lbs	1/11 - 3/1	112 lbs	4/1 -20/5

(* Valid for any distance 30 miles to 'above 200 miles'. From 15 lbs to 112lbs the 'above 200 miles' rate is also shown)[13]

with an owner's risk some 20-25% below this; not perhaps to be used as breakages by railway in those days seemed quite high.

Perhaps most useful was the effective lack of a higher weight limit, one hundredweight being as much as a sack of potatoes, which weighed twice the present day sack and was just about liftable once one was trained to it. Even then 'parcels' above 1 cwt. could be sent by passenger train on application.

The Railways did use adhesive (separate pot of glue with a stick in it, once a small brush from which the bristles had long worn off) labels and one from Dunton Green is shown. In early days every station handled parcels traffic. The grouping of the railway companies into four, LMS, LNER, GWR and SR in 1923, helped through parcels traffic, and in 1948 these four became British Rail. Now the number of stations handling parcels traffic has been rationalised and in this area the two stations concerned with the 'Red Star' service are Tubbs Hill on the Charing Cross Line and Wrotham and Borough Green on the run to Victoria.

Currently the Railways Red Star service handles packets, parcels and heavy parcels. The 'same day' service becomes a courier service or the consignee can collect from the station in the way it has always been done. Collection from consignor can also be arranged.

The current (1985/6) tariff (selected items only) is -

	Station to Station Per Package	Per Consignment Delivered to Door, Overnight		
		by noon	by 9 am	Same Day
Up to 1 kg. (2.2 lbs)	£7.50	£10.65	£15.50	£18.00
5	8.00	10.65	15.50	20.00
7	8.50	11.00	18.00	22.00
10	9.50	11.65	20.25	25.00
Selected higher items are				
25	£12.50	18.75	29.25	40.00
50	27.00	31.25	45.00	67.50
100	52.00	56.00	75.00	125.00 [14]

'*Sevenoaks Tubs Hill*' and '*Boro' Green and Wrotham*' are the two parcels stations remaining within the area.

Early days at 'Halstead Knockholt' station. (Unknown)

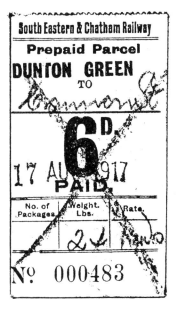

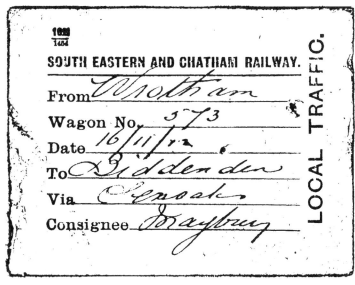

Above: 1917 South Eastern and Chatham Railway Parcel Ticket Dunton Green 6d.
Waggon Ticket for a full waggon load by Railway from Wrotham to Biddenden via Sevenoaks.

Over: Railway Parcel Rates 1920s. Such parcels normally travelled in the Guards van of passenger trains.
Sevenoaks was Scale B to London.

South Eastern and Chatham Railway.

RATES

FOR

CONVEYANCE OF PARCELS

BY PASSENGER TRAIN

Station	Rate	Station	Rate	Station	Rate
Bexley	A	Ham Street and Orlestone	D	Selling	D
Bexleyheath	A	Harrietsham	C	**Selsdon Road**	A
Bickley	A	**Hastings**	D	Sevenoaks (Bat and Ball)	B
Biddenden (K. & E. S. Rly.)	C	Hawkhurst	C	Sevenoaks (Tub's Hill)	B
Birchington-on-Sea	D	Hayes	A	**Shalford**	B
Bishopsbourne	D	Headcorn	C	Sharnal Street	C
Blackheath	A	Herne Bay	D	Sheerness Dockyard	C
*Blackheath Hill	A	Herne Hill	A	Sheerness East	C
Blackwater and Camberley	B	Higham	B	*Sheerness-on-Sea	C
Bodiam (K. & E. S. Rly.)	D	High Halden Road (K. & E. S. Rly.)	C	Shepherd's Well	D
Box Hill	B	Hildenborough	B	Shooter's Hill & Eltham Park	A
Brasted	B	Hither Green	A	Shoreham (Kent)	B
Bridge	D	Holborn Viaduct	A	Shorncliffe	D
†Brixton and S. Stockwell	A	Hollingbourne	C	Shortlands	A
Broadstairs	D	Honor Oak	A	Sidcup	A
*Brockley Lane	A	Horsmonden	C	Sidley	D
Bromley North	A	Hothfield (for Westwell)	D	Sittingbourne and Milton Regis	C
Bromley South	A	Hythe	D	Slades Green	A
Brookland	D	Kearsney (for River and Ewell)	D	Smeeth	D
†*Camberwell	A	Kemsing	B	Smitham	A
Cannon Street	A	Kenley	A	Snodland	C
Canterbury East	D	Kent House	A	Sole Street	B
Canterbury West	D	Kidbrooke	A	Southborough	B
Caterham	A	Kingswood & Burgh Heath	A	South Canterbury	D
Catford	A	Knockholt	B	Southfleet for Springhead	B
Catford Bridge	A	Lady Well	A	*Southwark Park	A
Charing	D	Lee	A	*Spa Road	A
Charing Cross	A	Lenham	C	Staplehurst	C
Charlton	A	Lewisham Junction	A	Strood	B
Chartham	D	*Lewisham Road	A	Sturry	D
Chatham	B	Leysdown	D	Sundridge Park	A
Chelsfield	A	London Bridge	A	Swanley Junction	B
Chilham	D	Lordship Lane (for Forest Hill)	A	Sydenham Hill	A
Chilworth and Albury	B	Loughborough Junction	A	Tadworth	A
Chipstead & Banstead Downs	B	Lower Sydenham	A	Tattenham Corner	A
Chislehurst	A	Lydd	D	Tenterden Town (K. & E. S. Rly.)	B
†*Clapham and N. Stockwell	A	Lyminge	D	Teynham	C
Cliffe	B	Maidstone Barracks	C	Ticehurst Road	C
Clock House	A	Maidstone East	C	Tonbridge Junction	B
*Coombe Lane	A	Maidstone West	C	Tovil	C
Coulsdon and Cane Hill	A	Malling	C	**Tunbridge Wells**	C
Cranbrook	C	Marden	C	Upper Sydenham	A
Crayford	A	Margate Sands	D	**Upper Warlingham**	A
Crofton Park	A	Margate West	D	Victoria	A
Crowhurst	D	Martin Mill (for St. Margaret's Bay)	D	Wadhurst	C
Croydon East	A	Maze Hill (for E. Greenwich)	A	Walmer (for Kingsdown)	D
Crystal Palace and Upper Norwood	A	Meopham	B	*Walworth Road	A
Cuxton	C	Merstham	B	**Wanborough**	B
Dartford	B	Minster Junction (Thanet)	D	*Wandsworth Road	A
Deal	D	Minster-on-Sea (Sheppey)	D	Warlingham	A
Denmark Hill	A	New Beckenham	A	Wateringbury	C
*Deptford	A	New Cross	A	Waterloo Junction	A
Dorking	B	New Eltham	A	Well Hall	A
Dover Harbour	D	Newington	C	Welling	A
Dover Priory	D	New Romney and Littlestone-on-Sea	D	**Wellington College**	B
*Dover Town	D	Northfleet	B	Westcombe Park	A
Dulwich	A	Northiam (K. & E.S. Rly.)	D	Westenhanger	D
Dungeness	D	Nunhead Junction	A	Westerham	B
Dunton Green	B	Nutfield	B	Westgate-on-Sea	D
Earley	C	Ore	D	West St. Leonards	D
Eastchurch	D	Orpington	A	West Wickham	A
East Farleigh	C	Otford	B	Whitstable Harbour	D
East Margate	D	**Oxted**	B	Whitstable Town	D
Edenbridge	B	Paddock Wood Junction	C	Whyteleafe	A
Eden Park	A	Peckham Rye	A	Winchelsea	D
Elephant and Castle	A	Penge	A	Wittersham Rd. (K. & E.S. Ry.)	D
Elham	D	Penshurst	B	**Wokingham**	C
Elmer's End	A	Pluckley	C	**Woldingham**	A
Elmstead Woods	A	Plumstead	A	**Woodside and South Norwood**	A
Eltham (for Mottingham)	A	Port Victoria	C	Woolwich Arsenal	A
Erith	A			Woolwich Dockyard	A
Etchingham	C			*Wrotham and Boro' Green	B
Eynsford	B			Wye	D
				Yalding	C

*These Stations are closed temporarily.   † Parcels for these Districts are dealt with at Herne Hill.

THE GENERAL PARCELS SCALES INCLUDE IN LONDON COLLECTION FROM THE RECEIVING OFFICES SHOWN ON COVER, AND DELIVERY WITHIN A RADIUS OF 2½ MILES FROM SOMERSET HOUSE; ALSO COLLECTION AND DELIVERY WITHIN THE ORDINARY AREA AT SUBURBAN, COUNTRY AND SEASIDE STATIONS WHERE THOSE SERVICES ARE UNDERTAKEN.

For Owner's Risk Scales arrangements, see Notes on page 6.

SPECIAL LONDON AND SUBURBAN "A" SCALE.

(Applicable between any two Stations marked " A " in list on page 2.)

	WEIGHT NOT EXCEEDING													
	3 lbs.	7 lbs.	11 lbs.	15 lbs.	20 lbs.	25 lbs.	40 lbs.	55 lbs.	65 lbs.	75 lbs.	80 lbs.	90 lbs.	100 lbs.	112 lbs.	Above 112 lbs.
	s. d.	s. d.	s. d.	s. d.	s. d.	s. d.	s. d.	s. d.	s. d.	s. d.	s. d.	s. d.	s. d.	s. d.	
General Parcels Scale ..	0 6	0 10	1 2	1 4	1 6	1 7	1 8	1 10	2 0	2 2	2 2	4 2	5 2	2 6	1d. per additional 4 lbs. or part thereof.
*Owner's Risk Scale ..	0 6	0 8	0 11	1 0	1 2	1 2	3 1	5 1	6 1	7 1	8 1	9 1	10 1	11	1d. per additional 5 lbs. or part thereof.

Fractions of 1 lb. are charged as 1 lb.

* Applicable only to Traffics shown on pages 4, 5 and 6. The signing of a General Owner's Risk Agreement, or an Owner's Risk Consignment Note, is an indispensable condition upon which these rates are applied.

STANDARD SCALE OF RATES.

Applicable with certain exceptions :—

(1) Between all Stations in Great Britain (subject to Scale " A " above) ;
(2) " " and Ports in Great Britain ;
(3) " " and Ports in Great Britain and all Stations and Ports in Ireland ;
(4) " " and Ports in the United Kingdom, and (A) Jersey and Guernsey, (B) Douglas, Isle of Man; } Where through bookings are in operation
(5) " " in Ireland ;

GENERAL PARCELS SCALE.

To or from London Scale.	Distance not Exceeding	WEIGHT NOT EXCEEDING												
		2 lbs.	3 lbs.	5 lbs.	7 lbs.	8 lbs.	11 lbs.	15 lbs.	20 lbs.	25 lbs.	30 lbs.	35 lbs.	40 lbs.	45 lbs.	50 lbs.
	Miles.	s. d.	s. d.	s. d.	s. d.	s. d.	s. d.	s. d.	s. d.	s. d.	s. d.	s. d.	s. d.	s. d.	s. d.
B	30	0 9	1 0	1 0	1 3	1 3	1 6	1 11	2 1	2 2	2 4	2 6	2 8	2 9	2 11
C	50	0 9	1 0	1 0	1 3	1 3	1 6	2 1	2 2	2 6	2 8	2 11	3 3	3 6	3 10
D	100	0 9	1 0	1 0	1 3	1 3	1 6	2 2	2 6	2 11	3 6	4 1	4 6	5 1	5 10
	200	0 9	1 0	1 0	1 3	1 3	1 6	2 6	3 3	3 10	4 6	5 3	6 2	6 10	7 7
	Above 200	0 9	1 0	1 0	1 3	1 3	1 6	3 1	4 1	4 10	5 10	6 9	7 7	8 7	9 8

To or from London Scale.	Distance not Exceeding	WEIGHT NOT EXCEEDING											
		55 lbs.	60 lbs.	65 lbs.	70 lbs.	75 lbs.	80 lbs.	85 lbs.	90 lbs.	95 lbs.	100 lbs.	105 lbs.	110 lbs.	112 lbs.	Above 112 lbs.
	Miles.	s. d.	s. d.	s. d.	s. d.	s. d.	s. d.	s. d.	s. d.	s. d.	s. d.	s. d.	s. d.	s. d.	
B	30	3 1	3 3	3 4	3 6	3 8	3 10	3 11	4 1	4 1	4 1	4 1	4 1	4 1	‡
C	50	4 3	4 6	5 0	5 3	5 10	6 2	6 7	6 10	7 4	7 7	8 0	8 2	8 2	
D	100	6 5	6 10	7 5	8 0	8 7	9 1	9 9	10 4	10 11	11 5	12 0	12 3	12 3	
	200	8 4	9 1	9 11	10 8	11 5	12 1	12 10	13 9	14 5	15 2	15 11	16 4	16 4	
	Above 200	10 6	11 5	12 5	13 5	14 4	15 2	16 2	17 3	18 1	19 0	20 0	20 5	20 5	

OWNER'S RISK SCALE.

Applicable only to certain Perishable and other Traffics shown on pages 4, 5 and 6. The signing of a General Owner's Risk Agreement, or an Owner's Risk Consignment Note, is an indispensable condition upon which these rates are applied.

To or from London Scale.	Distance not Exceeding	WEIGHT NOT EXCEEDING												
		2 lbs.	3 lbs.	5 lbs.	7 lbs.	8 lbs.	11 lbs.	15 lbs.	20 lbs.	25 lbs.	30 lbs.	35 lbs.	40 lbs.	45 lbs.	50 lbs.
	Miles.	s. d.	s. d.	s. d.	s. d.	s. d.	s. d.	s. d.	s. d.	s. d.	s. d.	s. d.	s. d.	s. d.	s. d.
B	30	0 7	0 9	0 9	0 11	0 11	1 2	1 4	1 6	1 7	1 9	1 11	2 1	2 1	2 2
C	50	0 7	0 9	0 9	0 11	0 11	1 2	1 6	1 7	1 9	1 11	2 2	2 4	2 1	2 4
D	100	0 7	0 9	0 9	0 11	0 11	1 2	1 7	1 9	1 11	2 1	2 2	2 6	2 8	2 11
	200	0 7	0 9	0 9	0 11	0 11	1 2	1 9	1 11	2 1	2 4	2 9	3 1	3 6	3 10
	Above 200 (except as shown below). } To Scotch and Interior Irish Stns. }	0 7	0 9	0 9	0 11	0 11	1 2	2 1	2 2	2 6	2 11	3 4	3 10	4 5	4 10
		0 7	0 9	0 9	0 11	0 11	1 2	2 1	2 9	3 4	4 5	5 1	5 10	6 7	7 4

To or from London Scale.	Distance not Exceeding	WEIGHT NOT EXCEEDING											
		55 lbs.	60 lbs.	65 lbs.	70 lbs.	75 lbs.	80 lbs.	85 lbs.	90 lbs.	95 lbs.	100 lbs.	105 lbs.	110 lbs.	112 lbs.	Above 112 lbs.
	Miles.	s. d.	s. d.	s. d.	s. d.	s. d.	s. d.	s. d.	s. d.	s. d.	s. d.	s. d.	s. d.	s. d.	
B	30	2 2	2 4	2 6	2 8	2 8	2 9	2 11	3 1	3 1	3 1	3 1	3 1	3 1	‡
C	50	2 4	2 6	2 8	2 9	2 11	3 1	3 4	3 6	3 8	3 10	4 1	4 1	4 1	
D	100	3 3	3 6	3 10	4 5	5 4	4 6	4 10	5 1	5 5	5 10	6 2	6 2	6 2	
	200	4 3	4 6	5 0	5 3	5 10	6 2	6 7	6 10	7 4	7 7	8 0	8 2	8 2	
	Above 200 (except as shown below). }	5 3	5 10	6 3	6 9	7 2	7 7	8 2	8 7	9 1	9 8	10 1	10 3	10 3	
	To Scotch and Interior Irish Stns. }	8 0	8 9	9 6	10 3	10 11	11 8	12 5	13 2	13 10	14 7	15 4	16 1	16 4	

Fractions of 1 lb. are charged as 1 lb.

In the case of Traffic with Ireland and the Isle of Man, Port Dues will be charged in addition to the above rates.
‡ Rates for weights above 112 lbs., also charges for Stations in the Isle of Wight, and on certain Light Railways, can be obtained at the Stations.

| 454 | SEVENOAKS | WEALD | HILDENBOROUGH | TONBRIDGE | 454 |

	NS		SSO	14	SSO		SSO	14	SSO	14	SSO		SSO		
SEVENOAKS (Tubs Hill Stn.)	7 9	9 14	1114	.....	1214	14	.....	2 14	3 14	.....	4 14	5 14	.....	6 14	7 14	.....	8 14	9 14	.....	1014	.....	Principal fares :
SEVENOAKS (Car Park)	7 12	9 17	1117	.....	1217	17	.....	2 17	3 17	.....	4 17	5 17	.....	6 17	7 17	.....	8 17	9 17	.....	1017	.....	Sevenoaks—
SEVENOAKS WEALD (Forge)	7 25	9 30	1130	.....	1230	30	.....	2 30	3 30	.....	4 30	5 30	.....	6 30	7 30	.....	8 30	9 30	.....	1030	.....	Tonbridge 10d.
WEALD TURNING	7 28	9 33	1133	.....	1233	33	.....	2 33	3 33	.....	4 33	5 33	.....	6 33	7 33	.....	8 33	9 33	.....	1033	.....	Sevenoaks—Weald 3d.
HILDENBOROUGH CHURCH	7 35	9 40	1140	.....	1240	40	.....	2 40	3 40	.....	4 40	5 40	.....	6 40	7 40	.....	8 40	9 40	.....	1040	.....	Weald—Hildenboro'4d.
TONBRIDGE (Star & Garter)	7 45	9 50	1150	.....	1250	50	.....	2 50	3 50	.....	4 50	5 50	.....	6 50	7 50	.....	8 50	9 50	.....	1050	.....	Hildenboro'—
TONBRIDGE STATION	7 50	9 55	1155	.....	1255	55	.....	2 55	3 55	.....	4 55	5 55	.....	6 55	7 55	.....	8 55	9 55	.....	1055	.....	Tonbridge 4d.

	NS		SSO		SSO		SSO		SSO		SSO		SSO			
TONBRIDGE STATION	7 50	1010	12 4	.....	1 4	2 4	.....	3 4	4 4	.....	5 4	6 4	.....	7 4	8 4	.....	9 4	10 4	.....	11 4	.....	For additional service
TONBRIDGE (Star & Garter)	7 55	1015	12 9	.....	1 9	2 9	.....	3 9	4 9	.....	5 9	6 9	.....	7 9	8 9	.....	9 9	10 9	.....	11 9	.....	between Sevenoaks
HILDENBOROUGH CHURCH	8 5	1025	1219	.....	1 19	2 19	.....	3 19	4 19	.....	5 19	6 19	.....	7 19	8 19	.....	9 19	1019	.....	1119	.....	and Tonbridge, via
WEALD TURNING	8 13	1033	1227	.....	1 27	2 27	.....	3 27	4 27	.....	5 27	6 27	.....	7 27	8 27	.....	9 27	1027	.....	1127	.....	Main Road, see
SEVENOAKS WEALD (Forge)	8 16	1036	1230	.....	1 30	2 30	.....	3 30	4 30	.....	5 30	6 30	.....	7 30	8 30	.....	9 30	1030	.....	1130	.....	route 403.
SEVENOAKS (Car Park)	8 28	1048	1242	.....	1 42	2 42	.....	3 42	4 42	.....	5 42	6 42	.....	7 42	8 42	.....	9 42	1042	.....	1142	.....	NS—Not Sunday.
SEVENOAKS (Tubs Hill Stn.)	8 31	1051	1245	.....	1 45	2 45	.....	3 45	4 45	.....	5 45	6 45	.....	7 45	8 45	.....	9 45	1045	.....	1145	.....	SSO—Sat & Sun only.

(SE 811)

PARCELS BY COUNTRY BUS

Parcels for conveyance by Country Buses should be securely wrapped and tied, and handed to an agent or conductor, with fees as follows: Weight not exceeding 7 lb., 3d.; 14 lb., 6d.; 21 lb., 9d. 28 lb., (limit) 1s. 0d. Agent's booking fee, 1d. Parcels will be delivered to the nearest agent, or may be collected from the conductor by consignees. (Country bus routes are those numbered 401 to 499)

AGENTS

Ash. Turner, White Swan.
Bessels Green. Mrs. Cooper, Confectioner.
Brasted. A. Evans, High Street.
Broadham Green. W. Worsfold Haycutter's Inn.
Chelsham. C. Peters, Hare and Hounds.
London Transport Garage.
Crawley. Kingham's Stores.
Crockham Hill. Baxter, Butcher
Dartford. T. Avis & Sons, 15 Lowfield Street.
Dormansland. Miss Glover, Plough.
Dunton Green. London Transport Garage.
East Grinstead. Miss Miller, Tobacconist.
Mrs. Spillman, 33 Lingfield Rd.

Edenbridge. Keeting, Bridge Bazaar.
Sawyer, Highfield Garage.
Eynsford. Munn, Grocer.
Farningham. Oxtoby, High St.
Gravesend. W. Croucher, New Road.
Green St. Green. Farnborough: Stead, Newsagent.
Near Dartford: C. Freeman, White Hart.
Halstead. Bayliss, Corner Stores.
Hextable. Hancock, Rose-doors, Plantation Road.
Horsham. Southdown Bus Office, Carfax.
Mrs. C. Denman, 175 Crawley Road.

Knockholt. Clifford Stores.
Lanesend (Green St. Green). B. Solomon Stores.
Leaves Green. Horwood, King's Arms.
Limpsfield. F. A. Potter, High Street.
Longfield. Mrs. Rich, Stores.
Marsh Green. G. Everest, Stores.
Northfleet. Windiate, Perry Street.
Otford. Knight, Grocer.
(New) Oxted. W. H. Spark, Station Road.
(Old) Oxted. Down, High Street
Redhill. London Transport Kiosk.
F. R. Melton, Hooley Lane.

Reigate. London Transport, Bell St
Riverhead. Mrs. L. Barrel, London Road.
Sevenoaks. Bennitt, Tobacconist, 136 High Street.
Shoreham. Bell, Central Mart.
Stanstead. Russell, White House Tea Rooms.
Sundridge. L. Smith, Square.
Sutton at Hone. C. F. Kimmer.
Swanley. Mrs. Collier, Station Rd.
Turners Hill. Fowler, Oven.
Westerham. C. J. Hollingworth.
Westerham Hill. H. Hall, Old Barn.
Wrotham. Besles, Greengrocer, Square.

| 464 | HOLLAND | OXTED | WESTERHAM | EDENBRIDGE | 464 |

PRINCIPAL FARES : Holland—Edenbridge 1/3., Holland—Oxted Station 3d., Oxted—Westerham 4d., Westerham—Edenbridge 8d.

HOLLAND (Post Office)	8126 9	8 9 50	12 0	1 0	03	05 2	66 0	08 30	1030	EDENBRIDGE (Star)	.....	.....	11 0	2 0	4 0	7 0	9 30
OLD OXTED (The George)	8134 9	16 9 58	12 8	1 8	83	85 3	46 8	08 38	1038	CROCKHAM HILL (Royal Oak)	.....	.....	1112	2 12	4 12	7 12	9 42
OXTED (Police Station)	8138 9	120 10 2	1212	1 12	123	125 3	86 12	8 42	1042	HOSEY COMMON	.....	.....	1120	2 20	4 20	7 20	9 50
OXTED STATION	.....	10 3	.....	1 13	33	.....	6 13	38 43	1043	WESTERHAM (Kings Arms)	7 52	.....	9 115	1126	2 26	4 26	7 26	9 56
LIMPSFIELD SCHOOLS	.....	1010	.....	1 20	3 20	.....	6 20	8 50	1050	LIMPSFIELD SCHOOLS	8 1	.....	9 124	1135	.....	2 35	4 35	.....	7 35	10 5
WESTERHAM (Kings Arms)	.....	1019	.....	1 29	3 29	.....	6 29	8 59	1059	OXTED STATION	8 8	.....	9 131	1142	2 42	4 42	.....	7 42	1012
HOSEY COMMON	.....	1025	.....	1 35	3 35	.....	6 35	.....	.....	OXTED (Police Station)	8 9	8143	9 32	1143	1243	2 43	4 43	4 3 5	4 3	7 43	1013
CROCKHAM HILL (Roy.Oak)	.....	1033	.....	1 43	3 43	.....	6 43	9 13	.....	OLD OXTED (The George)	8 11	8147	9 36	1147	1247	2 47	4 47	4 4 7	5	7 47	1017
EDENBRIDGE (Star)	.....	1045	.....	1 55	3 55	.....	6 55	9 25	.....	HOLLAND (Post Office)	8121	8155	9 44	1155	1255	2 55	4 55	5 5 5	5	7 55	1025

‡—Not Sunday.   †—Sunday only.

(SW & SE 704)

3 BOOKS FOR RAMBLERS   CHILTERNS 3d. SURREY & KENT 2d. BUCKS, BERKS, HERTS & ESSEX 2d.   On sale at Ticket Offices of Metropolitan Line and Bookstalls of other Underground Stations.

C5/36

| 471 | ORPINGTON | CUDHAM | KNOCKHOLT | ORPINGTON | . | 471 |

PRINCIPAL FARES : Orpington—Cudham 6d., Cudham—Knockholt 3d., Knockholt—Pratts Bottom Schools 3d., Pratts Bottom—Orpington 4d.

	NS	NS	S												NS								
ORPINGTON STATION	.....	8 7	.....	1052	1252	2 52	4 52	6 52	8 52	1052	ORPINGTON STATION	.....	9 52	1152	1 52	3 52	5 52	7 52	9 52
GREEN STREET GREEN	.....	6 15	.....	11 01	8 3	05	07	09	9 11 0	GREEN STREET GREEN	.....	10 0	12 02	04	0 6	08	0 10	0
CUDHAM	.....	8 35	.....	11 10	10 3	105	107	109	10 11 10	PRATTS BOTTOM	.....	10 4	12 42	44	4 6	48	4 10	4
KNOCKHOLT (Crown)	.....	8 35	.....	1120	1 20	3 20	5 20	7 20	9 20	1120	KNOCKHOLT POUND	.....	8 9	1012	1212	2 12	4 12	6 12	8 12	1012
KNOCKHOLT POUND	7 30	8 38	9 23	1123	1 23	3 23	5 23	7 23	9 23	1123	KNOCKHOLT (Crown)	.....	8 12	1015	1215	2 15	4 15	6 15	8 15	1015
PRATTS BOTTOM	7 38	8 46	9 31	1131	1 31	3 31	5 31	7 31	9 31	.....	CUDHAM	.....	8 22	1025	1225	2 25	4 25	6 25	8 25	1025
GREEN STREET GREEN	7 42	8 50	9 35	1135	1 35	3 35	5 35	7 35	9 35	.....	GREEN STREET GREEN	.....	8 32	1035	1235	2 35	4 35	6 35	8 35	1035
ORPINGTON STATION	7 50	8 58	9 43	1143	1 43	3 43	5 43	7 43	9 43	.....	ORPINGTON STATION	.....	8 40	1043	1243	2 43	4 43	6 43	8 43	1043

NS—Not Sunday.   S—Sunday only.

Parcels Rates London Country Buses.
Motor 'bus parcels. Maidstone and District Parcels Ticket.

MA 4206
The Maidstone & District Motor Services Ltd
PARCEL TICKET
4d
Name ....
Destination ....
Parcels only carried subject to the advertised conditions of the company.

49877—Willmepc, Printer, Ashtead

Motor Bus Services and Parcel Carrying

The motor bus services carried parcels along their own routes as part of the service they provided as a 'bus company, but were careful not to handle individual letters. Mailbags full of letters were carried on some routes particularly around Westerham under contract to the Post Office, but never the individual letter, only parcels which themselves were not supposed to include letters.

A horse omnibus from Sevenoaks to the station was running in 1891. George Humphreys & Co. of Sevenoaks were running motor buses to Westerham in 1908, but the main operators were to be based outside Sevenoaks. By April 1914 there were East Surrey Traction Company services from Reigate and Redhill to Westerham and Riverhead extending that same year to Tubs Hill Station and then Sevenoaks Market Place. Also in 1914 Maidstone and District Motor Services were running from Maidstone through Borough Green and Seal to Sevenoaks and by 1921 Autocar Services Ltd. of Tunbridge Wells, later Autocar and Redcar Services Ltd., were running hourly to Tonbridge and Sevenoaks. From Farningham where there had been a connection to Dartford from 1904, Wm. Allen extended to Sevenoaks in January 1917, when the rail link through Otford was suspended as a wartime economy measure. West Kent Motor Services Ltd. started local services covering Ivy Hatch, Ide Hill, Edenbridge in the 1927/1930 period.

Hawkins had founded East Surrey Traction Company in 1911 and ousted Humphreys on the Westerham route by 1914. In 1921 he took over the Autocar route to Farnborough by agreement basing his three buses for the route at the Railway Hotel, Bat and Ball, and in 1922 tookover the Dartford-Sevenoaks route from Allen. In 1929 ESTC became a subsidiary of the London General Omnibus Company and the next year Hawkins became Managing Director of Green Line Coaches. In 1932 the local London Services were renamed London General Country Services. The London Passenger Transport Board, in 1934, ran to Westerham, Croydon, Dartford, Gravesend, Bromley, Hilden and Tonbridge; the Green Line to Tunbridge Wells, Bromley, London.[15]

Parcel charges on London Transport Country Buses (Nos. 401-499) were as follows:[16]

	1936	*1961*
7 lbs	3d	1/-
14 lbs	6d	1/6
21 lbs	9d	2/-
28 lbs	1/- (limit)	2/6

Parcel to be collected from the conductor or delivered to nearest agent, generally a shop such as a Newsagent or Sweet and Tobacco shop, often open late. Agency Fees an additional 1d to 1936 and up to 1958, 2d in 1961.

The introduction of one-man buses and the demise of the conductor saw the end of the bus parcel service: on London County about 1970, on Maidstone and District a little later about 1975.

Road Delivery and Collection Services

After WWII came the concentration of Road Services. In the 1950's much small parcel delivery was carried out by British Road Services, including a Cash-on-Delivery service (COD) as shown in the illustration. Later came the National Freight Corporation. Once privatisation came into vogue in the 1980's, BRS was disbanded, or rather metamorphosed into The National Freight Corporation and then many private parcel-carrying firms sprang up. As of 1985/86 the locally based firms are shown as

A. D. Brett, West Kingsdown
A20 Couriers, Wrotham Hill Industrial Estate
CPS Delivery Services, Scotts Way, Riverhead
CWG Hawken, Edward Road, Biggin Hill
Ellis Transport, The Street, Plaxtol
Howard New, 14 Biggin Hill Airport
Norwood Transport Ltd., Platt Industrial Estate, Boro' Green
N & H Transport, Clarks Lane, Halstead. [17]

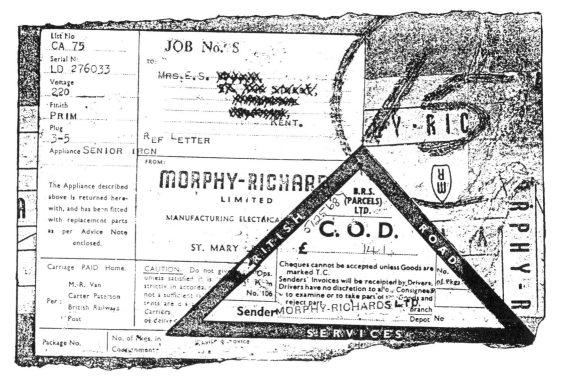

Top: C1955 Small parcel Cash-on-delivery service by British Road Services. Repair of Small Iron 14s/1d.
Bottom: Securicor parcel delivery labels of 1982/3.

Nationally based road parcel services also both collect and deliver throughout the area. These include Group 4 and also Securicor which started cash carrying in 1935 and developed parcel services in the 1960s, firstly as a service to their Bank Customers. Securicor, for example, offer 'Night Owl Swifty' for delivery of urgent documents by 9 am next day, Service A that delivers parcels by mid-day and Service B that delivers by 5 pm next day. TNT, the Australian-owned company, handles parcels, also a 'Mailfast' service. Interlink is based on Bristol. United Carriers, part of the Bunzl Group, handle 500,000 parcels a day. There are also the international carriers such as DHL and Federal Express, Lynx, Parceline and Amtrak which are also to be seen within the area.

Road Haulage   Locally based firms are shown as:-

S & A Bowen Ltd., Knockholt
Brown's Transport Ltd., Ash
CPS Delivery, Scotts Way, Riverhead
D. G. Cox, Seal
A. J. Hirst, Haulage Ltd., Ightham
Steve Lacey UK Continental Transport, Seal
J. MacLening, Shoreham
Norvan Express Transport, Boro' Green
D. R. Porter & Sons, Tatsfield
J. W. Salt, Boro' Green
Turners Transport, West Kingsdown
Taylor Pennell Transport Sevenoaks

W. H. Brown & Sons Ltd., Stansted
G. Burgess, Westerham
T. R. Clark & Son Ltd., Old London Road, Knockholt
Haven Haulage, Knatts Valley
Lavers Transport Ltd., Dunton Green
Geo. Malyon, West Kingsdown
Miles Bros., Otford Lane, Halstead
G. C. Nash, Sevenoaks
J. M. Rand, West Kingsdown
S. L. B. Transport Ltd., Sevenoaks
Mike Taylor Haulage, Boro' Green.

Again National Road Haulage runs throughout the area.

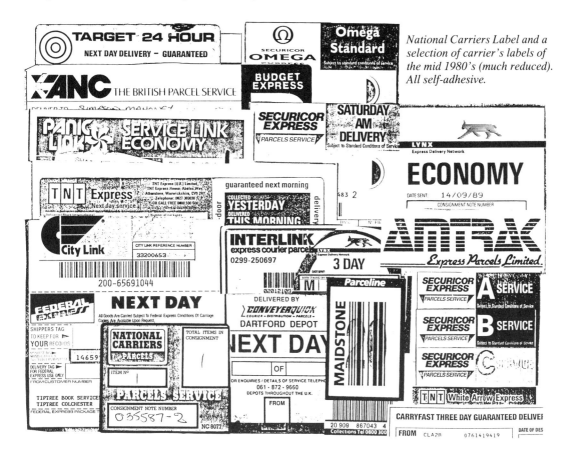

National Carriers Label and a selection of carrier's labels of the mid 1980's (much reduced). All self-adhesive.

If Answer ...

BOOK POST

This Card may be sent by Post (ABROAD or INLAND) with Halfpenny Stamp, provided nothing further than Sender's name is on it, in addition to the Address. If any communication is written Inland Postage is One Penny, and usual letter rate according to weight for Abroad. [Bent & Warwick, Art Printers, Bedford]

To

Master James Gilham

Linton

Nr Maidstone — Kent

From *Florence.*

Name

Address

OTFORD LANE

HALSTEAD

Postcode *TN1H 7EE*

Post·A·Book

A Royal Mail service in association with the Book Marketing Council & The Booksellers Association.

Post-A-Book is a post office trademark

Official G.P.O. Non-Letter Services

Whilst the Post Office has always jealously guarded its monopoly of letter-carrying, this has not been the case for parcels where it has no monopoly and where it is in direct competition with the railways and other load-carrying services. Parcels (with no written enclosures) can vary from a small packet of documents or a book up to goods weighing 20 lbs or more, and beyond to a whole lorry or railway truck load. At the lower weight end, there has always been the problem of defining the boundary between letters and small packets or parcels, but there is less difficulty in seeing the boundary when viewed by the customer in terms of £-s-d charges.

1 Victoria Cap 34 of the 12th July 1837 in Para xxvi gives the rates of Inland General Post as –

One sheet	Single piece of paper	Under 1 oz Single Rate)	
Two sheets	Two pieces of paper or	Under 1 oz Double Rate)	
	sheet with Inclosure	)	All under 1 oz
Three sheets	Three pieces of paper	Under 1 oz Treble Rate)	
	or two with Inclosures	)	

Over 1 oz whether single, double or treble.	Four times a Single
For every ¼ oz beyond	An additional Single Rate

So a 4 oz letter packet would be 16 times the single rate. This epitomises the pre-1840 charges. The high cost of sending even small packages by post forced private persons and businesses to use Stage Coaches and Carriers for the heavier and larger Letter Packets such as wills and other documents, let alone parcels. For example, a letter might be sent by the General Post to a solicitor asking him to meet a particular coach on which a packet of documents were being sent as a parcel, the parcel itself not being supposed to contain any current letters.

Examples of this practice are known for Sevenoaks, as also that of sending a letter along with the parcel of goods in which case the content of the letter was supposed to refer only to the goods in question.

Prior to 1883 the Post Office had no parcel service available to the general Public but there were services other than the normal letter post. There was Newspaper Post, Bankers Parcels, Book Post, Pattern and Sample Post, as also arrangements by which Members of Parliament could both send and receive letters free of charge - the frank.

Prices Current and Commercial Lists

Unstamped (i.e. without tax stamp on the printed page) items authorised by the PMG were allowed to pass through the inland post from an early date pre-1820 for 1d, providing they were unmarked. If found to have items marked to draw attention to them, then they were charged as letters. These might be said to be the start of the cheap printed paper rate.

Book Post, Halfpenny Packet Post, Printed Papers

Bookpost, which became in effect a parcel post for printed matter, started in 1848, (21 February) at 6d per lb with a maximum of 14 lbs. In 1855 the rate was reduced to 1d per ¼ lb and any type of printed matter could be sent. In 1870 the maximum weight was greatly reduced to 5 lbs at ½ d per 2 oz and the Pattern/ Sample Post (see below) was absorbed so that a wide range of articles could be sent, and in 1892 this list of articles was extended further.

Oversize Picture Post Cards could be sent by 'Book Post' for ½d if only the sender's name was written and there was no message. Many were sent from the seaside; but this one of 1906 is from Borough Green and measures 10½" x 9" approx. In the end it was delivered without bending. (Reduced)
The Post-a-Book Service was revitalised in 1982. This postage scheme was developed in conjunction with bookshops to send a book by mail for a standard fee depending on which of three sizes of padded envelopes fitted the book, rather than by weight. Book sent by W H Smith 1982. Envelope 12" x 10".

By now the normal Parcel Post was in operation so the Book Post concentrated on the lower end of the weight scale. In 1897 Bookpost had an effective maximum of 2 oz after which it became subsumed in the Letter Rate and so in 1904 there was a name change to 'Half Penny Packet Post'.

In 1915 the title 'Book Post' was resumed and at the same rate of ½ d per 2 oz it became effective up to 5 lbs, because of the increase in letter rate. In 1918 there was an increase to 1d per 1 oz and so once again the rate became effective only to 2 oz. In 1920 the final definitive name 'Printed Paper' post was achieved at ½ d per 1 oz with a maximum of 2 lbs. This maximum remained until 1968 with gradual first step increase in rate from ½ d per 1 oz to 3d per 2 oz. The 1968 change made the rate cost effective only in the range 1½ to 2 lbs and in 1971 was entirely abolished for inland mail.

Items posted were examined to see that no letters were enclosed. If any were found they were taken out and charged separately or the whole package might be charged at letter rate. The very large size picture postcards were carried under 'book post' and this is why they could carry no message but senders name and address.

Pattern/Sample Post

Again there was an early facility at least c1820 where patterns and samples up to one ounce together with name and address and price, paid the postage of a single letter. But over 1 oz the postage was the same as for a letter. Some greater facility was needed and this came with the Pattern/Sample Post, started in 1863 at the insistence of the Chamber of Commerce to allow traders to submit to clients a wide range of samples of no intrinsic value at 3d per 4 oz. with a maximum of 1½ lbs, the rate being reduced to 2d the following year and in 1870 it was absorbed into Bookpost.

Bookpost

In 1982 Bookpost returned in a modified form in that one can now buy a book together with pre-paid envelope in most of the larger bookshops and, having addressed the padded envelope, have the book posted by the bookseller without further ado. There is no weighing of the packet, the cost relates to the size of the book and hence the size of envelope required.

Newspapers

By 1711 Newspapers had to carry a Government Tax stamp printed onto the side of the paper itself. When this had been done the Newspaper was able to pass free for up to 7 days after publication in the General and 5th Clause Posts, though not the Penny Posts, in spite of the fact that they were bulky and took up more room and weighed more heavily than the letters carried. The theory was that as Newspapers had already paid a tax on each sheet they could not be taxed twice; and it should be noted that calculating the rate to be charged and writing it onto the letter is always referred to by the GPO as 'taxing'. In an age when no telegraph or wireless was available many papers were sent by mail and this free passage constituted a great burden on the Post Office. A separate Newspaper Office was set up by the Post Office in 1788. Most 'Clerks of the Road' became involved in this necessary and lucrative business of the distribution of Newspapers in a private capacity which subsequently became the subject of a Government Report.[18] Some obtained up to 4 times their salary in this way, others nearer the bottom of the payscale, a mere 5% but nearly all were involved until in 1834 their newspaper franking privilege was withdrawn.

Newspaper Tax Stamp applied to a Local Paper, the South Eastern Gazette and Surrey News 1865. Last Newspaper duty stamp was 30th September 1870: from 1st October 1870 Newspapers carried a ½d Adhesive stamp when posted.

By 1836 60,000 Newspapers per night were being sent, all being carried at no income to the P.O. As they were carried free of further charge once the compulsory tax stamp had been paid for, Newspapers were often sent as message bearers. For example, if some one were ill, a paid letter enquiring about their health could be answered by a newspaper if they were improving and only by another paid letter if they were getting worse and details were required.[19] Messages were also passed by a pre-arranged code in the address, Mr. Smith, Mr. S. Smith, S. Smith, Esq., etc. and after outside inspection an unpaid letter could be refused.

In 1855 the Newspaper Tax became optional and if not paid newspapers were carried at Book Post Rates with 1d minimum, using adhesive stamps.

> Tax *1711* ½d per sheet, up to 4d per sheet by *1815*, down to 1d by *1836*.
> Postage free in General and 5th Clause Posts, charged in Penny Post but made free in 1836.
> *1851* For taxation purposes, a surface of letterpress not exceeding 1530 sq. in. counted as one newspaper. 1530-2295 sq. in. as one and a half newspapers, over 2295 sq. in. as two.[20]
> *1855 June 22* was the last issue requiring a tax stamp impressed. But stamps could still be impressed to cover postage, and many were.

Newspaper Postage. 1855 1d; 1870 ½d per copy; 1915 ½d 6 oz; 1920 1d, 1940 1½d 4 oz; 1956 2d 6 oz; 1957 2½d 6 oz; 1961 3d 6 oz; 1965 3d 2 oz with a maximum weight of 2 lbs; 1968 Under the Two Tier post, Registered Newspapers given first class transmission on paying Second class rate if posted by publisher or his agent; 1971 Max weight 1½ lbs.

Bankers Parcels

Registration as now available to the General Public dates from 1841 and the Parcel Post service from 1883, but Bankers Parcels were certainly being dealt with during the 1750-1800 period. This service arose from the need when many Banks issued their own Bank notes to return Country banknotes to their Bank of origin. The notes were reissuable negotiable currency and as such were liable to be stolen. The quantity sent back from London to Provincial Banks were certainly large enough to constitute parcels and, being in quantity, they could hardly all be cut in half and sent each half separately as was the contemporary accepted practice for small quantities.

One such parcel was stolen from a mailcoach[21] in 1822 at a time when the London and County Bank in Sevenoaks might well have been transmitting paper currency to London, though the only recorded Sevenoaks banking difficulty concerned gold not notes and was stolen from a stagecoach not a mailcoach.

In 1825 such Bankers parcels had to exceed 6 oz in weight and were carried to the issuing Bank's address only, at one quarter the letter rate. Later there was a forfeit of £100 if any communication were to be enclosed. In 1840 Bankers parcels were charged at letter rate, but the 1 lb weight maximum for letter rate did not apply. The parcels were treated as registered mail. In the 1930's bankers parcels were posted as 'High Value Packets' with a bright red HVP label stuck on to distinguish them.

Though, of course, all these services would have been used in Sevenoaks few 'covers' remain of any of the above as proof of the early pre-1883 days. Certainly the writer has never seen any Bankers Parcels wrappings for Sevenoaks, though frequently walked through the streets himself in the 1930s to a Post Office with a large parcel of banknotes with several of the red HVP labels stuck onto it.

Parcel Post

It can be seen that by 1882 the Post Office had experience in carrying parcels in the form of books and newspapers, but perhaps not the variety and quantity to be expected once the floodgates had been opened to accepting all kinds of parcels.

A Parcel post had been proposed in 1839 by Henry Cole the Postal Reformer, and in 1840 Sir Roland Hill considered such a scheme but it was not pressed against the already established parcel carriers, the Railway companies and road carriers such as Pickfords. In 1867 the Royal Commision on Railways advocated such a plan.

Then in 1880 the Postal Union Conference in Paris discussed international parcel post and shortly

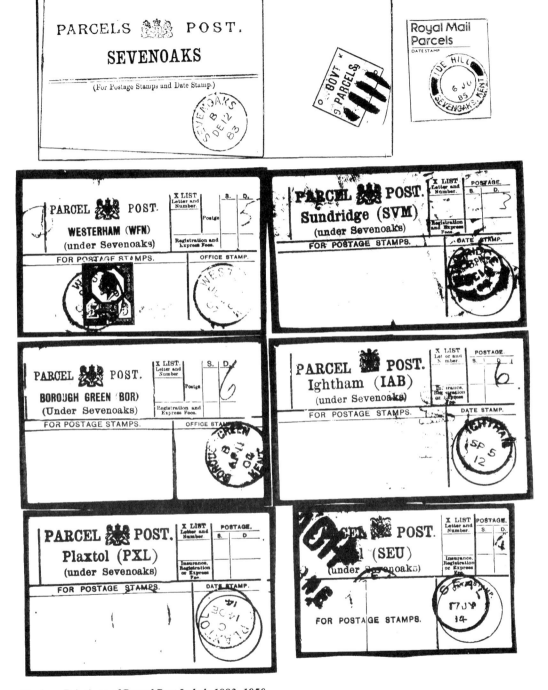

Various Printings of Parcel Post Labels 1883–1950
1883 GPO First Parcels Post label. Used from a Government Office in Sevenoaks with overprinted 9d stamp (4 lbs) cancelled by 5-bar cork stamp, used to avoid damage to contents of parcel when cancelling. (James A Mackay) Later, to avoid damage to contents, the stamp had to be stuck on the parcel label and cancelled (sometimes with a rubber but often with a steel handstamp) before the label was attached to the parcel. The labels attached to parcels went through at least six basic typesettings between 1883 and 1920.

afterwards the U.K., one of the few countries still without an inland parcel service, was given until April 1882 to develop such a service. An Act was passed (45 & 46 Vict. C 74) on 18th August 1882 and the service finally started on 1st August 1883. There had to be the additional time not only to make contractual arrangements but also to employ extra staff and to find space for the physical handling of the parcels.

The Railways, well entrenched in the parcels business themselves, proved a difficult body with whom to negotiate and they demanded a high price. For they were in effect contracting to carry as agent for the Post Office those very parcels that they would have carried themselves. Yet the Post Office was strong in its collection and delivery network, an area where the Railways were weak, and therefore the Post Office expected the number of parcels to increase greatly with its new service.

A Parcels Service with a 7 lbs limit, fixed with an eye to international requirements, was started on 1st August 1883.

Parcel Post, Local Arrangements

Sevenoaks Post Office spent 1882 and the early part of 1883 making a report on the Costs of Establishment and office accommodation expenses. There would be much paperwork in the accounting for parcels, the listing involved was quite complex and many forms were involved. But like everywhere else, the Sevenoaks office and the others opened for business on time, August 1st. An example of an early label emanating from one of the Sevenoaks government offices is shown opposite. The following year an advertisement appeared[22] in the Sevenoaks Chronicle being for that of the Postmasters own establishment.

New Parcels Post
Woolls Yarns etc at London & Birmingham Prices
All of the best qualities
Sent Free per Parcels Post
F. H. Hills 58 High Street
Sevenoaks

Of course the packets did not travel free; it meant the sender paid for the postage.

A special rule book was issued '*Inland Parcels Post Rules for Sub-Postmasters 1883*'. Much of it is taken up with the forms to be filled in and the way bags have to be sealed, even more pages cover the rules for rural letter carriers delivering parcels. They were now to be called postmen, not just letter carriers. But of course they were used to carrying parcels as a private enterprise venture from the households to the local railway station. This the old style letter carriers did from about 1840 onwards, 1844 on in this area, charging 1d per parcel and the P.O. turned a blind eye to the practice for it was a service that was needed yet not provided officially. Yet not so blind an eye for both the Plaxtol rural Postman and the Seal rural Postman were compensated officially by the Post Office for loss of income. How much is not shown but an allowance existed from August 1883 until late 1884 when it was withdrawn.

The 1883 Rules state that parcels must be kept separate from letters and that they normally are handled on a weekday only. The parcels must be prepaid in stamps and contain no forbidden articles that are listed. The person employed to deliver parcels '*must not smoke on duty; must not carry parcels other than the official ones; must not be connected in any way with an inn or public house; if drunk on duty is not only liable to dismissal, but punishment as well*'. He must wear his uniform. The parcel deliverer on entering a village must blow a horn or loud whistle; he is to deliver at houses within 70 yards of his walk and at all the houses in a village; his normal load of parcels, and letters if a joint delivery, being 35 lbs if on foot. If over 35 lbs it may be possible to engage a horse. All letters and parcels for houses beyond his walk must be left at a sub-office or a house according to the instructions from persons to whom they are addressed. If on foot he must not take up parcels from the public (as he can letters and registered letters) and if on horse he may not take up parcels except with the authority of the Surveyor of the District'. If he did take up parcels this entailed both weighing to calculate postage and measuring them to ensure that they were within the limits of size. There was a specially calibrated GPO tapemeasure. If he refused a parcel he had to explain why and report his action to the next sub-office.

Sevenoaks Diary Items   *1884 Trolley for Parcel Post work; 1885 Parcel Post delivery accelerated. Parcel Post delivery allowance converted to Auxiliary Postman Wages; 1899 Boro' Green Day mail delivery of Parcels; 1908 Westerham Parcel delivery established. Parcel hand cart provided. And in 1892: Errors in Parcel Post Accounts. Postmaster cautioned.*

Articles for the Blind   These often need to be fairly large packages. A special rate started on 1st September 1906 at ½ d for 2 oz rising to 1 ½d for 5 lbs and was altered in 1940 to ½ d for 2 lbs rising to 2 ½ d for 15 lbs. On 17th May 1965 the service became free of postage charges.

The London-Sevenoaks-Hastings Parcel Coach

The Post Office found their contracts with the railway companies most expensive and in an effort to handle their parcels traffic themselves and so to reduce costs, the way was paved for the reintroduction of the horse-drawn parcel coaches down the very roads where mailcoaches had ceased to run some forty years earlier.

First to start up was the London to Brighton Parcel Coach on 1st June 1887, later the London to Hastings Parcel Coach via Sevenoaks on a date not exactly recorded, but the London to Tunbridge Wells section was running by 1895.

These horse parcel coaches were four-horse drawn with driver and horses contracted out as before and a uniformed post office guard. The coach was a large rectangular box into which one could enter from the back. Parcels were also carried on the roof which had a deep guard rail. The guard's job was to sort parcels inside and then to take his seat at the front beside the driver. To protect the mails the guard had a revolver and sword bayonet. He also had a coach horn with which to warn off other users of the road, chiefly market garden waggons with their drivers half asleep for, like the previous mailcoaches, the parcel coaches travelled through the night.[23]

London-Hastings Parcel Coach. First Arrival of CC6613 Solid tyre motorised Milnes-Daimler Parcel van via Sevenoaks and Tunbridge Wells at St Leonards-on-Sea Sorting Office 3 July 1906. (Unknown, probably PO Official)

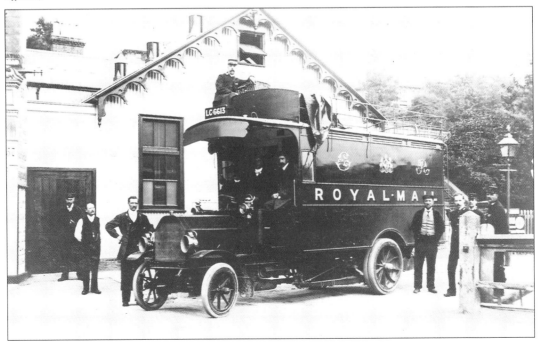

Motorisation of Parcel Coaches   About 1905/6 the parcel coaches were motorised and the photograph shows the first arrival of the London-Hastings or rather the London-St. Leonards Parcel Service motor van on its first arrival at St. Leonards-on-Sea sorting office on 3rd July 1906.

The following year[24] in the second half of 1907 in the 'Report on Working 1906/7' it is mentioned that the London and Hastings Motor Parcel Service was diverted from passing the Crown Hotel, Sevenoaks, because of a 'fracas' that was going on outside it. Research into the cause of this fracas in the Sevenoaks Chronicle of that year, 1907, finds that volume 'Wanting' in the British Library at Colindale and all other public libraries. One might be excused for thinking it was being hushed up.

The road to Hastings was becoming popular and an interesting sidelight is shown when in 1909 at the instigation of the Automobile Association, a Brigade of Guards was transported from London via Sevenoaks to Hastings and back, one of the first recorded large scale movements of troops by motor vehicle.

In that same year the Sevenoaks Post Office made use of the parcels van between the Post Office and Tubs Hill Station.

> 'London and Hastings Motor Parcel Coach'
> Saving 2 trips to Station   £ 31. 6. -
> Staff 1 hr at 7d daily   9. 2. 7
> Total savings p.a. £22

Normally the horse-drawn vehicle was referred to as a 'coach' and the motorised one as a 'van'. This nomenclature is shown on the special postmarks that they carried. As with coaches two vehicles were required to provide a full service, one travelling from each terminal each night. The motorised service continued into wartime and terminated in the spring of 1916.

Current GPO Parcels Situation

In 1963 Parcels distribution was reorganised, and 'Salfords' came into being. This is the large Parcel Concentration depot on an industrial estate just south of Reigate which handles parcels for the South East including those for Sevenoaks and now Tonbridge M.L.O. From the early need for simple trolleys a whole range of parcel handling equipment has been developed. Most obvious are the square-fronted articulated lorries painted red that ply the roads in great numbers showing in their unaerodynamic abandon not only the growth in business but also the reduction in dependence on the railways as carriers. One is given to wonder why Post Office lorries (in 1984) are among the few that do not have air deflectors fitted on cab roofs and what reduction in postage per parcel might be given through saving of fuel if they did. These lorries are built to a shape to accept the modern trollies, mates, that fit within and carry the sorted parcels. Parcels are now accepted up to 25 kg (about 55 lbs) a considerably higher weight than used to be the case. Heavy-weight parcels are supposed to have a green crayon stripe and the mates carry a green and white diagonally striped label to alert personnel and avoid possible hernias through incorrect methods of handling.

Local parcels for overnight delivery in the area Sevenoaks, Edenbridge, Crowborough, Cranbrook are dealt with within Tonbridge MLO and should bear a special yellow label to enable them to be picked out. Without this, they often escape to Salfords and four or five days passes before they are brought back again.

Rates

Parcel rates started in 1883 at 3d for 1 lb up to 1/- for 7 lbs; both rate and maximum weight allowed increased gradually to 2/- for 2 lbs up to 6/6d for 22 lbs in 1963. In 1983 it was £1.30 for 1 kg (2.2 lbs) up to £3.95 for 22 ½ kg, and now £4.60 for 25 kg (55 lbs) in 1986.

An area parcel service at a slightly reduced cost, 5p less, was started in 1966 and extended in 1977. Now there are the two parcel rates; one a national rate and the other an Area rate covering the S. East corner, Kent, East and West Sussex but not London. Most interesting was a parcel rate sale with '30% off' County parcels for a couple of months in the summer of 1982, advertised with its own special self-adhesive label '30% off/County Parcels' in green. This was for the general public and never to be repeated although

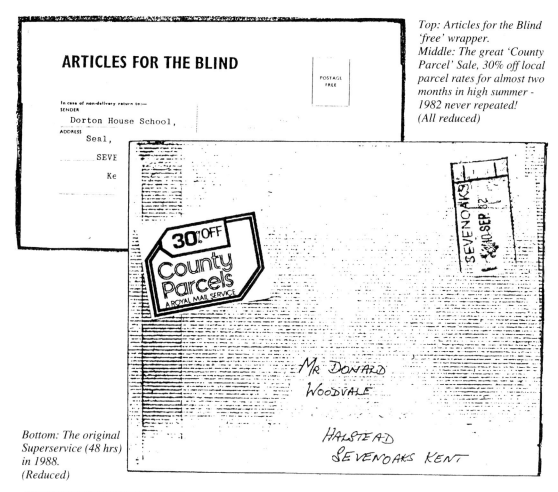

ARTICLES FOR THE BLIND

POSTAGE FREE

In case of non-delivery return to:—
SENDER
Dorton House School,

ADDRESS   Seal,

        SEVE

        Ke

Top: Articles for the Blind 'free' wrapper.
Middle: The great 'County Parcel' Sale, 30% off local parcel rates for almost two months in high summer - 1982 never repeated!
(All reduced)

Bottom: The original Superservice (48 hrs) in 1988.
(Reduced)

MR DONALD
WOODVALE

HALSTEAD
SEVENOAKS KENT

Royal Mail Parcels
SuperService

Consignment no.   557770SB.

Delivery address
Name
Full address   071382

XXXXXXXXXXXXXXXXXXXXXXXX
XXXXXXXXX
XXXXXXX
KENT
TN2X 2QP

Item no.

OF   2

of
2
total items

Sender

FLORAPAK LTD.
ST THOMAS'S ROAD
SPALDING
LINCS PE11 2YL

business customers received free parcel delivery labels 1kg and 25 kg in 1987 as part of the 'Business Programme' presentation.

Registration for Parcels was replaced by 1972 with Compensation Fee. Receipted Parcels has now been replaced, 1986, with 'Trackback', a method of tracking the records of delivery by means of a label bearing the lines of a bar code. Details of delivery are kept in a computer and can be immediately extracted when a customer makes a query.

Bar Codes and Trackback

There are several different specifications for Bar Codes, 'Trackback' being a little different to the Product Code (EAN) seen on groceries, but of the same general type. Bars are light-readable by a 'pencil' or wand drawn across them. Most bar code specifications require that as well as the light and dark bars the printed code also bears the number in arabic numerals of a specified format.

The light and dark bars digitalise the arabic number in a particular manner according to the system used, and in a manner almost impossible to convert back to arabic numerals by the eye. For this reason the

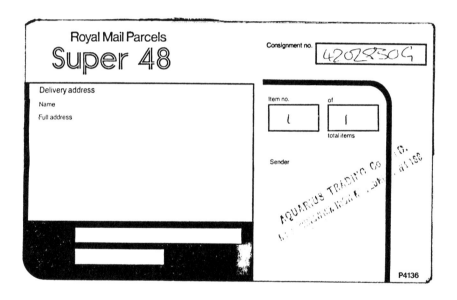

Royal Mail Parcel Delivery. In 1989 'Superservice' became Super 24 (one day) and Super 48 (two days) Service.

accompanying arabic number is normally considered part of the code specification, as applied by the printer.

Example. The Trackback bar codes consist of three groups of 4 Arabic numerals and would be seen by the customer for but a fleeting moment whilst he signs for the parcel.

So an example from the better-known EAN system may suffice as an indication of how the system works. After the usually longer (but not so in Trackback) 'guard bars' (101) at the beginning and at the end and also in the middle, the number is represented by the light and dark bars, giving the 'O' and '1' of computerised binary counting. Each character is 7 modules long with two dark bars and two light bars of varying width. The dark bars may be grouped up to four together, and so be 1, 2, 3, or 4 units thick. Dark bars give the '1', light bars the '0'. A single numeric digit is represented by the seven modules chosen from one of three possible sets (A, B, C). Thus '3' may be represented in European Article Numbering (EAN) as -

The figure '3' as represented by sets A,B,C   EAN.

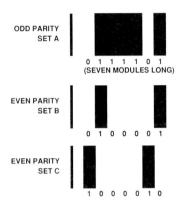

ODD PARITY
SET A

0   1   1   1   1   0   1
(SEVEN MODULES LONG)

EVEN PARITY
SET B

0   1   0   0   0   0   1

EVEN PARITY
SET C

1   0   0   0   0   1   0

Which set of binary symbols is used to represent a numeric digit depends on the odd/even parity pattern being used as a safeguard against inaccuracies and misreading. The pattern chosen might be, say, Sets AABBAB CCCCCC, which would be represented by the prefix 2 in the EAN-13 pattern. The method is straightforward, but complex, making visual interpretation of the bars difficult, almost impossible, as well it might be for they are meant to be read by a machine.

The arabic numbers and check digits so produced by the bars may then be split in any desired manner to carry information, forming a code with as many components as needed.

Superservice

Based on the Parcel Concentration offices and with the new administrative organization came improved parcel delivery for contract customers. The 'Rider' services gave overnight delivery in localities eg Thames Rider. 'Superservice' in February 1988 gave 48 hour delivery countrywide and when this was improved in 1989 the service was renamed 'Super 24' and 'Super 48'.

Contract Parcel, 'C' added in front of PPI, and Trackback label. The barcode part of the Trackback label has been transferred to the receipt sheet when the addressee signed for the parcel on receipt; When not delivered first time, a second lower half of label was used, 'to be collected'; 'Local Delivery' labels in yellow used in 1984 so that parcels were picked up before leaving Tonbridge for Salfords and delivered in the local area overnight. If not picked out they took five days or longer to achieve local delivery; Redirected parcels, unlike letters, may be charged for. PP38G label 'Free' applied at Salfords with 'Redhill and Reigate' postmark if for some reason a second charge was not to be collected; Sevenoaks was served by Salfords parcel sorting depot. International double label, large number applied to parcel, smaller similarly numbered label on documentation; small coloured label applied to all internal parcels during late 1980's and payment listed as a means of allocating income to 'RM Parcels'.

WOODVALE,

HALSTEAD,

SEVENOAKS,

KENT. TN14 7EE.

POSTAGE
PAID
PHQ
SERIAL NO 1

FROM FOAM FOR COMFORT LTD LEEDS TEL (0532) 673770

P.P. 38G

REIGATE Date Stamp
28 AUG. 74
H1 1AA

No charge to be
made on Delivery

Trakback

Royal Mail Parcels
Signed Delivery Service

Parcel Number 0004 5976 4601

Trakback
Royal Mail Parcels
Signed Delivery Service

Lift and Pull

live

To be collected 8000 2417 5112

This parcel was delivered

by the

Post Office

Royal Mail Parcel
For Local Delivery

Trakback

Royal Mail Parcels
Signed Delivery Service

Parcel Number 0009 0465 5198

0009 0465 5198

Lift and Pull ▶

Signature required on delivery

3416
KENT

2890
SEVENOAKS

Royal Mail Parcels

A02710

GPO Salfords, Redhill Parcel Concentration Office (PCO)
Handling parcels for the whole of Kent/Sussex (1987)

The Post Office has no monopoly status for parcel carrying and is in full competition with other operators. The 'National Parcel Plan' with organisation into PCO's started in the 1970s and now 'Parcels' is one of the two divisions into which 'Royal Mail' has been split under the 1986 re-organisation.

All Parcels for Kent/East and West Sussex (except local parcels, heavy parcels, pallet loads and datapost which is part of parcels) both inwards and outwards are handled through Salfords Mechanised Parcel Concentration Office located on the industrial estate beside the A23 a few miles South of Redhill. It is one of 32 strategically placed centres throughout the country.

Salfords depot is open seven days a week, 24 hours a day, but delivers on six days only; there is a shut-down on Saturday afternoons and Sunday afternoons when only a skeleton staff is on duty.

Up to 70,000 parcels a day are handled, inwards and outwards. Up to midnight parcels from Kent/Sussex are sorted outwards to the rest of the U.K. After midnight a switch is made to sorting for Kent/Sussex. All transport is by road except for a small amount of Railway Freightliner traffic where the contract has two years to expire. Then all traffic will be on the road, giving greater flexibility and control over its movement.

There are 183 operational staff of which 61 are drivers, mostly HGV drivers, 86 Postmen and the rest Postmen Higher Grade and Supervisors. In addition there are a small number of office staff. Shifts are 0600-1300, 1300-1800, 1700-0200, 2130-0600. There are on average 50 operational staff on duty at a time, but some shift overlap at busy times and less staff on duty at quiet periods. Ten to fifteen hours overtime per man per week is available. Overtime is worked because it would be difficult to convert these hours to full-time jobs. Postmen H.G. are used after midnight for the Kent/Sussex inward sort as a detailed knowledge of villages as well as Post towns is required. The target is 78% of parcels delivered within 3 days, 94% in 4 days.

The Sorting Operation

A mailbag, on average, can carry 4 parcels, a MATE (Mail All purpose Trailer Equipment) carries 80. Mates are about 4ft square and 6ft high with open tops, four small wheels and a handbrake. They can be pushed individually or towed up to three at a time.

The factory building - it was not purpose built - is therefore planned with a parcel sorting line down the centre for parcels arriving and departing in mates. There is also a single line overhead mailbag carrying rail with hooks that circles the perimeter of the factory and integrates with the mate centre line at the necessary points. Lorries that have been loose-loaded with parcels are unloaded by hand using a mobile conveyor which also integrates with the main line.

The lorries, many of them articulated vehicles with 40ft trailers, bringing in parcels for sorting are unloaded at one end of the factory, using the tail-shift on the lorry trailer to bring the loaded mate to ground level. A 40ft trailer contains 40 mates when full. The loaded mates are manually pushed one at a time the few yards to the 'lift and tip' machine which raises them about 25 feet and tilts 120°, so tipping all the parcels onto a conveyor. The bag parcels are manually unloaded and the loose parcels also join the conveyor which takes them to a storage glacis. Falling slowly down the gradual slope in the storage glacis, the parcels arrive at one of the four coding stations. Each station is manned by two postmen, the first faces the parcels right way up and removes to be dealt with manually those unsuitable by size, weight or shape to be handled automatically. The second man codes by sorting area. They can work at a speed of over 1,000 parcels an hour: 5,000 per hour can be coded by the four stations.

When coding no marks are put on the parcels but the information is fed to the controlling computer that, having measured the length of the parcel by electronic eye, knows its position on the conveyor slats. The parcel may occupy up to 5 slats and is tipped off left or right into the correctly coded bin. It slides down a chute to ground level where it is loaded into a mate. When filled up with loaded parcels these mates are towed by yellow Towmasters, a small indoor vehicle that all postmen are taught to drive, towing not more

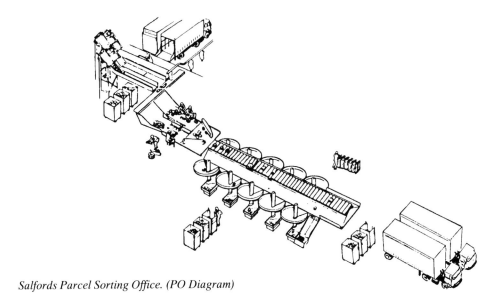

Salfords Parcel Sorting Office. (PO Diagram)

than three mates at a time, to the lorries at the loading bay at the other end of the factory. Lorries for set destinations are filled up at set times while large notices everywhere exhort the postal staff to do this quietly as this end of the operation is facing a residential area.

Heavier Parcels

This sorting line handles parcels up to 10kg, those 10-25kg which normally have a green crayon band or a turquoise and white diagonal stripe label, are handled manually using if need be small hand operated 'coolie' fork lift apparatus.

Heavier and awkward items are dealt with at another depot a mile down the road but many pallet loads turn up at Salfords to be loaded last at the back end of the trailer, nearest the door. Having extended the weight limit from 10 to 25 kg, the Post Office has a new service, 'Direct Pallet Service'. Pallet loads up to ½ ton can now be accepted on a negotiated contract. These are small pallets and fork lift equipment is available. An item such as a car engine is normally given a mate to itself and packed with wood.

Transport

Just as the old postboy spent his time carrying sacks for each post town and shifted much more deadweight than payload, so the mates in the trailers are both heavy and create deadspace both in themselves and above. It is said that a looseloaded 40ft trailer can hold as much as 3 trailers filled with mates. But, of course, loose-loading is only possible where all items are going to one place and there is no need to keep items separate.

Salfords depot is based mainly on 40ft trailers for articulated vehicles. There are also 20ft trailers and smaller vans, for the depot also has to deliver the local parcels for Reigate and Redhill as well as the main run. Vehicles are owned not leased. Main supplier is British Leyland but following the current interpretation of 'free market' and of European Community Regulations, there will be Renault and later Volvo and Daf to be seen soon.

Current Reorganisation under new Administration

After a three year planning stage the parcel sector, now under Mr. Nelson previously Managing Director of D.H.L., hived off completely on the 27th February 1990 with the Headquarters moving to Milton Keynes and renaming itself Royal Mail 'Parcel Force'.

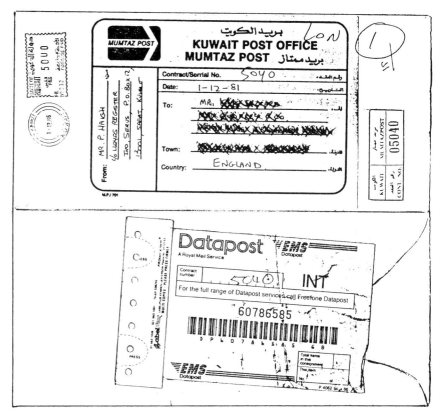

Datapost EMS (Express Mailing Service) Courier Service is a part of 'parcels', World wide and with different names in individual countries. Above: Kuwait Mumtaz Post/Datapost International. Below: Hong Kong Speedpost.

References

Chapter 1 1085–1625

1   K M E Murray, The Constitutional History of the Cinque Ports. Manchester Univ Press 1935.
      p1, 235; F W Jessup, Kent History Illustrated, Kent CC 1973 p38; A maritime History of
      Rye, John A Collard 1978. Watchbell St Rye.
2   Acts of the Privy Council. Aug 1546 p505.
3   Sevenoaks Preservation Society Historical Notes No4. c1962.
4   Acts of the Privy Council. 1589 p349.
5   East Sussex Record Office. Rye 47/50 (26 May 1594).
6   Historical Manuscript Commission. 13th Report Appendix Part IV. MS Rye Corpn 1580.
7   ESRO. Rye 1/4/158 (15 Feb 1574).
8   HMC. 13 Pt IV. 1573 p25.
9   Corsini Correspondance in The Philatelist & PJGB Nos 686/9 and Sept 84, Oct 84, June 86,
      Oct 88 auction catalogues. Christie, Robson Lowe; Corsini Correspondance at Guildhall Library.
10   Queen Elizabeth's visits to Sussex, W D Cooper, Vol 5 (1852) Sussex Archeological Collection. ESRO.
11   HMC 13 Pt IV.
12   Calendar of State Papers Domestic. 25 May 1549.
13   75 Warrants for the opening of letters in force at the end of 1988 under the Interception of
      Communication Act 1985. Report of Commissioners 1988 CM 652 HMSO.
14   Sir Cyril Hurcombe, Posts under the Tudors. The Antiquary 1914 and Postal History Society
      Bulletin No 7 1938.
15   ESRO. Original Letter 13 Sept 1589 47/39(3); HMC 13 Pt IV p88
16   Gentleman's Magazine. Vol 30 p539.
17   PRO. Pipe Rolls (Chancery Lane) E351/2736 Post Office audited Declared Accounts; Audit Office AOI
      Post Office D. A. Bundles Nos 1950-53 Rolls 1-28 (Kew). Both cover AD 1566-1637.
18   PRO. SP38.
19   Wm. Lewin, His Majesty's Mails p9 Sampson, Low Son & Marston 1864.
20   CSPD. 1597.
21   Ernest W Tilley, Kent Post. Vol 15 Nos 2/4.
22   HMC. 13 Pt IV. p127.
23   POR. Post 14/257. 29.10.1802
24   Wm Lambarde, A Perambulation of Kent. 1570.
25   Jack Cade, whose doings are reported in Calendar of Patent Rolls 1446-52 p460.
26   Sir John Dunlop, The Pleasant Town of Sevenoaks. Holmesdale & Caxton Press 1965 p78.
27   Phillips MSS12. Sevenoaks Library and Clarke and Stoyal, Otford in Kent 1975 p64.
28   Return to House of Commons. 10 Feb 1845 'Royal Messengers . . .'
29   Feudal Aids 1284-1431 p19.
30   Letter books of Christ Church. Canterbury Cathedral Archives.
31   Henry VIII Letters & Papers, Foreign & Domestic Vol 12/2 1537 ref 448 & 606.
32   Alfred Watkins. The Old Straight Track. Methuen 1925/ Abacus 1974.
33   Sir John Dunlop, Ibid p105.
34   Dr Gordon Ward, Sevenoaks Essays. Ashgrove Press 1980.
35   Petley deed 1588, mentioned in G H Warlow's History of Halstead 1934.
36   Domesday Book. King William I Winchester 1086/Ed John Morris. Philimore 1983.

Philip Symondson of Rochester's Great map of Kent 1596 can be found in Philipott's Villare
Cantianum 1659; also Ordnance Survey reprints.

Chapter II 1625–1695

1   Acts of the Privy Council of England. July 1626.
2   Lord de Lisle & Dudley m/s. Kent Archives Office 12.54. 1636.
3   Proclamation of 11.2.1637 in Appendix to the Report from the Secret Committee on the Post Office 1844.
4   Historical Manuscript Commission 13 Part IV; Jeremy Greenwood. Kent Post 3/1.
5   Marian Mills, letter to Sevenoaks Chronicle 23.1.1987.
6   A.M. Everitt, The Community of Kent and the Great Rebellion 1640-60 p111ff Leicester Univ Press 1966.
7   Ibid. p190, 204, 304.
8   Kent Post Vol 3, No 3.
9   PRO SP 18.42 (101) quoted in 'The Inland Posts 1392-1672' Ed J.M.W. Stone Robson Lowe 1987.
10   Edward Hyde, Clarendon State Papers Vol iv of 5vol edn p304.
11   Statutes at Large.
12   Vivien Sussex. The Norwich Post Office 1568-1980 East Anglian Postal History Study Circle 13 and Sevenoaks Library. A list of those paying Land Tax 1702.
14   Ed. B. Lubbock, Journal of Edward Barlow. London 1934.
15   Boyne, Trade Tokens of the 17th Century.
16   State of the Post Office as now managed 1660–1663. Papers of the First Lord Clifford Chudleigh. Michael Jackson. Postal History No 250 2/1989.
17   London Gazette 4-8 Oct 1666; London Gazette 22 Aug 1667.
18   Location of 'The Post for all Kent 1661' Postal History Society SS10.
19   Kent Archives Office Q/RLV Licenced Victuallers Recognizances. Membrane of 1665.
20   Post 94/11 'Kentish Road' Postmasters Salaries 1666/7; PRO SP 25/5.
21   Calendar of State Papers Domestic Sept 1666.
22   POR. Post 94 Whitley Letter Books Vol II p634: Jeremy Greenwood, The Posts of Sussex 1250–1840. Privately published Reigate 1972
23   Post Office Broadsheet 1669. PRO SP 29/263.
24   Ogilby, Britannia 1675.
25   London Gazette 28 Dec 1678.
26   London Gazette 26 July 1697.
27   David Smith, Antique Maps of the British Isles. Batsford 1982.
28   Kent Archives Office Q/LRV Licenced Victualler Recognizances gives Christian name.
29   Postal History Society SS10; POR Post 94.
30   Gentleman's Magazine Vol 85 p309. Account of the Post Office in 1677.
31   POR Post 3 Accounts 1685.
32   POR Post 2 Accounts p167 20 June 1694.
33   HMC Vol 13 Part IV p362.
34   G.H. Warlow, History of Knockholt 1934 p58.
35   Thomas de Laune, The Present State of London 1681/1690 edns.
36   David Mountfield, The Coaching Age Robert Hale 1976 p28.
37   POR Post 3 1673-1750.
38   C.W. Chaklin, 17th Century Kent. Longmans p36.

Chapter III 1695–1770

1   Sir John Dunlop, The Pleasant Town of Sevenoaks. Caxton & Holmesdale Press 1964 p107, 117, 118.
2   Extracted from POR Post 3 Accounts.
3   Statutes at Large. 1710 An Act for establishing a General Post Office 9 Anne c10.
4   J.T. Foxell & A.O. Spafford, Monarchs of all they surveyed. HMSO.
5   POR. Post 68/1 Ralph Allen's Book of Instructions (1730-40), also Ralph Allen's own Narrative 1720 - 1761. Postal History Society SS 8 1960.
6   POR. Post 14/1 Bye and Cross Letter Office Reports 1757-1831.
7   POR. Post 3 Accounts.
8   POR. Post 58/1 Order Book 1737-1774.
9   Kent Archives Maidstone U1007 Polhill.

10   Kent Archives Maidstone U2133 Fremlin.
11   Ogilby & Morgan Travellers Pocket Book 1755.
12   POR. Queen Anne's Establishment Book 1702.
13   POR. Post 58/1 Order Book 1737-1774 p192.
14   Sevenoaks Corporation Minute Book 1576-1719. Sevenoaks Library.
15   Louis Melville, Society at Tunbridge Wells. Eveleigh Nash 1912 quoting Celia Fiennes.
16   Hugh Barty-King, Quilt Winders and Pod Shavers. Macdonald and Janes 1979 p60 ff.
17   Sevenoaks Justices Minute Book. 1714-1726. Sevenoaks Library.
18   Sir John Dunlop, The Pleasant Town of Sevenoaks, Caxton & Holmesdale Press 1964. p121
19   The Case of the Deputy Postmasters c1706 POR ; The Norwich Post Office, Vivien Sussex.
20   Act mentioned in London Gazette 22 July 1780 ; Herbert Joyce, History of the Post Office,
          Richard Bently and Son p205.
21   Act for regulating the commencement of the year; and for correcting the calendar now in use   1751.
22   Tycho Wing, Almanack for the year 1752.
23   Phillips MSS 14 p18. Sevenoaks Library.
24   St James Chronicle and British Evening Post 2.11.1771.

Chapter IV 1770-1801

1   Jasper Sprange, Tunbridge Wells Guide Book 1780.
2   The Torrington Diaries, A tour into Sussex p340, Camden Historical Society.
3   Kent Archives Q/RLV Licenced Victuallers section.
4   POR. Post 58/1. Order Book 1737-1774. p192.
5   POR. PMG Reports Vol.19 Minute 528.
6   POR. PMG Reports Vol.14 Minute 63Q.
7   Ibid.
8   POR. PMG Reports Vol.14 Minute 90Q.
9   POR. Post 9/145A. 1791 (signed 31.1.93). An account of the annual salaries payable to the Deputies of the
          Bye and Cross Road.
10   POR. Post 2/107 (1793). Receipts by PO Revenues. Bye and Cross Rd Letter Office.
11   POR. Post 23/3.
12   John Copeland, Roads and their Traffic 1750-1850 p153, David and Charles 1968 .
13   London 'Evening Mail' 18 Feb 1795.
14   Guide to T Wells 1780 p158.
15   'Kalendar' year books London (1769-1788).
16   1783/4 Highway Diversions QRH2 / 15x, 23, 57 and Session Order Books QSO / W11, 12 Kent Archives.
17   POR. Post 61/1.
18   POR. Post 35. 1793 Minutes 196P, 5c, 19c, 86c, 105c.
19   POR. Post 35. October 1793.
20   GPO notice.
21   POR. Post 10/8. Plan for Arming Mails.
22   POR. Post 15/9. 10 Jan 1801.
23   Vale, Mail Coach Men p177. Cassell 1960.
24   Evening Mail, 18th March 1801.
25   Tonbridge Library Archival Section, Notes by an early researcher in P.O. Archives prior to its reorganisation.
          Detail quoted is probably among the Prosecution briefs in P.O. Archives, but these not yet catalogued
          officially.
26   E L S Horsborough, Bromley, Kent. Hodder & Stoughton 1929.
27   Women's Institute, Scrapbook of Farnborough 1955 (Bromley Library).
28   Postal History No 237 1986/1.

Chapter V 1801–1840

1   POR Post 42 1810.

2   B Austen, Impact of the mailcoaches on public coach service in England and Wales. Journal of Transport History 3rd ser II 1981.

3   Sussex Weekly Advertiser 25 June 1827.

4   Brett's Historico-Biography I p217 Hastings Library.

5   W G Moss, The History and Antiquities of Hastings 1824. Published by the author at Hastings.

6   John Copeland, Roads and their Traffic 1750-1850 p182, p172 David and Charles 1968.

7   Frank Chapman, Book of Tonbridge, Barracuda 1984.

8   P.O. Return 23 Aug 1843 Number of Stagecoaches etc used by the P.O. as Mails in England and Wales not being so originally.

9   Cinque Ports Chronicle 18 Dec 1839 quoted in Hastings and the Royal Mail, H Manwaring Baines, Hastings Museum 1951.

10   Evidence taken for new route Shoreham to Grinsted Green. Sevenoaks Library.

11   James Carley, The Gravesend to Wrotham Turnpike Road 1973.   Gravesend Public Library.

12   POR Post 42/110v 19 March 1799.

13   D Mountfield, The Coaching Age 1976, Robert Hale & Co.

14   Robson Mailcoach and Conveyance Lists 1831, 1837 Rp M S Todd Den of Antiquity Nether Stowey; Alan Bates, Directory of Stagecoach Services 1836. David & Charles 1969.

15   B Austen, Ibid.

16   Hastings Guide. P.M.Powell. 2nd Edn. c1815.

17   Kelly's Directories; Manwaring Baines, Hastings and the Royal Mail 1951.

18   7th Report from Commissioners on Management of the P.O. 1837.(mailcoach contracts) and 1st Report from the Select Committee on Postage 1837/8 appendix 45 Mailcoaches.

19   Report to Commons on Horsing of Mailcoaches 1837-41, 1842 and Commons Report 381 Mailcoaches (Horses, Passengers, Rates) 7 June 1841.

20   Commons Report 364 Relative to Mail Coaches (Horses) 23 June 1836.

21   Commons Reports 155 Names and Payments to Mail Coach Guards 19 March 1841 and 431 Mailguards: names and payments 22 June 1841.

22   E L Horsborough, Bromley, Kent.

23   POR Post 9/142 p84.

24   POR Post 10 Wheatley/Worcester 1841.

25   Charles G Harper, The Road to Hastings, Chapman & Hall 1906.

26   A Peal, Six days near Sevenoaks, Sevenoaks Library.

27   POR Post 58.

28   Dr Gordon Ward's notebooks. Book 12 p45, Sevenoaks Library.

29   E G Box, Old Sevenoaks p47.

30   G F Cavell, K A S xxiii p330/331.

31   E G Box, Sevenoaks and the neighbouring parishes. Typescript Sevenoaks Library; F Richards, Old Sevenoaks 1901, J Salmon.

32   Land Tax Assessments, Kent Archives Maidstone Q/RPI 331.

33   POR Post 68 Rules. Early (c1810-1820) Rulebook.

34   POR Post 14 26 Feb and 23 Nov 1807.

35   POR Post 14 3 Aug 1821.

36   Commons Return 293 Postage: Post town delivery charges. 26 April 1830.

37   PMG Report 680. Vol 56.

38   Commons Returns:
        264 Appointments of Deputy Postmasters, 4 June 1835.
        565 Appointments of Deputy Postmasters (Supplementary) 1835.
        155 Payment of Postmasters, 19 March 1841.

39   John Thomas Pocock, Diary of a London Schoolboy 1837-1839 Ed Holden, Camden Historical Society 1980.

40   7th Report, Comm on Management of P.O. 1837 Appendix.
        1st and 2nd Reports from Select Comm on Postage 1837/8.

41   The Times 19th September 1838 p5.

42   AA Touring Guide 1952.

43   Correspondance in Current Archaeology 1989/1990.

Chapter VI 1804–1840 Local

1   Christopher Wright, Kent through the years. B.T. Batsford Ltd., 1975 p147

Chapter VII 1839 - 1920

1   Archie Donald, Kent Post. Vol 10/4 1982
2   C. Devereux, Railways to Sevenoaks. Oakwood Press 1967.
3   POR Post 11/7 1986 July.
4   H.S. Wilson, Travelling Post Offices, Part 2 England - South. Railway Philatelic Group 1979.
5   D. Gould, Westerham Valley Railway. Oakwood Press 1974.
6   Illustrated London News 3 Aug 1889.
7   Driving. His Grace the 8th Duke of Beaufort p294. The Badminton Library of Sports & Pastimes 1890 /
       Ashford Press Publishing 1986.
8   POR Post 11/7.
9   Acts -   24, 25 Vict c70 1 Aug 1861   61, 62 Vict c29 2 Aug 1898
       Locomotives   28, 29 Vict c83 5 Jul 1865   3 Edw 7 c36 14 Aug 1903
       on Highways   41, 42 Vict c77 16 Aug 1878
                         59, 60 Vict c36 14 Aug 1896
10   John M.C. Wheeler, A Brief Guide to the Memento Rooms David Salomons House Southborough 1986.
11   Charles Jarrett, 10 Years of Motors and Motor Racing. Redcliffe Hutchings 1906.
12   POR Post 14.
13   Land Tax 1780-1828 Ref Q/RP1 331 Kent Archives.
14   Sevenoaks Land Tax Assessment Book 1838, Sevenoaks Library.
15   1841 Census of Sevenoaks.
16   POR Post 35 Vol 71 p528.
17   Maidstone Journal 16 Nov 1847.
18   1841 Census of Sevenoaks.
19   Wm Sedgewick and R. Ward, The Rural Postal Service over three centuries. 1982 Yorkshire Postal
       History Society.
20   Ibid.
21   Sevenoaks Preservation Society Transactions, Box 979 Sevenoaks Library.
22   Jane Edwards, Conversations with her Aunt (Jane Edwards Diary), Sevenoaks Library 1863.
23   S. Hyde Turner, Recollections (m/s), 1929 Sevenoaks Library.
24   POR Post 9/69 1865.
25   POR Post 38 Vol 185 Min 2521.
26   Sevenoaks Transactions M/s pencil list. Box 176 Sevenoaks Library.
27   Leslie Stephen, Life of Henry Fawcett, Smith Elder & Co. 1886.
28   Payne's Sevenoaks Almanack 1841.
29   POR Post 35 Vol 83 Minute 37S.
30   Post Office Circular 2 April 1866.
31   C. Hill, Our Priceless Day of Rest. Postal History Bulletin No 201 1977.
32   Letters of Queen Victoria 1837-1861. John Murray. In 3 vols 1908 Vol II p244 and Report to the
       Commissioners appointed to investigate the question of Sunday Labour in the Post Office 1850.
33   Post Office Circular 6th August 1859.
34   Post Office Circular 19 June 1871.
35   Post Office Circular 20 Jan 1885.
36   Post Office Circular 5th September 1893.
37   Post Office Circular 16th Nov 1874.
38   Tonbridge Mechanised Letter Office Local Archives.
       Itemised: No 9 Sevenoaks Post Office Allowances and Staff Records.1874-79
                   No 13 Sevenoaks Appointments Record.   1895-1900
                   No 18 Sevenoaks Allowances and Appointments Record.   1900-11
                   No 24 Sevenoaks Establishment Record.   1900-20

39   Report of P.M.G. 1909 List of Provincial Offices.
40   POR Post 64/13 and 64/14.
41   Post Office Circular 23 June 1896.
42   Alan Clinton, Post Office Workers: A Trade Union and Social History. 1984 Allen & Unwin.
43   Ref 'Social Clubs - P.O.' Sevenoaks Library.
44   As Ref 19, Rural Postal Services.
45   2nd Report of P.M.G. 1856.
46   Multiple Sources inc Directories; POR Post 35.
47   Tonbridge M.L.O. Archives, as Ref 38.
48   Salmon's Sevenoaks Directory 1903.
49   P.O. Circular 131 12 June 1891.
50   Sevenoaks Establishment Record, Tonbridge M.L.O. Archives.
51   POR Post 35 1909.
52   POR Post 9/69 ff.
53   17th Report of P.M.G. 1871.
54   Sevenoaks P.O. Returns of Traffic Volumes. 1894-1928 Tonbridge M.L.O. Archives.
55   Sevenoaks Rating Book 1838 Sevenoaks Library.
56   Sevenoaks Telephone Directories 1902-1920.
57   Knockholt Telephone Exchange - Subscriber Increases. Tonbridge M.L.O. Archives.
58   Westerham Diary. Tonbridge M.L.O Archives.
59   Francis J. Field, British Air Mails - A Chronology. 1935.
60   Gordon Anckorn, A Sevenoaks Camera No 86, Ashgrove Press 1979.
61   Sevenoaks Chronicle 1 May 1982, p10.
62   Gordon Anckorn, Sevenoaks Memories 85-87, Ashgrove Press 1984.
63   Graham Wallace, RAF Biggin Hill 1957, p23.
64   M.H. Gould, History of Royal Naval Air Services. 1983 Forces Postal History Society.
65   Robin J. Brooks, Sevenoaks Volunteers, Bygone Kent Magazine Mar 86, Vol 7/3; also Sevenoaks
        Library L456/7.
66   Post Office Circulars 1899 and 15 May 1901.
67   Transactions of Sevenoaks Preservation Society, Sevenoaks Library D979.
68   Sevenoaks Library Box 64a.
69   POR Historical Summary Sheet, Army.

Chapter VIII 1920–1985/6

1   Tonbridge MLO Archives. Westerham Diary 1927-1951.
2   Sevenoaks Chronicle 7 May 1926.
3   M. J. Daunton. The Post Office since 1840 p144 Athlone Press 1984.
4   POR Post 38 Minutes 10135, 11506, 3103.
5   Ton MLO L.A. Westerham Diary 1927-51.
6   Ton MLO L.A. Traffic Volumes; T L A Book 20.
7   Sevenoaks Chronicle and Courier 15 July 1927.
8   Sevenoaks News 11 July 1940.
9   Sevenoaks News 17 October 1940.
10   Andrew Rootes, Kent Front Line County 1986.
11   K. R. Gulvin, Kent Home Guard North Kent (Meresborough) Books 1980.
12   Sevenoaks News 19 October 1944.
13   Helmut Wolff, Die deutschen Kriegagefangenen in britischer hand. Verlag Ernst Werner Gieseling.
14   Mr. D. H. Bennett of Southborough. Verbal Communication 1984.
15   Boorman & Maskell, Tonbridge Free Press Centenary 1969.
16   Frank Chapman, The Book of Tonbridge. Barracuda 1980.
17   Mr. Coke Snr of Borough Green, Verbal Communication 1984.
18   Graham Wallace, R.A.F. Biggin Hill 1957 Putnam.
19   Bruce B. Halpenny, Action Stations 8 Military Airfields of Greater London, Patrick Stephens, Cambridge.

20   James Shaffer, Geographic Locations of U.S. Army Post Offices 1941-1978. War Cover Club U.S.A.
         W. J. Bailey and E. R. Toop. Canadian Military Posts. Vol. 2, E. B. Proud 1985.
21   Major W. J. Bailey, Canadian Military Postmarks, 1978, P.O. Box 5083, Ottawa.
22   Chris Ashworth, Action Stations 9 Military Airfields of N.W. Kent 1965, Patrick Stephens Ltd.
23   Zena Bamping, West Kingsdown 1983 West Kingsdown Parish Council.
24   Neil Griffiths, History of Fort Halstead.
25   Michael E. Corby, The Postal Business 1969-79; study in Public Sector Management, Kogan Page 1979.
26   Robert Albon, Privatise the Post; steps towards a competitive service, Centre for Policy Studies 1987.
27   M. J. Daunton, The Post Office since 1840, Athlone 1985 p353.
28   Archie Donald, Kent Post. Vol. 10/4 Dec 1982.
29   Edward Wells, Mailshot 1987 p189.
30   (Post Office) Courier Newspaper November 1983.
31   Visits to Sevenoaks Sorting Office pre-1984.
32   Visits to Tonbridge, Dartford, Canterbury Mechanised Letter Offices. 1984-86.
33   Correspondance Patrick G. Awcock 1986.
34   Sevenoaks Chronicle 27.1.1984.
35   Daily Telegraph 27 June 1981; Stamps and Postal History, 24th November 1982 and
         2 November 1983; Stamp Collecting 21 April 1983; (P.O.) Courier June 1984.
36   Privatise the Post (see 26).
37   Daily Telegraph 16 January 1984.
38   Kenneth Miles, Sevenoaks Branch Secretary Union of Communication Workers in Sev. Chron. 23.8.1985.
39   Daily Telegraph 27 June 1985.
40   Post Office Report and Accounts 1984/5 & 1985/6.
41   Return to H of C 3/1844. Names of P/masters and Towns to which ½ sheets of Postage Free paper will be sent.
42   (P.O.) Courier. February and April 1984.
43   Daily Telegraph 22 July 1986.

Chapter IX

1   Post Circular No. 5 - Postal Reform Movement.
2   Post Circular No. 8 - Postal Reform Movement.
3   Wrotham Local History Box D920. Sevenoaks Library.
4   Mary Waugh, Smugglers in Kent and Sussex 1700-1840, Countryside Books, Berkshire, 1985.
5   Daily Telegraph, 2nd April 1985.
6   'Queens Messengers', Return No. 98 to the House of Commons, 16 April 1844.
7   Sevenoaks Justices Minute Book, 1834, Sevenoaks Library.
8   Brett's Historico-Biography I. Hastings Library.
9   Sevenoaks Advertiser, 1 July 1843.
10   Sevenoaks Advertiser, 1 August 1842 and 2 January 1843.
11   Box D920, Sevenoaks Library.
12   POR Post 10/108, 1939.
13   Contemporary Parcels Handbill. 1920.
14   Contemporary Red Star Parcels Handbill. 1985.
15   Eric Baldock, The Motor Bus Services of Kent and E. Sussex. Meresborough Books, Gillingham 1985.
         John Hibbs, History of British Bus Services, David & Charles 1968, p136.
16   Contemporary Local Bus Timetables of 1936 and 1961.
17   Telephone Yellow Pages, Thompsons Local Directory 1984-6.
18   'Clerks of the Road' Report No. 706 to House of Commons, 1833.
19   Post Circular No 8
20   Illustrated London News 30.8.1851.
21   British Mail Coach (Journal) No. 11, 1976.
22   Sevenoaks Chronicle, 4 June 1884.
23   Stanley Johnson, The Royal Mail Parcel Coaches, Country Life. 28 December 1935.
24   POR Post 35. Minute 20832 1907.

Bibliography

Background reading for each period including books, acts, official notices and other sources of information.

Preface
E. E. Thoyts, How to decipher and study old Documents, Elliot Stock, London 1893.
   The 'y' can be seen in handwriting as early as 1413 in, for example, Revelation of Julian of Norwich (B.L. Sloan MS 3705 f 2v page reproduced) John Julian. DLT London. 1988

Chapter I 1085-1625
Chevening Cameo 1979.
J. Crofts, Packhorse, Waggon and Post. Routledge Kegan Paul 1967.
Howard Robinson, The British Post Office A History, Greenwood Press 1948/1970.
Statutes at Large.
Proclamation, 1603. Orders for Thorough-Posts and Couriers, riding on the King's Affairs.
Proclamation, 1609. 'to redress the disorders among the Postes of our Realme'.
Calendar of State Papers Domestic.
E. J. Brigstocke Sheppard, Rerum Britannicarum medii sevii scriptores No. 85
      Literae Cantuarienses. Letter Books of the Monastery of Christ
      Church Canterbury. 3 vols HMSO 1889.

Chapter II 1635-1695
Samuel Graveson, Posts of the 17th Century. Postal History Bulletin No. 20 1942 & ff.
R. M. Willcocks, England's Postal History to 1840. Privately published 1975.
Thomas Gardiner Ed Bond, A General Survey of the Post Office 1677-82 Postal History Society 1958.
Calendar of State Papers Domestic.
Acts of the Privy Council.
Ed. Lubbock, 'Barlow's Journal'.
Jeremy Greenwood, Kent Post Vol. 1 & ff.
C. Brewer and R. L. Hull, The Postal History of Tonbridge and Tunbridge Wells, Kent Post Vol 8 1985.

Acts, Ordinances and Proclamations
1635 Proclamation. 'for the setling of the Letter Office of England and Scotland'.
1654 Ordinance touching the office of Postage of Letters - Inland and Foreign.
1657 Act for setling the Postage of England, Scotland and Ireland.
1660 Act I Caroli II Cap 35 for erecting and establishing a Post Office.

London Gazette
4 Oct. 1666	Removal of Kent Office
2 July 1667	Overcharging
22 Aug. 1667	Removal of Office
2 Sep. 1667	Bad Addressing
17 Dec. 1668	Local Distribution
22 June 1669	Daily to the Wells
9 Aug. 1669	re Broadsheet
7 Apr. 1670	Half Post to Chester
20 Mar. 1678	Removal of Main P.O.
27 June 1687	Seven days a week from T'Wells

Post Office Records
Post	1	Treasury Letter Books 1686-
	3	Post Office Accounts 1685-
	94	Peover Papers
		Six Roads (94/11) 1666/7
		Whitley Letter Books 1672-77

Chapter III 1695-1770

J. T. Foxall & A. O. Spafford, Monarchs of all they Surveyed HMSO 1952.
Harry R. G. Inglis, Contour Road Book of England 1901 Gall and Inglis.
Louis Melville, Society at Tunbridge Wells in the 18th Century. 1912 Eveleigh Nash.
J. Manwaring Baines, Historic Hastings. F.T. Parsons Ltd., 1955.
Alan W. Robertson, Post Roads, Post Towns, Postal Rates 1635-1839. 1961. Published by author.

Post Office Acts
1710   9 Anne c10
1717   3 Geo I c7
1749   22 Geo II c25
1765   5 Geo III c25
1767   7 Geo III c50
1769   9 Geo III c35

London Gazette
22 June 1699 Daily Post to Tunbridge Wells during the season.
12 April 1720 Prepayment of Cross Post Letters.
28 July 1761 Ralph Allen Contract. By and Cross Letters.

Turnpike Acts
South
24 June 1709 8 Anne c20
24 June 1725 11 Geo I c15 Sevenoaks-Southborough
18 Nov. 1740 14 Geo II
          1762 2 Geo III c67 and c72 Sevenoaks-Flimwell and on to Rye.
North
29 Nov. 1748 22 Geo II c8 Farnboro, Riverhill, Sevenoaks
          1773 13 Geo III c92 Farnboro, Riverhill, Sevenoaks
          1785 Order. Closure of Chevening-Knockholt Road by J.Ps.
    also 1796 36 Geo III c128
          1816 56 Geo III c34
          1765 5 Geo III c68 Cross route

Chapter IV 1770-1801

John Copeland, Roads and their traffic 1750-1850, David and Charles. 1968.
Edward Hasted, History of Kent, E.P. 13 vols. 1797/1970.
T. W. Horsfield, History of Sussex. 1835 2 vols.
Bryan Keith-Lucas, Parish Affairs: the Government of Kent under George III [1760-1820] Kent County
Library 1986.
John Boyle, In Quest of Hasted, Phillimore 1984.

Post Office Acts
1782 22 Geo III c41
1784 24 Geo III c37
1785 25 Geo III c60
1787 27 Geo III c13
1803 43 Geo III c25

Stage Coach Acts
2 Geo III c15 1761 (Fish)
19 Geo III 1779
20 Geo III c51 1780
25 Geo III c51 1785
28 Geo III c57 from 1 Nov. 1788
30 Geo III c36 from 29 Sept 1790
46 Geo III c136 from 1 Sept 1806
50 Geo III c48 from 9 June 1810

Chapter V 1801-1840

Brian Austen, English Provincial Posts 1978 Phillimore & Co.
Brett's Historico-Biography I Ch. XXII History of Hastings P.O. Hastings Public Library.
John Copeland, Roads and their Traffic 1750-1850, David & Charles 1968
J. Manwaring Baines, Hastings and the Royal Mail, Hastings Museum 1951
Post Office Records,   Post 42 Freeling's Minute Books
                        Post 40 Reports from Surveyors, and supporting documentation.
G. F. Oxley, English Provincial Local Posts, 1765-1840 Postal History Society 1973
Christopher Wright, Kent through the years, Batsford 1975
A. Peal, Six Days near Sevenoaks or the Narrative of a Balloon Ascent 1825, Sevenoaks Library.
Anthony Bird, Roads and Vehicles, Longmans 1969.
W. Stitt Dibden, The Additional Half-Penny Mail Tax 1813-1839, SS14. PHS Soc. 1963.
Highways Act 1835   5&6 Gul IV c.50

Acts New Routes

50 Geo III c18 1810 Shoreham-Grinsted Green
51 Geo III c205 1811 Repeal of above
5 Gul IV c20   12 June 1835 Polhill Route
6 Gul IV c2   18 Mar. 1836 Polhill Route

Acts Turnpikes

6 Geo IV c50 2 May 1825 Gravesend and Wrotham

Acts Stagecoaches   - numbers on roof

46 Geo III c136 22 July 1806
50 Geo III c48   9 June 1810
3 & 4 Gul IV c48 28 Aug. 1833

            - To facilitate trials of felonies committed on Coaches passing through several Counties
59 Geo III c96 12 July 1819

            - Licencing
3 Geo IV c33   1822
7 Geo IV c33   1826

Chapter VI 1804-1840 Local

Actual Survey Records in Post Office Records, Post 42/40.

Postal Acts
1765   Postal Act
1801 41 Geo III c7

Chapter VII 1839-1920

Jean Farrugia, The Letter Box, Centaur Press 1969
Jean Newman, Dunton Green: Story of a Village in Kent. Privately published 1986
G. D. Kitchener, M.A., Halstead in Kent, an Historical Guide. Privately published 1978
Local Government Act 1888
Brian Stewart and Mervyn Cutten, The Shayer family of Painters, F. Lewis 1981
Postmasters Rulebooks as listed.
Directories as listed.

Chapter VIII 1920-1985/6

M. J. Daunton, The Post Office since 1840, Athlone Press 1984
Yearly 'Report and Accounts' of the Post Office

Chapter IX

Thos. East, Carriers Cosmographie, A.G. 1637

GENERAL BACKGROUIND REFERENCES

Directories
Baileys British Directory 1784
Universal British Directory Vol   12   1793
(No Sevenoaks detail)   13   1795
                          14   1799

Holden's Annual London & County Directory
(No Sevenoaks detail)   1811

James Pigot   1823/4
                 1826/7/9
                 1832/4
                 1839/40

Kelly's Post Office Directory for the Six Home Counties   1845   1866
                                                          1851   1870
                                                           1855   1874
                                                             1862   1878

Kelly's Directory of Kent, Surrey, Sussex   1882   1903   1913   1927

	1887	1905	1915	1930
	1890	1907	1918	1934
	1895	1909	1922	1938
	1899	1911	1924	

Guides
Post Office Directory 1850 (Reprint)
Post Office Guides 1856-1985

Local Directories
Payne's Sevenoaks Almanack 1841
Sevenoaks Telegraph and Kent Messenger Calendar   1901, 1909, 1911, 1914
Salmon's Directory of Sevenoaks 1903/4 yearly to 1919
Sevenoaks Directory, Caxton & Holmesdale Press 1920 yearly to 1940
Sennocke Almanack. W. Wicking, 54 High Street (from 1865) 1904   (only one available)
Westerham. C. Hookers Directory (from 1862)   1878, 1884, 1896, 1921, 1926, 1931, 1935 (only dates available)

Newspapers
Sevenoaks Free Press (printed Tonbridge)1879
Sevenoaks Chronicle and Kentish Advertiser   18.2.1881 - (continuing)
Sevenoaks Express and District Advertiser   21.7.1863 - 1902
    (local edition of Sussex Express printed in Lewes)
Kent Messenger and Sevenoaks Telegraph 1886 - 1930
Sevenoaks News 9.5.1935 - 8.10.84

Journals
The Kent Post Vols 1-11 (available Tonbridge Library)
Postal History Bulletin

Post Office Guide with List of Post Offices
The Guide has been issued yearly from 1856 with some hiatus over the war years, and is on sale to the public. Early guides contained a list of all Post Offices. Later on (1937) the *lists* were printed and sold separately and were discontinued altogether after 1977. The *guide*, giving details of services, was published yearly with a monthly update service until 1986. We now await the New Administration's Guide.

Postmasters Rulebooks available

c1794-1829 General Regulations relating to Postmasters and the Management of their offices.

1846 Instructions for the Guidance of all Postmasters in the United Kingdom.

1846 Instructions for the Guidance of all Letter Receivers in the United Kingdom, Hartnell and Co., Red Lion Court.

1856 Rules for Sub-Postmasters in the United Kingdom. Eyre & Spottiswood.

1869 Rules for Receivers at Provincial Towns in England. Eyre & Spottiswood.

1876 Rules for Sub-Postmasters and Letter Receivers in charge of Money Order Offices in the United Kingdom., Eyre & Spottiswood.

1883 Rules for Sub-Postmasters. Eyre & Spottiswood.

1911 Code of Instructions for Surveyors and Independent Postmasters.

1917 GPO Rules for Temporary Postmen and Postwomen.

1919 Postmasters Manual Vol. I (Amend to 1925).

1923 Postmasters Manual Vol. II (Amend to 1925).

Some Early Maps of Kent, Surrey, Sussex

1526 Philip Symondson, First Kent map showing roads.
  (Christopher Saxton 1569-1606; John Speed 1610-1629; Willem Bleau 1599-1638; William Kip 1598-1635; all show few or no roads).

1675 John Ogilby, strip road maps of the road from London to Rye

1622-73 Thomas Jenner, distance tables. Jacob Van Langaren's plates with the new maps by Jenner. John Garrett continued to use the plates until 1677.

1669-1703 Robert Morden, Kent and parts of Sussex (all the Rye road) 1696, 1702

1734-1762 John Rocque, Surrey, 1765. Large Scale. Reprint 1931 Surrey Arch. Soc. Guildford

1750-60 Eman(ual) Bowen, Kent (all Rye road)

1770 Andrews and Dury, Large Scale Kent.

1783-1835 John Cary, many maps of Kent, Surrey, Sussex showing roads.

1779-1785 Antonio Zatta, Venice. Kent, Surrey.

1754-93 Carington Bowles, strip map of London-Rye road 1781

1789 Hasted's 'Kent' with large scale maps of the Hundreds: Codsheath (Sevenoaks), Westerham, Wrotham Hundreds cover postal district.

1794-1812 Laurie & Whittle, noted for 'straightline' roads.

c1810 John Cary, 15 miles around London. Large scale of north half of Sevenoaks district.

1817-1834 Christopher and John Greenwood. Kent 1819/20 Sussex 1825/6

Ordnance Survey, Kent

c1800 1" Kent, 4 Sheet Lt. William Mudge, first edition Old Series, Published Faden, engraved Foot 1801, and Baker 1804. Reprint of 1801 map Harry Margary Lympne Castle 1990.

1819 David and Charles have reissued the 1" to mile O.S. maps for all England published by Col. Mudge, 1st January 1819, but with later additions (such as railways) to the plates.

1864 on The second edition of the 1" O.S. map commenced publication.

1868/9 Earliest Large Scale Ordnance Surveys of Sevenoaks were 6" (1868/9) and 25" (1869) according to British Library map Librarian. There does not appear to be **any** large scale map of the town prior to this date. [There was no 1837 Municipal Boundaries Map as Sevenoaks was not a municipality.]

1903 on. 1" O.S. map.. 3rd Edition; 1914 on, 4th Edition; 1931 on, 5th Edition; 1947 on, 6th Edition; 1952 on, 7th Edition.

The various editions of early O.S. maps are somewhat complex. The position is explained in

The Historian's Guide to Ordnance Survey Maps Published 1964 for The Standing Conference for Local History by the National Council of Social Service, 26 Bedford Square, WC1

Brig, H. S. L. Winterbotham (Sometime Director-General of the Ordnance Survey). A Key to maps 1939 Blackie.

Appendix

Appendix

Main office:	Sevenoaks, some additional details
Sub-offices:	Town (TSO) and village sub-office details
	Status, Postmasters, Postmen, History, Postmarks, Population
	Town Sub-Offices Index page 410
	Village Sub-offices, also Westerham and Edenbridge Towns. Index page 413

Population Growth of Local Main Towns
Coaches through Sevenoaks 1831 and 1837
Official Declaration. 1884 Version
Kings and Queens of England
Multiplying Factors for Inflation 1500-1987

Sources

This Appendix gives further detailed information not mentioned in the main text and also includes reference work and the recordings of original data of Messrs C Brewer, M M English, Jeremy Greenwood, R F J Grove, Ray Haffner, Derek Hamilton-Smith, Pat Harding, James Mackay, M A Porter, T E Smith, Tom Stevens, Norman Woods, F. West, Douglas Wilson and others whose information is incorporated, with their permission.

Sources of information are:

Post Office Records: Post 7, Post 30/35, Post 38, Post 55, Post 58, Post 68.
Establishment Book GPO 1939. List of Principal Officers in the Post Office.
Post Office Circulars, PO Guides, Postmaster's Manuals.
Sevenoaks Record Books at Tonbridge Head Office.
Post Office Directory 1850 (Rp London Postal History Group).
Pigot's directories, Kelly's directories.
Victoria County History, Kent and Surrey.
Guidebooks: Sprange, Blacks, Murray.
Robsons Mailcoach Conveyance Lists.
Newspapers.
Personal sight of original documents.
Postmarks on early letters seen.
The Place Names of Kent, Judith Glover. Batsford 1976 / Meresborough Books 1982.

Wherever possible information has been cross-checked using more than one source.

Sevenoaks Main Office, some additional detail.

Status

1635	Branch office under Chipstead.
1676	Sevenoaks Post Town office opened. Chipstead suppressed
1687-1711	Farmed.
c1750	A period as Sub-Post Town under Tonbridge.
By 1845	Money Order Office.
c1860	Now designated 'Head Post Office' rather than 'Post Town'.
1861	Nov 25 Savings Bank.
1865	Nov 6 Government Annuity and Insurance work (under 27/28 Vict c43 of May 1865).
1870	Feb Telegraph Office (SV).
1874	April 1st Receipt Stamps sold.
1880	Sept 13 Deposit 1d Savings Stamps sold.
1883	Parcels office.
1905	Became Crown Office. In 1939 designated class I.
1912	Telephones taken over; hived off 1981 (69 years).
1972	Under Tunbridge Wells (later Tonbridge) as a Salaried Sub Office.
1985	No longer a full Sorting Office, 'Sevenoaks' postmark on outgoing mail ceased. Mail sent to Tonbridge MLO.
1986	Split to 'Royal Mail Letters' and 'PO Counters' Ltd.

Location of Office

1717-1728	Crown Inn on same site as present main Post Office.
1729-1738	Old Crown Inn.
1743-1748	Crown Inn.
1797-1803	Duke of Dorset Arms.
1807-1837	Wheatsheaf Inn, London Road.
1837-1841	Movement from London Road to High Street, probably via Shambles.
1841	High Street. (more than one location).
1905	South Park. North Side. Crown Office Class II.
1976	South Park, South Side. Corner with London Road. Crown Office.

Opening Hours:(to public)

Alldays	Early 1840s	Everyday 7am - 10pm; later 8am - 9pm.
Weekdays	1930s	8am to 7.30pm.
	1940/50s	8.30.am to 6.30pm.
	1957	Shops are now closing earlier and only one or two customers in the Post Office between 6-6.30pm, so will be closing at 6pm.
	1987	Open 9am (Friday Staff Training 9.30) to 5.30 pm. Sat. 9.00 to 1.00 pm.
Sundays		At first open all Sunday; c1849 Morning and evening only; c1907 mornings only. 1958 Counter still open on Sundays 9-10.30am, 1959/60 Sunday counter opening ceased.

Postmaster Salary *(with 1987 value in brackets)*

1660 nil; 1678 £12 per annum (£565); 1717 £45 + £40 (2000 + 1800); 1728 £45 (2150); 1797 £16 + 4 (440); 1805 £28 (530); 1810 £50 (850); 1909 £370 (11,100); 1915 £390 (9,250); 1919 £390 (5,070); 1929 £455 (7,735); 1933 £480 (9,600); 1937 £641 (12,179); 1939 £650 (11,700) Head Postmaster class VII.

A salary of over £350 in 1911, for example, put the Sevenoaks Postmaster in the category of **Larger Postmasters** with the additional powers that gave.

Establishment
1897, 1899 Establishment, see p.258
1939 Class II B

Indoor	*Male* 1 Assistant Super.; 2 Overseers; 21 Sorting Clerks and Telegraphists.
	Female 3 Sorting Clerks and Telegraphists; 1S/H Typist; 2 Telephone Asst. Supers.; 21 Telephonists
Outdoor	1 Inspector; 1 Asst. Inspector; 1 Head Postman; 58 Postmen *(112 in all)*

TSO/Rural 18 Telephonists; 17 Postmen *(35 in all)*

Sevenoaks Postmen

1841	William Nall (40) Postman	**1871**	Edward Hever (60) Postman
	William Bennett (60) Postman		Richard Langridge (21) Postman
1851	William Bennett (now 70) Postman		Albert Bennett, Postman
	Jonathan Lee (64) Postman		John Albany (40) at St John Hill
	Thomas Longhurst (53) Postman	**1881**	William Bonner (17) Postman
	John Smeed (21) Postman		Frederick Law (17) Postman
	Chas Stamford (45) PO Keeper at St Johns Hill		Henry Reynolds, Letter Carrier
1861	George Heare (39) Letter Carrier		William T Reynolds (67) Letter Carrier
	Thomas Clout (57) Post Messenger	**1890** *to*	H Sawyer, Town Postman
	Wm Thompson (54) PO Messenger	**1910**	Gibson, Town Postman
	Charles Stamford (55) at St Johns Hill		*(In 1910 Mr Sawyer had 5 Good Conduct Stripes)*

Auxiliary Town Postmen (1889-1895)

Herbert Standen	age 16½	15/- week	Nov 1889-1897 Promoted
Charles Reynolds	age 16	15/- week	1892-1895 Appointed Rural Postman
Thomas Read	age 20	15/- week	June 1893-1897 App RP Cudham
George Goodhew	age 27	15/- week	June 1893-1898 Promoted RP
L Boorman	-	13/- week	1893-1895 Resigned
Wm Bartholomew	age 18	15/- week	June 1893
Wm Reynolds	age 17	14/- week	March 1894- Promoted RP
Thomas Walter Allen	age 17	13/- week	Nov 1893-1897 Promoted RP
Alfred Edward Allen	age 17	13/- week	March 1895-1897 Promoted RP
Charles Heath	-	14/- week	March 1895- Left
Ferguson Alexander	age 17	14/- week	Nov 1895-1897 Promoted RP

Assistant Town Postman 1
20 June 1898

Postman's Sunday Relief
For *Town Postmen* 7 Jan 1900

H Sawyer)   one week one, one week the other (ie work
Gibson   )   alternate Sundays)

For *Rural Postmen* working from Sevenoaks 1900

Sevenoaks to	Cudham, mounted.	Crittenden 6/-
	Plaxtol	W Sawyer 3/-
	Weald	H Read 2/-
	Underriver	G Read 2/6
	Shoreham	W Ring 2/6
	Godden Green	H Gunner 2/-

Deliveries

1891. Three weekday Town deliveries 7am, 11am, 6pm. Sunday one delivery 7am.
In 1901 there were four Town deliveries daily (7am, 10.30am, 4pm and 7.30pm), gradually reduced to two.
In 1958 the second Town delivery on Saturday ceased.

Delivery Routes

Sevenoaks to Hernwood Sept 1895
Sevenoaks to Shenden Sept 1895
Sevenoaks to Whitley Mill 1904 Cecil Brown R Aux
Gradually the delivery routes based on Sevenoaks Main office increased and detail is shown under each village.

Postage Rates: Sevenoaks to London

Single Letter 24 miles

Date		Rate	Reason
1635-	1660	2d	Under 80 miles
1660-	May 31 1711	2d	Under 80 miles
June 1 1711-	Oct 9 1765	3d*	Under 80 miles
Oct 10 1765-	Aug 30 1784	2d	Two Post Stages
Aug 31 1784-	Jan 4 1797	3d	Two Post Stages
Jan 5 1797-	Apr 4 1801	4d	15-30 Miles
Apr 5 1801-	Mar 11 1805	4d	15-30 Miles
Mar 12 1805-	1812	5d	15-30 Miles
1812-	Dec 4 1839	6d	20-30 Miles **
Dec 5 1839-	Jan 9 1840	4d	Universal Inland Rate
Jan 10 1840-		1d	Universal Inland Rate

* At the same time some archival and other letters to London from Sevenoaks that have been seen appear to bear a 2d charge, though it must be said that charge mark numerals took on a shape of their own, 2, 3 and 7 often appearing identically shaped. This did not matter too much as, at any time, everyone 'knew the rate' and what the squiggle represented. It is only historians that are troubled with the interpretation.

** In 1838 charged by distance along nearest public road, not distance by route actually taken; no change Sevenoaks to London.

Inflation effect on rate to London

Charges calculated at **June 1987** prices using RPI multipliers at end of Appendix.

Mileage rate for 24 miles

1635 2d x 49 =	98d =	41p
1660 2d x 42½ =	85d =	35½p
1711 3d x 42½ =	127½d=	53p
1765 2d x 38 =	76d =	31½p
1784 2d x 33 =	66d =	27½p
1797 3d x 23 =	69d =	29p
1801 4d x 16 =	64d =	26½p
1805 5d x 18½=	92½d =	38½p
1812 6d x 15½ =	93d =	39p
1839 6d x 22 =	132d =	55p

Universal rate for all inland distances

1840 4d x 21 =	84d =	35p
1840 1d x 21 =	21d =	9p
1920 2d x 13 =	26d =	11p
1930 1½d x 17 =	25½d =	10½p
1950 2½d x 12½ =	31½d=	13p
1960 3d x 8 =	24d =	10p
1970 5d x 5½ =	27½d =	11½p
1980 12p x 1½ =	=	18p
1987 18p x 1 =	=	18p

Sevenoaks Town Postmarks

Early Town Marks

1	1761-1763	Two line Seven/Oaks 28x14mm
2	1775	Two line Seven/Oakes 35x16
3	1778-1781	Two line Seven/Oaks 34x16
4	1786	Two line 24 Seven/Oaks 34x13
5	1788-1790	Two line Seven/Oaks 32x13
6	1792-1793	One line Sevenoaks 52x4
7	1793-1797	Curved arc Sevenoaks 47x4 and 54x4
8	1799-1801	Curved arc Seven-oaks 43x3½
9	1804-1828	Two line Seven-oaks/24 boxed 42x11
10	1829-1836	One line Seven-oaks (mileage removed)
11	1814-1829	Penny Post Mark. Unboxed two line Seven Oaks/Py Post
12	1837	Penny Post Mark. Boxed two line Seven Oaks/Py Post
13	1837-1844	Large dated Broken Circle Seriffed Sevenoaks

Universal Penny Post Marks

-	1840	Single Stroke 1x60mm
14	1840	Fancy 'P1'
15	1849-1850	'Paid P1' in circle
16	1840	'7 Oaks' in oval
17	1840-1844	Maltese Cross Obliterator

Date Cancellers

20	1849-1857	Medium dated broken circle. Seven-oaks sans- seriffed
21	1853-1857	Medium dated broken circle. Seven.oaks sans-seriffed
22	1857-1858	Small dated broken circle. Sans-seriffed

Obliterators (Killers)

23	1844-1862	3 bar Horizontal Oval Single. 697
-	1883	5 bar Dumb Vertical oval single. Cork for parcels
23a	1921-1932	2 bar Vertical oval single 697. For Newspapers

Duplex 697

24	1862-1868	3 bar Circular Seven.oaks
25	1864-1869	4 bar Circular Seven.oaks
26	1870-1876	4 bar Vertical Seven.oaks
27	1874-1887	4 bar Vertical Sevenoaks
28	1880-1893	3 bar Vertical Sevenoaks
29	1894-1895	3 bar Vertical Sevenoaks Time in asterisk code
30	1896	3 bar Vertical Sevenoaks in small letters. Time in clear

Square Circle

31	1881-1885	4 split arcs 22mm ring

Double Circle

32	1899-1910	Thick Arcs Cross Pattee at Bottom 24-27mm rings
33	1910-1929	Thick Arcs Figures 1 or 2 at Bottom 25-27mm rings
34	1926-1927	Thick Arcs V Large Letters. Kent at Bottom

(The more modern handstamps, not listed, have thin arcs at each side.)

Machine Postmarks

35	1928-1932	Krag. 5 wavy lines
36	1932-1936	Universal. Continuous 5 wavy lines
37	1937-1984	Universal. Broken 7 wavy lines

Single Circles (mainly used as receivers)

38	1858-1863	Seven.oaks 19-20mm
39	1858-1869	Seven oaks 20-21mm
40	1870-1876	Seven-oaks 21-23mm
41	1874-1893	Sevenoaks 19-22mm
42	1901-1903	Sevenoaks/MO & SB 21-22mm

Skeletons - loose type

45	1906, 07, 26	Sevenoaks

Rubber Packet/parcel stamps

50	1886	Seven Oaks Oval with horizontal bars
51	1887	Sevenoaks Oval with horizontal bars
52	1889	Sevenoaks Circle with bar above and below
53	1889-1891	Target. Sevenoaks seriffed
54	1892-1904	Target. Sevenoaks sans-seriffed
55	1917	Vertical Bars. Sevenoaks sans-seriffed
56	1930-1982	Modern Rubber Packet Stamps
57	1984	Modern Rubber Packet Stamp with Postcode

Parcel Rectangular Handstamps

60	1912	Parcel Post/Sevenoaks (SV)/date
61	1922	Parcel (SV) Post/Sevenoaks/date
61a	1935	Sevenoaks/Kent/date
62	1940	"Roller" Sevenoaks/Kent/Parcel Post/date
63	1984	Paid in Cash - red
64	1883-1920	Parcel Post Labels with Office name

Instructional

70	1878 on	Many explanatory marks, mostly boxed and with 697

    eg,   More to pay

          Not to be found

          Gone no address

Commemorative

80	1927	Agricultural Show
81	1966	Boy Scout Rally

Station

90	1892	Station Ovals -

          Tubs Hill

          Bat and Ball

    Station Telegraph Nos in circle 1221, 1222, 1223

Registered

95	1893-1984	Sevenoaks (Kent) registered ovals

SEVEN OAKS   1761–63   28 x 14 mm   1

SEVEN OAKES   1775   35 x 16 mm   2

SEVEN OAKS   1778–80   34 x 16 mm   3

24 SEVEN OAKS   1786   34 x 13 mm   4

SEVEN OAKS   1788–90   32 x 13 mm   5

SEVENOAKS   1792   52 x 4 mm   6

SEVENOAKS   1796/97   7

SEVEN-OAKS   1801   8

SEVEN-OAKS 24   1804–10   9

SEVEN-OAKS   1832–35   10

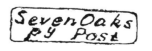

13

SEVENOAKES Penny Post   1829   11

SevenOaks By Post   1837   12

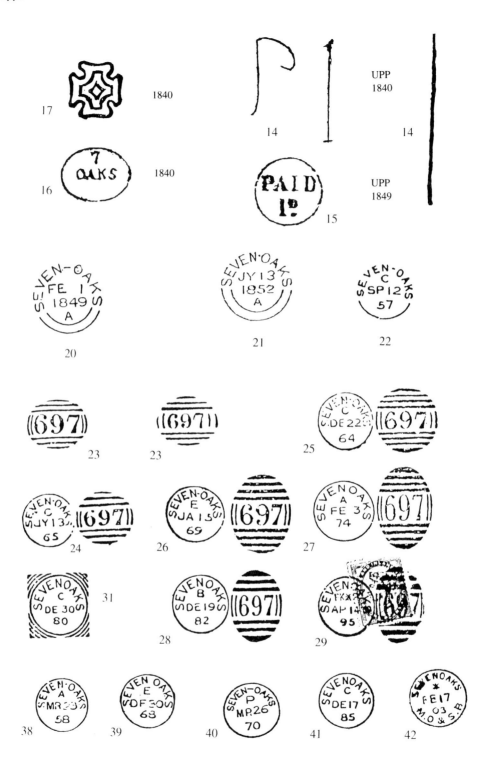

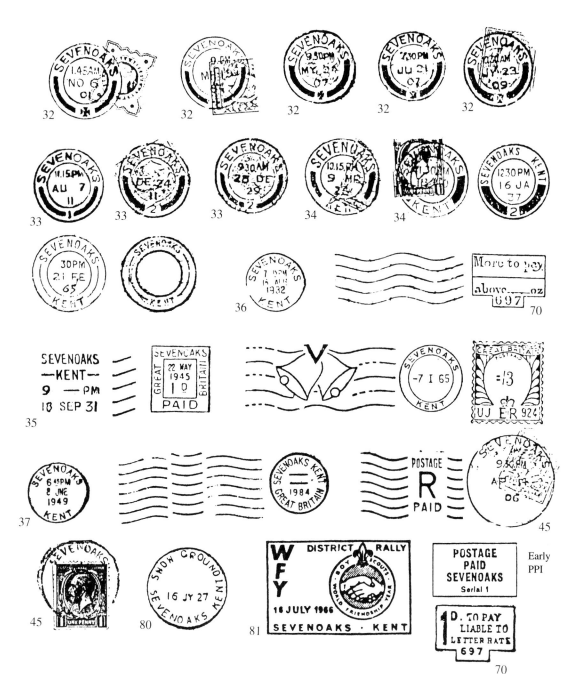

32   32   32   32   32

33   33   33   34   34

36   70

35

37   45

45   80   81

Early PPI

70

Town and Village Sub-Office Details

Receivers/Sub-Deputies/Sub-Postmasters and Sub-Postmistresses

Where a full date is given this has been taken from Post Office Records (Post 58) which can be considered a primary source. The remainder come from secondary sources such as directories, and may contain errors, but wherever possible dates have been crossed checked to a second source.

Sub-Postmasters and Sub-Postmistresses are contractors of services to the Post Office, not direct employees. In early days their records of engagement were at times kept in different sets of books to those of the deputy postmasters. A full run of the relevant books has not survived.

It must also be remembered that the person who is the sub-postmaster of a village office is not necessarily the person seen behind the counter. A note of some postmaster's occupations, nurseryman, schoolmaster, wheelwright is enough to show that the postmaster would be unable to attend to postal business all the time the office was open. So often it might be a spouse, a relative or an employee, full or part-time, who handled the counterwork.

Locations of Village Offices

The Post Office did not keep a record of the actual physical location of an office within a village. No doubt there was discussion with the local Surveyor as to the suitability of the location, but such records, if any, have not come down to us. Locations, where mentioned, have been taken from the series of 25" and 10" maps held in Sevenoaks Library and are for certain years only: 1867/9, 1896/8; 1909 also 1936 (1").

Populations of Villages Population figures are taken from many sources, Guide Books, Victoria County History, Cary, Pigot, Kelly or from 1841 the Census itself.

Note that the boundaries of areas tend to change as time goes on such that the figures may not be strictly comparable as relating to the same ground area. Nevertheless the figures are useful as they give an indication of size of growth and when the greatest growth of an area took place.

Some villages are even now only double the population they were in 1801; others may be ten times greater. The overall increase from 1801 to 1981 for the whole postal district, including towns, appears to be about fifteen times.

A Note on National Directories

Those available covering the area are:

Baileys British Directory 1784
Universal British Directory 1793, 1795, 1799 (No Sevenoaks data)
Holden's Annual London and County Directory 1811 (No Sevenoaks data)
James Pigot 1823/4, 1826/7/9, 1832/4, 1839/40
Kelly's Post Office Directory for the Six Home Counties
1845, 1851, 1855, 1862, 1866, 1870, 1874, 1878
Kelly's Directory of Kent, Surrey, Sussex
1882, 1887, 1891, 1895, 1899, 1903, 1905, 1907, 1909, 1911, 1913, 1915, 1918, 1922, 1924, 1927, 1930, 1934, 1938

The work of updating was too detailed to be attempted each year in full. In the intervening years a directory might be bound up in a different way and sold with a fresh date on the cover. It might contain minor revisions. If there have been changes, a directory, almost by definition, will be a year behind its issue date, possibly more. For an example see the Hever entry in the Post Office Directory 1850; the timings changed mid-1848 when Hever came under Edenbridge, the new Post Town, so the entry is 18 months out of date when issued.

A Note on the 'Post Office' Directories

The 'New Annual Directory' (First edition 1800) was compiled by two Post Office officials, Ferguson and Sparke, both inspectors of inland letter carriers, later joined by Critchett. In 1836 the Chief Inspector of inland letter carriers, Frederick Kelly, bought the patent from Critchett who by then appeared to be sold owner. Kelly greatly expanded the work using letter carriers, paid by commission on sales for the London edition and publishing it as a 'Post Office Directory of . . .'. This caused Pigot to adandon coverage of London and the Home Counties and to concentrate on provincial directories* of the North and West. It also incurred the wrath and opposition of one Jonathan Duncan (Proprietor of the 'Sentinel' newspaper) whose petition to Parliament was printed as a supplement to the votes and proceedings on 10th March 1846. In this petition Duncan claimed that the 1845 edition had nearly 16,000 errors and omissions and that it had only been carried through by causing grave injustice to the letter carriers who had been forced to work on it to the detriment of their own duties, and that some delays to mail resulted. In 1847 Kelly was prohibited from using Post Office accommodation, materials and staff in the compilation of his directory, which was a private venture. He continued to increase the staff he himself employed and the venture soon became firmly established.

* Jane E Norton. Reliability and Discrepancies in Directories. p16 of *Guide to National and Provincial Directories of England and Wales.* Royal Historical Society. 1950/1984.

General Notes Applying to Town and Village Receiving Houses and Sub-Offices

Long before there were officially recognised post offices outside the main route, there were places where letters could be left or accepted, sorted or passed on. Prior to 1800 such places were mostly Public Houses. The financial arrangements were private.

History: The person in charge of a Post Town Office was termed a 'Deputy' (Postmaster); a 'Sub-Deputy' being in charge of a Sub-Post Town Office, these were the smaller offices such as Sandhurst and Newenden on the Rye road, where the cost of a fully-fledged Post Town was not considered to be justified by the amount of business handled. There were no Sub-Post Towns in the Sevenoaks District. After 1803 with the development of 5th Clause and Penny Posts many small Receiving House Offices were set up in charge of a 'Receiver'. From the 1860's on many Post Towns developed into Head Post Offices with the officer in charge termed 'the Postmaster' and later from 1927 'the Head Postmaster'. This nomenclature became redundant in 1986. Those Post Towns that did not so convert, often because they were not strategically placed in relation to the new railway distribution network, together with the Sub-Post Towns and Receiving Offices developed into Sub-offices. These smaller offices increased in number greatly from 1860's on.

The Post Office has designated its offices in many ways, and continues so to do. By **Operational Function:** Railway Sub Office (1856-1905), Bag Receiving Office, Railway Station Telegraph Office, Postal Order Post Office, Money Order Office and Savings Bank, Telegraph Office, District Offices functioning as Postmens Sorting Offices. Not all these have counters available to the public. By **Location:** Town Receiving Offices, Town Sub-Offices from 1892 (ie near to the Head Office) as opposed to Sub-offices (ie rural). By **Type of building** and its maintenance: Crown Offices Class I and II which would both be with salaried staff. By **Administrative status:** Head Post Office, Branch Office (counter), Independent Sub-Office, Salaried Sub-Office (SSO). All with salaried staff. By **method of Financing** and payment of staff: Salaried staff (SSO) as before. Sub-Postmaster and staff employed by him/her. Scale Payment Sub-Office (SPSO), Credit Stock Offices (Community Post Offices). Perhaps the greatest division is between the Crown Office with its salaried staff, Crown employees to 1969 as minor civil servants, now Post Office employed, and the Contracted Sub-Postmasters Office in premises supplied by the Sub-Postmaster remunerated since the 1930's on a scale payment at so much per transaction with a basic minimum. Postmasters of Non-Crown Offices are officially appointed contractors to the Post Office for the supply of certain services to be performed in a particular way. The relationship has similarities with the present day franchise operation. All employees of Sub-Postmasters still subscribe the declaration, as do Crown employees.

The 1987 agreement with the National Federation of Sub-Postmasters made it possible to operate on a basis other than the Scale Payment, leading to a greater range of contracted offices. The smaller office (under 50,000 transaction units, £4,500pa) now being able to operate part-time, often two half-days a week (eg Cudham), as a Community Office and so remain open. At the other end the smaller Crown Offices can be taken over as a contracted Agency Office with the Crown office counter premises vacated and staff employed elsewhere having often been given the opportunity to contract the agency themselves. New Romney started to operate thus in mid-1989; Westerham and Tenterden are under disucssion.

1856   Postmaster cannot be the owner of a Public House or Inn, cannot hold a Newspaper agency or deliver any Newspapers not posted unless doing so prior to August 1846. This Newspaper regulation was

	rescinded 25.8.60. May not deliver items, circulars, letters not regularly posted. Salary paid quarterly.
1860	17th March. The practice of stamping letters is abolished at all sub-post offices at which undated stamps only have hitherto been used. 'The stamps'* were withdrawn and had to be returned, and were not reissued for up to 25 years according to work carried out; after 1861 for Savings Bank work, 1870 for Telegraph work and 1885 for Postal Orders. Even then instructions at first said such new dated stamps were not to be used for postal purposes. The offices at which such ruling applied were the smaller ones doing less than £1,000 of business a year. (* Stamp = handstamp, the village postmark.)
1869	No need for the office to open to the public on Sundays, but the Postmaster may, probably would, have letter delivery duties to organise. (Up to 1921.)
1869	Telegraph. The Railways had quickly installed the telegraph as an aid to running their own services safely and to time. In 1869 the various private telegraph companies were nationalised and came under the Post Office. Where there was already a telegraph office that could be made available to the public open at a local station, the PO was slow to transfer the facilities to the PO premises within that village.
1882/3	(Married Woman's Property Act 1870 & Amendments 1874 etc.) A married woman can hold the office of sub-postmistress but should inform the Surveyor if about to be married. (That is, if in post as a spinster and wishing to continue in post after marriage.)
1883	All offices handle Parcels business.
1884	No person under 14 years of age to be employed except in rural districts and for Telegraph business.
1884	After 3.6.84 all offices doing Savings Bank work did 'Government Annuity and Insurance' business.
1884	Insurance Policies allowed as Bonds in lieu of Guarantors. By 1900 the Standard amount was £200 (£6,600). Sevenoaks was £600 (£19,800), Westerham £300, small offices, Brasted Chart, Chevening, Toys Hill, Westerham Hill, Stansted, Hodsall St were only £20 or £30 (£990).
1884	For those offices that had started again to stamp letters: Abolition of stamping of Inwards letters (Receiving Stamps) in HO bags at Sub-Offices. TPO Direct bags still stamped.
1887	From January 1887 Town Postmen and Sorters had a fortnights Annual Leave. Rural Postmen 1 wk.
c1890	Village Sub-Postmasters salaries ranged from £7 to £35 per annum. Sub-Postmasters were given an allowance of a few shillings a week for making deliveries to houses in their area. With this they might make the delivery themselves or engage labour. If the work expanded they woud be allocated an auxiliary postman. Then, if more work, one or two Rural Postmen. Similar allowances were given for Telegraph work and Letter box Collection. Very small offices were not concerned with delivery.
c1880 -1910	Sub-offices that received the major portion of their mail from Travelling Post Offices (TPOs) were called **Railway sub-offices**. There were none such in this area.
	SO The Post Office Guide states that a Sub-Office (SO) is an office which receives part of its correspondance from some other office than its own Head Office. This refers to Independent Sub Offices. Such local offices were Wrotham, Brasted, Westerham. They added 'SO. Kent' to their address instead of 'Sevenoaks'. From 1905 as the Crown Offices came into being, all other village offices appeared to pick up the appellation 'sub-office', meaning **dependent** sub-office.
	TSO means Town Sub-Office (not Telegraph Sub-Office).
c1910	**Licenced Stamp Sellers** No commission is paid, and a bond is required. A licenced vendor is required to exhibit an enamelled plate, sent to him when his application is approved. There is no rule as to the size of stock held, but he is required to supply each applicant with a 'reasonable' number of stamps. Surveyors and Independent Postmasters deal with applications. Premises must be not less than 150 yards from Post Office unless it stays open longer, and not normally a place where intoxicating liquour is sold for consumption on the premises. A licence not necessary for sale of stamps at Hotels, Clubs and Boarding Houses or at bazaars etc open only for a few days. A licence is also needed for the sale of stamps through automatic machines other than at a post office.
1984	All village offices shut for lunch, normally 1-2pm. Most have two afternoons a week off, Saturday andthe local early closing day, so achieving a 5-day week. Offices are normally open on Saturday mornings.
1987/89	**New Style Agency Counter Office**s, taking over in many places often instead of Crown Office. First one at New Romney in April 1989. Open longer hours, 9-5.30 pm Six days/week and remain open at lunchtime. Operated on a contracted basis and provided a full range of services, in agency premises not the Crown Office.Small offices, now termed '*Community Offices*' open part-time, often two halfdays per week. Newsagents and many shops approved to sell postage stamps.

Village and Small Town Postmarks

A synopsis of postmarks recorded is shown with each office. This note explains the abbreviations used. Actual examples are shown after the list of offices. Items recorded in the proof books but not otherwise recorded are shown in parentheses.

The Proof Books cover some years only, many years are missing and destroyed. For Steel datestamps from 1825 about two-thirds only are available, 106 years available and 51 years missing. For Rubber stamps less than half are available, 45 years. The balance, from 1932, are not now being recorded; though some rubber stamps from 1970's on have been recorded.

Steel	**Available**	**Lost**
	1825-1887	1888-1905
	1906-1920	1921-1955
	1956-1982 & on	
Rubber	**Available**	**Not Recorded**
	1885-1931	Pre-1885
	Some 1970s on	1932-1970s

Some, but by no means all, of the proof books are indexed. At most the indexes are 95% accurate, so a full search is still needed.

For periods not covered by the proof books the only answer is personal search and the recordings of others.

Sub-Office Postmarks, Standard Types (Simplified)

1 Penny Post Numbers Most Receiving Houses had before 1839 an identifying number which was impressed on the letter. The 'Sevenoaks Penny Post' stamp was then put on when the letter got to Sevenoaks. These identifying numbers were used well after the penny posts ceased, right up to 1845 or so when the UBC Is were issued. Halstead and Ightham were in 1839 issued not with a number but with a full village identification.

2 UBC I Undated Broken Circle Type I Name in Seriffed letters.

3a UBC II Undated Broken Circle Type II Name in Sans-seriffed letters.

3b DBC II Dated Broken Circle, only in type II for villages. Larger towns were given dated stamps from 1837 when there is a DBC I for Sevenoaks.

4a & 4b ESC Early Single Circle. Mostly these were undated (4a) and had the village name in a straight line within the cicle. As they were mostly issued in 1858, they only lasted a few years before being withdrawn in 1860 and so are most difficult to find. Dated (4b).

5 No Stamp Period Small villages with less than £1,000 of business a year, £20 a week, were issued with undated stamps. Here this means all offices other than the Post Towns Sevenoaks and Edenbridge, and the two others Westerham and Wrotham. On 24th March 1860 there was an instruction to those offices with undated stamps not only withdrawing the stamp but asking for it to be returned. This left the office without any stamp and accounts for the occasional pen and ink cancellation on a local letter, or the use of the bag seal; as also even as late as 1883 pen and ink cancellations on Parcel Post labels. Officially letters went unstamped to the Post Town for cancellation there.

Gradually handstamps returned as offices from 1869 on became Money Order Offices or, if not that, Telegraph Offices or sold Postal Orders. Even though they might then have a stamp, the office was not necessarily authorised to use it for postal purposes. But gradually the practice of striking the village stamp at least beside the adhesive stamp if not cancelling it, became normal practice. All handstamps are now dated.

6/7 Single Ring Used throughout the period, mainly at first as a receiving stamp but later as the standard village steel datestamp. Locally there were issues of the 1870s (6) and 1880s (7).

8 Climax A cheaper form of rubber stamp with a moveable date, which was issued to thousands of the smaller offices.

9aKiller or obliterator. A barred numerical horizontal oval used to obliterate the stamp on the obverse. The datestamp was additionally applied to the back of the letter in a second operation. (Vertical barred ovals were later used mainly to cancel adhesive stamps on Newspapers.) Only Westerham and Edenbridge had these.

9b Duplex A double stamp, the datestamp and numerical obliterator together so that the adhesive stamp could be cancelled and the datestamp applied all in one operation.

10 Square Circle A circular stamp squared out at the corners. These corners were subject to wear and the design was subsequently dropped.

11 Single Ring Large/medium letters Unproofed 1895 series.

12 Single Ring Medium/small letters Unproofed 1910 series.

13 Single Ring Town at bottom (Sevenoaks, Westerham or Wrotham).
Double Ring - Thick Arcs. A standard design used throughout the world. At the bottom there might be a Cross Pattee (often misdescribed as a maltese cross), Sevenoaks, '1' or '2', Kent, Sevenoaks Kent or Westerham Kent or Edenbridge Kent.

14 Double Ring Thick Arcs. Cross Pattee, Kent, or Sevenoaks at bottom.

15 Double Ring Thick Arcs. 'Sevenoaks Kent' or 'Westerham' at bottom.

16 Double Ring Thin Arcs. 'Sevenoaks Kent' or 'Westerham Kent' at bottom.

17 Single Ring Counter 1960s - 1980s.

18 Single Ring Modern lettering (some very small, 1½ mm high).

19 Skeleton or Travelling stamp. Provided with loose type so that the office name can be made up on the spot. For temporary use when a stamp is lost or one is sent for repair.

20 Parcel Rectangles and (21) other **packet rubbers.**

22 Station Ovals

23 Commemorative

24 Instructional

25 Bag Seals (old type).

26 RAF - Postal Services and Despatch Rider Letter Service (DRLS).

27 Licenced Services - Christmas etc.

28 Temporary P.O.s (Biggin Hill Air Events).

30 Machine Marks Krag (30) and Universal (31) are two of the best known makes. The Krag machine was developed in Norway and sold by Krag Kaskin Fabrikk AS of Oslo. It is a continuous dater and canceller hence quieter in operation. Trials were in 1907 and machines bought in 1912. It has two dies, one of which is differnetiated by a '+' at the bottom, which give an unframed 4 or 5 line impression that looks square.

The Universal is sold by the Universal Stamping Machine Co of New York. It is a single impression dater and canceller, first purchased in 1912. The die gives a circular impression. As well as Sevenoaks, only Westerham and Edenbridge had machine marks.

Double Stamping As gradually village stamps were brought back into use, the larger villages such as Seal were cancelling the adhesive stamps on their letters by 1890 but others were placing the mark beside the adhesive stamp and the post town still cancelled the stamp. By April 1904 all offices were to sell Postal Orders and were provided with a stamp which could also be struck beside the adhesive stamp if they made up an outward despatch of mail. By 1905 the small office could cancel the adhesive stamp and the main office struck theirs beside. By 1906 the village office of whatever size could cancel the stamp and the main office stamp was not required. The three post towns Sevenoaks, Westerham and Edenbridge followed through this pattern, but at somewhat varying dates.

Right through to the 1960s letters and cards are to be found with the stamp cancelled by the village stamp. By the 1970s all are taken into Sevenoaks for machine cancellation and by mid 1980s they now go to the mechanized letter office and receive the Tonbridge postmark.

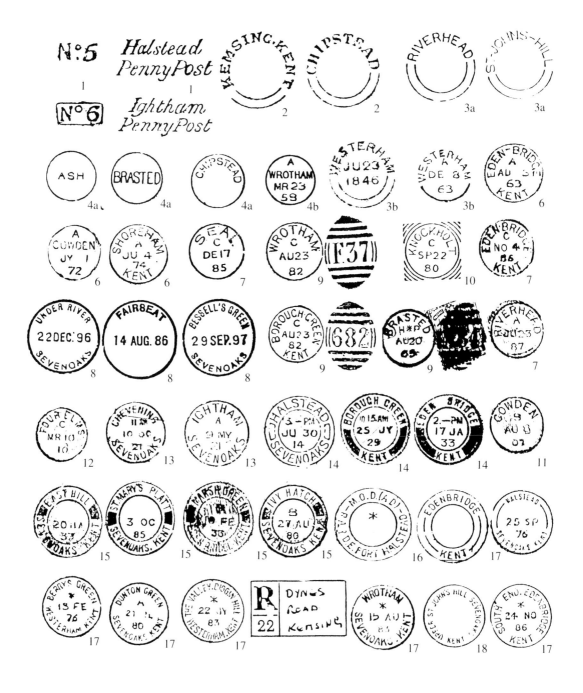

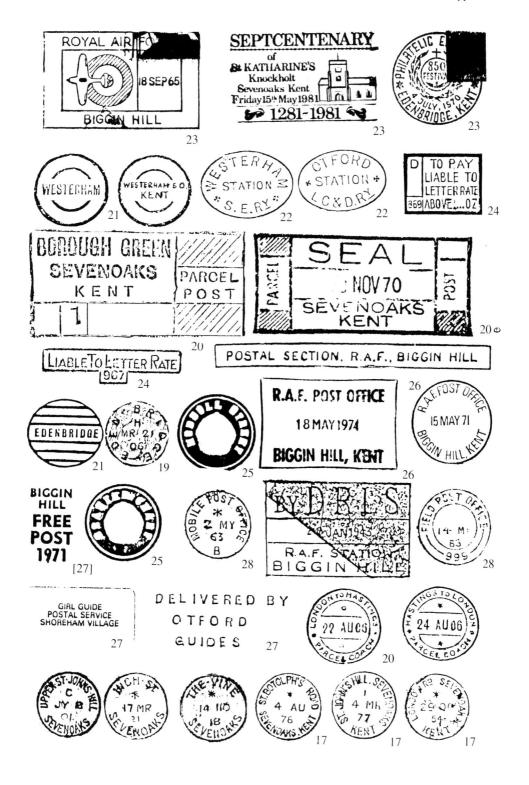

ROYAL AIR FO
18 SEP 65
BIGGIN HILL
23

SEPTCENTENARY
of
St KATHARINE'S
Knockholt
Sevenoaks Kent
Friday 15th May 1981
1281-1981
23

PHILATELIC E
850 FESTIVA
4 JULY, 1970
EDENBRIDGE, KENT
23

WESTERHAM
21

WESTERHAM & O.
KENT
21

WESTERHAM
STATION
S. E. RY.
22

OTFORD
STATION
L.C.& D.RY.
22

D TO PAY
LIABLE TO
LETTER RATE
369 ABOVE...OZ
24

BOROUGH GREEN
SEVENOAKS
KENT
1
PARCEL
POST
20

SEAL
NOV 70
SEVENOAKS
KENT
PARCEL   POST
20

LIABLE TO LETTER RATE
967
24

POSTAL SECTION, R.A.F., BIGGIN HILL

EDENBRIDGE
21

BR
H
MR 21
90
19

R.A.F. POST OFFICE
18 MAY 1974
BIGGIN HILL, KENT
26

R.A.F. POST OFFICE
15 MAY 71
BIGGIN HILL, KENT
26

BIGGIN
HILL
FREE
POST
1971
[27]

25

MOBILE POST OFFICE
2 MY
63
B
28

KYDRLS
4 JAN 43
R.A.F. STATION
BIGGIN HILL
26

FIELD POST OFFICE
14 M
63
999
28

GIRL GUIDE
POSTAL SERVICE
SHOREHAM VILLAGE
27

DELIVERED BY
OTFORD
GUIDES
27

LONDON TO HASTINGS
22 AUG
PARCEL COACH
20

HASTINGS TO LONDON
24 AU 06
PARCEL COACH

UPPER ST JOHNS HILL
C
JY B
01
SEVENOAKS

HIGH ST
17 MR
21
SEVENOAKS

THE VINE
14 110
18
SEVENOAKS

ST BOTOLPH'S ROAD
4 AU
76
SEVENOAKS, KENT
17

ST JOHNS HILL, SEVEN
1
4 MR
77
KENT
17

LONDON RD, SEVENOAKS
29 O
54
KENT
17

Town Sub-Offices (TSOs)

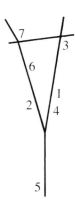

There have been seven permanent town offices, two of which are now shut.
1. Upper St Johns Hill (No 2) 1882- (Sevenoaks 1)
2. London Road (No 103) 1892-1977 (Sevenoaks 5)
3. St Johns Hill (No 120) 1846 open, within Town delivery 1866,
   Town Sub-Office 1893 June 27
4. The Vine (47 Dartford Road) 1897-1977 (Sevenoaks 3)
5. High St (No 13) 6.6.1898-
6. St Botolphs Road (No 3) 1904- (Sevenoaks 2)
7. Riverhead (listed under village offices) open 1808 Town Office 1955-
8. Special Occasion Post Offices (eg the 1927 Agricultural Show)
   (Sevenoaks 8, 9)

St Johns Hill Town Receiving Office later (1892) TSO

At the north end of Sevenoaks on the road to Otford a town area that had been developed from early times. With the arrival of a Branch Railway line in 1862 what is now known as Bat and Ball Railway station was placed more or less on top of the medieval St Johns Hospital. Further development came with the Railway and soon this became a Town Office.

Status
1846 Receiving House open
1866 Became within Town delivery
1872 March 1 Money Order Office and Savings Bank
By 1890 Telegraph Office (from July 1893 XVB)
1893 June 27 Became Town Office
1917 Telegraph closed 6 March, but reopened 24 April same year

Sub-Postmasters: Charles Stamford (-1851=1861-); William Thomas Reynolds (-1866=1867-); John Albany, grocer (-1871-); James Bradlaugh, corn dealer and stationer (23.3.1874=30.3.07); Gilbert Ellis, hair dresser (31.3.1907=1927); A L Groves (1928=1951).

History: 1862 Railway to St Johns open; 1863 Wallbox near to St Johns Station refused; 1863 Second daily delivery established St Johns Hill; 1867 Extension of Town delivery; 1879 Further extension of Town delivery. New Mail Truck and shelter. In 1869 the P.O. location was on the west side of St Johns Hill (Road) opp its present location.

Postmarks: UBC II (1846); ESC (1858); Probably no stamp 1860-1871; SR 1877-1901; SR 1937-1982. PP Rect 1982.

Upper St Johns Hill TRO later (1892) TSO

The present office is on the corner of St Johns Hill and Holly Bush Lane. In earlier times 1908 it was a few shops further north down St Johns Hill.

Status
1882 April Post Office open
1882 June 1 Money Order and Savings Bank
1890 Sept 23 Telegraph Office (SJH to June 1893, XVA after)

Sub-Postmasters: Miss Mary Ann Chalcroft (12.7.1889=1897); William Chalcroft, bookseller and stationer (1.10.1897=1924-); F Stroud (-1925=1926-); Mrs A Wooley, stationer (-1927=1938-); S J Huddle (-1939=1941-); H A Bowden (-1947=1957-).

Licenced Stamp Sellers: 1910 George William Orpin, Hartslands; 1917 T C Turk 9 St Johns Hill.

Postmarks: SRs (1882)-1979 (4 diff types). PP Rect 1981.

The Vine (3) TSO

Situated opposite the lower end of the Vine Cricket Club Grounds, at 147 Dartford Road. Now closed.

Status
1897 Office open. Town Sub-office (TSO)
1897 September 1st. Money Order Office and Savings Bank
1977 Closed

Sub-Postmasters: Mrs Charlotte Warren (1.6.1897=1899-); J Child (1899); James John Armsden (19.10.1899=25.3.02); James William Roberts (26.3.1902=3.3.09); George Alfred Wooldridge (4.3.1909=13.5.1909); John Harvey Logan Lorimer (14.5.1909=1930); William Cavell (1930=1957-).

Postmarks: Climax (1897); SRs 1895-1977.

13 High Street TSO

The only Town Office south of the main office in South Park, it is situated in the old part of the Town opposite Sevenoaks school. Opened as a Sub-Office on 6th June 1898 (PO Circular). It is not listed in Sevenoaks Almanacks prior to 1903 nor, strangely, in the PO Guide until mid-1901.

Early photographs show on the name board above the window the legend 'High Street Post Office'. After about 1956 photographs show a name change to 'The Old Post Office', but no-one can recall why and there are no written references. Peradventure it was thought to be the Town Main Post Office at some time.

For many years up to the 1970s this was the Sevenoaks School Tuckshop, 'Ma Browns', where boys wrote their names on the ceiling it was so low. Later the school opened its own canteen and so the High Street shop was not so well patronised.

Outside is one of the finest examples of a Victorian 'Ludlow' wall letterbox, well painted and well maintained.

Status
1898 June 6th Post Office Open. Town Sub-Office (TSO)
1901 Sept 2 Money Order Office and Savings Bank

Sub-Postmasters: John Jerome Wood (6.6.1898=17.6.02); John William Wood, confectioner (18.1.1902= 1937-); Mrs G Thornton (-1838=1954); Mr and Mrs Ridge (1954-56); Mrs J Brister (1956=60-).

Licenced Stamp Seller: 1910 Arthur Paine 30 High Street.

History: In 1986 there was concern about the continued viability of the shop and office as the new pedestrian crossing to Sevenoaks school cut down parking from 5/6 to 2/3. So far it remains open. The P.O. Counter has been moved to the right as one enters instead of opposite the door as it was for a long time.

Postmarks: Climax proofed 9.3.08, SRs 1902-1984 PP Rect 1940.

London Road TSO

The original London Road Office was situated well down Tubs Hill, past the Eardley Road corner and next to Camden Villas. After it had been open a few years building was started in St Botolph's Road and Mr Raven the postmaster found himself a premises there nearer to the station and moved in together with the Telegraph facilities.

An office remained in London Road but it was moved some way up the hill to the lower corner with Eardley Road.

Status
1892 Oct 1 open as Post Office only (MOSB business delayed)
1894 Jan 1 Money Order and Savings Bank (P.O. Circular 27.6.93)
1894 Aug 21. Telegraph Office (XVC) up to April 1904
1977 Closed

Sub-Postmasters: William Raven, confectioner (1.1.1894=1904); Harry Moore, stationer (2.4.1904=1941); V D Moore (-1947=1949-); W W Hosking (-1951=1957-).

Licenced Stamp Sellers: 1902 H Scarborough Tubbs Hill; 1922 Cyril Edwin Bertie Woods 87 London Road.

Postmarks: SRs (3 types) 1895-1977.

St Botolph's Road TSO

When building started in St Botolph's Road, Mr Raven saw the advantage of being nearer the station and left London Road to set up a Post Office with Telegraph work more or less where it is at present. He was a confectioner and his new business was styled 'W Raven and Sons'.
Elsewhere can be seen his advertisements for 'Teas in the Garden'.

Status
1904 Office open
1904 July. Telegraph Office (XVC)
1904 Money Order Office and Savings Bank
1990 April Temporary Closure

Sub-Postmasters: William Raven, confectioner (1.1.1904=1923-); Miss Jessie Marie Raven, confectioner (-1924=1938-); J C Harmston (1939=1949-); Miss A M Marchant (-1951=1957-). At present a grocers shop.

Postmarks: SRs (2 types) 1905-1977. PP Rect 1982.

Riverhead In village list.

Index to Village Offices

Sub-Offices may be found in three groups, in alphabetical order.   Offices in existance in 1840 are shown in CAPITALS.

West

Badgers Mount
Berry's Green
Bessels Green
Biggin Hill
Biggin Hill, Valley
Biggin Hill RAF PO
BRASTED
Brasted Chart
Chevening
CHIPSTEAD
Cudham
HALSTEAD
Ide Hill
Knockholt
RIVERHEAD
SUNDRIDGE
Tatsfield
Toys Hill, Brasted
Weald
*WESTERHAM
Westerham Hill

East

Ash
Borough Green
Dunton Green
East Hill
Fairseat
Godden Green
Hodsall Street
IGHTHAM
Ivy Hatch
KEMSING
Kemsing, Dynes Road
Kingsdown
     do   West, Hever Rd
Knatts Valley
OTFORD
Plaxtol
St Mary's Platt
SEAL
SHOREHAM
Stansted
Stone Street
Underriver
WROTHAM
Wrotham Heath

Edenbridge Group

Hever Road, Edenbridge TSO
Marlpit Hill, Edenbridge TSO
Marsh Green, Edenbridge TSO
South End, Edenbridge TSO
Bough (Bow) Beech
Chiddingstone
Chiddingstone Causeway
Chiddingstone Hoath
Cowden
Cowden Pound
Crockham Hill
*EDENBRIDGE
Four Elms
Hever
(Lingfield)
Mark Beech

*Subsequently became a Crown Office

Edenbridge Post Town (1848) covered Brasted, Ide Hill, Sundridge (all 1857-86), Westerham (1857-96).

S.O. Groupings:
Brasted S.O. (1886-1902) Brasted Chart, Sundridge, (?Ide Hill).
Westerham S.O. (1896-1927) Biggin Hill, Tatsfield, Westerham Hill.
Wrotham S.O. (28.4.1896-1922) Ash, Borough Green, Fairseat, Hodsall Street, St. Mary Platt, Stansted, Wrotham Heath.

Sub-Offices to East

Ash   Ashe (1845) Ash-next-Ridley (1922) Ashchurch

The northernmost point of the postal district. Closed in 1982, the newly built local post office is at New Ash Green (under Dartford) where a new village has been created a mile away.

Status
1845 Receiving House open
1889 Dec 2 Money Order and Savings Bank
1896 April 28 address 'Ash Wrotham S.O. Kent'
1897 October 19th Telegraph office (ASE)
1908 April 1st Telephone Exchange (3 subscribers)
1922 Address reverted to 'Sevenoaks Kent'
1980 Office closed

Sub-Postmasters: James Buggs, tailor (17.3.1845=1865); George Elcome, bricklayer (29.3.1865=1892); Mrs Amy Joyce (1.6.1892=19.7.05); Frank Fletcher (20.7.1905=1915-); Mrs Kate Jennor (-1918-); Mrs Hannah Whiffen, shop (-1922=1938-).

History: 1845 Letters 3 times a week (Sun/Wed/Fri); 1863 Improved arrangements *Wrotham to Ash* daily; 1894 Delivery Allowance converted to Rural Postman's wages; 1899 Allowance for Sunday Substitute; 1903 Ash daymail delivery established; 1906 *Wrotham to Horse & Groom* Sunday delivery established and allowance for substitute; 1908 *Ash to The Billett* delivery extended; 1908 Telephone Exchange opened with 3 subscribers including call office; 24.8.1910 Tel Exchange had 4 subscribers.

Postmen: Ash, 1894-6 G Pratt R Aux, 1897-98 Thomas Gilbert (age 16) R Aux, 1898 Edward Percy Pratt R Aux. *Wrotham to Ash* Frederick Higgins Law 1880 employed under allowance, 1883 Mail Driver, 1888 Daymail messenger, 1889 Acting R.P. 1890 R.P.; 1897 John Marchant; 1908 Alexander George Quaife; 1910 Frederick Griffin (previously a postman at Scarboro' and at Bedale N Yorks). *Ash to Fairseat* all by R Aux 1900 Edwin Pankhurst, 1901 Arthur Park, 1901 Benjamin Waters, 1903 Henry James Hoadley.

Postmarks: UBC II (1846); ESR (1858); No Stamp 1860-1891; SR 1904-29; DR Thick 1966-77.

Population: 1801 472, 1841 663, 1881 632, 1921 600, 1961 994, 1981* 5,583.
* Includes New Ash Green.

Borough Green   Boro' Green

On the cross route Westerham to Maidstone. Came into prominence with the opening of the station, Wrotham & Boro' Green, on the line to Maidstone. Boro' Green was where the station was, whereas Wrotham was two miles away. Basted Paper Mill finally in the ownership of Wiggins Teape Ltd lying one mile to the south on the River Bourne was closed in 1949 after some two hundred years working.

Status
1847 Receiving House open
1874 Railway Station opened
By 1881 Telegraph at Railway Station; closed to public 7.7.1885
1882 April 1st Money Order Office and Savings Bank
1885 July 7th Telegraph Office (BOR)
1896 Address 'Wrotham S.O. Kent'
1922 Now 'Sevenoaks Kent'
1977 Local delivery sorting ceased

Sub-Postmasters: James Semark, grocer (-1847=1852-); John Semark, shop (25.11.1852=1862-); George Henry Prior, stationer (18.5.1867=1882-); Jesse Callow, watchmaker (1.12.1884=1900-); Frank Callow, stationer (1900=1934-); Horace Callow, grocer (-1938-).

History: c1850 *Letter Carrier to St Mary Platt*; 1866 *Boro Green to Platt* extra walk; 1888 Boro Green delivery extended; 1889 *Boro Green to Great Comp* walk; 1892 *Boro Green to Great Comp* extended to Leybourne Wood; 1892 *Boro Green to house 'West Bank'* instead of Lodge; 1900 Boro Green evening delivery extended; 1909 *Boro Green to Claygate* cycle post.

Postmen: 1893 F Beavan Aux R.P.; 1893 F Callow Aux R.P., 1895 R.P. 1908 21/- week, later Postmaster; 1900 Borough Green to Crouch Joseph Albert Coles (age 15½). R. Aux; 1900 Jesse Callow the postmaster resigned Mar 1900 and became Aux Rural Postman. (PRO Post 58 and Kelly do not tally on dates), his brother Frank took over as PM.

Postmarks: UBC II (1847)-1859; No Stamp 1860-82; SR 1882; Duplex (1882)-1907; SR 1894-1905; DRs Thick 1909-53; DR Thin (1965); SRs 1971-83. Packet; Target (1911), Barred (1917). PP Rect (1931)-1983. Station Telegraph No 180.

Dunton Green Dunsten Green (1847)

Once the bridge was built in 1636 at Longford next the watermill which had been there since AD1200 or earlier, the hamlet of Dunton Green found itself on the main road to London. Administratively Dunton Green came under Otford until in 1908 it became a seperate civil parish and its Postal needs too came under Otford at first. A Turnpike gate here in 1800.

Prior to the village Post Office opening in 1889, Dunton Green had from 1873 one of the earliest wall letter boxes which is still in place opposite the 'Rose and Crown' at the north end of the village. It is near the 21st milestone, which also is still in place near Donnington. Along the footpaths and Telston Lane this box is only 1½ miles from Otford. The 'Green Line' bus garage in the now centre of the village opened by 1921 under the auspices of East Surrey Traction Co.

Brick and tile works 1862–1956. Claypits where now is West Kent Cold Storage. Limeburning at the Chalkpits by Polhill ceased in 1966. The name means 'Dunna's farmstead'.

Status

1862 Railway line passed through
1868 Railway Station open on Main Line
1873 Wall Letter Box, serviced from Otford
pre-1875 Telegraph at Railway Station; closed to public 5.11.1895
when post office telegraph opened
1881 Branch Railway line to Westerham open
1889 Post Office open
1893 January 2nd Money Order Office and Savings Bank
1895 November 5th Telegraph Office (DGN)
1915-8 Telegraph (despatch only) available at station all week and Sundays

Sub-Postmasters: Joseph Martin, grocer and draper (3.6.1889=1913-); Harold John Frayne, tailor and stationer (-1915=1924-); Ebenezer Barham, stationer (-1926=1930-); George A Bircham, shop (1931=1949); Mr & Mrs G Bircham, son (1949=Oct 1963).

Licenced stamp seller: 1909 Clay Bros Longford.

History: 1893 Dunton Green delivery established; 1895 Letterbox at Longford; 1900 *D.G. to Morants Court,* wages of Rural Postman in lieu of Rural Auxiliary Postman and allowance for delivery. Sunday substitute allowance; 1904 *D.G. to Rye House* extension; 1908 D.G. village made a cycle post with 2nd and 3rd deliveries *extended to Halstead and Knockholt.*

Some Locations of P.O.: 1908 East side of London Road on corner north of Duke's Head; 1960-80s same side further north.

Rural Postmen: 7.5.1893 E Martin; 15.12.1895 Thomas Ayres. *D.G. to Morants Court and Riverhead*: 1895 Walter Ashton R.P., 1899 Edwin Piper R.P., 1903 Fredk John Baddeley, 1904 Joseph Bashford R.P. 21/- week in 1908. Auxiliary Rural Postmen: 1893 E Martin, 1895-8 Thomas Ayres (Resigned and rejoined the Army), 1898 Walter Ashton. Village delivery: 1908 George Payne R. Aux, 1909 Robert Ball.

Postmarks: Climax (1891); SR 1897-1921; DR Thick 1928-76; Skeleton 1973; DR Thin (1974); SR 1981-85. SE Railway oval (1892); Telegraph No 463.

Population: Seperated from Otford at 1911 Census when D. G. 1,450; 1921 1,450; 1961 1,840; 1981 1,710.

East Hill/Knatts Valley

The office was originally at East Hill on top of the Downs two miles north east of Otford and so called. Later the office was moved half-a-mile down into Knatts Valley and the name was changed. However the office has now moved back, first to a house, now to the mobile home park at East Hill, but there has been no return to the original name.

Status
1931 July 8 East Hill. Post Office opened. Postal Orders sold
1934 Aug 8 East Hill office closed. Knatts Valley opened
By 1983 Limited opening, Tu and Th only

History: 1904 Two deliveries a week from Otford.

Postman: 1906 Leonard Richard Emery.

Postmarks: East Hill DR Thick 1933; Knatts Valley DR Thick 1937-85.

Fairseat   Faseyseat   Facy   Facey Street   Farsee Street
A Hamlet of Stansted.

Status
1871 Receiving House open
1886 Postal Orders sold
1896 April 28 Address 'Fairseat, Wrotham S.O. Kent'
1889 January 1st Money Order Office and Savings Bank
1905 June Telegraph Office (FAS) via Rochester
1922 Address now 'Stansted Sevenoaks'

Sub-Postmasters: Mrs Charlotte Smith (-1874-); Mrs Frances H S Jacques (12.2.1877=1882-); Edward (Edwin) Turbille (27.4.1883=1927-); Stella C Henden (-1945=1953-).

History: 1878 Wall Letter Box near Church; 1890 Day mail; 1897 Fairseat to Rose Farm delivery. 1985 on Culverstone & Vigo Boy Scout Christmas post delivered in village.

Postmen: 1904 F D Burgess R Aux; 1909 *Fairseat to Vigo*, Percy Hollands R Aux.

Postmarks: No Stamp 1871-86; Climax (1886); SRs 1896-1928; DR Thick 1936-86; PP Rect 1983.

Local To Fairseat

A village 1½ miles North East of Fairseat, **Culverstone**, postally under Gravesend, had local postal services run by the Boy Scouts which in theory covered the whole of the North East part of the Sevenoaks Postal District. In 1971 the Culverstone Strike Post issued 6d and 1/- stamps with a ten mile delivery service. There is also a Christmas Post in conjunction with Vigo village.

Godden Green
A largish village built round a large open village green, the sort of place where one would expect to find a post office but it is now closed.

Status
1873 Receiving House open
1892 Postal Orders issued, not paid
1896 March 2nd Money Order Office and Savings Bank
1934 Closed

Sub-Postmasters: Joseph Pomphret, farmer (-1874-); William Ransley (10.4.1875=1879); Mrs Sarah Ann Ransley (1879=1887-); Joseph Pomphret, farmer and shopkeeper (1.8.1888=30.9.03); Harry Kent, shop (1.10.1903=1938-).

History: 1845 Letters taken to Godden Green 3 times a week (Sun/Wed/Fri); By 1863 daily; 1874 Extn of delivery; 1877 Godden Green daymail established; 1894 Delivery allowance converted to Rural Post wages; 1898 *G.G. to Bowpits* rural delivery established 4 days/week; 1903 G.G. extra daymail to Hall Farm; 1905 G.G. Cycle post.

Postmen: 1892 *Sevenoaks to Godden Green* John Clayton R.P.; 1905 Thomas Smith R.P.

Postmarks: No Stamp 1871-1886; Climax (1892); SRs 1903-26.

Hodsall Street

A small village north of Fairseat. Name means Hod's hole or hollow.

Status
1890 Post Office open
1896 April 28 Address 'Hodsall Street Wrotham S.O. Kent'
1922 Under Sevenoaks
1973 April closed

Sub-Postmasters: Valentine Wellard (26.7.1890=4.2.97); John G Wellard, baker grocer and draper (10.4.1897=1902); John Algernon Slade (17.6.1902=1903); Frederick Augustus Foster* (30.4.1903=1904); Moses Diffey, grocer (30.2.1904=1906); Percy Stonham Cook grocer (7.5.1906=1908); Frederick Charles Cockett, grocer (21.3.1908=1.9.1909 Resigned); Clarence Leslie King 22.9.1909=1912-); Thomas H Burgess, grocer (-1913=1938-).
* Permission to sleep off the premises.

History: 1893 *Hodsall Street to The Haven* delivery established; 1908 *Hodsall St to The Hove* new delivery; 1910 *Wrotham to Hodsall* St walk.

Postman: Richard John Shepherd 1895 *Wrotham to Plaxdale Green*, 1910 *Wrotham to Hodsall Street*.

Postmarks: SR Sevenoaks 1900; SR Wrotham S.O. 1907-9; DR Thick: DR Thin 1978-82.

Ightham   Ightmam

On the main Westerham to Maidstone cross route, and near to Oldbury on Ightham Common, the pre-Roman campsite by Crown Point. Ightham is at the head of the old route south to Tonbridge along the river Bourne valley, later a Roman Trackway, which was used before the track through the wealden forest south of Sevenoaks was cut. In Armada days c1588, Ightham had a fire beacon in communication with Crowborough, Goudhurst and Birling.

Monuments to the Selby family in Ightham church include that to Dame Dorothy Selby to whom is ascribed the foiling of the Gunpowder plot to blow up Parliament. There is a famous herb garden here.

Name means Ehta's settlement.

Status:
1839 Receiving House. Sevenoaks Penny Post.
1877 February 1st. Money Order Office and Savings Bank.
1883 August 24th. Telegraph Office (IAB).
1984 Closed. (P.M. Retired).

Sub-Postmasters: Nancy Steer (-1844=1848-); Henry James Steer, linen draper (-1844=1848-); Reuben Martin (8.1848=1849); William Hackett (9.5.1849=1859); Thomas John Corman, grocer and baker (22.9.1859=1871-); Henry Larking, farmer Pet Ham Farm (-1874-); Daniel West Vennell, grocer (5.9.1876=1878-); Joshua Durling, wheelwright (15.10.1880=14.2.02 died); Miss Kate Eliza Durling, stationer (29.4.1902=1918-); Horace Callow, stationer (-1922=1938-).

History: 1881 Wall Letter Box Oldbury Hill; 1892 Ightham delivery extended; 1894 delivery allowance converted to Rural Postman's wages; 1895 RP Allowance for alternate Sunday substitute; 1900 Wages of RP instead of Rural Auxiliary and allowance for delivery with Sunday substitute allowance for *Ightham Common-Ightham* and *Ightham-Oldbury*; 1905 *Ightham to Crickets Farm* daymail extended; 1908 Cycle Posts *Ightham to Ightham Park* and *Ightham to Crickets Farm*; 1909 *Ightham to Plaxtol* cycle post; 1929 Ightham daymail extended.

Some Locations of PO: 1908 at the bottom of Trycewell Lane, North side; 1960s in Ightham Road, opposite the centre of Jubilee Crescent.

Postmen: Sevenoaks to Ightham, 1874 J H Reynolds RP (4 GC), 1902 David Saker RP (transferred to Weald Post), 1904 Reginald J Burges RP (1 GC), 1908 A G Y Hollman RP 21/- week. *Ightham to Cricketts Farm*: 1897 Alfred Hollman R Aux, 1899 John Meyers age 63 R Aux.

Rural Auxiliary Postmen: R Hardiman, 1895-7 Fred Holman, 1895-7 Albert Hollman, 1900 Thomas Dunn age 15¼, 1897 Guy Alfred Doggett, 1905 Charles Walkling, 1905 Wm Jesse Fowler; 1909 Charles William French

RP (having been Boy Messenger 1903-5 Town Aux 1905 Rural Aux 1905-6 Assistant Postman 1906-9).

Postmarks: 'Ightham Penny Post' 1839-41; UBCI (1842)-1845; ESR (1858); No Stamp 1860-77; SRs 1877-08; Skeleton 1909; SR 1910-1918; Skeleton 1921; SR 1924-32; DR Thick 1933-1983. PP Rect 1982-4.

Closure: Lt-Col Sidney Bow, after staying on extra time while great efforts were made in the village to find a replacement postmaster who could provide premises, finally retired in 1984 and the office closed.

Population: 1801 709, 1841 1,039, 1881 1,254, 1921 1,596, 1961 1,544, 1981 1,731.

Ivy Hatch

Nearest Post Office to Ightham Mote, a moated Grange dating back to Edward III, situated in a dip and said to be passed by soldiers during the civil war without them being able to find it. They were using early editions of the Van Langeren map shown in illustration on p45.

Name derived from 'Heavy Hatch' or gate.

Status:
1845 Daily delivery of Letters.
1873 Wall Letter Box.
1885 Post Office Open
1900 August 1st. Money Order Office and Savings Bank

Sub-Postmasters: Edward Love, grocer (22.2.1894=26.3.97); Charles William Honess (8.5.1897=16.3.99); Walter Henry Honess (5.5.1899=29.5.00); Charles Ernest Bowles, grocer (30.5.1900=1927-); Benjamin Taylor, grocer (-1930=1938-).

History: 1890 *Ightham Mote to Ivy Hatch* day mail; 1907 *Seal to Ivy Hatch*; 1905 Telegraph messenger.

Postmen: 1907 George A Ashdown.

Postmarks: SR (1885); Climax (1893); SRs 1904-28; DR Thick 1934-85.

Kemsing   Kemesinge   Kemsyng

At the foot of the North Downs, the Pilgrim's Way runs along the top of the village but not actually through it. Pilgrim's Way was the route taken by the foreign pilgrims to Canterbury who landed at Southampton and is not the Pilgrim's Road taken by travellers from London. 'The Bell' Inn became the bag exchange point for the Penny Post. Opposite the present Post Office is St Edith's Well. Heaverham and St Clere are in the neighbourhood. Baron Montague Norman, Governor of the Bank of England, lived at St Clere between the Wars. There is a Youth Hostel.

The name means 'place associated wiyh Cymesa' (OE).

Status:
1804 Receiving House Sevenoaks, 5th Clause Post Bag exchange point between
    Dartford post and Sevenoaks post.
1826 Receiving House Sevenoaks Penny Post.
1876 Railway station on Maidstone line at some distance beyond Noah's Ark.
1888 April 3rd. Money Order Office and Savings Bank.
1893 Jan 3. Telegraph at Kemsing Railway Station.
1904 July. Telegraph Office (KSG).
1911 Telephone Exchange (11 initial Subscribers) and Call Office.

Sub-Postmasters: 'The Bell' with John Brown 1795, Thomas Moody 1800-1818, William Harbour 1820, William Wigzall 1826, William Jeffrey 1840-1867 (in all 1795-1867-); Hezro Holden, blacksmith (-1871-); Andrew Holden (6.5.1872=1913-) age 75; Andrew Holden (? son), stationer (-1915=1927-); Mrs H M Walker (-1930=1931-); Archibald Fiveash (-1936-).

Licenced Stamp Sellers: 1905 H W Foster, Noah's Ark; 1923 E P Foster Noah's Ark; 1924 Ed Garfield Watton, East Hill; 1925 Sidney Herbert Alston, Woodlands Manor; 1925/7 John William Hunt, East Hill.

History: 1804 Bag exchange point for messengers on Sevenoaks/Dartford walk. c1850 Kemsing organised bag to Seal and delivery at Eversham (Heaverham). 23.8.1858 New walk *Seal S.O. to Kemsing, Heaverham, East and West Yaldham, Woodlands.* Geo Martin 12/- week; 1876 Kemsing day mail: 1877 Wall letter box at

Heaverham; 1885 *Kemsing to South View* new delivery; 1889 *Kemsing and Portobello* day mail; 1894 *Seal to Kemsing* rural postman was Richard Coles with 4 Good Conduct Stripes; 1899 *Kemsing to Kingsdown* Charles H Eastwood RP 21/- week; 1901 Wall Letter Box Noah's Ark; 1909 Alfred G Hider: 1910 William G Shaw, RP.

Some Locations of PO: 1869 North side of West End (Road) opposite road to Noah's Ark; 1897 still North side of West End, now house next to Landway; 1936 in West End, midway between the two; 1970 in village stores south of St Edith's Well with (1986) a distinctive 1980s type K Pillar Box, probably the first in the district.

Rural Auxiliary Postmen: 1892 C Young, 1897-00 Benjamin Russell; 1900 A Swaisland.

Postmarks: UBC I (1842)-1845; ESR (1858); No Stamp 1860-87; Climax (1888); SRs 1904-20 DR Thick 1928-44; SR 1971-85. PP Rect 1984; LC&D Railway oval (1892).

Dynes Road   Kemsing

The Housing development at Knave Wood between Kemsing and Otford by 1959 required a separate post office and this was provided in the parade of shops.

Status: 1959 Post Office open. Money Order Office and Savings Bank.

Postmarks: SRs 1959-83. PP rect 1984.

Population: 1801 320, 1841 433, 1881 443, 1921 685, 1961 3,907, 1981 4,086.

Kingsdown/West Kingsdown   Kings Down

The village is on the main route Maidstone-Malling-Wrotham-Farningham-London route with many coaches passing but no mailcoach. Postally the village is on the border between Dartford and Sevenoaks districts and each post town handled its mail at different periods. The smock windmill built about 1800 and relocated 1880 is one of the few windmills remaining in the area. Kingsdown is at 560 feet, the road rising to 700ft before reaching Wrotham. Meaning is Kings Hill. Brands Hatch motor racing circuit is nearby.

Fawkham Road

This first office was several hundred yards up the Fawkham Road turn-off in what was then the centre of the village. By1962 the village name changed to West Kingsdown to distinguish it from the Kingsdown near Sittingbourne and also near Deal.

Status:
1809-1850 Kingsdown letters via Farningham.
        Dartford 5th Clause Post to 1839 inc
1852-1858- Kingsdown letters via Sevenoaks.
1871-1889 Kingsdown letters via Dartford.
1878 Letter Box in village.
1885 Office open. Under Dartford.
1890 Office under Sevenoaks.
1892 October 1st. Money Order Office and Savings Bank.
1892 Feb 9. Telegraph Office (KDQ).
1976 Fawkham Road Office shut.

Sub-Postmasters: William Thomas Bodiam, grocer and baker (24.7.1890=9.9.98); Henry George Clifford, grocer and draper (10.9.1898=1904); William Warren Judge*, grocer and baker (25.10.1904=1913-); Albert Harry Crouch, grocer (-1914=1928 died); Alice M Crouch, grocer (5.1928=1933-); Frank Saml Kerrell, grocer (-1933=37-); Bertie James Land, grocer (-1938=1960); Mr McGurgan (1960=Nov 1975, closed ill-health).
* Permission to reside off premises on condition he provided a safe and insured against burglary to the extent of £250.

Postmarks: Kingsdown Climax (1885-1890); Skeleton 1907; SR 1907-1920; *West Kingsdown* SR 1962-71.

Hever Road

By 1973 a new office was provided at the opposite end of the village where the new houses had been built, together with a parade of shops. Late 1986 the pillar box was painted yellow, probably unauthorised but it made a change.

Status: 1973 Office open. Money Order Office and Savings Bank.

Sub-Postmasters: (-1989) Ron Ashman (died on duty).

History: Kemsing to Kingsdown, 1896 Charles H Eastwood RP 21/- week;
1909 Alfred George Hidon, 1911 William George Shaw.

Postmarks: Hever Road SRs 1977-86.

Population: 1801 337, 1841 466, 1881 411, 1921 427, 1961 3,382, 1981 4,864.

Otford   Otteford   Ottanford

Early battles took place near this ancient village situated two miles north of Sevenoaks at the entrance to the Darenth valley as the river turns sharply north. Belgic invaders entered from the north and in AD775 King Offa of Mercia defeated the men of Kent here. Otford also lies at the centre of the East-West Holmesdale valley which traditionally extends from Rochester castle in the east to Guildford castle in the west; the village lies on the Pilgrims Way from Winchester to Canterbury, itself an old trackway running parallel to but lower down south of the ancient ridgeway track.

About AD790 the area was given to Christ Church Canterbury and after the Norman Conquest the manor of Otford which extended to Tonbridge, Penshurst, Chevening, Eynsford and Shoreham came under the jurisdiction of the Archbishopric of Canterbury. The village contains the archibishop's palace, now in ruins, built originally in 1501 on an existing site and rebuilt and extended by Archbishop Wareham in the reign of Henry VIII who stayed there several times. One time was on his way to the Field of the Cloth of Gold in 1520 when he arrived with 4,000 men together with Queen Catherine who had a further 1,000 in her retinue, having travelled by boat to Greenwich and then come down the Darenth Valley.

Otford was the early administrative centre for the whole area prior to the dissolution of the monasteries (1536/8). In 1601 Queen Elizabeth sold Otford Palace to the Sidney family of Penshurst for £2,000. Subsequently it went in the early 1700s to the Smythes of Westenhanger, 1790 to Robert Parker and in 1837 to William Pitt, Earl Amherst.

The present village is centered round the well-managed duckpond at its cross-roads. The Beatles in their hey-day voted Otford their favourite village.

The name means Otta's ford, over the Darenth.

Status:
1669 On GPO broadsheet as a branch from Chepstow (Chipstead).
1673 On Ogilvy's list.
Pre-1804 Served from Sevenoaks.
1804 July 19th Receiving House Dartford Fifth Clause Post.
1847 Under Sevenoaks once again.
1883 Jan 3. Telegraph Office at Railway station (1028). Closed July 1885.
1885 July 7th. Telegraph Office (OTF).
1885 September 1st. Sale of Postal Orders.
1886 December 1st. Money Order Office and Savings Bank.

Sub-Postmasters: Charles Troughton, grocer and baker (-1840=1874-); Thomas Henry Knight, grocer and baker (23.4.1878=1903-); Henry Warren, grocer (29.9.1903=1927-); Miss Jessie Warren, draper (-1930=1934-); J M Rainsford, chemist (-1935=1938-).

History: 1841 Office closes 2pm; 6.3.1847 *St Johns, Otford and Shoreham* messenger 10/- a week; 1863 Second daily post refused; 1869 Second daily delivery of letters established; 1873 Clears Dunton Green box; 1888 Otford delivery *extended to Beechy Lees;* 1890 Otford daymail; 1896 *Otford to Shoreham Place* second daymail; 1901 *Otford to Twitton* Rural Post *extended to Lower Barn;* 1904 *Otford to Beechy Lees and on to East Hill* twice a week; 1906 *Otford to Twitton* daymail established; 1982 on, Christmas local post by Girl Guides village only, 1984 on joint with Shoreham.

Some Locations of PO: 1869-1908 North side opposite pond; 1936 High Street North side; 1960-80s shopping parade corner Bubblestone Road.

Postmen: Otford to Shoreham by Rural Aux 1901 George Alfred Bliss, 1902 Philip John Boniface, 1903 Alfred Ernest Frederick Saker; *Otford to Twitton,* by Rural Aux 1900 Edwin John Boyce age 16½, 1898 George Moon age 17.

Postmarks: UBC I (1841)-51; No Stamp 1860-85; Climax (1885); SRs (1885)-1910; Skeleton 1910; SRs 1912-40; DR Thick 1932-66; SR 1964-85. PP Rect 1983. LC&D Railway oval (1893).

Population: 1801 497, 1841 798, 1881 1,388, 1921 845*, 1961 3,179, 1981 3,565.
* Dunton Green hived off 1911 Census (1,450).

Plaxtol   Plaxtole   Plaxtool

To the east, Hurst Wood of smuggler fame extends as far as Mereworth. 'Fairlawn' is to the south, and Roughway Paper Mill which was in full operation in 1905 is to the east on the River Bourne. The village itself now houses one of the famous local bakeries of the Sevenoaks area and is on the edge of hop-growing country.

The name means a plegstow or 'play place', a place where villagers gathered for sport or to watch miracle plays.

Status:
1844 October 28 Receiving House open.
1872 February 1st. Money Order Office and Savings Bank.
1885 August 18th Telegraph Office (PXL).

Sub-Postmasters: 1845 Office set up, Surveyor to select Postmaster, Thomas Wood chosen; George Knight, land surveyor, vestry clerk, clerk to Wrotham Local Board (-1852=1871-); Mrs Frances Sophia Burtenshaw, draper and grocer (3.2.1873=1922-); Miss Elsie Bacon, draper and grocer (-1924=1927-); Burtenshaw and Bacon, drapers and grocers (-1930=1938-).

Licenced Stamp Seller: 1910 Charlton Gittes, High Street; 1912 Charles William Post, High Street.

History: 28 October 1844 *Godden Green, Ivy Hatch, Stone Street, Shipbourne and Plaxtol* Messenger 12/-; until October 1854 deliveries *via Plaxtol to Shipbourne*, subsequently under Tonbridge; 1866 Delivery *Extension to Flamswood*; 1876 *Wrotham to Plaxtol* delivery now 6 days/week; 1879 Plaxtol Main Street delivery accelerated; 1881 *Plaxtol and Ivy Hatch* delivery extended to Bradley; 1887 Pony Keep allowance for Plaxtol Rural Postman; 1894 Letter box near Rectory; 1897 Plaxtol Second daymail; 1909 Plaxtol mounted post abolished, cycle post substituted.

Postmen: *Sevenoaks to Plaxtol.* 1891 Charles H Reynolds RP (1 GC) with horsekeep allowance; Frank Edward Newman RP (2 GC) with horsekeep allowance. *Plaxtol to Seal Chart* 1901 James Deering R Aux; *Plaxtol to Long Mill* 1899 Alfred Thomas Wood R Aux, 1900 Frederick Newman R Aux age 161/2k, 1899-00 Charles Stephen Martin R Aux; Plaxtol 1894 A Kennard.

Postmarks: UBC II (1844)-1859; No Stamp 1860-1873; SRs 1901-31; DR Thick 1936-85.

Population: 1921 1,052, 1961 1,015, 1981 2,076.

St Mary's Platt   St Mary Platt   Platt

A village and ecclesiastical parish, south of Borough Green.

Status:
1897 Open under Borough Green/Wrotham
1898 Aug. Money Order Office and Savings Bank
1922 April. Address now 'Sevenoaks Kent'
1981-1983 Shut.
1983 Reopened.
1989 May 17. Closed.

Sub-Postmasters: Frank Perkins (9.8.1897=17.5.00); Reginald Children Pearson, grocer and draper (18.5.1900=1938-).

History: 1845 Letters to Basted 3 times a week, by 1862 daily; 1906 *Borough Green to St Mary Platt* daymail established; 1906 *St Mary Platt to Leybourne Wood* daymail established. 1989 both grocers shop and post office closed when Mr Cooper resigned through lack of support.

Postmen: *Boro Green to St Mary Platt:* 1890 Frank Callow RP (3 GC). *Boro Green to Little Comp:* 1910 Joseph Baldwin RP.

Postmarks: Climax (1897)-1898; SR 1904-1924; DR Thick 1978-1982.

Population: Separated from Wrotham. 1911 1,150; 1921 1,283; 1961 1,111; 1981 1,270.

Seal   Sele   St Lawrence Seal

A large village to the north of Sevenoaks and on the main east-west cross route. There is still a postbox called Paygate opposite the bottom of Seal Hollow Road where in Turnpike times there was a gate. Golf Course at nearby Wilderness on the road south to Godden Green.

The name means 'a hall' or 'a building'.

Status:
1826 Receiving House, Sevenoaks Penny Post.
1869 July 1st Money Order Office and Savings Bank.
By 1877 Telegraph Office (SEU).

Sub Postmasters: 'The White Horse' Richard Vincent 1788, William Thompson 1793, George Hughes 1803-1825 ; Receiving House at the 'White Horse' (1826=1839-); Richard Jones, 'The White Horse' Inn (-1840=1855-); James Barham, draper and grocer (-1858=1871-); George Dutt, draper and grocer (27.7.1871=1882-); Charles Sear Young, grocer (25.6.1884=1924-) age 75; Robert Burns Scott, grocer (-1927=1930-); R M Yeates (-1933-); Austin & Co, Stores (1934); P O Stores. Grocers, Cavendish and Robinson (-1938-).

History: 1840 closes 7pm; 26.8.1858 *Seal S.O. to Kemsing, Heaverham, East and West Yaldham, Woodlands,* G Martin, Runner 12/- week; 1877 *Seal to Kemsing* daymail extd; 1878 *Seal and Woodlands* post extended; 1883 second delivery Seal; 1885 *Seal to Noah's Ark* delivery extended, also *Seal to Yaldham;* 1889 Seal additional delivery; 1896 *Seal and Oakbank* daymail; 1894 Delivery Allowance converted to Rural Post wages; 1895 Seal and Seal Chart R.P. to convey bags to Godden Green; 1904 *Seal to Seal Chart* delivery; 1907 *Seal to Seal Chart* delivery extended; 1909 *Seal to Ivy Hatch* Cycle Post.

Some Locations of P.O.: 1869-1936 South side of High St opp. Church St Jcn; 1960-1980s moved to north side of High Street.

Postmen: 1885 Seal R.P. Parcel Post Compensation withdrawn; 1890 *Seal to Romney Street.* Richard Coles R.P.; 1908 Same man still at Seal on max pay 21/- week on *Seal to Kemsing* route; *Seal-Ivy Hatch*: 1905 Wm John Chandler R. Aux, 1909 Joseph Baldwin R. Aux; *Seal-Noah's Ark*: 1900 Charles Edward Stone R. Aux, 1899 Herbert Pearch R. Aux, 1896 Albert Ernest Ashdown R. Aux; *Seal-Yaldham*: 1899 William John Parr (age 16) R. Aux, A E Ashdown R.P.; *Village*: 1894-7 W Northcliffe (age 16).

Postmarks: Penny Post 'No 7' 1832-39; UBC I 1842-57; ESR (1858); No Stamp 1860-69; ESR (1869); SRs (1872)-1908; Skeleton 1909; SRs 1913-30; DR Thick 1933-62; DR Thin (1962)-71; SR (1962)-80. PP Rect 1970.

*Population:*1801 993; 1841 1,618; 1881 1,609; 1921 1,627*; 1961 2,687; 1981 2,337.

* Underriver separated 1911.

Shoreham   Schoram

A large village 3½ miles north of Sevenoaks and one mile north of Otford situated on the river in the Darenth Valley, a locality favoured by Samuel Palmer the artist who lived there from 1826 to 1833 where he was often visited by William Blake. Paper mills on R. Darenth, which closed in 1926. The village World War I memorial consists not of a stone cross but of a large cross cut into the turf on the hillside above the village to expose the white chalk. More recently Shoreham was defended from the ravages of the M25 by Spike Milligan and in 1984 a joint venture to make the one-man Railway station a Countryside centre for visitors was initiated.

The name means 'a settlement by a score or cut' (OE). Here the deep bed of a stream.

Status
1787/1793 On John Cary lists as a Receiving House under Sevenoaks.
1804 July 19th. Receiving House Dartford 5th Clause Post.
1839 Receiving House on Sevenoaks Penny Post new route to Halstead but still retaining connections with Dartford.
1847 Under Sevenoaks.
1862 Village has station on line to St John's Station (now Bat and Ball).

1874 June 1st Money Order Office and Savings Bank. Telegraph office at Railway Station until 7.7.1885.
1885 July 7th Telegraph Office (SHM) at Post Office.
1892 May 31 Telegraph Office also at Railway Station. Weekdays and Sundays.

Sub Postmasters: 'The George', Licencees Dorothy Day 1765 William Young 1785 John Day 1787-1829 (1765-1829); John Day (? son) The George (-1838=1845) but in 1840/41 Mary Booker was acting as postmistress and closing at 2pm; William Hawkins (-1845=1846-); Mrs Harriet Hawkins (-1851=1855-); Harriet Hunt (1858=1859); Samuel Walker, shop (27.8.1859=1867-); George Walker, baker (-1871-); George Spring, baker (18.10.1872=1901*-); Mrs Ann Walker, stationer (21.4.1901=1922-); Mrs Annie Elizabeth Spring, stationer (1924=1938-); Elsie Morse (-1945-).

* Resigned.

History: Early post work was all at the George, now The Old George; 1847 Shoreham new arrangements, after report (destroyed 1950s). 1855 Nov *Sevenoaks to Shoreham* messenger, Edward Flint, established once again; 1863 Second daily post refused; 1869 Second daily delivery established; 1869 Establishment of official delivery *to Prestwick House and Dunstall Priory*; 1884 Hand cart supplied for Rural Postman; 1885 *Shoreham to Hales Farm* dely. estab.; 1890 Improved service, rural post mounted; 1895 *Shoreham to Telstone* post extended; 1897 *Shoreham to Romney Street*; 1898 *Shoreham to Highfields delivery extended to Romney Street* (later via Seal); 1899 *Shoreham to Badgers Mount* delivery extended by Sub-Postmasters postman; 1902 *Shoreham to Coombe Hollow* daymail; WWI Dunstall Camp nearby with Army Post Office; 1982 Girl Guide Christmas post in village only, 1984 joint with Shoreham.

Some Locations of P.O.: 1869 High Street east side; 1897 Red brick house north side of Church St just west of bridge; 1980s Grocery store west side of High St well up.

Postmen: *Sevenoaks to Shoreham*, 1894 George Thomas Heath, 1897 William Reynolds with horsekeep, 1900 Frederick S Spring R.P. with horsekeep; *Shoreham to Badgers Mount Farm*, 1905 Samuel Yates age 26 Sub-Postmasters postman 2¼ hours weekdays and Sundays 15¾ hrs 6/- weekly wage; *Shoreham to Filstone and Cockenhurst*, 1896 Jack Cheeseman R.P. to 1901; *Shoreham to Paper Mills and Sevenoaks*: 1906 Francis A Booker R.P. with use of own cycle, 1911 Robert Thomas Ayres R.P.; *Shoreham to Romney Street* 1901 Ed F Cheeseman R.P. (2 GC). *Shoreham to Highfield*: 1898 Frank White R. Aux.

Postmarks: UBC I (1841); ESC (1858); No Stamp 1860-1874; SRs (1874)-1913; Skeleton 1918; SR 1920-29; DR Thick 1936-84. No station oval known; Station Telegraph No 1247. WWI Army P.O. (HD) 3.3/10 Middlesex; Christmas mail label 1982=1989-

Population: 1801 828; 1841 1,021; 1881 1,420; 1921 1,509; 1961 1,863; 1981 2,007.

Stansted

Main village of the area but the present post office which is well outside the village on the road to West Kingsdown is much smaller than that of Fairseat. The church yard yew tree is said to be well over 1,000 years old.
   Name means 'At the Stony place' (OE)

Status
1897 Post Office open. Postal orders sold.
1922 Address 'Stansted Wrotham Kent' became 'Stansted Sevenoaks'.
1983 Limited opening.

Sub Postmasters: William Webb, wheelwright (13.6.1897=1924-);
William Josiah Tanton, grocer (-1927=1934-); Jno Burgess Leaver, grocer (-1938-).

Licenced Stamp Seller: Florence Toole.

History: 1897 *Wrotham to Stansted* walk.

Postman: *Wrotham to Stansted*, 1908 Walter Lawrence R. Aux.

Postmarks: Climax (1897)-1901; SR 1907; DR Thin 1977-1985.

Population: 1801 249; 1841 427; 1881 408; 1921 426; 1961 562; 1981 476.

Stone Street

A mainly rural area.

Status
1845 Letters delivered to Stone Street 3 times a week, daily by 1862.
1870 Receiving House open.
1885 Postal Orders sold.
1893 April 1st Money Order Office and Savings Bank.
1899 August 22nd Telegraph Office (XEO).
1928 July closed.

Sub Postmasters: Frederick Litchford (22.11.1870=1887-); Sarah Annie Green (17.5.1888=8.11.97); Elizabeth Jane Green (9.11.1897=1911); Miss Emily Charlotte Green/Mrs E C Freed (8.4.1911=1924-); Mr F Freed (-1927=1930-).

History: 1877 Stone Street delivery extended and wall letter box at Chart; 1907 New delivery *Stone Street to Bitchet Green.* Old office still has a Ludlow box in use.

Postmarks: No stamp 1870-1885; Climax (1892); SR 1895-1910.

Underriver   Under River

An important mainly rural area to the southeast of Sevenoaks yet at times based postally on Seal to the north as Underriver lies on the Seal-Hildenborough-Tonbridge road. There was always difficulty in getting someone to look after the office on a regular basis. The river is the Hilden Brook which flows into the Medway.

Status
1856 Receiving House open.
1896 Postal Orders issued, not paid. Closed 1925.
1926 May 19 Reopened. Closed 1931 April.
1932 Jan 13 Open again. Closed 1933 Jan 11.
1935 Nov 13 Open. Closed 1944 Sept 30.

Sub-Postmasters: Anna Killick (28.5.1856-); Thomas Chappel,
farmer (-1874-); Miss Annie Ashby (1.6.1876=1878-); Alice Mary Thorpe, age 19
daughter of Richard Thorpe (-1881=1883-); Richard Thorpe, gardener (19.8.1883=1911-) age 81;
Mrs Harriet F Ashby (-1913=1924-); Arthur Wright (-1927-); Miss Wright (-1929-); "Vacant" 1933.

History: 16 Oct 1856 *Sevenoaks to Underriver* James Savage; 23.7.1858. Savage resigned, walk taken over by J Kemp; 1891 Underriver Rural Post based on Seal; 1894 Delivery *extended to Hollanden Rd*; 1896 Daymail extended; 1899 *Underriver S.O. to Starvecrow delivery extended to Rumstead Farm* 3 days a week; 1904 Shelter Hut for Postman 30/- pa; 1907 Underriver cycle post.

Some Locations of P.O.: 1869 South of Church on west side of road; 1908 Well north of church on east side of road before junction.

Postmen: Sevenoaks to Underriver, 1870-77 Edward Hever, 1892 Samuel Meekham, 1896-1903 George Henry Bateman R.P. (transferred to Town Postman); 1903-1908 Geo. Waters (ex Brasted Post) (2 GC). *Seal to Underriver*: 1893 John Henry Hutson.

Postmark: UBC II (1856); No stamp 1860-1896; Climax (1896)-1910; DR Thick (1978).

Population: Separated from Seal 1911. 1921 318; 1981 1,762.

Wrotham

A large village at the extreme east part of the Sevenoaks Postal District, through which the Maidstone and Malling Stagecoaches to London ran, on the Hythe Road. These coaches did not carry mail, except unofficially. They stopped at 'The Bull' which inn also provided posting facilities at least in the later days of posting. Officially all mail had to be taken into Sevenoaks by footpost, which must have appeared an incongruity to the local inhabitants. A branch of the London and Country Bank was open by 1845.

   Name means 'a settlement where trees have been uprooted'.

Status

1787/1793 On John Cary Lists. Under Sevenoaks.
1804 Receiving House. Sevenoaks 5th clause Post.
1826 Receiving House. Sevenoaks Penny Post.
By 1854 Money Order Office.
1861 October 30th Savings Bank.
1870 Telegraph Office (WPU).
1874 Add 'S.O.' to address. Station open to London, with working to Sevenoaks 1881.
 Telegraph at station on Suns.
1892 May 31 Telegraph Office at Railway Station Weekdays & Suns. Open on Suns up to 1918.
1922 July address reverted to 'Wrotham Sevenoaks'.
1985 Nov Local Delivery Sorting ceased.

Sub-Postmasters: 'Bull Inn' George Taylor (-1786-); Frederick Leney, maltster Bull Inn (-1804=1846-); John Ashdown, baker (-1846=1862-); Frederick Wales (17.10.1865=1878-); Charles Henry Kirk (-1882-); H D Fowler (-1887=1890-); Frances Jane Fowler (15.7.1891=23.5.1895); Henry John Collins (4.8.1895=1903); Miss Grace Collins* (22.11.1903=1922-); Miss Margaret Collins (-1924=1938-).

* Previously Assistant to Wrotham S.O. 1895-1903.

Salaries: 1895 £39, 1903 £57, 1908 £118 per annum.

History: All early postal work done at 'The Bull'; 6.4.46 *Wrotham messenger to Fairseat, Stanstead, Kingsdown and Ash* 12/- week; 1847 *Shoreham and Wrotham* new arrangements after the Surveyor's report (destroyed); 1 Feb 1850 *Sevenoaks to Wrotham*, William Smeed died and his walk taken over by John Smeed; Subsequent mailcart service from *Sevenoaks to Wrotham* (about 1852) was frequently out to tender and as often changed hands. In 1853 Mr Fitness' tender was accepted (at the same time he also gained the route to Westerham). In 1856 it was Mr Ashdown's tender that was accepted, and at the beginning of 1860 the service was placed in the hands of Mr Harris. Later that same year Mr Martin's tender was accepted, in 1861 Mr. GS Burr's and in 1862 Mr G Bennett's; 1863 Ash, improved arrangements; 1870 Wrotham has established Rural Postman attached; 1871 *Sevenoaks to Ightham and Wrotham*, Geo Ashdown mail Contractor; 1873 *Wrotham delivery extended to Horses & Groom, Ferry's Lodge Farm*; 1876 *Wrotham to Plaxtol* delivery now 6 days/week; 1877 delivery extended *to Wind mill Cottages*; 1887 *Wrotham to Ridley*, Post extended; 1892 Wrotham daymail delivery established; 1894 delivery extended to *Newhouse Farm*; 1896 *Wrotham and Plaxdale* post extended, Postman George R David Barham R.P.; 1900 *Wrotham to Plaxdale Green*. Wages of Rural Postman in lieu of Rural Auxiliary Postman and allowance for delivery. Sunday substitute allowance; 1903 Evening delivery *Wrotham to Nepicar*; 1905 *Wrotham to Ash* bicycle post; 1906 *Wrotham to Ash delivery extended to New House Farm*; 1907 Daymail *Wrotham - New Hunton*; 1907 *Wrotham to Grove Cottage* delivery established; 1910 *Wrotham to Hodsall Street, Wrotham to Fairseat* both from footpost to cycle post; 1922 *Boro Green and Wrotham Rural* Post Revision.

Postmen: 1888-1908 G R D Barham R.P. (5 GC); 1908 W J Rogers R.P.; 1900-1908 R Sheperd R.P. Wrotham Aux R.P. 1893-91 Albert Edward King (dismissed), 1894 R Meakins (disappeared), 1895 John Collings (resigned 1896).

Postmarks: Penny Post 'No 8' 1829-39; UBCI 1842-49; Dated ESR 1858-1879; Duplex F37 (1882); S.R. 1885-1920; DRs Thick 1903-1937; Skeleton 1918; SR 1945-63; DR Thick 1958-73; DR Thin 1965-68; SR 1977-82. PP Rect 1931, 1983. No early station oval known. Str line Wrotham Parcels Office 1927.

Population: 1801 1,989; 1841 2,949; 1881 3,296; 1921 1,914*; 1961 1,487; 1981 1,669.

* St Mary Platt hived off 1911 (1,150).

Wrotham Heath

On the Turnpike Road from London to Maidstone where the cross route from Westerham joins the London road. Many stagecoaches but no mailcoach. In 1810 there was a toll-gate here and the Royal Oak Inn. Previously a haunt and storage area for Romney March smugglers.

Status
1891 Post Office open.

1895 June 11th Telegraph Office (WVH).
1896 April 28 Address 'Wrotham Heath Wrotham S.O. Kent'.
1899 June 1st, Money Order Office and Savings Bank.
1922 Address now 'Sevenoaks Kent'.

Sub-Postmasters: Frederick Carlow, baker and grocer (23.2.1893=15.3.07); Mrs Elizabeth Ann Hyland, grocer and draper (16.3.1907=5.6.10); William Tipples Roberts, shop (6.6.1910=1922-); Arthur William Aldridge (-1924-); Frank George Taylor, shop (-1927-); Alfred Sinclair, shop (-1930=1938-).

Postman: *Wrotham S.O. to Wrotham Heath S.O.* 1895 Richard Jno Shepherd (age 16) R. Aux; 1896 William J Rogers R.P. (4GC).

Postmarks: SR 1904-1917; DR Thick 1954-83; SR 1985.

Sub-Offices to West

Badgers Mount

Office in London Road used to be on part of the busy A21, but the road is now diverted.

Status: 1936 Feb 12 Post Office open. Money Order Office.

History: 1890s deliveries from Shoreham. 1920s deliveries from Halstead.

Postmarks: SR 1965-83.

Berry's Green

Midway between Biggin Hill and Cudham, serving a moderately populated area. Temporary premises, now dismantled, were erected beside a private house at the corner of Jail Lane and Single Street.

The name relates to the old manor of Bertrey, extinct since c1380.

Status:
1951 April 1st. Money Order Office and Savings Bank under Sevenoaks.
1957 Under Westerham.
1976 October 29th closed.

Postmarks: SR Sev(1951); SR Westerham 1976.

Sub-Postmasters: Thomas Trevor (-1960=1964-); Leonard P Pope (-1964=1971-); Harry B Epps (-1972=1973-); Edward J Ward (-1974=1976).

Bessels Green   Vessels Green   Bessell's Green

A hamlet of Chevening to the south. The end of terrace house at the corner in which the office is located fronts onto the Green, not far from Packhorse Road, on the main cross route to Westerham. A turnpike gate here in 1800. Handles Postal Business only.

Status:
1897 Sept Post Office open.
1899 April closed.
1905 Wall Letter Box, under Chipstead.
1939 Post Office open.

Postmen: *Riverhead to Bessels Green*, 1902 C H Pelling, Frederick Kimble R Aux.

Postmarks: Climax (1897); SR 1977-83.

Biggin Hill

With the development of Aperfield Estate at the turn of the Century and later the establishment of the Airfield, a local office was required rather than service from Cudham which necessitated a steep walk down into valley and then a walk up again. Much house building in the area necessitated the construction of a telephone exchange opened in 1931, a specialized house in London Road standing on its own and next to Aperfield Court Garage. This was used until the late 1960s when a new telephone exchange was built. The original 'house' stood empty for a short while and was then converted to a sorting office as from 1970/71.

Status:
1898 Wall Letter Box (under Cudham)
1899 Office open under Sevenoaks via Cudham
1899 October 10th. Telegraph Office (QWL).
1900 June 1st. Money Order Office and Savings Bank
1905 June 1st. Under Westerham.
1970 Local sorting office in converted telephone exchange.

Sub-Postmasters: Charles Smither, stationer (17.2.1899=1927-); James Clark Jn, grocer (-1930=1938-).

Licenced Stamp Sellers: 1923 William Henry Nelson, Melrose Road; 1927 E A C Marshman, Berry's Green.

History: 1899 *Biggin Hill to Skid Hill* delivery established; 1899 *Cudham and Biggin Hill* day mail at Crown Ash and Saltbox; 1899 Cudham delivery extension to Portlands; 1904 *Cudham to Biggin Hill* changed to *Westerham Hill to Biggin Hill*; 1906 Biggin Hill Sunday delivery established; 1971 Strike. Biggin Hill Free Post.

Sub-Postmasters Postmen: 1910 William Arthur Whitehead. *Biggin Hill SO to Berries Green.* 2hrs 10mins Weekdays and Sundays 15hrs, 5/- week.

Postmen: 1904 Alfred George Fuller RP; Cecil Martin Brown (Boy Messenger 1903-4), Aux RP 1904-10, Asst Postman 1910, Rural Postman 1911.

Postmarks: Climax (1899); SRSev 1902; SRWest 1906; DR Thick (1918)-49; DR Thin 1957-1983; SRs 1958-1984. Packet Rubber 1965. PP Rect 1983, Special RAF Biggin Hill Rect 1965.

Population: 1951 Separated from Cudham (3,675); 1961 4,086; 1981 11,112.

Biggin Hill, Valley

The development of an estate at Norstead Lane in the valley although only 500 yards west of the existing Biggin Hill office necessitated another post office in the parade of shops at the bottom of the very steep Stock Hill.

Status: 1967 Money Order Office and Savings Bank under Westerham.

Postmarks: SRs (1967)-1983 (two). PP Rect 1983.

Biggin Hill RAF PO

Wartime necessity produced a GPO post office on the Airfield site said to be a Class B office manned by RAF staff and under Westerham PO. When this fullscale office closed at the cessation of hostilities, an RAF postroom continued to handle mail, and still does for special events.

Status:
1943 Open.
1947 Closed.

Postmark: DR Thick 1944; RAF Postroom S.R. rubber stamps, used as receivers 1969-83; RE Field Post Office 1982.

Brasted   Bradestede

The village is four miles west of Sevenoaks. Being on the road to Westerham and through to Reigate, some premises in the village must have been used from an early date for handling letters. Brasted is first mentioned as a Receiving house under Sevenoaks in the 1787 and 1793 lists of John Cary. Between 1882 and 1895 letter boxes were placed at the hamlets of Brasted Chart one mile up the hill due south of Brasted and Toys Hill a mile further on just over the brow of the hill. The river Darenth flows beside the village, supplying water for the paper mills. The open air swimming baths were opened 24.6.1914. A railway station connecting with Dunton Green and Westerham was opened in 1881 until 1961. There is a pumping station run by Thames Water.

The name means 'a broad place' (OE).

Status:
1787/1793 Receiving House on John Cary lists.
1809 Receiving House Sevenoaks Penny Post.
1857-1886 Linked with Edenbridge Post Town.
1872 Aug 1. Money Order Office and Savings Bank.
1881 Railway station open.
1886 Independent Sub-Office 'Add "SO Kent" to address', ie Brasted SO Kent.
1892 August 16th Telegraph Office (BRK), Express Delivery Office.
1902 August 1 under Sevenoaks, address 'Brasted Sevenoaks Kent'.
1905 April. Telephone Exchange opens with 13 Subscribers and Trunk communication via Sevenoaks, inc Call Box.
1957 Office grouped under Westerham.

Sub-Postmasters: Reginald Norton, butcher with his daughter Mrs James, draper (-1810-); John Whiffen, linen draper (1825=1829-); Sarah Whiffen, draper (-1832=1852-); William Adams, grocer (7.8.1852=1859-); William James Edmed, grocer (-1862-); Mary Ann Withers (24.6.1863=6.3.00 dec'd); Wm Withers, grocer (24.5.1900=1907-)age 74; John Sturge Withers, grocer (1.1.1908=1918-); A H Bond (-1920-); Harry H Bond, motor engineer (-1922=1938-); Adcock (-1945-).

History: 1809 Sevenoaks Penny Post; 1840 served from Sevenoaks; Letter Carrier 17.3.1857 New appointment Jas Holland 14/- per week *Edenbridge to Crockham Hill, Brasted and Sundridge* and to deliver at all villages en route; *Brasted to Phillipines* delivery established 1868, *extended to Foxwold and to Toys Hill* 1885; *Brasted to Hogtrough* extended 1893; *Brasted-Phillipines extended to Henden* 1907; 1907 *Brasted-Phillipines* cycle post and cycle cleaning allowance 1/- week; 1909 Brasted mounted post converted to mailcart service.

Postmen: 1893 Albert Edward Standen R Aux, C Withers.

Rural Postmen based at Brasted: *Sevenoaks to Brasted:* 1902 George Waters RP with horsekeep; 1903 Edwin Bates RP (3 Good Conduct stripes) with horsekeep; T J J Dunn RP 21/- week. Rural Auxiliary Postmen: 1890 W Stevens: 8.8.94 A E Standen; 1893 C Withers. 1905 E Bates granted £20 loan to purchase a horse:

Sub-Postmasters Postman: 1899 William Thomas Parrett.

Some Locations of PO: 1897 North side of main road opp Chart Lane. 1985 South side of main road east end of village opp Rectory Lane.

Postmarks: Penny Post 'No 4' 1819; UBC I 1843-1850; ESR (1858); No Stamp 1960-72; SRs 1872-1907; Duplex A84 (4 types) 1884-1908; SR 1908-20; DR Thick Sevenoaks 1908-1957; Skeleton 1916; DR Thin Westerham (1958)-82. PP Rect 1983, SE Railway oval (1893).

Population: 1801 750, 1841 1,130, 1881 1,292, 1921 1,327, 1961 1,500, 1981 1,313.

Brasted Chart

In Kent the word 'chart' denotes an area of rough often higher ground outside a village. Such ground is often subsequently built on.

Status:
By 1891 Letter Box, cleared from Brasted.
1898 Post Office, under Sevenoaks via Brasted.
1902 Postal Orders issued
1930 Public Telephone.
1957 Office under Westerham
1982 Open Mon/Thurs only
1983 Open Thur only, shop closed.

Sub-Postmasters: John Wynn, shop (26.10.1898=29.8.09) dec'd; Mrs Ellen Matilda Wynn, shop (23.9.09=1922-); Mrs Leonard Matthews, shop (-1924-); John Kent, shop (-1925=1934-); William Cowlard, shop (-1938-); Annie C Kent (-1945=1951-).

Postmarks: Climax (1898)-1914; DR Thick 1950-78; DR Thin 1980-82.

Brasted, Toys Hill

An agricultural area, with houses at the cross-roads. Toys Hill Farm School was located here Pre WWI.

Status:
By 1895 Letter Box, cleared from Brasted.
1906 Post Office, under Brasted/Sevenoaks.
1930 Public Telephone.
1957 Post Office under Brasted/Westerham
1973 Closed.

Postmasters: Mrs Eliza Heath, grocer, born 1843 (1.1.1906=1924-); Mrs Alice Tidy, grocer (-1927=1956-).

History: *Brasted to Toys Hill* daymail started 1892.

Postmen: *Brasted to Toys Hill* 1899-03 Robert Cole RP; 1904 Thomas J J Dunn RP (1 GC Stripe).

Postmarks: Climax (1906)-1915; DR Thick 1980-82. At Christmas 1987 a special postmark for Toys Hill was granted. This was sponsored by Benhams of Folkestone and applied to commemorative covers at Sevenoaks main PO. A further special postmark occurred in 1989.

Chevening   Chyvening

With its hamlets of Chipstead and Bessels Green. All the parishes to the west of Sevenoaks are elongated North-South strips, Chevening parish being eleven times as long as it is in parts wide.

There was a village here before the Saxons came, that is the village has Celtic origins. In 1551 John Lennard had the manor. His grandson became 12th Baron Dacre and his son built a new house at Chevening, and the family held the property until in 1717 it was acquired by the Stanhopes, a family originating in the north of England. It was Charles, the 3rd Earl Stanhope who closed the Road. He was mildly eccentric and an inventor whose first iron printing press had some commercial success. An amount of Stanhope correspondance is currently extant in private hands.

The house and property of Lord Stanhope was later offered to Prince Charles but not taken up. In 1785 the North/South London road and the East/West Pilgrims Way were officially closed, and the village became a 'dead-end' for vehicular traffic, turning into an 'estate' village. PO in Cottage No8 Chevening village street. Famous postally for having, like Dunton Green, an early 1861 type wall letter box still in use.

The name means 'People living by the Ridge (Celtic), but some say it means 'Cifel's people' (OE).

Status:
1870 Wall Letter Box.
1901 Office Open. Telegraph Office (ZVN).
1904 June 1st. Money Order Office.
1906 Chevening Halt appears in Westerham Branch time table.
1945 Closed.

Postmasters: William Thomas Smith, estate plumber (9.2.1903=1905 resigned); Mrs Gertrude Mary Gunn, stationer (25.6.1905=1945).

Postmarks: Climax (1902); SR 1904-1921; DR Thick.

Population: 1801 756; 1841 1,003; 1881 1,086; 1921 1,031; 1961 2,113; 1981 3,034.

Chipstead   Chepstow   Chepsted

A hamlet of Chevening, two miles south on the Darenth ford. At one time the main centre of activity for posting and trade. After a lull of 150 years emphasised by the closing in 1785 of Chevening road as a through route to London, reopened as a local village receiving house. But again closed 1989 and premises a private house.

Status:
1635/1660 Main London to Rye Stageing Post with Branch posts up to Sevenoaks and to Otford, also past Westerham to Reigate.
1676 Stage shut. Now routed via Longford Bridge to Sevenoaks.
1824 Receiving House, Sevenoaks Penny Post.
By 1886 Telegraph Office (CPT).
1891 February 2nd. Money Order Office and Savings Bank. 1989 closed.

Sub-Postmasters: William Eastwood (-1840=1862-); Mrs Jane Eastwood (-1866=1867-); Thomas Ingram, boot and shoemaker (-1871-); Benjamin Corke, grocer and draper (27.12.1873=1878-); William Robert Gibson, grocer (-1882-); Thomas William Miller, grocer (21.4.1887=1911-); John Bramley Ball, grocer (-1912=1918-); Thomas George Joyce, confectioner (-1920=1924-); G A Hughes (-1925-); P H Hann (-1926-); G A Bircham (-1927=1930-); George K Hancock, confectioner (-1931=1960-); Harry Clarke (-1964=1988-), newsagent.

History: 1841 Office closes 8pm; 26 Feb 1857 *Sev to Riverhead and Chipstead* and deliver both villages; 20 May 1857 *Sev to Chipstead* Geo Bennett; 1889 *Chipstead and Halstead* post improved; 1896 *Chipstead to Chevening Park* delivery extended; 1898 Delivery extended; 1901 *Sundridge, Brasted and Chipstead* daymail; 1905 *Chipstead to Chevening* Cycle Post.

Some Locations of the PO: 1869 Middle of High St, North side; 1897 East end of High Street, north side; 1980s west end of High Street, still north side.

Postmen: Chipstead to Chevening. 1897 Charles Henry Eastwood, 1899 Frederick G Eastwood age 19½ R Aux; 1903 Benjamin G Baker, 1908 John Marchant RP earning 21/- week in 1908. *Chipstead to Knockholt*: 1892 A McManns. *Chipstead to Sevenoaks*: 1893 Charles Henry Pelling.

Postmarks: Penny Post 'No 5' 1840; UBC I 1843-1864; ESR (1858); No Stamp 1860-1886; SR 1886-1921; DR Thick 1928-71; DR Thin 1971-82.

Cudham

An old established Receiving House to the North of the Postal District. Previously under Bromley/Orpington, transferred to Sevenoaks in 1896. Was the office from which the Biggin Hill expansion was handled until a separate office opened in 1899 and until that office went under Westerham in 1904.

Status:
Pre 1840 Receiving House under Bromley; by 1872 under Chislehurst; by 1883 under Orpington.
1885 Postal Orders issued.
By 1889 under Chislehurst and served from Orpington RSO.
1896 Aug 1 transferred to Sevenoaks as Money Order Office and Savings Bank Office.
1937 Telegraph Office.
1989 Community Office open 2 mornings Mon & Thur 8-1.

Sub-Postmasters: John Yeates, grocer (-1844=52); Richard Yeates, grocer (25.11.1852=1890-); William Roberts, grocer (28.6.1892=1915-); Mrs Mary Howard, shop (-1918=1934-); J Clark, grocer and draper (-1935-).

Licenced Stamp Seller: 1910 C H A Howard, Horns Green.

History: 1844 Letters via Bromley; 1872 Letters via Chislehurst; 1895 Letters via Farnborough and Orpington RSO; 1896 *Cudham (from Chislehurst) and Biggin Hill* daymail; 1896 Allowance for horsekeep; 1896 Delivery from Sevenoaks; 1898 *Cudham to Letts Green* daymail established; 1904 *Cudham to Biggin Hill* Cycle Post and *Cudham to Royal Oaks* (? Green Street Green) walk merged into *Halstead to Colgates* with bicycle supplied.

Postmen: 1890-1920 *Sevenoaks to Cudham via Halstead*, George Harry Atkins, mounted post (mailcart); 1893 *Cudham to Biggin Hill* Thomas Read (1 GC); 1901 Charles Henry Gardner; 1902 David Saker; 1903 Alfred George Fuller.

Postmarks: SR 1904-31; DR Thick 1943-1982.

Population: 1801 514; 1841 776; 1881 1,029; 1921 2,247; 1961 1,243*; 1981 4,620**.
* Biggin Hill separated 1951 (3,675).
** inc Downe and Leaves Green.

Halstead

An early North Downs settlement at 600 feet with a church foundation first mentioned in the 'Textus Roffinus' of AD1150.
   Name means 'a place of shelter for cattle'.

Status:
1839 Receiving House, Sevenoaks Penny Post.
1876 May. Telegraph at Railway Station (to at least 1887, probably 1892).
1892 July. Telegraph Office (HTD) at Post Office.
1892 October 1st. Money Order Office and Savings Bank.

Sub-Postmasters: George Slaughter, baker and grocer (1839=1854); Mrs Elizabeth Slaughter, baker (20.7.1854=1862-); Philip Shewbridge, fruitgrower, married Widow Slaughter 13 yrs older (6.4.1863=1882-); William Jarvis, shop (-1887-1889-); Charles Jarvis, grocer age 22 (22.11.1889=1928-); Frank Henry Hughes (-1929=1930-); Frederick James Lloyd (-1931-); Sidney Baker Payne, shop (-1932=1957-). James and Margery Fitzjohn (-1976=1986-); Susan Burtenshaw (1986=1987); Mr & Mrs Jones (1987=1989).

History: 1809 Mail via Sundridge for collection, many writers used Chelsfield via Bromley; 1840 close 5pm: Delivery to Halstead was Walk via Chipstead and Knockholt by Henry Bartholomew who died 24.6.1850 and Walk taken over by James Francis at 12/- week. On 24 October 1857 J Francis died and Walk taken over by

T Clout who often used a pony to carry the mailbags; 1878 *Chipstead and Halstead* post extended and allowance for Sunday relief to RLC; 1890 George Harry Atkins, mail cart up Polhill along Otford Lane to Halstead, Knockholt and Cudham, dismounted Sept 1923, 'it was said that he'd never been late although he used to get to Sevenoaks at five o'clock in the morning, deliver at Riverhead, Dunton Green, up Polhill and along to Halstead, Knockholt and Cudham, do odd jobs there and then return to Sevenoaks leaving Cudham at 7pm'.*

1873 Halstead post improved; 1874 Day mail sanctioned; 1878 *Chipstead and Halstead* post extended with allowance for Sunday relief to Rural Letter Carriers; 1889 *Chipstead and Halstead* post improved; At some time between 1891-4 Wall Letter Box placed at Railway Station; 1894 *Curry Wood delivery* established; 1896 *Colgates delivery*; 1896 *Halstead delivery to Polhill Arms* daily; 1898 *extended to Shepherds Barn* 3 days/week; 1899 Shepherds Barn delivery increased to six days a week; 1904 Station Service, shelter of truck ceased; 1907 *Extended delivery to Henshaw's Caravan*; 1908 Daymail Otford Lane; 1908 2nd and 3rd delivery to Halstead by bicycle from Dunton Green; 1928 Badger's Mount daymail delivery extended. Old office on corner still has a Ludlow box in use.   (* Frank Bond recording 1970 quoted Sevenoaks Chronicle 14 August 1982.)

Location of Offices: Early to 1927 Corner stores, flint cottages at corner Church Lane and Knockholt Road: By 1929 Jessemine Cottage almost opposite Village Hall in Knockholt Road, to 17th August 1989 when the office moved to Gowers Stores on same side of the road but nearer the crossroads.

Postmen: *Halstead to Station*; 1896 A McManns, 1899 RP with Sunday sub, 1899 dec'd. *Halstead to Colgates*: 1896 William John Playford; F G Eastwood RP 21/- week (2 GC). *Halstead to Plaxtol*: 1895 Charles Henry Reynolds with Horse Allowance (the reason for this cross route is not known). *Halstead to Polhill*: 1905 William Jarvis R Aux with permission to deliver without wearing uniform, possibly because he had previously been the postmaster but left the appointment in favour of Charles Jarvis.

Postmarks: 'Halstead Penny Post' (1839)-1840; UBC I (1842)-1856; UBC II 1855; No Stamp 1860-1880; Square Circle (1880)-1913; Climax (1891); SR 1893; DRs Thick 1915-1971; SR with arcs 1976-85. SE Railway oval (1892); Station Telegraph No 614.

Population: 1801 145; 1841 303; 1881 474; 1921 565; 1961 1,582; 1981 1,591.

Ide Hill   Edythshyll   Hide Hill

A hamlet of Sundridge situated two miles to the south, with the Sevenoaks Union Workhouse, a plain stone buliding erected in 1845 to house 400 (in 1882 it held 194) and now a hospital, halfway along the route. Ide Hill village being also on the route from Sevenoaks to Edenbridge assumed an importance after Edenbridge became a post town in 1848.

Status:
1850 Open as a post office based on Sundridge.
1857 Link with Edenbridge until 1886.
1892 August 16th Telegraph Office (IHL) and Express Delivery Office.
1892 October 1st Money Order Office and Savings Bank.
1914 Public Phone Booth.
1926 Telephone Exchange.

Sub-Postmasters: John Mace*, tailor (27.2.1850-); Edward Sears, shoesmith (30.3.1850-); William Kirby, carpenter (16.1.1868=1909); Miss Mary Ann Kirby/Mrs Lynch**, shop (12.1.1909=1922); Jeremiah Lynch, caterer (1922=1931-); William Percival Farrell, caterer and stationer (1932=1938-).
* John Mace is shown in Directories as postmaster as late as 1866, but PO records (Post 58) shows the appointment of Mr Sears after only five weeks.
** The Secretary sanctions her marriage to Mr J Lynch 1909.

Licenced Stamp Sellers: 1924 Albert Percy Green, Coopers Corner; 1925 Mrs Lily Levings, Goathurst Common.

History: c1853 on Main run Sevenoaks-Tonbridge, mail also delivered to Sundridge; 16 April 1857 Westerham (under Edenbridge) and Ide Hill Runner W Thompson 12/- week; 1858 Arrivals from Edenbridge 7am and 3pm, departure 8.45am and 6.30pm, from Sundridge arrive 8pm depart 8am; 1867 *Ide Hill to Sundridge* Sunday post discontinued; 1875 *Ide Hill to Sundridge*, Mailcart instead of Mounted. *Sevenoaks and Ide Hill* service combined with the Tonbridge and Sevenoaks mail service and the Ide Hill messengership abolished; 1881 Collecting from Goathurst Common; 1896 *Ide Hill to Sevenoaks* John Legg; 1900 *Ide Hill to Coopers Green* daymail; 1903 Daymail to Goathurst Common; 1906 New dely established *Ide Hill to Yorks Hill*; 1906

Sundridge to Ide Hill and *Ide Hill to Goathurst Common* combined and bicycle provided; 1937 Outside stamping vending machines installed.

Some Locations: PO 1869 east side of road to Sundridge well down; present opp Green to west of P.H.

Postmarks: UBC II 1855; No Stamp 1860-1891; Climax (1891); SR 1901-13; Skeleton 1914; SR 1915-29; DR Thick 1952-85.

Population: 1921 803; 1961 1,840; 1981 Not given separately.

Knockholt

A Village on the North Downs at the top of Marams Court Hill and Rushmore Hill on the old route to London, five miles north west of Sevenoaks. The part of the village on the old route 'Knockholt Pound' where stands the post office and village hall is now more populous than the original Knockholt village area around the old established church standing in what is said to be a Druid's grove with the school opposite, both three-quarters of a mile to the west of the Pound and where also stand the 'Knockholt Beeches'. 'As wild, romantic and sequestered as the backwoods of America' says Black's guide book of 1895. 'Knockholt House' belonging to the Vavasseurs, and demolished in 1942 for its copper, stood near here.

Nearby is Fort Halstead, the Armament Research and Development Establishment, made 'Royal' in 1962 and now expanded to sit astride the old western main road holloway as it reaches to the top of the north downs, together with its counterpart at Badgers Mount.

Status:
1851 Receiving House.
1880 Telegraph Office (KEF).
1880 May 1st. Money Order Office and Savings Bank.
1911 March 1st. Telephone Exchange (11 Subscribers) and call office.

Sub-Postmasters: New Receiving Office, Surveyor to select (10.2.1851-); William Forge, boot and shoemaker (29.6.1856=1891-); Miss Mary Elizabeth Forge, stationer (18.6.1894=1913-); William Jesse Fowler, stationer (-1915=1938-). Fowler sisters (daughters) to 1988.

History: Prior to 1844 Mail officially left at Sundridge on the 'Penny Post' route for collection; 28.5.1844 Knockholt's messenger Hall retired through ill-health; 24 June 1850 James Francis; 24 October 1857 T Clout, of whom Frank Bond says in his tape recording (Sevenoaks Chronicle 14.8.82) 'Old Clout had a pony. He used to come from Sevenoaks up through Chipstead and leave the mailbag at Chevening. Then he would come on up through the Park, down Chevening Lane to the Post Office at Knockholt, leave a bag there, and go on to Halstead and leave a bag there . . . he'd got a sideline of some sort, I think it was boot repairing. At half past five in the evening he'd start off back, Halstead, Knockholt, Chevening, Chipstead, Sevenoaks. All he'd got was a little pony and he'd walk beside the pony because he'd got the bags slung across the saddle. Then we had a two wheeled cart via Halstead' (Atkins). Local Delivery, 1856 recorded by G F Warlow in his History of Knockholt (1934) p51 as an extract from an 'old paper', dated AAB 17 July 1856 that the postmaster at Knockholt will receive his letters in a sealed bag, and must despatch in like manner and will receive an allowance for delivery. Delivery at Knockholt Church, Shellys Farm, Burlyns, Knockholt Wood, Portlands Farm, Stonings Farm, Brasted Hill Farm, Sundridge Hill Farm and all houses on the line £12; Delivery at Horse Shoes, Ashgrove Cottage, Castle House, Park Corner, The Harrow, Chevening Lane, Singles Cross Lords Wood Farm and all houses on the line £6. Postmasters Salary £3 p.a.; Once Halstead station opened 1.5.1876 after much discussion and a public contribution to the total cost was made; a horse drawn omnibus went from the 'Royal Oak' now 'Tally-Ho' to Halstead Station twice daily (subsequently renamed Knockholt Station in 1900 to avoid confusion with Halstead Essex); 1874 Day Mail sanctioned; 1878 Unsuccesful attempt in Quarter Sessions to close the Knockholt–Chevening footpath beside the old road; 1892 Delivery *extension to the Grange*, also *Knockholt to Letts Green* delivery; 1893 Further delivery extensions; 1903 Extension *Knockholt to Shamrock House*; 1.6.1904 Official Cycle at Knockholt; 1904 Edward Wells, aged 59, Sub-postmasters postman *Knockholt SO to Rushmore Hill Farm and Colts* 2 1/2 hours weekdays and Sundays 17 hours 7/6 a week; 1908 2nd and 3rd delivery from Dunton Green by Cycle Post; 1909 *Knockholt to Melrose* Henry Burr R Aux; 1988 Closed on retirement of Fowler sisters.

Location of PO: Forge Cottages on north side of road to Knockholt, at the western end of Knockholt Pound.

Postmen: 1893 J Durling age 48 R Aux.

Postmarks: UBC II 1855; No Stamp 1860-1880; Square Circle (1880)-1909; DR Thick 1915-1971; SR 1973-78. PP Rect 1970-1983 SE&C Railway oval (1900), Special event St Katherines 1981. Fort Halstead: MOD(AD) RARDE DR Thin (1967).

Population: 1801 257; 1841 539; 1881 769; 1921 908; 1961 1,112; 1981 1,235.

Riverhead   River Head   Rethereth

Was a liberty of Sevenoaks, until recently separated by the Glebe field, now built on and so contiguous with the town, its physical independence has gone but not so its spiritual. It is not the head of the river (Darenth) but a source of one of the feeding waters. Recently in an outburst of plebianism, the owners renamed the Amhurst Arms 'The Dog and Duck', but some of the locals felt the pendulum had swung too far and threw the name out in favour of 'The Riverhead'. The newly-painted inn sign of a dog and a duck, however, remains, and real ducks continue to fly in and land on the rivulet by the Bank.

Status:
1809 Receiving House Sevenoaks Penny Post.
1871 June 1st. Money Order Office and Savings Bank.
By 1877 Telegraph Office (REA).
1906 Feb National Telephone Company Sub-Exchange opened
   with trunk lines connecting with Sevenoaks.
1955 Transferred from Country to Town Office Status.

Sub-Postmasters: Benjamin Pawley, Amherst's Arms (-1840=1846) Mrs Mary Ann Pawley was LV at Amherst's Arms, now The Riverhead; Frederick and Elizabeth Burgess, grocer (-1851-1862); John Williams (-1866=1874-) Samuel Saxby, grocer and draper (15.6.1875=1886); Frank Hayter, grocer and draper (24.11.1886=1909*); Mrs Eleanor Hayter, (1.7.1909=1922-); Arthur G Anderson, draper (-1912=1918-); A Townsend (-1918-); L Ellis, stationer (-1920-); J F Ellis (-1923-); Miss Lillian Ellis, stationer (-1924=1949-).
* Deceased 19 May 1909.

Licenced Stamp Seller: 1913 William Saxby Bassett, The Square.

History: 27 Feb 1857 *Sevenoaks to Riverhead and Chipstead* and delivery both villages, George Bennett 6/-week: 26 October 1857 Will Eastwood took over at the same salary. 1890 *Riverhead to Bessels Green*, Charles H Pelling Rural Auxiliary 1890 Temp RP 1894 (4 GC stripes); 1889 *Riverhead to Dunton Green* delivery extended; 1899 *Riverhead to Brasted*, Albert Valentine Palmer age 16 R Aux, Charles Phillips, age 17 R Aux; 1905 *Riverhead to Dunton Green* Cycle Post; 1906 *Riverhead to Bradbourne* delivery estab; 1908 Sunday evening collection at The Square Riverhead; 1908 C H Pelling Rural.

Postman: Riverhead to Bradbourne Hall, 1909 Henry James Heath R Aux.

Postmarks: Penny Post 'No 1' 1814-1829; UBC I (1842); UBC II (1846)-1857; No Stamp 1860-1871; SRs 1871-1921; DR Thick 1924-53; SRs 1944-84.

Population: 1921 943; 1961 1,762; 1981 1,772.

Sundridge   Sundrish   Sondresshe   Sonderesshe

A mile east of Brasted on the road from Sevenoaks to Westerham and beyond, this village also must have had early postal availability, though not mentioned on the John Cary lists. As with Brasted, the river Darenth supplied paper mills situated east of the village with water. The area Brasted/Sundridge/Chevening was referred to as the 'Archbishop's Garden' as although the churches are located in the diocese of Rochester, their livings were in the gift of Canterbury.

Status:
1809 Receiving House Sevenoaks Penny Post.
1857-1886 Link with Edenbridge Post Town via Brasted.
1875 Telegraph Office (SVM).
1882 April 1st. Money Order and Savings Bank Office.
1894 Express Delivery Office.
1896 Apl 28 to 1902 Address changed from 'Sundridge Sevenoaks'
   to 'Sundridge Brasted SO Kent'.

1902 Aug 1 under Sevenoaks. 1.1.03 Address Brasted, Sevenoaks.
1915 Public telephone.

Sub-Postmasters: Caroline Watts (-1841=1844-); Joseph Watts, tailor (-1845=31.7.1859); Joseph (? son) Watts, assessor and collector of taxes, road surveyor, newsagent (-1862=1890-); William Jarvis Nicholls, grocer (8.9.1892=18.9.99); William Burton, baker (16.12.1899=1918-); Samuel Prentice, baker and grocer (-1920=22-); Frederick Ballard, grocer and agent for the Westerham Herald (-1924=1938).

History: 1809 Sevenoaks Penny Post; 1840 Served from Sevenoaks; 6.3.1847 *Sundridge to Knockholt Beeches and Pound* 12/- week; c1853 Mail came down from Ide Hill on Sevenoaks-Tunbridge run; 1857 on walk from Edenbridge (see Brasted); 1883 Ovingden Green walk transferred to Sundridge; 1890 *Sundridge to Manor Green* dely; 1885-1920 Local walks; *Sundridge to Ide Hill* (recommencement of early service) John Legg 1888-1903; RP One GC Stripe retired old age, replaced in 1904 by Wm Humphrey RP two GC stripes; *Sundridge to Stanhope Lodge* by rural auxiliary postman (part-timer); *Sundridge to Manor Farm and Colts* by subpostmasters postman; 1896 *Sundridge to Ide Hill* Rural postman in lieu of *Ide Hill to Coopers Green*; 1908 W Humphrey RP 21/- week; 1909 Arthur Ring (age 17) subpostmasters postman *Sundridge to Manor Farm and Colts*, weekday 2hrs 55min, Sunday 11/2hrs = 19hrs earning 7/3 per week.

Some Locations of PO: 1869 on main road, east of village crossroads south side; 1897 west side of road to Ide Hill, second block of houses. 1960-80s Main road north side, west of crossroads.

Postmen: Sundridge to Union (Workhouse): 1904 John Quittenden Gallop R Aux, 1905 Albert Sales R Aux.

Postmarks: Penny Post 'No 2' 1828; UBC I 1842, UBC II (1847)-1850; No Stamp 1860-1875; SRs 1875-1921; Skeleton 1913; DR Thick 1927-71; DR Thin 1977-85.

Population: 1801 715; 1841 1,254; 1881 1,627; 1921 1,814; 1961 2,248; 1981 1,891.

Tatsfield (Surrey)   Tatesfield

On the North Downs ridge, with Botley Hill gong up to 800ft. Previously in Godstone Union. Only part of the Postal District not in Kent.

Status:
1852 Letters through Limpsfield.
1859 Letters through Westerham.
1883 Letterbox Westmoor Green under Westerham.
1891 Office opened under Westerham/Edenbridge.
1896 Under Westerham/Sevenoaks. Postal orders issued not paid.
1897 Telegraph Office (TFX).
1898 Mar 1. Money Order Office and Savings Bank.
1911 Telephone Exchange open January 11th and Call Office.

Sub-Postmasters: Joseph Mullens*, grocer and tobacconist (3.1.1891=1921-); Percy J Parker, grocer (-1924=1930-); William J Harris, grocer (-1934=35-).
* Tfrd from Edenbridge 1.4.1897.

Licenced Stamp Seller: William Lugton, Ship Hill 1910.

History: 1859 Letters by footpost from Westerham, also to Titsey; 1898 *Westerham and Tatsfield* daymail extended to the Stud Farm; 1901 Tatsfield evening collection and despatch to Betsome Hill established; 1902 *Westerham to Tatsfield* delivery extended to the Herries; 1904 *Tatsfield to Ken Court* delivery; 1904 *Tatsfield to Ricketts Hill* dely, and further extended 1906 to Parkwood Road; 1906 *Single Street Tatsfield* daymail established; 1907 *Tatsfield to Kings Cote* cycle post; 1908 Rural Postman E B Abraham 21/- week; 1909 E Blowden RP on *Tatsfield Ken Court* delivery.

Postmen: Tatsfield to Betsomes Hill, 1902 Harry E Painter R Aux; Village 1902 Ernest Ebenezer French R Aux; 1906 *Tatsfield to Parkwood Road*, 1906 John Harding R Aux.

Postmarks: Climax 1894; SRs 1901-25; DR Thick 1936; SR 1982.

Population: 1801 153; 1841 172; 1881 168; 1921 832; 1961; 1981 1,784.

Weald   Sevenoaks Weald

A liberty of Sevenoaks, situated to the south.

Status:
1853 Receiving House open.
1893 March 1st. Money Order Office and Savings Bank.
1893 October 24th. Telegraph Office (WXD).

Sub-Postmasters: Samuel Waters, shop (-1858-); Mrs Elizabeth Waters (1859=1862-); Edwin Read, baker and grocer (5.4.1864=1890-); Thomas Smithers (22.6.1892=1902); Miss Emmeline Mercy Rye/Mrs E M Fowler, stationer (1.3.1902=1913-); Henry James Hart (-1915=1918-); Mrs Mary Jane Wood (-1920=1938-).

History: 1845 Letters taken to Weald three times a week (Sun/Wed/Fri); 1850 daily, 26.4.1853 Runner *Sevenoaks to Sevenoaks Common and the Weald* J Lee 10/- per week; 1899 *Weald to Brickworks* daymail established; 1907 *Weald Height to Blackhall* delivery extended; 1909 *Sevenoaks to Weald* Cycle Post; 1914 *Weald to Halls Green.*

Some Locations of PO: 1869 North side of road opp extreme western point of green; opp eastern end of green, NW corner of road to Sevenoaks 1908-36; Across road to NE corner of road 1960-80.

Postmen: Sevenoaks to Weals: 1892 Francis Snashall, 1893 Henry Lower, 1894 Thomas Smithers (age 53) Aux RP 1897 George R Goodhew, 1898 Geo A Fletcher RP age 27 called up for reserve 7.12.1899, 1903 William F Freelove RP (1 GC) transferred from Dorking and later became Town postman, 1904 Ernest Wingfield West and David Seker (2 GC), 1905 *Weald to Bushes Farm* Cecil Brown R Aux.

Postmarks: UBC II (1853); No Stamp 1860-1892; Climax (1892); SRs 1897-1908; Skeleton 1906; DR Thick 1977-82.

Population: 1921 872; 1961 1,279; 1981 1,015.

Westerham   Oisterham

A town in the Darenth valley five miles west of Sevenoaks on the route to Reigate and Croydon. The main headwater of the Darenth rises from a spring in Squerries Court.

A Parliamentarian defensive area to prevent King Charles coming from Oxford, skirting London and joining with sympathizers in Kent. Birthplace of General James Wolfe 1727, hero of Quebec. Winston Churchill lived at nearby Chartwell. The railway line was given building reapproval in 1876 and opened 1881. Branch line trains were run through Brasted and Chevening Halt to connect with the main line at Dunton Green until 1961 closure. Around 1906 the SE & CR operated a through train to Cannon Street. Later in the 1920s, Westerham became a good motor bus communication centre with the Reigate-Westerham-Biggin Hill-Bromley and Sevenoaks-Westerham-Croydon routes passing through.

Status:
1669 GPO Broadsheet, Chipstead-Reigate route passed through.
1787/1793 On John Cary Lists. Receiving House under Sevenoaks.
1809 Receiving House Sevenoaks Penny Post (No 3).
1821 Receiving House Godstone Penny Post - as well.
1849 Money Order Office.
1857-1897 Under Edenbridge Post Town.
1861 December 30th Savings Bank Office
1870 Telegraph Office (WFN).
1881 Railway Station opened. Wall letter box installed. Line closed 28 Oct 1961.
1891-1927 Independent Sub-office, address 'Westerham SO Kent'.
1897 March 1 Transferred from control of Edenbridge to Sevenoaks.
1902 Salaried Sub-office.
1904 August. Telephone Exchange with Trunk Communication via Sevenoaks.

1905 Crown Office* Class II. Salaried sub-office, in 1939 listed as Class I. (Closed for lunch 12.30 to 1.30pm)
1957 i/c Brasted office.
1983 Currently the Office has three parcel positions and a parcel counter position. Sorting office at the side with bicycles, 4 small vans and 2 Sherpas. (Closed for lunch 1.30 to 2.30pm, closed Wed and Sat afternoons 1985).
* Class I Crown Offices were maintained by the Ministry of Works, Class II by the Department.

Postmasters & Sub-Postmasters: George Barton, licenced victualler Kings Arms 1810-1817 (-1809-); William Bennett (-1825=1852-); Thomas Thompson, grocer and ironmonger (25.11.1852=1862-); William Ray, collector of Rates (-1866=1871-); Miss Emily Ray (-1874-); Thomas Newton* (4.3.1879=1899-); Thomas Frederick Deakin age 66 (18.3.1900=1901-); Mrs Susan Fanny Norwood, ex Staplehurst (8.3.1902=1905-); Mrs Ellen Hatherall ex Freshwater Bay (26.10.1905=1927-); R C W Simmonds ex Ramsgate (11.5.1927=1935-); Miss C Coster ex Eastbourne (12.11.1935=1945-); Miss D K Champion ex Rochester (12.12.1945-); Miss E M Mullins (21.4.1952); T F Buckle (20.9.1959); Mr T A Archer (27.5.1962); R A Turner (30.7.1967); Mr Griffiths (6.1974=1985-).

Sub-postmaster salary: 1899 £80, 1921 £141, 1927 £151 pa.

* Transferred from Edenbridge 1.4.1897, dismissed 1899.

Licenced Stamp Sellers: Miss Emily Ashby, South Bank Stores, Westerham 1909; Walter E Bennett, High Street 1915; William J Parsons, Vicarage Hill 1924.

History: 1840/1845 Letters from all parts arrive from Sevenoaks and Godstone at 0830 and despatched to Godstone 5pm Sevenoaks 6pm both ways by mailcart; 1849/50 Mailcart *Sevenoaks and Westerham* Mr Bennett's tender accepted; 1853 Mr Fitness' Mailcart tender accepted: 1856 again Mr Bennett's mailcart tender; 1857 3.00pm under Edenbridge, Runner to Ide Hill William Thompson; 1859 Mailcart *Edenbridge to Westerham*: 1877 Westerham office open 7am to 8pm Sunday 7am to 10am, MOSB 9am to 6pm, Telegraph 8am to 8pm, Sunday 8 to 10am; 1883 open 7am to 7.50pm, Sunday 7.30am to 10am, MOSB 9am to 6pm, Receive parcels 8am to 7.45pm, Postal Orders issued to 7.50pm paid to 6pm; 1896 New Mailcart Service *Sevenoaks to Westerham* as now under Sevenoaks again; 1900 Feb Official bicycle at Westerham; 1905 Crown Office Class II. Rent £68 pa; 1909 Dec 25 premises rented for 21 years @ £68 pa from Landlord Thomas Henry Walker of High Street Westerham; 1990 Same building used but change in image.

Sevenoaks-Westerham: 1901 Railway new contract, bag ex Westerham at 5.33pm estab.

Westerham-Tatsfield: 1879-98 George Camber, Rural Postman (2 Good Conduct Stripes); 1899 John Palmer RP (3 GC); 1901 Ernest Bugler Abraham RP; 1904 Frederick Walter Cull; 1905 Philip John Boniface RP; 1906 Frank Holderness. 1905 Mounted Rural Post; late 1905 Horsekeep allowance raised; 1907 Mounted post abolished and mailcart service extended; 1918 Mounted Post substituted for mailcart.

Westerham-Westerham Hill: 1893 William Thomas Bartholomew RP (1 GC); 1896-1908 George Goose Camber RP (3 GC); 1910 Alfred George Fuller RP (1 GC).

Westerham to Mariners: 1892 Job Joseph Izzard; 1894 Howard Wallace Dell RP; 1898 Israel William Sandles; 1900 Frank Edward Newman RP; 1902 James Cosgrove RP; 1911 Alfred George Fuller RP (2 GC).

Westerham to Edenbridge: 1843 Footpost, about ten miles each way. London mail arrives at Westerham 6.30am Sorted, departs 7.30am, Edenbridge 9.30, Hever 10, Chiddingstone 11. Return 2pm, Hever 3pm, Edenbridge 4pm, Westerham 6pm; 1857-1896 London mail by train, mailcart arrives from Edenbridge at 6am.

Westerham to Biggin Hill: 1911 Walk; 1927 Use of Motor Bus (S10 Reigate-Westerham-Biggin Hill-Bromley).

Westerham to Ken Court 1909, to Ricketts Hill 1913, to Charts Edge 1918, to Toys Hill delivery by Motor post 1936, to Redhill by Motor Bus 1937.

Sub-Office Auxiliaries: John Palmer Westerham-Tatsfield 1896-9 then promoted RP: George Henry Bateman 1896-9 then promoted RP Sevenoaks; William James Sayers (age 16 1/2) 1899. Town Auxiliary: 1905 Horace Smith.

Some Locations of PO: 1869 Eastern row of houses facing green, house nearest church; 1897 Midway, houses on North side of green; East side of London Road: 1905 West side of London Road, Crown office.

Postmarks: Penny Post 'No 3' 1822-1838; UBC I 1842-43; DBC II 1846-57; DBC II (small) 1863)-1864; SR 1870-1914; J22 Duplex 1890-1908; Skeleton 1903 & 1906; DR Thick 1904-13; Skeleton 1917 & 1923; DR Thick 1915-1927; DR Thick 1933-1950; DR Thin 1984-85; SRs (1958)-1983. Machine Krag 1959-73. Universal 1982-3 (Xmas with Sevenoaks die). Packet: Target (1904) Rubber SC 1939-72 PP Rect 1930-3; Instructional 1956. SE Railway station oval (1893).

Population: 1801 1,344; 1841 2,162; 1881 2,301; 1921 3,162; 1961 4,228; 1981 4,315.

Westerham Hill

Top of the North Downs above Westerham on the road to Biggin Hill and Bromley.

Status:
1883 Letterbox Westerham Hill under Westerham.
1891 Letterbox Westerham Hill. Letters via Orpington RSO to 1895.
1892 Office open under Westerham. Postal Orders issued.
1902 January 1st. Money Order Office and Savings Bank.
1975 Shut.

Sub-Postmasters: Dougal Marmaduke Thompson* (17.8.1892=1899); William Abraham Hallam (28.4.1899=1901); Edward David Abraham, grocer and draper (2.7.1901=1913); James Clark, tobacconist (-1915=1924-); Ellen Barrow (-1925).
* Transferred from Edenbridge 1.4.1897.

History: 1898 *Westerham to Westerham* Hill Day Mail established; 1899 *Westerham to Westerham Hill SO.* Relief for Sub Office postman also Branch delivery established to Hanley Corner; 1901 Westerham Hill delivery extended also *Westerham Hill to Northfield* delivery extended to Childsbridge Cottage; 1904 *Westerham Hill and Silverstead* delivery established; 1905 *WH to Biggin Hill* Cycle Post; 1907 *WH to Norheads* delivery established.

Postmen: 1903 Alfred George Fuller; 1904 Cecil Martin Brown: 1908 R P Fuller RP on 21/- week. *Westerham Hill to Beacon Lights:* 1903 E B Abraham R Aux, 1905 Albert Dewsnap RP, 1905 Robin Cuthbert Jackson R Aux.

Postmarks: Climax (1892) and (1894); SR 1904-28; DR Thick 1933-75.

Temporary Post Offices in the area

Army Post Office	HD 3 Dunstall Camp near Shoreham	SR June to Sept 1916
(Home Defence)	HD35 Wildernesse	SR 7 to 14 July 1916
	MD11 Wildernesse	SR July to Sept 1917
	FPO 999 Biggin Hill	DR 1977 and 1983
GPO Mobile PO 'B'	Biggin Hill Airshow	SR 2.5.1963
RAF Postroom	Biggin Hill	SR May & Sept events 1969-85

Edenbridge District

Edenbridge   Eaton Bridge   Eton bridge

From Roman times there was a road from London through Edenbridge to the iron works of Sussex, passing through the Paygate to Holtye and Lewes.

    In the 1700s mail was often taken to Godstone and put direct into the General Post there, this was not very much further than taking it to Westerham which at that time was not yet officially connected to Sevenoaks.

    Named after the River Eden that flows into the Medway. Edenbridge, like Tunbridge Wells also has chalybeate springs. Of the two railway bridges going north from the town centre, the first station Edenbridge Town is on the LB & SCB via Croydon to Uckfield, the furthest Edenbridge on the South Eastern line to Tonbridge and Dover. In 1968 the town was badly flooded which somewhat disrupted postal communications for some days.

Status:

1810 Official Receiving House with private connection
    to Sevenoaks Penny Post at Westerham.
1837 Sub-Post Town (so shown in Appendix
    to Select Committee Report, no 25).
1839 Receiving House Sevenoaks Penny Post.
    Connection to Westerham now officially paid.
1842 Railway Station. SE Railway.
1848 Sept 1. A separate Post Town, but <u>not</u> listed as a Provincial Branch Office.
    By 1849 Money Order Office.
1857-96 Westerham under Edenbridge: also Sundridge and Brasted until 1886.
1861 November 11th. Savings Bank Office.
1870 Telegraph Office (EB) also TO at SE Rly Station pre-1875, TO at LB & SC Rly Station 7.2.1888.
1903 Salaried Office.
1919 July. As from 1 Sep Edenbridge Head Office converted to a Salaried Sub-office and transferred with its subordinate offices to the control of Tonbridge. No change in circulation of mails and address "Edenbridge Kent".
1934 New Building. Crown Office (MOW). Designated Class I in 1939.
1976 Ceased to cancel outgoing mail.

Subsequent affiliations were with Tonbridge/Tunbridge Wells, for circulation of mail, being concentrated on Tunbridge Wells for outgoing deliveries in May 1976, later Tonbridge MLO. In 1986 Mr Clancy of Sevenoaks was in overall charge for 'Royal Mail'. 1990 Crown Office shut, building used by R.M; Agency office next door.

Sub-Postmasters & Postmasters: Robert Parsons, grocer (1805=1832-); John Chandler, grocer (-1839 = 15.11.40); Post filled by Surveyor, no name recorded (17.12.1840=1844-); William Saxby, parish clerk and schoolmaster (1842=1852-); James Reynolds, ex Chiddingston messenger (30.4.1852=1854-); John Wickenden (25.10.1854=1855-); Thomas Thompson, grocer, ironmonger and insurance agent (1855); John Norman, collector of Poor Rate, agent to Govt. Emigration, commissioners stamp distributor (19.8.1855=1882-); William E Norman, Collector of Poor Rate (-1887-1896-); (? George Chandler 1896-1903) N D Watts, ex Bath office (2.3.1903=1906); Evan S Jones ex Pwllheli office (15.9.1906=1920); Frederick T Barnes ex Tonbridge Office (2.1.1920=1925); Harold Fuller ex Ramsgate Office (13.9.1925=1931); W G Howe ex Sidcup office (17.6.1931=1936); A E Doughty ex Whitstable office (29.4.1936=1938-).

Salary: 1844 £40 inc conveyance of bags from station and delivery. Assistant £10. 1925 £170pa. 1938 £275pa.

History: Pre 1795 most letters taken to General Post at *Godstone* 8½m; by 1800 5m, *to Westerham*: 1845 Letters by footpost arrive from Westerham 9.30am despatched 4pm; 1848 Letters arrive by train from London - 1856 5 Apr Edenbridge Night Mail Messenger Clement Sparrowhawk; 1856 Delivery to Gabriel Farm £12; 1859 Mailcart to Westerham 0500, Mailcart to East Grinstead 0420; 1857 Jas Hillard Runner (14/- week) New Post. *Edenbridge-Crockham Hill-Brasted-Sundridge* to ECBS; 1853 Messenger *Edenbridge-Four Elms* 8.12.53 John Mitchend; 1854 Messenger *Edenbridge to Chiddingston*, 23 Oct 54 William Kemp.

Some Locations of PO: 1869/97 East side of High Street opp Lingfield Road. 1936 West side of High street opp Croft Lane, Crown Office.

Messengers: 1.9.1848 *Edenbridge to Chiddingstone*; 6.4.1850 *Edenbridge to Common* 12/- week, and *to Crockham Hill* 12/- wk; 12.1.1853 *Edenbridge to Four Elms* 10/- week, later 14/-; 13.2.1856 Day Mail to Railway 9/- week.

Postmarks: Penny Post No 6; UBC I (1842); UBC II 1849-50; DBC II 1850-54; DBC II small 1859; 967 Killer 1850-67; SR 1863-67; 967 Duplex 4-bar 1868-1889; 967 Duplex 3-bar 1882-1902; 697 Duplex error 1892-1894; SR 1904; DR Thick 1904-1906; Skeleton small 1906, large 1917; DRs Thick 1906-1921; DRs Thick 1932-1947; DRs Thin 1965-1985. Rubber Target 1904-7; SR 30mm -1966=1967-; PP Rect ;1982. Machine Krag -1953-Universal -1961=1972-. Special Event Phil Exhib 1970.

Population: 1801 910; 1841 2,029*; 1881 1,942; 1921 2,890; 1961 5,242; 1981 7,866.
* Railway Workers.

Hever Road/South End   TSO
Hever Road at South end of Edenbridge, on south side of Hever Road.

Status:
1882 Wall Letter Box
Mid 1905 Post Office open. Town Sub-Office.
1907 Money Order Office and Savings Bank.
1920 March. Closed.

Sub-Postmasters: William Smith (-1905=1913-); Robert Keyte, wife Mary was a draper, (1914=1919-).

Postmarks: None seem.

South End: A few years after Hever road office closed the need for a Town office at the south end of the long High Street was again felt. South End was opened on the east side of the High Street midway between Hever Road and the River.

Status: 1935 Post and Money Order Office open. Town Sub-Office.

Sub-Postmasters: Smith Bros, Grocers and Post Office. High Street (-1938-).

Postmarks: SR 1986=89

Marlpit Hill TSO
To the north of Edenbridge situated to the west of the main road.

Status:
1882 Wall Letter Box.
1893 Post Office open TSO (Town Sub-Office).
1899 June 1st. Money Order Office and Savings Bank.

Sub-Postmasters: Stephen Robson, grocer (-1899=05-); Edward J Orpin, grocer and baker (-1907=1911-); Frederick Salmon Anderson, grocer (-1913=1938-).

Postmarks: Climax (1895); SRs 1908-86.

Marsh Green TSO
A hamlet to the south south west of Edenbridge on the road to Lingfield.

Status:
1882 Wall Letter Box
1894 Post Office open. Town Sub-Office. Postal Orders issued, not paid.
By 1905 Money Order Office and Savings Bank.
1905 May 16. Telegraph Office (MEE).
1984 Closed.

Sub-Postmasters: William Edward Divall (-1899-); Walter Walter, shop (-1902=1922-); Alfred Knight-Latter, shop (1923=1938-).

Postmarks: Climax (1894); SR 1909; DR Thick 1933; SR 1965; Special Event 1982 St Johns Marsh Green.

Village Sub-Offices

Bow (Bough) Beech

In 1841 the village was effectively split in two by the new railway line sunk into a fairly deep cutting with only a single road bridge to make the connection. The nearest station is a few miles away at Chiddingstone Causeway and called Penshurst station, on the line to Tonbridge.

There is now a large reservoir to the north of Bough Beech.

Status:
1846 Within the delivery of Tonbridge.
1853 Receiving House open under Edenbridge.
By 1887 Telegraph Office at Penshurst Station.
1891 Oct 13. Telegraph Office at Post Office (BOW).
1904 Money Order Office and Savings Bank. 1989 Shut.

Sub-Postmasters: Richard Butcher, Nurseryman (26.10.1853=1872-); George Winter, shop (-1882=1895-); William Jenner, shop (-1899=1938-).

Messengers: 1856 *Bow Beech to Hever*.

Postmarks: UBC II (1853); No Stamp 1860-90; SRs 1906-32; DR Thick 1948; SR 1965-86.

Chiddingstone

The Chiding Stone is a mass of sandstone 18 feet high. The village has the appearance of an 'estate' village, but unlike Chevening the road is no dead-end, it turns sharply and diverts around the estate of Chiddingstone Castle which now is a 'modern' castellated house. There is a non-standard Ludlow-type wall posting-box.

Status:
1829 Letters from Sevenoaks via Westerham.
1845 Receiving House under Westerham and Sevenoaks.
1846 Under Tonbridge.
1848 Under Edenbridge once it became a Post town.
By 1895 Telegraph Office and Express Delivery Office.

Sub-Postmasters: Under Richard Brook as acting postmaster (1840=1844-);
Richard Brook, shop (2.6.1845=1846-); William Brook, grocer draper and tallow chandler (-1851=1871-); Richard Crandall, grocer and draper (-1874=1887-); George Chandler, grocer (-1890=1913-); William John Tassell (-1918=1922-); Charles Frederick Wells, shop (-1924-); Mrs K Wells, shop (-1927=1938-).

Salary: 1845 £18.5.- pa (high compared with other Receiving Houses).

History: 20.2.1854 Messenger *to Stone Wall* 14/- week.

Postmarks: UBC I (1845); No Stamp 1860-86; Climax 1891; DR Thick 1944; SRs 1965-86.

Population: 1801 910; 1841 1,405*; 1881 1,292; 1921 1,061; 1961 915; 1981 812.

* Railway Navigators in the district.

Chiddingstone Causeway

A village in low-lying country, near to 'Charcotts'. The railway is on an embankment and the station called 'Penshurst'. Cricket ball and bat-making country. Dukes originated at Penshurst and moved here in 1841; still going under the name of British Cricket Balls Ltd.

Status:
1871 Wall letter box.
1884 Post Office open under Edenbridge.
By 1887 Telegraph Office at Penshurst Station.
1894 June 1. Money Order Office and Savings Bank.
1896 Nov 29. Under Tonbridge.
1905 May 16. Telegraph Office (ZWY).

Sub-Postmasters: John Crowhurst, shop (-1887=1890-); Josiah Cole, shop (-1895=1907-); Frank Martin, shop (-1909=1938-).

Postmarks: No Stamp 1884-89; Climax (1889).

Chiddingstone Hoath   The Hoath

A hamlet 1½ miles east of Mark Beech but in Chiddingstone parish.
Hoath is a Kentish synonym for heath. Stonewall is a mile east of the Hoath.
   The office is now shut.

Status:
1846 Within delivery of Tonbridge. Stonewall.
1853 Receiving House open (at Stone Wall, by 1862 at The Hoath). Postal only. Under Edenbridge.
By 1936 Telegraph office.
1983 Shut.

Sub-Postmasters: Mrs Alice Scott, shop (3.2.1854=1862-); John Scott, shop (-1871=1878-); Mrs Clifford Baker, grocer and draper (-1886=1899-); Mrs Betts, grocer and draper (-1902=1903-); Charles Tassell, grocer and draper (-1905=1909-); William John Tassell, shop (-1911=1922-); Leslie Wells, grocer (-1923=1938-).

Salary: 1854 £3 pa.

History: c1850 Stonewall served by foot messenger from Tonbridge. 20.2.1854 Messenger from *Chiddingstone to Stone Wall* 14/- week; 1856 Dely to *Bassetts Mill.*

Postmarks: UBC II (1853); No Stamp 1860-80; Climax (1892); SRs 1965.

Cowden   Cowdham

A village west by 1½ miles of the main Edenbridge to Hartsfield road. Cowden station on the line to Tunbridge Wells is about 2½ miles away, to the east of the main road. During the Civil War ordnance from the furnace at Cowden was among the munitions supplied by John Brown to the Parliamentarians. At times (c1850) the village was under East Grinstead, five miles distant as Post Town.

Status:
1844 Receiving House open under East Grinstead.
1844-1849 Mail from East Grinstead. Subsequently under Edenbridge.
1867 Jan 1. Post Office and Savings Bank.
1887 Money Order Office.
1890 Telegraph Office at Cowden Railway station.
1893 Sept 5. Telegraph Office at Post Office (CNL).

Sub-Postmasters: Thomas Bold (Boles) Wiles (Wills), grocer and draper (1844=1847-); Nicholas Arnold, shop (-1852=1855-); William Newton, draper grocer surveyor of roads farmer (-1862-); James Piper (-1874-); John Shoesmith, grocer (-1878=1887-); Henry Shoesmith, grocer (-1890-); Mrs Fanny Shoesmith, grocer (1895=1918-); Miss Mabel Baines, grocer (-1921=25-); Mrs Jessie Amy Igglesden, grocer (-1927=1930-); Miss Maud Igglesden, grocer (-1933=1938-).

History: 1850 Mail received (from E Grinstead) 9am, box closes 4.30pm.

Postmarks: UBC I (1844); USR straight line (1858); No Stamp 1860-1871; ESR str line (1872); SRs 3 types 1903-86.

Crockham Hill

North of Edenbridge on the main road through the town as it
begins to ascend the hill. There is a sandy common at 600 feet.

Status:
Between 1862 and 1865. Receiving House open.
1882 April 1st. Money Order Office and Savings Bank.
By 1887 Telegraph Office (COS).

Sub-Postmasters: William Gooding, grocer and baker (-1871-); William Latter, shoemaker (-1878=1899-); Frederick Gooding, grocer and baker (-1902=1903-); William Cox, blacksmith (-1905=1907-); Mrs Frances Mary Scarlett, confectioner (-1909=1938-).

Postmarks: No Stamp up to 1880, probably 1882; SRs 1899-1985.

Four Elms

Four Elms is a country cross-road village where the Edenbridge to Ide Hill and the Penshurst to Crockham Hill roads cross.

Status:
1852 Receiving House open.
1893 August 29th. Telegraph Office (FEE).
1894 June 1. Money Order Office.
1987 Shut.

Sub-Postmasters: William Winter, wheelwright (25.11.1852=1878-); William Gooding, draper and rate collector (-1887=1927-); Samuel Lavers, draper (-1930-); William Mycroft, general dealer (-1933=1938-).

Messenger: 12.1.1853 Messenger from Edenbridge.

Postmarks: UBC II (1855); No Stamp 1860-1889; Climax (1890); SR 1900-1910; DR Thick 1934; SRs (1965)-1986.

Hever   Hevre

Hever with its moated castle on the banks of the River Eden which flows into the Medway, has early associations with Henry VIII and Anne Boleyn and later the Astors. The name derives from that of an early owner William de Hevre, a one time village near Northfleet.

Hever station is on the LB&SC Rly line to Tunbridge Wells.

Status:
Sometime between June 1840 and June 1841, opened as a Receiving House under Sevenoaks and Westerham.
1848 Under Edenbridge.
By 1895 Money Order Office and Savings Bank.
1923 Shut.

Sub-Postmasters: William Best, schoolmaster (-1844=1862-); George Paine, parish clerk (-1867-1871-); Emmanuel Duke, smith (-1874=1882-); John Harrington, blacksmith (-1887=1922-).

Messenger: 1856 *Hever to Bow Beech* 9/- week.

History: Pre mid-1848 letters arrive 10.15am. Box closes 3.15pm.

Postmarks: UBC I (1843)-1850; No Stamp 1860-1889; Climax (1890); SR 1904-1913.

Population: 1801 187; 1841 582; 1881 670; 1921 718; 1961 1,062; 1981 1,033.

(Lingfield)

To the west of Marsh Green and with the address 'Lingfield RSO Surrey' from -1885=1900- was in 1889 despatching out some mail through Eden-bridge (Lingfield backstamp, Edenbridge cancel).

Mark Beech/Cowden Pound

Cowden Pound is a hamlet south of Edenbridge on the main road to Hartsfield. Mark Beech is a village a couple of miles away on the east side of that road. Throughout the years there was a single office located either at Mark Beech or at Cowden Pound. The wall letterbox at the pub has an internal flap to keep out the wet, the only one in the district so accommodated.

Status:
Office at Mark Beech open about 1858 as a Receiving House.
Office at Cowden Pound open 1882 as a Post office in 'Queens Arms'.

Cowden Pound 1901-6 July near Cowden Pound at Jessops House.
1901 May 1. Money Order Office and Savings Bank.
Office at Mark Beech 1906 July 8.
Dec 1906 on (recorded 10.9.07), Telegraph Office as well as MOSB.

Sub-Postmasters: John King (-1862-); No name (1874-8); Robert Morse, Queens Arms Public House and grocer (-1887-); G Langridge, Queens Arms and grocer (-1890-); George Pennifer, Queens Arms and grocer (-1900-); William Day, wheelwright and builder (-1902=1906-); Albert William Turk (-1907=1927-); Jack Seymour, stationer (-1930-); Mrs Ada E Seymour, confectioner (-1935=1938-).

Postmarks: Mark Beech. USR Curved name (1858); No Stamp 1860-80; SR 1907; DR Thick 1846; SR (1965)-86.

Postmarks: Cowden Pound Climax (1900); SR 1905.

Any additional information or corrections may be sent to the author via the publishers and will be gratefully received.

Population growth along the Road

	1660	1695	1801	1841	1881	1921	1961	1981
Bromley	-	-	2,700	4,325	15,154	35,070	68,252	294,451[†]
Orpington	-	-	500	907	3,050	7,000	80,300	-
Sevenoaks	800	# 891	1,403	5,061	*8,035	**9,058	17,645	17,212

#1695 Riverhead 371, Weald 310 not included.
* inc Riverhead & Weald.   *† Now includes Orpington*
** Riverhead (943) and Weald (872) now separate.

	1660	1695	1801	1841	1881	1921	1961	1981
Tonbridge	600	-	4,371	12,530	35,919	*15,929	22,146	30,530

* Southboro 20,000 now separate.

	1660	1695	1801	1841	1881	1921	1961	1981
T Wells	-	-	(2,000)	8,302	24,309	35,568	39,869	44,992
Rye	-	-	2,187	4,031	4,220	3,920	4,438	4,434
Hastings	-	-	2,982	11,781	42,258	66,495	72,169	75,294

In 1695 Sevenoaks had 206 houses and in 1801 Sevenoaks had 416 houses, Rye 397 and Hastings 562.

For comparison:

	1660	1695	1801	1841	1881	1921	1961	1981
Dartford	-	-	2,406	5,619	10,163	26,000	46,100	44,003
Maidstone	-	-	8,027	18,086	29,632	37,300	59,800	72,494

There are now at least 600,000 persons in the Tonbridge MLO area.

1831 Coaches passing through Sevenoaks, based on Robson's key to Mail and Coach Conveyance List 1831

Yearly Licence No.	From	Proprietor	Miles	No Inside	Journey	Destination
1 mail	Bolt-in-Tun, Fleet Street	Rob Gray & Co	66	4	Single	Hastings
1 mail	Golden Cross, Charing Cross	B W Horne & Co	66	4	Single	Hastings
2376	Golden Cross, Charing Cross	B W Horne & Co	66	4	Single	Hastings
2377	Golden Cross, Charing Cross	B W Horne & Co	66	4	Single	Hastings
2378	Golden Cross, Charing Cross	B W Horne & Co	66	4	Single	Hastings
2007	Bolt-in-Tun, Fleet Street	Rob Gray & Co	66	4	Single	Hastings
2008	Bolt-in-Tun, Fleet Street	Rob Gray & Co	66	4	Single	Hastings
2228	La Belle Sauvage, Ludgate Hill	R Nelson & Co	65	4	Single	Hastings
2229	La Belle Sauvage, Ludgate Hill	R Nelson & Co	65	4	Single	Hastings
2014	Bolt-in-Tun, Fleet Street	Rob Gray & Co	64	4	Single	Rye
2015	Bolt-in-Tun, Fleet Street	Rob Gray & Co	64	4	Single	Rye
2817	Bolt-in-Tun, Fleet Street	J Stephens & Co	24	6	Return	Seven Oaks
2016	Bolt-in-Tun, Fleet Street	Will Eastland	36	4	Return	T Wells
2592	Golden Cross, Charing Cross	B W Horne	36	4	Return	T Wells
2644	Golden Cross, Charing Cross	B W Horne	36	4	Return	T Wells
Others						
2738	Green Man & Still Oxford St	Alex Mills	24	6	M, Tu	Westerham
2780	Boar & Castle, Oxford St	Will Pauley	27	4	Return	Sundridge

To Maidstone via Wrotham from Golden Cross Charing Cross (2), La Belle Sauvage (2), Blossoms Lawrence Lane (2), Saracens Head Friday Street (2), George Boro' (1). Total 9 coaches, inc two vans, with five doing return journeys, so 14 passages a day in all.

1837 Coaches passing through Sevenoaks, based on Robson's key to Mail and Coach Conveyance List 1837

Yearly Licence No	From	Proprietor	Miles	Passengers In/Out	Destination	Name
691	Hatchett's, Piccadilly	R Gray & Co	67	4/11	Hastings	
692	Hatchett's, Piccadilly	R Gray & Co	67	4/11	Hastings	
1 mail	Charing Cross	R Gray & Co	68	3/3	Hastings	
1 mail	Charing Cross	B W Horne & Co	68	4/2	Hastings	
731	Charing Cross	B W Horne & Co	66	4/11	Hastings	*The Express*
732	Charing Cross	B W Horne & Co	66	4/11	Hastings	*The Express*
737	George & Blue Boar, Hbn	B W Horne & Co	67	4/11	Hastings	*The Despatch*
768	New Inn Old Change	T Moore & Co	64	3/3	Hastings	
771	New Inn Old Change	R Sisley & Co	64	3/1	Hastings	
766	La Belle Sauvage	T Breeds & Co	66	4/11	Hastings	*The Paragon*
767	La Belle Sauvage	T Breeds & Co	66	4/11	Hastings	*The Paragon*
769	Talbot, Borough	Stanbury & Co	63	4/2	Hastings	
693	Bolt-in-Tun, Fleet Street	R Gray & Co	64	4/8	Rye	*The Sovereign*
694	Bolt-in-Tun, Fleet Street	R Gray & Co	64	4/11	Rye	*The Sovereign*
744	Catherine Wheel, Borough	W Harris	32½	9/-	Southboro	
690	Bolt-in-Tun, Fleet Street	J Stephens & Co	24	4/11	SevenOaks	*United Friends*
641	Bolt-in-Tun, Fleet Street	R Gray	37	4/11	T Wells	*Morning Star*
643	Charing Cross	B W Horne & Co	37	4/11	T Wells	*Telegraph/Sx*
738	George & Blue Boar, Hbn	B W Horne & Co	38	4/11	T Wells	*The Union*
679	La Belle Sauvage	R Nelson & Co	36½	4/11	T Wells	
763	British Hotel Coffee House, Cockspur Street	T Skinner & Co	40	4/11	T Wells	*The Age*

Those coaches going as far as Tunbridge Wells did a return journey, the rest only a single. Licence numbers changed every year, some named coaches shown by Bates in 1836, eg Churchill's 'The Independent' to T Wells were not licenced in 1837.

Others

650	Green Man & Still, Oxford St	A Mills	24	12/6	M, Tu only	Westerham
689	Old Bell, Holborn	J Nicholson & Co	25	4/11	Sundridge	*The Times*

To Maidstone via Wrotham from Charing Cross (2S), Saracens Head (Martins van 1S), La Belle Sauvage (3R), Blossoms (1R), The George Aldermanbury (1R), 15 passages a day.

As well as Robson's lists secondary data may be found in Alan Bates, *Directory of Stagecoach Services 1836*, David and Charles 1969 and the *Geographical Pattern of Coaching Services in Kent in 1836*, Terence Paul Smith in *Archaeologia Cantiana* Vol XCVIII 1982.

Official Declaration taken from 1884 Regulations

On entering the service of the Post Office, it is necessary to make a declaration before a magistrate in a prescribed form, which must be obtained from the Head Postmaster; and no person, whether on temporary or permanent service, can be permitted to have access to the letters, or to perform any official duty, either Postal or Telegraph, until this declaration shall have been duly made and signed. The following is a copy of the declaration referred to:

I   (name)   do solemnly and sincerely declare that I will not wittingly or willingly open or delay, or cause or suffer to be opened or delayed, contrary to my duty, any letter or anything sent by the Post, which shall come into my hands or custody by reason of my employment relating to the Post Office, except by the consent of the person or persons to whom the same shall be directed, or by an express warrant in writing, under the hand of one of the Principal Secretaries of State for that purpose, or except in such cases where the party or parties to whom such letter, or anything sent by the Post, shall be directed, and who is, or are, chargeable with the payment of the postage thereof, shall refuse or neglect to pay the same; and except such letters, or anything sent by Post, as shall be returned for want of true directions, or when the party or parties to whom the same shall be directed cannot be found; and that I will not in any way embezzle any such letter or anything sent by the Post as aforesaid; and I make this solemn declaration conscientiously intending to fulfil and obey the same, and by virtue of the provisions of an Act, passed in the first year of the reign of Her Majesty Queen Victoria, intituled "An Act for the Management and Regulation of the Post".

This declaration was made before me,
at   in the
of   the   day
of   18

The declarations of a Sub-Postmaster, and of all persons employed under him, must be forwarded to, and will be preserved by, his Head Postmaster.

Kings and Queens of England

19 Dec 1154-1189	Henry II	35 years	30 Jan 1649-1660	Commonwealth	11 years
8 Sep 1189-1199	Richard I	10 years	29 May 1660-1685	Charles II	25 years
27 May 1199-1216	John	17 years	6 Feb 1685-1689	James II	3 years
28 Oct 1216-1272	Henry III	56 years	13 Feb 1689-1694	William III and Mary II	5 years
20 Nov 1272-1307	Edward I	35 years	1694-1702	William III alone	8 years
8 July 1307-1327	Edward II	20 years	3 Mar 1702-1714	Anne	12 years
25 Jan 1327-1377	Edward III	50 years	1 Aug 1714-1727	George I	13 years
22 June 1377-1399	Richard II	22 years	11 Jun 1727-1760	George II	33 years
30 Sep 1399-1413	Henry IV	14 years	25 Oct 1760-1820	George III	60 years
21 Mar 1413-1422	Henry V	9 years	29 Jan 1820-1830	George IV	10 years
1 Sep 1422-1461	Henry VI	39 years	26 Jun 1830-1837	William IV	7 years
4 Mar 1461-1483	Edward IV	22 years	20 Jun 1837-1901	Victoria	64 years
9 Apl 1483-	Edward V		22 Jan 1901-1910	Edward VII	9 years
26 June 1483-1485	Richard III	2 years	6 May 1910-1936	George V	26 years
22 Aug 1485-1509	Henry VII	24 years	20 Jan 1936	Edward VIII	
22 Apr 1509-1547	Henry VIII	38 years	11 Dec 1936-1952	George VI	16 years
28 Jan 1547-1553	Edward VI	6 years	6 Feb 1952-	Elizabeth II	
1553	Jane				
6 Jul 1553-1558	(Philip and) Mary	5 years			
17 Nov 1558-1603	Elizabeth I	45 years			
24 Mar 1603-1625	James I	22 years			
27 Mar 1625-1649	Charles I	24 years			

Multiplying Factors to Jan 1987
To bring historic amounts to retail price index 398 (1987 change)

AD

1500 x 270	1810 x 17	1850 x 29	1890 x 32	1930 x 17	1970 x 5.5
1510 x 270	1811 x 17	1851 x 30	1891 x 32	1931 x 19	1971 x 5
1520 x 270	1812 x 15	1852 x 30	1892 x 32	1932 x 19	1972 x 5
1530 x 210	1813 x 15	1853 x 28	1893 x 33	1933 x 20	1973 x 4.5
1540 x 180	1814 x 17	1854 x 24	1894 x 34	1934 x 20	1974 x 4
1550 x 175	1815 x 19	1855 x 23	1895 x 35	1935 x 20	1975 x 3.5
1560 x 110	1816 x 21	1856 x 23	1896 x 35	1936 x 19	1976 x 3
1570 x 95	1817 x 19	1857 x 25	1897 x 34	1937 x 19	1977 x 2.5
1580 x 97	1818 x 18	1858 x 27	1898 x 34	1938 x 18	1978 x 2
1590 x 83	1819 x 19	1859 x 27	1899 x 34	1939 x 18	1979 x 2
1600 x 70	1820 x 21	1860 x 26	1900 x 33	1940 x 17	1980 x 1.6
1610 x 55	1821 x 24	1861 x 26	1901 x 33	1941 x 15	1981 x 1.4
1620 x 53	1822 x 27	1862 x 26	1902 x 32	1942 x 14	1982 x 1.3
1630 x 50	1823 x 26	1863 x 27	1903 x 32	1943 x 14	1983 x 1.2
1640 x 48	1824 x 24	1864 x 28	1904 x 32	1944 x 14	1984 x 1.15
1650 x 42	1825 x 20	1865 x 27	1905 x 32	1945 x 14	1985 x 1.11
1660 x 42	1826 x 21	1866 x 26	1906 x 32	1946 x 14	1986 x 1.05
1670 x 47	1827 x 23	1867 x 24	1907 x 31	1947 x 14	1987 x 1.00
1680 x 47	1828 x 24	1868 x 25	1908 x 30	1948 x 13	
1690 x 50	1829 x 24	1869 x 26	1909 x 30	1949 x 13	
1700 x 44	1830 x 25	1870 x 26	1910 x 30	1950 x 12.5	
1710 x 43	1831 x 23	1871 x 26	1911 x 29	1951 x 12	
1720 x 47	1832 x 24	1872 x 24	1912 x 29	1952 x 10.5	
1730 x 48	1833 x 26	1873 x 24	1913 x 29	1953 x 10	
1740 x 48	1834 x 28	1874 x 25	1914 x 29	1954 x 10	
1750 x 48	1835 x 27	1875 x 26	1915 x 25	1955 x 9.5	
1760 x 42	1836 x 25	1876 x 26	1916 x 21	1956 x 9	
1770 x 35	1837 x 24	1877 x 26	1917 x 17	1957 x 8.5	
1780 x 35	1838 x 24	1878 x 26	1918 x 15	1958 x 8.5	
1790 x 31	1839 x 22	1879 x 28	1919 x 13	1959 x 8	
1800 x 18	1840 x 21	1880 x 27	1920 x 13	1960 x 8	
1801 x 16	1841 x 22	1881 x 28	1921 x 11	1961 x 8	
1802 x 21	1842 x 24	1882 x 28	1922 x 15	1962 x 7.5	
1803 x 22	1843 x 27	1883 x 29	1923 x 16	1963 x 7.5	
1804 x 22	1844 x 27	1884 x 29	1924 x 16	1964 x 7.5	
1805 x 19	1845 x 26	1885 x 30	1925 x 16	1965 x 7	
1806 x 19	1846 x 25	1886 x 32	1926 x 16	1966 x 6.5	
1807 x 20	1847 x 23	1887 x 33	1927 x 16	1967 x 6.5	
1808 x 19	1848 x 26	1888 x 33	1928 x 17	1968 x 6.5	
1809 x 17	1849 x 27	1889 x 32	1929 x 17	1969 x 6	

(Calculations and Approximations by A.G.D.)
Based on Bank of England Consumer Price Indices which are themselves based on several sources including the work of Phelps Brown, S V Hopkins, Sir P Harland, Crowther and British Labour Statistics.

Example: Rate of 1s/8d in 1710

(1710) 1/8 = 20d x 43 = 860d

$860d = \dfrac{860}{2.4}p = 358p = £3.58$ (1987)

Divisor for converting 'd' to 'p'

$\dfrac{240d \text{ in } £}{100p \text{ in } £} = 2.4$

A new series of indices started at 100 in Feb 1987 when the 1974 index had reached 398. All 'present day' figures in this book have been related to this point and require for comparisons in years to come to be further lifted by the amount the new 1987 index rises. (May 1991 133.5)

Index to Main Text

Archie DONALD
BSc(Econ) MEd FCCA FCMA FCIS FBIM JDipMA

An Honours Graduate in Economics and Social Anthropology of the University of London, Archie Donald studied Educational Psychology at Durham University for his Masters Degree. Married with two sons, he lives at Halstead in Kent on the North Downs where this book was written.

To earn a living in this life, he has been Photographer, Salesman, Banker's Clerk, Sapper RE, Gunner, Lance Bombardier (paid) and Lieutenant Royal Artillery, Spice and Rubber Broker, Company Secretary, Company Director, Group Chief Accountant, Management Trainer and latterly Head of Department of Business and Administrative Studies at South East London College, Lewisham.

As well as travels in Europe he has visited parts of Africa, India, Ceylon, Burma, Thailand and Singapore, some as a civilian. More recent visits include Iceland, Canada, Mexico, the USA, Hong-Kong and also to the People's Republic of China to liaise on Management Training. He is a member of The Kent Archaeological Society, The Sevenoaks Society, the Postal History Society, and the Kent Postal History Group – a gathering of individuals who study the early history of the Posts in Kent and contiguous parts of Sussex.

Other published works include *Management, Information and Systems* which was later published in Swedish and Japanese; and *Toward Consciousness III*, a book of poetry.

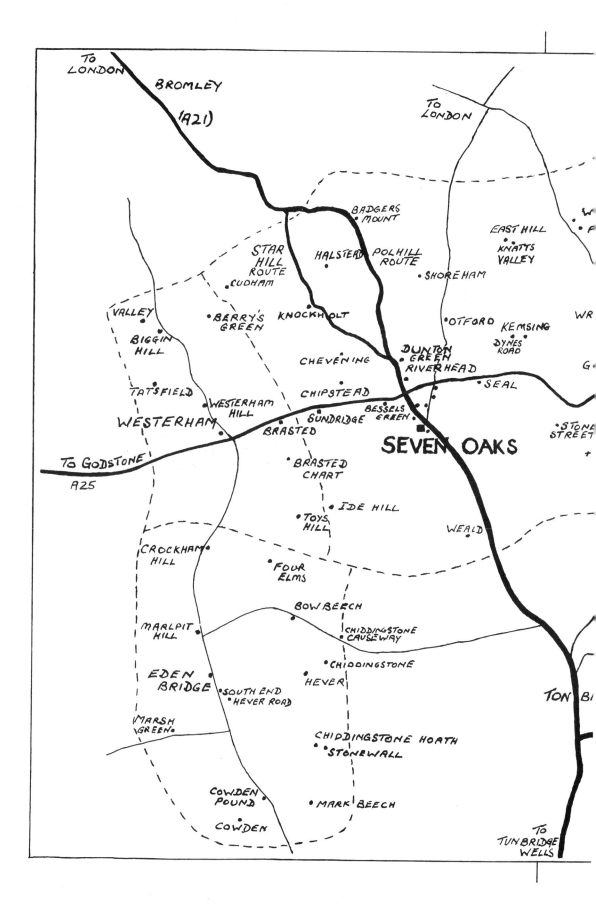